CASEBOOK ON RENT REVIEW AND LEASE RENEWAL

FOR MALCOLM, NIGEL, CATHERINE AND GARETH
Diana

FOR LIDIA AND MY PARENTS
Mark

CASEBOOK ON RENT REVIEW AND LEASE RENEWAL

DIANA BRAHAMS
of the Middle Temple, Barrister

AND

MARK PAWLOWSKI
LLB(Hons), BCL(Oxon), of the Middle Temple, Barrister
Senior Lecturer in Law, School of Surveying, Thames Polytechnic

COLLINS
8 Grafton Street, London W1

Collins Professional and Technical Books
William Collins Sons & Co. Ltd
8 Grafton Street, London W1X 3LA

First published in Great Britain by
Collins Professional and Technical Books 1986

Distributed in the United States of America
by Sheridan House, Inc.

British Library Cataloguing in Publication Data
Brahams, Diana
Casebook on rent review and lease renewal.
1. Landlord and tenant—England
I. Title   II. Pawlowski, Mark
344.2064'34   KD899

ISBN 0-00-383195-7

Typeset by Columns of Reading
Printed and bound in Great Britain by
Mackays of Chatham, Kent

Contents

CONTENTS

Publisher's note

The publishers plan to issue in due course a supplement to this book to include new cases. Those readers wishing to receive details of future supplements are invited to write to the publishers to record their interest:

Collins Professional and Technical Books
8 Grafton Street
London W1X 3LA

Foreword

It was an honour and privilege to read the proofs of this extremely valuable publication, the need for which I can clearly identify.

The last decade has seen a substantial increase of case law on rent reviews and business tenancy renewals, probably due to the earlier period of massive inflation to which was attributable an exceptional rental growth. Inevitably both landlords and tenants then sought recourse to the law and to valuers, whereas in times of moderate inflation, tenants—particularly in the provinces—were tempted to settle their own cases.

It follows that these highly important and searching topics now require considerable professional expertise from both valuers and lawyers. It is rare indeed for the modern practitioner to draft a lease without holding a full conference with both client and surveyor. Even 'ancient' practitioners like myself treat the subject matter of leases as being a 'legal minefield'.

This casebook will be invaluable to lawyers, valuers and property owners because it is a virtual mini-library, encapsulating the entire subject matter in a well indexed publication. All too often the busy practitioner may miss a case important to him because that case has not been reported in any of the usual sources readily available to him, despite the extensive number of property journals already published.

The casebook falls easily into its two sections—firstly on rent reviews and secondly on lease renewals—both with clear references under main subject headings.

Diana Brahams and Mark Pawlowski are to be commended to practitioners in this particular field. We should not forget the students of property law, and indeed our clients, to whom the publication must also appeal.

February 1986 **Vincent Kenneally, FSVA, FRVA**
President
Incorporated Society of
Valuers and Auctioneers

Preface

This casebook is, we believe, the first of its kind to deal with both rent review and lease renewal. For the first time, surveyors and lawyers alike are provided with a broad selection of judicial decisions in these subject areas.

Each leading case has its own summary of facts and decision and the relevant extract of the judgment is reproduced, thus providing the reader with his own portable mini-library at the office, on the site, at conferences and meetings with other professional advisers.

Each of the two sections has a full table of contents, and for easy reference the cases are grouped into various subject areas and are linked by guide notes and cross references. Other useful cases of lesser general importance are summarised in notes (often with their own extracts of the judgments), or alternatively they are to be found in the fuller extracts of the main authorities.

We think this book will be of value to both the practitioner and student alike. It is designed to be used in conjunction with one or more of the standard texts on the subject.

This is a complicated and technical area of the law and we hope this case book will shine a beam of light in a dark tunnel! Unfortunately due to limitations on space, it has not been possible to incorporate every case, and we are conscious of the difficulties of excluding any case of relevance to the subject.

We would also like to point out that many cases especially in cases of rent review turn on their own particular facts and it is often difficult, therefore, to extract any principle of general application but they may indicate the court's approach which may be helpful to others in similar circumstances.

In our view topics such as time limits, validity of notices, hypothetical assumptions, lease renewal terms and interim rent applications will be of particular concern to the practitioner. Indeed, some of the hypothetical assumptions that are called for, especially in rent review clauses, call for entry 'into a dim world peopled by the indeterminate spirits of fictitious or unborn sales' (see Peter Gibson J in *Daejan Investments Ltd* v. *Cornwall Coast Country Club* [6.3 (c)], quoting from Danckwerts J in *Re Holt (deceased)* [1953] 1 WLR at page 1492. It is obvious that 'marrying the hypothesis to the real world (in which the hypothesis must of course be set) may involve difficulties, depending on the subject matter ...' We hope that this casebook will in some measure facilitate this difficult process.

In the hope of avoiding future disputes, and even litigation, we would draw readers' attention to the 1985 edition of the Law Society/RICS Model Forms of Rent Review Clause which is currently available and was

published in the *Law Society's Gazette*, 18 December 1985, pages 3664-9.
The selection of cases is from material available to us at 14 February 1986.
Because a number of important recent cases were decided while the book
was going through the press, these have been included in an Appendix.

Diana Brahams and Mark Pawlowski
5 New Square
Lincoln's Inn
London WC2

Acknowledgments

We are grateful to the Incorporated Council of Law Reporting for England
and Wales, the All England Law Reports, Property and Compensation
Reports, Estates Gazette, Estates Times and Sweet & Maxwell's Current Law
series for giving us permission to use their reports in this Casebook. We also
wish to thank the School of Surveying, Thames Polytechnic for making their
library and photocopier available to us, and to Mr Joe McClenaghan MSc,
ARICS, DipTPl for reading the text and providing useful comments. We are
also indebted to John Baker for compiling the table of cases and the index so
efficiently, and to Malcolm Brahams for reading the proofs and commenting
on the text.

DJB
MP

PART I
RENT REVIEW

Chapter 1

Time limits

1.1 The general rule

The general rule is that time will not be of the essence in a rent review clause unless there are clear contra-indications.

UNITED SCIENTIFIC HOLDINGS LTD v. BURNLEY BOROUGH COUNCIL
and
CHEAPSIDE LAND DEVELOPMENT CO. LTD AND ANOTHER v. MESSELS SERVICE CO.

House of Lords   [1978] AC 904

In the first of these two appeals, which were heard together, the respondents leased adjoining properties from the appellants for 99 years at a rent of £1000 a year each. A rent review clause provided that, *inter alia*, during the year preceding the second and each succeeding 10 year period the parties should either agree or determine by arbitration the sum total of the properties' current rack rent and that one quarter of that sum, or £1000, whichever was the greater, would be the rent of each property for the next 10 years. The first 10 year period ended on 31 August 1972, and by that date the new rent had neither been agreed nor referred to arbitration and the respondents sought a declaration that, since time was of the essence of the contract, the appellants had lost their chance of increasing the rent for the second 10 year period. Pennycuick V-C held that although the review clause was expressed merely as a provision for the quantification of additional rent, it constituted a unilateral right to increase the rent vested in the appellants alone; that time was of the essence of the contract and that, since the appellants had not exercised that right promptly in accordance with the requirements of the review clause, the rent reserved for each property would remain at £1000 for the second 10 year period. On appeal the Court of Appeal dismissed the appeal.

In the second appeal the respondents leased property from the appellants for a term of 21 years. For the first period of seven years the rent was £117,340 a year. For the second and third periods of seven years the respective rents were to be determined in accordance with a rent review clause which contained a definition of the 'market rent' and defined the 'review date' as meaning, in respect of the second period, 8 April 1975. The procedure laid down for determining the market rent had to be initiated by a 'lessor's notice' specifying the proposed new rent. The notice had to be served between 12 and six months before the review date. The appellants gave the requisite notice in respect of the period starting on 8 April 1975, within the time specified, but no agreement was reached either as to the new rent or upon a valuer to determine it. Accordingly, as provided by the lease the appellants on 25 June 1975, applied for the appointment of a valuer to the President of the R.I.C.S., who was unwilling to comply with that request without a ruling by the court that it was a valid and effective application since the rent review clause stipulated that the valuer must notify both landlord and tenant of his valuation not less than 14 days before the review date. On a summons issued by the appellants, Graham J held (i) that the time for the service of a lessor's notice was of the essence of the contract, but that that stipulation had been complied with; (ii) that the time for applying for the appointment of a valuer was not of the essence; and (iii) that the market rent as determined by the valuer if higher than £117,340 a year, would be recoverable retrospectively to the review date. On appeal, the Court of Appeal reversed that decision.

On the appellants' appeals:

Held, allowing both appeals, that there was nothing in either of the leases in question to displace the presumption that strict adherence to the time-tables specified in their respective rent review clauses was not of the essence of the contract, and that therefore the new rents should be determined in accordance with the procedures specified in the respective leases.

Samuel Properties (Developments) Ltd v. *Hayek* [1972] 1 WLR 1296, CA overruled.

LORD DIPLOCK: So upon the question of principle which these two appeals were brought to settle, I would hold that in the absence of any contra-indications in the express words of the lease or in the interrelation of the rent review clause itself and other clauses or in the surrounding circumstances the presumption is that the time-table specified in a real review clause for completion of the various steps for determining the rent payable in respect of the period following the review date is not of the essence of the contract.

LORD FRASER OF TULLYBELTON: If a tenant felt himself prejudiced by the landlord's delay in serving a triggering notice, it would be open to him after the time for serving it had expired, to give notice prescribing a further time within which the triggering notice must be served. Provided that the further time was reasonable, he could thus make time of the essence.

... I am of the opinion that the equitable rule against treating time as of the essence of a contract is applicable to rent review clauses unless there is some special reason for excluding its application to a particular clause. The rule would of course be excluded if the review clause expressly stated that time was to be of the essence. It would also be excluded if the context clearly indicated that that was the intention of the parties—as for instance where the tenant had a right to break the lease by notice given by a specified date which was later than the last date for serving the landlord's trigger notice. The tenant's notice to terminate the contract would be one where the time limit was mandatory, and the necessary implication is that the time limit for giving the landlords notice of review must also be mandatory. An example of such interlocked provisions is to be found in *C. Richards & Son Ltd* v. *Karenita Ltd* (1971) 221 EG 25 where the decision that time was of the essence of the landlord's notice could be supported on this ground, although not, as I think, on the ground on which it was actually rested.

1.2 (a) Rent review procedures to be carried out inside time limits—'but not otherwise'

Where the lease lays down machinery which is subject to time limits, time will be of the essence if there is a clear indication of this in the clause. Where, therefore, the lease provides for a landlord to serve a notice invoking the rent review processes within a certain time 'but not otherwise', a failure to serve the notice within the time will, apparently, disentitle the landlord from serving the review notice.

DREBBOND LTD v. HORSHAM DISTRICT COUNCIL

Chancery Division   (1979) 37 P & CR 237

A lease provided *inter alia* that the landlord would be entitled to call for a rent review by giving the tenant notice in writing within the last six months before the expiration of the seventh and 14th year of the term. Clause 2 (c) provided that if, within three months after the date of the landlord's notice calling for review of rent there was no agreement between the parties as to various aspects of the revised rent, the matter 'shall if the landlord shall so require by notice in writing given to the tenant within three months thereafter but not otherwise be referred to arbitration'. The landlord gave notice to review the rent, but following abortive negotiations, the landlord did not serve an arbitration notice on the tenant until 18 months after the original notice. Meanwhile, the tenant had written to the landlord asserting that the landlord had lost his right to review.

Held: Clause 2 (c) of the lease was so worded, particularly having regard to the words 'but not otherwise', as to make time of the essence for the arbitration notice, since the object of the clause was clearly to permit three months for negotiations after the landlord's review notice had been served, and then to allow a further three months for service of an arbitration notice where no agreement had been reached; accordingly, since the time for serving the arbitration notice had expired the landlord had lost his right to serve a notice under clause 2 (c). *United Scientific Holdings Ltd v. Burnley Borough Council* [1978] AC 904 applied.

SIR ROBERT MEGARRY V-C: The starting point is the approach laid down in *United Scientific Holdings Ltd v. Burnley Borough Council* [[1978] AC 904; (1977) 33 P & CR 220] [counsel for the tenant] accepted, as he was obliged to do, that under rent review clauses time was presumed not to be of the essence, and that it was for him to establish that in this case there was enough to rebut the presumption. In the forefront of the contention on each side was, of course, the language of clause 2 (c) [4] of the lease. The question of the rent is to be referred to arbitration 'if the landlord shall so require by notice in writing given to the tenant within three months thereafter but not otherwise.' [Counsel for the landlord] understandably resorted to the dictionary. 'Otherwise,' he said, referred to manner or way or respects, and not to time. The phrase 'and not otherwise' related solely to the landlord making his requirement by a particular method, namely, by a notice in writing given to the tenant: the landlord must do it thus, and in no other way. The phrase had no reference to the words 'within three months thereafter,' for they laid down a period of time rather than a manner of doing something. [Counsel for the landlord] accepted that if these had been the only words governed by 'and not otherwise,' that phrase was wide enough in its meaning to be able to operate on them. But whereas here the phrase was preceded by words both of manner and of time, it applied only to the words of manner and not to the words of time.

For [counsel for the tenant], this approach was a selective disregard of the nearest antecedent. The phrase 'but not otherwise' immediately followed the words 'within three months thereafter': why should it leap over those words and attach itself only to the preceding words? In any case, the phrase came at the end of a compound expression, beginning with the word 'if,' and it was wide enough in its meaning to govern the whole of the compound phrase. The one way in which the landlord could obtain an arbitration was by making a requirement which in all respects (including time) satisfied clause 2 (c) [4]; he could not do it 'otherwise' or 'differently.' For good measure, [counsel for the tenant] pointed to one of the illustrations of 'otherwise' given in the *Shorter Oxford English Dictionary* on which [counsel for the landlord] relied. This was 'I went at once; otherwise I should have missed him'; and this, said [counsel for the tenant], displayed 'otherwise' as doing duty in relation to time.

[Counsel for the tenant] further contended that if the phrase 'but not otherwise' governed only manner and not time it had little or no practical effect. If the landlord made a requirement of arbitration orally or by some document not given to the tenant, he could, if the three months' time limit did not apply, cure his default as soon as it came to his notice by giving the tenant a suitable piece of paper. Why insert the emphatic 'but not otherwise' merely for this purpose? On the other hand, if those words of emphasis applied to the time limit as well, then there was some point in including them; and their purpose must be to make time of the essence.

[Counsel for the landlord] emphasised that once the trigger notice had been given in due time, both landlord and tenant knew that the rent revision machinery would operate so that if the commercial yearly rent exceeded the initial rent, there would in due course be an increase in the rent. Even if it took a long time to settle the new rent, clause 2 (a) made it run from the end of the seventh year or the quarter day next after the giving of the trigger notice, whichever was the later. There was therefore no need for the arbitration notice to be subject to a strict time limit.

Certain other points were discussed, but in the end they did not seem to me to have any great cogency. I think that I have to decide the case mainly on the basis of the arguments that I have indicated above. So far as grammar and the use of the English language is concerned, I prefer [counsel for the tenant]'s approach. The phrase 'but not otherwise' seems to me to have the broad sense of excluding all that is not comprehended in what lies between the word 'if' and the phrase 'but not otherwise,' whether it relates to manner or to time. I think that [counsel for the landlord] ascribes to the phrase too delicate and selective an import in picking on manner and rejecting time.

There also seems to be considerable force in [counsel for the tenant]'s contention that the phrase, with its inherent emphasis, has little significant function if [counsel for the landlord] is right. If it does make time of the essence for the arbitration notice (as I think it does), a sensible scheme emerges from clause 2 (c). Once the landlord has given his trigger notice, clause 2 (c) [2] allows three months for negotiation. Once that three months has run, the landlord can serve an arbitration notice. He may do it at once or he may leave the negotiations to continue. Much may depend on what the landlord thinks his prospects are from what has emerged from the negotiations. But if he is going to refer matters to arbitration, he must do so within the next three months. The time limit may well concentrate the minds and efforts of the parties and their valuers so as to avoid the expense and expenditure of time that all arbitration entails. Remove the time limit, and leisurely negotiations may well become more leisurely still, and the tenant may have the prospect of an arbitration being required left hanging over his head indefinitely. I do not for a moment say that without the time limit the clause is unworkable, but I do say that I can see why the parties might wish to impose time limits that mean what they say, and so I can see why the words 'but not otherwise' should be inserted in order to produce that result.

I should add a word on the meaning and effect of the phrase 'and not otherwise' on the footing that, as I have held, it applies to the time limit. [Counsel for the landlord] said that the 'time to be of the essence' was well-known to solicitors, and that, of course, is so. Doubtless it is in the same select gallery as 'subject to contracts,' 'without prejudice' and many other phrases sanctified by long usage in the law. If the intention was to make time of the essence, said [counsel for the landlord], it would have been easy enough to say so; but that was not done, and the phrase in fact used did not suffice. No authority, I may say, has been put before me on expressions which do suffice to make time of the essence. However, I do not think that the fame of the expression 'time to be of the essence' means that nothing else will do, and I did not understand [counsel for the landlord] to contend for so far-reaching a proposition. As far as the express wording of the document is concerned, all that seems to me to be needed is some expression which shows that the time limit is to mean what it says, and is to be obligatory and not merely indicative. The phrase 'and not otherwise' seems to me to do just that. If it does not, then it is difficult to see what it does do; and it is plainly an insertion into the normal flow of the sentence, made for emphasis, and not a phrase which has just slipped in, as it were.

In the result, the landlord's claim fails, and I dismiss the claim for the declaration sought by the originating summons.

1.2 (b) Incorporating the 'Rent Acts' into review procedures

Where a lease of residential premises contains a rent review clause providing for a 'fair rent' as at a stated date to be ascertained in accordance with the provisions of the Rent Act 1968 or its amendment or re-enactment, time will be of the essence and any assessment made some time after the stated date will be ineffective and the former rent will be payable.

McCLEOD RUSSELL (PROPERTY HOLDINGS) LTD v. EMERSON AND ANOTHER

Court of Appeal   (1985) 1 ETLR 149

The defendant tenants occupied premises under a lease dated 13 August 1975, as their home. The property was let to the tenants from 1 August 1975, for a term of seven years and thereafter from year to year at a rent of £570 pa for the first three years. The lease further provided *inter alia* that after the first three years the rent should be the fair rent as at 1 August 1978, to be ascertained in accordance with the provisions of the Rent Act 1968 or any statutory amendment or re-enactment thereof on the application of either party to the lease.

The then landlords failed to activate the review provisions. Subsequently the plaintiffs purchased the freehold and on 6 September 1979, applied for the registration of a fair rent for the property. A new fair rent was eventually fixed at £1300 pa but the tenants continued to pay at the original rent of £570 pa, contending that the notices of increased rent were totally ineffective. The plaintiff landlords brought proceedings in the county court for arrears. The county court judge gave judgment for the landlords. The tenants appealed.

Held: The appeal would be allowed. The parties had specifically agreed that from 1 August 1978, the rent should be 'the fair rent as at the first day of August 1978 to be ascertained in accordance with the provisions of the Rent Act 1968 or any statutory amendment or enactment thereof'. Therefore the parties had in effect incorporated into the lease the procedure set out in the Rent Acts in order to arrive at a fair rent, and the Rent Officer had to assess a fair rent as at the time of the application, see *Metropolitan Properties Co. (FGC) Ltd* v. *Lannon and Others* [1968] 1 All ER 354 per Widgery J at p 368. It was agreed that the fair rent as at 1 August 1978, would be substantially different from the fair rent 13 months later and the Rent Officer had no power to, and could not, assess the fair rent as at 1 August 1978, in September 1979.

Although there was a presumption that time was not of the essence in a rent review clause in the absence of any contra-indications, and here there was no time table stipulating that time should be of the essence in the lease, in order to make the review clause work it was clear that time was of the essence, because unless application for registration for a fair rent was made on or before 1 August 1978, the

Rent Officer could not assess the fair rent as at 1 August 1978. The application should have been made timeously or not at all.

HOLLIS J: It may be that an application made shortly after 1 August 1978, would have sufficed, for the fair rent would have been unlikely to have altered within a short period of time, but September 1979 was clearly too late.

The Rent Act 1977, which was in force when the applications were made to register a fair rent in 1979 and 1980, do not alter the provisions of the 1968 Act materially (see sections 67, 70 and 72 of the 1977 Act).

It therefore seems to me that the parties have in effect incorporated into the lease the procedure set out in the Rent Acts in order to arrive at a fair rent. Further the rent officer must assess a fair rent as at the time of the application—see *Metropolitan Properties Co. (FGC) Ltd* v. *Lannon and Others* [1968] 1 All ER 354 at page 368 where Mr Justice Widgery (as he then was) said:

'... I think that the principle is clear, namely, that the assessment should be made as at the date on which it is to take effect and that, therefore, it is proper to make one's calculations on the footing that what is sought to be achieved is a fair rent as at the date of the application on which registration will be effected.'

Thus the rent officer's duty was to assess a fair rent as at 6 September 1979, and it is agreed that that fair rent would be substantially different to the fair rent as at 1 August 1978. The Rent Officer had no power to, and could not, assess the fair rent as at 1 August 1978 in September 1979.

But, says [Counsel] for the appellants, time is not of the essence of such a contract as this unless the lease specifically says so, and he refers to the decision of the House of Lords in *United Scientific Holdings Ltd* v. *Burnley Borough Council* [1978] AC 904, Lord Diplock at page 930 says:

'So upon the question of principle which these two appeals were brought to settle, I would hold that in the absence of any contra-indications in the express words of the lease or in the interrelation of the rent review clause itself and other clauses or in the surrounding circumstances the presumption is that the time-table specified in a rent review clause for completion of the various steps for determining the rent payable in respect of the period following the review date is not of the essence of the contract.'

In this case there is no clause in the lease laying down a timetable or stipulating that time should be of the essence. But in order to make clause 1 work it is clear that time was of the essence, because unless the application for registration of a fair rent was made on or before 1 August 1978, the rent officer could not assess the fair rent as at 1 August 1978.

It may be that an application made shortly after 1 August 1978, would have sufficed, for the fair rent would have been unlikely to have altered within a short period of time, but September 1979 was clearly too late. The delay was not the fault of the plaintiff company itself, but it can stand in no better position than its predecessor in title.

The learned Judge held that time was not of the essence of this contract and furthermore that the application for registration of a fair rent could have been made at any time during the period of four years following the 1 August 1978. Speaking for myself I conclude that he fell into error and that in consequence his order must be set aside.

But [Counsel] for the plaintiff put forward an ingenious and attractive argument that the substantive contract was to produce a fair rent as from the 1 August 1978, and that everything else was simply machinery by which the fair rent could be assessed. As the machinery had broken down, he argued, the court could and should assess, with the help of valuers if need be, what the fair rent would have been as at 1 August 1978. He relies upon the majority decision of the House of Lords in *Sudbrook Trading Estate Ltd* v. *Eggleton and Others* [1983] 1 AC 444 in support of his submission.

That was a case where lessees exercised their option to purchase properties but the owners refused to appoint a valuer to agree a fair price in accordance with the contract. At p483 Lord Fraser of Tullybelton said this:

'I recognise the logic of the reasoning which has led to the courts' refusing to substitute their own machinery for the machinery which has been agreed upon by the parties. But the result to which it leads is so remote from that which parties normally intend and expect, and is so inconvenient in practice, that there must in my opinion be some defect in the reasoning.

I think the defence lies in construing the provisions for the mode of ascertaining the value as an essential part of the agreement. That may have been perfectly true early in the 19th century, when the valuer's profession and the rules of valuation were less well established than they are now. But at the present day these provisions are only subsidiary to the main purpose of the agreement which is for sale and purchase of the property at a fair or reasonable value.

In the ordinary case parties do not make any substantial distinction between an agreement to sell at a fair value, without specifying the mode of ascertaining the value, and an agreement to sell at a value to be ascertained by valuers appointed in the way provided in these leases.

The true distinction is between those cases where the mode of ascertaining the price is an essential term of the contract, and those cases where the mode of ascertainment, though indicated in the contract is subsidiary and non-essential: see *Fry on Specific Performance*, 6th edition (1921) p167, 169, para 360, 364. The present case falls, in my opinion, into the latter category.

Accordingly when the option was exercised there was constituted a complete contract for sale, and the clause should be construed as meaning that the price was to be a fair price. On the other hand where an agreement is made to sell at a price to be fixed by a valuer who is named, or who, by reason of holding some office such as auditor of a company whose shares are to be valued, will have special knowledge relevant to the question of value, the prescribed mode may well be regarded as essential.

Where, as here, the machinery consists of valuers and an umpire, none of whom is named or identified, it is in my opinion unrealistic to regard it as an essential term. If it breaks down there is no reason why the court should not substitute other machinery to carry out the main purpose of ascertaining the price in order that the agreement may be carried out.'

However [Counsel] for the appellants referred us to a decision of Mr Justice Fox (as he then was), *Weller* v. *Akehurst and another* reported in The Times Law Report for 28 November 1980, where he referred to *Sudbrook Trading Estate Ltd* v. *Eggleton and Others*, and then went on to say:

'Therefore, although the lease in the present case provided that the rent should be the open market value and defined that term with sufficient precision, the lease also required that its ascertainment should be effected in a particular way and stipulated that time should be of the essence in that procedure.

The parties could not have intended that if the lessor failed to observe the time provisions she should still be able to obtain the determination of the open market value by the court. For the court to take upon itself the determination of the open market value would be to fly in the face of the clearly expressed requirement of strict compliance with the time provisions. The rent review procedure was to be carried out timeously or not at all.'

I would have liked to have made an order which did justice between the parties. However I have come to the conclusion that on the facts of this case the application for registration of a fair rent should have been made timeously or not at all.

1.2 (c)   Clear words are needed to make time of the essence

THORN EMI PENSION TRUST LTD v. QUINTON HAZELL PLC

Chancery Division   (1984) 269 EG 414

A rent review clause provided that if within two months of the service of such notice the landlord and the tenant were not able to agree on a fair market rent, then, the question should 'as soon as practicable and in any event not later than four months' before the expiry of the landlord's trigger notice be referred to a surveyor for decision. The clause also permitted the landlord to serve a review notice after the review date had passed. The four months time limit expired without the parties agreeing the rent or the name of a surveyor to be nominated to act as an expert. Subsequently the landlord requested the president of the Royal Institution of Chartered Surveyors to nominate a surveyor to act. The tenant contended that time was of the essence and that the time limit for implementation of the review procedures had expired. The landlord sought a declaration that, *inter alia*, time was not of the essence.

Held: The declaration would be made. There were no contra-indications in the lease to displace the general rule that time was not of the essence. *United Scientific Holdings* v. *Burnley Borough Council etc* [1978] AC 904 and *Touche Ross & Co* v. *Secretary of State for the Environment* (1982) 265 EG 982 applied.

GOULDING J: Of course, one reported decision on a question of the interpretation of a legal instrument is never binding authority, in the absolute sense, in respect of another and different instrument. But in this case I have some unexpected guidance. Unhappily worded as the clause appears to be, it evidently has been used in a number of cases. There is a reported decision of the Court of Appeal on a rent review clause differing only in a few respects from the present case, namely, *Touche Ross & Co.* v. *Secretary of State for the Environment* (1982) 265 EG 982.

The Court of Appeal had to consider a clause which very closely resembled that now before me, though there are certain differences to which I shall refer ... Having considered and expounded the *United Scientific Holdings* decision, Dillon LJ considered the arguments before him. He paid attention to the words 'in any event', which, in that case, were in the phrase that the fair market rack rental 'shall as soon as practicable and, in any event, not later than three months after the service of the said notice' be referred for decision to a surveyor.

In the present case, of course, the same words 'in any event' occur, only here the phrase is 'not later than four months'. The learned lord justice clearly saw some force in the argument but he did not consider it decisive, particularly in view of the fact that what had to be done was reference made to a surveyor, not (he said) the service of a notice on the president, but a reference to a surveyor to be mutually agreed between the lessor and the lessee or nominated by the president.

The learned lord justice pointed out that there would be some time, necessarily, before the identity of the surveyor could be known. Therefore, in a 'fairly tight timetable' (as he called it), the ability to comply with the time-limit passed out of the hands of the parties. That, the learned lord justice thought, was some indication that time was not of the essence. He then dealt with another argument which had been addressed to him, which I do not need to repeat, and referred to certain authorities that had been cited. He concluded:

'Obviously it is undesirable that questions of whether time is of the essence in a rent review clause should depend on minute differences of language. Since there is no magical formula it is possible that small differences of language will lead in some cases to opposite conclusions.'

He declined to express any view on whether or not a certain earlier case (*Drebbond* v. *Horsham District Council* (1979) 37 P & CR 237) had been correctly decided.

The decision of the Court of Appeal in the *Touche Ross* case seems to have depended on two points: first, the 'presumption' (as Lord Diplock called it) that in such a context time is not of the essence, as established by the *United Scientific Holdings* case and, secondly, the fact that it would be difficult for a party to be sure of complying with the time-limits, since not merely had an application for the nomination of a surveyor to be made, but the question had to be referred to that expert within a short period of time. That latter element in the case persuaded the court that it was impossible to find an agreement expressed to take the matter out of the general principle laid down in the *United Scientific Holdings* case.

[Counsel] for the defendant in this case, submits that the second element is not present here. There is, indeed, a difference of language. In the *Touche Ross* case the language was that the question, in default of agreement and within a specified time

'... be referred for decision to a Surveyor to be mutually agreed between the Lessor and the Lessee or in default of agreement to be nominated on the application of either party by the President for the time being of the Royal Institution of Chartered Surveyors.'

The lease in the instant case, in the corresponding passage in clause 5 (2) (b), uses this language:

'be referred for decision to a Surveyor to be mutually agreed between the Landlord and the Tenant or in default of agreement to be nominated by the President for the time being of the Royal Institution of Chartered Surveyors.'

It will be observed that the words 'on the application of either party', which were present in the *Touche Ross* case, are absent in the instant case. Therefore, Mr Reynolds submits, it was impossible in the *Touche Ross* case to interpret the words 'referred ... to a Surveyor' as being satisfied by a request to the president to nominate a surveyor. In the instant case, those words being absent, it is possible and (Mr Reynolds submits) quite natural to interpret the word 'referred ... to a Surveyor' as being satisfied by a request to the president to nominate one.

I am unable to accept that submission. It seems to me that the language that I have interpreted in accordance with the ordinary meaning of English words clearly contemplates an actual reference within the time-limit to a surveyor whose identity is known. I do not think that the preliminary step of requesting the president to nominate a surveyor falls within the meaning of the phrase. Accordingly it seems to me that the argument based on the difficulty of complying with the time-limit where a nomination has to be obtained is available in the present case as it was in the *Touche Ross* case.

There is, however, another and more important difference between the language of the two clauses. In the *Touche Ross* case the rent review clause began:

'If the Lessor shall desire to review the rent herein before reserved on the First day of November 1981 and of such desire shall give to the Lessee not less than five calendar months' previous notice in writing ...'

In the instant case it begins:

11

'If the Landlord shall desire to review the rent hereinbefore reserved at or after the expiration of the eighth sixteenth and twenty-fifth years of the term hereby granted (or any of them) and of such desire shall give to the Tenant not less than six calendar months' previous notice in writing ...'

Those words 'or after' enable the landlord, if the 16th year already expired, still to serve a notice and not miss the opportunity of rent review altogether, although, as I read the language of the clause the revised rent will not operate retroactively. I do not want to speculate on other points of difficulty arising from those words 'or after', because they may at some time in the future become of practical importance ...

I have been unable to see why the extended right given to the landlord by the words 'or after' should make it necessary to exclude the *United Scientific Holdings* principle when one comes to consider the machinery that follows upon the trigger notice.

I think the plaintiff is right in saying that time is not of the essence in the clause in question, and that the determination of a revised rent pursuant to the notice given in the instant case can proceed.

Note: Compare *Drebbond's* case (1979) 37 P & CR 237 at 1.2 (a) above, at page 5.

1.2 (d) Collection of existing or alternative rent after review date no bar to late service of review notice if time is not of the essence

If time is not of the essence, the collection of the existing pre–review or alternative rent will present no bar to the late service of a review notice. The landlord may still be entitled to invoke the provisions of the review clause and charge the increased rent retrospectively. Mere delay will not debar the landlord from invoking the review provisions.

LONDON & MANCHESTER ASSURANCE CO. LTD v. G.A. DUNN & CO,

Court of Appeal   (1983) 265 EG 39

The tenant occupied business premises under a 21 year lease granted in 1971, which provided that the rent for the first seven years of the term should be fixed sums; for the next five years, ('the first review period'), the rent was to be £18,000 or the open market rental value. Clause 5 (2) of the lease provided that the open market rental should be specified by the lessor in a notice which was to be 'served at any time not earlier than 12 months prior to the expiration of the period of seven years in the case of the first review period'; there were then included provisions for assessment of the market rent by an independent surveyor in default of agreement, and for retrospective payment of the revised rent so fixed, should the revised rent not be ascertained by the commencement of the review period. The first review period expired on 25 December 1977 but the landlord failed to serve his notice and he subsequently sent the tenant nine quarterly rent demands based on the figure of £18,000 p.a. In March 1980 he served a notice on the tenant under clause 5 (2) and sought declarations from the court that he was entitled to have the open market rent assessed by a surveyor and charge it retrospectively. The tenant claimed that the correct rent for the first review period must be £18,000 p.a. Peter Gibson J made the declarations sought by the landlord (reported (1982) 262 EG 143). The tenant appealed.

Held: The appeal was dismissed by majority, with Lawton LJ dissenting and Oliver LJ and Slade LJ varying in their approach. Oliver LJ agreed with Peter Gibson J that the lease did not require the landlord to serve the review notice earlier than they did, but Slade LJ held that the review notice properly construed did require service before 25 December 1977, i.e. the commencement of the review period, but that as time was not of the essence it did not prevent the landlord from serving the notice late. The tenant's submissions based on common law election, estoppel, delay and alleged abandonment by the landlord of its right to seek review of the rent were rejected.

SLADE LJ: The facts of this case have been set out in the judgment of Lawton LJ. On the basis of those facts, three principal issues in my opinion arise: (1) Did clause 5 (2) (a) of the lease, on its true construction, specify a latest date by which a notice thereunder had to be served in relation to the first review period? (2) If the answer to question (1) is 'yes', was time of the essence in relation to such time-limit?

The first issue

In argument before Peter Gibson J it appears to have been accepted by counsel on both sides that the wording of clause 5 (2) (a) of the lease contains no express statement of the latest date by which a notice has to be served. The relevant phrase is 'at any time not earlier than 12 months prior to the expiration of the period of seven years in the case of the first review period immediately preceding the first review period ...' Before the learned judge it seems to have been assumed that, on a bare reading of the wording, the last 29 of these words had to be read as one composite, adjectival phrase qualifying the first three of them and that the phrases 'at any time' and 'prior to the expiration of the period of seven years' could not possibly be read together. The submission made before him on behalf of the defendants as to the point of construction, and dealt with in his judgment, was that a term should be *implied* in clause 5 (2) (a), to the effect that any notice under that subclause should be given not later than the expiry of the 12 months immediately preceding the rent review period. Peter Gibson J rejected that argument. He accepted that it would be entirely fair and reasonable for the parties to the lease to have agreed that the lessor's notice should be served by the start of the relevant review period. But, as he pointed out, it is not permissible for the court to imply a term merely because it is fair and reasonable, necessity being the appropriate test. The test is thus a difficult one to satisfy.

There is, however, another way of reading the relevant words of clause 5 (2) (a) of the lease, which does not appear to have been ventilated before Peter Gibson J in argument. This is to read the phrase 'not earlier than 12 months' as a separate adjectival phrase qualifying the phrase 'at any time'. Thus, in my opinion, the relevant words are, as a matter of language (without the need to supply any words by implication), capable of meaning either (1) at any time whatsoever in the future, provided only that such time is not earlier than 12 months before the expiration of the designated period of seven years or (2) at any time, not earlier than 12 months, before the expiration of that period.

This lease, like many other legal documents, contains no commas, but, with all deference to the contrary view held by Oliver LJ, I can see no sufficient reason why the phrase 'not earlier than 12 months' cannot as a matter of language be read as if it had been introduced and immediately followed by commas. On this footing, the relevant words would specify both an earliest date and a latest date for service of a lessor's notice.

[Counsel for] the plaintiffs pointed out that the second limb of clause 5 (2) (a), which begins with the words 'or not earlier than 12 months ...', and deals with the second and third review periods, is not prefaced by the words 'at any time'. Thus, he submitted, the phrase 'at any time', which introduces the first limb of clause 5 (2) (a), must be treated as also governing the whole of the second limb, dealing with the second and third review periods. This, he contended, made it grammatically impermissible to treat the phrase 'not earlier than 12 months', appearing in the first limb, as a separate adjectival parenthesis qualifying the phrase 'at any time'.

Skilfully though it was presented, I do not think that there is any substance in this point. If any sense is to be made of clause 5 (2) (a) as a whole, an expanded meaning has on any footing to be given to the second limb, which reads 'or not earlier than 12 months prior to the expiration of the periods of five years in the case of the second review period and the third review period as the case may be'. This second limb manifestly represents a form of abbreviation adopted by the draftsman in an attempt to avoid cumbersome repetition. On any footing the words have to be expanded in the course of construction. First, 'the periods of five years' there referred to are not explicitly defined; it is clear that the words 'immediately preceding the first review period' have, with appropriate amendments, to be read into the second limb of the subclause with reference to the second review period and the third review period respectively. Secondly, it is clear that the word 'or' has to be read into the second limb of the subclause, so that it introduces the reference to the third review period. In my opinion, the draftsman was clearly treating the words 'at any time' as being similarly read into the second limb of the subclause in relation to the second and third review periods, but similarly qualified in each case.

The subclause is not very well drafted and a process of minute grammatical analysis does not greatly advance the argument either way. The crucial words of the opening limb, as I have said, are in my opinion open to two possible interpretations. They are ambiguous and one has to look to the context to decide which of them is correct.

This lease was one of commercial premises. Its provisions relating to the payment of rent contained in the reddendum in clause 1 have already been set out in the judgment of Lawton LJ. These rents were payable by quarterly payments in advance on the four usual quarter days. Under clause 2 (1) the lessee covenanted to pay such rents 'on the days and in manner aforesaid'. Clause 3 (4), which I think should have been numbered clause 4, gave the lessor a right of re-entry 'if the rents hereinbefore reserved or any part thereof shall at any time be in arrear and unpaid for 14 days after the same shall become due (whether legally demanded or not) ...' The *reddendum* in clause 1 provided that the reviewed rents were to be 'determined in accordance with the provisions in that behalf contained in clause 5 hereof'. Clause 5 (2) contained a number of provisions which will be referred to later in this judgment and were designed to ensure that the rent review machinery, having once been set in motion, should operate with due expedition.

Against this background, without prejudice to the question whether time is of the essence for the purpose of the service of a lessor's notice under clause 5 (2) (a), the alternative construction of that subclause which in its context is more likely to represent the intention of the parties to the lease is that which treats it as designating a latest date (namely, the expiration of the previous rent-paying period) as well as an earliest date (12 months before such expiration) for the service of the notice. I think it inherently unlikely that the parties would have intended expressly to provide that the lessor should have an open-ended right 'at any time' after the stated date to serve a notice setting the rent review process in operation.

[Counsel for the plaintiffs] conceded or contended that the lessor would lose the right to serve a notice in respect of one review period as soon as the earliest date for service of a notice in respect of the next review period had arrived. While I appreciate the wisdom of this concession as a matter of advocacy, I do not see how it can be derived from the wording of clause 5 (2) (a), if that wording bears the construction which the plaintiffs place upon it. On such construction, I find it very diff.cul to place any limit on the apparently open-ended phrase 'at any time' by a process of implication, save perhaps by limiting it to the duration of the lease. The difficulties of attributing to the parties an intention to contract in the terms for which the plaintiffs contend are to my mind really insurmountable. For these reasons, I conclude that clause 5 (2) (a) on its true construction does specify a latest date by which a notice thereunder has to be served in relation to the first review period, such date being the expiration of the period of seven years therein referred to (24 December 1977).

The second issue

The conclusion just stated, if correct, of course puts a rather different complexion on the case from that which it bore as presented to Peter Gibson J. He naturally dealt with the case throughout on the footing on which it was presented to him, namely, that the lease specified no latest date for service of the relevant notice. On the footing which I think is the correct one, the lease specified a latest date; and the plaintiffs in serving their notice on 19 March 1980 were nearly 2¼ years late. Nevertheless this is far from the end of the matter.

In *United Scientific Holdings Ltd* v. *Burnley Borough Council* and *Cheapside Land Development Co. Ltd* v. *Messels Service Co.* [1978] AC 904 (which together I will call 'the *United Scientific* case') the House of Lords laid down clear rules to guide the courts in determining whether a failure to keep strictly to the timetable laid down in a rent review clause will deprive a landlord of his right to have his rent reviewed during the relevant review period. Lord Diplock stated the principle thus (at p 930 G):

'I would hold that in the absence of any contra-indications in the express words of the lease or in the interrelation of the rent review clause itself and other clauses or in the surrounding circumstances the presumption is that the timetable specified in a rent review clause for completion of the various steps for determining the rent payable in respect of the period following the review date is not of the essence of the contract.'

In the present instance, therefore, the question is whether there are sufficient contra-indications of this nature to rebut the presumption that time is not of the essence of the contract in relation to the service of a lessor's notice under clause 5 (2) (a) of the lease. For this purpose, I think it necessary to analyse the nature of the machinery for rent review embodied in clause 5 (2) (a) of the lease. The timetable envisaged by that subclause may be summarised as follows:

(1) In respect of any of the three review periods, the rent review process is to be initiated by a notice in writing served by the lessor proposing a rent for the relevant period.

(2) If, during the three months following such notice, a rent agreed between the parties in writing, in substitution for the sum proposed in the lessor's notice, that agreed sum will be the rent payable in respect of the whole of the reviewed period.

(3) If at the expiration of that three-month period no such substituted rent has been agreed between the parties, and the lessee has not served on the lessor a counternotice requiring the rent to be determined by an independent surveyor, then the rent proposed in the lessor's original notice will stand as the rent payable in respect of the whole of the reviewed period. This must be the effect of clause 5 (2) (c) and, in particular, the words 'time to be of the essence hereof'.

(4) If, during that three-month period, the lessee has served on the lessor a counternotice of the nature just mentioned, the parties then have one month within which to attempt to agree on the appointment of an independent surveyor. If during that one-month period they have failed to agree upon such appointment, then either party has the right to apply to the president of the Royal Institution of Chartered Surveyors to make the appointment so that determination may finally proceed.

The timetable envisaged by clause 5 (2) thus clearly contemplates that, in respect of any rent review period, the process of determining the open market value will have been completed within three months following the service of the lessor's 'trigger' notice under clause 5 (2) (a), unless the lessee has served a counternotice requiring the rent to be determined by an independent surveyor. In that contingency, a further delay of some weeks may elapse before the surveyor has made his determination and communicated it to both parties; but even then the delay is not likely to be a long one.

The care with which the parties to the lease stipulated for a strict timetable, once the rent review machinery had been set in motion, arguably affords some indication that they would have likewise contemplated that the lessor should adhere to the timetable which, at least on my construction, the lease specified in respect of the service of his initiating notice. There are some further possible pointers in the same direction. The form of the rent review clause was, at least in my experience, unusual in one respect. It has, I think, been common ground throughout the argument in both courts that, in view of the wording of clause 5 (1), there is no question of the surveyor, if and when appointed, being required to make an *ex post facto* determination of the rent as at the commencement of the relevant review period. He is required to determine it in accordance with the clause 5 (1) formula, but otherwise *in the light of market conditions prevailing when he makes his determination.* In this important respect, the form of the particular rent review clause is distinguishable from the superficially similar clause under consideration in *Accuba Ltd* v. *Allied Shoe Repairs Ltd* [1975] 1 WLR 1559, where it appears to have been common ground that an *ex post facto* determination of the rent as at the commencement of the review period would be required: see at p 1564 D-E per Goff J. This is a significant factor in the present case, because it means that any delay in the determination of the rent is likely to be prejudicial to the lessee, because of the customary continuing rise of market rents caused by inflation. Furthermore, the effect of the proviso to clause 5 (3) will be to render the increased rent when demanded payable retrospectively to the commencement of the review period. This is not, therefore, a case where delay is likely to provide any compensating economic advantage to the tenant such as was referred to by Lord Diplock in the *United Scientific* case at p 935 F. *Prima facie* the longer the lessor delays the greater may be the prejudice to the lessee, though I will have some further obervations to make in this context.

In the *Accuba* case it was held that time was not of the essence in regard to the service of the lessor's notice. That decision was approved by the House of Lords in the *United Scientific* case: see [1978] AC at p 936 E per Lord Diplock, at p 940 D per Viscount Dilhorne and at p 947 A per Lord Simon of Glaisdale. However, despite the superficial similarity between the rent review clauses in the *Accuba* case and the present instance, I think that a close examination of the two clauses reveals a number of material differences, of which I have already referred to one. I do not regard the approval by the House of Lords of the *Accuba* decision as by itself compelling a decision in favour of the plaintiffs on the facts of the present case.

In view of all the matters already referred to, I have found myself strongly attracted to the view that time *is* of the essence for the relevant purpose in the present case. But in the end I think this conclusion would be incorrect, for reasons which can be quite shortly stated.

To reach it would involve saying that the lessor would be wholly excluded from invoking the rent review machinery in respect of a particular review period even if it was only a day late in the service of its notice. In my opinion, however, there are at least three points which militate against such a draconian construction: First, unlike many other rent review clauses, the rent review provisions in the present case are not drafted in such a form as to suggest that the lessor is to have the right, exercisable or not at his own choice, to demand a rent review. The wording of the reddendum in clause 1 appears to assume that in respect of any review period the rent review procedure provided by clause 5 will, *in any event*, have been gone through. It refers to the reviewed rents in mandatory language. They are 'to be determined in accordance with the provisions in that behalf contained in clause 5 hereof'. And indeed, according to the strict wording of clause 1 (d), the provisions for the ascertainment of the rent payable during the second review period and the third review period will, on the face of them, be unworkable unless there has been 'a reviewed rent' governing the immediately preceding review period.

Secondly, the fact that the lease expressly provided that time was to be of the essence in respect of a lessee's counternotice under clause 5 (2) (c) but did not similarly expressly provide that time was to be of the essence in respect of a lessor's notice under clause 5 (2) (a), gives a quite powerful indication that time was not regarded as being of the essence for the latter purpose.

Thirdly, if for the reasons already stated delay in the setting in motion of the rent review machinery is likely to be prejudicial to the lessee, it can be said that the remedy lies in its own hands. As soon as a rent review period had arrived without the lessor having served the appropriate 'trigger' notice, it would, I think, be open to the lessee to give the lessor a notice specifying a period within which he required the lessor to serve a lessor's notice if he intended the 'open market value' to be determined and payable, instead of the rent of £18,000 for the first review period or the immediately preceding rent for the second and third review periods, as the case might be: see and compare *United Scientific* case at pp 933 F-934 per Lord Diplock and at p 946 E per Lord Simon. The period so specified, provided that it was reasonable, would then become of the essence of the contract and the lessee would have the means of finally ascertaining what rent he had to pay for the relevant review period.

The decision in the *United Scientific* case, I think, shows that, save in a case where a rent review clause is associated with a break clause, which gives the tenant the right to the surrender of the term on any rent review day by giving prior notice (see at p 936F), the court should be slow to construe all or any part of the timetable specified in a rent review clause as being of the essence of the contract. On balance, I do not think that the contra-indications in the present lease are sufficient to displace the presumption that time is not of the essence for the purpose of the lessor's notice under clause 5 (2) (a) and I would so hold.

1.3 (a) Procedures to appoint a valuer to ascertain the revised rent—whether time is of the essence—whether effective without service of trigger notice

Even though a rent review clause may provide a strict timetable for a part of the rent review provisions, e.g. the earlier stages in a rent review provision, if there is a subsequent provision (in regard to which time is not of the essence), and which is to operate after the time allowed for in the earlier strict stages has passed, the landlord is entitled to invoke it at that point without having in fact complied with the earlier stages in time and without serving a trigger notice.

LAING INVESTMENT CO. LTD v. G.A. DUNN & CO.

Chancery Division   (1982) 262 EG 879

A lease had a three-stage process for ascertainment of revised rent. The first two stages of the machinery contained strict time limits and those time periods had to have passed before the third stage, an application to the president of the Royal Institution of Chartered Surveyors for the appointment of a surveyor to fix a new rent, could commence. This third stage was not subject to a specified time limit, nor was a time specified for the determination of the rent by the surveyor appointed. The landlords did not go through the procedures contemplated for the first two stages, but applied to the president of the RICS for the appointment of a surveyor. The tenants contended that neither party was entitled to disregard the first two stages with their strict time limits and then to initiate the third stage of the process. The landlords sought a declaration that they were entitled to apply for the appointment of a surveyor to determine the rent under the review machinery.

Held: The landlord was entitled to invoke the application for a surveyor since express provisions would have been necessary if the initiation of the rent review procedures was a matter of crucial importance, so as to make it clear that the lessor or lessee wanting a review would lose his rights if no step were taken by that date. There was no express provision in the third stage and indeed there was a striking contrast between express provisions making time of the essence and what was sought to be implied. *Amherst* v. *James Walker Goldsmith & Silversmith Ltd* [1983] 3 WLR 334 followed (see later page 28); *Beer* v. *Bowden* [1981] 1 WLR 522 considered, [see later, page 22]).

PETER GIBSON J: *Amherst* v. *James Walker Goldsmith & Silversmith Ltd* also concerned the construction of a rent review clause. The lease was for a term of 28 years. The rent for the first 14 years was fixed at £2500 per annum, but for the second period of 14 years beginning on 24 June 1975 it was provided that the annual rent should be either £2500 or such higher yearly rent as should be ascertained in accordance with a proviso which provided for an assessment to be made in the following manner, that is to say:

'(a) Such assessment shall be made in the first instance by the lessor and submitted to the lessee for approval in writing on or before the twenty-fifth day of December one thousand nine hundred and seventy-four; (b) In the event of the parties hereto failing to reach such agreement as aforesaid on or before the date appointed (in respect of which time is to be deemed to be of the essence of the contract) then the yearly rent for the second period shall be fixed or assessed by an independent surveyor appointed for that purpose by the parties hereto failing agreement as to such appointment by the twenty-fifth day of January one thousand nine hundred and seventy-five (time in this respect to be deemed to be of the essence of the contract) then by an independent surveyor appointed for that purpose by the President for the time being of the Royal Institution of Chartered Surveyors.'

The second sentence in proviso (b) was similar to the second sentence in proviso (b) of the lease before me. The report in the *Amherst* case does not show what was proviso (c) in that clause. So it is not clear whether it contained a forfeiture provision as in proviso (c) in the present case. But proviso (d) was similar to proviso (e) in the present case.

As is apparent, the rent review provisions in the *Amherst* case differed from those in the present case in that there was an express provision that the rent review was to be initiated by the lessor submitting an assessment to the lessee and that that submission was to be by a particular date which the court held was the same date as 'the date appointed', that is to say 25 December 1974. The lessor on 25 June 1975 wrote to the lessee asking for agreement as to the surveyor but indicating that he was applying to the president for the examination of a surveyor and the lessor also suggested negotiating the rent. The question in that case was whether time was of the essence of the time-limit for the submission by the lessee of his assessment.

The provisions of that lease resembled those of the present case in that (1) the assessment provisions are introduced by the prefatory words 'in the following manner' as with the present lease, (2) a three-stage procedure is laid down, in respect of two of which stages time is expressly made of the essence, and in the last stage of which no time-limit is prescribed. Again these exactly match the present case. Again time is made of the essence of two matters to be agreed between the parties by a particular time.

Judge Mervyn Davies QC (sitting as a deputy High Court judge) held that time was not of the essence of the time-limit for the submission of the lessor's notice. On appeal the Court of Appeal agreed with him. Sir David Cairns, giving the leading judgment, first found significance in the fact that time had been made of the essence of some provisions but not of others. Second he rejected as inconsistent with the speeches of the majority of the House of Lords in the *United Scientific Holdings* case a submission by the tenants advanced by their counsel, that the fact that the trigger notice could be operated by the landlord alone made time of the essence of the time-limit in respect thereof. He then continued thus, at p 125:

'So far as other matters are concerned, I think that the most effective part of Mr Moshi's argument before us was to this effect that, unless we hold that the taking of the first step was one which had to be taken by a specified date, the lessee was put in difficulty in relation to the later steps, because there was a fixed date which could not be departed from, because it was provided to be of the essence of the contract, up to which he was entitled to agree either as to the amount put forward by the landlord for the rent or as to the surveyor who was to be appointed to fix that rent. The difficulty of that argument appears to me to be this, that, putting it at its highest assuming that it could be said that the period for the 'trigger' notice was subject to an absolute limit of December 25, there is certainly nothing in the agreement to say that it must be given before 25 December. If the date is to be of the essence of the contract at all, it is on or before 25 December; it is quite impossible to put it at a reasonable time before 25 December. So that, in effect, even if it were regarded as being of the essence of the contract, the position is that, if the notice were given by the landlord at the last moment, one would immediately be into what may be called the second stage.

It seems to me that the true meaning of this lease is that, if the notice is not given by 25 December, it can still be given at a later date. It may well be that the later date would have to be within a reasonable time, but as to that I express no more than a tentative opinion. But if notice is given thereafter and if it is not given so late that it can be said it was not given within a reasonable time and that that makes it invalid, then the position would be that, indeed, in effect, the second and third stages are concertinaed and we come straight on to the position where either party can go straight to the president of the RICS and ask for the appointment of an independent surveyor.

That I think is the meaning and effect of the agreement between the parties ...'

Eveleigh LJ agreed, saying that he found some difficulty in seeing that in a case like the one before him a trigger notice had any real part to play, certainly once the date specified in the lease had passed. Megaw LJ also agreed. He said, at p 129:

'I should have expected that, if the intention had been that for which [counsel for the tenants] contends, the latest date by which the lessor was required to give his assessment would have been expressly stated and not left to be, by implication, a reasonable time before 25 December; and the clause would, by its express terms, have made it clear that, if that action was not taken within that time, the lessor would lose his rights.

Thus in the *Amherst* case, although the parties had expressly agreed that the initiating step should be taken by 25 December 1974 and all that was being asked of the court was to imply a term that time should be of the essence in respect of that time-limit, the court refused to do so. In the present case, as I have said, [counsel for the tenant] is asking the court to imply not only that the initiating step should be taken by 19 July 1980 but also that time is of the essence thereof.

[Counsel for the tenant] distinguishes the *Amherst* case by saying that it was simply an application of the principle of *expressio unius exclusio alterius*. In effect, he says, the lease in the *Amherst* case spelt out that there was to be a trigger provision exercisable by the lessor at any time and he says that is very different from a case such as the present where no trigger notice at all is provided. He says that the justification for implying a term for an initiating step, that is to say that otherwise the stipulations as to time would be pointless and the forfeiture provision could cause severe hardship on the tenant, is also the justification for implying a term that time should be of the essence thereof. The two go together. He cited *Beer* v. *Bowden* [1981] 1 WLR 522 as an illustration of the court's approach to implying terms in a rent review clause. In that case the relevant provision of the lease was 'such rent as shall thereupon be agreed between the landlords and the tenant'. The court implied the word 'fair' between the words 'such' and 'rent'.

As Buckley LJ put it at p 528 D:

'If some such implication is not made, it seems to me that this would be a completely inoperative rent review provision, because it is not to be expected that the tenant would agree to an increase in the rent if the rent to be agreed was absolutely at large. Clearly the parties contemplated that at the end of five years some adjustment might be necessary to make the position with regard to the rent a fair one, and the rent review provision with which we are concerned was inserted in the lease to enable such an adjustment to be made. The suggestion that upon the true construction of the clause it provides that the rent shall continue to be at the rate of £1250 a year unless the parties otherwise agree would, in my opinion, render the provision entirely inoperative, because, as I say, one could not expect the tenant voluntarily to agree to pay a higher rent.'

I do not see how in the present case one could say that the rent review provisions would be rendered completely inoperative if [counsel for the tenant]'s terms were not implied. The rent review provisions would of course work if the express time-limits were adhered to and if they were not there is the fail-safe procedure for determining a rent, that is to say either party could go to the president for the nomination of a surveyor to assess the rent, and the landlord can compel the tenant's concurrence in such a step. In my judgment, therefore, *Beer* v. *Bowden* does not provide any principle that is applicable in the present case.

It seems to me that it would be a very surprising consequence if in a lease containing such similarities of language to the *Amherst* lease the lessor would find itself in a worse position than the lessor in the *Amherst* case who failed to comply with an express provision as to time, whereas the lessor in the present case was under no express obligation to take an initiating step. Like Megaw LJ in the *Amherst* case, I would have expected express provisions if the initiation of the rent review procedure by 19 July 1980 was intended to be a matter of crucial importance, so as to make it clear that the lessor or lessee wanting a review would lose his rights if no step were taken by that date. Again as in the *Amherst* case the contrast between what is sought to be implied and the express provisions making time of the essence is very striking. Further there is the same difficulty in the present case in implying that the initiating step should be made by the date by which agreement had to be reached between the parties as to rent as there was in the *Amherst* case in respect of the trigger notice. To serve a trigger notice or to take an initiating step on or shortly before the date in question as a practical matter makes it impossible to reach agreement by that date.

Of course the Court of Appeal did not have the benefit of the arguments that [counsel for the tenant] has put with such skill and lucidity to me but that court does not appear to have been troubled by the fact that time-limits in respect of which the parties had laid such heavy emphasis by making time of the essence thereof could in effect be ignored by the concertinaing of the successive stages. In the light of the approach of the Court of Appeal and consistently with the *Amherst* case it seems to me that I would not be justified in holding that necessity requires the implication of a term.

In the result I shall make the declarations requested in the originating summons in the following form:

1. A declaration that upon a true construction of clause 1 of the subunderlease the plaintiff is now entitled to apply and to require the defendant to concur in applying to the president of the Royal Institution of Chartered Surveyors to appoint an independent valuation surveyor to assess the fair market rent for the premises thereby demised for the period of seven years following 19 March 1981.

2. A declaration that the rent so assessed by the said surveyor or £2750, whichever shall be the higher, shall be the yearly rent payable by the defendant for the said period.

The plaintiffs were awarded costs.

Where the provisions in a review clause provide that there is a time limit for the application of the parties for the nomination of an expert valuer and the question has to be referred to the expert within a short period of time, the court will find it impossible to infer that such provisions are outside the general rule that time is not of the essence.

TOUCHE ROSS & CO. v. SECRETARY OF STATE FOR THE ENVIRONMENT

Court of Appeal   (1983) 265 EG 982

The review clause in a lease provided machinery for revising the rent payable and further,

> 'if within two calendar months after service by the lessor ... the lessor and lessee have been unable to agree upon a fair market rack rental ... the question of what is a fair market rack rental ... shall as soon as practicable and in any event not later than three months after service of the ... notice be referred for decision to a surveyor'

to be mutually agreed between the parties or nominated by the President of the Royal Institution of Chartered Surveyors. No reference was made to any surveyor within the three months' time limit referred to. In the High Court, Judge Finlay QC held that time was of the essence and that the landlords had lost their rent review by failure to comply with the time limit. The landlords appealed.

Held: The appeal would be allowed. If the clause had simply said that 'the question shall as soon as practicable be referred for decision to a surveyor', there would have been no doubt that time was not of the essence. Equally, if the clause had simply said that 'the question shall within three months after the service of the landlords' notice be referred' time would not have been of the essence. The running of those two phrases into a composite phrase as used in the clause therefore did not suggest that time was to be of the essence. Further, against any conclusion that the time limit was to be obligatory, was the fact that the clause provided for a reference to a surveyor, not service of a notice on the president. This procedure could take some time and would be out of the control of the parties. *Drebbond Ltd* v. *Horsham District Council* (1979) 37 P & CR 237 distinguished, (see earlier, page 5).

DILLON LJ: Subclause (a) reads as follows:

> 'if the Lessor shall desire to review the rent hereinbefore reserved on the first day of November 1981 and of such desire shall give to the Lessee not less than five calendar months previous notice in writing then on the first day of November 1981 for the residue of the term hereby granted the rent shall be revised and shall be such an annual sum as may be agreed between the Lessor and the Lessee or as may be determined as provided by the following subclauses of this present clause

to be the fair market rack rental of the demised premises Provided that in no circumstances shall the rent payable hereunder following such review be less than the rent payable by the Lessee at the date of the Lessor's notice calling for the review.'

In fact the Lessor duly gave a notice under subclause (a) on 22 May 1981 which was in due time.

Subclause (b), which is the most important subclause for present purposes, reads as follows:

'if within two calendar months after the service by the Lessor of the notice referred to in subclause (a) of this present clause the Lessor and the Lessee have been unable to agree upon a fair market rack rental (as defined by subclause (c) of this present clause) then the question of what is a fair market rack rental of the demised premises shall as soon as practicable and in any event not later than three months after the service of the said notice be referred for decision to a Surveyor to be mutually agreed between the Lessor and the Lessee or in default of agreement to be nominated on the application of either party by the President for the time being of the Royal Institution of Chartered Surveyors.'

It is then provided that the surveyor is to act as an expert and his decision is to be binding. The subclause ends by saying:

'The fair market rack rental as so agreed or determined shall subject to the proviso contained in subclause (a) of this present clause be the annual rent payable hereunder for the residue of the term in lieu of the rent payable immediately before the said review.'

What happened is that no reference was made to any surveyor within the three months' time-limit referred to in that subclause. The question is whether time is of the essence of that time-limit. The learned judge held that it was of the essence, and that the landlords (the plaintiffs) had lost their rent review by the failure to comply with that time-limit. It is against that decision that the landlords appeal.

The reason why the House of Lords (in *United Scientific Holdings Ltd* v. *Burnley Borough Council* [1978] AC 904) reached the conclusion that *prima facie* time is not of the essence under a rent review clause was that the detriment to the landlord of losing his review altogether by failure to adhere strictly to a time-limit was wholly disproportionate to the disadvantage to the tenant of a delay in the assessment of the rent. However, the House of Lords recognised that it was competent to the parties to a lease to agree that time should be of the essence either of the whole timetable or of any particular stage or step under the timetable. [Counsel] for the Secretary of State, has pointed out correctly that there is no magical formula which alone achieves the result of making time of the essence of a contract and he has said, again I think correctly, that what is necessary is something which shows that the time-limit is obligatory and means what it says.

In the present case the relevant words in subclause (b) are that

'the question of what is a fair market rack rental of the demised premises shall as soon as practicable and in any event not later than three months after the service of the said notice be referred for decision to a Surveyor to be mutually agreed between the Lessor and the Lessee or in default of agreement to be nominated on the application of either party by the President for the time being of the Royal Institution of Chartered Surveyors.'

As against any conclusion that the time-limit is obligatory, there is the factor that what has to be done is a reference to a surveyor—not the service of a notice on the president but a reference to a surveyor to be mutually agreed between the lessor and lessee or nominated by the president. If the surveyor is mutually agreed he is an identified person from the moment of agreement and the reference is then to be to him after there has been agreement that he is to be the surveyor to decide the question. If there is to be reference to a surveyor to be nominated by the president then the president has to name a surveyor and there can be no reference to that surveyor until he has been named. This means that matters pass, on a fairly tight timetable, out of the hands of the parties, because, apart from any question that the president may not be immediately available to act on the parties' request to him to nominate a surveyor, he has to find a surveyor who will be willing to undertake the task. That of itself may take a certain amount of time and is wholly outside the control of the parties.

It has been submitted that in the present case the detriment to the lessee, if time is held not to be of the essence and there can be a late reference to a surveyor, is greater than it could have been in either of the cases which the House of Lords had to decide in the *United Scientific Holdings* case, because under the definition of 'fair market rack rental' in subclause (c) of the rent review clause the rent is to be fixed at the date of determination. If, therefore, there is delay in a period of inflation the surveyor will fix a higher rent than would have been fixed if the reference to him had been at an earlier date before the latest assumed advance in inflation. But that is partly, at any rate, mitigated by the fact that the reference to the surveyor can be made by the lessee alone if the lessor is not prompt to act, at any rate where, as here, the lessor has instituted the rent review procedure by serving a notice under subclause (a). It is a factor to be taken into account that there may be detriment to the lessee from a delay in invoking the clause but it is only one factor. Taking the clause as a whole, I conclude that the wording of the clause is by no means enough to make time of the essence of this step in the procedure. Therefore, with all respect to the learned judge, I think he reached a wrong conclusion on the construction and effect of this clause ...

The other case to which we were referred was the decision of the present Vice-Chancellor in *Drebbond Ltd* v. *Horsham District Council* decided in 1979 and reported in (1979) 37 P & CR 237 [reported also at (1978) 246 EG 1013]. That is a case that was concerned with the interpretation of a rent review clause after the decision in the *United Scientific Holdings* case. The clause in question provided that the landlord should be entitled by notice in writing given to the tenant within the last six months before the expiration of the seventh and 14th year respectively of the term, to call for a review of the yearly rent payable under the lease and there was provision as to what was to happen if upon any such review it should be found that the commercial rent was greater than the initial rent. The clause went on to provide that the review should, in the first instance, be made by the landlord and the tenant, or their respective surveyors, in collaboration, but if no agreement as to the adjustment (if any) which should be made in the yearly rent should have been reached between the parties or the surveyors within three months after the date of the landlord's notice calling for such revision, the question as to the commercial yearly rent of the demised premises, and certain other questions, should

'if the landlord shall so require by notice in writing given to the tenant within three months thereafter but not otherwise be referred to the decision of a sole arbitrator to be appointed, in default of agreement between the parties, by the president for the time being of the Royal Institution of Chartered Surveyors'.

The learned Vice-Chancellor held that the words 'if the landlord shall so require by notice in writing given to the tenant within three months thereafter but not otherwise' had the effect of making time of the essence for taking that step and as the landlord failed to give the notice within the three months' time-limit the landlord had lost his rent review.

Naturally [counsel] for the Secretary of State, submits that there is not really very much difference between a phrase 'if the landlord shall require within a certain time but not otherwise' and a phrase that 'there is to be a reference in any event by the expiration of a certain time'. However, there are considerable differences in the schemes of the clauses in these two cases. In particular it was the landlord who had to give the notice in the *Drebbond* case and the tenant could do nothing about it. The notice which the landlord had to give within the time-limit was merely a notice to the tenant which did not expose the landlord to losing his review because of factors outside his own control and the limits of the timetable were more relaxed than in the present case. Obviously it is undesirable that questions of whether time is of the essence of a rent review clause should depend on minute differences of language. Since there is no magical formula it is possible that small differences of language will lead in some cases to opposite conclusions. I do not need to express any view either way on whether the *Drebbond* case was rightly decided on the terms of the lease which the court had to consider in that case. I merely say that I find nothing in the *Drebbond* case to lead me to the conclusion that the time-limit in the present case in subclause (b) is obligatory and of the essence of the contract.

I would allow this appeal.

LAWTON LJ and GRIFFITHS LJ agreed and did not deliver separate judgments.

In Lewis v. Barnett and Another (1982) 264 EG 1079 a rent review clause in a lease provided that in the absence of agreement on a new rent by a certain date the landlord was entitled to apply for the appointment of a surveyor to the President of the Royal Institution of Chartered Surveyors. The clause stated that if the landlord failed to make such an application in time the original trigger notice was void and of no effect; the lease had to be construed as a whole and it was clear that time was of the essence.

STEPHENSON LJ: This appeal arises out of rent review clauses in two leases which were granted by the respondent, Mr Barnett, to a Mr Lewis (that was a lease granted in 1970) and a lease granted to the predecessors in title of Mr and Mrs Scarborough.

The two leases set out a time-table in similar terms for the procedure of reviewing the rent and it is therefore only necessary to deal with one lease and one appeal. At [Counsel's] invitation on behalf of all three appellant tenants we take Mr Lewis' lease and what we decide about that determines what is done about the other lease.

What is asked for in [Counsel's] notice of appeal on behalf of these tenants is a declaration:

'that a notice dated 23 June 1977 given by the defendant as landlord to the plaintiff as tenant under a lease dated 10 December 1970 for the purposes of a rent review to have effect from 1 December 1977 is void having regard to the failure of the defendant to procure the President of the Royal Institution of Chartered Surveyors of (*sic*) an arbitrator for the purposes of determining the said rent by 1 September 1977 ...'

The question for decision arises on the terms of the two leases.

The first relevant provision is clause 1, which demises the premises for a term of 21 years from and including 1 December 1970 at a rent during the first seven years of £1380 and during the remainder of the said term the yearly rent (that is £1380 a year) or such other rent or rents as may become payable under and by virtue of the provisions of the third schedule thereto by equal quarterly payments in every year without any deduction, the first of such payments being due and payable on 1 December 1970.

Turning to the third schedule, by para 1 that gives the following meanings to two expressions. The 'rent review dates' are 1 December 1977 and 1 December 1984 and 'the open market rent' is:

'The yearly rent for which the demised premises might reasonably be expected to be let with vacant possession on the rent review dates in the open market by a willing lessor for a term equal to the unexpired residue on the rent review dates of the term hereby granted and otherwise upon the terms and conditions (save as to the amount of rent payable) contained in this deed ...'

Then there are three matters disregarded. Paras 2 and 3 provide:

'2. If at any time not more than twelve and not less than nine months before the rent review dates the landlord shall give notice in writing to the tenant of his desire to vary the yearly rent payable hereunder as from the rent review dates such yearly rent shall from and after the rent review dates be whichever is the higher of:
(a)   the yearly rent reserved hereunder immediately before the rent review dates and—
(b)   the open market rent.
3.   If the landlord and the tenant shall not have agreed the open market rent not less than six months before the rent review dates the open market rent shall be determined by a surveyor (hereinafter called 'the appointed surveyor') to be agreed upon in writing by the landlord and the tenant not less than four months before the rent review dates and in default of such agreement to be nominated by the President for the time being of the Royal Institution of Chartered Surveyors upon the application of the landlord to be made not less than three months before the rent review dates.'

Para 4 is immaterial. Paras 5 and 6 provide:

'5.   If on the rent review dates the open market rent shall not have been agreed or determined as aforesaid the yearly rent reserved hereunder immediately before the rent review date shall continue to be payable until the determination of the open market rent by the appointed surveyor but so that immediately on demand after such determination the excess difference (if any) over the amount actually so reserved and the amount which would have been payable had the determination been made before the rent review dates shall be paid by the tenant to the landlord and if not so paid shall be recoverable as rent in arrear.
6.   If the landlord and the tenant shall not have agreed the open market rent at least six months before the rent review date and the landlord shall neglect to make the application referred to in para 3 hereof then (unless the parties hereto shall in writing agree otherwise) any notice already given by the landlord to the tenant under the provisions of para 2 hereof shall be void and of no effect.'

It is conceded that the first notice, the notice under para 2 of the landlord's desire to vary the yearly rent, was not given in time. It should have been given by 1 March 1977, but it was not given until 23 June 1977, when it was given by letter in a form which was conceded to be adequate. The procedure that had then to be followed after the notice had been given of the landlord's desire to vary the yearly rent was, under para 3, that the open market rent should be agreed. That had to be done not less than six months before the rent review date. If it were not done, then a surveyor had to be appointed. If he could not be appointed by agreement not less than four months before the rent review date (in this case 1 December 1977) he had to be nominated by the president of the Royal Institution of Chartered Surveyors and, to be nominated by the president, there had to be an application by the landlord to the president to nominate a surveyor and that application had to be made by the landlord not less than three months before the rent review date. Again, it is common ground that the earlier of the two dates on which the application was made to the president was 13 March 1978—again, not in time. The application ought to have been made not later than 1 September 1977.

It was argued on behalf of the tenant before the learned county court judge and has been argued before us that, on those uncontradicted facts and on the true construction of the lease, the notice which the landlord gave under para 2 was void and of no effect, not because it was given out of time but because, first of all, the landlord and the tenant had not agreed the open market rent at least six months before 1 December 1977 and, secondly, the landlord had neglected to make the application to the president to appoint a surveyor before the three months from 1 December 1977 expired. It was submitted that, on the plain words of para 6, that para showed an agreement before the parties that the landlord's neglect to make that application until too late invalidated his notice under para 2 of his desire to vary the rent. The learned judge rejected that submission and was persuaded by [counsel for the landlord], in what must have been an extremely able argument, to achieve that result by regarding not the notice to vary the rent as void and of no effect but para 6 as void and of no effect.

The learned judge was rightly referred to the decision of the House of Lords in *United Scientific Holdings Ltd* v. *Burnley Borough Council* reported in [1978] AC 904. That decision reversed two decisions of this court and held that there was a presumption that the time-table provided in leases for reviews of rent did not make time of the essence of the contract. . .

The learned judge then went on to consider para 6 and said: 'The question is, are these two periods ...' that is the period of at least six months before the rent review date for agreeing the open market rent and the period of not less than three months before the rent review date for making the landlord's application to the president of the Royal Institution of Chartered Surveyors

'... of the essence of the contract? If you cut out para 6, time was not of the essence, in view of what Lord Diplock said. Does para 6 make time of the essence? In view of the recent House of Lords' finding in *United Scientific* v. *Burnley Council* I feel that in the absence of an express term in paras 2 and 3 of the third schedule, stating that time shall be of the essence, and in the absence of any common law notice, clause 6 must be of no effect. Therefore, with some regret, I find for the landlord.'

With all respect for the learned judge it seems to me that, in posing the question 'are there any express terms in the lease which make time of the essence?', he was not asking the right question; nor was he right to look in consequence at paras 2 and 3 for an express term there stating that time shall be of the essence. What he had to do was to construe the lease as a whole and to direct his mind to the question what the effect of para 6 was, read with all the other provisions of the lease, including, in particular, paras 2 and 3 to which it expressly refers.

I have not the smallest hesitation in saying that no principle of construction and no authority of any court compels or even justifies a judge in finding one paragraph in a written document (in this case a sealed lease) to have no effect. Effect must be given to the paragraph if it possibly can be. That was the basis on which the learned judge rejected the tenant's application. I am not surprised that [counsel for the landlord], without a respondent's notice (though I do not think he needs one: it is just a question of construction), asks this court to affirm the judge's judgment on a less paradoxical ground. [Counsel for the landlord] says that some effect must be given to para 6, but he submits that para 6 is careful to refer to the period of 'at least six months' in the opening words 'If the landlord and the tenant shall not have agreed the open market rent at least six months before the rent review date'; but is careful to omit any reference to the period of 'not less than three months' from the following words importing the second condition for nullifying and voiding any notice under the provisions of para 2, namely, that the 'landlord shall neglect to make the application referred to in para 3 ...'. He says that omission is deliberate and it is a necessary condition of a notice being voided by para 6 that the landlord should have neglected to make the application referred to in para 3 at any time, or at any reasonable time, or at any time which will not prejudice the tenant. He submits that if that construction is given to the paragraph it will still take effect where the landlord fails to make any application to the president when the circumstances for making that application arise, or fails to apply to the president after the tenant has given a common law notice making time of the essence, such a notice as indicated by Lord Diplock and Lord Salmon in the *United Scientific* v. *Burnley Council* case to be necessary to make time of the essence in a rent review time-table. Their lordships there suggested that the best way for tenants in the future to secure that time was of the essence for a time-table for a rent review was to say so in express words in the lease. It is no doubt that expression of opinion by Lords Diplock and Salmon in the *United Scientific* v. *Burnley Council* case which led the learned judge in this case to put the question he had to consider and his judgment in the way in which he did.

These leases were, of course, drawn up and executed before the decision of the House of Lords in that case, but nevertheless the tenants may have achieved indirectly the result that express words would have achieved by, in Lord Diplock's words, 'contra-indications in the express words of the lease'.

In my judgment, in spite of [counsel for the landlord]'s submissions, that is exactly what they have done. I cannot regard the omission of the reference to time from the reference to the landlord's application as having the effect for which [counsel for the landlord] contends. It seems to me that when the draftsman of this paragraph referred to the landlord's neglect to make the application referred to in para 3, he was referring, without setting out all the words, to his application to make it not less than three months before the rent review dates, because that is the application which the landlord has to make in para 3. He might have omitted the words 'at least six months before the rent review date' in the second line of the para if he had wished to be equally concise. In my judgment para 6 means what it says and what it says is that, if the landlord neglects to comply with para 3 in respect of the application there referred to in a case where he and the tenant have not been able to agree the open market rent in the time required, or at all, then any notice already given by the landlord to the tenant under the provisions of para 2, including the all-important opening notice, shall be void and of no effect. In my judgment, neither on the basis of the learned judge's judgment that para 6 was of no effect nor on the more plausible basis of [counsel for the landlord]'s construction of the para, can the learned judge's judgment be upheld.

For these reasons I would allow both appeals, set aside the learned judge's judgment in both cases and make the declarations asked for in both notices of appeal, stopping at the word 'void'. In other words the declarations in each case should be that a notice dated 23 June 1977 given by the defendant as landlord to the plaintiff as tenant under the lease for the purposes of a rent review to have effect from 1 September 1977 is void. [Counsel for the landlord] made the point that the notice of appeal added the words 'having regard to the failure of the defendant to procure the president (it must be "to appoint") an arbitrator for the purposes of determining the rent', without mentioning the date at which the application to appoint the president was made or ought to have been made. I do not think the addition helps the landlord and I would omit it.

Note: This case was considered and followed in *Henry Smith's Charity Trustees* v. *AWADA Trading and Promotion Services Ltd* (1984) 269 EG 729, CA at page 60, later.

1.3 (b) An application for the appointment of an expert is valid even though manifestly only made to comply with time limits while negotiations continue

An application to the President of the RICS which is made to comply with strict time limits in a review clause will be effective even if this intention is manifested in the application letter and the application is unaccompanied by the fee required by the RICS for processing of the application to begin, and thus made contrary to RICS Guidance Notes: *Staines Warehousing Co. Ltd* v. *Montagu Executor & Trustee Co. Ltd and Another* (1986) 277 EG 305— see Appendix).

1.4 (a) Delay—the right to review cannot be lost by 'abandonment'

Mere delay, however lengthy, does not bar the landlord from implementing his rent review procedures; the right cannot be lost by 'abandonment'.

AMHERST v. JAMES WALKER GOLDSMITH & SILVERSMITH LTD

Court of Appeal [1983] 3 WLR 334

A lease provided for a rent review to be initiated by the landlord serving a rent assessment notice on the tenants by 25 December 1974. The landlord failed to serve a notice by that date and the tenants refused a request by the landlord to extend the time and allow the rent review to proceed. But in proceedings commenced by the landlord in October 1978 it was held that time was not of the essence in regard to the initiation of the rent review, and in May 1979 the landlord served the tenants with a notice assessing a revised rent. The validity of that notice being disputed, the landlord sought a declaration that he was entitled to such rent as was determined pursuant to the rent review provisions of the lease notwithstanding the delay in serving a notice. The judge held that in the absence of prejudice to the tenants the delay, though unreasonable, did not prevent the landlord from relying on the rent review provisions and he granted the declaration. On appeal by the tenants:

Held: Dismissing the appeal, that, time not being of the essence, mere delay, however lengthy, could not preclude the landlord from exercising his contractual right to invoke the rent review provisions; and that (*per* Lawton and Oliver LJJ) there was no justification for reading into the lease any implied term that, the time stipulation in regard to the rent assessment notice not being of the essence, the landlord had to serve the notice within a reasonable time.

Telegraph Properties (Securities) Ltd v. *Courtaulds Ltd* (1980) 257 EG 1153 overruled.

Dicta of Slade LJ in *London & Manchester Assurance Co. Ltd* v. *G.A. Dunn & Co.* (1983) 265 EG 39 (see later, page 30) applied.

Per Lawton and Oliver LJJ. (i) Even delay plus hardship to the tenants would not disentitle the landlord to exercise the right which he has, on the true construction of the contract, unless the combination amounted to an estoppel.

(ii) The concept of abandonment is not apt in rent review cases.

OLIVER LJ: Essentially, as it seems to me, the question is one of construction not of remedies and what one has to ask is whether, as a matter of construction of the contract, compliance with the time stipulation is so essential to the contract that any

28

failure to comply with it entitles the other party, without more, to treat the contract as repudiated. Of course, that does not mean either that the contract is to be treated for all purposes as if the time had never been mentioned or that, when it comes to exerting any remedies for breach of contract, the ordinary rules of specific performance are suspended or abrogated. Thus, albeit the contract is not to be construed as if time were essential, damages may still be obtained for failure to comply with the fixed date for completion if damage can be shown: see *Raineri* v. *Miles* [1981] AC 1050.

Equally where, as a matter of construction, time is not of the essence, it does not follow that the party in default may not, by extensive delay or other conduct, disentitle himself from having it specifically performed: see, e.g., *Cornwall* v. *Henson* [1900] 2 Ch 298 and *M.E.P.C. Ltd* v. *Christian-Edwards* [1978] Ch 281.

But the question of how the contract should be construed and the question of whether a party in default may have deprived himself of a right to rely on the contract must now, in my judgment, be treated as logically distinct and separate questions, whatever may be the historical origin of the rule of construction.

[Counsel for the tenant]'s submission treats the service of a renewal notice after the time stipulated as a submission to the court of the issue whether or not the contract should be performed. But the landlord, in serving notice, is not invoking the aid of the court to perform the contract. He is exercising the right which the contract, as properly construed, confers upon him. If it is to be construed in the sense that time is of the essence, he has no right to serve the notice. If it is not, then the right subsists, unless the tenant can show either that the contract, or that part of the contract, has been abrogated or that the landlord has precluded himself from exercising it. He may do that by showing that the contract has been repudiated—for instance, where he has served a notice calling upon the landlord to exercise his right within a reasonable time or not at all and such notice is ignored—or that some event has happened which estops the landlord from relying on his right. But I know of no ground for saying that mere delay, however lengthy, destroys the contractual right. It may put the other party in a position where, by taking the proper steps, he may become entitled to treat himself as discharged from his obligation; but that does not occur automatically and from the mere passage of time. I know of no authority for the proposition that the effect of construing a time stipulation as not being of the essence is to substitute a fresh implied term that the contract shall be performed within a reasonable time and even if such a term is to be substituted the passage of a reasonable time would not automatically abrogate the contract. It is, I think, important to distinguish between that which entitles a party to treat the contract as at an end and that which entitled the party not in default to enforce it. No one contests that, once the stipulated date is passed, proceedings may be instituted to enforce the agreement (see, e.g., *Woods* v. *Mackenzie Hill Ltd* [1975] 1 WLR 613), but that is quite a different question.

In my judgment, therefore, the deputy judge was right in the conclusion at which he arrived, although I would in fact go further and suggest that, despite what Lord Salmon said in *United Scientific Holdings Ltd* v. *Burnley Borough Council* [1978] AC 904, even delay plus hardship to the tenants would not disentitle the landlord to exercise the right which he has on the true construction of the contract unless the combination amounted to an estoppel. In my judgment, the contractual right continues to exist unless and until it is abrogated by mutual agreement or the contract is discharged by breach or, to adopt the example of Lord Diplock in the *United Scientific* case, by the obligor being substantially deprived of the whole benefit that it was intended that he should have (which I take to be a reference, in effect, to frustration or failure of consideration and which I cannot envisage as arising in this sort of case). Apart from these circumstances, the only way in which I can envisage the landlord as being precluded from relying upon the clause is by an estoppel and I think that that must have been what Lord Salmon had in mind in the passages to which I have referred.

In particular, I cannot, speaking for myself, see how the right can be lost by 'abandonment.' So far as I am aware, this is not a term of art but I take it to mean the unilateral signification of an intention not to exercise the contractual right in question. If that is right, then I cannot see how it could bind the landlord save as a promise (promissory estoppel) or as a representation followed by reliance (equitable estoppel) or as a consensual variation of the agreement or as a repudiation accepted by the other party. I know of no ground for importing into the law of contract the notion that mere non-exercise of a contractual right is to be treated as analogous to an abandonment of chattels or of an appurtenant right such as an easement. It follows that, in my judgment, *Telegraph Properties (Securities) Ltd* v. *Courtaulds Ltd*, 257 EG 1153 in so far as it rests (as I believe that it does) on simple delay or, alternatively, on abandonment was wrongly decided.

Finally, I should add that I am not, for my part, persuaded that in fact the instant case is one where 'unreasonable' delay has occurred. The expression 'unreasonable delay' does, I think, require some definition. It must, I think, mean something more than 'prolonged delay' and it may, I suppose, be used to express the notion either of delay for which no acceptable reason can be advanced or delay which no reasonable man would incur acting in his own interest. But if this is its meaning then the absence of reason has no necessary relation to duration. If on the other hand, as I suspect, the phrase is used to describe such delay as it would not in the circumstances be reasonable to expect the other party to put up with, then it seems to me that it contains within it, by necessary implication, the notion of hardship or prejudice, for how otherwise is the other party harmed by it?

Note: In *United Scientific Holdings Ltd* v. *Burnley Borough Council* Lord Salmon said that

> 'if the lessors had been guilty of unreasonable delay which had caused prejudice or hardship to the lessees they would have forfeited their rights to be paid a market rent'

from the period in which the delay occurred. This statement which was made, *per curiam*, has now been considered and explained above. For cases on delay, see also *Chrysalis Properties Ltd* v. *Secretary of State for Social Services* (1983) NLJ 473, and *James* v. *Heim Gallery (London) Ltd* (1980) 41 P & CR 269, where a delay of five years out of a seven year review period was held not to be too long.

The question of delay was also considered by Slade LJ in **London & Manchester Assurance Co. Ltd v. G. A. Dunn & Co.** (1983) 265 EG 39.

SLADE LJ: It remains to consider whether, even so, the plaintiffs are precluded from relying on the rent review provisions in respect of the first review period, by reason of delay in serving their 'trigger' notice. On the construction which the learned judge placed upon clause 5 (2) (a) of the lease, namely, that there was no time-limit specified for the service of the notice, he found no difficulty in concluding that it was not meaningful to describe the interval of time between the start of the review period and the service of the notice as a 'delay', still less that it should be categorised as unreasonable. However, on the construction which I have placed upon clause 5 (2) (a), a clear delay of some 2¼ years did occur between the date thereby designated for the service of the lessor's notice and the actual service of it.

Though some decisions given before that in the *United Scientific* case (for example, the *Accuba* case) contained observations as to the effect of delay in the service of a landlord's 'trigger' notice, I do not, with all respect to the judges who made them, think they are now of much assistance. For the *United Scientific* decision overturned what had previously been the commonly held view as to the legal effect of timetables designated by rent review clauses.

In argument in the present case, counsel have been able to refer the court to very few, more recent, authorities giving guidance on this question. In the *United Scientific* case itself Lord Salmon accepted, [1978] AC at p 956, that 'if the lessors had been guilty of unreasonable delay which had caused prejudice or hardship to the lessees', they would have forfeited their rights under the rent review clause. But I think that none of the rest of their Lordships in that case said anything directly relating to this particular point. In *James* v. *Heim Gallery (London) Ltd* (1981) 41 P & CR 269 [also reported at (1981) 256 EG 819] Buckley LJ (at p 278) left open the question whether a party who unreasonably delays in asserting his right under a rent review clause can be held to have abandoned that right so as to be debarred from asserting it. In *Telegraph Properties (Securities) Ltd* v. *Courtaulds Ltd* (1981) 257 EG 1153, where a landlord had delayed for more than six years before invoking a rent review clause, Foster J, without making any statement of principle, held (at p 154) that 'the plaintiff has been guilty of such delay as to make it unreasonable for it to call on the defendant for a rent review and to do so would be of necessity unfair for the defendant'. Finally, in *Amherst* v. *James Walker (Goldsmith and Silversmith) Ltd* (1982) 262 EG 442, Mr John Mowbray QC, after a careful review of the authorities, held in effect that in a case where time is not of the essence (a) a landlord's delay can disentitle him to serve a 'trigger' notice, if it is not only unreasonable but so long and inexplicable as to amount to sufficient evidence that he has abandoned his right to a review; (b) subject to point (a), even unreasonable delay by the landlord does not invalidate the notice, unless the delay has prejudiced the tenant or caused him hardship.

In the absence of binding authority compelling a different conclusion, I am satisfied that delay on its own, even if unreasonable, will not in general disentitle a landlord from invoking a rent review clause in a case where time has not been made of the essence of the contract. There is, I think, no general principle of the law of contract that *mere* delay in the enforcement of a contractual right, or in the performance of a contractual duty, by one party to a contract ('A') will entitle the other party ('B') to regard himself as discharged from the obligation to recognise such right or from the contract as a whole (as the case may be). If in such circumstances A has been guilty of unreasonable delay, than, ordinarily, the prudent and proper course for B to adopt, if he wishes to bring matters to a head, will be to serve a notice on A fixing a reasonable period within which A must exercise his right (if at all) or must perform his part of the contract (as the case may be). In some circumstances, of course, the delay on the part of A may be so gross and inexplicable as to make it so clear that he does not intend to exercise his right or to perform his part of the contract that any such notice is unnecessary. But, ordinarily, it will be necessary for B to serve a notice on A or at least to have some communication with him before he can properly and safely regard himself as being absolved.

Subject to the position that may arise where the tenant can demonstrate that the landlord's delay in serving a 'trigger' notice has caused him prejudice or hardship, I can see no reason why similar principles should not apply in relation to a rent review clause where the original lease has not made time of the essence for the relevant purpose. Subject as aforesaid, therefore, I would for my own part be prepared to hold that in such a case mere delay, even of unreasonable length, in serving his 'trigger' notice will not disentitle a landlord from relying on a rent review clause unless the delay is so long and inexplicable as to amount to sufficient evidence that he has abandoned his right to a review.

However, some of the decisions to which I have referred, or dicta in those decisions, suggest that, even in the absence of evidence of final abandonment by the landlord of the relevant right and of any communication by the tenant with the landlord designed to clarify the situation, a landlord may forfeit the right if his unreasonable delay has caused prejudice or hardship to the tenant: see the *United*

Scientific case at p 956 per Lord Salmon; the *Telegraph Properties* case; and the *Amherst* case. I am bound to say that, with the greatest respect to all those concerned, I find rather more difficulty in accepting this suggestion.

In some cases the delay of a landlord in applying for a rent review might entitle the tenant to rely on the doctrine of equitable estoppel, if the delay had been coupled with an express or implicit representation by the landlord that he did not intend to invoke his rights and the tenant had relied on this representation to his detriment. In the absence of such representation, however, it is not entirely clear to me what principle of law or equity would debar the landlord from still relying on the contractual right conferred on him by the lease.

Nevertheless, for the purpose of this judgment, I am content to assume in favour of the defendants, without deciding, that the plaintiffs could have lost their rights to enforce the rent review provisions in regard to the first review period if the defendants had proved to the reasonable satisfaction of the court that the delay had both been unreasonable and had caused them prejudice or hardship.

What then is the evidence on this point? The plaintiffs' application to the court was supported by one brief affidavit sworn by Mr S J T Turnbull, the chairman of the company which acts as managing agent to the plaintiffs. This affidavit set out very briefly the circumstances in which the relief was sought by the summons. It exhibited the lease and the relevant correspondence. It was answered by an equally brief affidavit sworn by Mr L E Fretten, the manager of the estate department of the defendants. In the course of this affidavit, he asserted that the plaintiffs had, since 25 December 1977, demanded and received from the defendants rent at the rate of £18,000 per annum and were therefore estopped from seeking to demand rent at the alternative rate. He submitted as follows, in para 7 of this affidavit:

'If on the true construction of the lease the plaintiff's contention is correct that the notice is a valid notice and can be given outside the said twelve month period the defendant company is advised that it must be given within a reasonable time of the expiration of the said twelve month period. The giving of the notice in March 1980 is not notice within a reasonable period.'

These two affidavits, as I understand the position, were the only affidavits before the court and there was no cross-examination on them. The affidavit of Mr Fretten explicitly referred to no prejudice or hardship whatsoever alleged to have been suffered by the defendants as a result of the plaintiffs' allegedly unreasonable delay in serving their notice.

In the absence of specific evidence of prejudice or hardship, I think that there is only one point of any substance that can be invoked by the defendants in this context. The determination by the surveyor, if and when it now takes place, will assess the reviewed rent by reference to values appertaining at the time of the determination: see clause 5 (1) of the lease. As invited by the defendants' counsel, I think it right that the court should take judicial notice of the fact that, due to the impact of inflation, rents of commercial premises in London rose between December 1977 and the spring of 1980. There is, however, no evidence at all as to the extent of this rise or as to the specific effect it will have on the amount of the reviewed rent ultimately payable by the defendants. As [counsel for the landlord] pointed out, there are other respects in which delay would appear to produce at least some compensating benefits for the defendants. First, the determination when made will, under clause 5 (1), fall to be made by reference to the annual value in the open market of a hypothetical lease for a term equivalent to the number of years unexpired, of the actual term granted by the lease of 1971, *at the time of the determination*. Fewer years will now remain unexpired than remained unexpired in 1977. Secondly, even on the assumption that the determination produces a figure substantially higher than £18,000 per annum which will be payable retrospectively to the start of the first review period, the resulting sum will be payable in inflated currency, and without interest, by the defendants, who will have had the benefit of the money during the intervening period. In the circumstances and in the absence of any clear evidence to support the inference, I do not think that it would be right for the court to infer that the defendants will on balance have suffered any substantial financial loss or other hardship by the delay. This is not, in my opinion, a case where *res ipsa loquitur*.

Similar comments as to the dearth of evidence apply in relation to the defendants' submissions based on alleged abandonment by the plaintiffs of their right to seek a rent review for the first review period. There is no firm evidence whatever that the defendants believed that the plaintiffs had abandoned this right. True it is that the correspondence exhibited to Mr Turnbull's affidavit contained a letter dated 25 March 1980, written by the defendants to the plaintiffs, which appeared to show that the defendants thought that the plaintiffs had chosen to abandon their right to seek a rent review when they demanded rent at the rate of £18,000 per annum. But Mr Fretten did not depose to any such belief on behalf of the defendants in his affidavit, so that no opportunity was given to the plaintiffs either to test the assertion of such belief by cross-examination or to adduce evidence to rebut it. In the absence of any further evidence as to the dealings between the parties, beyond those referred to in this judgment and that of Lawton LJ, I feel wholly unable to conclude that the lessor's delay (though admittedly unexplained) is so long and inexplicable as to indicate that the plaintiffs had abandoned the relevant right. Once again, in my opinion, this is not a case where *res ipsa loquitur*.

Accordingly, I think that the third principal issue in this case must be decided in favour of the plaintiffs by a negative answer.

Note: Another case in which time was held not to be of the essence in the service of a landlord's trigger notice, applying the general principles laid down in *United Scientific Holdings Ltd* v. *Burnley Borough Council* etc. [1978] AC 78 and the decision of the Court of Appeal in *Amherst* v. *James Walker Goldsmith & Silversmith Ltd* [1983] 3 WLR 334 (earlier), was *H. West & Son Ltd* v. *Brech and Others* (1982) 261 EG 156, where Cantley J held that unreasonable delay could not, of itself, preclude a landlord from serving an effective review notice, and that a delay of 18 months in relation to a review period of seven years was not so unreasonable as to preclude the landlord from relying on his trigger notice.

In **Printing House Properties v. J. Winston & Co.** (1982) 263 EG 725 Dillon J held that under a seven year lease with a review in the fourth year, a delay of 22 months was not so inordinate as to lead to any inference of abandonment or implied agreement not to operate the clause which accordingly remained enforceable.

In **Million Pigs Ltd v. Parry and Another (No. 2)** (1983) 268 EG 809, Goulding J held that though the landlords delay in implementing rent review provisions had been unreasonable, there had been no allegation or proof that the delay had prejudiced the tenant, and the tenant had not served a notice making time of the essence. Accordingly, the landlord's had not lost their rights to a review; where a rent review clause was 'silent', it was not possible to import the requirement for the landlord to implement the rent review provisions within a reasonable time irrespective of whether the tenant was prejudiced by the landlord's delay.

1.4 (b)   Election and estoppel—the right to review can be forfeited on these grounds

In principle, election and estoppel can prevent a landlord from implementing a rent review clause, but in practice this may be difficult to establish as illustrated by the facts of **London & Manchester Assurance Co. Ltd v. G. A. Dunn & Co.** (1983) 265 EG 39 (for facts see earlier, page 12).

SLADE LJ: Before considering whether the plaintiffs have, in one way or another, now precluded themselves from demanding a rent review in respect of the first review period, I think it necessary to take stock of the position of the parties as at the start of the first review period, in the light of the conclusions which I have reached as to the construction of the lease. On the basis of those conclusions, their position as at 25 December 1977 was this. The latest date specified by the lease for the service of the lessor's notice under clause 5 (2) (a) in respect of the first review period had passed. But time was not of the essence for the purpose of that notice. So the defendants should have appreciated that unless and until the plaintiffs gave a clear indication to the contrary they were still retaining the right to serve a lessor's notice, initiating the rent review process for that period, at some later date. In fact what happened was that, on or about 25 December 1977, the plaintiffs' agents served on the defendants a notice demanding rent in advance for the ensuing quarter, at the yearly rate of £18,000, and served on them eight similar notices in respect of eight more quarters before they finally served the notice of 19 March 1980, requiring the rent payable in respect of the premises to be reviewed and stating that in their opinion the open market rental value of the premises was, at the date of the notice, £140,000 per annum.

As [counsel for the defendants] pointed out, the service of the first of these demands clearly indicated that the plaintiffs or their agents had looked at and were conscious of the provisions of clause 1 (c) of the lease, since rent for the period of three years immediately preceding the first rent review period had been payable at the lower rate of £14,600 per annum. On the other hand, it was equally obvious that the first of these demands was not intended to constitute a lessor's notice of the nature referred to in clause 5 (2) (a) of the lease. What then was the proper inference to be drawn from the service of these demands?

The answer to this question must considerably depend on the answer to another question. Assuming, as I have concluded, that time is not of the essence for the purpose of the service of the lessor's notice under clause 5 (2) (a) of the lease, what were the obligations imposed by the lease on the defendants in regard to the payment of rent during the interim period between the beginning of the first review period and the setting in motion by the lessor of the rent review machinery? There are, I think, three possible answers to this question, namely, that the lease on its true construction either (1) provided for the payment of rent at the rate of £18,000 per annum during this interim period (see clause 1 (c)) or (2) provided for the payment of rent at the rate of £14,600 per annum during this period (see clause 5 (3)) or (3) made no provision at all for the payment of rent during this period.

[Counsel for the] plaintiffs argued in favour of the first of these constructions. [Counsel] on behalf of the defendants argued in favour of the second. On the assumption that the court rejected his argument that time was of the essence for the purpose of the service of a lessor's notice, he submitted in effect that, as soon as the first review period arrived, the plaintiff landlords had a choice. One course open to them was to reserve the right to initiate a rent review in respect of that period, in which case, as he contended, they would have been entitled to receive interim rent at the rate of £14,600 per annum under clause 5 (3) of the lease. The other possible course was finally to give up their right to initiate a rent review in respect of that period in which case (and only in which case, as he contended) they would have been entitled to receive rent at the rate of £18,000 per annum under clause 1 (c) of the lease. In [counsel for the defendants'] submission, the plaintiffs, by demanding rent in December 1977 and succeeding quarters at an annual rate of £18,000, had unequivocally demonstrated their decision to take the second of these two courses and had thereby induced the defendants to pay rent at that annual rate, which was a larger amount than the defendants would have been bound to pay if the plaintiffs had still been reserving to themselves the right to invoke the rent review procedure in respect of the first review period.

I hope that this summary adequately represents the substance, though not the

34

form, of [counsel for the defendants'] submissions in this context, which led on to the further submissions that the plaintiffs, by serving the nine demands for quarters' rent at a rate of £18,000 per annum, had precluded themselves, either by the doctrine of common law election or by estoppel, from demanding rent at a higher rate in respect of the first review period.

Election and estoppel

As [counsel for the defendants] accepted, both his submissions based on election and those based on estoppel rest entirely on the premise that the plaintiffs had no right to receive rent at a rate of £18,000 per annum, so long as they wished to reserve the right to invoke the rent review provisions in respect of the first review period. The correctness or otherwise of this premise depends on the construction of clauses 5 (3) and 1 (c) of the lease.

[Counsel for the defendants] submitted in effect that the provisions for the payment of an interim rent, embodied in clause 5 (3) of the lease, are on their true construction capable of operating even at a time when the lessor has not yet served the necessary notice setting the rent review process in operation. I do not think that this construction of clause 5 (3) is the correct one.

Clause 5 (3) is prefaced by the words 'In the event of the determination by such independent surveyor not having been made and communicated to both parties hereto prior to the commencement of the first review period ...' The period during which the interim rent is to be payable under the subclause, beginning with the commencement of the review period, is expressed to end 'on the quarter day immediately following the date on which such determination shall have been made'. The whole of the subclause thus presupposes that a situation has been reached in which a determination by a surveyor is bound to be made in due course. In these circumstances, I agree with the learned judge that clause 5 (3) is not apt to apply at a time when the rent review procedures have not been initiated at all, or when they have been initiated but have not yet reached the stage of the lessee's election to have a determination by an independent surveyor. In my opinion, he was right in concluding (see p 14 C of the transcript of his judgment) [see (1982) 262 EG 143 at p 145] that clause 5 (3) can apply only when the lessee has, pursuant to clause 5 (2) (c), elected for the determination by an independent surveyor, but the surveyor has not yet made his determination and the review period has commenced.

It follows, therefore, in my opinion, that until the defendants served their counternotice of 6 June 1980, clause 5 (3) had no operative effect at all. What then were the defendants' obligations in regard to the payment of rent during the interim period between the commencement of the first review period and 6 June 1980? Disregarding any legal consequences that may have flowed from the plaintiffs' demands for rent at a rate of £18,000 per annum, [counsel for the defendants], as I understood his argument, submitted that, if clause 5 (3) had no operative effect during this interim period, the defendants were under no obligation to pay any interim rent at all. This, as I understand it, was an alternative basis upon which he submitted that these demands for rent by the plaintiffs constituted a final abrogation of their rights to seek a rent review for the first review period, because they were inconsistent with the reservation of any such rights.

[Counsel for the plaintiffs] met this argument by submitting that clause 1 (c) imposed an obligation on the defendants to pay rent at the rate of £18,000 per annum during this interim period, until clause 5 (3) began to operate. [Counsel for the defendants'] answer to this submission was that, as a matter of principle, rent does not fall to be payable until it is certain and ascertained. He accepted that a lease may provide for the payment of a fixed sum on account of rent or a guaranteed minimum rent, and that in that event the fixed sum or guaranteed minimum can be sued or distrained for even before the final aggregate amount has been ascertained: compare *Walsh* v. *Lonsdale* (1882) 21 ChD 9 and the *United Scientific* case at p 935 E-F per Lord Diplock. He pointed out that clause 5 (3) of the lease in the present case did provide for the payment of a fixed sum on account in the contingency to which it applied. He submitted, however, that clause 1 (c) itself could not properly be construed as obliging the lessee to pay anything at all until the open market value of the demised premises for the first review period had been determined or the lessor had finally abrogated his right to seek a rent review for the first review period (in which case rent at the rate of £18,000 per annum would of course be payable).

I confess that I do not find this point easy. While I have been driven to the conclusion that time is not to be regarded as being of the essence for the purpose of a lessor's notice under clause 5 (2) (a), I strongly suspect that the draftsman did not direct his mind to the situation that might arise if a rent review period arrived but the lessor had not yet set in motion the rent review machinery or indicated whether he intended to do so. Nevertheless, I think that clause 1 (c) is capable of being read as imposing on the lessee an obligation to pay a guaranteed minimum rent of £18,000 per annum and this, in my opinion, is how it should be read, since the alternative construction of the subclause, suggested on behalf of the defendants, would leave an obvious lacuna in the lease. The construction which I thus place on clauses 1 (c) and 5 (3) of the lease is substantially the same as that placed on them by Peter Gibson J. At pp 14 F-15 D of the transcript of his judgment he referred to certain incidental difficulties which he recognised as being attendant on his construction of clause 5 (3). The same difficulties, I think, attend his and my construction of clause 1 (c). I do not think it necessary to refer further to them, beyond saying that I agree with him that they are not sufficient to outweigh the other considerations pointing towards the construction which he favoured.

It follows that the plaintiffs, in serving the successive rent demands at a rate of £18,000 per annum from December 1977, were doing no more than they were, in my opinion, entitled to do under the lease, in the circumstances then appertaining. It cannot be said that these demands either were necessarily inconsistent with the reservation by the plaintiffs of the right to serve a 'trigger' notice in respect of the first review period or implied any clear representation that they did not intend to do so. The defendants' submissions based on election and estoppel accordingly must, in my opinion, fail, since the premise on which they are founded is incorrect.

1.5   Discussions between surveyors retained by the parties and the landlord's entitlement to serve a review notice

Discussions as to the level of rent payable between the parties' surveyors may not amount to an agreement as to the revised rent and the landlord may still be entitled to serve a review notice thereafter.

ESSO PETROLEUM CO. LTD v. ANTHONY GIBBS FINANCIAL SERVICES LTD

Court of Appeal   (1983) 267 EG 351

A rent review clause in the underlease of commercial premises provided for a rent review subject to the landlord's giving formal notice during a two-year review period, and further stated that if the landlord failed to serve such a notice he could, at any time after the review period have the rent reviewed by giving the tenant one month's notice. The landlord failed to serve a notice within the review period, and separate discussions proceeded with the landlord and his head landlord, during which the landlord's surveyors agreed with the tenant's surveyors that no increase in the rent would be required to raise the rent payable under the underlease to market level. Subsequently, the landlord served the tenant with one month's notice to operate the review clause. The tenant brought proceedings claiming that the agreement reached between the surveyors earlier precluded the landlord from operating the review procedures. In the High Court the judge found the tenant's case made out. The landlords appealed.

Held: The appeal was allowed. When the parties' surveyors had their discussions they had not been purporting to operate the review clause or to waive the need for a review notice. Accordingly, the landlord was entitled to serve one month's notice and review the rent.

OLIVER LJ: This is a simple and effective review clause giving the landlord an option to call for review within a year either side of the review date and with a provision for arbitration in default of agreement within two months of notice given. But the clause does not end there, for there is a very important additional subclause and it is this that has given rise to the present proceedings, although it is common ground that, at the time when the question of a rent review for the year 1978 arose, everybody had overlooked its existence. It is in these terms:

'(f) Notwithstanding subclause (a) of this Clause if the Landlord fails to give notice calling for a review of the yearly rent payable hereunder during the review period the Landlord shall at any time thereafter have the right to review the said rent upon giving to the Tenant not less than one month's notice in writing of its intention so to do and if the Landlord shall give to the Tenant a notice as aforesaid then from and after the date therein specified (which shall be a date not earlier than one month from the date of service of the said notice) the yearly rent then payable shall be increased to an amount which shall represent the commercial yearly rent of the demised premises at the date specified in the said notice and the amount thereof shall be agreed between the Landlord and the Tenant or determined in accordance with the provisions of subclause (d) of this Clause;'

...

The plaintiffs' case, both before the learned judge and before the court, has been that although it is accepted that the precondition to the operation of clause 5 (x) (f) has been literally satisfied, in that no notice calling for a review of the rent of the third and fourth floors had been given during the review period, yet the sense of the clause as a whole is to preclude a further review until the next review period if a review has actually taken place in relation to the previous review period. A 'review' merely means that the rent has been examined to see whether it corresponds with the market rent and, it having been agreed between the surveyors that the market rent for the building at 6 July 1976 was £11.50 (a figure subsequently accepted by both sides in relation to the second floor), the rent for the third and fourth floors had been reviewed, the absence of any notice being accounted for by the fact that it would have been an entirely academic exercise. This was the contention which the learned judge accepted. The discussions between Mr Rose and Mr Larkin, he held, resulted in their agreeing a nil increase for the third and fourth floors and that meant that they had reviewed the rent. The learned judge expressed himself as satisfied

'that the parties proceeded with their review of the rent of the third and fourth floors on the basis that they had clause 5 (x) in mind and on the basis that: (1) prior to their agreeing on a nil increase, no notice was necessary, notwithstanding the opening words of 5 (x) (a), and (2) that no notice was necessary after so agreeing'. 'In short', he said, 'in conducting their review of the rent of the third and fourth floors, the parties implicitly waived the provision respecting notices that was intended to initiate the review.'

Accordingly, he held that the defendants were precluded from initiating any further review prior to 6 July 1983 and that the notice given under clause 5 (x) (f) was invalid and ineffective.

For my part, therefore, I do not find it possible to regard the parties in July 1978 as if they were mutually agreeing to dispense with formality of a notice under clause 5 (x) (a) and to proceed straight to a determination under clause 5 (x) (d). One has only to consider what the position would have been if the surveyors had not, in fact, concurred in their view of the acceptable market rent. Clearly there would then have been no room for a submission to arbitration unless and until the defendants had taken the step of serving notice under clause 5 (x) (a). Similarly, when one comes to the stage of 'agreement' between the surveyors, it becomes, I think, obvious that neither surveyor envisaged himself as operating under the review machinery of the underlease.

The agreement was, in fact, hedged about with every safeguard that either of them could think of to ensure that it did not achieve finality and bind the clients on either side—and indeed in writing to his clients on 28 July Mr Rose drew attention to the possibility that either the plaintiffs or the Legal and General might change their minds. Thus, at the stage when notice was served in respect of the second floor, all that had happened was that the surveyors, without committing their clients, had reached a conclusion about what they would respectively recommend. In fact, their recommendations were subsequently accepted and the revised rent for the second floor was agreed but at and after the date when notice was served it remained open to the defendants, if they wished, to seek a higher rent than £11.50 per sq ft and to the plaintiffs to seek a lower rent.

The essential question is whether, when the two surveyors, in the course of reaching what could, in the nature of things, be only a preliminary agreement on the level of market rent for the building as a whole, agreed on what was the obvious factual corollary of their assessment, namely, that, if their recommendation were accepted, there would be no increase in the rent currently payable for the third and fourth floors, that latter agreement constituted a 'review' of the rent as contemplated by the underlease of those floors. On this question, I find myself unable to reach the same conclusion as the learned judge, and for my part I accept [counsel for the landlord]'s submissions that the position can be tested by asking the question 'When did the review take place?', bearing in mind that subclause (e) clearly envisages that the review is not complete until an agreement has been reached or a decision by the arbitrator has been made. Clearly at the date when the notice in respect of the second floor was served, there had been no final agreement. All that had occurred was an agreement by the surveyors of a rental level which they would be prepared to recommend to their clients—no doubt with a fair degree of confidence that their recommendations would be accepted—and an acceptance of the fact that if their recommendations *were* accepted, a notice to review the rents of the third and fourth floors would be an academic exercise. The learned judge expressed it as an agreement that no notice was 'necessary', but that is an inaccurate use of language. A notice was necessary if a review was to be carried out under the terms of the underlease (as was done in the case of the second floor), but having regard to what the surveyors had agreed between themselves and what they confidently expected their clients to accept it was inappropriate to serve a rent review notice in respect of the third and fourth floors, since it would achieve nothing. Clearly there was not, at that stage, any determination of the matter for the purposes of clause 5 (x) but merely a decision by the defendants, on the strength of Mr Rose's assessment of the probabilities, to serve notice in respect of the second floor. In respect of that there was subsequently a binding agreement which was formalised by the signature of the memorandum which accompanied the notice. In respect of the third and fourth floors, however, there was then nothing to agree and no proposal submitted by the defendants for consideration. It is perfectly true that, in reporting to the plaintiffs on 8 August 1978, Mr Dawson informed them that Mr Larkin had 'recommended' 'that the rent of the third and fourth floors remains at the existing level of £197,225 per annum, as the current rental value, and the rent review provisions in the lease are upwards only'. That was, however, no more than a statement of the consequence of an acceptance that the rental value of office accommodation in the building at that time was £11.50 per sq ft and cannot, in any event, be evidence against the defendants with regard to the intention with which they—or Mr Rose on their behalf—had entered into the discussions.

Short of some form of estoppel, therefore—and none has been contended for in this court—I can for my part see no evidence which could legitimately lead to the conclusion that the parties were conducting or thought that they were conducting a review of the rent of the third and fourth floors under the provisions of the underlease nor in my judgment does such a conclusion follow from the facts as found by the learned judge. If they were not, then in my judgment it follows that it remained open to the defendants to call for a review subsequently under the provisions of clause 5 (x) (f), and the fact that, at the time, none of the persons concerned in the discussions was conscious of the existence of such a right is immaterial.

I would allow the appeal.

Agreeing, SIR DENYS BUCKLEY said: I only wish to add these short observations. It is clear that the objective of a rent review under the relevant provisions of the underlease of the third and fourth floors of 7 Hanover Square to which my Lord has referred is to determine what shall be the amount of the rent to be paid under the underlease from the relevant review date in respect of the premises demised by that underlease. If as the result of such a review the commercial yearly rent as defined in the underlease is found to exceed the yearly rent which is for the time being under review, that commercial yearly rent becomes the amount of the rent to be paid as from the relevant review date; if on the other hand that commercial yearly rent is found not to exceed the yearly rent under review, the latter rent continues to be the rent payable under the underlease. The ascertainment of the amount of the commercial yearly rent for the premises as at the review date is an essential part of the operation; indeed I think that it is the crucial part.

It is common ground between the parties that the parties and their respective agents never found it necessary in the present case to determine or even to discuss what is the measure of the relevant square footage of the premises comprised in the third and fourth floors. It necessarily follows, as is again common ground, that they never evaluated what the commercial yearly rent for the premises as at 6 July 1978 precisely was. Mr Rose and Mr Larkin were content to take for granted that it would work out at less than the £197,225 which was currently payable in respect of the third and fourth floors. Upon that footing a review of the rent payable for the third and fourth floors would have been a barren exercise. That both Mr Rose and Mr Larkin realised this seems to me to be clear from their conduct.

In my judgment no review of the rent payable for the third and fourth floors within the terms and for the purposes of the underlease was ever embarked upon or, if it was, was ever concluded.

Chapter 2

Interrelation between review clauses and break clauses and the effect on time limits

2.1 Time is of the essence when break and review clauses are interrelated

Where a break clause in the lease is interrelated with the rent review provisions this may amount to a contra-indication to the general rule that time is not of the essence in a rent review clause. However, where the two clauses are not fully interrelated the general rule is not displaced. If the machinery provides for steps to be taken which are outside the parties' control it is less likely that time will be of the essence.

AL SALOOM v. SHIRLEY JAMES TRAVEL SERVICE LTD

Court of Appeal   (1981) 259 EG 420

By an underlease the lessee had the right to give the lessor notice to determine the term prematurely; the lessee, by giving notice had the right to review the rent payable. 23 or 24 December 1978 was the last day on which either the notice to determine the underlease prematurely or the notice to review the rent could be given. The lessor purported to serve a rent review notice on 5 January 1979. The lessee claimed the rent review notice was invalid. By an originating summons the lessor sought a declaration that the rent review notice was validly exercised. The question for the court was whether time was of the essence. John Mills QC, sitting as a deputy High Court judge (1980) 255 EG 541, refused to grant the declaration. The lessor appealed.

Held: The appeal was dismissed. When the provisions relating to the break clause and rent review are inter-related time will be of the essence.

WALLER LJ: The general principles relating to rent review clauses were laid down by the House of Lords in the case of *United Scientific Holdings Ltd* v. *Burnley Borough Council* [1978] AC 904. It is unnecessary to read in any detail the speech of Lord Diplock, because his conclusions are conveniently summarised at p 930, where he said this:

> 'So upon the question of principle which these two appeals were brought to settle, I would hold that in the absence of any contra-indications in the express words of the lease or in the interrelation of the rent review clause itself and other clauses or in the surrounding circumstances the presumption is that the time-table specified in a rent review clause for completion of the various steps for determining the rent payable in respect of the period following the review date is not of the essence of the contract.'

In the passage that I have quoted from Lord Diplock's speech, he spoke of interrelation; in another passage he dealt with the status of a break clause, and at p 929 he said:

'My Lords, although a lease is a synallagmatic contract it may also contain a clause granting to the tenant an option to obtain a renewal of the lease upon the expiration of the term thereby granted. Such a clause provides a classic instance of an option to acquire a leasehold interest in futuro, and it is well established that a stipulation as to the time at which notice to exercise the option must be given is of the essence of the option to renew. Although your Lordships have not been referred to any direct authority upon the converse case of a "break clause" granting to the tenant an option to determine his interest in the property and his contractual relationship with the landlord prematurely at the end of a stated period of the full term of years granted by the lease, there is a practical business reason for treating time as of the essence of such a clause, which is similar to that applicable to an option to acquire property. The exercise of this option by the tenant will have the effect of depriving the landlord of the existing source of income from his property and the evident purpose of the stipulation as to notice is to leave him free thereafter to enter into a contract with a new tenant for a tenancy commencing at the date of surrender provided for in the break clause.'

As I have already said, both provisions about break and rent review in this case were in the same clause and closely allied to each other. The words 'not less than six months' notice in writing prior to the expiration of the said third year of the term' were used for both break and rent review. Whether the word 'interrelated', 'correlated' or 'associated' is used, the implication of the use of the same phrase in the same clause is overwhelming. The phrase must mean the same in each case, either that in both time was of the essence, or in neither. In my view the phrase could not change its meaning in the course of 10 lines unless there were some qualifying phrases to make such a change clear. I have no doubt that in both cases here time was of the essence.

This decision was applied in:

LEGAL AND GENERAL ASSURANCE (PENSIONS MANAGEMENT) LTD v. CHESHIRE COUNTY COUNCIL

Court of Appeal   (1984) 269 EG 40

DILLON LJ: In the *Al Saloom* case the rent review clause was introduced expressly by the words 'subject to the lessee's right of determination'. There are no such express words in the present case, but it is plainly implicit that the rent review clause will not take effect if the lessee duly exercises his right of determination because the term will not go on beyond the review date.

There is no significant difference between the wording in the present case in subclause 3 (a),

'at the expiration of the Seventh and Fourteenth years of the term hereby granted ... the Landlord shall have the right to review the yearly rent ... on giving to the Tenant not less than six months notice in writing prior to the date of review of its intention so to do'

and the wording in subclause (b), 'If the Tenant shall desire to determine the present demise at the expiration of the seventh or fourteenth years of the said term and shall give not less than six months previous notice in writing.' Therefore, as it seems to me, the decision of this court in the *Al Saloom* case is indistinguishable from the present case and binding on us, and that is enough to dispose of this appeal.

But I would add this. It is pointed out, and stressed, by [counsel for the landlord] that where the dates of a break clause and a rent review clause are coincidental, there is always a possibility that the landlord's service of a rent review notice may come too late—even if in time—for the tenant to be able to take into acount and act on it in serving a break notice. That is theoretically possible if the astute landlord wants to take the chance of serving his rent review notice at the last possible permitted moment, or if by some accident a notice properly served in accordance with the notice provisions of section 196 of the Law of Property Act 1925 does not come into the tenant's hands in due time. But most landlords who wish to invoke rent review procedures are apt to serve in comfortable time before the expiration of the permitted period. Therefore the learned judge in the present case was fully entitled, in my view, to say, as he did in his judgment: 'I think the tenant could reasonably expect that the notice would be given in sufficient time for him to decide whether he wanted to break or not.'

The reason for having coincident dates is obviously that the tenant should have in mind, when he decides whether he is going to break or not, whether or not the landlord is going to invoke rent review procedure, and the reasoning which has led the courts to hold that time is of the essence of a rent review clause where the tenant's break clause in the same lease is geared to a date later than the date prescribed for the service of the landlord's rent review notice leads equally, I think, to the conclusion which this court reached in the *Al Saloom* case and I would reach in this case, that time was of the essence of the rent review clause in this lease.

Note: See also *Lahman* v. *Kenshire* (1981) 259 EG 1074, and for more cases on the point see below.

These cases where the break clause and the review clause were held to be interlinked should be contrasted with *Edwin Woodhouse Trustee Co. Ltd* v. *Sheffield Brick Co. PLC* (1984) 270 EG 548 where they were held not to be fully interrelated, see below at 2.1 (d), page 48.

2.2 An interval between the issue of the trigger notice and exercise of the break clause is irrelevant if they are interlinked

Where there is a triggering off of a rent review provision started by the landlord followed by an option given to the tenant to break the lease if he so wishes, time is presumed to be of the essence unless there are contra-indications. It is irrelevant that there is an interval of time provided for between the triggering action and the date when a decision has to be made about breaking the lease. Where the break clause and the rent review provisions are interrelated time will be of the essence.

COVENTRY CITY COUNCIL v. J. HEPWORTH & SON LTD

Court of Appeal   (1985) 265 EG 608

Lawton LJ: The only additional point which it is necessary for me to mention is this. [Counsel for the plaintiffs] submitted that where you have a lease which provides for triggering action followed by a break clause and there is an interval of time provided for between the triggering action and the date when a decision has to be made about breaking the lease, the tenant can always serve upon the landlord a notice making time of the essence of the agreement. He says that makes a difference and it was a difference to which their Lordships did not put their minds when making the observations which they did about the interrelation of the triggering-off provision and the break provision. The fact is they all did: in the course of their speeches they all considered the possibility in these rent review cases of the tenant making time of the essence of the contract if he wished to do so. Indeed in Lord Fraser's case he mentioned that aspect of the matter immediately before he made his observations about the interrelation of the triggering-off procedure and the break clause. In any event, in my judgment, it is unrealistic to talk about tenants in this sort of situation serving this kind of notice. No landlord and no tenant, in my judgment, when making a lease of this kind, would have contemplated such a possibility.

Note: Where there is an interrelation between a rent review clause and a break clause the presumption is that time was of the essence of the rent review clause regardless of whether the rent review can be triggered only by a landlord's notice or whether it can be invoked by either the landlord or the tenant.

Compare the decisions in *William Hill (Southern) Ltd* v. *Govier and Govier* (1984) 269 EG 1168 and *Metrolands Investments Ltd* v. *J. H. Dewhurst Ltd* [1985] 3 All ER 206 where time was held to be of the essence, with *Woodhouse (Edwin) Trustee Co. Ltd* v. *Sheffield Brick Co. Plc* (1983) 270 EG 548, where the clauses were held not to be interrelated and time was not of the essence. In these cases the question of correlation between the time limit in the break clause and the review clause did not involve a landlord's trigger notice.

2.3   The lease may provide that the tenant should be in a position to know whether the landlord can obtain an increase of rent before the tenant is out of time to exercise his option to determine the lease

WILLIAM HILL (SOUTHERN) LTD v. GOVIER AND GOVIER

Chancery Division   (1984) 269 EG 1168

A lease of business premises contained a review clause with two review dates, and further provided that if the revised rents were not agreed by the parties nine months before the review dates then either the landlord or the tenant could have the question referred to arbitration by an independent surveyor. The clause further provided for the tenant to have the option to determine the lease by giving three months notice to expire on either of the review dates. The landlord sought to invoke the review clause a month out of time.

Held: Time was of the essence because the rent review provisions and the break provisions were interrelated and linked and as such amounted to a sufficient contra-indication to displace the general rule that time was not of the essence in a rent review clause as stated in *United Scientific Holdings* v. *Burnley BC* see earlier, page 3. The landlord was therefore not entitled to have the rent reviewed. *Coventry City Council* v. *J. Hepworth & Sons Ltd* considered and followed, (1982) 46 P & CR 170 (see page 42 earlier).

E.C. EVANS-LOMBE QC: The important clause is clause 4 of the lease which is headed 'Rent and Rent Review'. The material provisions of this clause are as follows:

4. *Rent and Rent Review*
(1) The yearly rent is £325 per annum from the 29th day of September 1977 to the 3rd day of November 1978 and thereafter the yearly rent is £800 per annum (subject to the provision for review mentioned below) ...
(2) The rent shall be reviewed at the 25th December 1982 and at the 25th December 1987 each of which such review dates are hereinafter called "the Review Date" and from each such review date the yearly rent shall be the greater of:—
   (a) the rent hereinbefore reserved
   (b) the rent payable following any previous review
   (c) the best rack rent of the demised premises obtainable in the open market ...

If the landlord and the tenant shall fail to agree such rent 9 months before the review date then either party may within a further period of one month refer the question of the amount of rent to be determined on the foregoing basis to a chartered surveyor nominated in default of agreement between the landlord and the tenant by the President for the time being of the Royal Institution of Chartered Surveyors on the application of the landlord ... and in the meantime the tenant shall continue to pay rent at the same rate as before the review date and any increased rent following the review date shall be paid in one sum on the quarter day next following its determination in respect of the period from the review date until such quarter day ...

(3) If the tenant shall be desirous of determining this present lease at the end either of the fifth or tenth year as the case may be of the term hereby granted and of such desire shall give to the landlord at least 3 months previous notice in writing in that behalf to expire on the 25th day of December either in the year 1982 or 1987 and if the said rent for the time being reserved hereunder shall have been paid then at the end of each fifth or tenth year as the case may be the said term hereby granted shall cease but without prejudice to the rights and remedies of either party ...'

It is to be observed that notwithstanding the heading of the clause, clause 4 deals with three subjects: the rent payable at the commencement of the term, the machinery for reviewing that rent and the machinery for the tenant determining the lease before the expiry of the term. The juxtaposition of dates by which the various steps comprised in this machinery were to be taken is of importance. The rent from 3 November 1978 onwards is to be £800 unless reviewed. The review provisions provide for an 'upwards only' review. The first line of subclause (2) is expressed so as to make a review of the rent on 25 December 1982 and 25 December 1987 mandatory. It uses the words 'the rent shall be reviewed' on those dates. Those dates are also the dates upon which the tenant's notices to determine the term in its fifth or 10th year must expire, the time of notice being a minimum of three months. The machinery for solving what the new rent shall be in default of agreement between the parties is that, in default of such agreement, by nine months before the review date, either party may within the next month refer the question of the new rent to an arbitrator (that expression not being used in its strict legal sense). Subclause (2) clearly envisages that the process of arbitration may not be complete by the review date and accordingly provides for backdating of the new rent from the date when it is determined to the review date and payment in arrear by the tenant.

Looking at the provisions of clause 4 as a whole and without applying to those provisions any special rules of construction which may arise from the authorities, the clause provides a machinery that the parties should have either agreed a new rent or put in motion the machinery for resolving their disagreement five months before the last date upon which the tenant could serve notice to determine the lease early. It is clear that the clause does not provide that the tenant shall know the new rent positively before he has to take the decision whether to determine or not. He ought to know, however, that the landlord is insisting on an increased rent and that the question of the amount has been sent to an arbitrator. It is highly likely that he will know the parameters of the dispute between him and the landlord as to future rent.

I will now summarise briefly what has happened and which events give rise to the dispute in this case. Prior to the first review date no steps were taken by either side to attempt to agree a new rent and there was no reference by either side. The first indication that the landlords were looking for an increase of rent came in a letter dated 27 January 1983. The tenants' response to that letter was that it was by then too late to review the rent before the next review date on 25 December 1987. The reason why the tenants say that it is now too late to review the rent is that, there being no agreement between the parties as to a new rent, the time for referring that dispute for solution to an 'arbitrator' is now passed. The landlords contend that, properly construed, time is not of the essence of the provisions of clause 4 of the lease and, the tenants not having taken any steps to make time of the essence, it is open to them (the landlords) to put the machinery for review into operation. The tenants contend that, properly construed, time is of the essence of the provisions of clause 4 and there can be no relaxation of the dates contained in it.

In *Coventry City Council* v. *J. Hepworth & Sons Ltd* (1981) 261 EG 566, Warner J was confronted with a very similar problem. At p 568 in the left-hand column he summarises the effect of the provisions of the lease which he had under consideration as follows:

'So that clause laid down an elaborate and precise time-table. On or before 31 December 1973 the corporation might give to the tenants notice of its desire to increase the rent in respect of the period from 1 April 1975 until the expiration of the term created by the lease, that is, roughly speaking in respect of the second 21 years of it. I shall call that a "rent review notice". If the corporation gave such a notice and no agreement had been reached by 28 February 1974 (that is within two months) there was to be a reference to arbitration. Clearly, what was envisaged was that, in the two months before 31 December 1973 and 28 February 1974 there would be negotiations between the parties which would either produce agreement on a new rent or be abortive. Then if the negotiations proved to be abortive, the parties were given one month in which to agree upon a single arbitrator. If they failed to do so, each must appoint an arbitrator. The last day for doing that was 30 April 1974. The provisions of sections 7 and 8 of the Arbitration Act 1950 would then apply. On or before 30 September 1974 the tenants might give notice of their intention to determine the lease as from 31 March 1975, that is the day before any increase of rent might take effect. At that time, that is on 30 September 1974 assuming that the corporation then served a rent review notice, the tenants might not know precisely what the new rent was going to be. Clause 4 (3) (c) expressly envisaged that the new rent to be determined by arbitration might not be known before 1 April 1975. Nonetheless, obviously, the tenants would, in the contemplation of clause 4 (3), be in a good position to know, by 30 September 1974, at least roughly what the new rent was likely to be. They would have been parties to the negotiations envisaged by the clause and parties also to any subsequent arbitration. By 30 September 1974 any such arbitration would be well under way. So the tenants would be aware of the upper and lower figures envisaged in negotiations and in the subsequent arbitration.'

Warner J was therefore considering a lease the scheme of which was substantially similar to the lease which I have to consider. Later in his judgment Warner J says:

'The general principle laid down by the House of Lords in the *Cheapside* case was stated by Lord Diplock in these terms at p 930: "so upon the question of principle which these two appeals were brought to settle I would hold that in the absence of any contrary indications in the express words of the lease or in the interrelation of the rent review clause itself and other clauses or in the surrounding circumstances the presumption is that the timetable specified in a rent review clause for completion of the various steps for determining the rent payable in respect to the period following the review date is not of the essence of the contract".'

The important words there for the purposes of this case are: 'in the absence of any contrary indications in the interrelation of the rent review clause itself and other clauses'.

Warner J then goes on to quote extensively from the judgments from the House of Lords in *United Scientific Holdings Ltd* v. *Burnley Borough Council* and *Cheapside Land Development Co. Ltd* v. *Messels Service Co.* both cases reported at [1978] AC 904. I will not repeat his quotations in this judgment but they are all relevant here.

Finally at p 569 in the second column he deals with the landlords' arguments in this way:

'Mr Cripps submitted that it was not in every case where a rent review clause was associated with a tenant's option to break that time was of the essence of the rent review clause. That is manifestly right, as the House of Lords treatment of the *Hayek* case illustrates. I do not think, however, that the features of the present case to which Mr Cripps pointed are sufficient to negative the presumption that, where a rent review clause is linked to a tenant's option to break, time is of the essence of the rent review clause. The length of the term and the fact that the lease provided for only one break in 21 years are, I think, sufficiently explained by the circumstance that it was granted in 1953, at a time when inflation was at a much lower rate than now. The fact that substantial sublettings by Hepworth was envisaged seems to me neutral. The period of 9 months between 31 December 1973 and 30 September 1974 was, I think, intended, not to give the tenant an opportunity to serve a notice making time of the essence, but to enable any necessary arbitration to have been completed by 30 September 1974 or at least to be sufficiently advanced by that date to give the tenant a good idea of what the revised rent was likely to be. Lastly I do not think that it matters that there could be no certainty that the tenant would know the precise amount of the revised rent by that date.'

I gratefully adopt the approach of Warner J in my approach to this case. Earlier decisions on the construction of other documents cannot bind a court construing a document save where its terms are virtually the same. However, where the documents in question present substantially the same pattern the earlier decision can be of the greatest persuasive force to the court of construction in the later case. Warner J's decision in the *Coventry* case was affirmed in the Court of Appeal [at (1982) 265 EG 608].

In the present case, as in the case before Warner J, provisions for rent review and determination of the lease by the tenant appear closely associated in the lease. As I have said, the dates present a pattern which seems to indicate that the provisions are linked. It is now clearly established by authority that the court would almost always construe time being of the essence of provisions for the early determination of leases. As Warner J and the Court of Appeal have held, where such provisions are linked with provisions for rent review, *prima facie* the court will construe the provisions to make time of the essence of those relating to the review.

The question therefore is, is there in the lease in the present case, by contrast with the lease in the *Coventry* case, any feature which, notwithstanding their appearance in the same clause, may indicate that the provisions for review and determination are not linked? And, secondly, are there features of the case which, notwithstanding linkage, leads the court to a conclusion contrary to Warner J's *prima facie* rule?

The main thrust of [counsel]'s argument for the landlords is to contend that there was no link between the review provisions and those for determination of the lease. He pointed to a distinction between the provisions for review in the present case and those in the *Coventry* case, namely that in the present case the provisions of subclause (2) made the review mandatory. It therefore takes effect without any requirement of a 'trigger-notice' on the landlord's part. The tenant's decision whether or not to determine the lease early will not be affected in any way by the operation of the review provision. There will be no room for doubt as to whether a review is to take place or not. The only question that he will need to know before deciding whether to give notice to determine is the amount of increase, if any. Even if strictly operated in accordance with the time schedule the tenant has no guarantee that he will know what the new rent is to be before the time for the service of the notice is upon him and the lease expressly acknowledges this.

[Counsel] for the tenants contended this was no valid distinction. He drew my attention to the fact that, albeit mandatory, the review provisions contain a time schedule. In particular, a fixed date is provided for the time by which the parties must refer any dispute as to rent to arbitration. He said that although the provisions for review were mandatory the rent did not review itself. If the parties did not agree as to the rent and they let the time for referring their dispute to arbitration go by, the old rent stood.

It seems to me that where one finds, as in the present case and as in the *Coventry* case, provisions for review and determination by the tenant in the same clause with a time schedule which seems to indicate an intention by the parties that the tenant shall know whether the landlord is seeking an increase of rent, it is not conclusive of the question, whether time is of the essence of the review provisions, that these provisions are automatically activated by mandatory words in the lease or are optionally activated by provisions giving the landlord an option whether by a certain date to serve a trigger-notice. Obviously where a lease contains provision for a mandatory review as at a certain date, and nothing else, time will not be of the essence of that provision. Where a lease provides for a mandatory review and then sets up a machinery for concluding that review which seems to be geared to providing the tenant, either with the answer as to what the future rent shall be or with a shrewd idea of what it should be, or at least with the knowledge whether or not the landlord is going to ask for an increase before he has to take a decision whether to give notice to terminate, time is of the essence of the provisions for review. I do not therefore see any general basis for the distinction which [counsel for the landlords] put forward.

[Counsel for the landlords] further contended that the provisions as to time in the review machinery were too imprecise to make time of the essence. In particular he pointed out that the vital words in subclause (2) are 'if the landlord and the tenant shall fail to agree such rent 9 months before the review date then either party *may* within a further period of one month refer the question ...' The permissive nature of the provision, he said, militated against the court finding time of the essence. When I put to [counsel for the landlords] that use of the word 'may' might be argued to indicate that the parties were not contemplating the arbitration machinery as the only way of solving any dispute as to future rent and that the court might retain a residuary jurisdiction itself to determine the appropriate 'rack rent' he conceded that on the authorities that argument was not open to him. It seems to me that once that concession is made the use of the word 'may' ceases to be of importance. In default of agreement the parties have the option to put in train an arbitration within a fixed period of one month from a certain date. If they do not take that opportunity, then the only avenue for solving the dispute contemplated by the lease is lost and the old rent must stand. It seems to me, in the present case, that the lease gives to the tenant the right to sit back and watch whether or not the landlord will in the time specified refer the question of future rent to arbitration. It matters not that there has or has not been anything in the nature of negotiations leading up to such a reference. Once, however, the time for referral is gone by, the tenant can decide whether or not to terminate the lease knowing whether the landlord is in a position to seek an increase of rent or not.

Contrast the *Woodhouse* case below with *William Hill* above, and the further case of *Metrolands* at page 52. In *Metrolands* the decision in *William Hill* was followed, and also the earlier Court of Appeal decision of *Coventry City Council* v. *J. Hepworth* (see at page 42) which affirmed Warner J's decision at first instance ((1981) 261 EG 566). The *Coventry City* case involved the correlation of a rent review clause which was initiated by a trigger notice and a break clause. Warner J expressed the applicable presumption as the presumption that, where a rent review clause is linked to a tenant's option to break, time is of the essence of the rent review clause (at page 569). In the Court of Appeal he confined his reasoning to following Lord Fraser (in

United Scientific Holdings, for facts and judgment see 1.1 page 3) in referring to a rent review initiated by the landlord's trigger notice correlated with a break clause. Griffiths LJ agreed, but stated that he found the reasoning of Warner J compelling and did not wish to give reasons of his own.

2.4 Even a day's interval between the operation of the review clause and break clause will prevent them from being interlinked

EDWIN WOODHOUSE TRUSTEE CO. LTD v. SHEFFIELD BRICK CO. PLC

Chancery Division   (1984) 270 EG 548

In 1968 a 21-year lease was granted by the plaintiff landlord to the defendant tenant's predecessor in title. The lease had a rent review clause which provided for two seven-year reviews, with the review periods commencing on 25 December 1975 and 1982 respectively. By clause 5 of the lease there was an option for the tenant to determine the lease at the end of the seventh or fourteenth year of the term by giving the landlord six months' notice in writing the last dates for which were 24 June 1975 and 1982. The two review periods expired without the tenant giving notice to break the lease. In September 1982, the landlord gave the tenant notice of its intention to invoke the rent review provisions. It was agreed that time was of the essence in relation to the break clause. The tenant contended that the review provisions and the break clause were inter-linked so that time was of the essence in invoking the review clause and that there was an implication that the landlords should give the tenant more than six months' notice before the review period in order for the tenant to know the likely level of the revised rent and to give the tenant time to consider whether or not he wished to exercise his option to determine the lease, or that there was an implication that the landlord had to give the tenant notice of intention to review a reasonable time in advance of the date namely, 'the six months next before the appropriate relative date' by which the parties had to reach agreement if the subsequent mechanics of determination by a valuer were not to be brought into effect.

Held:
(1)   There was a fatal difficulty both in the submission that the landlord's notice had to be given at least six months next before the appropriate relative date and the alternative implication that it must be given a reasonable time before that date. The difficulty in relation to the suggestion that it should be given at least six months next before the appropriate relative date was, that meant, on the proper construction of the lease, that the landlord's notice would have to be given by or on 25 June 1982, that being the date by or on which agreement between the parties had to be reached if the subsequent mechanics were not to operate. But the break clause in clause 5 required notice to be given *before* midnight on 24 June 1982, a day before. This arose because, whereas notice under the break clause had to be given at a date determined in relation to the end of the 14th year of the term, the rent review agreement provision was linked not to the end of the 14th year but to the day of the commencement of the 15th year of the term, so that there was necessarily a difference of one day between the clause 5 break date and the date in the rent review provision. There was no direct correlation between the two dates.
(2)   The concept of a 'reasonable time' before the appropriate relative date gave rise to at least two further difficulties, in that there was no longer correlation between the review and the break notices; and if the implication of the proviso was that the landlord had to give some notification a reasonable time before the six-month date, then all the force of the suggestion that break clause and review clause should either both, or neither, make time of the essence disappeared because the

concept that time should be of the essence in relation to a provision, whether express or implied, that imposed an obligation to do something a reasonable time before the happening of some event was a concept of insuperable difficulty. If time was of the essence, then the date as to which time was of the essence had to be a date which was either specified or able to be spelled out by a process of necessary implication. Here there was an insuperable difficulty for the tenant because there was nothing in the rent review provisions which indicated with any kind of certainty, what the landlord had to do or when he had to do it, in that there were no clear terms stating that the landlord had to serve anything in the nature of a trigger notice and there was no implication that he was under a duty to do so. Accordingly, there was nothing to displace the presumption that time was not of the essence in the review provisions as laid down in *United Scientific Holdings Ltd* v. *Burnley Borough Council* (see page 3 earlier). *Re Essoldo (Bingo) Ltd's Underlease, Essoldo Ltd* v. *Elcresta Ltd* (1971) 23 P & CR 1 and *Wrenbridge Ltd* v. *Harries (Southern Properties) Ltd* (1981) EG 1195 considered in detail with approval. *Al Saloom* v. *Shirley James Travel Service Ltd* (see above page 40) (1981) 259 EG 420 distinguished.

JUDGE FINLAY QC (sitting as a High Court judge): The lease is dated 16 December 1968. By that lease the plaintiff company granted to the original lessees a lease of the fifth floor of the premises of 112 Jermyn Street for a term of 21 years from 25 December 1968 'paying therefore during the said term the yearly rent specified in the first schedule to the lease'. The first schedule is in these terms:

'The rents reserved by and payable under this lease are and shall be as follows ...:
(1) during the first seven years of the said term (hereinafter called "the first period") a yearly rent of ONE THOUSAND SIX HUNDRED POUNDS ...
(2) during the next seven years of the said term (hereinafter called "the second period") a yearly rent amounting or equal to the greater of the two undermentioned rents or amounts namely:
    (i) the yearly rent payable hereunder during the first period.
    (ii) the yearly value (agreed or determined as hereinafter provided) of the demised premises at the appropriate relative date and
(3) during the remainder of the said term (hereinafter called "the third period") a yearly rent amounting or equal to the greater of the two undermentioned rents or amounts namely:
    (i) the yearly rent payable hereunder during the second period
    (ii) the yearly value (agreed or determined as hereinafter provided) of the demised premises at the appropriate relative date
PROVIDED and it is agreed that in this Schedule the expression "the appropriate relative date" means in relation to the second period the first day of that period and in relation to the third period means the first day of that period and the expression "the yearly value" means such sum or amount as the parties shall agree as being or (failing agreement at least six months before the appropriate relative date) as a Valuer appointed by the parties or (failing appointment at least two months next before the appropriate relative date) nominated at the request of either party (a) by the President [of the RICS etc] . . .'

then further provisions follow as to the mode of valuation and to the duties of the valuer or arbitrator.

There was an assignment by the original lessee in 1978, and a further assignment on 9 September 1982, whereby the premises became vested in the defendants. It will be observed that the first rental period expired in 1975 and the second came to an end at midnight on 24 December 1982.

There was also provision made in clause 5 of the lease that—

'If the Tenant shall be desirous of determining this Lease at the end of the seventh or fourteenth year of the term hereby granted and of such his desire shall give to the Landlords not less than six months notice in writing and shall pay all rent and perform and observe all the covenants and conditions herein before contained and on its part to be performed and observed up to such determination then and in such case immediately after the expiration of the said period of seven or fourteen years as the case may be this Lease shall cease and be void but without prejudice to any claim by the Landlords against the Tenant in respect of any antecedent breach of any covenant or condition herein contained ...'

It will be observed that a notice determining the lease at the end of the 14th year of the term consequently required to be served by not later than 24 June 1982.

The then tenant did not break the lease at the end of the seventh year, nor was any notice given by the present defendants, or their predecessors, prior to 24 June 1982.

By a letter dated 27 September 1982 the plaintiff landlords by their agents gave notice to the defendants that it was the plaintiffs' intention to review the rent payable under the lease at 25 December 1982, that date being the first day of the third period within the meaning of the third schedule.

The defendants contended that that notification was inoperative on the ground that time was of the essence in relation to the rent review provision in the sense that notice had to be given by the landlord of its desire to operate the rent review provisions at least six months next before the appropriate relative date, that is, before 25 December 1982, and, the notice of 27 September falling within the six months next before the relative date, the notice was of no effect ...

There are two cases upon which reliance was placed, to which I must refer, namely, *Re Essoldo (Bingo) Ltd's Underlease, Essoldo Ltd* v. *Elcresta Ltd* (1971) 23 P & CR 1. There, was a provision that the rent should be a fixed sum during the first three years of the term, and during the remainder of the term whichever shall be the greater of the following alternative rents, namely the amount payable during the first three years (£6000).

'or a yearly rent of such amount as the respective surveyors of the landlord and the tenant shall before the last quarter day of the third year of the ... term agree upon in writing as being the then current market rental value for the letting of the demised premises as a whole with vacant possession for a term of four years commencing on the aforementioned quarter day upon the terms of this under-lease,'

with provision, in default of such agreement, for determination of the rent by a surveyor to be nominated by the president of the Royal Institution of Chartered Surveyors. The three years expired on 24 August 1969. The last quarter day was 24 June, but neither party took any steps towards determination of the second alternative until 9 July and at that point the landlord claimed to have the rent determined in accordance with the second alternative, that is, by a surveyor appointed by the Royal Institution of Chartered Surveyors. The tenants' contention was that, if no attempt was made at the proper time to reach agreement, then the provisions in default of agreement did not come into operation but only came into operation if an attempt had been made and failed. The Vice-Chancellor, Sir John Pennycuick, said at p 4:

'I think it is clear that the contention raised on behalf of the tenant was not well founded. The provision for determination by a surveyor appointed by the president of the institution is simply expressed to operate in default of agreement between the parties' surveyors before the specified date, and I do not see any reason to qualify the plain meaning of those words.

[Counsel] for the tenant, conceded that this construction involves writing in after the words "in default of said agreement as aforesaid" the words "after an attempt has been made to make it". I do not see any justification for writing in these or comparable words.'

In *Wrenbridge Ltd* v. *Harries (Southern Properties) Ltd* (1981) 260 EG 1195, Lloyd J followed the *Essoldo* decision and held that the question before him was determined by the decision of the Vice-Chancellor in that case. He said at p 1196:

'... it seems to me that if there is some step which is to be taken in the course of operating a rent review clause and if the parties wish to make the taking of that step a condition precedent, then they must do so in clear terms, or by necessary implication. Here, in my judgment, the words are not sufficiently clear to require the parties to attempt to reach agreement on either of the two preliminary matters as a condition precedent to their right to go for the appointment of an arbitrator under the third limb of the clause.

As to the second of the two grounds of distinction, it is difficult to know what the draftsman of this clause had in mind by making time of the essence.'

(that was time of the essence in relation to the two earliest modes of determination provided for by a rent review provision which provided for a third mode of determination if the first two failed)

'The time-limit in this clause is quite unlike the time-limit considered by the House of Lords in the case of *United Scientific Holdings Ltd* v. *Burnley Borough Council* ... The time-limit is a time for *completing* negotiations between the parties. That leaves open the question when negotiations were to be commenced. In order to answer that question it would be necessary to imply some term into the clause such as, for instance, that the negotiations were to be commenced a reasonable time before the date in question.'

...

There appears to be a fatal difficulty both in the submission that the landlord's notice has to be given at least six months next before the appropriate relative date and the alternative implication relied upon that it must be given a reasonable time before that date. The difficulty in relation to the suggestion that it should be given at least six months next before the appropriate relative date is that that means, and I find on the construction of the lease it has the result, that the landlord's notice, which he is impliedly obliged to give, would have to be given by or on 25 June 1982, that being the date by or on which agreement between the parties has to be reached if the subsequent mechanics do not come into operation. But the break clause in clause 5 would have to be given before midnight on 24 June 1982, a day before. This arises because, whereas the break clause has to be given at a date determined in relation to the end of the 14th year of the term, the rent review agreement provision is linked not to the end of the 14th year but to the day of commencement of the 15th year of the term, so that necessarily there is a difference of one day between the clause 5 date and the date designated in the proviso to the first schedule. Consequently, there not being any direct correlation between the two dates, much of the force in the submission that there is an interrelation is taken away.

The alternative suggestion that there is an implication that the landlord should give notice of his intention to operate the rent review provision a reasonable time before the date which falls at least six months next before the appropriate relative date gives rise to at least two further difficulties. One is that the introduction of the concept of a reasonable time before (what I call for convenience) the six-month date means that there is no longer correlation between the rent review notice and the break clause notice. On the other hand it could be said that the implication that the landlord must give notice a reasonable time before introduces the possibility that the tenant will then have a reasonable time to consider whether or not, in the circumstances that the landlord wishes to operate the rent review provisions, he ought, or ought not, to exercise the break clause option.

But the second difficulty appears to be this. If the implication of the proviso is that the landlord has to give some notification a reasonable time before the six-month date, then all the force of the suggestion that break clause and rent review clause should either both, or neither, make time of the essence disappears because the concept that time should be of the essence in relation to a provision, whether express or implied, that imposes an obligation to do something a reasonable time before the happening of some event appears to me to be one of insuperable difficulty. If time is to be of the essence, then the date as to which time is of the essence must, it appears to me, be a date which is either specified or able to be spelled out by a process of necessary implication.

In the end it appears to me that the insuperable difficulty which the tenant faces is that there is nothing in the proviso to the first schedule which does, with any kind of certainty, indicate what the landlord has to do, or when he has to do it. The fact that there are alternative suggestions that he has to give a notice at least six months next before the appropriate relative date, or alternatively a reasonable time before it, indicates the lack of precision in the implication that the tenant has to rely upon. It would have to be implied, first that there is to be an attempt by the parties to reach agreement, and that that in turn implies a necessity that the landlord should give a notice, and in turn that that implies a need to give a notice in time to permit the conducting of the attempt.

These pointers of implication are all, it appears to me, of far too indefinite a character. There are no clear terms which indicate that the landlord is under a duty to serve anything in the nature of a trigger notice nor, in my judgment, is it possible to find within the four corners of the lease, reading it as a whole, anything which, by necessary implication, imposes on the landlord any such duty.

The result in my judgment is that there is nothing here which militates against the application of the presumption referred to by Lord Diplock in the paragraph from his speech which I have already read. Accordingly, time is not of the essence in relation to any implied obligation upon the landlord to serve a notice to bring into operation the rent review provisions of the first schedule and accordingly the notice given on 27 September 1982 was, in my judgment, effective to bring those provisions into operation. The date at least six months before the appropriate relative date having by then passed, the provisions as to the appointment of a valuer by the president for the time being of the Royal Institution of Chartered Surveyors, and, failing that being done in due time, by the president for the time being of the Chartered Auctioneers' and Estate Agents' Institute, therefore come into operation. It is, of course, at any time open to the tenant and the landlord to reach agreement as to what the revised rent should be.

William Hill was followed and the *Woodhouse* decision was distinguished in *Metrolands* below.

METROLANDS INVESTMENTS LTD v. J. H. DEWHURST LTD

Chancery Division [1985] 3 All ER 206

A lease made in 1968 for a term of 21 years provided that the yearly rent for the first three years was to be £1500, for the next eleven years £1800 and for the remaining seven years the rent at which the demised premises might reasonably be let at the

commencement of that period on the open market on terms similar to those in the lease or, failing agreement between the parties, the rent that was determined by an arbitrator appointed by both parties. The arbitrator's determination was required to be obtained before the expiration of the first half of the fourteenth year. The rent review clause further provided that in any event the yearly rent for the last seven years was not to be less than £1800. The lease also contained a break clause entitling the tenant to terminate the lease at the end of the fourteenth year by serving at least three months' notice within the second half of that year. The period during which the tenant could serve a notice operating the break clause therefore commenced after the expiration of the period during which an arbitrator's award could be obtained, with the result that the rent review clause and the break clause were so correlated as to enable the tenant to know the rent that would be payable for the last seven years before deciding whether to terminate the lease at the end of the fourteenth year. The parties took no steps to implement the rent review clause during the period provided therefor, nor did the tenant attempt to operate the break clause in the time provided by it. Two weeks after the expiration of the period during which the tenant could serve a notice terminating the lease the landlord served notice on the tenant requesting a rent review. The tenant contended that the notice was invalid because it had been served after the expiration of both the rent review time limit and the time limit for operating the break clause, and that time was of the essence in regard to both time limits. The landlord sought a declaration that the rent payable for the last seven years was the yearly rent at which the premises could be let on the open market at the commencement of that period, alternatively an inquiry as to what was the rent payable in that period, or in the further alternative a declaration that in default of agreement the landlord was entitled to have the rent determined by arbitration. The tenant submitted that time was of the essence of the reddendum,
. that it was therefore not open to the landlord to obtain a determination of the rent by machinery not provided for in the lease and that accordingly the yearly rent payable for the last seven years was £1800, even though it was common ground that such a rent was far less than the open market rental value of the premises at that time. The landlord conceded that time was of the essence where there was a correlation between a break clause and the time limit in a rent review clause which was triggered by a landlord's notice, but submitted that time was not of the essence of a rent review clause where the tenant as well as the landlord had the option to initiate the rent review.

Held: (1) Where there was an interrelation between a rent review clause and a break clause the presumption was that time was of the essence of the rent review clause regardless of whether the rent review could be triggered only by a landlord's notice or whether it could be initiated by either the landlord or the tenant. Accordingly, time was of the essence of the rent review clause in the reddendum by reason of its correlation with the break clause; dicta of Lord Diplock, Lord Simon and Lord Fraser in *United Scientific Holdings Ltd* v. *Burnley BC* [1977] 2 All ER at 77, 85, 98 applied; *Coventry City Council* v. *J. Hepworth & Sons Ltd* (1982) 46 P & CR 170 and *William Hill (Southern) Ltd* v. *Govier & Govier* (1984) 269 EG 1168 followed.

(2) Since time was of the essence of the rent review, the arbitration machinery for that review was an essential part of the contract and the landlord was not entitled to obtain the court's determination of the fair market rent for the last seven years of the term in place of an arbitration award once the time limit for obtaining an arbitration award had expired. Nor, in all the circumstances, was it possible to imply a term that on a failure to obtain an arbitration award within the time limit the rent for the last seven years was to be a fair rent. Since the parties had chosen the procedure for rent review with precision and had made time of the essence, the review procedure was to be followed timeously or not at all; and since a rent of £1800 per annum was not only the rent payable for the period immediately preceding the last seven years but also the minimum rent contemplated by the parties if the machinery for a rent review had

been implemented it was to be assumed that the parties had intended that the rent for the preceding period of the term should continue to be the rent for the last seven years of the term. The court would accordingly declare that £1800 per annum was the rent payable for the last seven years of the term; *Weller* v. *Akehurst* [1981] 3 All ER 411 applied [4.4 page 94; *Beer* v. *Bowden* [1981] 1 All ER 1070 [page 221] and *Sudbrook Trading Estate Ltd* v. *Eggleton* [1982] 3 All ER 1 distinguished.

Note: At time of going to press this case had gone to appeal and the appeal was allowed: see pages 59 and 78.

PETER GIBSON J: Counsel for Dewhurst relies on what he says are two contra-indications, first in the express terms of the lease, second in the interrelation of the reddendum and other clauses, in particular the break clause.

Counsel founds himself for his first contra-indication on the words of the *reddendum*. He relies on limb 4, 'but such yearly rent shall not in any event be less than £1800', which, as he points out, comes after limb 3 containing the time limit for obtaining the decision of the arbitrator. Therefore, he says, the draftsman must have had the proviso in mind in drafting limb 4 and the possibility that the time limit might not be met, and the intention of the parties can be inferred to be that in that event, as well as any other event such as the rent being determined at a figure lower than £1800, the yearly rent should be £1800. I cannot accept this argument. Limb 4 relates to 'such yearly rent'. That, as counsel for Metrolands pointed out, can only refer to the yearly rent on the hypothetical basis set out in limb 1 or on that basis and agreed or determined in limb 2. All that limb 4 does is to put a minimum figure on the yearly rent on that basis or on that basis and agreed or determined. It does not refer to the rent not ascertained by reference to limb 1 or limb 2. In my judgment, therefore, limb 4 cannot be construed as a default clause to operate on the failure to go to arbitration at all or to obtain the decision in time.

I turn then to counsel for Dewhurst's second contra-indication. He relies on the interrelation between the time limit in limb 3 of the reddendum and the break clause. It is clear from the *United Scientific* case that in the absence of the break clause time is not of the essence of limb 3. Save for the break clause the facts of the *United Scientific* case are very similar to those of the present case. In that case the only reference to time was a requirement that on a failure to agree the rent the rent should be determined during a one-year period prior to the period to which the rent was to relate and that it should be so determined by arbitration.

Counsel for Dewhurst submits that time is of the essence in respect of the break clause containing a time limit and that there is a correlation between the break clause and limb 3 of the reddendum. I did not understand counsel for Metrolands to dispute either part of that submission. It is clear from the *United Scientific* case that time is of the essence of a break clause. As Lord Diplock stated ([1977] 2 All ER 62 at 72, [1978] AC 904 at 929):

'... there is a practical business reason for treating time as of the essence of such a clause, which is similar to that applicable to an option to acquire property. The exercise of this option by the tenant will have the effect of depriving the landlord of the existing source of income from his property and the evident purpose of the stipulation as to notice is to leave him free thereafter to enter into a contract with a new tenant for a tenancy commencing at the date of surrender provided for in the break clause.'

Further, it is to my mind clear that there is a correlation between the time limit in limb 3 and that in the break clause. The timetable in the lease envisaged that the arbitrator's award would be known at the latest by 18 August 1981 and the period in which Dewhurst had the right to serve a notice operating the break clause commenced the next day. To my mind it is immaterial that the break clause is not in the same clause as the provision for rent review. It is trite law that a document must be construed as a whole. Counsel for Metrolands does not dispute that the obvious purpose of the correlation between the time limit in limb 3 and the break clause was to enable Dewhurst to make its decision whether or not to exercise its right to determine the lease in the knowledge of what the new rent would be if it continued in possession after the review date. He also does not dispute that where there is such a correlation between a break clause and a time limit in a rent review clause containing a landlord's trigger notice, the prescribed procedure requiring the landlord to initiate the rent review by serving a notice, time is of the essence of the rent review clause. But, he submits, the same does not apply to a rent review clause when it is open to the tenant as much as it is to the landlord to initiate the review. In the latter case, he submits, time is not made of the essence of the rent review clause. Counsel's concession in relation to rent review clauses with a landlord's trigger notice is plainly correct. In the *United Scientific* case Lord Diplock commented on the previous authorities and referred to two in which there had been a break clause correlated with the rent review clause, C Richards & Son Ltd v. *Karenita Ltd* (1971) 221 EG 25 and *Samuel Properties (Developments) Ltd* v. *Hayek* [1972] 3 All ER 473, [1971] 1 WLR 1296.

In the *Richards* case there was a lease for 14 years with a provision for rent review for the final seven years. Such review was to be triggered by a landlord's notice given at any time during the first three months of the seventh year. There was also a break clause for the tenant to determine the lease at the end of the seventh year exercisable by the tenant giving three months' previous notice. The landlord's trigger notice was nearly six months out of time but it still left the tenant about a week to operate the break clause. Goulding J held that time was of the essence for the rent review clause, but for reasons which were disapproved by the House of Lords in the *United Scientific* case. However, Lord Diplock said of the case that it was rightly decided because the timetable of the rent review clause for the determination of the rent review was obviously correlated with the time for operating the break clause (see [1977] 2 All ER 62 at 77, [1978] AC 904 at 936). In the *Samuel Properties* case the lease for 21 years provided for rent reviews at the end of the seventh and fourteenth years such reviews to be initiated by a landlord's trigger notice not later than two quarters before the expiry of the seventh and fourteenth years. There was also a break clause enabling the tenant to determine the lease at the end of the seventh and fourteenth years on giving at least one quarter's prior notice in writing. That was subject to a proviso that if the rent had not been reviewed by the beginning of the quarter before the expiration of the seventh and fourteenth years the lessee's right to terminate the lease should be extended until one month after notification to the lessee of the reviewed rent. The Court of Appeal held that time was of the essence. Lord Diplock said that but for that proviso by necessary implication time would have been made of the essence of the rent review clause because of its interrelation with the time by which notice was to be given under the break clause, but because of the proviso the implication that would otherwise have arisen from the association of the rent review clause with the break clause was negatived. Lord Simon said ([1977] 2 All ER 62 at 85, [1978] AC 904 at 946]:

'However, where a rent review clause is associated with a true option (a "break" clause, for example), it is a strong indication that time is intended to be of the essence of the rent review clause—if not absolutely, at least to the extent that the tenant will reasonably expect to know what new rent he will have to pay before the time comes for him to elect whether to terminate or renew the tenancy (cf *Samuel Properties (Developments) Ltd* v. *Hayek*. That situation stands in significant contrast with those in the instant appeals.'

Lord Simon also agreed with Lord Diplock's analysis of, inter alia, the *Richards* and *Samuel Properties* cases.

Lord Fraser, referring to the equitable rule against treating time as of the essence of a contract, said ([1977] 2 All ER 62 at 98, [1978] AC 904 at 962-963):

'It would also be excluded if the context clearly indicated that that was the intention of the parties—as for instance where the tenant had a right to break the lease by notice given by a specified date which was later than the last date for serving the landlord's trigger notice. The tenant's notice to terminate the contract would be one where the time limit was mandatory, and the necessary implication is that the time limit for giving the landlord's notice of review must also be mandatory. An example of such interlocked provisions is to be found in *C Richards & Son* v. *Karenita Ltd* where the decision that time was of the essence of the landlord's notice could be supported on this ground, although not, as I think, on the ground on which it was actually rested. *Samuel Properties (Developments) Ltd* v. *Hayek* is not in this class because, although there was a tenant's break clause, the time allowed to the tenant for giving notice was automatically extended until one month after the notification of the reviewed rent to the lessee.'

Those remarks to which I have referred were all strictly obiter, but they were followed by Warner J in *Coventry City Council* v. *J Hepworth & Sons Ltd* (1981) 261 EG 566 and by the Court of Appeal affirming his decision (see (1982) 46 P & CR 170). The *Coventry City Council* case again involved the correlation of a rent review clause which was initiated by a trigger notice and a break clause. Warner J expressed the applicable presumption as 'the presumption that, where a rent review clause is linked to a tenant's option to break time is of the essence of the rent review clause' (at 569). In the Court of Appeal Lawton LJ confined his reasoning to following Lord Fraser in referring to a rent review initiated by a landlord's trigger notice correlated with a break clause. Griffiths LJ agreed, but stated that he found the reasoning of Warner J compelling and did not wish to give separate reasons of his own.

There are only two reported cases where the question of the correlation between the time limit in a break clause and that in a rent review clause, not involving a landlord's trigger notice, has been considered. One is the decision of his Honour Judge John Finlay QC sitting as a judge of the High Court in *Edwin Woodhouse Trustee Co. Ltd* v. *Sheffield Brick Co plc* (1983) 270 EG 548. In that case the judge held that time was not of the essence, but that case turned on somewhat peculiar wording of a rent review clause which is dissimilar to that in the present case and I do not think it assists me. The second case is a decision of Mr Evans-Lombe QC sitting as a deputy judge of this division in *William Hill (Southern) Ltd* v. *Govier & Govier* (1984) 269 EG 1168. In that case the lease provided for reviews of rent on review dates at the end of the fifth and tenth years. If the landlord and tenant failed to agree the best rack rent obtainable in the open market for the premises nine months before the review date, then either party might within a further period of one month refer the question of the amount of the rent to a chartered surveyor nominated in default of agreement by the president of the Royal Institution of Chartered Surveyors on the application of the lessor. There was a break clause which the tenant could operate by giving three months' notice to terminate the lease at the end of the fifth and tenth years. The deputy judge found similarities between that case and the *Coventry City Council* case, and in particular relied on Warner J's statement of the applicable presumption. He rejected an argument based on the distinction between a landlord's trigger notice case and a mandatory review case. He said (at 1171-1172):

'It seems to me that where one finds, as in the present case and as in the *Coventry* case, provisions for review and determination by the tenant in the same clause with a time schedule which seems to indicate an intention by the parties that the tenant shall know whether the landlord is seeking an increase of rent, it is not conclusive of the question, whether time is of the essence of the review provisions, that these provisions are automatically activated by mandatory words in the lease or are optionally activated by provisions giving the landlord an option whether by a certain date to serve a trigger-notice. Obviously where a lease contains provisions for a mandatory review as at a certain date, and nothing else, time will not be of the essence of that provision. Where a lease provides for a mandatory review and then sets up a machinery for concluding that review which seems to be geared to providing the tenant, either with the answer as to what the future rent shall be or with a shrewd idea of what it should be, or at least with a knowledge whether or not the landlord is going to ask for an increase, before he has to take a decision whether to give notice to terminate, time is of the essence of the provisions for review. I do not therefore see any general basis for the distinction which [counsel for the landlord] put forward.'

He summarised the position as he saw it as follows (at 1172):

'In default of agreement the parties have the option to put in train an arbitration within a fixed period of one month from a certain date. If they do not take that opportunity, then the only avenue for solving the dispute contemplated by the lease is lost and the old rent must stand. It seems to me, in the present case, that the lease gives to the tenant the right to sit back and watch whether or not the landlord will in the time specified refer the question of future rent to arbitration. It matters not that there has or has not been anything in the nature of negotiations leading up to such a reference. Once, however, the time for referral is gone by, the tenant can decide whether or not to terminate the lease knowing whether the landlord is in a position to seek an increase of rent or not. It follows from the above that in my judgment the provisions for review of the rent and premature termination of the lease at the instance of the tenant are in this lease linked. I have not had placed before me any special circumstances which may, none the less, drive me to conclude that Warner J's *prima facie* rule does not here apply. Accordingly, in my judgment, time is of the essence of the provision requiring reference to arbitration in default of agreement of the amount of the new rent within the month succeeding the commencement of the ninth month before the review date.'

Counsel for Metrolands submitted that that case was distinguishable on the ground that the relevant time limit there involved was within the control of the parties, being that in respect of the reference to the so-called arbitrator (described by the deputy judge as 'not being [an arbitrator] in the strict legal sense' (at 1170)); whereas in the present case the time limit was in respect of the act of a third party, the arbitrator. Counsel pointed out that under the Arbitration Act 1950 there were many possibilities for delays which were not within the control of the parties and that in the present case to allow an ample period for the arbitration would involve commencing negotiations far in advance of the rent review date. I see that there is that difference between the two cases, and it is of course true that each case turns on the construction of the wording of the lease and it must be decided on its own particular facts. But I would be very reluctant to treat the *William Hill* case as distinguishable on so narrow a ground, when there is the major point of similarity between the two cases that the tenant, no less than the landlord, had the right to refer the matter to the arbitrator. The decision in the *William Hill* case is of a judge, albeit a deputy, of equal jurisdiction on a point on which there is no other direct authority by way of a decided case; and whilst it is not binding on me I would not wish to introduce further uncertainty into this difficult area of the law by a decision inconsistent with his unless I was convinced that the deputy judge reached the wrong conclusion.

Counsel for Metrolands submitted that the case was wrongly decided. He said that the deputy judge had wrongly treated the *Coventry City Council* case (a landlord's trigger notice case) as similar to the *William Hill* case and had completely failed to give adequate weight to the fact that the tenant wanting to know what the rent would be before operating the break clause had the means to find out. To my mind it is clear from the judgment (at 1170-1171) that the deputy judge did consider the difference between a landlord's trigger notice case and a case such as that before him where the tenant as well as the landlord could refer the matter to the arbitrator, but the deputy judge considered the difference as being of no importance. Counsel for Metrolands also submitted that the deputy judge went wrong because of an incorrect concession by counsel for the landlord (at 1172) that the court had no residuary jurisdiction to determine the rack rent. But as the point turns on specific wording not present here, and it does not relate to the question of time being of the essence, and in any event it related to an argument which the deputy judge rejected albeit of the landlord who was successful on other grounds, viz the correlation between the rent review clause and the break clause, the error (if it be such) does not to my mind matter.

Counsel for Metrolands' main submission was that in the *United Scientific* case itself the House of Lords had reached the conclusion that time was not of the essence, *inter alia*, because the tenant as well as the landlord had it in his power to initiate the rent review. He submitted that for the very same reason it was wrong to treat the mere correlation of the rent review clause with the break clause as conclusive of time being of the essence of the rent review clause. The only justification for treating time of the essence was that the tenant needed to know what the rent would be before operating the break clause, and he had the means to find out himself. Add to that, he said, the other factors that the House of Lords found so weighty, such as the injustice to the landlord if denied his right to a fair rent for a period of years by a delay, even of a day, and the absence of any real prejudice to the tenant other than what could have been avoided by the tenant's own action to ascertain the rent before the expiry of the time limited for the operation of the break clause, and the fact that the observance of the time limit in the present lease was in the third party's hands. The result, he submitted, was that the court, weighing what he accepted was the contra-indication of the correlation of the reddendum with the break clause, should hold that the parties must have intended that time was not of the essence of the *reddendum*.

I very much feel the force of these submissions. But the difficulty in the way of my accepting them is that it seems to me that the arguments of counsel for Metrolands apply with equal force to some at least of the trigger notice cases, such as the *Richards* case. He accepts that in a landlord's trigger notice case the correlation between the rent review clause and the break clause is itself enough to make time of the essence of the rent review clause. In a case like the *Richards* case, as counsel pointed out, it is not what actually happened that is important; the question whether time is of the essence must be judged at the moment of the lease. But in the *Richards* case there was a period of six months between the time for the service of the landlord's notice and the latest date for the exercise by the tenant of the break clause. If time was not of the essence the tenant could, as the House of Lords held in respect of *Cheapside Land Development Co. Ltd* v. *Messels Service Co.* [1977] 2 All ER 62, [1978] AC 904, heard together with the *United Scientific* case, have served a notice on the landlord specifying a period, which Lord Diplock said could be short, within which the tenant could require the landlord to serve a notice instigating the rent review, and the tenant could make time of the essence. This could be done as soon as the time for the landlord's notice had expired. Thus there would have been time enough, and this could have been seen at the date of the lease, for the tenant to have known the actual rent for the period under review, or at least have known the upper and lower figures, before the tenant had to decide whether to operate the break clause: see in particular Lord Diplock in the *United Scientific* case [1977] 2 all ER 62 at 75-76, [1978] AC 904 at 933-934. In other words, in many landlord's trigger notice cases it would be open to the tenant to find out the likely rent, just as much as in a case where he has an express right to refer to arbitration; and yet that was not treated by Lord Diplock, Lord Simon and Lord Fraser as relevant. The simple correlation between the rent review clause and the break clause was enough, save where there was a specific inconsistent provision such as the proviso in the *Samuel*

Properties case. Moreover, I think that Lord Diplock in referring, as he did, to the necessary implication as to time being of the essence where there was an interrelation between a rent review clause and a break clause, and Lord Simon to the like effect, were intending to lay down general guidelines. I confess that, for the reasons so attractively advanced by counsel for Metrolands, I do not find the simple correlation approach completely satisfying logically. But I am unable to say that Warner J was wrong to state the applicable presumption in the way that he did, nor am I able to say that the deputy judge in the *William Hill* case was wrong to follow that statement.

Accordingly, I shall follow the decision in the *William Hill* case in holding that here, too, time is of the essence of the *reddendum* by reason of the correlation with the break clause.

[The landlords further submitted that even if time was of the essence the landlord could obtain a determination by the court on the rent. This was rejected by the judge, who said:]

It would to my mind again be absurd if, although time was of the essence for the arbitration award because of the correlation with the break clause, the landlord could now obtain a determination of the market rent from the court when the tenant is too late to operate the break clause.

Another similar line of attack employed by counsel for Metrolands was based on *Beer* v. *Bowden* [1981] 1 All ER 1070, [1981] 1 WLR 522. He submitted that on the basis of that authority a term was to be implied that the rent was to be a fair rent. But in that case the term of the relevant rent review clause was that the rent was to be 'such rent as shall ... be agreed between the Landlords and the Tenant ... and in any case not less than the yearly rent [of £1250] payable [under the lease]'. The Court of Appeal rejected an argument that £1250 should be the rent, for the obvious good reason that a tenant by the mere expedient of refusing to agree a higher rent would not have to pay more than £1250. Accordingly, the court implied a term as to a fair rent, to give the agreement business efficacy. That case is clearly distinguishable from the present case, which does not allow the tenant to frustrate the rent review.

What then is the result? Counsel for Dewhurst does not submit that no rent should be payable. Instead, he submitted that the court should apply the principle adopted in *Weller* v. *Akehurst* [1981] 3 All ER 411. In that case a lease provided that there should be a rent review to govern the rent for the second half of the term of the lease. A procedure was laid down for the rent review, and time was made of the essence. But there was a failure to observe the timetable and nothing was said in the lease as to what was to be the rent in that event. Fox J held that, as the parties had chosen the procedure for rent review with precision and made time of the essence, the procedure was to be followed timeously or not at all. He further held that in the lease the provision for rent for the first half of the term should be taken to have been intended by the parties to continue for the second half of the term. So, counsel for Dewhurst said, in the present case, where not only was £1800 the rent for the immediately preceding period but also it was the minimum rent which the parties had contemplated if there had been a rent review. Counsel for Metrolands pointed to the difference between the language of that case and the present case, but, in my judgment, the differences in language are not significant, and I think that that principle ought to apply here. I shall therefore declare that £1800 is the rent payable for the last seven years of the term.

Note: On appeal (judgment 21 February 1986) the court held that although there was a clear correlation between the break clause and the rent review provisions this was not a sufficient contra-indication to make time of the essence because in this case (i) the relevant date by which a valuation had to be made was substantially outside the lessor's control; (ii) any potential hardship to the tenant arising from the lessor's delay could be mitigated by the tenant initiating the rent review procedures. These two factors had to be taken in conjunction with one another.

Chapter 3

Deeming provisions

3.1 A 'deeming provision' in a rent review provision may be a contra-indication to the presumption that time is not of the essence

A 'deeming provision' in a rent review clause which provides the level of rent payable in default of implementation of review procedures by prescribed dates may be a contra-indication to the presumption that time is not of the essence. Whether or not it is a contra-indication making time of the essence will depend on the terms of the clause itself. If the machinery provides for steps to be taken which are beyond the control of the parties it is less likely that time will be of the essence.

HENRY SMITH'S CHARITY TRUSTEES v. A.W.A.D.A. TRADING AND PROMOTION SERVICES LTD

Court of Appeal (1984) 269 EG 729

A lease contained rent review provisions which were both detailed and comprehensive in providing for the determination of a revised rent. The clause also contained 'deeming' provisos which included clause 7 providing that

'If on the expiration of two months from the date of service of such (the tenant's) counter-notice the Landlords and the Tenant shall not have agreed in writing an amount to be treated as the market rent and the Landlords shall not have applied for the appointment of a Surveyor in accordance with paragraph 6 of this Schedule the amount stated in such counter-notice shall be deemed to be the market rent.'

The landlords initiated the rent review procedure by a notice dated November 1980, which proposed a market rent of £29,000 p.a. The tenants served a counter-notice dated 3 December 1980 expressing the view that the market rent was £8000 p.a. This was within the one month time limit specified. Thereafter the parties entered into negotiations but failed to reach agreement on the level of the revised rent. In June 1981, four months after the time limit provided in the lease had expired, the landlords applied to appoint an independent surveyor to determine what the market rent should be. The tenants contended that the application was ineffective and out of time and that the deeming provisions of clause 7 applied, that clause 7 and other deeming provisions in the lease were sufficient contra-indications to rebut the presumption that time was not of the essence in a rent review clause. In the High Court Vinelott J held that the landlords' application was valid and effective. The tenants appealed.

Held: The appeal was allowed. The parties had not only set out a timetable but had in terms provided what was to happen in the absence of strict compliance with that timetable. The presumption of elasticity would undoubtedly have been acceptable if clauses 3 and 6 had stood alone but the deeming provisions of clause 4 and 7 made it clear that something quite different was intended. It was highly undesirable that decisions of this type of dispute should turn upon fine distinctions and there was no difference between a rent review scheme which, in the event of default in adhering to the timetable, avoids the whole process (see *Lewis* v. *Barnett* (1982) 264 EG 1079 (CA)) and one which automatically resolves the dispute, albeit in a somewhat draconian way as in the present case. Both schemes had made precise (and in the present case, elaborate) provisions for exactly what should happen if one of the parties should fail to exercise his rights within the specified period of time. In neither case would it be possible seriously to write into the clause after each specified period of time words such as 'or such longer period as shall elapse before the expiration of reasonable notice making time of the essence of the contract'. Accordingly, the parties must be deemed to have intended in the case of this lease the general rule should not apply and that time should be of the essence of the contract. The contractual rent was £8000 p.a. Dictum of Lord Diplock in *United Scientific Holdings Ltd* v. *Burnley Borough Council* [1978] AC 904 at page 930 (see earlier page 3) applied. *Lewis* v. *Barnett* (1982) 264 EG 1079 (see earlier page 24) followed.

SIR JOHN DONALDSON MR: The issue is whether, as Vinelott J held, the landlords are entitled to have the market rent for the period from 24 June 1981 determined by an independent surveyor, notwithstanding that they made the relevant application four months after the expiry of the two months' period specified in clause 7.

It is, I think, unfortunate that the learned judge was not referred to a decision of this court on not dissimilar rent review provisions in *Lewis* v. *Barnett* now reported in (1982) 264 EG 1079 but then unreported ... The application to the president for the appointment of a surveyor was made six months after the latest date calculated in accordance with clause 3.

A division of this court, consisting of Stephenson LJ, Brandon LJ and Sir Stanley Rees, held that (per Stephenson LJ at p 1080):

These leases were, of course, drawn up and executed before the decision of the House of Lords in that case, but nevertheless the tenants may have achieved indirectly the result that express words would have achieved by in Lord Diplock's words, "contra-indications in the express words of the lease".

In my judgment, in spite of Mr Davidson's submissions, that is exactly what they have done. I cannot regard the omission of the reference to time from the reference to the landlord's application as having the effect for which Mr Davidson contends. It seems to me that when the draftsman of this paragraph referred to the landlord's neglect to make the application referred to in para 3, he was referring, without setting out all the words, to his application to make it not less than three months before the rent review dates, because that is the application which the landlord has to make in para 3. He might have omitted the words "at least six months before the rent review date" in the second line of the para if he had wished to be equally concise. In my judgment para 6 means what it says and what it says is that, if the landlord neglects to comply with para 3 in respect of the application there referred to in a case where he and the tenant have not been able to agree the open market rent in the time required, or at all, then any notice already given by the landlord to the tenant under the provisions of para 2, including the all-important opening notice, shall be void and of no effect.

[Counsel] for the landlords submits that the principles laid down in the *United Scientific* case require us to treat the time-limits specified in the rent review clauses with which we are concerned as being elastic, unless and until a notice is served making time of the essence. On this view, clause 3 allows the tenant an unlimited time in which to serve a counternotice, unless and until reasonable notice is given making time of the essence. If and when such a notice makes time of the essence and there is non-compliance, clause 4 deems the landlord's view to be correct and to determine the market rent. Clauses 6 and 7 operate similarly. The landlord has an unlimited time in which to apply for the appointment of a surveyor, unless and until time is made of the essence. If the failure continues, clause 7 comes into operation.

I am quite unable to accept this construction. The parties have not only set out a timetable but have in terms provided what is to happen in the absence of strict compliance with that timetable. The presumption of elasticity would undoubtedly be acceptable if clauses 3 and 6 stood alone with minor alterations in language to make that possible. But clauses 4 and 7 make it clear that something quite different is intended.

It is highly undesirable that decisions of this type of dispute shall turn upon fine distinctions and I reject the suggestion that there is a difference between a rent review scheme which, in the event of default in adhering to the timetable, avoids the whole process (*Lewis* v. *Barnett*) and one which automatically resolves the dispute, albeit in a somewhat draconian way (the instant appeal). Both make precise and, in the case of the instant appeal, elaborate provision for exactly what shall happen if one of the parties shall fail to exercise his rights within the specified period of time. In neither case would it be possible seriously to write into the clause after each specified period of time words such as 'or such longer period as shall elapse before the expiration of reasonable notice making time of the essence of the contract'. Accordingly, in my judgment, the parties must be deemed to have intended that in the case of their lease the general rule should not apply and that time should be of the essence of the contract.

It may well be thought unwise to have a strict timetable review clause which, in the event of default, may have the effect that an unreal rent put forward for negotiating purposes becomes the contractual rent. This I would accept, but it is for the parties to make their own contract. One modification which may commend itself is to borrow from the procedure in what is sometimes known as a 'flip-flop' arbitration. Each party is free to put forward a figure (in this context a figure for the market rent) which they say is the 'right' figure. In default of agreement, an arbitrator or expert decides what is the "right" figure, but, and this is the significant feature, his award or determination takes the form of confirming whichever of the parties' suggested figures is nearest to the 'right' figure. The practical result is, of course, that each party is forced to put forward a highly realistic figure, since any exaggeration in either direction is likely to lead to the other party's figure being accepted. This approach has, I understand, been used in wage bargaining and will be equally appropriate— indeed perhaps even more appropriate—in rent review.

For the reasons which I have given, I would allow the appeal and declare that in the events which have happened the contractual rent is £8000 per annum.

Agreeing, **Griffiths LJ** said: The construction, so benevolent to the landlords, which [counsel for the landlords] seeks to place on para 7, involves the submission that if the two-month period expires before the landlords have applied for the appointment of a surveyor to determine the market rent, the process of its ascertainment is to remain in a state of total suspense until the tenant stimulates the landlords into activity by serving a notice making time of the essence, and a 'reasonable time' expires thereafter. The 'deeming' provisions in para 4 must, I think, inevitably stand on the same footing. Accordingly, the landlords' submission, in my opinion, likewise involves the proposition that if the one-month period referred to in para 4 expires before the tenant has served its counternotice, the whole process of ascertainment of the market rent is to be frozen until the landlords have stimulated the tenant into activity by serving a notice making time of the essence for the purpose of para 4.

Despite its attractive presentation, I find myself wholly unable to accept [counsel for the landlord's] argument on these points in the context of the present lease. I think that the 'deeming' provisions of para 4 of this particular rent review clause are quite inconsistent with the survival of any right of the tenant to serve a counternotice after the expiration of the one-month period designated in that paragraph. Likewise, I think that the deeming provisions of para 7 are quite inconsistent with the survival of any right in the landlords to apply for the appointment of a surveyor after the expiration of the two-month period therein specified. While in other contexts 'deeming' provisions may not necessarily connote finality, they do so in the context of this lease.

As will be observed from the definition of the 'variation date' contained in para 1 (i) of the Third Schedule, a period of at very least six months must elapse between the service of the landlords' trigger notice and the arrival of the 'variation date'. The provisions of the rent review clause are very carefully drafted so as to ensure that, save in one exceptional contingency, the 'market rent', and thus the 'revised rent', must in any event be ascertained before the 'variation date' arrives. There was a very good reason for the draftsman's care in this respect. Para 8 provides that, save in the one exceptional contingency, 'on and from the variation date the revised rent shall be substituted for the current rent and the provisions of this Lease as to payment of rent shall apply to the revised rent'. The application of the mandatory provisions of para 8 would have been obviously likely to present difficulties if there was a possibility of the 'variation date' arriving before the market rent had been ascertained. The draftsman was rightly concerned to avoid such difficulties. The one exceptional contingency to which I have referred is the case where the landlords have duly applied for the appointment of a surveyor in accordance with para 6, but the surveyor has not yet made his determination before the variation date arrives; in this contingency the interim provisions of para 9 will apply. However, the draftsman plainly did not contemplate that the interim provisions of para 9 would have any application where the tenant had omitted to serve a counternotice or the landlords had omitted to apply for the appointment of a surveyor within the respective specified time-limits. These two contingencies had already been covered by the deeming provisions of paras 4 and 7 respectively.

The structure of the Third Schedule is thus one under which the respective parties are given carefully defined rights exercisable within carefully defined time-limits and in which the consequences of any failure to exercise such rights within those limits are no less carefully defined. The interrelation of the various paras of the rent review clause is, in my opinion, quite inconsistent with any necessity for the tenant to serve on the landlords a 'time of the essence' notice of the nature suggested, before he can rely on the provisions of para 7 according to their terms. This para, when read with the other paras of the schedule, is, in my opinion, too explicit a 'contra-indication' within the relevant principles to allow the ordinary presumption against time being of the essence to operate in the landlords' favour; it serves clearly to rebut the presumption. As the decision in *Lewis* v. *Barnett* well illustrates, one cannot invoke the *United Scientific* principles for the purpose of rejecting or modifying a provision which clearly indicates the parties' intention that time *is* to be of the essence for the purpose of a rent review clause. There is nothing to prevent the parties from contracting on this basis if they so choose and, if they do so choose, to entitle the court to rewrite the contract which they have made.

3.2 Whether or not a 'deeming provision' does amount to a contra-indication to the rule that time is not of the essence depends on the proper construction of the clause concerned

The case of *Henry Smith's Charity Trustees* v. *AWADA Trading and Promotions Services Ltd* was distinguished and a deeming clause was held not to be a firm indication that time was of the essence in the following case.

MECCA LEISURE LTD v. RENOWN INVESTMENTS (HOLDINGS) LTD AND ANOTHER

Court of Appeal   (1984) 271 EG 989

A rent review clause in a lease contained machinery and a timetable and a 'deeming provision' in the event of non-compliance with the review procedures which provided that if the tenants failed to serve a counter-notice within the prescribed time 'they shall be deemed to have agreed to pay the increased rent specified in the rent notice as from the review date'. The landlords served a notice but the tenants failed to deal with it in the time provided in the review clause. The landlords demanded the rent stated in their review notice on the basis that the deeming provision was a sufficient contra-indication to make time of the essence and accordingly that the tenants had lost their right to challenge the rent proposed by the landlords. The tenants commenced proceedings contending that time was not of the essence. Bristow J found for the tenants. The landlords appealed.

Held: The appeal was dismissed by Eveleigh and May LJJ, with Browne-Wilkinson LJ dissenting. The mere presence of a deeming clause was not a firm indication that time is of the essence. The clause had to be read as a whole bearing in mind that there was a presumption to be displaced and that the parties were intending to arrive at a fair rent amicably if possibly. To hold otherwise in this case would be to make the clause a trap and the chosen machinery dangerous.

EVELEIGH LJ: In this appeal a number of cases have been cited to the court showing on the one hand where time has been of the essence and on the other hand where it has not. In particular the tenant relied upon *Davstone (Holdings) Ltd* v. *Al-Rifai* (1976) 32 P & CR 18 and *Touche Ross & Co.* v. *Secretary of State for the Environment* (1983) 265 EG 982. In the former case the clause provided:

'If the lessee shall raise no objection to the increased rental proposed by the lessor within 28 days of receiving such notice the lessee shall be deemed to have accepted and agreed the same.'

Goulding J held that the tenant was not precluded by his delay from objecting to an increase of rent.

Foremost among the cases referred to by the landlords was *The Trustees of Henry Smith's Charity* v. *AWADA Trading & Promotion Services Ltd*, a decision of this court dated 2 December 1983. The clause in that case contained an elaborate time-schedule and provided that the rent stated by the landlord be deemed to be the rent if the tenants' counternotice was not served in time, and, on the other hand, if a counternotice was duly given and the landlord did not apply for the appointment of a surveyor to determine the rent within a specified period, then the rent stated by the tenants' counternotice should be deemed to be the rent payable. There was also an important provision for the payment of a provisional rent at the figure stated in the landlord's notice pending a determination of the market rent by a surveyor. There was also a provision to adjust the position between the landlord and the tenant once the market rent was determined, but no interest was recoverable by the party who had been out of pocket. In that case time was held to be of the essence. I find no help at all from the facts of other cases where there is a deeming provision, as in the present case, but other terms in the review clause and the lease are different.

In accordance with *United Scientific* v. *Burnley Council* we have to start with the presumption that time is not of the essence, then, on a consideration of the lease itself and the surrounding circumstances, to determine whether the parties have shown an intention to make time of the essence. As Lord Fraser said at p 957:

'... it is proper to recall that the application of any general rule may always be excluded if the intention to do so is expressed or clearly implied.'

It is clear from the review clause taken as a whole that the parties intended to provide machinery for the determination of a fair rent. They clearly regarded it as desirable if that rent could be determined by mutual agreement. They were to 'use their best endeavours to reach agreement as to the amount of the rent.' It is 'within twenty-eight days after service of such counternotice (or within such extended period as the Lessor and the Lessee shall mutually agree) ...' No time is laid down for the appointment of the arbitrator and no time is laid down for the announcement of his decision. As Dillon LJ pointed out in *Touche Ross & Co.* at p 983:

'Lord Fraser at p 960 took into account in relation to one of the particular cases before their Lordships' House there, as a factor tending against time being of the essence of the rent review clause, that steps fell to be taken which were not under the control of the parties.'

It is only from the words of the deeming clause itself that any argument can be raised in support of the contention that time was intended to be of the essence.

In *The Trustees of Henry Smith's Charity* Griffiths LJ said:

'I do not accept that the mere presence of a "deeming" provision in a rent review clause will in all cases be sufficient to make time of the essence of the contract.'

Slade LJ referred to the 'comprehensive and stringent nature' of the clause under consideration in that case and he said: 'While in other contexts "deeming" provisions may not necessarily connote finality, they do so in the context of this lease.' I cannot regard the mere presence of the 'deeming' clause as a firm indication that time is of the essence. I read the clause as a whole and bear in mind that there is a presumption to be displaced, and the parties are clearly intending to arrive at a fair rent to be determined amicably if possible. It seems to me that to hold otherwise would make the clause a trap and the chosen machinery dangerous. In my opinion time is not of the essence in this case.

My conclusion does not mean that a 'deeming' provision is of no effect. It entitles the landlords to make time of the essence by giving notice to that effect once the 28th day has expired. It is a useful part of the machinery in the hands of the landlords.

We were referred to the case of *Raineri* v. *Miles* [1981] AC 1050. The fact that a purchaser may sue for damages resulting from delay in completion by the vendor, even though time for completion is not of the essence, has no relevance to the present case. In that case there was no issue as to whether or not there was an agreed and binding obligation to complete. We, on the other hand, are concerned to determine whether there is a binding obligation to pay a rent as stated in the landlords' notice. Moreover, the deeming provision forms part of the machinery devised to produce a fair rent and must be viewed in that context. It is not to be seen as an independent clause creating a binding obligation upon the happening of a particular event.

I therefore would dismiss this appeal.

Agreeing that the appeal should be dismissed, **MAY LJ** said: While I respectfully agree that decisions on this type of dispute should not turn upon fine distinctions (per the Master of the Rolls at p 12B of the transcript of the *Henry Smith's Charity* case), it is I think also important in deciding questions of construction to distinguish between principle on the one hand and argument on the other. That there is a presumption against time being of the essence in rent-review clauses is principle; that where a particular rent-review clause contains 'deeming' provisions this will nevertheless suffice to make time of the essence of that clause is argument. As such, it can validly be used in respect of any rent-review clause containing similar provisions: it does not necessarily follow that it will succeed in every such case ...

The effect, therefore, of the *Henry Smith's Charity* case is in my opinion that, although the fact that a rent-review clause does contain a 'deeming' provision is a contra-indication which may be sufficient to rebut the general principle, whether it does so or not remains in the end a matter of the proper construction of the particular clause concerned.

Dissenting, **BROWNE-WILKINSON LJ** said: There must now be many thousands of leases containing rent-review clauses in many different forms which provide for a default rent. It would in my judgment be most undesirable if in every case where a notice is served out of time the parties were in doubt as to the legal consequences. In commercial and property law it is in my judgment of the highest importance that the parties should know the legal consequences of their acts without having to go to court for them to be determined. Therefore, with regret, I cannot agree that the matter depends in each case on the exact detailed drafting of the rent-review clause, the existence of a provision for a default rent being merely one of the factors to be taken into account in deciding whether time is of the essence.

For myself, in order to avoid the fine distinctions in this field which the Master of the Rolls deplored in the *Smith's Charity* case (at p 12B), I am not prepared to distinguish this case from the *Smith's Charity* case. I accept, of course, that the rent-review clause under consideration in the *Smith's Charity* case was much more detailed than that in the instant case and had certain features which are not present in the instant case. But, for the reasons I have given, I do not think that the right answer can depend on comparatively small differences in drafting. As I read the *Smith's Charity* case, Griffiths LJ did not treat the provisions for a default rent as being a very important, let alone decisive, factor, ie he preferred what I have called the first view. The Master of the Rolls, on the other hand, adopted what I have called the second view and treated the default rent as being decisive. Slade LJ, although looking at all the features of the rent-review clause in that case in coming to the view that time was of the essence, undoubtedly treated the provisions for default rents (which he called 'the deeming provisions') to be of 'critical' importance (p 23F) and 'quite inconsistent with the survival of any right' to serve a notice out of time (at p 27). In my judgment the *ratio decidendi* of the decision of the majority was that the provision for a default rent was a decisive, or virtually decisive, contra-indication displacing the presumption that time was not of the essence.

Therefore, although I differ with considerable diffidence, for myself I would not have been prepared to draw narrow distinctions between this case and the *Smith's Charity* case and would have allowed the appeal in the hope that clarity and consistency in the relevant law would be maintained.

However, in the case below, a deeming provision in the rent review clause was held to be a sufficient contra-indication to the general rule that time is not of the essence in rent review clauses and *Mecca Leisure Ltd* v. *Renown Investments (Holdings) Ltd and Another* (above, page 64) was distinguished.

GREENHAVEN SECURITIES LTD v. COMPTON AND ANOTHER

Chancery Division   (1985) 1 ETLR 105

The rent review clause in a lease of commercial premises provided that the rent was subject to review on specified dates. Paragraph 1 of the First Schedule offered three alternative methods of fixing the revised rent: (1) by agreement between the parties (2) in default of agreement then the rent should be the greater of (a) the rent payable immediately before the review date and (b) the rack rent defined by an arbitrator appointed during a period commencing three months before and expiring twelve months after the review date, or (3) in default of agreement and application for the appointment of an arbitrator 'then a sum equal to the rent payable immediately before the review date'. The first review date was 25 March 1983. No new rent had been agreed but neither party applied to appoint an arbitrator not later than 12 months after that date. Subsequently, the landlord made a belated application on 20 June 1984. The tenant contended that time was of the essence and that the application was too late and ineffective and that the rent payable was the rent payable immediately before the review date. The landlord sought to persuade the court to construe the review clause on the basis that the review provisions did not make time of the essence.

Held: Although there was a presumption that time was not of the essence in the provisions of a rent review clause of a lease, and that presumption could only be displaced by a clear indication to the contrary, there was such a clear contra-indication in the material clause under consideration. Although the fact that a rent review clause did contain a deeming provision was a contra-indication which might be sufficient to rebut the general principle, whether or not it did so would depend on the construction of the clause concerned. Here, there was a sufficient contra-indication because the three alternatives of paragraph 1 of the first schedule clearly defined the future rent by strict time limits embracing every point. Dictum of Lord Diplock in *United Scientific Holdings Ltd* v. *Burnley Borough Council* (1978) AC 904 at p 930 and 932 applied; *Lewis* v. *Barnett* 264 EG 1079, *Henry Smith's Charity Trustees* v. *Awada Trading and Promotion Services* 269 EG 729 followed; *Mecca Leisure Ltd* v. *Renown Investments (Holdings) Ltd and Another* distinguished.

GOULDING J: That I think enables me to go at once to the first schedule, which is the part of the lease in dispute. It consists of four paragraphs, of which the most important for present purposes is para 1. I will read it in full. It is headed—and also marked in the margin—'Review of rent' and it reads:

'1. The rent as from each review date until the next review date, or in the case of the last or only review date from that review date until the end of the term, shall be ...'

and then there are three subparas numbered (1), (2) and (3).

'(1) The sum agreed in writing between the Landlord and the Tenant at any time before the new rent shall have been ascertained under subparagraphs (2) or (3); or
(2) If no such agreement shall have been reached then a sum equal to the greater of (a) the rent payable immediately before the review date and (b) the rack rental value of the property (as defined in paragraph 2) determined by a single arbitrator, appointed in default of agreement by the President of the Royal Institution of Chartered Surveyors in accordance with the Arbitration Act 1950 or any Act amending or replacing it, on the application of the landlord or the tenant made during a period commencing three months before and expiring twelve months after the review date; or
(3) If within the said period the Landlord and the Tenant shall not have agreed in writing who shall be the arbitrator for the purpose of subparagraph (2) and neither the Landlord nor the Tenant shall have applied to the President of the Royal Institution of Chartered Surveyors for the appointment of an arbitrator for the purpose of that subparagraph, then a sum equal to the rent payable immediately before the review date.'

Para 2 of the schedule contains an elaborate definition of the rack rental value of the property, which is to be determined if necessary by arbitration. Para 3 is in these words:

'3. As soon as may be after a new rent has been agreed or determined under subparagraphs (1) or (2) of paragraph 1 the Landlord and Tenant shall sign in duplicate a memorandum in writing (the cost of which shall be borne by the Tenant), recording the amount of the new rent so agreed or determined.'

Para 4 consists of two sentences; the first sentence says:

'4. If a new rent is not ascertained under paragraph 1 until after a review date, then the rent which was payable immediately before the review date shall continue to be payable until the new rent has been so ascertained, after which the new rent shall be payable.'

The second sentence provides for the payment of any excess due from the tenant with the first instalment of rent falling due after the new rent has been ascertained.

The material facts are very short and simple. The first of the review dates was 25 March 1983, so that no new rent having been agreed either party was at liberty to apply for the appointment of an arbitrator not later than 12 months after that date. However, neither party did apply. The landlord made a belated application on 20 June 1984 and the landlord maintains that the late application is none the less effective because time is not of the essence of the provision contained in para 1 (2) of the first schedule to the lease which I read. The landlord says correctly that as one starts off with a general rule that time is not of the essence in the machinery provisions of rent-review clauses, the whole of the provisions of the first schedule are to be regarded as machinery before achieving the object of a reasonable rent from time to time that will be fair as between the parties, and that the expiry of the period commencing three months before the expiring 12 months after a review date does not extinguish the right of either party to apply for the appointment of an arbitrator; it merely marks the end of the period contemplated by the parties as the proper time in which to apply and it gives either party the ability to serve on the other a notice fixing a further reasonable time as to which time will be of the essence, so that if such further time notified is reasonable and has expired, then it will indeed be too late for the dilatory party to apply. In practice, of course, it is only the landlord that is ever likely to apply for an arbitrator because the provisions of the schedule show that review can never result in an actual reduction of rent.

That is the attitude of the landlord. The tenants say, on the other hand, that the language of the first schedule is perfectly clear; the parties have agreed that if no application has been made within the specified time, then the new rent is to be the same as the former rent payable immediately before the review date. And the tenants maintain that there is no reason for departing from what, according to them, is the clear contractual provision in the lease. They say that the court would, in effect, be making a new bargain for the parties and setting aside the bargain they had made if it were to apply the equitable doctrine that relaxes time-limits in the way that the landlord here desires.

Now, I can best approach the decision of the matter by examining the three propositions on which the landlord's contention was founded. They are, first, that there is a presumption that time is not of the essence in the provisions of a rent-review clause in a lease. Second, that that presumption can be displaced only by a clear indication to the contrary and, third, that in the clause now under scrutiny there is no such indication.

The first two propositions, in my judgment, are correct, the difficult one being the third. The first two propositions are established, I think, by what is now the leading authority in this field, the decision of the House of Lords in *United Scientific Holdings Ltd* v. *Burnley Borough Council* [1978] AC 904. Lord Diplock there said at p 930 of the report:

'So upon the question of principle which these two appeals were brought to settle, I would hold that in the absence of any contra-indications in the express words of the lease or in the interrelation of the rent-review clause itself and other clauses or in the surrounding circumstances the presumption is that the timetable specified in a rent-review clause for completion of the various steps for determining the rent payable in respect of the period following the review date is not of the essence of the contract.'

And the same noble and learned lord said, at p 932:

'So far from finding any contra-indications to displace the presumption that strict adherence to the timetable specified in this rent-review clause is not of the essence of the contract, the considerations that I have mentioned appear to me to reinforce the presumption.'

I read that later citation to show that [counsel] for the landlord, was justified in using the word 'presumption', which he did.

I also think that the same case of *United Scientific Holdings* makes good [counsel for the landlord]'s second proposition that the presumption can be displaced only by a clear indication to the contrary. The language of Lord Diplock in the first of the passages I cited was that time would not be of the essence in the absence of any contra-indication in the expressed words of the lease or the interrelation of the rent-review clause and other clauses or surrounding circumstances. I may say that in the present case there is no evidence to send the court anywhere but to the expressed words of the lease itself to look for a contra-indication. That the contra-indication must be clear I have no doubt.

Lord Simon, in the same case of *United Scientific*, at p 944 approved as correctly summarising the modern law in the case of contracts of all types a sentence from the 4th ed of *Halsbury's Laws of England*, which says:

'Time will not be considered to be of the essence unless: (1) the parties expressly stipulate that conditions as to time must be strictly complied with; or (2) the nature of the subject matter of the contract or the surrounding circumstances show that time should be considered to be of the essence ...'

In giving that approval, I do not think Lord Simon could have meant to interpret the passage as requiring an expressed stipulation that time should not be of the essence, for that would be contrary to the general current of authority, both in *United Scientific* itself and elsewhere. The stipulation of the parties that time is not to be of the essence can, of course, be put in those very words, or it can be put in any provisions that are inconsistent with time not being of the essence. I think the requirement of an indication to make time of the essence is well explained, if I may say so with respect, by Slade LJ in a case I shall be referring to in a moment, *Henry Smith's Charity Trustees* v. *AWADA Trading and Promotion Services Ltd* reported (1983) 269 EG 729, Slade LJ observed at p 735:

'Though the best way of rebutting the presumption is to state expressly that stipulations as to the time by which steps provided for by the rent-review clause are to be taken is to be treated as being of the essence ... this is not the only way. Any form of expression which clearly evinces the concept of finality attached to the end of the period or periods prescribed will suffice to rebut the presumption. The parties are quite free to contract on the basis that time is to be of the essence if they so wish.'

And the lord justice referred to certain authorities.

Those being the two general propositions asserted by the landlord and derived from the *United Scientific* case, I propose first of all to express my own first impression of the matter, applying those rules to the case before me, and then to see how far that first impression ought to be modified having regard to reported authorities decided in the Court of Appeal since the House of Lords' judgment in the *United Scientific* case.

Para 1 of the first schedule says that: 'The rent as from each review date until the next review date ... shall be (1) or (2) or (3)' that is one or other of three alternatives which are clearly intended to be between them clearly separate from one another and together exhaustive. The first is the sum agreed in writing between the landlord and the tenant. No time-limit is prescribed for such agreement except that it must be before either of the two other alternatives has fixed a new rate.

The second alternative is the former rent, if it be greater, the rent determined by arbitration. There is a time-limit expressed for that—a period of 15 months expiring 12 months after the review date in which either party can apply for the appointment of an arbitrator unless, of course, although unable to agree on a new rent the parties have agreed on the individual to determine it. In which case no application is necessary.

Then comes the third alternative, which is introduced by a protasis, an 'if' clause. It begins: 'If within the said period ...' and I interpolate that the said period quite clearly means the period of 15 months during which application can be made for the appointment of an arbitrator

'... the Landlord and the Tenant shall not have agreed in writing who shall be the arbitrator for the purpose of subparagraph (2) and neither the Landlord nor the Tenant shall have applied to the President of the Royal Institution of Chartered Surveyors for the appointment of an arbitrator for the purpose of that subparagraph, then a sum equal to the rent payable immediately before the review date.'

Grammatically there is no doubt about that whatever. The said period is a period that expires on a fixed date—that is 12 months after the review date. At that point it is perfectly clear whether or not there has been any agreement as to the rent or the personality of the arbitrator and whether there has been any application in default of agreement to the president. If not, then unambiguously, the third alternative comes into play and a sum equal to the old rent is to be the new rent.

It seems to me, going straight from the *United Scientific* case to the lease, abundantly clear that the tenants' contentions are justified. If subpara (3) were not in para 1 of the first schedule then, indeed, it would be strongly arguable that time was not of the essence. The clause would have said that either party could apply during a certain period expiring 12 months after the review date but would not have said in terms what was to happen if application was not made. It would then be arguable 'Ah well, that is a machinery provision limiting the time and the parties have not said what is to happen if it is not strictly made; therefore on *United Scientific* principles it will be taken to give a reasonable further time to either party to apply.' But subpara (3) is there; the parties have said in expressed terms what is to happen if the time-limit is not observed. To my mind they have therefore clearly indicated that time is to be of the essence in respect of that period and the court would indeed be making a bargain for the parties they never made for themselves—and writing into subpara (3) qualifying words that are not there if the court were to accede to the landlord's application.

Now, that is my personal view founded simply on an attempt to apply the principles of *United Scientific* to the document before me. I have to consider now three cases that have been decided in the Court of Appeal since the House of Lords' decision. The first of them was *Lewis* v. *Barnett* reported at (1981) 264 EG 1079. Now, that was a case in which there was a division—I do not want to go through the facts at unnecessary length. There was a vital provision that:

'If the landlord and the tenant shall not have agreed the open market rent at least six months before the rent-review date and the landlord shall neglect to make the application referred to in paragraph 3 ...'

and that was an application for the appointment of an arbitrator. '... then' the provision went on

'(unless the parties hereto shall in writing agree otherwise) any notice already given by the landlord to the tenant under the provisions of paragraph 2 hereof . . .'

and that was the notice triggering the rent-review clause '... shall be void and of no effect.' Now, the landlord had not made his application for the appointment of a surveyor to arbitrate until six months after the latest date provided by the clause, and the judgment of Stephenson LJ, with which the other two members of the court agreed, held that the tenants had achieved indirectly the result that expressed words would have achieved by, in Lord Diplock's words in the *United Scientific* case, contra-indications in the expressed words of the lease.

Stephenson LJ also said (at p 1080):

'I have not the smallest hesitation in saying that no principle of construction and no authority of any court compels or even justifies a judge in finding one paragraph in a written document (in this case a sealed lease) to have no effect. Effect must be given to the paragraph if it possibly can be.'

So the case of *Lewis* v. *Barnett* I find a powerful encouragement to my view of first impression that I cannot accede to a construction of the rent-review clause which would make subpara (3) of para 1 without effect.

The second case in the Court of Appeal is that, to which I have already given the reference, of *Henry Smith's Charity Trustees* v. *AWADA Trading and Promotion Services Ltd*. Then there was provision for the service of an initial notice by the landlord and a counternotice by the tenant and then, in default of agreement, the landlord was to apply to the president of the Royal Institution of Chartered Surveyors for the appointment of a surveyor to determine the new rent, and then there was this time provision:

'If on the expiration of two months from the date of service of such counternotice, the Landlords and the Tenant shall not have agreed in writing an amount to be treated as the market rent and the Landlords shall not have applied for the appointment of a surveyor in accordance with paragraph 6 of this Schedule the amount stated in such counternotice shall be deemed to be the market rent.'

Now, the question before the court was whether time was of the essence of that stipulation or whether, the landlords' application for appointment of an independent surveyor being four months late, the rent demanded by the tenants' counternotice which was, in effect, the previously existing rent, was inevitably fixed until the next review date should come.

The first judgment was given by Sir John Donaldson MR and he took a view very similar to that taken by the court in *Lewis* v. *Barnett*, to which case he referred. He said that he was quite unable to accept the landlords' construction under which time was not of the essence and he continued at p 731 of the report:

'The parties have not only set out a timetable but have in terms provided what is to happen in the absence of strict compliance with that timetable. The presumption of elasticity would undoubtedly be acceptable if clauses 3 and 6 stood alone with minor alterations in language to make that possible. But clauses 4 and 7 make it clear that something quite different is intended.

It is highly undesirable that decisions of this type of dispute shall turn upon fine distinctions and I reject the suggestion that there is a difference between a rent-review scheme which, in the event of default in adhering to the timetable avoids the whole process (*Lewis* v. *Barnett*) and one which automatically resolves the dispute, albeit in a somewhat draconian way (the instant appeal). Both make precise and, in the case of the instant appeal, elaborate provision for exactly what shall happen if one of the parties shall fail to exercise his rights within the specified period of time. In neither case would it be possible seriously to write into the clause after each specified period of time words such as "or such longer period as shall elapse before the expiration of reasonable notice making time of the essence of the contract". Accordingly, in my judgment, the parties must be deemed to have intended that in the case of their lease the general rule should not apply and that time should be of the essence of the contract.'

Griffiths LJ did not take the same view. He, I think because of the hardship to the landlord in the particular case, only reluctantly held that time was of the essence and he said in terms that he did not accept that the mere presence of such a provision as that relied on by the Master of the Rolls would in all cases be sufficient to make time of the essence. But, on examining a number of other detailed provisions of the clause, in which it differs from the one that I have to examine, Griffiths LJ reluctantly agreed that time was of the essence.

Slade LJ mainly relied, I think, on *Lewis* v. *Barnett* and the view taken by the Master of the Rolls. He said (at p 735) that the paragraphs referred to by the Master of the Rolls:

'(apparently unlike the two forms of lease under consideration in the *United Scientific* case, so far as one can gather from the report of that decision) set out in addition, specifically and clearly, what is to happen in default of the exercise of the rights given to the respective parties within the permitted periods of time.'

And he said that he thought the provisions of the two paragraphs particularly in question were quite inconsistent with the survival of any right to take the necessary steps after the expiration of the periods specified. He also said that while in other contexts such provisions might not necessarily connote finality (so far agreeing with Griffiths LJ) he said they clearly did so—well, he said they did so—he obviously thought it clear in the context of the lease before him.

Thus the decision in the *Henry Smith's Charity* case and the reasons given by two of the three members of the court are entirely on all fours with *Lewis* v. *Barnett* and, as I think, confirm the view which I should have arrived at without any authority except that of *United Scientific*. However, the latest interpretation of the *United Scientific* decision by the Court of Appeal creates some difficulty. It was the case of *Mecca Leisure Ltd* v. *Renown Investments (Holdings) Ltd* (1984) 271 EG 989. The clause provided for the service of what was called a rent notice by the landlord setting out the figure that he thought the future rent should be and then for the service of a counternotice by the tenant within 28 days and on that followed an express provision as to what should happen if time were not observed, for the clause said:

'If the lessee shall fail to serve a counternotice within the period aforesaid it shall be deemed to have agreed to pay the increased rent specified in the rent notice as from the review date.'

There was then provision for arbitration if a counternotice should have been served, and no time-limit (I think I am right in saying) was set for the application for appointment of an arbitrator, except that a period of 28 days was to elapse for attempts for the landlord and tenant to reach agreement. But after that 28 days, failing agreement on an arbitrator, both or either of the parties might apply and no limit was set as to the time of application. And what had happened was that the tenant had been late in serving the counternotice and the landlords contended that the time specified for the counternotice (28 days) was of the essence and that on the expiration of that period accordingly the figure stated in the landlords' notice became absolute. The landlords, of course, relied on the cases that I have already cited and primarily, as appears from the first of the judgments in the *Mecca Leisure* case—that of Eveleigh LJ—the landlords relied on the *Henry Smith's Charity* case.

Eveleigh LJ dismissed that in very general terms. He said (at p 990):

'I find no help at all from the facts of other cases where there is a deeming provision, as in the present case, but other terms in the review clause and the lease are different.'

So he went back to *United Scientific* and he read the words requiring the counternotice within 28 days and the 28 days after service of the counternotice for agreement. Then he said: 'No time is laid down for the appointment of the arbitrator and no time is laid down for the announcement of his decision ...' and he said: '... It is only from the words of the deeming clause itself' that was the clause that said if the lessee failed to serve a counternotice within the period the lessee was deemed to have agreed to pay the increased rent specified in the rent notice 'that any argument can be raised in support of the contention that time was intended to be of the essence.' And he concluded:

'I cannot regard the mere presence of the "deeming" clause as a firm indication that time is of the essence. I read the clause as a whole and bear in mind that there is a presumption to be displaced and the parties are clearly intending to arrive at a fair rent to be determined amicably if possible. It seems to me that to hold otherwise would make the clause a trap and the chosen machinery dangerous. In my opinion time is not of the essence in this case.'

May LJ agreed with Eveleigh LJ. He gave somewhat more consideration to the *Henry Smith's Charity* case and agreed with the Master of the Rolls in that case that decisions on this type of dispute should not turn upon fine distinctions. But he came to the conclusion that the Master of the Rolls had been wrong in giving such very strong weight to what had come to be referred to as deeming provisions and preferred the less weight put upon such clauses by Griffiths LJ and, to some extent, by Slade LJ. So, May LJ said (at p 992):

'The effect therefore of the *Henry Smith's Charity* case is in my opinion that, although the fact that a rent-review clause does contain a "deeming" provision is a contra-indication which may be sufficient to rebut the general principle, whether it does so or not remains in the end a matter of the proper construction of the particular clause concerned.'

And he said that in the case before him he did not think that one did any real violence to the machinery to enable the parties to arrive at the fair market rent if one construed the subclause as entitling the lessee to serve a counternotice even after the stipulated 28 days had expired. He felt also that there would be far greater hardship to the tenant if time was held to be of the essence than to the landlord from any tardiness on the tenant's part. So, on balance, he agreed with Eveleigh LJ that the indication that time was intended to be of the essence was not strong enough to outweigh the general presumption laid down by the *United Scientific* case.

From those opinions Browne-Wilkinson LJ dissented. He thought it impossible to distinguish the case from the *Henry Smith's Charity* case without introducing the fine distinctions which the Master of the Rolls had deplored in that case and he thought that the *ratio decidendi* of the majority decision in *Henry Smith's Charity* was that the provision for a default rent was a decisive, or virtually decisive, contra-indication displacing the presumption that time was not of the essence.

So I have to reconsider in the end my own view based simply on *United Scientific* but fortified by two subsequent decisions in the Court of Appeal—I have to reconsider it in the light of the *Mecca Leisure* case. Now, it seems to me that the indication that time is of the essence is far stronger in the present case than it was in the *Mecca Leisure* case; in the present case the three alternatives of para 1 of the first schedule clearly define the future rent by strict time-limits, embracing every point, whereas in the *Mecca Leisure* case, although there was a strict time-limit with a deeming provision as regards the lessees' counternotice, there was nothing as regards the appointment of an arbitrator or the time of decision by the arbitrator. It seems to me that accepting, as I must, that there was an insufficient contra-indication in the *Mecca Leisure* case I am still at liberty on the language of the case before me to hold that there is a sufficient contra-indication. I think, applying the *United Scientific* principles and bearing in mind all the observations of the Court of Appeal in all three of the cases, that I am still bound to hold that the language of the lease in the present case is inconsistent with the presumption that time is not [*it would appear that, having regard to the context, the word 'not' is missing from this sentence*] of the essence. I am not prepared, in effect, to jettison a whole subparagraph or alter its effect by inserting words that are not there in order to apply a presumption which is, by the authority of the House of Lords, rebuttable if a sufficient contra-indication is shown. Accordingly, the tenants succeed and I must dismiss the originating summons. [Landlord's originating summons dismissed.]

Contrast the decision below where B.A. Hytner QC sitting as a deputy judge of the Queen's Bench Division elected to follow the decision in *Mecca Leisure Ltd* v. *Renown Investments (Holdings) Ltd*, if it was not properly distinguishable from *Henry Smith's Charity Trustees* v. *A.W.A.D.A. Trading & Promotion Services* (see earlier, page 60).

TAYLOR WOODROW PROPERTY CO. LTD v. LONRHO TEXTILES LTD

Queen's Bench Division   (1985) 275 EG 632

The tenant served his counternotice (in response to the landlord's trigger notice), outside the time limits provided in the rent review provisions of the lease. There was no express provision making time of the essence and the tenant contended that time was not of the essence under the general rule. The rent review clause, however, contained a one-way 'deeming provisions' to the effect that:

'if the tenant shall fail to serve a counternotice within the period aforesaid it shall be deemed to have agreed to pay the increased rent specified in the rent notice'

which the landlord contended was a sufficient contra-indication to displace the general rule that time was not of the essence.

Held: In so far as there were dicta suggesting that a deeming provision was virtually decisive, these had to be read in the context of a case where the deeming provisions were two-way, see *Henry Smith's Charity Trustees* v. *A.W.A.D.A. Trading & Promotion Services Ltd* (1984) 269 EG 729, (CA) (see above). The ratio in *Mecca Leisure Ltd* v. *Renown Investments (Holdings) Ltd* (1984) 271 EG 989 (see above) seemed to be that the existence of a deeming provision was, not without more, to be regarded as sufficient to render time of the essence. Therefore, (with some hesitation), any reconciliation between the two decisions appeared to lie in the difference between the two deeming provisions in the cases. Therefore, because in the present case the deeming provision was one-way, it came within the ambit of *Mecca* and therefore time for service of the counternotice of the tenant was not of the essence of the contract. The warning against fine distinctions given both in *Mecca* and *Henry Smith* should, however, be heeded in the future.

If, however, *Mecca* and *Henry Smith* were not reconcilable then the later decision should be preferred, see *Colchester Estates (Cardiff)* v. *Carlton Industries plc* [1984] 2 All ER 601.

B.A. HYTNER QC (sitting as a High Court judge): On 6 September 1973 Myton Ltd entered into an underlease with Fludes Carpets Ltd in respect of premises known as Unit A4, 64 Churchill Square, Brighton, as from 7 January 1970 for a term of 21 years at an annual rent of £5000. As a result of subsequent assignments, the present plaintiffs became the landlords and the present defendants became the tenants.

The underlease contained a detailed provision for rent review, and this is to be found in Part II of the third schedule, which I think ought to be read in full:

'Not more than Twelve months and not less than Six months before the expiration of the Fourteenth year of the term hereby granted the Landlord may serve on the Tenant a notice in writing (hereinafter called a "Rent Notice") providing for the increase of the rent payable hereunder as from the expiration of the year of the term then current to an amount specified in the Rent Notice based upon the terms as if referred to an arbitrator as hereinafter mentioned and in such notice the Landlord shall specify that the Tenant may serve a counter-notice in accordance with paragraph (a) of this Part and that in default the provisions of paragraph (b) of this part will operate and thereupon the following provisions shall have effect—

(a) the Tenant within one month after the receipt of the Rent Notice may serve on the Landlord a counternotice calling upon the Landlord to negotiate with the Tenant the amount of rent to be paid hereunder as from the expiration of the said year

(b) If the Tenant shall fail to serve a counternotice within the period aforesaid it shall be deemed to have agreed to pay the increased rent specified in the Rent Notice

(c) If the Tenant shall serve on the Landlord a counternotice calling upon the Landlord to negotiate with the Tenant as aforesaid then the Landlord and the Tenant shall forthwith consult together and use their best endeavours to reach agreement as to the amount of the rent to be paid hereunder as from the expiration of the said year but failing agreement within two months after service of such counternotice the question of whether any and if so what increase ought to be made in the rent payable hereunder as from the expiration of the said year shall be referred to the arbitration of a single arbitrator to be agreed between the Landlord and the Tenant or should there be failure of agreement application shall be made by the Landlord for an Arbitrator to be appointed by the President for the time being of the Royal Institution of Chartered Surveyors whose valuation shall be made as an expert and not as an arbitrator and the decision of such arbitrator shall be final and binding on the Landlord and the Tenant

(d) The Arbitrator shall determine the question so referred to him by ascertaining the annual rack rental value of the demised premises at the date of the Rent Notice that is to say the highest annual rent at which the demised premises might reasonably be expected to be let without premium in the open market as between willing landlord and willing tenant with vacant possession and upon the terms of this Lease (save as regards rent) and for the purposes for which the demised premises are at the date of rent review permitted to be used Provided always that in no event shall the rent payable after each rent review be less than the rent payable immediately before such rent review.

(e)   Such increased rent shall be payable by the Tenant to the Landlord as from the expiration of the year of the term then current for the residue of the said term

(f)   A note of the increased rent payable pursuant to this Part shall when agreed or determined be endorsed on this Underlease and on the Counterpart thereof

... The defendants deny liability and rely on the counternotice of 19 December 1983, and consequently the only issue before me is the validity of that counternotice. The landlords say that it is out of time and that that is fatal, since time was of the essence of the contract. The tenants say that the counternotice was valid, since time was not of the essence. The counterclaim is not pursued.

[Counsel for the landlords] submitted that Part II of the Third Schedule—the rent-review clause—could not be clearer. The parties had legislated for two means of determining the rent, a long route and a short route. The long route involved, at the end of the day, determination by an expert, the short route being a rent fairly calculated by the method which would be adopted by an expert and accepted by failure to serve a counternotice within time by the tenants.

[Counsel for the landlords] conceded that the starting point for determining whether time for service of the counternotice was of the essence of the contract was *United Scientific Holdings Ltd* v. *Burnley Borough Council* [1978] AC 904 and the well-known dictum of Lord Diplock at p 930G:

'So upon the question of principle which these two appeals were brought to settle, I would hold that in the absence of any contra-indications in the express words of the lease or in the interrelation of the rent-review clause itself and other clauses or in the surrounding circumstances the presumption is that the timetable specified in a rent-review clause for completion of the various steps for determining the rent payable in respect of the period following the review date is not of the essence of the contract.'

Reliance was also placed on the manner in which this principle was expressed by Lord Salmon, which is to be found at p 950 F:

'The time provision in a rent-revision clause of the present kind, even in a lease concerning a commercial transaction, is however different in character and I regard it as not being of the essence of the contract unless it is made so expressly or by necessary implication'

and in the manner in which the same principle was expressed by Lord Fraser at p 962 F:

'I am of the opinion that the equitable rule against treating time as of the essence of a contract is applicable to rent-review clauses unless there is some special reason for excluding its application to a particular clause.'

[Counsel for the landlords] then relied on four matters, to which he later added a fifth:

1   the fact that the rent-review clause contained a 'deeming' provision;

2   that by para (b) of the rent-review clause there was an obligation placed upon the landlord to put a figure in his notice based on the method which would be adopted by an arbitrator;

3   that the landlord was required to inform the tenant in the notice of his right to serve a counternotice;

4   that the landlord was required to draw to the tenant's attention in the notice the consequence which would follow his failure to serve a counternotice;

5   that if time was not of the essence the operation of para (e) of the clause could involve substantial savings to the tenant in the event of a determination by an expert, of a late determination by an expert, or presumably by protracted negotiations not being finalised until well into the following year.

All these factors, submitted [counsel for the landlords], were factors which constituted, in Lord Diplock's words, a contra-indication to time not being of the essence of the contract, or, in Lord Fraser's words, were special reasons for holding time to be of the essence, or, in Lord Salmon's phrase, should cause me to draw the necessary implication that time was of the essence.

It is convenient to deal with these matters in reverse order. As to the fifth, [counsel] for the tenants, submitted that it was based on a misreading of para (e): whenever the new rent is determined, it is to be paid as from 7 January 1984. [Counsel for the tenants] agreed, however, that a tenant called upon in, say, July 1984 to pay substantial arrears would save interest, but, taken as a whole and bearing in mind that a landlord could, if he felt that the tenant was dragging his feet in relation to the negotiation process, serve a time notice, I do not regard the provisions of para (e) as an indication that the parties intended to displace the presumption against time being of the essence. I will, however, return to this point later.

As to the second, third and fourth factors, [counsel for the tenants] submitted that a notice which failed to comply with these requirements would nevertheless have been a valid notice, relying on the case of *Dean and Chapter of the Cathedral Church of the Holy Trinity in Chichester* v. *Lennards Ltd* [1977] 35 P & CR 309 in which it was held that a provision in a rent-review clause requiring that the landlord's written notice should state the suggested new rent was not of the essence of the contract:

'Applying these principles, it seems to me that this notice should not fail because it does not name the actual figure of suggested new rent. It gives the tenants perfectly good notice that the landlords desire that the rent should be raised to correspond with the new market value: and it was courteously suggested that the surveyors of the parties should decide what the new rent should be. That was a perfectly proper notice per Lord Denning MR (p 314).

On the basis of that decision it is difficult to sustain an argument that the notice would have been valid if the landlord had suggested a figure which was calculated by a method wholly different from one utilised by an arbitrator. The stipulation that some figure should be stated in the landlord's notice was regarded as 'a little bit of machinery' by Lord Denning MR (at p 314) and accordingly I so regard the method of calculating the figure which was to be inserted in the instant case.

[Counsel for the tenants] submitted that precisely the same principle should be applied to the requirement for the counternotice to be referred to in the notice. Here it is to be observed that the tenant was simply being referred to his own lease. There was no provision that the consequences of failure had to be spelt out in simple language to the tenant. As we have seen, that was not done by the landlords here. The notice simply referred in formal terms to schedules and parts etc. If the requirement to state the proposed new rent in a notice is regarded as a little bit of machinery, the requirement to refer in the most formal manner to some of the terms of the document already held and signed by the tenants would, in my view, merely constitute a minor cog in that machinery.

I am consequently driven to the conclusion that requirements in a rent-review clause which may be flouted with impunity by a landlord cannot have the substance to lead to a necessary implication that they were intended to displace an equitable presumption nor to amount to a contra-indication nor a special reason.

[The deputy judge then considered in detail the decisions in *Henry Smith's Charity* and *Mecca Leisure* (see earlier for full facts and *ratio*) and concluded:]

On analysis, it would appear that the court as a whole in the *Henry Smith's* case, starting from the standpoint of *United Scientific Holdings Ltd* v. *Burnley Borough Council*, regarded both deeming provisions and the detailed nature of the review machinery as capable of making time of the essence of the service of a notice. However the stringency of the machinery was to a large extent based on the existence of two separate deeming provisions. In so far as there are dicta suggesting that a deeming provision is virtually decisive, these are to be read in the context of a case where the deeming provisions were two-way. The ratio in *Mecca Leisure* certainly appears to be that the existence of a deeming provision is not without more to be regarded as sufficient to render time of the essence.

I am therefore driven, albeit after much hesitation, to accept [counsel for the tenants'] submission that the reconciliation between the two decisions lies in the different deeming provision, that since in the instant case the deeming provision is one-way it comes within the ambit of *Mecca*, and therefore time for service was not of the essence of the contract. In so far as the facts of this case may be different from those in *Mecca*. I should heed the warnings given in both the *Mecca* and *Henry Smith's* cases against making fine distinctions. Some, but not, I think, decisive, support for this conclusion may be found in the decision, never overruled and never disapproved, of Goulding J in the *Davstone* case.

I am, however, not so confident of the correctness of this conclusion as to leave the matter there. Assuming that I am wrong and that the two decisions are in irreconcilable conflict, ought I then to accede to [counsel for the landlord]'s submission that *Mecca* was wrongly decided? That submission is not immediately attractive. The majority judgment set out correctly and applied to the particular facts of the case the principles clearly laid down by the House of Lords in *United Scientific* v. *Burnley*. In my view, the correct approach to this problem is to be found in the general rule that where there are conflicting decisions of courts of co-ordinate jurisidiction the later decision is to be preferred if it is reached after full consideration of the earlier decision. (See *Minister of Pensions* v. *Higham* [1948] 2 KB 153 per Denning J at 155, recently applied by Nourse J, as he then was, in *Colchester Estates (Cardiff)* v. *Carlton Industries plc* [1984] 2 All ER 601.) If this conclusion be wrong, it should be added in fairness to counsel, to both of whom I am indebted, that no argument was advanced on the point and, [counsel for the tenant] not appearing on the judgment, I did not think it right to invite argument at that stage.

Consequently, whether the *Henry Smith's* and *Mecca* cases can or cannot be successfully reconciled, I reach the same result. Furthermore, any conflict between the two cases in respect of the weight to be attached to interest lost or gained on a late determination should be reconciled in the same way, the later case prevailing, and consequently leading to the conclusion that little weight is to be given it.

In my judgment, therefore, time for service of the tenants' counternotice was not of the essence of the contract. The counternotice served on 19 December 1983 was valid, and this claim consequently fails.

Note: *Greenhaven Securities Ltd* v. *Compton* (see earlier page 66) as then unreported and decided one month before, was not cited during argument.

The Court of Appeal judgment (unreported, 21 February 1986) in *Metrolands Investments Ltd* v. *J.H. Dewhurst Ltd* (above at page 52) upheld Peter Gibson J in finding that the reddendum of the lease did not amount to a contra-indication to the general rule. The material words used are set out on page 54 above.

Chapter 4

Trigger notices

4.1 (a)   A trigger notice must give a clear indication of intent

There is no magic formula, but trigger notices must be clear. They must give
to the other party plain indication of their intent to exercise a right and must
not be expressed to be 'subject to contract' if they are to be effective and
implement rent review provisions.

SHIRLCAR PROPERTIES LTD v. HEINITZ AND ANOTHER

Court of Appeal   (1983) 268 EG 362

The rent review provisions under the lease in question were subject to strict time
provisions with time expressly made of the essence. The landlords' agents wrote a
letter to the tenants headed 'subject to contract' and indicating that 'the rent
required as from the review date is £6000 p.a. exclusive, and we look forward to
receiving your agreement'. It was sent by recorded delivery. The tenants contended
that the letter was ineffective to trigger the rent review provisions in the lease. The
landlords brought proceedings claiming an increased rent. In the High Court,
Michael Davies J dismissed the landlords' claim (decision reported in (1982) EG 266,
EG 126). The landlords appealed.

Held: The appeal would be dismissed. The letter did not express a clear intention
and was not a notice within the terms of the rent review clause of the lease
setting out the first stage of the rent review machinery. As such it was ineffective for
the purposes of the rent review clause in the lease. In particular, the words 'subject
to contract' made it unclear whether the letter was a preliminary step before the rent
review machinery was put in motion.

KERR LJ: It is perfectly clear that this letter was written in the context of the rent
review clause, and to that extent, to use the words of Templeman J (as he then was)
to which I come in a moment, but only to that extent, the tenant who received it
would understand what the landlord was up to. The question, however, is whether it
is a sufficiently clear notice within the terms of clause (iii) (A), the first stage of the
rent review machinery. As to that I have no doubt that the words 'subject to
contract', which are in capital letters and underlined after the signature, must govern
the whole of this letter.

In those circumstances it seems to me that the passage from the judgment of
Templeman J in *Keith Bailey Rogers & Co. v. Cubes Ltd* (1975) 31 P & CR 412 is
apposite, and the learned judge in fact cited it in his judgment. Templeman J there
said at p 415, and I leave out immaterial words:

> 'If it is clear ... that each of the recipients could be in no doubt as to what the
> landlord was up to and what the notice and the letter meant as far as he was

concerned, it does not seem to me that the court is entitled or bound to be perverse and invent imaginary difficulties which might have arisen in other cases.'

I therefore ask myself whether the recipient of this letter, governed as it is by the words 'subject to contract', could be in no doubt. To my mind the answer to that is in the negative. I think any recipient might ask himself whether the words 'subject to contract' have the effect that the landlord is indeed bound by the figure of £6000 put forward in the letter. Similarly, if the tenant is minded to accept that figure, and is therefore minded to write back and agree to it, he would be left in doubt, and that doubt would remain if he consulted his solicitor, as to whether any such agreement would be binding. In my view, therefore, this is not a sufficiently clear specification of the required rent under the rent review clause to fulfil the requirements of it, and I would dismiss this appeal.

DILLON LJ: The question is, then, as to the effect of the words 'subject to contract'. They are wholly inapposite to a trigger notice given by landlords under this particular rent review clause. My initial inclination, therefore, was that they should be disregarded and that a reasonable tenant would take the view that they were merely meaningless. On consideration, however, I think that these time-hallowed words 'subject to contract' would leave the tenant in doubt as to whether the figure of £6000 a year was being put forward as a firm figure specified by the landlords under the rent review clause or was merely being put forward as a provisional figure which, if not agreed by a binding contract such as is envisaged by the words 'subject to contract', the landlord might reserve the right to revise. If it is merely a provisional figure, then it is not enough to trigger the rent review clause.

On the whole I feel that a reasonable tenant might regard this as merely a provisional figure. Therefore the meaning of the notice is not so plain that the notice can be taken as a valid stipulation of a rent which sets the review provisions in operation. I, too, would therefore dismiss this appeal.

The appeal was dismissed with costs.

4.1 (b) 'Without prejudice' notices are inappropriate for triggering rent reviews

The mere fact that a notice is headed 'without prejudice' will not prevent it from being admissible in evidence if there was no dispute or negotiations in progress when it was sent, but it is inappropriate on a notice triggering a rent review. A communication which is equivocal and does not comply with strict time limits imposed cannot operate as an effective trigger notice. The problems of an equivocal notice were considered below in *Norwich Union Life Insurance Society* v. *Tony Waller Ltd* where Harman J approved and followed the earlier decision of Megarry V-C in *Drebbond Ltd* v. *Horsham District Council* (1978) 37 P & CR 237.

NORWICH UNION LIFE INSURANCE SOCIETY v. TONY WALLER LTD

Chancery Division   (1984) 270 EG 42

By a lease, dated 29 July 1969, certain property was demised by the plaintiff to a Mr Solomons for a term of 21 years from 29 September 1968, at a rent of £1600 per annum exclusive during the first 14 years of the term and during the remaining years that rent or such increased rent as may be payable in accordance with the provisions of clause 2 of the lease, which *inter alia* provided as follows:

'The Landlord shall be entitled by notice in writing given to the Tenant at any time after the commencement of the fourteenth year of the term hereby granted to call for review of the initial market rent payable and if the then current market rent (as hereinafter defined) at the end of such fourteenth year or at the date of the Landlord's notice (if later) is greater than the initial market rent then as from the end of such fourteenth year or as from the quarter day next following the giving of such notice whichever shall be the later the initial market rent shall be increased to the then current market rent.'

In November 1981, a chartered surveyor, acting for the plaintiff, wrote a letter to the defendant stating that he had been instructed in respect of the forthcoming rent review and asking for an inspection of the property. On 4 August 1982, the plaintiff's surveyor wrote the defendant a second letter, headed 'without prejudice', calling for a review of the rent and proposing a rental of £11,500 per annum exclusive from 29 September 1982. (The letter is given in full in the judgment.) Subsequently, the matter was put into the hands of the plaintiff's solicitors who, on 20 June 1983, served a 'trigger' notice on the defendant, which was properly framed and complied with the time limit contained in clause 2 of the lease, to operate from Midsummer Day 1983.

By an originating summons, the plaintiff sought against the defendant determination of two questions. First, whether the plaintiff had given to the defendant a valid notice in writing under the lease and, secondly, whether time was of the essence of the provisions of clause 2 of the lease.

Held:
(1) The letter headed 'without prejudice' was admissible in evidence since there was no dispute or negotiations in progress between the parties when it was served. The letter was written at a time when no view was emanating from the defendant; it was, therefore, not governed by the rubric 'without prejudice' and was not privileged from disclosure.
(2) While no specific form had to be adopted in order to constitute a 'trigger' notice, nevertheless, the letter in question was wholly ineffective as a trigger notice under the rent review clause since the terms in which it was written were equivocal.
(3) Even if the letter had been written in unequivocal terms, it would still have been ineffective because it failed to comply with the time limit, which was of the essence, in the relevant portion of the rent review clause.
(4) The subsequent trigger notice (served by the plaintiff's solicitors on 20 June 1983), which complied with the time limit and was properly framed, was effective to bring the rent review into operation, although the increase of rent resulting from it would necessarily begin from a later date, namely, Midsummer Day 1983.

HARMAN LJ: In essence the important averments in the lease can be extracted as follows:

'The Landlord shall be entitled by notice in writing given to the Tenant at any time after the commencement of the fourteenth year of the term hereby granted to call for review of the initial market rent payable and if the then current market rent (as hereinafter defined) at the end of such fourteenth year or at the date of the Landlord's notice (if later) is greater than the initial market rent then as from the end of such fourteenth year or as from the quarter day next following the giving of such notice whichever shall be the later the initial market rent shall be increased to the then current market rent,'

with a so-called proviso effectively saying upwards only.
(b) defines the current market rent at the date of review, otherwise its terms have not been and did not need to be considered in any detail. The relevance of 'at the

date of review' is only that it is plainly contemplated by this structure that the landlord's notice triggering the review will operate either from the end of the 14th year or from the quarter-day following the landlord's notice, and this form is not therefore one which involves substantial retrospection or back-dating in its procedure.

Subclause (c) of clause 2 provides the machinery for working out the review: 'Such revision' it is called

'as aforesaid shall be made by the landlord and the tenant in collaboration, but, if no agreement shall have been reached between the parties within three months after the date of the landlord's notice calling for such review, the question'

and I skip over several lines

'shall, if the landlord shall so require, by notice in writing given to the tenant within three months thereafter but not otherwise be referred to the decision of a surveyor'

in brief, as an expert appointed by the RICS.

(d) is the machinery for endorsing a memorandum of the reviewed rent on the lease.

The matter was handed to well-known West End agents, Messrs Edward Erdman, who proceeded to write a letter in November 1981, saying that they had been instructed in respect of the forthcoming rent review which was due on 29 September 1982 and asking for inspection of the premises. The first paragraph is somewhat misleading, since no rent review was due on 29 September 1982 at the time the letter was written, since there was no rent review machinery triggered by any trigger notice.

That letter was followed, some eight months or so later, by a letter of 4 August 1982. Like the first, this is somewhat inapt. I will refer to the whole of it, since a great deal of argument has turned upon it. It gives the young lady in Messrs Edward Erdman's reference at the top, and dates it '4 August 1982', and marks it 'PRIVATE & CONFIDENTIAL RECORDED DELIVERY', and addresses it to 'T Waller Esq, Messrs Tony Waller Shoes'—not, it is to be noted, to the tenant by its proper title at all—gives the address, and then puts the words

'Without Prejudice.
Dear Sir, *19 Fawkon Walk, Hoddesdon.*
We have been instructed by your landlords, the Norwich Union Insurance Group to negotiate with you in connection with the rent review contained in your lease which becomes operative as at September 29 1982.
It is our clients proposal to increase the rental to £11,500 per annum exclusive as from this date.
We trust that this increase is acceptable to you and would be obliged if when replying you would enclose the name and address of the solicitors who will be acting on your behalf.
Yours faithfully.

What is anyone to make of that document? It is headed 'Without prejudice', and any lawyer meeting a letter like that at once starts back and says 'I cannot look at this', because it is claimed to be privileged. I have been urged to look at it, although privilege is claimed for it, in order to determine whether the label 'Without prejudice' can appropriately be attached to it. If it is appropriately attached to it, then the letter is inadmissible and cannot be referred to in any matters proceeding between these two parties.

I was referred to *Halsbury's Laws*, vol 17, which is of no assistance at all, and to a series of cases, *Walker* v. *Wilsher* (1889) 23 QBD 335, *Re River Steamer Co.* (1871) 6 Ch App 822 and *Re Weston and Thomas's Contract* [1907] Ch 244. None of these seems to me to really bear upon the question, which, as I rather pressed [counsel for the plaintiff] to agree and eventually he did agree, was: is there here a position where 'Without prejudice' can properly be used as invoking the privilege which goes with the phrase? It seems to me that the decision which gives one the most help on the matter is a decision cited by [counsel for the defendant], *Re Daintrey* [1893] 2 QB 116, which was a bankruptcy case and a decision of the Queen's Bench Division in bankruptcy which in those days took bankruptcy appeals. It shows the judgment of the court given by Vaughan Williams J (as he then was) on a document headed 'Without prejudice', and there is set out, on p 119 on the judgment, what in the opinion of that court the rule was:

'In our opinion the rule which excludes documents marked "without prejudice" has no application unless some person is in dispute or negotiation with another, and terms are offered for the settlement of the dispute or negotiation, and ... the judge must necessarily be entitled to look at the document in order to determine whether the conditions, under which alone the rule applies, exist.'

The rule is, as [counsel for the plaintiff], in my view, absolutely correctly submitted, a rule of public policy based upon the proposition that it is better to settle than to fight—I paraphrase [counsel for the plaintiff], but I think that is not unfair as a way of putting what he was submitting. It is, in my judgment, an accurate description of the purpose of the rule, and it also, in my judgment, illuminates the occasions on which the rule arises, and they are entirely in accordance with Vaughan Williams J's formulation. The rule has no application unless some person is in dispute or negotiation with another. Here, the letter of 4 August 1982 was written, not quite out of the blue, because there had been that rather inept inspection letter written eight months earlier, but written at a time when there was, so far as anything before me goes, no view, position, attitude or anything else emanating from or evidenced by the tenant. The matter at that stage was, in my view, entirely an opening shot, and an opening shot in a situation where no war had been declared and no dispute had arisen. Indeed 'shot' may be an inapt word to apply to it. As it seems to me, this letter was not written in the course of negotiation, which must imply that each side has expressed a view and that a *modus vivendi* between them is being proposed, nor had a dispute been constituted, whether by litigation, arbitration or mere verbal or oral threats over the back fence of two neighbouring properties. It seems to me beyond any question that this rubric 'Without prejudice' can only be effectively used where one has an extant disagreement—dispute, issue, call it what you will—or extant negotiations with both sides having set up their own position in them. As it seems to me, this letter, being the initiating letter, could not appropriately be so headed, and I therefore hold against [counsel for the plaintiff]'s first argument. In my view it is not governed by the rubric attached to it 'Without prejudice', which words remain part of it and are material as part of its writing for the purpose of understanding what it really says but which do not have the effect of validly claiming privilege.

The letter is, as I have already observed, inapt. It refers to 'a rent review contained in your lease which becomes operative', as if the rent review was already triggered by something in the lease. That is of course a complete misunderstanding by the young woman who wrote it. There was a need, under this well-known precedent, to fire a trigger notice. The question which is raised by [counsel for the defendant] is whether this is not in fact itself a trigger notice. It is quite clear that the tenant took some steps in response to it, because the next letter in the bundle is of 23 August by surveyors acting for the tenant, rejecting the figure of £11,500. In my judgment, the figure is not the only important part of the letter and one cannot, as was suggested by [counsel for the defendant] at one point, regard the letter as severable into parts and to regard the first part of it as an attempt to invoke clause 2 (a) and the second part of it as an attempt to settle the dispute raised by that invocation to which the term 'Without prejudice' could properly be applied. It seems to me quite impossible to separate this letter out into parts. Its whole constitution is of one continuous thought, and, whether it be a trigger notice or whether it be no such thing, it is not severable into separate bits.

In my view, the document contains no reference whatever to clause 2 (a), contains no reference to the procedures which would normally be followed under a trigger notice referring to the definition of 'current market rent' in the lease and going on to deal with the way in which it should be dealt with under clause 2 (c). It does not ask for the names of surveyors to be appointed by the tenant, as is envisaged by the third line of clause 2 (c), and indeed the letter is really that written by a muddle-headed person not truly appreciating what they were doing at all.

I have been much impressed by [counsel for the defendant]'s argument that this document was in truth equivocal. It is common ground between the parties that no specific form has to be adopted in order to constitute a trigger notice. [Counsel for the plaintiff]'s submission was that it should be a clear and unequivocal notice giving plain intimation to anyone receiving it of what it was. Certainly, that is, in my view, the desirable state of all such notices. But it being common ground that no special form of words is necessary—no magic formula is involved—the question is: trying to read it as a whole, looking at its confused terminology, its meaningless heading 'Without prejudice' and its general ineptitude, is this a document which a tenant looking at it would think was a trigger notice? If so, [counsel for the defendant] would say, the fact that the landlord has chosen to use inept agents who write equivocal notices does not entitle a landlord to disown his own notices and say they are not what they might reasonably be thought to have been. For that purpose, both [counsel for the defendant] and [counsel for the plaintiff] referred to the decision of the Court of Appeal in *Shirlcar Properties Ltd* v. *Heinitz* (1983) 268 EG 362, where Lawton LJ summed up his judgment on a notice headed 'Subject to contract' with the proposition that 'Since there is an argument both ways about this matter' that is to say, the meaning of the notice

'and as, in my judgment, it is an argument which is reasonable on both sides, it seems to me that it cannot be said that the tenants on receiving this letter would necessarily and reasonably have inferred it was an effective trigger notice for the purpose of the lease. There is doubt about its meaning, and as there is doubt it seems to me the letter was ineffective for the purpose of the rent review clause in the lease.'

[Counsel for the defendant] urges that that is not an applicable set of words to apply to this garbled document of 4 August, because, he says, if it is equivocal (as it undoubtedly is) and it could reasonably have been thought to have been a trigger notice, if the tenant so receiving it acted upon it, the landlord cannot go back, as it were, and deny his own document. In my view, that, attractive as it is, is wrong. In my view, in the end one has to construe the letter, and this letter is far more equivocal and obscure than that contained in the notice referred to in *Shirlcar Properties*. Further, it seems to me that the principle of the decision in *Shirlcar Properties* is that, although there are no magic words or magic formulae to be required before a rent review clause is invoked, yet the document does have to be clear and plain to the recipient. This document, in my view, would not have been plain to any recipient. I have stared at it now for a day and a half and I still do not know what it means. I find it bemusingly confused in its whole construction and attitudes. In my view, the only proper conclusion one can come to upon this document is that, although it is admissible and I am against [counsel for the plaintiff] on his 'Without prejudice' argument of privilege, yet I conclude that, upon reading the whole, it is wholly ineffective to act as a trigger notice.

If I were wrong on that, it would be necessary to go on to consider what happened under it. If the notice were an effective notice because, equivocal as it is, it is yet enough to entitle the tenant to accept it as being a trigger notice, is plain beyond any question that the machinery envisaged by clause 2 (c) of the lease was not complied with. Clause 2 (c), is, as I have said, in the well-known precedent form, and it required, after the trigger notice, a notice of reference to the expert. It is required by a formula, which I have already read and I shall repeat, that the question 'shall, if the landlord shall so require, by notice in writing given to the tenant within three months thereafter but not otherwise be referred to the decision of a surveyor'. As it seems to me, the words 'within three months thereafter but not otherwise' are only consistent with that time-limit being strictly and precisely adhered to. It is not, to my mind, so much a question of the ordinary rules about time being of the essence in so many contracts affecting the sale of or dealing with land, but of the particular construction of this special clause in its own true reading.

[Counsel for the plaintiff] argued gallantly that the words 'but not otherwise' cover not only the time phrase but also the requirement that the notice shall be in writing and shall be given to the tenant. He said that those varying matters were all comprehended in the words 'but not otherwise'. So, I agree, they are. But equally so each of them separately, to my mind, is. And I would have no hesitation or doubt in concluding that the force of those emphatic, unequivocal and clear words 'within three months thereafter but not otherwise' amount to an express stipulation between the parties that that time-limit must be complied with.

In fact, that conclusion which I would reach upon the construction of the document accords precisely and exactly with the conclusion reached by the Vice-Chancellor upon the self-same clause from the self-same precedent in a case called *Drebbond Ltd* v. *Horsham District Council* (1978) 37 P & CR 237 [also reported at (1978) 246 EG 1013]. The Vice-Chancellor held that time, as he put it, was made of the essence by this phrase in this very self-same clause. In such circumstances it would be my duty to follow the Vice-Chancellor unless convinced beyond any peradventure that his decision must be wrong. Far from so feeling, I would independently of that decision have reached precisely the same conclusion myself and I am confronted and gratified to find that really supports the conclusion which I reached independently.

The *Drebbond* decision has been before the Court of Appeal in a case called *Touche Ross & Co.* v. *Secretary of State for the Environment* (1982) 265 EG 982, where the matter was mentioned by Dillon LJ in his judgment allowing the appeal on that case, but the lord justice is very careful to make no observations at all about the correctness or otherwise of the *Drebbond* case. He distinguishes it from the formula which was before the court in the *Touche Ross & Co.* case and he says that he finds nothing in *Drebbond* which compels him to the conclusion that the different words made the time-limit in that case obligatory and of the essence of the contract. He says that there is no magical formula and, given such, it is possible that small differences of language may lead in some cases to opposite conclusions. Upon that basis, it seems to me plain beyond a peradventure that the Court of Appeal, having considered the very matter and having expressly and specifically not made any reflections upon the *Drebbond* decision, the *Drebbond* decision stands and is unaffected by the decision in *Touche Ross* upon differing words.

Thus, in my view, this clause 2 (c) which lays down machinery is a clause requiring specific compliance with its time-limits and, those time-limits not being complied with, had I been of the view that the letter of 4 August was a valid trigger notice I would hold that it had now come to no effect by reason of the failure to comply with the limits of clause 2 (c).

However, I have, as I have said, come to the conclusion that the letter of 4 August is a thing writ in water and of no effect at all. Upon that basis there is therefore no difficulty whatever in the landlord now invoking clause 2 (a) and saying that 'I am entitled by notice in writing at any time after the commencement of the 14th year to call for a review. I now call for a review'. Fortunately, at last the matter was handed to the lawyers and a sensible letter with a proper trigger notice was drafted by them and sent on 20 June 1983, which will obviously operate from Midsummer Day 1983. It is a relief to come to a document that is decently drafted in this case. The result is that there is now a review, which will operate from that midsummer quarter-day last year and the rent will be reviewed as at that date and will be payable as from that date. The landlord by its failure, as I hold, to serve a proper notice, and, further and in any event by its failure to take the expert-invoking steps after serving such notice as it did, will have lost some three quarters of increased rent, being the rents due at Michaelmas 1982, Christmas 1982 and Easter 1983. That seems to me an entirely satisfactory and appropriate commercial result to reach, and it in a sense reinforces my view that clause 2 (c) in this precedent does lay down strict time-limits which must be complied with, because, as it seems to me, the whole matter, given the reference in 2 (a) to notice in writing at any time but which notice will only operate from the quarter-day following if later than the end of the 14th year, it is a reasonable commercial pattern for that result to follow. The tenant is not penalised by the landlord's delay. The landlord suffers for his own delay, if indeed 'suffering' is the right word, because of course the rent when reviewed may be reviewed to a higher level because rent levels may have changed between Michaelmas 1982 and midsummer 1983, but that seems to me all perfectly natural and entirely contemplated by the form of clause 2 and its four subclauses of this lease.

Had I been of the view that the letter of 4 August was a notice, would that entitle the tenant to say: 'You have served a notice. You failed to proceed diligently under 2 (c). You are out of time. That is an end of it'? In my view, it would not. This may be an *obiter* conclusion upon my part, but, as it seems to me, this whole rent review clause, from beginning to end, is contemplating a review of the initial market rent which is not a complete act until the current market rent has been defined by the surveyor to whom it is referred, if indeed it is not agreed earlier. It was postulated in argument, what would happen if a landlord served an undoubtedly valid trigger notice, served an undoubtedly in time notice of reference, a surveyor was appointed and proceeded to embark as an expert on his assessment of the rent, and then, through some ordinary vicissitude of life (which is all too present before all of us), was killed or died? The tenant's argument, as it seems to me, that the landlord having given a valid notice and having embarked upon the review cannot further give another notice, would lead to a result of a most bizarre and uncommercial kind which I cannot believe would be required by anything except the clearest possible words. But in my judgment, upon the words of this clause, no such result follows. The landlord, as I say, in my view is entitled to require his review at any time, and, if he has not got his review after the end of the 14th year, he is entitled to require it as from the next following quarter-day after service of a trigger notice. It seems to me that that is a perfectly sensible commercial result. It is quite true, as [counsel for the defendant] observed, that the landlord is not to blame if the unhappy accident occurs that the expert to whom the matter is referred is killed in a car smash. That is true. None the less it is a risk which must exist in the world—no special provisions are made for—and it seems to me that that does in truth bring the process which had been initiated to a grinding halt incomplete and that the right thing to do and the commercially sensible thing to do is to go back and start again with a new trigger notice and, if necessary, a new reference. As far as I can see, no great hardship is caused other than that (what is undoubtedly true) the landlord will lose the increased gales of rent due to this accident. But accidents do cause loss and it in no way causes a substantial frustration of the commercial contract or a substantial prejudice to either party. In my view, the matter is quite simple to operate in that way, and the reference which I was given to *Pollock* v. *Brook-Shepherd* (1982) 266 EG 214, where a notice of reference was required under the so-called Leasehold Reform Act 1967, which notice was held could be given once only, is a reference to a set of statutory provisions so remote from any contemplation of this sort which arises in rent review cases that it is of no guide to me at all. The words are plainly quite different and the whole context of the matter, and the approach of the courts to expropriatory statutes, is so substantially different that I find no guidance in the *Pollock* case.

I therefore answer the questions raised by the originating summons as follows. I answer the first part of question 1 Yes, and that was given on 20 June 1983, and the effective date for any increase in the rent payable under it is midsummer day 1983. As to question 2, whether time is of the essence in clause 2 (c), I hold that the answer is Yes. I do not believe that there is any further answer needed to question 2.

No order was made as to costs.

The principle that a notice or counter notice must be demonstrably clear and not a mere expression of disagreement was laid down in *Amalgamated Estates Ltd* v. *Joystretch Manufacturing Ltd* (1980) 257 EG 489, in the Court of Appeal, (considered more fully on a different point below at page 91), where Templeman LJ held there was 'no magic formula' and Lawton LJ construed the tenants' letter as little more than an expression of disagreement.

AMALGAMATED ESTATES LTD v. JOYSTRETCH MANUFACTURING LTD

Court of Appeal   (1980) 257 EG 489

LAWTON LJ: The first step is to construe the letter of 12 December 1978. It was a letter expressing disagreement with the figure put forward by the landlords. But it was a little more than that because, in the final paragraph, there was a request for an explanation as to how the landlords had reached the figure of £10,000. On receipt of this letter the landlords would not have known with certainty what attitude the tenants were taking up. They had made it clear that they disagreed. On the other hand, by asking for particulars as to how the figure was made up, they may have been inviting the landlord to convince them that the figure of £10,000 or some figure near £10,000 was perhaps a reasonable figure in all the circumstances.

There is nothing, in my judgment, in the letter to indicate that, on 12 December 1978, the tenants wanted to go to arbitration. The landlords were left without any clear indication as to what the tenants wanted to do. They might, perhaps, have got some further information about the tenants' intentions had they answered the letter and given their reasons for fixing the figure at £10,000 per annum; but they did not. They were under no obligation to give any explanation. They were, in my judgment, entitled to sit back and wait to see what action the tenants took under clause 3 (c) of the proviso and, when the tenants did not take any steps to call in aid the provisions of that clause, they were entitled to assume that they did not want to take advantage of it.

TEMPLEMAN LJ: It is true that no magic formula is required but, in my judgment, the tenant must make it clear to the landlord that he proposes to have the rent decided by arbitration in accordance with the provisions of the lease. The landlord and tenant may reach a compromise before arbitration has been reached, but, nevertheless, on the plain words of the lease it seems to me that the tenant is directed to serve a counternotice making it clear to the landlord that he proposes to go to arbitration if that is his intention. I cannot spell that out of the tenant's letter, which simply said he did not agree with the landlord's £10,000 and asked for an explanation.

Note: This decision was applied in *Sheridan* v. *Blaircourt Investments Ltd* (1984) 270 EG 1290. Similar views were expressed by Goulding J in *Bellinger* v. *South London Stationers Ltd* (1979) 252 EG 699 and by Michael Wheeler QC, sitting as a deputy judge of the Chancery Division, in *Oldschool* v. *Johns* (1980) 256 EG 381.

However, the test that a counter notice should be clear and 'unequivocal' expressed by McNeill J in *Edlingham Ltd* v. *MFI Furniture Centres Ltd* (1981) 259 EG 421 and Nicholls J in *Sheridan* v. *Blaircourt Investments Ltd* (1984) 270 EG 1290 is too stringent if unequivocal means 'incapable of bearing any other meaning'. The test is that laid down and applied by the Court of Appeal in *Amalgamated Estates Ltd* v. *Joystretch Manufacturing* (1980) 257 EG 489, above page 87, per Lawton LJ and Templeman LJ, namely, that the counter notice must be 'a clear indication' to the landlord as to the tenant's intention, or must make it 'clear to the landlord that he proposes to go to arbitration', per Sir Nicholas Browne-Wilkinson VC in *Nunes and Another* v. *Davies Laing & Dick Ltd* (1986) 277 EG 417 — see Appendix.

In **Glofield Properties Ltd v. E B Tobacco Ltd and Another** (1985) 275 EG 74, it was held by Cantley J (1) that the tenant's letter querying the amount of rent specified on review by the landlord did not amount to a valid counter notice in that it failed clearly to convey the tenant's intent to go to arbitration; (2) that the landlord was not estopped from relying on the rent review provisions because they had not indicated by act or word that they would not rely on them. It was the tenant's self-induced belief that the letter in response to the trigger notice amounted to a valid counter notice which was responsible for the failure to act within the time limits provided in the lease.

CANTLEY J after reviewing the authorities, and in particular Templeman LJ's remarks that there was 'no magic formula' in *Amalgamated Estates* (see above at page 87), said: The letter of 22 March fell far short of informing the landlord that the tenant elected to have the rent determined by an independent surveyor appointed under clause 5 (2) (c), or even that it was intended to be a counternotice of any sort under the clause. The only point of contest in the trial has been the issue of estoppel. The relevant law on estoppel is well established and it is admirably stated in *Halsbury's Laws of England* 4th ed. I quote from vol 16 at para 1505:

> 'Where a person has by words or conduct made to another a clear and unequivocal representation of fact, either with knowledge of its falsehood or with the intention that it should be acted upon, or has so conducted himself that another would, as a reasonable man, understand that a certain representation of fact was intended to be acted on, and that the other has acted on the representation and thereby altered his position to his prejudice, an estoppel arises against the party who made the representation, and he is not allowed to aver that the fact is otherwise than he represented it to be.'

There are three elements: (1) the words or conduct must amount to a clear and unequivocal representation of fact, or at least be such that the other party reasonably understood them to be a clear and unequivocal representation, intended to be acted upon, (2) the other party must in fact have acted on the representation, and (3) he must have been prejudiced by so doing.

[Counsel for the landlord], in effect, submitted that the plaintiff company so acted as to lead the tenant reasonably to believe that if no new rent was agreed within the three months and negotiations for a new tenancy or for a new rent failed, they would then be entitled to have the rent determined by an independent surveyor. He relies on the correspondence between the parties culminating in the landlord's agent's letter of 4 June and on the fact that at about the same time the landlord's office sent a rent notice for 4 June for the original rate of rent. He also relies on the fact that, as [counsel for the tenant] admitted, the landlord was well aware at all times of the terms of clause 5 (2) and was waiting to see if the tenant served the appropriate notice under clause 5 (2) (c) within the three months. I have already referred to the rent notice and the way in which, as I accept, it came to be sent. No witness called for the defendants has said or suggested that he was thereby led to believe, or that he ever did believe, that the rent was not going to be altered at all. It would have been quite unrealistic, after the landlord's letter of 9 March, to expect that the rent would not be increased at least to some extent. [Counsel for the landlord] is on somewhat better ground when he relied on the letter of 4 June because among other things it did mention a future discussion of a revised rental and by then time was running out, but the letter has to be considered in its context. The solicitor's letter of 3 June told the landlord's agent that he would shortly be hearing from the tenant's valuer. The letter was dealing with the proposal for a new lease and did not refer to anything else.

A new lease was what Mr Kennedy, the tenant's solicitor, really wanted, as he made clear in his evidence, and as he had already made clear in his letters of 10 May and 3 June. The landlord's agent was replying to the letter of 3 June. He was dealing with a solicitor, as the solicitor knew, and for all the landlord's agent knew his letter of 4 June might be crossed in the post by the necessary counternotice under clause 5 (2) (c). It is not suggested, and I would not accept it if it were, having seen him, that Mr Gyngell, the landlord's agent, was intending to lead Mr Kennedy into thinking that he had complied with clause 5 (2) (c) or that as far as the landlord was concerned there was no need to comply with it. He was simply replying to the letter of 3 June. His reply did not alert the tenant's solicitor to the need to comply with the conditions of clause 5 (2) (c), but the landlord had no duty to do that. I do not find in the correspondence any clear and unambiguous promise expressly or by implication that the landlord would not seek to rely on non-compliance with clause 5 (2) (c), nor do I find the letters and conduct of the landlord and its agent such that the tenant and its solicitor would reasonably understand them as clearly and unequivocally representing that clause 5 (2) (c) would be treated as having been complied with or that its provisions would not be relied upon.

However, in the end, all this discussion completely ignores the oral evidence. No witness called on behalf of the defendants has said that the failure to give an appropriate counternotice under clause 5 (2) was caused by anything written or done by or on behalf of the plaintiff company, or that anything written or done by or on behalf of the plaintiff company led him to believe and act in the belief that the plaintiff would not rely on the provisions of clause 5 (2). The fact is that the defendants acted throughout the three-month period in the self-induced belief that the requisite counternotice had been given by the letter of 22 March. Mr Buckley, the controlling director of the defendant company, and Mr Kennedy, the defendant's solicitor, were witnesses of striking integrity and candour.

Mr Buckley told me that he was well aware of the provisions of clause 5 (2) and during the three-month period he asked Mr Kennedy if the steps Mr Kennedy had taken were sufficient to cover the defendants under the lease. Mr Kennedy assured him that they were. He had done what was required. Mr Kennedy unhesitatingly confirmed this evidence. He believed that his letter of 22 March had protected his client and he so assured Mr Buckley. He believed that it was a sufficient counternotice for the purpose of clause 5 (2) (c). That was still his belief on 29 June 1982, as can be seen from the letter which he wrote on that date. He told me that when he received the letter of 4 June what he visualised next was that in about the second week of June the parties would get together to discuss the terms of a new lease and if they could not ultimately agree on that they would then have to arbitrate on the terms of the old lease. He now realises he made a mistake as even the best of men sometimes do.

In the circumstances it seems to me to be quite hopeless to seek to rely on the alleged estoppel. Accordingly, the rent of the premises became a rent of £11,000 per annum from the review date and the plaintiff's money claim on that basis must succeed.

The plaintiffs were awarded costs. A stay of execution was granted pending an appeal. Liberty to apply was given to enable tenants to decide whether to seek relief against forfeiture.

4.2 (a)   Landlord's trigger notice not invalidated by omission of suggested revised rent

A landlord's trigger notice which is in accordance with the terms of the lease is not invalidated by the omission of a statement of suggested new rent. The requirements of a review clause are directory rather than mandatory.

DEAN AND CHAPTER OF CHICHESTER CATHEDRAL v. LENNARDS LTD

Court of Appeal   (1977) 244 EG 807

The landlord had served a notice in accordance with the review provisions of the lease save for the fact that no suggested rent was specified. The tenant contended that the notice was invalid. The landlord took out a summons for a declaration that the notice was valid. Graham J held that it was bad because, though it was given in time, it did not state the new rent to be reserved. The landlord appealed. Pending the appeal the House of Lords gave judgment in *United Scientific Holdings Ltd* v. *Burnley Borough Council* (etc) (1978) AC 904 see earlier, page 3.

Held: The appeal would be allowed. The provisions in the rent review clause were not mandatory but directory and the landlord's letter should not fail because it did not state the actual figure of the suggested new rent. It gave the tenants good notice that the landlord desired the rent to be raised to correspond to the market values of September 1975 and the tenant was not misled by it. The letter should not be invalidated because of the omission of one bit of machinery.

Principle enunciated in *United Scientific Holdings Ltd* applied.

LORD DENNING: The court had to look at rent review clauses afresh. Lord Salmon in the House of Lords had said that

'each lease constitutes, among other things, an agreement between the parties that, at stated intervals, the rents shall be revised so as to bring them into line with the then open market rent; the rent revision clauses specify the machinery or guidelines for ascertaining the open market rent. These provisions as to time are not, in my opinion, mandatory or inflexible; they are only directory.'

A mandatory provision was one which must be fulfilled in all its strictness, and failure to perform it meant that the whole thing failed; whereas a directory provision did not require that degree of strictness; even though it was not complied with, the whole did not fail; it could still be regarded as valid and effective. That was how the House of Lords regarded the time provision in the rent review clause in those cases.

Did that new approach apply to the provisions about the suggested new rent? He (his Lordship) though that it did. That was confirmed by the Judicature Act in 1873 when Parliament had enacted that

'stipulations in contracts, as to time or otherwise, which would not before the passing of this Act have been deemed to be or to have become of the essence of such contracts in the Court of Equity, shall receive in all courts the same construction as they would have heretofore received in equity';

and that was repeated in substantially the same words in section 41 of the Law of Property Act 1925.

Applying those principles, the letter of September 1975 should not fail merely because it did not state the actual figure of the suggested new rent. It gave the tenants good notice that the landlords desired that the rent should be raised to correspond to the market values of September 1975. The tenants were not in the least misled. It should not be held invalid simply because of the omission of one bit of machinery.

4.2 (b)   Landlord's trigger notice need not specify a sum equal to genuine pre-estimate of revised rent

There is no implied term that the rent specified in the landlord's review notice has to be a *bona fide* genuine pre–estimate of the market rental of the premises.

AMALGAMATED ESTATES LTD v. JOYSTRETCH MANUFACTURING LTD

Court of Appeal   (1980) 257 EG 489

The lease provided that the open market value should be arrived at in a rent review clause as first specified by the landlord; if the tenant did not accept the figure, then the parties should agree a new open market rent; if the parties could not agree a figure, then, if they should agree on an independent surveyor who would act as arbitrator; in the event of failure to agree on a surveyor, a surveyor should be appointed by the president of the Royal Institution of Chartered Surveyors. The landlord served a notice specifying an unrealistically high figure of £10,000 pa. The tenant disputed the figure but did not serve a specific counter notice by the time limit provided (time being of the essence), and the landlord accordingly demanded the reviewed rent of £10,000 p.a. The tenant refused to pay contending that (1) there was an implied term that the figure specified in the landlord's notice had to be a *bona fide* genuine pre-estimate of the open market rental; (2) that the letter rejecting the landlord's rental figure and asking for an explanation of it amounted to a counter notice within the provisions of the review clause.

Held:
(1) There was no room for implying that the figure specified by the landlord must start with a *bona fide* and genuine pre-estimate of the rent. *Davstone (Holdings) Ltd v. Al-Rifai* (1976) 32 P & CR 18 applied.
(2) The letter expressing disagreement was not a sufficiently certain notification to the landlord that the tenant wished to go to arbitration and was not effective as a counternotice under the review clause.

LAWTON LJ: There are two questions, therefore, for decision in this case: (1) should there be implied into clause 3 (a) of the proviso words to the effect set out in the defence, namely, that the sum specified by the landlords should be a *bona fide* and genuine pre-estimate of the open market rental value?; (2) was the tenants' letter of 12 December 1978 a counternotice under clause 3 (c) of the proviso?

As to the first point, I have no doubt at all that the words which, it was submitted, should be read into clause 3 (a) cannot be so read. The proviso deals with definitions and procedure. Clause (1) of the proviso provides that the open market rental must be a rent which might reasonably be demanded by a willing landlord, etc. Clause (3) sets out how that reasonable rent is to be fixed and it is to be done in three stages. First, the landlord is to specify his figure; then there are to be negotiations for an agreement if his figure is not at once accepted. That is clear from clause 3 (b). If there is no agreement then there is to be arbitration. It is after all those steps have been taken that a reasonable rent is to be ascertained; and I can see no room at all in this lease for implying that the figure specified by the landlord must start with a *bona fide* and genuine pre-estimate of the rent. The whole purpose of the lease is to decide what that rent should be and, as Templeman LJ pointed out in the course of argument, if there was such an implied term to be written into clause 3 (a), disputes would inevitably follow as to what was a *bona fide* and genuine pre-estimate of the rent. There would be no certainty at all and the lease must have intended the procedure in the proviso to deal with such uncertainties as there were.

My judgment in that respect is supported by the decision of Goulding J in the case of *Davstone (Holdings) Ltd* v. *Al-Rifai* [1976] 32 P & CR 18. The lease in that case was differently worded from the one in this case, but the issue in that case was the same as in this case; and Goulding J held that there was no room for the kind of implied term which [counsel] on behalf of the tenants submitted should be read into this lease.

Note: See also *Wolverhampton and Dudley Breweries Plc* v. *Trusthouse Forte Catering Ltd* (1984) 272 EG 1073.

Where the parties have agreed a new rent in accordance with the terms of the lease, the landlord may not necessarily rely on his error in proposing the new rent (which was lower than that already payable) even if the tenant had not changed his position and merely considered the landlord's proposal and accepted it. See *Centrovincial Estates PLC* v. *Merchant Investors Assurance Co. Ltd* [1983] Comm LR 158, CA, where the tenants resisted the landlords' summons for a declaration but at trial subsequently the landlords were successful.

4.3 (a) Requirements of method of service of notice not mandatory but a matter of interpretation

YATES BUILDING COMPANY LTD v. R.J. PULLEYN & SONS (YORK) LTD

Court of Appeal   [1976] 237 EG 183

The holders of an option exercised their rights to purchase a portion of land but the notice was sent by ordinary post and not by registered or recorded delivery post as specified in the option agreement. The sellers contended that the option was not validly exercised. The buyers sought a declaration that a contract for sale had been brought into existence by the notice under the option agreement and claimed specific performance. Templeman J dismissed the buyers' claims. The buyers appealed.

Held: As a matter of interpretation, if the seller received the notice to exercise the option in time it was a valid exercise of the option.

LORD DENNING MR: But the question is whether the words 'such notice to be sent by registered or recorded delivery post' are mandatory or directory. That test is used by lawyers in the construction of statutory instruments, but it can also be used in the construction of other documents. The distinction is this: a mandatory provision must be fulfilled exactly according to the letter, whereas a directory provision is satisfied if it is in substance according to the general intent (see *Howard* v. *Bodington* (1877) 2

PD at 210-211). In applying this rule of construction, you must look to the subject-matter, consider the object to be fulfilled, and then see whether the provision must be fulfilled strictly to the letter or whether the substance of it is enough. So in the present case the question is whether the letter of acceptance *must* be sent by registered or recorded delivery post, else it is bad; or whether it is sufficient if it gets there in time, as, for instance, by ordinary post or by special messenger. Orr LJ gave this instance in the course of the argument. Suppose there were a postal strike during the last week, and the buyer, to make sure it was in time, sent the letter by special messenger, would this not be sufficient? Looking at the object of this provision, it seems to be this. It is inserted for the benefit of the buyer so that he can be sure of his position. So long as he sends the letter by registered or recorded delivery post, he has clear proof of postage and of the time of posting. But if the buyer sends it by ordinary post, he will have no sufficient proof of posting, or of the time of posting. In that case, if the seller proves that he never received it, or received it too late, the buyer fails. None of those reasons apply, however, when the seller does receive it in time. So long as he gets the letter in time, he should be bound. So I would hold, simply as a matter of interpretation, that if the letter did reach the sellers in time, it was a valid exercise of the option.

Orr LJ agreed with Lord Denning. However, Scarman LJ took a slightly different view.

SCARMAN LJ: I agree, subject, however, to one minor point. I am not convinced that the term 'directory' has any application to the field of contract. Contractual provisions seem to me to be either obligatory or permissive, and the term 'directory'—which is, of course, borrowed from the statute law—does not seem to me to be helpful in this context. I agree with the Master of the Rolls that the one question before the court is the interpretation of clause 2 of the option agreement. I read that agreement as requiring the option to be exercised by a notice in writing which is to be actually received by Pulleyns or Pulleyns' solicitors. When later in the clause one comes to the words which have to be construed in this case 'such notice to be sent by registered or recorded delivery post,' I think they are a clear indication, and are intended as such to the offeree, that if there is to be any issue as to whether or not the notice has in fact been received, he had better use registered or recorded delivery post if he wishes to put it beyond doubt. Of course, if there was any such issue, the burden would be upon the party seeking to exercise the option to prove that his notice had been received. The clause is a clear indication that one would most easily and most efficaciously discharge that burden by using registered or recorded delivery post. I wholly agree with the rest of the judgment of the Master of the Rolls.

4.3 (b)   The position of an agent and a subsidiary company

A subsidiary company may act as agent for the lessor and lessee and a notice from one subsidiary company to another for determination of a lease is effective.

TOWNSENDS CARRIERS LTD v. PFIZER LTD

Chancery Division   (1977) 242 EG 813

A lease contained a break clause which provided that either the lessor or lessee could determine the lease by giving notice to the other party in writing. Notice was given by a letter from the lessee's associated company and addressed to an associated company of the lessor. The lessor sought a declaration that the letter was not a valid notice to exercise the option to determine the lease.

Held: The claim failed. Although the demise was to the associated company, the premises were used and operated by the company giving the notice and from early days the lessor had corresponded with the associated company and sent rent demands to it. Subsequently the lessor's associated company on whom the notice had been served had taken over the functions of lessor and had dealt with correspondence and rent demands. Thus, the two associated companies had been clothed with the authority to act as agents and thus, since the letter of notice was sent to the landlord's authorised agent it was valid.

MEGARRY V-C: If a landlord and a tenant had expressly or by implication each respectively consigned the management of the reversion and the tenancy to agents on their behalf, what was done in relation to the tenancy as between the landlord's and tenant's agents would be as validly done as if it had been done between the landlord and the tenant themselves. And in a case where one party had acted to its detriment, the other party would be precluded from asserting that it was not bound by what had been done.

When those principles were applied to the facts of this case, it followed that the plaintiffs' claim failed and would have to be dismissed.

4.4   The consequences of missing the review date where time is of the essence

If the landlord misses the review date where time is of the essence in the rent review clause then the old rent is payable.

WELLER v. AKEHURST AND ANOTHER

Court of Appeal   [1981] 3 All ER 411

A 14 year lease provided for a specified rent for the first seven years with a rent review for the remainder of the term. The rent was to be the open market rental which was to be either (a) a sum specified in a notice in writing to the tenant at any time before the commencement of a clear period of two quarters immediately preceding the review date, (b) a figure agreed between the parties before the expiration of three months immediately after the posting of such a notice, or (c) a figure determined by an independent surveyor whom the parties had appointed. The lease provided by clause 1 (4) that if the surveyor's determination was not published before the review date then the tenant was to pay rent at the yearly rate payable immediately before the review date. The lease further provided that all stipulations as to time in the rent provisions of the lease were to be of the essence and incapable of enlargement save by agreement by the parties. The landlord purported to give the tenant notice specifying the revised annual rent for the second seven years of the term but the notice was served late and did not leave the clear period of two quarters of a year, and accordingly the notice was out of time. The landlord sought a declaration of the rent payable for the second seven years of the term. The tenant contended that the landlord's failure to observe the timetable had made the rent review provisions inoperative, and that the rent payable for the remainder of the term was the rent payable immediately before the review date, pursuant to clause 1 (4).

Held: The court would give effect to the strict requirements of time laid down in the lease. Thus, although the lease had provided that the reviewed rent was to be the open market rental, it required that the ascertainment of the market rental had to be effected in a particular manner, and if the strict timetable was not adhered to then it could not apply.

Clause 1 (4) did not deal with the provision since it was applicable only where an independent surveyor had been appointed under the review provisions, and was not directed to the current situation where no surveyor had been or could be appointed.

However, since the review provisions were inapplicable the court would infer that the old rent would continue for the rest of the term.

Fox J: The position therefore in the present case is that although the lease provides that the rent shall be the open market value and defines that term with sufficient precision, the lease also requires that the ascertainment of the open market value shall be effected in a particular way and stipulates that time shall be of the essence of the provisions in that procedure.

In my judgment, the parties cannot have intended that if the landlord failed to observe the time provisions she could still be free to obtain the determination of the open market value by the court. The parties chose the procedure for rent review with precision and made it plain that the procedure was only to be available on a strict timetable. The landlord having failed to observe that timetable, it seems to me that there is thereafter no room for the operation of any procedure to determine the open market value. If the open market value cannot 'be determined in manner following' (to use the language in cl 1 (3)) it cannot, in my view, be determined at all. Clause 1 (3) states in terms that the open market value shall be 'such annual sum as shall be ...' There then follow paras (a), (b) and (c). That language, coupled with the direction for determination 'in manner following', excluded, I think, the possibility of it being any other sum or determined in any other way. For the court now to take on itself the determination of the open market value would, I think, be to fly in the face of the clearly expressed requirement of strict compliance with the time provisions. I think that the rent revision procedure was intended to be carried out timeously or not at all. The provision for revising the rent was in the landlord's favour; only the landlord could invoke it. But the landlord could only invoke it on strict terms. I see no reason to suppose that the parties intended that the landlord should get a rent increase in any other way ...

The question is whether, in view of the provisions that time is of the essence, any other mode of working out the formula is permissible. For the reasons which I have given, I do not think that it is.

I should add this. If the landlord gave a *bona fide* notice under cl 1 (3) (a) stating an amount which was in fact above the open market value and the tenants failed to give a counternotice in due time, the tenants could not, I think, invoke the definition to redress the position. The tenants would have to accept the amount stated in the landlord's notice. It would be a curious result if the tenants, having failed to observe the timetable, are bound by the cl 1 (3) procedure but if the landlord fails to serve notice in time, the landlord can still get the open market value determined by the court.

I should mention that the expression used in the opening sentence of cl 1 (3) is 'open market *rental* value' not 'open market value', but that, I think, was merely a slip and the contrary was not contended.

The result in my view is that the provisions of cl 1 (3) are wholly inoperative and that the provisions of the lease do not permit the open market value to be determined in any other manner than that specified in cl 1 (3).

In those circumstances, the tenants assert that the rent for the second seven years is £850 per annum. Two arguments are advanced in support of that. First, it is contended that the position is expressly dealt with by cl 1 (4). It is said that the language of that provision is very wide. It begins: 'In the event of the determination of such independent surveyor not having been published prior to the review date for any reason whatever ...' While I agree that that language is indeed wide, it seems to me that cl 1 (4) is assuming that an independent surveyor has been duly appointed under cl 1 (3). The provision, I think, is simply dealing with the period which elapsed after the review date until the quarter day after the determination of the rent by the surveyor. The whole provision, I think, assumes that the surveyor will issue a determination, but that there will be an interval before he does so. Thus the proviso begins: 'PROVIDED that at the expiration of the said interval ...' I do not think that cl 1 (4) is dealing at all with the present circumstances where no surveyor has been or can now be appointed.

In my view, therefore, the lease contains no express provisions to deal with the present case.

What then is the position? That the parties should, in the circumstances, have contemplated that no rent at all should be payable for the residue of the term, I reject altogether. The lease grants a term for 14 years and it is inconceivable that the parties contemplated that no rent might be payable during the second period of seven years.

A liability on the part of the tenant to pay rent must have been intended. The question is how much. In my opinion, if the parties had been asked at the time of the grant of the lease what was to happen if the lessor chose not to serve a notice under cl 1 (3), or failed to serve such notice in time, it is wholly reasonable to suppose that they would have said that the old rent of £850 per annum was to continue. Thus, I do not think that the parties could have been contemplating any reduction of the rent at all. The lease was granted during a period of inflation, and it is clear that only the landlord could set the cl 1 (3) procedure in motion. It was a provision for the landlord's benefit.

On the other hand, I see no reason to suppose that they would have contemplated that the rent should be increased in the event of no valid notice being given under cl 1 (3) by the landlord. The landlord was adequately protected by cl 1 (3) if he wished to increase the rent in line with the market. But, it having been agreed that time was of the essence of those provisions, it cannot, in my view, have been contemplated that, having failed to operate cl 1 (3), the landlord should still be free to get the rent increased by a quite different machinery not expressed in the lease at all. Clause 1 (3) was in general for the benefit of the landlord but the time provisions in cl 1 (3) (a) were for the protection of the tenant.

What I am dealing with is a rent review provision containing strict requirements for its operation. It did not operate because the person at whose option the rent review was to be made did not comply with the requirements. I think that in those circumstances the reasonable and necessary inference is that the old rent continues. I will so declare.

Note: This decision was applied in *Metrolands* above at page 52.

Chapter 5

Surrendering the lease

5.1 A lessee's liability to pay rent in accordance with a rent review clause is not discharged if the lease is surrendered after the rent review date has passed and the lessor is entitled to sue for a declaration that the lessee is liable to pay the revised rent when it is determined

A lessee's liability to pay rent in accordance with a rent review clause in his lease is not destroyed or discharged by a surrender of a lease which occurred after the rent review date, because when a lease contained such a clause, the lessee covenanted he would pay rent fixed in accordance with that clause from the review date, so that his obligation under that covenant took effect from the review date. Similarly, the lessor had a corresponding right from that date to sue for a declaration that this was the lessee's obligation. Accordingly, when the revised rent was fixed by an arbitrator (albeit after the surrender date) but took effect before the date of surrender of the lease, i.e. the review date, the lessee remained liable for the increased rent payable from the review date until the date the lease was surrendered. If the lessee was unable to pay that rent at the new rate, his sureties would be liable to pay it.

TORMINSTER PROPERTIES LTD v. GREEN AND ANOTHER

Court of Appeal   [1983] 2 All ER 457

STEPHENSON LJ: The question raised by this appeal is whether the surrender of the lease has extinguished, discharged or released the lessee's liability (and thereby the sureties' liability) to pay two quarterly payments of increased rent for which there would have admittedly been liability if the lease had not been surrendered. The surrender took place after the first review date and during the next five years of the term of the lease, but before the open market rental value of the demised premises at the review date had been determined by an independent surveyor in accordance with the rent review clause in the lease. It is common ground that the sureties are in the same position as the lessee and that there was no reference to liability to pay the increased rent in the terms of surrender and no express agreement as to that liability. The question is therefore one of law depending on the true construction of the terms of the lease and the legal effect of its surrender in the light of authorities which are not directly in point.

There are cogent arguments for and against the judge's view that the sureties are liable to pay the increased rent and charges claimed and that their liability is not extinguished by the surrender of the lease. And the arguments on both sides have been very well put.

Counsel for the sureties submits that the wording of para (B) (4) of the fourth schedule is such as to show that the surrender put an end to liability for any rent. The authority of decided cases shows that a surrender puts an end to the lease itself, not merely to the term of years granted by the lease. All the tenant's liabilities are thereby extinguished except those which have already accrued or have been expressly reserved. There was no reservation in the letters exchanged on 4 April 1979, and the language of para (B) (4) does not preserve an accrued liability or corresponding right to sue but negatives it. Where, as here, there has been a 'delay period' because there has been a failure to agree or the determination of the independent surveyor has not been published prior to the review date, it is (I quote from the fourth schedule) 'at the expiration of the delay period' that there shall be due as a debt payable by the Lessee to the Lessor on demand a sum of money equal to the amount whereby the yearly rent agreed or determined by such independent surveyor shall exceed' the previous rent. That means that that excess is not due before the expiration of the delay period, and until then there is no debt due or payable, there is no yearly rent agreed or determined and nothing which can be (I quote again from the schedule) 'duly apportioned on a daily basis in respect of the delay period'. The only accrued right is to have an arbitration, not to be owed or paid a debt. There is no right of action vested in the lessor before the surrender enabling the lessor to sue for the increase.

Counsel for the lessor emphasises the basic obligation of the lessee under cl (1) and the fourth schedule, para (B) to pay as rent for the next five years after the review date the open market rental value of the demised premises at that date by equal quarterly payments in advance; and he contrasts that with the machinery for ascertaining that rent and open market rental value provided by sub-paragraphs including sub-para (4). That basic obligation exists at the review date as an obligation to pay the increased rent when it is determined, like the contractual obligation to pay the price of goods to be fixed by a third party. The debt is due at the review date, though it waits to be payable until the expiration of the delay period and the determination of its amount. It is owed from the review date until surrender, and nothing in para (B) (4) indicates that it is not; after surrender it becomes payable retrospectively and would be so payable without the provisions of para (B) (4). Counsel for the lessor might not be able to say that there was a debt before 25 January 1980; but he does say that there was a liability. Even if the debt does not exist until quantified, the contractual obligation to pay it when quantified does exist from the review date until surrender of the lease, perhaps rather as on an interlocutory judgment for damages to be assessed the judgment 'debtor' is under a present liability to pay unliquidated damages to be assessed in the future. Or, another imperfect analogy, as a party ordered to pay costs to be taxed if not agreed owes a duty to pay them but cannot be sued for them until they are agreed or taxed.

There is authority for the following propositions. (1) Rent payable in arrear which has not accrued or become due at the date of surrender of a lease is not recoverable in full; until the Apportionment Act 1870 it was not recoverable pro rata for so long a time as the tenant occupied the premises before surrender: *Grimman* v. *Legge* (1828) 8 B & C 324, 108 ER 1063, *Slack* v. *Sharpe* (1838) 8 Ad & El 366, 112 ER 876. (2) Rent which has accrued or become due at the date of surrender is recoverable: *Walker's Case* (1587) 3 Co Rep 22a, 76 ER 676, *A-G* v. *Cox, Pearce* v. *A-G* (1850) 3 HL Cas 240 at 275, 10 ER 93 at 106. (3) A surrender of a lease operates only to release the tenant from liability on covenants taking effect after the date of the surrender, leaving him liable for past breaches, eg of repairing covenants: *Dalton* v. *Pickard* (1911) [1926] 2 KB 545, [1926] All ER Rep 371, *Richmond* v. *Savill* [1926] 2 KB 530, [1926] All ER Rep 362, in which the court followed *Dalton's* case, *Walker's* case and *Cox's* case. Statements in cases of disclaimer of the lease by a trustee in bankruptcy deemed to have been surrendered by s 23 of the Bankruptcy Act 1869, which suggested that the surrender of a lease destroys all its provisions and every liability under it (*Re Latham, ex p Glegg* (1881) 19 Ch D 7, *Re Fussell, ex p Allen* (1882) 20 Ch D 341, *Re Morrish, ex p Sir W Hart Dyke* (1882) 22 Ch D 410) are to be taken as limited to future breaches and rights of action not yet accrued. The proposition derived from them that the mere surrender of a tenancy precludes the landlord from further enforcing against the tenant any of his obligations under the lease, whether those obligations had already accrued before the date of the surrender or had not, was stated to be wrong by this court in *Richmond* v. *Savill*, and does not appear to have been revived since it was laid to rest in 1926. Counsel for the sureties does not seek to revive it.

Now the rent which the lessor has recovered from the sureties is rent payable in advance in respect of two quarterly periods which had in fact expired before the date of surrender. The amount would have been different had the independent surveyor fixed a different open market rental value. If he had found that that value was no higher than £7100 a year, that would have been the rent for which the lessee would have continued to be liable. And, once the amount of the rent payable for the second period of five years has been determined, it is payable retrospectively from the review date and the start of that period: *C H Bailey Ltd* v. *Memorial Enterprises Ltd* [1974] 1 All ER 1003, [1974] 1 WLR 728, *United Scientific Holdings Ltd* v. *Burnley BC, Cheapside Land Development Co. Ltd* v. *Messels Service Co.* [1977] 2 All ER 62, [1978] AC 904.

In the *Cheapside Land Development Co.* case Graham J had granted the landlords a declaration that the market rent as determined by the valuer for the second and third periods of seven years in a lease for a term of 21 years, if higher than the annual rent payable in arrear on the usual quarter days for the first period of seven years, would be recoverable with effect from the start of the second period at the review date. The Court of Appeal reversed his decision, apparently on the ground that the rent was not, and had to be, certain. The House of Lords restored the order of Graham J, holding that to be distrainable rent had to be certain, that a contractual money payment made by a tenant to his landlord in consideration for the use of the latter's land was rent and that it need not be certain at the date from which it became payable: see the speeches of Lord Diplock, Lord Simon and Lord Fraser ([1977] 2 All ER 62 at 72, 76, 86, 99, [1978] AC 904 at 930, 934-935, 947, 964). (When Lord Fraser speaks of the rent as the contractual sum due which 'need not be certain at the date on which it becomes payable', I think he must mean 'at the date from which it becomes payable when ascertained'.) In the first of these passages Lord Diplock points out ([1977] 2 All ER 62 at 72, [1978] AC 904 at 930):

'The determination of the new rent under the procedure stipulated in the rent review clause neither brings into existence a fresh contract between the landlord and the tenant nor does it put an end to one that had existed previously. It is an event on the occurrence of which the tenant has in his existing contract already accepted an obligation to pay to the landlord the rent so determined for the period to which the rent review relates. The tenant's acceptance of that obligation was an inseverable part of the whole consideration of the landlord's grant of a term of years of the length agreed. Without it, in a period during which inflation was anticipated, the landlord would either have been unwilling to grant a lease for a longer period than up to the first review date or would have demanded a higher rent to be paid throughout the term than that payable before the first review date. By the time of each review of rent the tenant will have already received a substantial part of the whole benefit which it was intended that he should obtain in return for his acceptance of the obligation to pay the higher rent for the succeeding period.'

Counsel for the lessor naturally relies on what Lord Diplock there said as supporting his submission that the obligation precedes the surrender and is therefore enforceable once its extent has been determined. So did the deputy judge in support of his statement ([1982] 1 All ER 420 at 423-424, [1982] 1 WLR 751 at 755-756):

'Here, at the surrender, the landlord was entitled to be paid as a contract debt the difference, if any, between the old rent and the review rent for the period after the review date. It was a present right based on a partly executed consideration ... But it was a present right not yet actionable, to a future payment, because the difference was not payable until the quarter day after the arbitrator fixed the new rent and there might be no difference; but again, the landlord could, apart at least from the surrender, compel the arbitration to be carried through ... It seems to me that the tenant's duty to pay the difference between the old and the review rent for the period after the review date is correlative with the tenant's right to possession during that period and so it should be paid, even though the surrender intervenes before its amount is fixed. As the lessee here continued in possession during the period after the rent review date, it ought to pay the difference between the arbitrator's rent and what the lessor has received for that period.'

He then gave judgment for that rent and the undisputed service and insurance charges claim.

It may be said that the tenant who pays rent in arrear will have already received when he pays it a substantial part of the benefit of the occupation for which he has agreed to pay it, yet his liability does not survive a surrender. But in my judgment the liability to pay rent determined in accordance with a rent review clause is a liability which is not destroyed or discharged by a surrender after the period for which it will ultimately be paid has started to run. There is, when that period has started, a right to sue, not for the as yet undetermined rent but for a declaration that the tenant is liable to pay it when determined, as the *Cheapside Land Development Co.* case shows. There is not an antecedent breach of an obligation, indeed there could not be until the quarter day immediately following 25 January 1980; but there is an antecedent obligation accruing before surrender puts an end to the lease. The lessee has no right to occupy the premises after the review date rent-free: he owes a contractual duty to pay at least the initial rent as long as he holds the lease, however long the determination of the new rent may be delayed. It is the prior existence of that contractual obligation, that covenanted liability, of the tenant which differentiates such a claim as this from a landlord's claim to recover rent payable in arrear after the date of surrender, for there the tenant is under no obligation or liability to pay any rent before that date.

I would accordingly uphold the lessor's submission, affirm the judgment of the deputy judge and dismiss the appeal.

5.2 Even after surrender, a lease exists as a document and its terms can be acted on if they are to determine the basis for fixing a reviewed rent in a sublease

Where an underlease contains a rent review clause which provides that the reviewed rent is to be ascertained in accordance with the relevant terms of the headlease, the fact that at the material date the headlease had been surrendered did not affect the validity of the rent review. The headlease, though it was no longer effective, still existed as a document, and its terms could be acted upon for the determination of the reviewed rent under the sublease, see *Lorien Textiles (U.K.)* v. *S.I. Pension Trustees* (1981) 259 EG 771.

Chapter 6

Interpreting review clauses

6.1 (a) Problems of construction, examples of the court's approach

Generally, each case will depend on its own facts and the wording of an individual clause, but the following cases are an indication to the court's attitude to construction. For instance, sometimes the court will favour a literal approach even where it does not reflect the likely intention of the parties and in Philpot's case below the Court of Appeal rejected the landlord's argument that the parties must have intended that the review rent was to be the rack-rental value when construing an ambiguously drafted review clause.

PHILPOTS (WOKING) LTD v. SURREY CONVEYANCERS LTD AND ANOTHER

Court of Appeal   (1986) 277 EG 61

The rent review clause in a lease provided that the rent on review should be:

'A sum equal to the aggregate of £8000 plus the amount (if any) by which the fair rack-rental value ... at the time of review shall exceed the sum of (1) £8000 or (2) the yearly rent fixed at the previous date of review as the case may be ... and so that in no event should the rent payable ... after the date of review be less than the rent payable by the lessee to the lessor immediately before the date of review.'

The landlord contended that the clause should be construed as providing a sum equal to the aggregate of £8000, the initial yearly rent, plus the amount by which the fair rack-rental value at the time of review should exceed £8000. By contrast, under the tenant's construction one took the initial rent of £8000 and added to this the amount by which the rack-rental value exceeded the previous rent. If this construction were correct, then, if one assumed that the fair rack-rental was always increasing, the rent payable on the first review would be its equivalent, but that payable on every subsequent review would always fall short of it. This was because the addition to be made to the initial £8000 was not the difference between the sum and the rack-rental value, as contended for by the landlord, but the difference between the previous rent and the rack-rental value. Michael Wheeler QC, sitting as a deputy High Court judge rejected the tenant's construction as unascertainable and capricious and made a declaration based on the landlord's construction. The tenant appealed.

Held: The appeal was allowed. Although when he had accepted the landlord's construction, the deputy judge had probably correctly assessed what the parties had indeed believed and desired to be the effect of the review clause, a court of construction could only hold that they intended it to have that effect if the intention appeared from a fair interpretation of the words which the parties had used against the factual background known to them at or before the date of the lease, including its genesis and objective aim. Here it was not suggested that there was any material background beyond the fact that the lease was a commercial lease between commercial parties. The landlord's argument contained an inherent proposition that commercial parties to a commercial lease *invariably* intended that the rent should not, in real terms, fall below the market rent initially agreed upon, but this proposition was unacceptable. It was perfectly possible for the parties to assume that the fair rack-rental value will always increase, but nonetheless to intend that the rent payable on the second review shall always be less. Unless such a construction led to such absurd results that the parties could not be credited with an intention to achieve them, (and this was not the case here), the clause should be construed to give full effect and meaning to the words actually used. Here the results, though unpredictable and possibly capricious, were not unascertainable, and the tenant's construction would prevail. By employing the words 'as the case may be' the rent review clause indicated that the second alternative sum was to be used where the previous rent was not £8000.

NOURSE LJ: I think it very probable that, in accepting the landlord's construction, the learned judge has correctly assessed what the parties did indeed believe and desire to be the effect of clause 5 (1) (iii) of the lease. But a court of construction can only hold that they intended it to have that effect if the intention appears from a fair interpretation of the words which they have used against the factual background known to them at or before the date of the lease, including its genesis and objective aim. It is not in this case suggested that there is any material background beyond the fact that the lease is a commercial lease between commercial parties.

Inherent in [counsel for the landlord]'s principal argument is the proposition that commercial parties to a commercial lease *invariably* intend that the rent should not in real terms fall below the market rent initially agreed upon. I cannot accept that proposition. It is perfectly possible for them to assume that the fair rack rental value will always increase, but nonetheless to intend that the rent payable from the second review onwards shall always be less. There is nothing in the words of the lease to exclude that possibility, unless it be that the tenant's construction of them leads to results so absurd that the parties cannot be credited with an intention to achieve them. I do not think that it does. The learned judge described the results as unascertainable and almost capricious. By the first of these he meant that they were unpredictable. So indeed they are. But that is not, I think, enough. I am not sure whether I would describe them as capricious. They may be. It is a word which means different things to different people. But for myself I would not think that capriciousness was enough. I think that [counsel for the landlord] must show that the results are absurd, and of that he has failed to persuade me.

Once [counsel for the landlord]'s principal argument has been rejected, so that the words of clause 5 (1) (iii) can be examined without any preconceptions as to their intent, I find that the arguments of [counsel for the tenant], as I have stated them, must prevail. His primary argument is a formidable one which speaks for itself. The tenant's construction gives full meaning and effect to the words 'as the case may be'. Those words do not mean 'whichever is the higher' and the rejection of [counsel for the landlord]'s principal argument defeats an implication to that effect. The tenant's construction finds employment for the words introduced by 'and so that ...' and prevents them from being a mere repetition of what has gone before. The only point which is left to sustain the landlord's construction is the explanatory, not restrictive, meaning of those words. I have felt the force of that point, but not strongly enough for it to overgo the points which are against it.

For these reasons, although in a full understanding of how the learned deputy judge came to be of the contrary view, I am of the opinion that the tenant's construction is correct. I would therefore allow this appeal.

6.1 (b)   The court may apply a missing term to give business efficacy to an agreement

But contrast *Guys 'n' Dolls Ltd* v. *Sade Brothers Catering Ltd*, below, where the Court of Appeal found that a literal interpretation of the clause did not give business efficacy to the intention of the parties.

GUYS 'N' DOLLS LTD v. SADE BROTHERS CATERING LTD

Court of Appeal   [1983] 269 EG 129

A 13-year lease of business premises provided that after 28 September 1980, the first review date, the rent for the premises should be £7500 p.a. in excess of the fair rack market rental. The rack rental was to be determined 'in all other respects on the terms and conditions of this lease'. The landlords sought a declaration against the tenants that the yearly rent payable from 28 September 1980 until the second review date in 1985 was the aggregate of (a) £7500 and (b) the market rent of the premises to be determined without taking account (i) either the obligation of the defendant to pay rent at a rate of £7500 p.a. above such fair rack market value, or (ii) the amount of rent payable under the said lease from and after the second review date of September 28 1985.

It was accepted by the landlord that in assessing a hypothetical fair rack rental market value for the first five years of the remaining 10-year term, the valuer had to take into account the *existence* of the rent review clause in the lease and the manner in which the amount of rent payable from 1985 would fall to be assessed by virtue of that clause. The question before the court was whether, when determining the rent payable at the first review, the valuer had also to take into account the £7500 p.a. excess which would fall to be paid under para (2) of the lease during the second rent review period. In the High Court, Walton J had held that in ascertaining the market rent at the first review date (a) no account should be taken of the obligation to pay the extra £7500, but (b) account should be taken of the tenant's obligation to pay the extra £7500 during the second review period. The landlords appealed.

Held: The plain and obvious intention of the parties was that the annual rent should be maintained at a figure £7500 in excess of the market level. The one way effect could be given to this intention was to construe the provisions of the lease on the basis that, in determining the amount for the fair rack market rental value on the occasion of any review, no account whatsoever was to be taken of the fact that the actual rent payable under the lease following the review, during either the first or second review period, was to be £7500 above the market value. By a process of necessary implication it was necessary further to exclude from the ambit of the phrase a reference to pay the annual £7500 during the period of the second review. There was not sufficient justification for construing the crucial words 'and in all other respects on the terms and conditions of this lease' as being wide enough to include the £7500 excess payable during the second review, but (as was now agreed) *not* as including the £7500 excess payable during the first review period. It would be ridiculous to add on the premium of £7500 only to then immediately take it away again by reducing the fair market rent by that amount.

Lister Locks Ltd v. *TEI Pension Trust Ltd* (1984) 264 EG 827 approved (see below for facts and extract, page 152).

SLADE LJ: The fifth schedule, so far as material, reads as follows:

'(1) After the 28th day of September 1980 the yearly rent payable in respect of the demised premises until the 28th day of September 1985 shall be £7,500 above such sum as shall be agreed between the Landlord and the Tenant as representing a fair rack market value of the demised premises ...'

I interject that it is common ground that the word 'rental' should be read into the middle of the phrase 'fair rack market value' as a clerical omission

> '... for a term of years equivalent to the then unexpired residue of the term hereby granted as between a willing lessor and a willing lessee with vacant possession and taking no account of any goodwill attributable to the premises by reason of any trade or business carried on therein by the tenant and in all other respects on the terms and conditions of this lease and if the Landlord and the Tenant shall be unable to agree on the amount of such rent as aforesaid the same shall be decided by some competent person to be agreed to by the Landlord and the Tenant and in the event of failure so to agree by a person to be appointed by the President for the time being of the Royal Institution of Chartered Surveyors ...'

Thus the point of construction falls to be determined by reference simply to the four corners of the lease itself. Nevertheless, when the lease, in particular the fifth schedule, is read as a whole, it seems to me that, as [counsel for the landlord] has submitted, the plain and obvious intention of the parties was that at all times, throughout the periods of both the first rent review and the second rent review, the annual rent payable should be maintained at a figure representing a steady £7500 above the market rental value of the premises—such market rental value being assessed without regard to the obligation to pay the £7500 excess itself. That is the clear and unmistakeable intention I derive from a general reading of the fifth schedule to the lease, and, in so doing, I do not disregard the point made by [counsel for the tenant] that the intention of the parties has to be gleaned without forgetting that the lease itself might be assigned, and that the obligations thereunder might devolve on parties other than the original tenants or landlords.

There is, in my judgment, one way in which effect can be given to such an intention. In my judgment the provisions of the lease can properly be construed on the basis that, in determining the amount of the 'fair rack market rental value' on the occasion of any review, no account whatsoever is to be taken of the fact that the actual rent payable under the lease following the review—be it the first review or the second review—is to be £7500 above the sum determined to be the 'fair rack market rental value'. I respectfully disagree with the conclusion of the learned judge that there is no method of reaching this result on the basis of the words used in the lease. As I have already pointed out, I think that he himself, by a process of construction, implicitly restricted the strict literal meaning of the crucial phrase 'and in all other respects on the terms and conditions of this lease', by excluding from its ambit any reference to the obligation to pay the annual £7500 excess during the period of the first rent review. For my part, I am satisfied that by a similar process of necessary implication, it is not only proper but necessary further to exclude from the ambit of the phrase a reference to the obligation to pay the annual £7500 excess during the period of the second rent review. To do otherwise would seem to me to lead to a result which would have the effect of frustrating rather than giving effect to the commercial object of the parties. The speech of Lord Wilberforce in *Prenn* v. *Simmonds* well illustrates that the court is justified in taking such considerations into account in any process of construction (see [1971] 1 WLR 1381 at p 1385 A-B).

It may be that one could reach the same result by saying, contrary to my view, that even on its literal meaning, the crucial phrase on which the tenants' argument has to be based, is not wide enough to include a reference to the obligation to pay the £7500 excess at any time during the lease. However, whichever way one reads this phrase, I think that on any footing it cannot be reasonably supposed that the parties intended that, in carrying out his functions in 1980, the valuer should reduce the 'fair rack market rental value' falling to be assessed by him, on account of the annual excess of £7500 which the tenants would have to continue to pay during the second rent review period, any more than he should reduce such figure on account of the annual excess of £7500 which they would have to pay during the first rent review period.

In this context, my thinking is broadly on the same lines as that which is to be found expressed in a passage from a judgment of Mr Michael Wheeler QC in *Lister Locks Ltd* v. *TEI Pension Trust Ltd* (1982) 264 EG 827, the passage being at p 832—though the particular provisions of the lease in that case were not, of course, the same as those in the present case.

In short, I cannot see sufficient justification for construing the crucial words 'and in all other respects on the terms and conditions of this lease' as being wide enough to include the £7500 excess payable during the second rent review period, but (as is no common ground) *not* as including the £7500 excess payable during the first rent review period.

Note: A literal approach defeating the probable intentions of the parties has often been taken in the context e.g. of 'reviewing without review': see pages 124-34, but contrast the decision in *Datastream International* at page 134.

6.2 Whether rent should be reviewed on the basis of deemed vacant possession

The question of whether rent should be reviewed on the basis of deemed vacant possession of the premises or should have regard to the factual position where premises may be wholly or in part sublet, will depend on the wording of the lease. The parties can impose what valuation assumptions they choose. Where this point is unclear then the court must take into account the intentions of the parties and all the circumstances surrounding the letting.

In the *Avon* case, the court held that valuation was to be on the basis of vacant possession notwithstanding the existence of sub-tenants when the lease was taken.

AVON COUNTY COUNCIL v. ALLIANCE PROPERTY CO. LTD

Chancery Division   **(1981) 258 EG 1181**

JUDGE MERVYN DAVIES QC (sitting as a High Court judge): By the lease the council demised to the tenants the plot of land, buildings and premises described in the First Schedule to the lease and it was declared that the said plot of land, buildings and premises 'with any alterations or additions' were in the lease referred to as 'the demised premises'. The term of the lease was 125 years from 21 December 1974. The demise was made subject to and with the benefit of the leases and licences mentioned in the Third Schedule to the lease. These leases and licences are hereinafter referred to as 'the scheduled leases and licences'. The lease reserved 'the yearly rent following that is to say during the first five years of the said term the yearly rent of £55,200-00 and during the twenty-four successive periods of five years of the said term each a yearly rent to be assessed in accordance with Clause 6 (iv) hereof' together with a further rent in respect of insurance expenditure.

The clause 6 (iv) already mentioned is in these terms:

'6 (iv) (a) The Council shall have the right to review the yearly rent for the time-being payable hereunder at or after the end of the fifth year and also at the end of each subsequent fifth year of the term hereby granted (the date when such review takes place being hereinafter referred to as "the date of review") on giving to the Tenants not more than twelve nor less than three months notice in writing prior to the date of review and after the date of review this Lease shall be read and construed and shall take effect in all respects as if the yearly rent for the time-being payable hereunder instead of being the sum of £55,200-00 had been 70 per cent of the rack-rental market value (as hereinafter defined) of the demised premises but without prejudice to any of the other terms and conditions contained in the Lease and so that in no event shall the yearly rent payable by the Tenants to the Council after the date of review be less than the yearly rent payable by the Tenants to the Council immediately before the date of review.

(b) The rack-rental market value of the demised premises shall (subject as hereinafter provided) by the amount which shall be agreed between the Council and the Tenants to be the best rent at which the whole of the demised premises might reasonably be expected to be let in the open market by a willing landlord to a willing single tenant for a term of years equal to the unexpired residue of the term granted by this Lease and subject to similar covenants and conditions (other than the amount of the rent) to those contained in this Lease there being disregarded:

(i) any effect on rent of the fact that the Tenants or their predecessors in Title have been in occupation of the demised premises or any part thereof.

(ii) Any goodwill then attaching to the demised premises or any part thereof by reason of the carrying on thereon whether by the Tenants or by their predecessors in Title or by an under-Tenant of the Tenants or their predecessor in Title of any business or businesses.

(iii) Any improvements made to the demised premises by the Tenants with the consent of the Council or the Court.

(c) In the event of the Council and the Tenants failing to agree as to the rack-rental market value of the demised premises at the date of review within three months of such date of review, then and in any such case the dispute shall as soon as practicable be referred to the award of some competent person to be agreed upon by the Council and the Tenants (or in default of agreement) to be nominated by the President for the time-being of the Royal Institute of Chartered Surveyors ...

Put shortly, the question is whether the rent is to be fixed on the basis of vacant possession or on the basis that the scheduled leases and licences subsist.

[Having considered the circumstances in which the lease came to be granted, the judge continued:]

Between the date of the agreement (4 February 1972) and the date of the lease (5 March 1975) the scheduled leases and licences were granted on the dates already mentioned. No doubt all five were executed pursuant to clause 17 (b) of the agreement. The initial rents payable under the scheduled leases were (1) £34,500, (2) £23,450 and (3) £15,830. I note that the three scheduled leases begin with the words 'This underlease' but they are in fact leases. I suppose they were looked upon as underleases because the rents were to be handed over to the developer and had the lease been in existence the terms of years granted by the schedule of leases would have been granted by the developer and so would have been true underleases. The terms of the scheduled leases are, as I have said, 35, 25 and 25 years. The lease refers to the scheduled lease dated 29 March 1974 as having a term of 25 years. That is a mistake. In fact its term is 35 years. The scheduled leases contain rent review provisions. All three provide for new rents at successive intervals being fixed by reference to an assumed letting 'with vacant possession'.

So I come to the question whether the phrase 'rack-rental market value' in clause 6 (iv) of the lease means a value determined on a vacant possession basis or on some other basis such as that indicated in the second limb of paragraph 1 of the amended originating summons.

[Counsel] for the tenants contended for a non-vacant possession value. The main points of his argument were:

'(1) clause (iv) does not contain the words "with vacant possession"; such words could be read into the clause only if it was necessary in order to make sense of the valuing provision and that was not the case. He contrasted the rent review provisions of the scheduled leases where the words "with vacant possession" do appear. There is perhaps some justification in the circumstances of this case for supposing that the words of the scheduled leases may throw some light on the lease and vice versa.

(2) clause (iv) came into operation at a time when the demised premises were not in vacant possession. The scheduled leases had already been granted. They will continue for many years and may well be extended by virtue of the Landlord and Tenant Act 1954. Accordingly, the lease was drafted on the footing that the rent arising under the lease would be a rent based on a recognition of the fact that the scheduled leases existed; and that meant that the rent would not be fixed on any vacant possession basis. The lease was, he said, a reversionary lease.

(3) It was suggested that the main reason for the constitution of the (reversionary) lease was to bring into being an intermediate single managing tenant. This single tenant would relieve the council from the risk and trouble of management in that the single head lessee would attend to the superintendence of the common parts, etc.'

In light of these considerations, [Counsel for the tenants] said that the meaning of clause 6 (iv) was that a new rent would be fixed not on any vacant possession basis but with a recognition of the fact that the council's interest in the land was burdened by the scheduled leases and licences.

In my view the absence from subclause (iv) of the words 'with vacant possession' is not fatal to the claim that subclause (iv) contemplates a vacant possession valuation. The words quoted may be implicit in the clause. I see the strength of [counsel for the tenants'] second point but it must be tested by reference to the actual words of subclause (iv) in the whole context of the lease.

I therefore turn to subclause (iv). First, paragraph (a) says that the new rent is to be '70 per cent of the rack-rental market value (as hereinafter defined) of the demised premises'. Then paragraph (b) defines 'rack-rental market value of the demised premises'; I have already read paragraph (b) in full.

[Counsel] for the council, pointed out that '(b)' is concerned with a rent of the 'demised premises', a phrase defined in the lease as being the buildings and land described in the First Schedule to the lease. Thus, it was submitted, subclause (iv) does not call for a rent that is in any way related to the scheduled leasehold interests that subsist; the rent is to be related to the land and buildings and that implies a rent based on vacant possession. I see great force in that submission. In conjunction with this submission, [counsel for the landlords] said that if [counsel for the tenants'] construction is to be upheld one has to alter or disregard the words 'of the demised premises'. [Counsel for the landlords] said that the [counsel for the tenants'] construction required the deletion from paragraph (b) of the words 'the whole of the demised premises' and the insertion of some such words as 'the reversion immediately expectant on the determination of the leases to which the demised premises are subject at the date of the review'. I note too the use of the phrase '*the whole* of the demised premises' in connection with the phrase 'a willing *single* tenant'. Those phrases together certainly seem to suggest that no account is to be taken of the scheduled leases. Continuing with the wording of (iv) (b) I come to the words 'and subject to similar covenants and conditions (other than the amount of the rent) to those contained in this lease'. So paragraph (b) does not say specifically that the notional letting is to be regarded as subject to the scheduled leases and licences. Then come the 'disregard' provisions of subparagraphs (i), (ii) and (iii). These seem to me to be appropriate to a rent fixed by reference to vacant possession rather than by taking account of the scheduled leases.

These considerations taken together lead me to the conclusion that the words 'with vacant possession' are implicit in subclause (iv) (b). It is to be read as though those words followed the words 'expected to be let'. I have reached this conclusion simply by considering the words of subclause (iv). The circumstances that existed at the date of the lease do not seem to me to make this construction in any way doubtful. I add that the conclusion that it is right to be able to construe '(iv)' as I have is I think satisfactory for three reasons. In the first place, the phrase 'rack-rental market value' of itself suggests to me a vacant possession valuation. I say that because a rack-rent is the best rent that can be reasonably obtained and the best rent would ordinarily be obtained in respect of premises in vacant possession. Secondly, the initial rent under the lease was not intended to be fixed by any reference to the scheduled leases: see agreement dated 4 February 1972, clause 22. In making this comment I appreciate that such rents were not intended to be fixed by reference to vacant possession either. Thirdly, the rents of the schedule leases had to be approved by the developer, ie the person about to become the tenant under the lease: see 1972 agreement, clause 17. That being so, it is difficult to see why the rent of the lease should be tied in any necessary fashion to the rents of the scheduled leases.

Accordingly the originating summons is answered as to paragraph 1 in the vacant possession sense.

As to paragraph 2 of the summons, I was told that on a vacant possession basis there was agreement that the new rent of the demised premises is to be £92,000 a year.

The defendants were ordered to pay the costs of the application.

However, *Avon County Council* v. *Alliance Property Co. Ltd* was distinguished in:

SCOTTISH & NEWCASTLE BREWERIES PLC v. SIR RICHARD SUTTON'S SETTLED ESTATES

Chancery Division   (1985) 276 EG 77

The defendant landlords owned a valuable freehold site which was ripe for development in 1960. In June 1960, following a building agreement, the landlords granted a development company a 99 year lease, who in turn granted a lease of the whole building (which was in the course of construction), to the plaintiff tenants, for a term of 42 years commencing on completion of the works. The underlease contained a single rent review after 21 years of the term and various covenants restricting user, assignment and alterations etc. While the building was being constructed, the tenants sought and obtained a modification of the design of the downstairs with the result that a dividing wall was erected on the ground floor premises separating off the area. This was done so that part of the ground floor could be sublet separately by the tenants. Ultimately, the development company surrendered its headlease to the landlords who became the plaintiffs' direct landlords. It was always contemplated that the tenants would sublet most of the building, and all the upper floors were in fact let to a single tenant on terms almost identical with those of the tenants themselves with a notional reversion between. The landlords served a notice triggering the rent review, and the matter was to be arbitrated. For this purpose, the lease provided guidance as to the basis for fixing the increased rent.

The clause was silent on the question of whether valuation was to be on the basis of vacant possession or not. A dispute arose as to the basis on which the arbitrator was to fix the rent, and the tenants sought the guidance of the fact on the following questions:

(1) What assumption is the arbitrator to make as to the terms in the notional letting other than as to rent?

(2) Is the arbitrator to assume that the notional letting is with vacant possession, or is he to assume that it is subject to the existing underlettings? and

(3) Is he or is he not to assume that a wall dividing part of the ground floor occupied by the lessees from part occupied by sublessees is an improvement or

additional building carried out by the tenant, with the consequence that its effect on rent is to be disregarded?

Held:

(1) The rent was to be reviewed on the terms of the existing lease other than as to rent for the period of 21 years.

(2) When the lease was granted to the tenants it was known that the underleases were going to be created, and the original rent payable under the lease was calculated with reference to the rents payable under the subleases and the formula then adopted found its place for certain purposes in the rent review provision, and further, the sublettings, if continuing beyond the review date, were themselves subject to review at that date. That was a requirement which was imposed by the landlords in the lease and consequently the tenant would then be in receipt of the full rack rents following such reviews and his interest would be correspondingly enhanced. The landlords could thus be considered to be offering a lease of the whole, vacant possession of a part and leases at full rents of the remainder. This being established there should be no assumption of vacant possession of the whole, including the upper floors as well as the ground floor, which everybody knew was not going to occur. The premises would be valued subject to the existence of the sublettings. *Avon County Council* v. *Alliance Property Co. Ltd* (1981) 258 EG 1181 distinguished (see page 105).

(3) The dividing wall was a modification of the building during the course of its construction and as such was an improvement of the design of the building but was not an improvement to the building, even though the tenant had contributed to the cost of its construction. *Per curiam*: However, had the wall been an improvement as such, it would have been carried out in anticipation of the grant of a lease to the tenant and, as the review clause provided that any improvement made by the tenant was to be disregarded on review, it would have approached an unconscionable attempt by the landlord to profit by it, decision of Scott J in *Hambros Bank Executor & Trustee Co. Ltd* v. *Superdrug Stores Ltd* (1985) 274 EG 590 approved. (See 12.6, page 257.)

JUDGE PAUL BAKER QC (sitting as a High Court judge): But what I am concerned with is what the arbitrator is to do in regard to the determination of the question to him, the question being whether any, and if so what, increase ought to be made in the rent payable as from the expiration of the 21st year of the term. He is directed by subclause (d) to determine that question by:

'(i) ascertaining the annual rack rent of the demised premises including any buildings thereon at the date of the rent notice that is to say the annual rent at which the demised premises and any such buildings might reasonably be expected to be let as a whole without premium in the open market as between a willing landlord and a willing tenant if the tenant undertook to pay all usual tenant's rates and taxes and to bear the cost of repairs insurance and other expenses (if any) necessary to maintain the same in a state to command such rent and assuming that the tenant has observed and performed all the covenants and conditions by it to be observed and performed hereunder but disregarding (a) any effect on rent of the fact that the tenant or any persons deriving title under it had been in occupation of the demised premises (b) any goodwill attached to the demised premises since the commencement of the term hereby granted by reason of the carrying on thereat of the business of the tenant or of any person deriving title under it and (c) any effect on rent of any improvement or additional building carried out by the tenant or any person deriving title under it.'

One notices that there is no reference to vacant possession there, as there is in some of these clauses, and that question has come up here. Then one notices that 'the disregards' obviously have been taken to some extent from the statutory disregards in the Landlord and Tenant Act 1954, but there are very important differences. They have certainly been tailored to the particular situation here, but the three disregards are those which are to be found in the 1954 Act, that is to say the effect of the occupation, goodwill and, important for present purposes, the effect of any improvement or additional building. But clause (c) goes beyond the disregard in the statutory provision in that it refers to 'additional building' and 'any persons deriving title under it'.

That is the main provision, but I should just deal with the rest of the clause. Subclause (ii) directs what the arbitrator is to do. He is to determine the question and then having got that decision made, he is to go on:

'(ii) calculating the amount which bears to the annual rack rental value ascertained under paragraph (i) above the same ratio that the rent payable hereunder at the date of the rent notice bears to the original gross annual rent (hereinafter defined). And if the amount calculated under paragraph (ii) above exceeds the rent payable hereunder at the date of the rent notice the difference shall be the increase in the rent payable hereunder.'

Then there is a covenant on behalf of the tenant to pay that increase from the 21st year, and I need not read that out, but go on to (f):

'For the purpose of this clause the expression "Original Gross Annual Rent" shall have the same meaning as that assigned to it by an agreement dated the thirteenth day of March One thousand nine hundred and sixty-one made between the same parties as the parties hereto and in the same order.'

That is a provision which has the effect of reducing the rent which has been determined by the arbitrator, because he has to calculate the amount which that bears to the value that he has ascertained by the same ratio that the rent under the lease bears to the original gross annual rent, and as the gross annual rent is larger than the rent payable under the lease, as we noticed as I went along, then, of course, that will necessarily mean a reduction, of not very large proportions because it was not a very big reduction, but a reduction of the rent so ascertained by the arbitrator under clause (d) (i).

Assumption as to terms of natural letting

That is the clause, and now I can deal with the first question: what are the terms of the hypothetical lease which the arbitrator is to assume when he is making his award or determining what increase in rent there should be?

The landlords' position is this, that he should assess the rent payable for the residue of the term, that is 21 years, on the same terms and conditions as are in the existing lease other than as to the rent. There should be, among other things, no further review; there is no provision for further review, this is the one and only, and that will no doubt result in a higher rent being awarded than would be if the arbitrator was to assume a notionally shorter lease, or perhaps a lease for the rest of the term, the 21 years, with shortish reviews—which is the common feature of leases of this type of property being granted today. So that is the landlords' view, that except for the amount of the rent it is on exactly the same terms as in the current lease but without any review at all.

To some extent there is support in the authorities for that view. In the case of *Ponsford* v. *HMS Aerosols Ltd* [1979] AC 63, there are some dicta of the House of Lords which bear on this question. They were concerned with fixing the reasonable rent for demised premises—that was the phrase in question, 'What was the reasonable rent for the demised premises?', and that led to a judicial opinion which happily I am not concerned with in this case. It is simply some *dicta* which shows the approach of at least some of their lordships, certainly two of those in the majority, on the matter. I was referred specifically to the speech of Viscount Dilhorne at p 76 at G, where his lordship said:

'In the present case and in many others provision is made for the assessment to be made by an independent surveyor. What is he to do? Surely it is to assess what rent the demised premises would command if let on the terms of the lease and for the period the assessed rent is to cover at the time the assessment falls to be made.'

Then he goes on: 'That rent may depend to some extent on local factors such as deterioration of the neighbourhood.' But the point is what it would command if let on the terms of the lease and for the period the assessment is to cover. That is how Viscount Dilhorne saw it.

Lord Fraser at p 83 has a sentence in his speech which says this, dealing with the question of what is meant by a reasonable rent:

'Regard must, of course, be had to the terms of the lease, because its provisions with regard to duration, responsibility for repairs and other matters may affect the rent, but their effect would be the same whoever the landlord or the tenant might be.'

So his lordship also directed his attention to the terms of the existing lease other than as to rent.

In a more recent case in 1984 Harman J in *Sterling Land Office Developments Ltd* v. *Lloyds Bank plc*, reported in (1984) 271 EG 894, had some observations about this. He was dealing with the effect of a user clause which had a very restrictive effect in the lease his lordship was concerned with, but he had some observations which are of assistance here. The arbitrator there was directed simply to find 'an amount equal to the market rental for the demised premises with vacant possession'. There, of course, the vacant possession point—which is the second point I have to deal with—was expressly dealt with, but the point at the moment is that it is as to the market rental of the demised premises. There is no indication there of what terms the arbitrator is to assume in the hypothetical lease. Harman J says this:

'Mr Gaunt, for Lloyds Bank, submitted that no valuation could ever be made without knowing the terms on which the property to be valued was to be disposed, that is to say, freehold or leasehold, the length of term, user, and others. There were here, he submitted, as Mr Poulton's motion raised the question, three possible sets of terms: first, on the terms of this lease; second, on the "usual covenants"; third, the terms likely to be available at the time of the valuation in the open market. He urged that the first was the correct implication, and that that meant all the terms of this underlease, including the user covenant as presently standing.

Then he goes a little into that, and then he analyses that and dismisses the idea that it should be on the usual covenants basis. He ends up by saying:

'On this point, I am wholly convinced by Mr Gaunt that any valuation should, if possible, not be on the terms of the "usual covenants." I am also content to accept that a valuer should not be asked to determine what covenants might be expected in the open market at the date of valuation.'

By a process of elimination his lordship obviously accepted that the right approach was on the terms of the lease.

So that is how the matter stands on the landlords' submissions and the supporting authority.

The tenants say that whatever may be the position generally in regard to this, in this case guidance is given in the review provision itself. [Counsel for the tenant] called my attention to the phrase

> 'in the open market as between a willing landlord and a willing tenant if the tenant undertook to pay all usual tenant's rates and taxes and to bear the cost of repairs insurance and other expenses necessary to maintain the same in a state of command such rent ...'

So there is an express direction as to what covenants are to be included and that excludes the rest of the covenants and provisions of the lease itself. He accepted that the length of term was 21 years, that is to say the whole of the outstanding residue, and that he did not feel able to put forward an argument that the arbitrator should assume that it should be any other term than the outstanding unexpired portion of the term. But he said this: 'The terms of the lease should be the terms specified in clause (d) (i) and those which the property is most likely to be let at in the open market at the due date.' So that is the third of the possible bases that Harman J considered. 'One can leave the arbitrator to decide on what terms the property would be let for on a 21-year lease, and such an arbitrator', so the submission goes,

> 'would say that no one would let on review for 21 years without some review date. It is not possible that it should be on the same terms as the existing lease because of the express provisions of the rent review clause which do not follow the words of the lease'.

He said:

> 'It was not in contemplation that it would be those terms and it must be contemplated that the arbitrator was to judge what the market would be at a review in regard to those other terms including a review provision.'

He distinguished the authorities on the basis that in those cases, as we have seen, 'there was no guidance whatever in the submission to the arbitrator as to what he was to do in regard to the terms of the lease'.

I am bound to say I see some logical difficulty in that submission. It would be possible to say that only the terms mentioned in the review clause should be regarded as forming part and parcel of the hypothetical lease, but if that is so, then there would be no rent review provision in it. I cannot myself see how the expression of some terms in the review provision leaves the rest of the provisions at large to be incorporated or not as the arbitrator might decide. It seems to me the choices open are either no terms at all other than those indicated in the review provision, or those in the existing lease in so far as they are not inconsistent with the express terms in the review provision. In fact they are not inconsistent with the terms in the lease, because under the lease the tenant, as one might expect, does pay the tenant's rates and taxes and bears the cost of repairs and insurance.

So on that ground it seems to me that the landlords' submission should be accepted and that the arbitrator should be directed to review this lease on the basis that it is to be on the terms of the existing lease other than as to rent for the period of 21 years.

There are certain other considerations that have led me to that view. One depends on the history of the phrase that is in the review provision,

> '... a willing tenant if the tenant undertook to pay all usual tenant's rates and taxes and to bear the cost of repairs insurance and other expenses necessary to maintain the same in a state to command such rent ...'

because that has its origin, so far as this case goes, in the agreement of March 1961, and particularly in clause 4, where one finds that phraseology set out in relation to assessing the rents of the parts that are unlet in order to assess the initial rent of the lease and that does just seem to have been copied into the rent review provision which, as I have said, was in fact formulated first in clause 5 of that agreement without properly considering its due effect.

Then a point which [counsel for the landlord] made when he called my attention to the following words in the clause '... and assuming that the tenant has observed and performed all the covenants and conditions by it to be observed and performed hereunder ...'. It would be strange, though not impossible, if the arbitrator was to assume that all the terms of the lease up to the review date had been observed and performed, even if the fact was otherwise, in other words that the tenant was fully abreast of his covenants, but, on the other hand, then going on to the hypothetical lease, to assume that some of those covenants were not going to find any part in it whatever. As I see it, having been directed to make that assumption, one infers from that that he is to assume that those covenants and conditions are to continue.

Accordingly on that part of the matter I propose to answer the question I put to myself at the outset, that the assumption he is to make as to the term is that he is to assume that all the terms presently in it, other than the amount of the rent, are to be offered for 21 years without any further review.

Assumption as to letting with vacant possession or subject to existing underlettings

Now I come to the question of vacant possession. What the arbitrator has to ascertain is the annual rack rent of the premises including any buildings, that is to say the annual rent at which the demised premises must reasonably be expected to let as a whole without a premium in the open market. If it stood alone I think one would assume that it meant with vacant possession. It is the normal assumption: if premises are offered for letting one assumes what is being offered is the possession of those premises and not a lease subject to an existing lease. One is not being offered a lease of the reversion. But the question I have to consider is a much more complex one, because here underleases are known to exist or are going to be brought into existence. What is the position if underleases are known to exist and a lease is granted subject to them? That was the position in a case before Judge Mervyn Davies (as he then was) sitting in this court, *Avon County Council* v. *Alliance Property Co. Ltd* (1981) 258 EG 1181. The learned judge in that case held that there, in the circumstances that he had, the 'rack rental market value' (and I do not see any difference between that phrase and the one I have got to consider, 'the annual rack rent') was to be determined on the basis of a deemed vacant possession of the whole. That was despite the fact that there were existing subleases of parts of the premises and the lease had been granted subject to those subsisting subleases.

Now neither counsel suggested that I can derive any general principle from this case, indeed each of these cases turns on the particular provisions of the rent review provision under consideration, but nevertheless I have had a meticulous examination of the learned judge's judgment by both counsel—and I make no complaint about it, indeed I have been greatly assisted by both counsel in this case generally. In the end I found that it is not really of great assistance to me in resolving the problems that I have here. It helps to clarify one's ideas, but it is not of great assistance. The points that seem to me so remote from this case are these. In that case the provision was for a 125-year lease but with five-yearly reviews throughout the whole term. It was subject to a number of underleases which ranged into the term, but nothing like half of it; I think 35 years was the longest one and some were 25 years and some shorter periods. One can see that if there were to be five-yearly reviews with subleases of that nature throughout a long term one would see that it would lead to very great variations on each five-yearly review if it had to depend on the state of the underleases which would vary from year to year. There was no provision that I could see for linking those subleases with the review of the head lease at any point. I can well understand the decision that the learned judge came to in dealing with the facts of that case. Nevertheless, the conclusion I have come to on this is that on this review the subleases are to be taken into account at the review. There is only one review at mid-term and that, of course, at once sets it apart from the *Avon* case, though that in itself is not conclusive of the question. But it is a point.

Then, second, the subletting of all the other floors and the part of the ground floor was contemplated and agreed to from the outset, and, indeed, the original rent was calculated by reference to the rents receivable from subletting, and the formula then adopted finds its place for certain purposes in the current review provision.

Third—and I think this is what has really weighed with me—that the sublettings, if continuing beyond the review date, are themselves subject to review at that date. That was a requirement which was imposed by the landlords in the clause that I have referred to, and consequently the tenant will then be in receipt of the full rack rents following such reviews and hence his interest will be correspondingly enhanced. The landlords could thus be considered to be offering a lease of the whole, vacant possession of a part and leases at full rents of the remainder. Having established that, why, I ask, should there be an assumption of vacant possession of the whole, including the upper floors as well as the ground floor, which all know is not going to occur? It is for those reasons that I find, on this part of the case, in favour of the tenants' submissions.

[Counsel for the tenant] supported his submissions with a reference to the case of *Oscroft* v. *Benabo* [1967] 1 WLR 1087. This was a case where the court was concerned with an application under the Landlord and Tenant Act 1954 for a new lease. In the premises—which were mixed business and residential—there was a residential flat. When the new lease came to be considered it would appear that the landlord had required the tenants, or was requiring the tenants, to take a new lease of the entirety of the premises which had been the subject of the previous lease, that is to say both the part occupied by the tenant for business purposes and also the upper floor which was sublet for residential purposes. The tenant's right to demand a new lease is confined to the holding, which is the part he is himself occupying for his business or for his own residence and, therefore, he cannot insist on other parts of the premises which are not so occupied being included in the lease. But the landlord is entitled to require that under section 32 of the Landlord and Tenant Act. The landlord can require the new tenancy ordered to be granted to be a tenancy of the whole of the property comprised in the former tenancy, and in that situation how is the property to be valued? Is it to be valued on the basis that the tenant is taking possession of the whole of the property, or is account to be taken of the sublease? The court was of opinion that the latter was the right decision. I put it in that way because the opinion of the court on this matter was *obiter*, their having decided on another point and the point could not be opened in the Court of Appeal, not having been taken in the court below.

My attention was called to the *dictum* of Willmer LJ on p 1094 of the report, where his lordship said:

'Assuming (if I may anticipate the third point) that Thomas is the tenant of the upper floor, he is the tenant of the partners, and not of the landlords. It seems to me that if he is a tenant and if his tenancy is a protected one, that must be a relevant circumstance to consider when deciding the rent at which the premises as a whole might reasonably be expected to be let in the open market by a willing lessor; which is what the judge has to decide in the pursuance of section 34 ... In fixing that rent, it seems to me that all the circumstances of the particular case, including the fact of any existing subtenancy, must necessarily be taken into consideration.'

And Harman LJ said, on p 1097:

'The point is whether, when finding the market value, the county court judge is to take into account all the factors. If, for instance, there is a statutory tenant in possession of part of the premises, is that a matter which he can take into account in arriving at an open market value? It seems to me that he clearly is entitled to look at the open market value of the premises in the condition in which they are and with such disadvantages as they possess as between a willing lessor and a willing lessee. There is no rule, so far as I can see, to bar the judge from taking into account the fact that there is a statutory tenancy.'

Of course those *dicta* do lend some support for the view which has been pressed on me by [counsel for the tenant] and I have accepted that here in this case one does look at the position as it stands, although I am bound to say that I do not find the case in any way conclusive of this case and it is not on the ground of any sort of authority that I am deciding it. Looking at the position in that case, it would indeed be strange if the landlord could insist on the tenant taking a sublet part under section 32 and at the same time make him pay for the vacant possession value of it. So to that extent it seems to me that the case is not conclusive of the matter.

In deference to [counsel for the landlord]'s submission on this important point I ought to say a few words on his most careful argument in support of the proposition that the arbitrator is to assume that it is with vacant possession. [Counsel for the landlord] said that vacant possession valuation is likely to be the intention unless it is expressed to the contrary, and in general I would accept that; as I said, I think one starts with that. Were it otherwise the landlord would be in the position on a review of rent of being in the hands of the tenant if the tenant decides what terms he is to arrange with the subtenants.

I think to my mind, with respect, there are two answers to that. The first is that it is in the common interest of the landlord and tenant, as [counsel for the tenant] put it, to get the best rent and, second, in this particular case the landlord has expressly protected himself by the provisions of the assignment clause.

Then, still on this point, it was pointed out that the arbitrator is put in a curious situation, since he would have to value the subleases in existence and therefore has to assess what they would get under the subleases. That does not seem, with respect, to be a great drawback in the matter. Indeed, valuers are continually having to assess interests subject to other interests, and in this case he is assisted by the fact that all those subleases are themselves under review by a similar formula.

Then it was suggested to me that with regard to the first disregard, he has got to disregard any effect on rent of the fact that the tenant or any person deriving title under it has been in occupation of the demised premises, and if that requires him to assume that it is with vacant possession it ignores any sort of occupation that has been or is going on. That, in my judgment, is not a legitimate use of that disregard, indeed not the purpose of it, which is limited to negating the special effect of the tenant's own occupation, because that might either enhance the value in that he is likely to make a special bid and thereby increase it, or his occupation might diminish the value of the premises in that he had been in any way unsatisfactory in his occupation and thereby the premises had deteriorated. It is really directed at those sort of considerations and not to conclude the question as to whether it is with or without vacant possession that the arbitrator is to review the rent.

The next point was based on the *Avon* case but, as I say, I do not really get much guidance from it or feel that that case is a very great help here.

Then, based on the assumption that I was, as I have, to decide that the arbitrator was to assume that it was on the other terms, then it was said, well those terms do presume that the lease is granted with vacant possession. That was, I think, the way it was put, on the hypothesis of everything I have decided, that those are the terms on which the arbitrator is to proceed in valuing this hypothetical lease as to rent. That, as it seems to me, does not really answer the question at all, whether it is subject to underleases or not. Quite frequently if there are subsisting underleases then the lease refers to them, but it does not necessarily have to do so without thereby vitiating some parts of the covenants of the lease and there is no need to state that it is subject to underleases.

Then [counsel for the landlord] had a special point on clause 4 of the agreement in relation once again to the formula we looked at in relation to other points, the formula of the tenants' bearing costs of all repairs and insurances and other expenses, pointing out that that occurs, indeed is the fact, in clause 4 of the agreement of 1961 in relation to unlet premises and thereby by incorporating it into the rent review it has the same consequence, and that was an indication that that, too, was to say that one was to assume that the hypothetical lease was with vacant possession.

I have already dealt with this to some extent. In clause 4 it was necessarily with vacant possession because that was the only occasion on which it could operate. It did not in itself determine it because that was dealing with, and only with, those parts of the premises that were unlet after the lapse of a period of one year after the lease had been granted, and I think it is putting too much on that, if I may say so, by copying that into the rent review clause itself that thereby it is also to be assumed that the premises are unlet. The expression 'part of the building which is unlet' is expressly defined in clause 4 but, of course, is not to be found in clause (d) (i).

I think the next point that was taken was that one must ignore the actual lease with the actual rent in the hypothetical lease. The natural corollary is to assume that any interest which is under it also does not exist. That, as it seems to me, is simply another way of putting the first major point about vacant possession and is not an additional way, and I do not really see that as adding in any way to the first submission.

Then another point was that as the initial rent was calculated by reference to a formula based on rent receivable, if they had intended to follow the same matter here, that the valuation was to be by reference to rent receivable, they would have said so. Again I find that unacceptable as a point, persuasively as it was put, because initially what was being taken was the rent actually being received on the open market; these were the first rents of the property and they were, therefore, actual open market rents being received. Here it is a question of valuation and it is quite a different situation on review where it must be either notional vacant possession or, as here, where the subleases themselves are under review.

Finally there was a point based on the formula, the reduction exercise based on the formula. This point to me has potency, I think because the formula itself is ambivalent. It was initially an uplifting arrangement to give the landlord a share of the profit rentals and it has been introduced in the review clause, not altogether happily in my judgment, as a reducing formula to allow for the burdens and risks in the management of a multi-occupied building. Then it is said: 'Well, if it is valued subject to subleases and then reduced the tenant then gets a double reduction.' But I think that is an oversimplification of the situation. First of all, as I see it, on general grounds, the introduction of the original gross annual rent and the rent payable into the review clause, clause 2 (d) and (f), to my mind underlines the connection with the underlettings rather than the reverse. Second, as the underlet rents were themselves subject to review, it may have been thought at the time that there was no difference between the value with vacant possession and the value of the head lease subject to leases which are themselves going to command a full rent. Having dealt with those two considerations, although I was impressed with this point of [counsel for the landlord], I do not find it sufficient to upset the conclusion which I came to on general grounds at the outset of this discussion, based mainly on the provisions of clause 2 (22).

Assumption as to dividing wall

So I propose to answer that point by saying he is to assume that the notional lease is subject to the existing underlettings.

I have, lastly, to deal with the dividing wall. It was at one time thought that this was going to be a point of real significance and, indeed, it was put in the forefront of the originating summons, but it is agreed now not to have very much bearing on value, because if the subtenancies are to be ignored—that is to say the vacant possession point was right—then the hypothetical tenant taking on the existing terms could remove the wall, the landlord not being able reasonably to withhold his consent and thus possess himself of the entirety of the ground floor which it seems commands a higher rental value as a whole than when divided. As I have heard full argument and it may have some bearing on the rent and being one of the disregards I propose to deal with it.

The question is: is it an improvement or additional building carried out by the tenant or any person deriving title under it? I can ignore the last words 'person deriving title under it'; there is no question of any such person here. It breaks down into three questions: (1) Was it an improvement or additional building? (2) Was it carried out by the plaintiffs? and (3) Were they the tenants at the time?

I leave the first one on one side for the moment and deal with the other two first. To answer the second question: 'Was it carried out by the plaintiffs?' I am firmly of the view, in my judgment, that they did carry it out. They ordered it and paid for it, even though it was actually carried out by the landlords' contractors with the landlords' approval.

On the third point: 'Were they the tenants at the time?', that is not quite so straightforward and indeed there is a certain amount of authority about this. The point is that when it was carried out, as I have explained in my review of the facts, they had not then taken the lease, though they were under an agreement to take the lease. It was done before the lease was granted. I have been referred to a number of cases on this point, but I think I need only refer briefly to two of them.

The first is the decision of the House of Lords in *Re 'Wonderland', Cleethorpes* [1965] AC 58. There was an application for a new lease under the 1954 Act and there had been an improvement by the tenant some years before the time had started; he had done it when he had been holding under a previous lease and then he had taken a new lease and that had expired, and then he sought to say that the value of improvements that he had done under the former lease were to be disregarded. The House of Lords held that it had to be effected during the term of the current lease to qualify to be disregarded. The harshness of that decision did in fact lead to some statutory amendment, but that has no bearing on what I have to decide in this case.

The other case is a very recent decision early this year of Scott J in *Hambros Bank Executor and Trustee Co. Ltd* v. *Superdrug Stores Ltd* (1985) 274 EG 590. There the position was that Superdrug were proposing to take a lease of some premises that were in bad need of renovation and adaptation and before they took the lease—they had not had any previous lease of the premises, but before they took them they had done substantial fitting-out work during the period immediately prior to the grant of a lease and clearly in contemplation of that grant and in the expectation that it would be granted to them, as in fact it was. Scott J held for the tenants on a number of grounds. The first was that they were literally the tenants; as we have here, Superdrug were defined as the tenants, and on the factual matrix that it was in clear contemplation that the lease would be granted to them. Then, faced with the *Wonderland* case which I have just mentioned, the learned judge distinguished it in this way:

'I am not clear that the *dicta* and principles expressed by their lordships in that case indicate what their view would have been had the improvements been carried out shortly before the current tenancy by the person shortly becoming the current tenant and with a view to the grant of the current tenancy. The example I am contemplating is that of a tenant who negotiates a tenancy with a landlord and is allowed into possession before the grant of a lease in order to carry out various improvements to adapt the premises for his use as tenant. Let it be supposed that the term originally granted expires, that there is no provision in the lease for renewal or rent review and that the tenant, relying on his statutory rights, applies for a new tenancy. I do not think the *Wonderland* case is any authority for the proposition that in assessing the rent for the new tenancy the improvements made by the tenant in those circumstances fall to be taken into account on the ground that they were improvements carried out before the grant of the lease. That was not the factual situation with which the House of Lords in the *Wonderland* case was concerned. It is a factual situation which raises, to my mind, quite different considerations from those with which the House of Lords was concerned. I do not regard the dicta by Viscount Simonds and Lord Morris to which Mr Reynolds referred me as having any bearing on the facts in the present case.

For myself I am perfectly happy to follow the approach of the learned judge in that case and apply them to this case. The way I would put it is: are the improvements referable to the grant of a tenancy under consideration, or are they referable to some former interest of the tenant, as in the *Wonderland* case? Here they were done in anticipation of the grant of a lease and the occupation by the plaintiffs for the first time of these premises.

I return, then, to the first of the questions on this part of the matter: 'Was it an improvement or additional building?' Here I have not got any guidance from the authorities that have been referred to me. I am sure they would have been pointed out had there been such guidance. The work in question here was a modification of the landlords' building in the course of erection, and the modification concerned the wall and the drains, as I have already called attention to. That and other variations not in evidence resulted in certain savings of works in not doing other works and resulted in a net charge to the plaintiffs. As I would see it, in the case of an improvement or an additional building what is being looked at is the alteration of or addition to a building that the landlord has provided. That is what is contemplated here: the landlord provides a building and then the tenant adds something to it or improves it in some way. But if a building is built according to the design of a tenant, or to some extent according to the design of a tenant, and it is never built by the landlord in some other way, then, in my judgment, it is not an improvement or additional building. It is part of the original building, and it is none the less so even though the tenant contributes to the building cost. What he has improved in those circumstances, in my judgment, is the design of the building; he has not improved the building itself. The building that went up is all that ever went up, as [counsel for the tenant] put it to me. I recognise, of course, that in some cases it may be difficult to sever out what is a genuine improvement which is added in as a building is going up as originally designed, on the one hand, which would be an improvement, and, on the other, what we have here, which is a modification resulting in some parts of the building not being built according to original plans but being built according to some other plan.

Having formulated that test and applied it to this case, it seems to me that this wall and *a fortiori* the drains which are mentioned in that variation are not an improvement or additional building carried out by the tenant.

I think that disposes of the questions I have been asked to answer.

[The defendants were ordered to pay half the plaintiffs' taxed costs.]

6.3 Requirements for tenant's compliance with planning permission and lawful user

It is trite law that the letting of premises for a particular purpose does not give rise to any implication, or any warranty on the part of the lessor, that the premises can be lawfully used for that purpose, see *Hill* v. *Harris* [1965]

2 QB 601. It is common to provide in leases a covenant on the part of the tenant to the effect that he will obtain planning permission and otherwise comply with legislation (as required by the lease in *Daejan Investments*, below). There is no justification for assuming, in the absence of words requiring such assumption, that the hypothetical letting on the terms and conditions of the lease (including the user clause), should put the hypothetical lessor and lessee in a different position from that of an actual lessor or lessee.

DAEJAN INVESTMENTS LTD v. CORNWALL COAST COUNTRY CLUB

Chancery Division   (1985) 273 EG 1122

Premises which had been used as a gaming club or casino were let under a lease with a rent review clause which provided that the rack-rental value should be the highest rent at which the premises might be let at the material date with vacant possession for the residue of the term on the terms and conditions of the lease, disregarding certain matters which might otherwise have added to the letting value. A dispute arose between the parties as to whether the hypothetical letting envisaged under the review clause involved a hypothesis that the premises were let lawfully for the use of a casino from the date of the rent review, with the implication that the lessee had obtained all necessary permissions and consents. The matter came before the Court under the Arbitration Act 1979, section 2 (1) and arose in the course of a reference to arbitration.

Held: There was no binding authority to the effect that a rent review clause such as the present required the rent to be fixed on the assumption that the permitted user was lawful. *Bovis Group Pension Fund Ltd* v. *G.C. Flooring & Furnishing Ltd* [1984] 269 EG 1252, (see 7.1 (a), page 247, later), distinguished because in that case the parties had gone out of their way to introduce an artificial assumption into the rent review clause as a basis for valuation, and it was the emphasis of the parties on this point that was at the root of the decision. However, this did not mean the arbitrator could not take into account evidence tending to show the existence in the market of persons who might stand a good chance of obtaining the necessary consent and gaming licence and also the uncertainty that attaches to any such applications.

PETER GIBSON J: Clause 6 contains the rent-review provisions. It provides for the review to be initiated by a notice served by Daejan on the tenant and, if there be a failure to agree the rack rental value, for a reference to an arbitrator. 'Rack rental value' was defined in clause 6 (5) as follows: 'In this clause "rack rental value" shall mean the highest rent at which' and I interpose (as is common ground) two words 'as at' there omitted

'the rent-review date the premises might reasonably be expected to be let in the open market by a willing lessor with vacant possession for the residue of the term hereby granted and upon the terms and conditions (including provision for rent review) of this lease, it being assumed that the demised premises have been put into a state of repair and condition consistent with full performance of the obligations of the Tenant under this lease but there being disregarded:
(a) any effect on rent of the fact that the Tenant or his predecessor in title or some associate of the Tenant has been in occupation of the holding;
(b) any goodwill attached to the holding by reason of the carrying on thereat of the business of the Tenant or some associate of the Tenant (whether by him or by a predecessor of his) in that business;
(c) any effect on rent of any improvement carried out by the Tenant;

(d) any addition to the value of the demised premises attributable to the Gaming or Justices' Licence which may be held in respect of such premises if it appears that having regard to the terms of the current tenancy and any other relevant circumstances the benefit of the Licences belongs to the Tenant or some associate of the Tenant:

provided that in this context "associate" means any other company being at the time a subsidiary of the Guarantor [Ladbroke] as defined by section 154 of the Companies Act 1948.'

...

The envisaged letting involves a hypothesis, and in the light of some of the arguments advanced I am reminded of the language of Danckwerts J in *Re Holt (dec'd)* [1953] 1 WLR 1488 (a case concerned with a share valuation for estate duty purposes) at p 1492, where he said that he had to 'enter into a dim world peopled by the indeterminate spirits of fictitious or unborn sales'. Marrying the hypothesis to the real world (in which the hypothesis must of course be set) may involve difficulties, depending on the subject-matter. But the concept of such a hypothetical transaction is one that is now familiar in a number of contexts apart from rent reviews—for example, estate duty, capital gains tax and compulsory purchase—and there is a good deal of helpful guidance to be obtained from the authorities. It is clear that the matter must be treated as a valuation exercise in which one postulates a hypothetical lessor and a hypothetical lessee who in neither case has the attributes of the actual lessor or the actual lessee. The lessor is to be treated as being in a position to grant a lease of the relevant term and to be a willing lessor, that is to say that he is prepared to let the premises for whatever is the highest rent that he can obtain without a premium. He cannot refuse to let the premises or defer the letting of the premises on the ground of some supposed under-value, provided that the rent is the highest rent reasonably obtainable in the open market. Because the letting is with vacant possession, any existing tenancy or right to occupation must be assumed to have ended before the hypothetical letting. Although nothing is expressly stated in clause 6 (5) about the hypothetical lessee, he must, I think, be taken to be a willing lessee; and he, too, cannot refuse to take the letting because he might think that the rent is too high.

The open market is one that includes all possible lessees each of whom has had an equal opportunity of bidding to become the lessee on the letting. It must also be assumed that the lessor has taken all necessary steps to obtain the best rent on the open market for the premises in their actual condition, subject to the expressed assumptions and directions in clause 6 (5) and any necessary consequences thereof. Thus one must assume that adequate publicity has been given to the prospective letting. However, even if established in evidence that a particular description of property is, in the real world, actually sold or let in a particular way, it does not follow therefrom that such a sale or letting satisfies the hypothesis of an open market sale or letting on a particular day ...

The matter has been argued before me on the footing that the highest rent that is likely to be obtainable is from a lessee wanting to use the premises as a casino. The central issue between the parties is whether the hypothetical letting is on the footing that the lessee is able to use the premises lawfully for the purpose of a casino from the rent review date, with the implication that the lessee must be assumed to have a certificate of consent and a gaming licence in respect of the premises by that date. [Counsel for the landlord] submits that the assumption must be made to make the rent-review clause workable. He submits that it is wrong to postulate a speculator as the lessee, not knowing what use he can lawfully make of the premises. He says that it must be assumed that the lessee will have taken all the necessary steps to obtain the certificate of consent and a gaming licence before the rent review date and for that purpose have entered into a conditional contract with the lessor which became unconditional on the rent review date. [Counsel for the tenant] submits that the hypothesis in clause 6 (5) does not permit of any such assumption. He says that the only contract the hypothesis permits is a letting on the rent-review date itself, and that an unconditional one; and that it is not a letting on the open market on that date when the terms have been conditionally agreed between the lessor and a favoured lessee long before that date.

In some respects the arguments between the parties, particularly in the pleadings, touched on the metaphysical, disputing as they were how to reconcile the hypothesis with dates in the real world. To my mind, much of such disputation misses the point. If the hypothesis requires one to assume that the casino user is lawful, then it is necessary to assume that all preliminary steps, however complex, enabling such lawful user to be made will have been taken in a dateless continuum of time immediately before the letting. To this extent I agree with [counsel for the landlord]. But the more uncomfortably Procrustean the task of fitting the suggested assumption to the real world, the more one is entitled to expect the assumption to have been made explicit. In the case of a casino user there are undoubtedly (as [counsel for the tenant] pointed out) difficulties in fitting that assumption. The long preliminaries to the letting, and the determination at an early stage of a conditional contract of what person (albeit chosen out of the rival bidders in the open market) should be the lessee, and what rent should be paid, are markedly different from any operation of the open market hypothesis.

It is obvious that there is no such assumption expressly contained in clause 6 (5). [Counsel for the tenant], however, submits that the assumption is required by the words 'the highest rent' at which the premises might reasonably be expected to be let. He says that if a lessee would pay the highest rent for a casino user, it must be inferred that the user is a lawful user for the lessee on taking possession on the letting. I cannot accept that the words have the significance for which [counsel for the landlord] contends. Even without the word 'highest', the rent at which the premises might reasonably be expected to be let in the open market by a willing lessor is the highest rent obtainable, just as the price which shares would fetch on a sale in the open market is, for estate duty purposes, the highest price; and I have already quoted the words of Lord Reid on that. The word 'highest' adds no more than emphasis.

[Counsel for the landlord] accepted in opening that without the reference to the highest rent, the review valuation might be expected to reflect the full range of possible uses for the premises. I agree. Of course, the valuation will reflect the fact (if it be such) that a would-be lessee wanting the premises for a casino user to which he knows that the lessor does not object would pay more than a lessee wanting the premises for some other (less profitable) use. But it does not follow that the parties intended any assumption that the valuation was to be on the basis that casino user was a lawful user.

There are to my mind several indications to the contrary. First, it is trite law that the letting of premises for a particular purpose does not give rise to any implication, or any warranty on the part of the lessor, that the premises can lawfully be used for that purpose: see *Hill* v. *Harris* [1965] 2 QB 601. Indeed, it is common to provide in leases a covenant on the part of the tenant to the effect that he will obtain planning permission and otherwise comply with legislation (as the present lease does). I cannot see any sufficient justification, in the absence of words in the rent-review clause requiring such assumption, why the hypothetical letting on the terms and conditions of the lease (including the user clause) should put the hypothetical lessor and lessee in a position different from an actual lessor and lessee.

Second, there is a clear indication from clause 6 (5) (d) that the parties realised that there might be no current gaming licence at the time of the rent review. So, too, in clause 2 (2) it was envisaged that the works to be carried out by the tenant might be for any of the purposes permitted by the user clause. If it be a fact that a rent for a casino user is higher than the rent for some other user, then, in view of the somewhat precarious nature of a gaming licence, in my judgment, viewing the matter objectively, it seems unlikely that the parties would, without any express words requiring the assumption, have intended that the tenant be bound to pay a rent based on a user which he may not enjoy, the more so in a lease with 20 years to run and including three further rent reviews.

The third indication is in clause 6 (5) (d), requiring, as it does, the valuer to ignore the gaming licence only if the benefit of it belongs to the tenant or some associate (as defined) of the tenant. [Counsel for the tenant] has advanced an argument in relation to question 4 of the amended notice of motion giving a wider meaning to those words than their defined terms would allow. For reasons that I shall explain later, I reject that argument, and I accept what [counsel for the landlord] himself submitted by way of an alternative argument, that the gaming licence which someone other than the tenant or some associate of the tenant in fact holds is not to be disregarded in assessing the rent. The parties therefore must be taken to have envisaged the possibility that there would be an actual gaming licence holder at the time of the rent review whose licence could be taken into account. That means that no one else would be assumed to have such a licence at the same time. It follows that unless it is permissible to treat the actual gaming licence holder as the hypothetical lessee, it must have been envisaged that the hypothetical lessee might not be the holder of a gaming licence. In my judgment it would be wrong to treat the actual licence holder as the hypothetical lessee. Indeed, I did not understand [counsel for the landlord] so to submit. He submitted, in my view rightly, that the actual licence holder (in this case Crockfords) would be a special purchaser in the sense of a person who had a special interest over and above any other bidder to obtain the letting. Any other bidder would have to outbid the special purchaser. If authority were needed for the proposition that the hypothetical lessee is not to be treated as having the attributes of an actual lessee or occupier, it can be found in *F R Evans (Leeds) Ltd* v. *English Electric Co. Ltd*, a decision of the Court of Appeal [(1978) 245 EG 657] in the judgment of Browne LJ.

[Counsel for the landlord] submitted that *Bovis Group Pension Fund Ltd* v. *G.C. Flooring & Furnishing Ltd* (1984) 269 EG 1252 was on all fours with the present case, the differences between the cases being immaterial. If he is right, then *Bovis* lays down a principle of general application, that wherever there is a rent-review clause, and whether or not there is an express mention of the user on which the valuation is to be based, the valuation must proceed on the footing that every permitted user is a lawful one. I cannot agree. I do no more than repeat that statements of high judicial authority emphasise over and over again that each case must be looked at in the light of its own facts. In *Bovis* the parties had gone out of their way to introduce an artificial assumption into the rent-review clause as a basis for valuation, and it was because of the emphasis of the parties on this point that the majority in the Court of Appeal were able to find, as an attribute of the demised premises, that planning permission was in effect attached to it. In the present case there is nothing comparable. The gaming and justices' licences attach to a person (albeit in respect of premises), but in no way can they be said to be attributes of the premises. Further, as I read Eveleigh LJ, he was specifically distinguishing the case where property is let merely permitting a use, for example, as offices as distinct from being let as offices. In my judgment, it is quite impossible to say that the premises were let as a casino, as distinct from being let with use as a casino as one of the permitted uses.

Despite the deployment by [counsel for the landlord] of his very considerable powers of persuasion, I have no doubt that clause 6 (5) does not require or permit the arbitrator to assume that the hypothetical lessee will take possession with a gaming licence already in his possession. That does not, however, mean that the arbitrator cannot take into account evidence tending to show the existence in the market of persons who might stand a good chance of obtaining a certificate of consent and a gaming licence if they obtained an interest in the premises. The arbitrator's valuation will no doubt reflect that fact, if established. He will also, no doubt, take account of the uncertainty that attaches to any application for a certificate of consent and a gaming licence.

Where review provisions in a lease provide that the amount of the increase in the rent should be determined 'having regard to all the circumstances then existing' including planning permission, any potential planning permission may be included as a factor to be assessed.

RUSHMOOR BOROUGH COUNCIL v. GOACHER AND ANOTHER

Chancery Division   (1985) 276 EG 304

The tenant under a 99 year lease and supplemental lease occupied land subject to periodical rent reviews. The lease provided *inter alia* that

'The amount of the increase shall be such as shall increase the amount payable by way of rent hereunder to the amount for which the said piece of land hereinbefore described and hereby demised might reasonably be expected to be let in the 15th, 29th, 43rd, 57th, 71st, or 85th year of the said term (as the case may be) in the open market by a willing lessor to a willing lessee having regard to all the circumstances then existing including any permission for the carrying out of any development of the said piece of land granted pursuant to the Town and Country Planning Acts 1962 to 1968 or any subsequent legislation or any regulations thereafter.'

The landlord contended that regard should be had to the development potential of the land as 'an existing circumstance' whereas the tenant argued that planning could only be taken into account if there was planning permission in existence.

Held: All circumstances then existing at review were to be taken into account, and in particular, but without excluding the generality, one may take into account any existing planning permission. In that situation, if development potential exists as a fact proved in evidence, then it may be taken into account. However, it could be that such development potential would be of little importance in the matter of fixing the rent since the rent was to be fixed in accordance with all the circumstances which included the existing user in the planning sense and the user provisions of the lease, but that was a matter for the arbitrator to decide. *Plinth Property Investment Ltd* v. *Mott, Hay & Anderson* (1979) 39 P & CR 361 distinguished.

MERVYN DAVIES J: Reading clause 1 of the schedule to the supplemental lease, one sees that in fixing a new rent one has to have regard:

'to all the circumstances then existing including any permission for the carrying out of any development of the said piece of land granted pursuant to the Town and Country Planning Acts 1962 to 1968 or any subsequent legislation or any regulations thereunder.'

[Counsel] for the corporation said that that meant that in fixing the rent regard may be had to the development potential of the land. That, he said, is an existing circumstance, and the fact that the wording in question makes specific reference to an existing planning permission does not mean that there is any implicit direction that development potential is a circumstance not to be taken into account. He said all the circumstances had to be taken into account and that the reference to planning permission was an illustrative reference only.

[Counsel] appeared for the respondents, and among other submissions his most persuasive argument was, to my mind, that the reference to planning after the phrase 'all the circumstances then existing' showed the extent to which planning was to be taken into account as a circumstance. It was plain, he said, that planning was a circumstance only if there was a planning permission in existence. By inference that meant that the possibility of planning permission by reason of development potential was to be disregarded. [Counsel for the respondents] referred to *Plinth Property Investment Ltd* v. *Mott, Hay & Anderson* (1979) 39 P & CR 361. That case, it was said, showed that the arbitrator is not to speculate about planning permission. He is to look at settled circumstances. To my mind the *Plinth* case does not greatly assist [counsel for the respondents]. I say that because the arbitrator plainly has to take account of the permitted user of the premises, not only in the light of planning permission but also in the light of clause 3 (12) and clause 3 (14) of the lease; but that does not necessarily mean that the arbitrator must ignore the development potential if it be a fact shown to exist by professional evidence, and if it be a fact that it is not excluded from consideration by the wording of clause 1. So one turns to the wording of clause 1.

The point is short and to be decided by the impression made on the mind by the words. I do not accept [counsel for the respondents'] suggestion that the words

'including any permission for the carrying out of any development of the said piece of land granted pursuant to the Town and Country Planning Acts 1962 to 1968 or any subsequent legislation or any regulations thereunder'

mean there is there defined or explained the extent to which planning matters can be taken into account. To my mind clause 1 is not saying 'to this extent and to this extent only is the planning position a "circumstance"' within the phrase 'all the circumstances then existing'. The impression in my mind made by clause 1 is that all circumstances then existing are to be taken into account, and in particular, but without excluding the generality, one may take into account any existing planning permission. In that situation, if development potential exists as a fact proved in evidence, then it may, in my view, be taken into account. I add that while I think the arbitrator is not prevented from having regard to development potential, it may be that such development potential will be of little importance in the matter of fixing the rent. I say that because the rent is to be fixed by reference to all the circumstances. The circumstances include the existing user in the planning sense and the user provisions of the lease, including clauses 3 (12) and 3 (14). In the face of those circumstances, it may be that development potential will be of little importance, but that, I think, is a matter for the arbitrator, who will no doubt be assisted by professional evidence.

6.4 (a)   Review disregarding the review clause—the general principles

Although a lease may contain a rent review clause, when it comes to determining the new rent on review, the fact that it exists may fall to be disregarded for the purposes of fixing the new rent. Reviewing without review will increase the level of rent payable by the tenant. Whether this is the case depends on the wording of the lease which must, however, be interpreted so as to give effect to the underlying commercial purpose of the lease if this is not overridden by clear words or other circumstances. See the very recent cases (decided *after* the cases reported below) and new guidelines on page 134 and in the Appendix.

SAFEWAY FOOD STORES LTD v. BANDERWAY LTD

Chancery Division   (1983) 267 EG 850

The rent review clause in a 90-year lease of business premises provided that the revised rent should be determined on the basis of a hypothetical lease for a term equivalent to the unexpired residue of the actual term, disregarding certain matters but 'in all other respects on the same terms and conditions as are in these presents contained (save for this proviso)'. It was agreed by the parties that 'this proviso' meant the whole of the rent review clause. A dispute arose as to whether at the first review date the then fair market rent was to be a fixed rent with no review for the 69 year residue, or whether it should be assumed that the rent would be subject to periodical reviews as provided by the review clause.

Held: A literal construction was the correct approach. At the first review date, the rent should be determined on the basis of a proper rent for a 69-year lease without review at a fixed rent throughout.

GOULDING J: The clause which contains the provisions for rent review foreshadowed by the reddendum is clause 5 of the lease. It begins as follows:

'IT IS HEREBY AGREED AND DECLARED by and between the parties hereto that if during the continuance of this demise the Lessor shall not earlier than six months nor later than three months immediately preceding the expiration of the twenty first forty second sixty third and eighty fourth year of the term hereby granted serve upon the Lessee a notice in writing requiring a review of the yearly rent first hereby reserved (meaning the said yearly rent of Sixteen thousand five hundred pounds) then within ten days thereafter each party shall appoint a duly qualified valuer to negotiate and endeavour to reach agreement with the valuer of the other part as to the fair market rack rent of the demised premises at that time for a Lease for a term equivalent to the then unexpired residue of the said term and taking no account of any goodwill attributable to the premises by reason of any trade or business carried on therein by the Lessee or any effect on rent of any rebuilding alteration or addition to the demised premises or change of user of the demised premises connected with any such rebuilding alterations or additions which may be carried out by the Lessee or any sublessee in accordance with the terms and conditions of any licence granted by the Lessor and in all other respects'

and here I come to the point of controversy

'on the same terms and conditions as are in these presents contained (save for this proviso).'

There then follow provisions for the determination of a revised rent if the valuers do not agree. I need not read those provisions at this point. The clause concludes in these terms:

'If in the event of the fair market rack rent so agreed or determined at the expiration of each respective period as aforesaid shall be more than the rent then currently payable either under Clause 1 hereof or by virtue of a previous application of this clause the figure so agreed or determined as aforesaid shall be substituted for the amount of the rent then currently payable as from the commencement of the twenty second forty third sixty fourth and eighty fifth year of the said term (as the case may be) and thereafter such substituted rent figure shall be deemed to be the rent hereby reserved for the remainder of the said term or until the next review under the provisions of this clause.'

Just before the point at which I broke my reading of the rent review clause there is a direction that the revised rent is to be determined by the valuers on the basis of a hypothetical lease for a term equivalent to the unexpired residue of the actual term, disregarding—to put it shortly—goodwill and improvements effected by the tenant, and then it continues: 'in all other respects on the same terms and conditions as are in these presents contained (save for this proviso).' It is not disputed on either side that 'this proviso' means the whole of clause 5. It is clear—I think it is also not really in dispute—that, literally interpreted, the effect of the saving is to prevent the valuers from taking the existence of a rent review clause into account when fixing a revised rent. In other words, at the end of the first 21 years they are to ask what would be the fair market rack rent for a lease for the remaining 69 years (and a bit) of the term at a fixed rent throughout—that is, without putting in the hypothetical new lease any provision for further review. But the tenant, for obvious reasons, does not think that that is a satisfactory interpretation and asks for a declaration that, for the purposes of revising the rent under clause 5 of the lease, it ought to be assumed that the rent payable under the hypothetical term is capable of upward revision at intervals of 21 years.

[Counsel] for the tenant, submits that the basis of valuation arrived at on a literal construction of the clause is artificial, inconsistent with the scheme of the lease as a whole, and inconsistent with the practice of the true market in such premises. He says the lease itself requires periodical reviews of the rent and the parties cannot have intended that essential feature of the lease to be ignored in working under the rent review clause itself. [Counsel for the tenant] suggests that there are two possible ways of construing the words in question. One is the bold step, which is authorised if it is necessary to give effect to a manifest intention of the parties, of simply ignoring the parenthesis containing the words 'save for this proviso' and treating it as something that has to be rejected as inconsistent with the rest of the document. The court can of course adopt such a course if satisfied that what is rejected is in truth repugnant to what can be inferred from the instrument as a whole.

If that seems too bold, then [counsel for the tenant] suggests that the words 'save for this proviso' need not be read as 'except and excluding the whole of this proviso' but may be given some effect by treating them as requiring adjustment to meet the altered date at which revision takes place. If 'save for this proviso' is read as 'subject to necessary adjustment of this proviso', then the rent review provision can be incorporated into the hypothetical lease on which the valuation is made, but on the first occasion not referring to the 84th year but only to the three preceding occasions and on a second review not referring either to the 63rd or the 84th year, and so on.

[Counsel] for the landlord, does not dispute that the court can if necessary do violence, in construing a document, to the literal meaning of some part of it, but insists that that can only be done where one can see plainly what the true intention of the parties was and that the words that are to be rejected or distorted are words plainly not intended to be taken in their most literal sense. [Counsel for the landlord] referred me to two cases decided in 1982 where a more or less similar question arose on the wording of other leases, in each of which the literal construction prevailed. One was a case decided by McNeill J. It appears to be unreported. Its name is *French Kier Property Investments* v. *Marconi Co*. The other was decided a little subsequently (but in ignorance of my brother's decision) by myself, and that was *Pugh and Others* v. *Smiths Industries Ltd and Others*, reported at (1982) 264 EG 823.

I agree with [counsel for the tenant] that I do not get any great help from those decisions, because I do not think that one can solve questions of construction by comparing more or less similar but by no means indentical cases on documents differently worded, so I come back to the first principles of the matter. I am content to go back to one of [counsel for the tenant]'s authorities, *Key* v. *Key*, decided by the Court of Appeal in 1853. It is reported in 4 De GM & G 73, and there Knight Bruce LJ said:

'There are many cases upon the construction of documents in which the spirit is strong enough to overcome the letter; cases in which it is impossible for a reasonable being, upon a careful perusal of an instrument, not to be satisfied from its contents that a literal, a strict, or an ordinary interpretation given to particular passages, would disappoint and defeat the intention with which the instrument, read as a whole, persuades and convinces him that it was framed.'

A little later in his judgment he cited the test from an earlier case in these terms: '... an implication so probable that the mind could not resist it.' Those citations are from pp 84 and 85 of the report.

When I apply that test, I am of opinion that [counsel for the landlord] must prevail. There is nothing absurd or insensible in the literal construction that requires the valuers at the end of the 21st year to consider the proper rent for a lease for approximately 69 years at a single rent throughout. It may not be what one would think most probable, but there is nothing absurd about it, nothing insensible about it. For all that I am entitled to know in a construction case, the matter may have been so arranged as the result of bargaining on various points between the original landlord and the original tenant. If I assume that they had a common intention different from what the words express, I think I am merely guessing, and accordingly on this point the defendant must succeed.

In *Pugh*'s case below, the existence of the review clause which provided for periodical rent reviews had to be disregarded when valuing the revised market rent because the drafting of the lease required that the provisions of the rent review clause had to be disregarded for this purpose. See *British Gas* later in the Appendix where *Pugh* was considered in the light of general principles of interpretation.

PUGH v. SMITHS INDUSTRIES LTD AND OTHERS
F.A. WELCH v. SMITHS INDUSTRIES LTD AND OTHERS
SMITHS INDUSTRIES LTD v. PUGH AND OTHERS

Chancery Division   (1982) 264 EG 823

A lease for a term of 23 years provided for the rent to be reviewed after three years and subsequently every five years. The review clause indicated the revised rent should be the 'full yearly open market rent', and defined this as the rent which would be obtainable on

'a letting with vacant possession of the property for the residue of the term hereby granted, and on the basis that the lessee would be obliged to perform and observe the covenants and conditions on the part of the lessee contained herein, but excluding therefrom the provisions of this clause ...'

The landlord contended that when reviewing the rent the fact that the lease contained provision for later rent reviews during the remainder of the term should be ignored. The tenant submitted that the purpose of rent review clauses is to meet the problem of acute inflation and relied on Lord Salmon's speech in *United Scientific Holdings Ltd v. Burnley Borough Council etc.* [1978] AC 904 at p 948 that it was totally unrealistic to regard such clauses as conferring a privilege on the landlord or a burden on the tenant. The tenant also asked for rectification on the ground that it was the common intention that the review clause should not unduly burden the tenant.

Held: The landlord's construction of the review clause was the correct one. This meant that the reviewed rent was £36,750 p.a. instead of the lower figure of £30,600 p.a.

While there was a common intention that the rent should be reviewed, there was no common intention discernible as to the form the review should take, and rectification of the review clause should therefore be refused.

Per curiam: Lord Salmon's views in the *United Scientific* case and those of Lord Dilhorne in *Ponsford* v. *H.M.S. Aerosols* (see later) as to purpose and character of rent review clauses were not rules of construction to determine the meaning of a particular clause in a lease.

GOULDING J: [Counsel for the tenant] said that rent review clauses in leases of business premises are now very well known and recognised by the courts and their purpose and intent are equally well known. He referred me to part of the speech of Lord Salmon in *United Scientific Holdings Ltd* v. *Burnley Borough Council* [1978] AC 904 at p.948, where his lordship explained the purpose of rent review clauses as being to meet the problem of acute inflation when what is a fair market rent at the date when a lease is granted will probably become wholly uneconomic within a few years. His lordship also said that it was totally unrealistic to regard such clauses as conferring a privilege upon the landlord or imposing a burden upon the tenant. He continued:

'Both the landlord and the tenant recognise the obvious, viz that such clauses are fair and reasonable for each of them. I do not agree with what has been said in some of the authorities, namely, that a rent revision clause is for the benefit of the landlord alone and not at all for the benefit of the tenant. It is plainly for the benefit of both of them. It is for the benefit of the tenant because without such a clause he would never get the long lease which he requires; and under modern conditions, it would be grossly unfair that he should. It is for the benefit of the landlord because it ensures that for the duration of the lease he will receive a fair rent instead of a rent far below the market value of the property which he demises. Accordingly the landlord and the tenant by agreement in their lease provide that, at stated intervals during the term, the rent should be brought up to what is then the fair market rent. The revision clause itself lays down the administrative procedure or machinery by which the fair market rent shall be ascertained.'

[Counsel for the tenant] referred me for the same purpose to what was said by Lord Dilhorne in *Ponsford* v. *H M S Aerosols Ltd* [1979] AC 63 at p.76 and 77 where the noble and learned lord explained rent review clauses in much the same way as Lord Salmon had done, as being a protection against inflation . . .

So here, if the House of Lords in the two cases thought of rent review clauses as clauses operating in a balanced way to counteract inflation of the currency as between landlord and tenant, it does not follow that in this particular lease such a balance was aimed at or achieved. It may be, looking at nothing outside the terms of the document and admissible evidence, that this bias of the clause in favour of the landlord was stipulated for in negotiation against other advantages allowed to the tenants. One just does not know from the document. Or, again, it may well be that neither side gave any thought to this point. If that be so, I am not, I think, to jump to the conclusion as a matter of construction that had it been raised Smiths Industries Ltd would have been content to have the alternative favoured by Young & Brown.

In the case below, Walton J interpreted the words 'subject to the provisions of this [lease] other than the rent hereby reserved' quite literally—with the 'unfortunate' result that 'the rent hereby reserved' was held not to apply merely to the rent originally agreed—or that agreed on a later review—but to the *provisions generally relating to rent, i.e. the rent review clause.* His approach was heavily criticised and has now been expressly disapproved in *Datastream International Ltd* v. *Oakeep Ltd* (1986) 277 EG 66, (page 134 and Appendix), *MFI Properties Ltd* v. *BICC Group Pension Trust Ltd*, The Times 7 Feb 1986, (Appendix) and most importantly, *The British Gas*

Corporation v. *Universities' Superannuation Scheme* (unreported but for full text see Appendix).

NATIONAL WESTMINSTER BANK PLC v. ARTHUR YOUNG McCLELLAND MOORES & CO.

Chancery Division   (1985) 273 EG 402

A lease contained a review clause which provided for the fixing of a fair market rent etc 'subject to the provisions of this (lease) other than the rent hereby reserved ...' The question before the court was whether, when the arbitrator decided what was to be the fair rent for the next review period, he was to do so on the basis that he was to ignore the possibility of a rent review notwithstanding that the actual lease contained a rent review clause.

Held: There was no presumption one way or the other. Every case depended on the precise wording of the lease. In this lease, the words were odd and something appeared to be missing; further, since rent was not a 'provision' the clause should be rewritten to run: 'subject to the provisions of this (lease) other than the provisions relating to the amount of rent payable'. What was quite clear was that, however unfortunate, and whether it was intended or not, in this particular lease the fair market rent was to be ascertained on the assumption that there was no rent review provision. A market rent has to be fixed on a set of abstractions which may be actual, may be hypothetical, and in most review clauses were a mixture of the two. There was no such thing as a market rent in the abstract.

WALTON J: The first and I think probably the main question which arises here is whether, when the arbitrator is deciding what is to be the fair market rent for the next rent period, he is to do that upon the basis that the lease contains (as, of course, we know it does in fact contain) a rent review clause or whether, on the other hand, he is to fix the fair market rent on the basis that there is no such clause in the lease. I do not think that there is a presumption one way or the other. I think that in every case that must depend upon the precise terms of the lease, because it must be very much borne in mind that there is no such thing as a fair market rent of any premises in the abstract. There is only a fair market rent upon a set of abstractions which may be actual, may be hypothetical and in most cases under rent reviews are a mixture of the one and the other. For example, here we have that the premises are expected to be let with vacant possession, which is, of course, something which we know as a fact just is not the case because the tenants are actually in possession and are certainly not just going to move out for the purpose of a rent review.

So the attempt by [counsel for the tenant] to poison my mind in advance to achieve the lower of the two values by defining the fair market rent as something which favours the tenant, as in fact he was attempting to do, I do not think impresses me very much.

The words here are unusual and seem to me to be very odd, because, repeating the relevant ones, they are

'to a tenant without a premium with vacant possession and subject to the provisions of this Subunderlease other than the rent hereby reserved ...'

Quite clearly, something is missing from that phrase and why I say something is missing is because it starts off 'subject to the provisions of this Subunderlease other than the rent ...' Quite clearly, 'the rent' is not a provision. The rent is something which is payable under, or reservable by, or covenanted to be paid as a result of, a provision in the lease and, therefore, something has got to be put in. The simplest (and it may in fact be the most correct) is to put in the words 'other than the provisions relating to the rent hereby reserved' and if that were put in, as [counsel for the tenant] quite correctly and forcefully pointed out, one would have some rather odd suppositions. One might have the supposition that there is no direct covenant to pay the rent. One might have the supposition that there was no power of re-entry for non-payment of the rent. Be it so, if those have any effect on the valuation of the rent, I should be surprised, but I think that it is much simpler to think that the missing words are something along the lines of 'provisions relating to the amount of rent payable'. But, whatever it is, it seems to me quite clear that, however unfortunate it may be and whether it was intended or not, in this particular lease the fair market rent is to be ascertained upon the somewhat curious assumption that there is no rent revision clause contained in the hypothetical terms which the arbitrator is considering. In the present case, that is stated by the arbitrator, who told us what the effect of that would be. It would be very considerable because it would put up a not inconsiderable rent by no less than 20.5%; but it is a simple point and it seems to me an inescapable one in view of the way the definition of 'fair market rent' is drawn. [Counsel for the tenant] did try to draw a distinction between 'rent' and 'rents' throughout the lease, but it does not seem to me that such a distinction in fact exists and I do not think that even if it did exist, it would really assist me in construing what is a very simple clause defining what is to be taken for this purpose as the fair market rent.

Note: Walton J refused to certify that there was a point of general public importance as provided by section 1 of the Arbitration Act 1979 and refused to give leave to appeal. On an application by the tenants who were dissatisfied with the result of Walton J's judgment, the registrar decided that the failure by the tenants to obtain a certificate of leave from the trial judge was a fatal bar in the jurisdiction of the Court of Appeal. The tenants application to the Court of Appeal was dismissed. The provisions of section 1 (7) of the 1979 Act made it clear that the Court of Appeal had no jurisdiction to consider an appeal from the refusal by a judge of a High Court to grant a certificate under the 1979 Act: see Practice Note [1985] 1 WLR 1123.

National Westminster Bank Plc v. *Arthur Young McClelland Moores & Co.* (above) was followed by Peter Gibson J in *Equity & Law Life Assurance Society Plc* v. *Bodfield Ltd* (1985) 276 EG 1157, when he held that, for review purposes, a term which provided that the hypothetical letting should be on the same terms as those provided for in the lease 'other than as to duration and rent' meant that the terms as to future rent reviews should be excluded and the rent should be reviewed on the basis that there were no review periods in the lease. However, there was an additional factor to be considered in *Equity & Law Life* (below) as the review clause *inter alia* also provided for a discount of 15 per cent on the market rent payable on review but his approach followed that taken in *National Westminster Bank* above.

EQUITY & LAW LIFE ASSURANCE PLC v. BODFIELD LTD

Chancery Division   (1985) 276 EG 1157

A lease (of industrial premises) for a term of 70 years commenced in 1968. The rather complex review provisions provided *inter alia* that for the first three years the rent was to be £22,500 p.a., for the next seven years £27,000 p.a. and thereafter £28,500 p.a. or such rent should be determined under the rent review clause which provided that a review should take place every 14 years and that there should be payable as additional rent the sum equal to the amount by which 85 per cent of the current open market rent exceeded £28,500 p.a., namely that the tenant was in effect to be given a discount of 15 per cent on the current market value. The open market rent was to be fixed on the basis of a lease equal in length to the unexpired residue and 'upon the terms of this lease other than as to duration and rent'. The landlords sought a declaration claiming that in fixing the revised rent the valuer had to disregard the effect on the market rent of any provisions in the lease relating to the quantification of rent and since these included the rent review clause itself, the revised rent had to be fixed on the assumption that there were to be no future reviews for the remainder of the term, which meant a revised rent on the basis of a 56 year term without review. The tenants argued that the phrase 'other than as to duration and rent' excluded only those terms under the existing lease which actually quantified the rent, i.e. those fixing the first staged rents; obviously they did not wish the 15 per cent discount to be disregarded, thus they contended that while the express words of the review clause required only the terms of the lease which actually quantified the rent to be ignored, the court should then, as a matter of necessary implication, require the discount to be disregarded, citing *Guys 'n' Dolls Ltd* v. *Sade Brothers Catering Ltd* (1983) 269 EG 129 (and see above) where the court held that a term providing for the payment of a premium rent should be disregarded by implication.

Held: An interpretation of the rent review clause which excluded only the provisions which actually quantified the rent payable and then excluded the 15 per cent discount by implication made little sense. The more natural way to approach the matter was to seek a meaning for the words 'other than as to rent' which comprehended all the terms to be taken as excluded from the hypothetical letting. There was no feature of the lease which differentiated it very significantly from that in *National Westminster Bank* (above) other than clause 4.2 which provided for the discount, namely that the reviewed rents were to be limited to the greater of £28,500 p.a. and 85 per cent of the net rental value so ascertained by way of additional rent.

PETER GIBSON J: Clause 4 contains provisions for rent reviews every 14 years of the term. The reviews are triggered by a notice to be served by the landlord, whereupon the landlord and the tenant are to endeavour to agree what is termed the net rental value of the demised premises and, if they fail to agree, the net rental value is to be determined by a valuer.

Clause 4 (2) is an elaborate clause, the effect of which is to limit the rent payable following such review to the greater of £28,500 and 85 per cent of the net rental value so ascertained. The method provided by the clause is to require a sum equal to the amount by which 85 per cent of the net rental value exceeds £28,500 to be paid by way of additional rent or, if at the time of a later review an additional rent is already being paid, then by way of an increased additional rent.

Clause 4 (4) is the critical clause defining, as it does, the net rental value in this way:

'The "net rental value" means the best rent which the premises hereby demised might reasonably be expected to fetch on the open market upon the following assumptions that is to say (i) that they are vacant and to let as a whole without a premium or other capital payment for the residue unexpired of the term hereby granted upon the terms of this lease other than as to duration and rent (ii) that the premises have been kept in good repair and condition in all respects in accordance with the Lessees' obligations hereunder. There shall be disregarded (a) any goodwill attached to the premises by reason of the carrying on thereat of the business of the Lessees (b) any effect on the rent of any improvement carried out by the Lessees hereunder otherwise than in pursuance of an obligation to the Lessors.'

The scheme of the rent review as provided by that clause is therefore that, to ascertain the net rental value, a hypothetical letting of the premises is postulated and for that various assumptions there specified contrary to reality are made. They include the assumption that instead of the 70-year lease continuing for the remainder of the term a new lease for the unexpired residue of the term is to be granted, and that instead of the actual rents payable under the lease the best rent obtainable on a letting on the specified assumptions will be payable. But the rents that will in fact be paid by the actual tenant in the real world are governed by clause 4 (2).

Save for the meaning of the words 'other than as to duration and rent' there is no difficulty in construing the rent review clause, which has plainly been drafted with care, professional skill and precision. One conceivable meaning of the words if taken in isolation is that they refer to all the terms of the lease which in any way relate to duration or rent. But [counsel] for the landlord and [counsel] for the tenant are at one in rejecting that meaning and I think they are right to do so. The basic terms which can be said to relate to duration, for example the forfeiture clause, or to relate to rent, for example the tenant's obligation to pay rent quarterly in advance on the usual quarter days, must be taken to have been intended to be terms of the lease in the hypothetical letting. A narrower meaning must therefore be found for the words.

[Counsel for the landlord] submits that the natural meaning to be given to the words is that they refer to terms which quantify duration and rent. On that construction, therefore, the rent review clause is excluded from the terms of the hypothetical letting.

[Counsel for the tenant] gives an even narrower meaning to the words. He says that they refer to the terms of the lease which give the duration of the lease and the quantified amounts of the rents initially reserved or, as he puts it, £X. Thus the terms he says that are excluded are the terms that the lease is for 70 years and that the rents of £22,500, £27,000 and £28,500 are the operative rents.

I shall deal with [counsel for the tenant's] submission first. On his construction, as it seems to me, rather more of the lease would in fact have to be excluded from the terms of the hypothetical lease than in his submission which I have just described. In effect the whole of the reddendum so far as it provides both for rents payable and periods for which they are payable would fall to be excluded. Far more significantly, however, [he] accepts that clause 4 (2) could not sensibly be treated as a term of the hypothetical lease providing, as it does, for payment of a rent less than the net rental value, the ascertainment of which is the whole object of the hypothetical exercise.

He submitted on the authority of the decision of the Court of Appeal in *Guys 'n' Dolls Ltd* v. *Sade Brothers Catering Ltd* (1983) 269 EG 129 that where a lease provides for a rent review on the basis of a hypothetical lease on the terms of an actual lease and the actual terms provide for the payment of rent at a discount to or a premium over the market value ascertained on the rent review, the court will as a matter of necessary implication exclude that term from the terms of the hypothetical lease. I of course accept that is so where the terms of the lease are explicit in requiring the hypothetical letting to be on the terms of the actual lease. But in the case of a lease such as this which does not contain such explicit terms, to my mind it is a very odd process of construction to construe the words 'other than as to rent' as in the first place limited only to the rents initially reserved, but then to exclude clause 4 (2) by a process of necessary implication. The more natural way to approach the matter is, in my view, to seek a meaning for "other than as to rent" which comprehends all the terms to be taken as excluded from the hypothetical letting.

[Counsel for the tenant], however, advanced several contentions in support of his submission. First he submitted that only if rent reviews were included in the hypothetical letting could references to increased rents in other parts of the lease which are incorporated in the hypothetical letting be given any meaning. But even on his own construction in the hypothetical letting at the final rent review there would be otiose references to increased rents. In any event, the point is, in my judgment, answered in the way that Goulding J dealt with a similar argument advanced in *Pugh* v. *Smiths Industries Ltd* (1982) 264 EG 823 at p 826: 'If the valuer is to exclude the provisions of the rent review clause, naturally he disregards references to it in the other parts of the lease.'

Second, he submitted that a rent review clause such as this which contains words of ambiguity should be construed by the court in such a way as leans in favour of giving effect to what he described as the general purpose of such a clause. By reference to *Ponsford* v. *HMS Aerosols Ltd* [1979] AC 63, and the remarks of Viscount Dilhorne at p 76 and Lord Fraser at p 83, he described this as to up-date rent at regular intervals so that the landlord obtains the increased rent the demised premises would command if let on the terms of the lease for the residue of the term. I do not doubt that that is generally the commercial purpose of a rent review clause even in a lease granted in 1968 before the days of high inflation. I accept that it is surprising to have a valuation on the footing that the lease will run for 56 years without a rent review clause, as is the case when one is considering the first rent review. But I do not understand the *Ponsford* case to lay down any presumption or rule of construction to govern the interpretation of a rent review clause.

Walton J in *National Westminster Bank plc* v. *Arthur Young McClelland Moores & Co.* (1984) 273 EG 402 made this observation on the question of whether a rent review clause is to be treated as included in the terms of a hypothetical letting:

'I do not think that there is a presumption one way or the other. I think that in every case that must depend upon the precise terms of the lease, because it must be very much borne in mind that there is no such time as a fair market rent of any premises in the abstract. There is only a fair market rent upon a set of abstractions which may be actual, may be hypothetical and in most cases under rent reviews are a mixture of the one and the other.'

So in my judgment here.

In the present case there is the particular difficulty that unusually a discount from the net market value is given to the tenant, for what reason it is not known. It may or may not have been intended to compensate the tenant for not including rent review clauses in the terms of the hypothetical letting. In the circumstances the only safe course is to construe the actual words used without regard to such general considerations as those advanced by [counsel for the tenant].

The same comments can be made in respect of [his] next submission that the court should construe the rent review clause so as to achieve the position that the rent should be fair to both parties. This submission was made on the basis of the recognition by Goulding J in the *Pugh* case that a rent review which excluded a rent review clause from the terms of the hypothetical letting involves a one-sided assumption in favour of the landlord. But Goulding J in *Pugh's* case, in rejecting a similar submission to that advanced by [counsel for the tenant], commented (264 EG 823 at p 826):

'It may be, looking at nothing outside the terms of the document and admissible evidence, that this bias of the clause in favour of the landlord was stipulated for in negotiation against other advantages allowed to the tenants. One just does not know from the document. Or, again, it may well be that neither side gave any thought to this point.'

[He] then submitted that support for his construction could be derived from the words of section 34, Landlord and Tenant Act 1954 (as amended) and certain judicial comments thereon. By that section the court in granting a new business tenancy both determines the rent (section 34 (1)) and has the power to include a rent review clause in the new lease (section 34 (3)). The rent is to be that at which, having regard to the terms of the tenancy '(other than those relating to rent)' the holding might reasonably be expected to be let on the assumptions specified in the section. Both Stamp J in *Regis Property Co. Ltd* v. *Lewis & Peat Ltd* [1970] Ch 695 at p 699 and Megarry J in *English Exporters (London) Ltd* v. *Eldonwall Ltd* [1973] Ch 415 expressed the view that the words in parentheses in section 34 (1) were intended to prevent the nonsense that would arise if the terms relating to rent were not ignored.

It is common ground between [both counsel] that the court must take into account for the purposes of section 34 any rent review clause that it decides to include when determining the rent, and therefore the words in parentheses in the subsection must be construed as not referring to the rent review clause.

I accept that section 34 provides an illustration of the use of words similar to those which I have to construe as not referring to a rent review clause. But I do not think it provides a compelling argument that in the present lease the words 'other than as to rent' do not refer to a rent review clause. The context and the circumstances of the application of section 34 are entirely different from the present. Under the Landlord and Tenant Act the court at the same time as it fixes the rent determines whether or not there is to be a rent review clause, and it would be a nonsense if it were to ignore the review clause it decides to include when it fixes the rent. In the present case the valuer is not deciding whether or not to include a rent review clause. The only question is what did the parties agree? Did they agree that the rent review clause was to be included in the terms of the hypothetical letting or not?

I turn to [counsel for the landlord's] submission. He says that if one poses the question: 'What are the terms of the lease as to rent?', the answer that would naturally be given would not be limited to the terms reserving the fixed quantified rents but would be bound to include a reference to the terms as to the revised rent payable on a rent review. I agree. There are no difficulties or inconsistencies with other parts of the lease when the words are so construed. Further, support for this construction to my mind can be found in the decision of Walton J in the *National Westminster Bank* case, to which I have already referred. In that case the hypothetical letting for the purposes of a rent review was to be 'subject to the provisions of this subunderlease other than the rent hereby reserved'. Those words of exclusion might perhaps more readily than in the present case be taken to refer simply to the quantum of rent. Walton J had no difficulty in construing them as meaning something along the lines of provisions relating to the amount of rent payable, and he reached the clear conclusion that the rent review clause was thereby excluded.

[Counsel for the tenant] has rightly pointed out that each lease turns on its own wording. I accept that, but my attention has not been drawn to any feature of the lease before me that differentiates it very significantly from the lease in the *National Westminster Bank* case other than clause 4 (2), which, as I have indicated, tends to be a pointer against the construction advanced by the tenant. In these circumstances, therefore, I am assisted by Walton J's decision in reaching the conclusion that I have stated.

But contrast the decision of Warner J in *Datastream International* v. *Oakeep Ltd* (1985) unreported, (but see Legal Notes, *Estates Gazette*, 21 December 1985, p 1357). In *Datastream*, Warner J held that the words 'subject to the provisions of this lease (other than as to the amount of rent hereby reserved)' did not indicate that in fixing the market rent the valuer should disregard the existence of rent reviews in the lease and that he was therefore to take them into account.

DATASTREAM INTERNATIONAL LTD v. OAKEEP LTD

Chancery Division   5 November 1985

A lease provided that the rent should be reviewed and the sum fixed should be equal to the market rental value. This was to be determined on the basis of a term equal to the unexpired residue and 'subject to the provisions of this lease (other than as to the amount of rent hereby reserved)'. The question before the court was whether any reviewed rent should be determined on the basis that the valuer should ignore the existence of rent reviews or not.

Held: Any interpretation should, where possible, be on the basis that it does not produce an unfair and unreasonable result, namely that did not require the tenant to pay for a benefit it did not enjoy, here, a lease without a rent review clause in it. Here the wording of the lease should be read as obliging the valuer to take account of future reviews: *Pugh* v. *Smiths Industries Ltd* (1982) 264 EG 823, *Lister Locks Ltd* v. *TEI Pension Trust Ltd* (1981) 264 EG 827, and *Pearl Assurance plc* v. *Shaw* (1984) 274 EG 490 considered; *National Westminster Bank plc* v. *Arthur Young McClelland Moores & Co.* (1984) 273 EG 402 and *Equity & Law Life Assurance Society plc* v. *Bodfield Ltd* (1985) 276 EG 1157 distinguished.

Note: Although Warner J chose to distinguish the wording in the review clause in *Datastream* from the similar provisions in *National Westminster Bank* and *Equity & Law Life*, and did not expressly disapprove of the decisions in those cases, they do conflict in their approach to the same problem. As a matter of common sense and commercial fairness the decision in *Datastream* is to be preferred, (for the extract, see Appendix). *Datastream* was followed and amplified in the most recent two cases of *MFI Properties* and *British Gas*, and must be seen as authority for rejecting the literal approach adopted by Goulding, Walton and Peter Gibson 'JJ' and others in earlier cases. The further cases of *MFI Properties* and *British Gas* are set out together with a full editorial note in the Appendix.

Compare the case below in the light of the more recent decisions of *Datastream*, *MFI Properties* and *British Gas* (see Appendix).

SECURICOR LTD v. POSTEL PROPERTIES LTD

Chancery Division   (1985) 274 EG 730

A 25-year lease provided for periodical rent reviews. The review clause defined the revised rent to be the market rent, as defined by the rent review clause and providing for certain matters to be disregarded in ascertaining the rental value, and continued: 'and there being disregarded this clause'. The landlords contended that the clause had to be construed literally and the rent had to be assessed on review on the basis of a lease for a term as long as the residue, i.e. 20 years without review. The tenants contended that the words 'and there being disregarded this clause' should be struck out.

Held: The clause clearly provided that the market rent for the notional term was to be ascertained disregarding the rent review provisions in the lease and the rent should be determined on that footing.

JUDGE BLACKETT-ORD (sitting as a High Court judge): Pausing there, it is the reasonable open market rent, at the review date, for the balance of the term; as we have now got to the first review date, we contemplate a lease for a term of 20 years, with vacant possession—and I suppose with a willing landlord, whatever that means.

Having got so far, the clause goes on to say that the rental value is to be ascertained on the basis of the supposition—if not the fact—that the tenant has complied with the repairing covenant in the lease. I think that is a summary of that provision. Then it goes on to say that certain things are to be diregarded if otherwise applicable. First, certain matters set out in section 34 of the Landlord and Tenant Act 1954; second, any work carried out by the tenant before the commencement of the present actual lease—that being, of course, aimed at a sitting tenant who has taken a new lease, and work which he has carried out is disregarded if it is before the lease with which I am now concerned; third, so far as may be permitted by the law, all restrictions whatsoever relating to rent or to security of tenure—so we are back in the open market; and fourth, the wording is: 'and there being disregarded this clause'.

Then I think one must assume a full stop, and the clause continues: 'Such lease being on the same terms and conditions (other than as to amount of rent) as this present demise without the payment of any fine or premium.'

The landlord's contention is that the notional lease which has to be considered is one for 20 years with a rent fixed at the market rent at the review date and payable for the whole of the 20-year term. The tenant's contention is that the rent under the notional lease should be subject to review in the same way as the rent under the actual lease. The tenant, I think, does not dispute—it is difficult to see how he could dispute—that the words 'and there being disregarded this clause' (and this clause being the only clause in the lease dealing with rent review) must bear their literal meaning. And indeed I have referred to certain authorities in which that view has been taken by the court: that is to say, that the provisions of rent-review clauses are normally to be taken, as one might say, at their face value. There were two cases decided by Goulding J and reported in the Estates Gazette: *Pugh* v. *Smith Industries* (1982) 264 EG 823 and *Safeway Foodstores Ltd* v. *Banderway Ltd* (1983) 267 EG 850, but I do not find them of assistance except that they do indicate—as indeed does also the case decided by Walton J (to a transcript of which I was referred) of *National Westminster Bank plc* v. *Arthur Young McClelland Moores & Co.*, a judgment given on November 26 last [reported at (1984) 273 EG 402]—that the court construes these clauses literally unless, of course, the circumstances are extremely exceptional. I find it difficult to think what circumstances those could be, because if one is forced to the conclusion that something has gone so far wrong with the clause that the court should endeavour to interpret it in some different way, then really there is no question of taking it literally. But apart from that—and that sort of circumstance is not found in the present case—I would only refer to what Goulding J said in the *Safeway* case, at the bottom of the first page of the report:

> 'I do not get any great help from those decisions because I do not think that one can solve questions of construction by comparing more or less similar but by no means identical cases on documents differently worded.'

But [counsel for the tenant] exhorted me to strike out the words 'and there being disregarded this clause'. He conceded that this would be a bold course for me to adopt, but he prayed in aid the last sentence of subclause (3) of clause 6 containing in brackets the words 'other than as to amount of rent'. He referred to two cases on the Landlord and Tenant Act 1954, Part II, as amended: the decision of Stamp J, as he then was, in *Regis Property Co. Ltd* v. *Lewis & Peat* [1970] Ch 695 and a decision of Megarry J in *English Exporters (London) Ltd* v. *Eldonwall Ltd* [1973] Ch 415. In each of these there are observations suggesting that the rather similar wording in the Act, referring to the new lease to be granted to a tenant or the interim tenancy pending the final determination of the application as being on certain terms and conditions 'other than as to amount of rent', is simply excluding the amount of the existing rent from consideration. Because, obviously, the court is being asked to fix a different rent and it would be absurd to bring into account as binding the provisions determining the existing one. And so [counsel for the tenant] says that that means that the reference in the last sentence of subclause (3) to 'other than as to amount of rent' means simply that the court should disregard the original rent figure but still allow the proposed notional lease to contain the rent-review provisions of clause 6; that, he said, being fair because—and it is mentioned in the affidavits—the landlord's formula will give them a greater rent than they would get initially if the notional rent were to be subject to review.

But it is necessary to construe clause 6 as a whole, and in the statute there is no such provision as the direction in clause 6 that the provisions of the clause are to be disregarded. That must cover the subsequent reference in the clause to the lease being on the same terms and conditions 'other than as to amount of rent'.

In my judgment the clause clearly provides that the market rent for the notional term is to be ascertained disregarding the rent-review provisions in the lease. Accordingly, the landlord's contention is correct, and the rent should be decided by the expert or arbitrator on that footing.

6.4 (b)   Seeking the determination of the court on the question of review without review before going to arbitration

In *Chapman* v. *Charlwood Alliance Properties* (1981) 260 EG 1041, the plaintiff tenant of industrial premises applied under section 2 (2) of the Arbitration Act 1979 for leave to allow the High Court to determine two questions of law before the case went to arbitration. The issues arose from a rent review clause which required that the residue of the term of 106 years was to be valued, and were (i) whether the rent had to be fixed on the basis that there were to be no reviews during the residue of the term; (ii) whether the demise had to be valued as a whole or at the aggregate of the rent of the industrial parts. Hodgson J held that the first issue of whether the rent should be assessed for the residue of the term without review was a matter of law, but that it should be answered with the aid of the relevant extrinsic evidence which would be produced at the arbitration hearing, and the second issue was a matter of fact and valuation rather than law. Further, there was no clear evidence that it was probable that there would be a substantial saving of costs so that in all the circumstances the judge's discretion to give leave should not be exercised.

6.5   There is no irresistible presumption that a rent review clause will produce an upward movement for the landlord

BODFIELD LTD v. CALDEW COLOUR PLATES LTD

Chancery Division   (1985) 1 ETLR 110

The landlord of an underlease of premises forming part of a much larger area let on a 125 year headlease sought a declaration that the rent review clause in the underlease should be construed on the basis of an irresistible presumption that a rent review clause produced an upward movement for the landlord. The matter arose because the wording of the headlease did not anticipate that the headlessee would occupy the premises himself and the underlease with some modification was designed to cover a situation where the tenant was in actual occupation of the whole or part of the premises, followed the same format, providing:

'... the gross rental value of the demised premises shall be the aggregate amount of rents actually paid or received by the lessee in respect of the demised premises or in respect of any sub-letting of the demised premises at the commencement of the relevant review period, provided that if any part or parts of the demised premises are at the commencement of such relevant review period vacant or unoccupied by the lessee or let on sub-lease commencing more than three years before the commencement of the relevant review period there shall be attributable to such part or parts the best rent determined by a surveyor as specified at which such part or parts might reasonably be expected to be let in the open market ...'

The tenant was and had been in possession of the whole of the premises at the commencement of the review period. Literally construed, the clause therefore did not allow for the landlord to receive any increase in rent. The landlord contended that this result was so unfair that the judge should in effect read the word 'unoccupied' by the lessee as 'occupied' by the lessee.

137

Held: As it stood the clause made sense. The landlord's submission was totally incompatible with the one change from the headlease that the parties had made themselves, namely by putting in the words 'actually paid by the lessee'. Once it was certain (as it was) that the proportion of rent actually paid by the lessee in respect of the portion of the premises which it occupied had to be taken into account, it was wholly specious to argue that it was so absurd and wrong to deprive the landlord of increases in rent that some totally different meaning had to be given to it. There was no irresistible presumption that a rent review clause produces an upward movement for the landlord and if it does not there is something wrong with it.

WALTON J: Now we come to the underlease of 11 September 1968, which is the one that falls here to be construed, made between Crown and Commercial Properties Ltd, the predecessor in title of the plaintiffs, as landlords, and the defendants as tenants. The crucial part that has to be looked at here is clause 7 (6) of the underlease. That provides that:

'If the lessor shall at any time after the end of the seventh and fourteenth years of the term, the period between the end of such year and the beginning of the next such year so specified in which any such notice shall be given being referred to as "the relevant review period", give to the lessee at least three months' written notice (hereinafter called "the lessor's notice") specifying the revised rent and if the lessee shall not give ...'

A counter-notice, then that specified rent becomes the revised rent. That, of course, follows very closely indeed the language of the head lease. Then (b) deals with giving a notice of objection by the lessee, which was duly given, and there is similar provision to those contained in the head lease for the appointment of a single surveyor to be appointed in default of agreement by the president for the time being of the Royal Institution of Chartered Surveyors, and he has to calculate the revised rent.

Now we come on to the clause which has given rise to all the trouble, and this is quite clearly an adaptation of the clause contained in the head lease.

'For the purposes of this clause, the gross rental value of the demised premises shall be the aggregate amount of rents actually paid or received by the lessee in respect of the demised premises or in respect of any sub-letting of the demised premises at the commencement of the relevant review period, provided that if any part or parts of the demised premises are at the commencement of such relevant review period vacant or unoccupied by the lessee or let on sub-lease commencing more than three years before the commencement of the relevant review period ...'

Pausing there, that is exactly the same as in the head lease.

'... there shall be attributable to such part or parts the best rent determined by the surveyor as specified at which such part or parts might reasonably be expected to be let in the open market by a willing lessor to a willing lessee with vacant possession',

and so on and so forth. Then (b):

'It is hereby agreed that in respect of any sub-lease, leases of part or parts of the demised premises commencing less than three years before the date of review in respect of which the lessee receives a premium, then the rental equivalent to such premium shall be added to the rent actually reserved by such sub-leases when the gross rent is calculated.'

So it will be seen that with a minor change—but an important one—the language of the sub-lease does indeed reflect the language of the head lease and, at any rate *prima facie*, produces a rent review clause along the same lines precisely as the head lease. The relevant change which is made arises from the circumstances that whereas it was quite clear from the head lease that the head lessee was not expected in any way to go into occupation—and so far as I know has not gone into occupation—in the case of the under lease it was expected that the tenant would, or at any rate might, go into occupation—and indeed the tenant has gone into occupation, and apart from the fact that it shares with a subsidiary company (which for present purposes is entirely immaterial), it has throughout been in occupation of the whole of the premises.

Therefore, some other version of the clause as contained in the head lease was required in the under-lease in order to cater for that fact, and it has been done by the draftsman—and I can see why he did it although, I regret to say, I do not think it was very skilfully done—by referring, when defining the gross rental value of the demised premises, to the 'aggregate amount of rent actually paid or received by the lessee in respect of the demised premises'.

Now that is quite clearly—having regard to the matrix of fact which is available to me in this present case—a portmanteau phrase, because he does not mean, I think, at all the amount of rent actually paid by the lessee.

Let me give a very simple example which did not happen: let it be supposed that the lessee had let exactly half of the premises to a sub-tenant so that it itself was only occupying one-half of the premises. Then I think that the way the draftsman quite clearly intended sub-clause (c) to operate would be that the gross rental value of the demised premises would be the amount of the rent notionally paid by the lessee in respect of the half of the premises which it was occupying and the rent received by it in respect of the one-half of the premises which it was not occupying from the sub-lessee.

That is the only way I can give those words, 'amount of rent actually paid or received by the lessee in respect of the demised premises or in respect of any sub-letting of the demised premises at the commencement of the relevant review period', any sense. Therefore, in accordance with the ordinary principles of construction, where I can see quite clearly what the draftsman must have meant and that he cannot have meant anything else, that is what quite clearly he did mean to provide.

The alternative would be to say 'the aggregate rent paid by the lessee for the whole of the premises and also the amount he received in respect of half of them which he had sub-let to the under-lessee' and that, in my view, would be a totally absurd construction to be placed upon those opening words when one can quite clearly see what the clause is aimed at.

That being the state of the game, when one reads on one discovers that it is provided as a proviso to sub-clause (c) that 'if any part or parts of the demised premises are at the commencement of such relevant review period vacant'—that is to say nobody in them at all—'or unoccupied by the lessee'—but occupied by somebody else not a sub-tenant—'or let on sub-lease commencing more than three years before the commencement of the relevant rent review period, there shall be attributed to such part or parts the best rent ascertained ...'

So it seems to me that the draftsman has covered—not very elegantly, but covered—all the possible positions. He has covered—which was not necessarily covered in the head lease because it was not necessary to do so—the case of the tenant who was in possession of all or some of the premises, in which case you take the whole or an apportioned part of the rent proportionate to the part occupied by the tenant. He has covered, in exactly the same way as is covered in the head lease, those portions that are vacant, unoccupied by the lessee or let on sub-lease, and, indeed, he has split up the three years provision into the two similar parts, dealing separately with those leases granted within the three years and those granted without the three years, as provided by the head lease.

What, then, is there to argue about on the construction of the clause? What [counsel for] the landlord, has said is if that is the true construction of the clause, then, since the tenant has remained in possession and is in possession of the whole occupation of the premises at the commencement of the review period, the landlord is not going to get any increase in his rent, and that is dreadfully unfair. It is so unfair that I ought to read the word 'unoccupied' by the lessee in clause (c) as 'occupied' by the lessee.

Well, if [counsel for the landlord] will permit me, I have listened to some surprising submissions in my time, but I think that submission about takes the biscuit. It is totally and utterly incompatible, as [counsel] for the defendants pointed out, with the one change from the head lease that the parties have themselves made, namely by putting in the words 'actually paid by the lessee', and once you are certain— and you cannot possibly be anything other than certain from the very beginning of the terms—that you have to take into account that proportion of the rent which is actually paid by the lessee in respect of the portion of the premises which it occupies, it is wholly specious to argue to the effect that it is so absurd and so totally wrong, depriving the landlord of increases in rent, that some other totally different meaning must be given to it.

I am afraid those arguments do not hold water for five minutes. Of course if one sees in the document a total nonsense from the construction of the document or any other admissible documents themselves, one may read the document correctly in order to make it make sense. And, indeed, I have applied that principle myself in reading 'the amount of rent actually paid by the lessee' as having, on its true construction, the meaning—as it quite clearly has—'amount of rent actually paid by the lessee in respect of such portions if any, of the premises which at the relevant date he occupied'.

[Counsel for the landlord] cited to me *Slough Estates Ltd* v. *Slough Borough Council* [1969] 2 Ch 305; [1969] 2 All ER 988. There there was a manifest error in a planning permission which was granted in that it was granted for the wrong portion shown on the map, the coloured instead of the uncoloured portion on a particular map, but when one looked at the application of the planning permission one saw quite clearly what was meant.

Here it seems to me that really on the true construction of clause 7 (6) (c) there can be no argument, and indeed it is fair to [counsel for the landlord] really to say that as a matter of construction he had no argument to offer. What he was really trying to say was that there must be an irresistible presumption that a rent review clause produces an upward movement for the landlord and if it does not there is something wrong with it and it must therefore be tinkered about with until it does produce a certain result seen from the landlord's point of view.

There is no such presumption of any description whatsoever. This clause, inartistic as it is and needing explanation as I have explained it, nevertheless in the crucial part, where it refers to the portions of the premises vacant or unoccupied by the lessee or let on sub-lease, means exactly what it says. When it says 'vacant' it does not mean 'occupied'. When it says 'unoccupied' it does not mean 'occupied'. And when it says 'let on sub-lease' it does not mean 'not let on sub-lease'.

6.6 Where a lease dates back prior to its execution there is no reason why the review period should not be calculated from the earlier date if that was the intention of the parties

BEAUMONT PROPERTY TRUST v. TAI

Chancery Division (1982) 265 EG 872

A lease provided for five yearly rent reviews. The term commenced some three years and nine months before the date on which the lease was executed. A dispute arose as to whether the first review was five years from the date of execution (as contended for by the tenant), or from the date the term commenced (as submitted by the landlord).

Held: The intention of the parties had to be taken from the wording of the lease as a whole. Although there had been no payment to the landlords until the date of execution, the first five-year period referred to in the review provisions ran from the date expressed as the commencement of the term. Guidance laid down by Sir Robert Megarry V-C in *Bradshaw* v. *Pawley* [1980] 1 WLR 10 applied.

VIVIAN PRICE QC (sitting as a deputy High Court judge): In this case the lease relates, as I have said, to Unit 6 in a shopping centre and for reasons which are not apparent upon the face of the documents, the lease being executed on 17 December 1979, the term of the lease is expressed in clause 1 of the lease to be for a period of 25 years, not from 17 December 1979 but from 25 March 1976.

The dispute between the parties stems from that simple matter, because the reddendum to the landlords is (and I shall read the *habendum* as well):

'TO HOLD the same (Except and Reserved as aforesaid) unto the Lessee for a term of 25 years from the 25th day of March 1976 yielding and paying therefor to the company:—(a) during the first five years (from the date of the lease) of the said term a yearly rent of two thousand five hundred pounds (£2,500) (b) for each subsequent five years of the said term such rent as shall be determined as hereinafter provided being the full market rental value of the demised premises at the beginning of each period of five years or the yearly rent of two thousand five hundred pounds (£2,500) whichever shall be the greater.'

Then subclause (b) goes on in terms about which there is some dispute:

'the rent in respect of each year to be paid in advance without any deduction on the usual quarter days the proportion thereof for the period from the said [blank] day of [blank] one thousand nine hundred and seventy-nine to the [blank] day of [blank] one thousand nine hundred and seventy-nine having been paid on the date hereof.'

The matter in fact in dispute was very clearly expressed in the correspondence that was exhibited to an affidavit of Mr John Lawrence, sworn on behalf of the plaintiffs, and also appears in the affidavit of Mr Malcolm McGuinness, solicitor, acting on behalf of the defendant. I do not think I need read that correspondence, nor do I need read that affidavit, because again the points emerged very clearly and succinctly in arguments of counsel appearing before me.

What it was in effect was this: that the landlords' claim that on the true construction of the lease, the rent review provision being for equal five-year periods, the first rent review would be on 25 March 1981, which is of course under five years from the date of execution of the lease, but is for five years from the date from which the term of the lease was expressed to run, namely 25 March 1976. The subsequent reviews would be at five-year intervals thereafter, namely 25 March 1986, 25 March 1991 and finally on 25 March 1996, the lease itself coming to its full term on 24 March in the year 2001. About that latter date there is no disagreement. Essentially the disagreement is about when the one-and-a-quarter-year first audit period shall be: shall it be at the beginning of the actual running of the lease, as the landlords assert, or should it be at the end of the full period, as the tenant asserts, because the tenant asserts that the clear meaning of the words that I have already read out, expressed in clauses 1 (a) and (b) of the lease, is that the first rent review date is to be five years from the date of the lease. The date of the lease there can be no doubt about—17 December 1979. So, says the tenant, five years from the date of the lease, which is what the words state in clause 1 (a), means that the first review date is 17

December 1984, and thereafter there would be five-year intervals expiring on 17 December 1989, 1994 and 1999, leaving the one-and-a-quarter-year period from 1999 to 24 March 2001.

What is the correct approach to this matter? Of course one has to read the document as a whole in order to find what the intention of the parties was when they executed the lease. I was referred, if I may say so with great respect, to a very helpful authority, and indeed it was relied upon both by [counsel] for the plaintiffs and [counsel] for the defendant tenant, and that is the judgment of the learned Vice-Chancellor, Sir Robert Megarry, in *Bradshaw* v. *Pawley* [1980] 1 WLR 10. I do not need to go through the details of the case and I do not need to refer in detail to the judgment, because at the end of his judgment, after reviewing the law, the learned Vice-Chancellor at the bottom of p 16 sets out the principles of law which I should follow, and so far as they are relevant to the circumstances of this case those are the principles that I do follow. I shall read them out (p 16H):

'In the result, I think that where a lease creates a term of years which is expressed to run from some date earlier than that of the execution of the lease, the relevant law may be summarised as follows. (1) The term created will be a term which commences on the date when the lease is executed, and not the earlier date.'

So, applying this here, there is no doubt that in law the term created by this lease was created on 17 December 1979 and not on the date where the term is expressed to run from in clause 1, 25 March 1976.

(2) No act or omission prior to the date on which the lease is executed will normally constitute a breach of the obligations of the lease. (3) These principles do not prevent the parties from defining the expiration of the term by reference to a date prior to that of the execution of the lease,

So applying that here, the principles that the learned Vice-Chancellor is expressing do not prevent the parties from defining the expiration of the term of the lease, that is 25 years, by reference to a date prior to the execution of the lease, that is 25 years from not 17 December 1979 but 25 March 1976, making, as I have said, 24 March 2001. Then continuing with principle (3), which is of course very relevant here,

'or from making contractual provisions which take effect by reference to such a date, as by defining the period for the operation of a break clause or an increase of rent.'

Of course that is the very point that is for my decision here.

'(4) There is nothing in these principles to prevent the lease from creating obligations in respect of any period prior to the execution of the lease. (5) Whether in fact any such obligations have been created depends on the construction of the lease; and there is nothing which requires the lease to be construed in such a way as to avoid, if possible, the creation of such obligations.'

As will be seen, of those principles there set out by the Vice-Chancellor it is (3) that principally occupies me and my attention.

As I said, the arguments on behalf of both parties were very clearly and very succinctly put to me, and I should first of all try to summarise those respective approaches.

First of all, as must be quite clear, on both sides I was taken through the lease as a whole in an attempt to see whether support could be given for one side's contention or the other. I start, of course, with the words of clause 1 itself. The contention on behalf of the landlords is essentially that the words 'from the date of the lease' in clause 1 (a) are there for the purpose of making it clear that the payment to the landlords did not begin until the date of the lease, that is 17 December 1979, but had no other effect upon the meaning of the expression 'the first five years'. In other words, say the landlords, the term expressed in the earlier words of clause 1 is 25 years from 25 March 1976, and the first five years of that term obviously run from 25 March 1976 until 24 or 25 March 1981. The words that I am dealing with are concerned with providing for a payment to the landlords, and there is no other purpose in these words but providing for payments. The payment that they are concerned with in clause 1 (a) is payment during the first five-year period of the 25-year term. So the payment is to be a yearly one of £2500, but the words 'from the date of the lease' are there in order to make absolutely apparent and beyond doubt that the requirement for payment does not arise until the date of execution of the lease in December 1979. I hope that I am summarising the way in which the landlords' argument was so admirably expressed, with a clarity that I do not hope myself to achieve.

Then, say the landlords, once you have decided that as being the intention of the parties, you go through the lease and everything you then find is consistent with the contention. It is not, of course, a matter of construing the words so much as trying to find out what is the intention of the parties as expressed in these words at the time when the lease was executed. And, say the landlords, if you then go through the remaining terms of the lease you will find consistently that, as I have said, the first five-yearly period for payment in fact ends no more than one-and-a-quarter years after the date of execution of the lease. Although I was taken through the lease it does not seem to me that any useful purpose is to be served by now going through the various points and places in the lease where one finds the use of the said term and other matters which reinforce or support the landlords' contention, because this is exactly the exercise that was carried out again so succinctly and clearly by [counsel] on behalf of the tenant. What seems to me at the time to be the position was that once you have made up your mind what the meaning of the words were in clause 1 (a) then that view was reinforced by the remaining portion of the lease. Of course one is construing the document as a whole and it is very important that, having formed a view, then you should review that preliminary conclusion which you have formed by going through the rest of the document. The tenant, of course, relies upon the plain words of clause 1 (a) in its first five lines, which read as follows: 'Yielding and paying therefor to the company (a) during the first five years (from the date of the lease)' ... Reading it in that way, as I have done, it is of course quite clear that in the first line they are defining, says the tenant, the first five years as running from the date of the lease, and he rejects the contention of the landlords that 'from the date of the lease' is there to make it clear that there is no obligation to pay rent prior to the execution of the lease.

Argument was also addressed to me on this basis: that if I was in any doubt about what the words mean, in other words that there is an ambiguity, then the words should be construed against the grantor. Not surprisingly, both parties relied upon that principle. On the one side, says [counsel] on behalf of the landlords, of course this is the sort of case in which it is not the landlords who are the grantors, it is the tenant who is the grantor in the particular case of these words in the lease. No, says [counsel] on behalf of the tenant, you have got it quite the wrong way round, and it is in fact the landlords' grant here, and the words must be construed against them. I was referred to a number of cases and to *Halsbury's Laws of England* and other authorities, which seem to me to provide a fascinating subject to debate. But in the end, and I am bound to say in my judgment at the beginning, there is no ambiguity in the words of this lease at all. In my judgment although they could have been more felicitously expressed the intention of the parties emerges very clearly from the words that are used, namely that the term of the lease at its maximum will expire 25 years after 25 March 1976, but within that total period of 25 years there will be possible breaks at five-yearly intervals. It so happens that the lease is executed after the date when that 25-year term was expressed to be possibly beginning, namely 25 March 1976, but the first five-year period up to the break point, or possible break point, is not affected by the later execution of the lease, the first five-year period still expires five years after 25 March 1976. The trouble is caused by the words in brackets, 'from the date of the lease', in my judgment being put in the wrong place; they should have been put earlier on in the *reddendum*, 'Yielding and paying (from the date of the lease) therefor to the company', and so on. Whether there would still have been a dispute between the parties if the words had been moved from the place where they are to that possible place I do not know, but in either case in my judgment the intention of the parties clearly emerges, and in my judgment the plaintiff landlords are entitled to the declaration they seek, namely that the first five-year period referred to in clause 1 (a) of the said lease ran from the commencement of the term of the lease, namely 25 March 1976.

6.7   Unless there is a clear indication to the contrary, a review clause will be construed as protecting the rental value of the landlord's premises in their actual condition for the time being against inflation.

TRUST HOUSE FORTE ALBANY HOTELS LTD v. DAEJAN INVESTMENTS LTD

Chancery Division   (1980) 256 EG 915

An underlease of premises in the Strand, which included the Strand Palace Hotel, was vested in the plaintiffs. Clause 1 (i) provided for the rent to be reviewed on the basis that certain defined areas which were in fact used as part of the hotel and were physically adapted for that purpose were to be valued 'on the basis that those areas are actually let for or are available for letting for shopping and retail purposes'. The plaintiff tenants contended *inter alia* that the material areas should be valued in their existing physical state and condition, while the landlords submitted that the rental valuation required to be made under clause 1 (i) thereof, so far as it related to those parts of the relevant area not actually let for shopping and retail purposes at the relevant date, was to be made on the footing of those parts being treated as being at the relevant date in a state reasonably appropriate for such use.

Held: The clause merely required the premises to be valued at the relevant date. There was no requirement or supposition as to the state of the premises at all. The areas were to be valued in their actual condition at the relevant date.

Fox J: The issues, I think, may be summarised thus: is the valuation to be made on the basis of the premises in their actual physical state, or is it to be made on the basis that such part of the premises as is not now let as shops is (as is said in the defendants' formulation) to be treated as being in a state reasonably appropriate for such use? The dispute is limited to those parts of the premises not already in use as shops. It is agreed that the latter must be valued in their actual physical state.

I come then to the construction of the clause. Omitting immaterial words, the clause provides that

'the rental shall be the aggregate of (a) the excess of the rental value on the relevant date ... of those areas ... on the basis that those areas are actually let for or are available for letting for shopping and retail purposes.'

I should mention that it is common ground that the expression 'rental value' gives rise to no difficulty of interpretation. It seems to me that, as a matter of the ordinary usage of the English language, the clause merely requires that the premises are to be valued at the relevant date. There is no requirement or supposition as to the state of the premises at all. The clause simply deals with 'areas' and requires that the rental value of those areas at a particular date be ascertained. In my judgment, the ordinary meaning of the language of the clause is that the areas are to be valued in their actual condition at the relevant date.

The defendants' construction involves the insertion of words requiring that the premises be treated as being at the relevant date in a state reasonably appropriate for the specified use. No such language forms part of the clause, and it would, it seems to me, be improper to insert it unless there are circumstances which compel me so to do.

It is pointed out by way of preliminary on behalf of the defendants that the clause does require certain suppositions to be made if sensible effect is to be given to it; for example, that any necessary planning permission to enable user for shopping or retail purposes has been given, and that any provisions in the underlease which might prevent such user or alteration of the premises for such user have been suitably varied or waived or appropriate consents given. These considerations do not, I think, advance the defendants' contentions. The clause requires one to assume that the areas in question, which are now used for hotel purposes, should be available for letting for shopping and retail purposes. Any question of contravention of planning control or of the provisions of the underlease goes directly to availability. I do not think that the premises are 'available' for a purpose if there are in existence lawful prohibitions, whether statutory or contractual, against the user of the premises for such purpose. But it seems to me that premises can be available for shopping and retail purposes irrespective of their physical condition. Availability, I think, does no more than assume that the premises are on offer with vacant possession and that they can be used for the specified general purpose without illegality or breach of covenant. The supposed new lessee may or may not need physical alterations of the premises to carry out the shopping or retail uses which he contemplates, but the premises are available for shopping and retail purposes, and it is a matter for the lessee how he utilises that availability. The degree of alteration which is appropriate will vary widely according to the precise nature of the user.

The defendants go on to contend, however, that the purpose of the clause is to protect the landlord against inflation, and that the purpose will be frustrated if every seven years the expert, in fixing the rent in respect of any part of the premises which are not, on the relevant date, used for shopping or retail purposes, will have to take into account the fact that a tenant would or might have to expend large sums on the premises to make them suitable for the shopping and retail purposes which he has in mind. I do not, however, think that that is a consideration which compels me to read words into this clause which are not there. No doubt the construction for which the tenant contends is financially less favourable to the landlord than the landlord's own construction, but it seems to me to be the ordinary meaning of the clause, and it can be given effect to without difficulty and without altering the language at all.

As to the protection of the landlord against inflation, I accept that such is the purpose of the clause, but what is it that is being protected against inflation? In the absence of clear language to the contrary, I would assume that it is the rental value of the landlord's premises in their actual condition for the time being. The rent review clause, on the plaintiffs' construction, achieves exactly that, it seems to me.

I cannot see any satisfactory basis upon which I should read in words to give the landlord the rental benefit of physical premises other than those actually contained in the underlease. You protect the landlord against inflation by reassessing every seven years the rent of the actual premises which he owns and not of other premises. I do not see why the landlord should get the benefit of assumed alterations which the landlord has not made.

6.8 A market rent may be automatically substituted for the existing rent

C.H. BAILEY LTD v. MEMORIAL ENTERPRISES LTD

Court of Appeal [1974] 1 WLR 728

A review clause provided that if on 21 September 1969 the market rental value exceeded the rent reserved in the lease 'there shall be substituted from such date for the yearly rent ... an increased yearly rent equal to the market rental value so ascertained'. In September 1970 the landlords gave the tenants notice that they intended to increase the rent in accordance with the provisions of the lease. The landlords claimed a declaration that they were entitled to increase the rent. Eveleigh J held that the market rental value on 21 September 1969 could be ascertained after that date had passed but that the increased rent only became payable on the quarter day after its ascertainment. The landlords appealed and the tenants cross-appealed.

Held: The appeal was allowed and the cross-appeal dismissed. The rent review clause should be construed according to its natural meaning, and that since the rent review clause provided for the increased rent, when ascertained, to be substituted from 21 September 1969, it was payable retrospectively from that date. *In re Essoldo (Bingo) Ltd's Underlease* (1971) 23 P & CR 1 overruled.

LORD DENNING MR: The time and manner of the payment is to be ascertained according to the true construction of the contract, and not by reference to out-dated relics of medieval law.

So I think these rent review clauses are to be construed according to their natural meaning. The clause in the present case says that the increased rent, when ascertained, 'shall be substituted *from* such date' that is, from 21 September 1969. It was, it is true, not ascertained until 23 March 1973; but, once ascertained, it is substituted *from* 21 September 1969. It must be paid *from* that date. I know this means it operates retrospectively. But that is the plain intention of the clause. And effect must be given to it.

It was said: suppose the landlords did not apply for the rent review for months or years after the date when they became entitled to it. Would not this operate unfairly on the tenant? In most cases it would not do so. The tenant has benefited because he has not had to pay the increased rent, and meanwhile he has had the use of the money, or, if he would have had to borrow it, he has not had to pay interest on it. But, if there was a case where the delay of the landlord did prejudice the tenant, then I should think the tenant might well pray in aid the principle of equitable estoppel to hold up the increase. It is to be remembered, too, that it is always open to the tenant himself to take steps to ascertain the increased rent. Howsoever that may be, I am quite clear that the case depends on the true construction of this rent review clause. Even though the increased rent was not ascertained until 23 March 1973, nevertheless it operates as from and is payable as from 21 September 1969.

6.9 Fixing a 'fair rent as between the parties' in default of agreement

This means as between the particular parties and the test will be subjective; see later, 10 (b) at page 224, *Lear* v. *Blizzard* [1983] 3 All ER 662.

Chapter 7

Common hypothetical assumptions and common words and phrases

Determining a rent on review may be subject to a number of common but hypothetical assumptions, and certain words and phrases have been judicially defined. For example, 'a reasonable rent for the demised premises' does not mean a rent which it would be reasonable for the tenant to pay in all the circumstances but a rent which was reasonable for the premises. (See further in *Ponsford and Others* v. *HMS Aerosols Ltd* [1979] AC 63 and *Cuff* v. *J & F Stone Property Co. Ltd* [1979] AC 87, see below under 'tenants' improvements' page 237, Chapter 12).

7.1 (a) Notional user and planning permission

Assumptions as to the use which may be made of the premises: the court is prepared to construe a rent review provision on the artificial basis that a hypothetical assumption must be made as to the use of the premises in order to determine the level of the revised rent with some certainty. Each case, however, will depend on the wording of the lease in question, and the following cases are included to give examples of the court's approach and attitude to these issues.

BOVIS GROUP PENSION FUND LTD v. G.C. FLOORING & FURNISHING LTD

Court of Appeal   (1984) 269 EG 1252

The rent review clause of a lease provided that the revised rent was to be at the current rack rental which was defined as

> 'the rent at which having regard to the terms hereof (other than as to rent and user) the demised premises might reasonably be expected to be let for office purposes without premium in the open market by a willing lessor to a willing lessee ...'

No planning permission had ever been given for the use of the building as a whole and the building was actually used partly as showrooms and stockrooms with ancillary offices and partly as offices. It was agreed between the parties that the revised rent of the premises should be £85,000 p.a. related to full office user or £75,000 p.a. if based on the actual user. The landlords claimed that the clause had to be construed on the basis that there was planning consent for the notional user, namely offices. The tenants contended that the actual user had to be taken at the time of the rent review. Lloyd J held that the landlords' contention of a notional planning consent should succeed. The tenants appealed.

Held: The appeal would be dismissed. The purpose of the rent revision clause was to provide for an upward revision with a reasonably certain formula enabling the parties to anticipate what the revised rent should be in the future. The review clause indicated that the rent was to be fixed by the yardstick of the going rate for office space in the area, which presupposed that the use was lawful and that there was planning permission granted for office use of the whole premises; such a notional assumption would present no difficulties for an experienced surveyor.

EVELEIGH LJ: Bearing in mind in this case that these premises at the date of the lease—and that is an important date to consider—were let for a variety of purposes to tenants holding subunderleases, it seems to me that the intention which emerges is to provide some yardstick that will lead to certainty when the day arrives in the future for the rent revision clause to be applied, and the parties chose as that yardstick something for which the premises were not in fact being used at the date of the lease, namely office premises. They were choosing in effect an agreed use, namely office use, as the basis for rent which was to be assessed in 10 years' time, and they envisaged, as I see it, for that assessment premises which would be in a state of being used as offices—and that must mean lawfully used: in other words, premises which had the character of office premises capable of being used as such—planning permission would be one attribute of those premises. In that way it seems to me the parties strove to achieve certainty. The clause indicates to me that the valuer has to assume that there are these premises in use as offices. The clause uses the phrase 'let for office purposes'. That, to my mind, is another way of describing the premises as office premises. The object is to value the premises on the basis that you are able to let them for office purposes. It seems to me that that is saying that we are concerned to determine the value of these premises as office premises. If estate agents were to advertise premises with an announcement, 'These valuable premises are to be let for office purposes' and stipulated a rent, that would convey, to my mind, to any prospective purchaser the message that he could lawfully use those premises for office purposes.

We are not seeking here to value a lease with a user clause permitting office use when in fact it may or may not have real office value, and the fact that a property can be let with a permitted purpose that requires planning permission does not, to my mind, show it is being let as such premises. It is a different case.

The appellants here say that the clause literally read means that you must take the premises as you find them, you must assume a lease which says 'for use as offices' *inter alia*, and you must take a lessee who takes the lease with a chance of obtaining planning permission, or maybe with the intention of obtaining planning permission, for use as offices. To my mind that produces uncertainty, which I cannot think that the parties to this lease ever intended, As was said in argument, 'They have chosen a yardstick, but it would be made of elastic'.

Note: This case was distinguished on its facts in *Daejan Investments Ltd* v. *Cornwall Coast Country Club Ltd*, see 6.3, page 119.

7.1 (b) 'Full current market rack rental value' and the hypothetical 'willing landlord' and 'willing tenant'

ROYAL EXCHANGE ASSURANCE v. BRYANT SAMUEL PROPERTIES (COVENTRY) LTD

Chancery Division   (1985) 273 EG 1332

A large warehousing estate comprising 32 units was let on a 99-year lease. At the date of the lease 18 units had been sublet, and all of them were sublet by the time of the hearing. The review clause provided that the revised rent should be '75% of the full current market rack rental value of the premises at the rent review date commencing such period'. The parties agreed that 'full market current rack rental value' meant the rent for which the whole premises would be let on a single lease by a hypothetical willing landlord to a hypothetical willing tenant for a term of years commencing on the relevant review date, and that such rent was to be fixed on the basis that the premises were being let with vacant possession and disregarding any sublease which was actually in existence at the time. A dispute arose between the parties because the landlord contended that the hypothetical tenant would probably be an investor seeking income from the sublettings of the units and therefore, to avoid, in effect, a double discount the rent on review should be 75% of the *gross* rents which the hypothetical tenant would receive from the subtenants, without further deductions such as costs, fees, expenses and profits etc.

Held: The landlord's contention was rejected. It was impossible to say that the clause was framed on the basis that an investor would be the lessee. In ascertaining the rental value of the premises, the expert should have regard to all likely tenants, whether or not they were investors or persons who wished to occupy all or some of the premises for their own purposes, and no-one should be excluded. The highest rent obtainable on this basis would be the 'full current market rack rental value'.

PETER GIBSON J: What the parties cannot agree is a fourth proposition put forward by Royal Exchange, as to the meaning of the expression 'full current market rack rental value'. In its final form the proposition advanced by [counsel] on behalf of Royal Exchange was this: 'the full current market rack rental value' means an aggregation of the market value of the individual units of the demised premises as they form part of the demised premises at the rent revision date, whether or not such units are sublet at that date, and no further deductions from such total sum for the purposes of landlords' costs, fees, expenses, profit or other matters may be made other than the 25% deduction allowed for in clause 6 (a) (iii). [Counsel for the plaintiffs] submits that the court should make a declaration in that form.

The reasoning underlying that submission is this. The demised premises consisted of a warehousing estate of 32 units, rather more than half of which were, at the date of the lease, sublet. On the hypothetical letting required by the rent-review clause, the hypothetical lessee would be likely to be an investor seeking an income from the subletting of the units. Such an investor would, in bidding for the demised premises, take account of the gross income receivable from the sublettings of the units and would not be prepared to pay to the landlord a rent equal to that gross income. He would want a discount therefrom to cover such matters as his own costs and expenses in making the sublettings, the risk that there might be periods when units were not let, the risk of defaults, and the lessee would want to make a profit on the transaction. The 25% discount must be taken to cover those matters. To avoid a double discount for the same matters, the full current market rack rental value must refer to the gross rent receivable by the hypothetical lessee from sublettings.

[Counsel for the plaintiffs] submitted that that proposition was justified, having regard to:
(1) the factual context for which he relied only on the facts as to the state of the demised premises at the time of the lease, which facts appeared in the lease;
(2) the context in which the phrase 'full current market rack rental value' appears in the lease, that is to say that it follows the words 'seventy-five per cent of'; and
(3) the use of the word 'full' which, it is suggested, meant 'undiscounted'.

[Counsel] for Bryant Samuel submitted that the words of the lease were clear and the position was simple. The 'full current market rack rental value' of the demised premises had its ordinary meaning of the rent which the hypothetical tenant taking the entire demised premises under a single lease would pay. It is for the expert to determine on ordinary valuation principles what that amount is. Once that amount is ascertained, Bryant Samuel must pay 75% thereof as rent.

Attractively though [counsel for the plaintiffs] presented his submissions, I am satisfied that [counsel for the defendants'] submissions are to be preferred. What clause 6 (a) (iii) requires to be ascertained first is the full current market rack rental value of the demised premises at the relevant rent revision date. The demised premises are the entire premises let by the landlord to the tenant, regardless of whether the tenant has in fact sublet all or any of the units forming part of the demised premises, as the parties are agreed that the premises are to be valued with vacant possession. It is common ground that the valuation exercise contemplated by the clause involves a hypothetical single letting by a hypothetical lessor to a hypothetical lessee. The value is measured by the rent payable by the lessee to the lessor on that letting. It is well established that the market in which such hypothetical letting takes place is the open market, from which no one is excluded. Investors seeking an investment income may well be in such market and will, no doubt, measure their bids having regard to the income they will receive and the costs, risks and profit to which [counsel for the plaintiffs] referred. But I find it impossible to say that clause 6 (a) (iii) was framed on the footing that an investor would be the lessee. Why should not the hypothetical lessee be a person wanting to occupy the whole or part of the demised premises for his own purposes when the lease itself expressly contemplates that the tenant might occupy the holding (clause 6 (b) (iii)) and might carry on business thereat (clause 6 (b) (iii))? In this context it must be borne in mind that the lease is for a term as long as 99 years and that the lease expressly contemplated that there might be changes both in user and to the state of the buildings, albeit only with the landlord's consent. The parties cannot be taken to have contemplated that, throughout the term, the premises would only be sublet by the tenant for warehousing use to provide the tenant with an income.

Note: In effect, what the landlord was trying to do was to introduce the realities of the factual situation into the hypothetical requirements of the review clause.

7.1 (c) 'Fair rack rent'

For a full discussion of the meaning of 'fair rack rent' which is 'payable' on review, see Chapter 8.2, *Compton Group Ltd* v. *Estates Gazette Ltd* (1978) 36 P & CR 148, CA and compare *Rawlance* v. *Croydon Corporation* [1952] 2 QB 803, and *Newman* v. *Dorrington Developments Ltd* [1975] 1 WLR 1642 which were distinguished.

7.1 (d) 'Fair yearly rent'

A 'fair yearly rent' does not necessarily mean fair between the particular parties concerned, but what a hypothetical tenant would fairly be expected to pay if taking premises from a hypothetical landlord.

99 BISHOPSGATE LTD v. PRUDENTIAL ASSURANCE CO. LTD

Court of Appeal   (1985) 273 EG 984

A review clause provided that the revised rent should be

'a fair yearly rent for the ... premises ... having regard to rental values current ... for property let without a premium with vacant possession and to the provisions of this lease ... The demised premises were a substantial modern tower block in the City of London.'

The arbitrator had before him evidence from both sides as to the levels of office rents but it was common ground that there was no precisely comparable building and the evaluation of rent payable for the whole building had to be approached on a floor–by–floor basis. The evidence showed it was unlikely that, if the whole building were vacant, that a tenant would be found who would require it all for his own occupation, and that the most likely lessee would be a tenant requiring a substantial part of the building for his own purposes who would sublet the remainder. The arbitrator made an award which did not allow for a rent-free period; he also made an alternative award which assumed the entire building was vacant and that a 16-month rent free period would be required to allow for marketing the excess space to prospective subtenants. Both parties were dissatisfied. The tenants appealed contending *inter alia* the alternative award should stand. Lloyd J allowed their appeal (1984) 270 EG 950 and upheld the arbitrator's alternative award. The landlords appealed.

Held: The appeal was dismissed. The arbitrator's task was to determine a fair yearly rent for the premises at the valuation date. Fair meant fair as between a hypothetical tenant and hypothetical landlord of similar large vacant office premises and not fair as between the particular parties involved. In determining the fair yearly rent the arbitrator had to have regard to hypothetical comparable property let without a premium with vacant possession. He had to have regard to the provisions of the lease other than provisions for rent. The arbitrator was not entitled to disregard the rent–free period which would be required to induce a letting of the premises when determining the sum for the yearly rent. The fact that he was calculating rent on a floor–by–floor basis made no difference.

Oliver LJ: [Counsel for the tenants] in his argument says: what one has to look at is the rental value of property let without a premium with vacant possession. It may be true that that is simply something to which you have to have regard, but you *are* compelled to have regard to it because the lease says so. You are compelled also to have regard not only to that but to the actual term of the lease.

The arbitrator agrees, apparently, as appears from the passage in his award to which I have referred, that had there been a comparable building which had been let recently with vacant possession, that would have been the best evidence of what the fair rent was. He says—and I do not think this can be controverted—that undoubtedly, if there had been such a comparable building and one which had been let recently, then the rental value would have to allow for a discount for any rent-free period which had been allowed to the tenant.

Why, then, [counsel for the tenants] asks forensically, should the court feel compelled to approach the matter on a different basis when, by necessity, the building has to be looked at on a floor by floor basis? One could put it in two ways. One could take the discount into account floor by floor, by allowing against the comparables a discount for a notional rent-free period for each floor; or one could take it into account, as the arbitrator did in his alternative award, at the end; and since what one is doing is in fact arriving at a fair rent not for each floor separately but for the building as a whole, the way in which the arbitrator approached it was the correct way.

At the end of the day, the point is a fairly short one and, I suppose, to some extent a matter of impression, but speaking for myself, I have come to the clear conclusion that the learned judge was right in the conclusion to which he came. The salient features of this clause, as it seems to me, are, first, that what has been fixed is the fair yearly rental for the premises as a whole; secondly, that 'fair', of course, means not 'fair' between these particular parties, circumstances being as they are, but what a hypothetical tenant would fairly be expected to pay if taking the premises from a hypothetical landlord. Thirdly, the lease directs that that is to be ascertained by reference to the vacant possession rental values of property at the relevant date. In other words, one has to look not at property generally but property of a particular type—let without a premium and with vacant possession.

I cannot see for my part that if one is compelled to have regard to that in arriving at a fair rental for the whole premises, one is then, as it were, entitled or obliged to throw that consideration away at the second stage when one comes to consider what the fair rental is.

For these reasons, therefore, I would hold that the learned judge came to the right conclusion, and I would dismiss this appeal.

Agreeing, **NEILL LJ** said: The arbitrator's task was to determine the amount which, in his opinion, represented a fair yearly rent for the demised premises as at what can conveniently be called the 'valuation date'.

In carrying out this task, the arbitrator had to have regard to two factors, to disregard two other factors, and to make an assumption about the covenants in the lease.

It is only necessary for me to refer to the words 'having regard to' in subclause 1 (d). First, the arbitrator had to have regard to rental values current as at the valuation date for a property let without a premium with vacant possession. Secondly, he had to have regard to the provisions of the lease other than the provision for the rent.

I accept [counsel for the landlords'] argument that the arbitrator had to look at the matter in two stages. He had to examine the evidence of comparables and consider the other criteria to which his attention was directed. Then he had to make his assessment of the fair yearly rental. But, as it seems to me, when making this assessment at the second stage, the arbitrator had to give full effect to the fact that the comparables to which his attention was directed were current rental values for property let with vacant possession. This was one of his guidelines, and I am unable to accept that the arbitrator, in determining a fair yearly rental, could adjust this guideline to eliminate the element which reflected the discount applicable to a rent-free period.

Note: Compare the meaning of fair rent as between the parties and a reasonable rent see Chapters 10.3 (a) and 11.4 (b) respectively.

But compare the decision in *Lister Locks* below which suggests that when construing the basis on which a 'fair rack market rental' should be determined on review, and where there is some uncertainty, there are cases where the court has regard to the history of the negotiations between the parties, as showing the commercial purpose of the contract, and the background and context of the transaction, notwithstanding the caveat given by Lord Wilberforce in *Prenn* v. *Simmonds* [1971] 1 WLR 1381, ([1971] 3 All ER 237 HL(E).)

LISTER LOCKS LTD v. T.E.I. PENSION TRUST LTD

Chancery Division   (1982) 264 EG 827

A 25-year lease of business premises provided for an initial rent which was made up of the sum of a 'Basic Initial Rent' and an 'Extra Initial Rent'. The rent review clause provided in effect that every five years the Basic Initial Rent should be reviewed so as to be equal to the fair rack rental market value of the premises, and that the Extra Initial Rent should be reviewed in the same proportion (the Extra Reviewed Rent). The tenant submitted that when the fair rack market rent was determined, the additional obligation to pay the Extra Reviewed Rent should be taken into account.

Held: The tenant's case failed. Notwithstanding the doctrine which restricts the extent to which surrounding circumstances can be brought in as an aid to ascertaining what were the intentions of the parties, a more liberal approach may be helpful where there were continuing negotiations and it was not possible to say at what stage a consensus was reached. There was here an exchange of letters which recorded the history of the term which ultimately appeared in the lease. However, the tenant's submission would fail because his construction would make nonsense of one of the lease's provisions, namely, in taking away with one hand what was given with the other. For, if the rent review of the basic rent was to take into account the obligation to pay the extra rent, that would result in a reduction of the figure which would otherwise be obtained; but once that figure was obtained, the formula for ascertaining the rent review of the extra rent required that figure to be taken into account, and it virtually made the rent review for the extra review of rent formula of little use. When regard was had to the background against which the lease was entered into, and the purpose of the 'extra reviewed rent', it was right and proper, and necessary to give business efficacy to the lease, to add in the words so as to exclude the extra rent review provision from the calculation of the fair rack rental value.

MICHAEL WHEELER QC (sitting as a deputy judge of the Chancery Division): On 9 December 1974, the defendants, T E I Pension Trust Ltd, let two units on a commercial estate, referred to as units 3 and 3a, at Ipswich, in Suffolk, to Howard Rotavator Company Ltd for a term of 25 years from 2 December 1974. On 27 March 1979 the original tenants assigned the residue of the lease to the plaintiffs, Lister Locks Ltd.

The summons before me concerns the true construction of the rent review provisions in the lease.

The yearly rent is expressed in clause 1 of the lease as follows:

'YIELDING AND PAYING THEREFOR yearly during the first five years of the term hereby granted the clear rents of Fourteen thousand nine hundred and eighty-two pounds (£14,982) ("the Basic Initial Rent") plus One thousand six hundred and eighty pounds (£1,680) ("the Extra Initial Rent") and after the first five years of the term hereby granted and every subsequent period of five years throughout the said term the fair rack rental market value as hereinafter defined together with the Extra Reviewed Rent as hereinafter defined or the rents previously payable under the provisions of this Lease whichever shall be the greater'

all such rents were to be paid quarterly in advance.

I should here add that clause 1 of the lease also provided for other payments, expressed to be by way of further rent or by way of additional rent in respect of insurance, interest on arrears of rent, and service charge ...

I hope I shall not be thought to be over-critical if I say that there are, on the face of it, minor defects in the wording of this proviso. It uses the words 'rent' and 'rents' more or less indiscriminately. It starts by dealing with a proviso for ascertaining the fair rack rental market value and then proceeds to use at least once a quite different term—'the current market rent,' and so on, but basically it will be seen:
(i) that the lease provides for a 'basic initial rent' of £14,982 per annum and an 'extra initial rent' of £1680 per annum for the first five years;
(ii) that for every subsequent five years the 'basic initial rent' is to be replaced by 'the fair rack rental market value' and the 'extra initial rent' by 'the extra reviewed rent', in each case 'as hereinafter defined';
(iii) The fair rack rental market value is to be ascertained in accordance with paragraph (ii) of the proviso, part of which I will read again, namely:

'... the best rent at which the premises might reasonably be expected to be let for a term of years equivalent to the then unexpired residue of the term hereby granted in the open market by a willing Landlord to a willing Tenant and'

and these are the critical words

> '*subject to similar covenants and conditions* (other than the amount of the rent) to those contained in this Lease ...'

I should here add that both sides agree that nothing turns on the use in the proviso to clause 1 of the term 'current market rent' in addition to the expression 'fair rack rental market value';

(iv) It will be seen from paragraph (v) of the proviso to clause 1 that once the 'fair rack rental market value' has been ascertained for any subsequent period of five years, '*the extra reviewed rent*' is merely a straightforward mathematical computation and (in respect of the first rent review, the one with which I am concerned) is simply the fair rack rental market value over the 'basic initial rent' multiplied by the 'extra initial rent'; in other words, the 'extra initial rent' is to increase in the same proportion as the 'basic initial rent'.

The question I have to consider is whether, in ascertaining the fair rack rental market value in accordance with paragraph (ii) of the proviso, one of the covenants and conditions which the valuer has to take into account is the obligation to pay the 'extra reviewed rent'.

The plaintiffs say 'yes'—and it is what the lease says—and the obligation *is* one of the covenants and conditions, and I must give effect to the unambiguous words of paragraph (ii) of the proviso to clause 1.

Not surprisingly, the defendants say 'no'. They argue that on a true construction the words 'subject to similar covenants and conditions (other than the amount of the rent) to those contained in this Lease' do *not* include the obligation to pay the 'extra reviewed rent'.

I should here emphasise that what I am concerned with in this case is construction and not rectification. That assumes an added importance because, as we shall see when I refer briefly to the authorities, if it had been a question of rectification, a good deal more would have been admissible in the terms of surrounding circumstances, and so on, than is permissible on a purely construction approach.

The defendants have three answers to the plaintiffs' claim for a literal approach. First they argued—perhaps a little faintly, but they put it first because if it was accepted it was conclusive—that the words 'other than the amount of the rent' exclude the obligation to pay the 'extra reviewed rent'. Secondly, they say, approaching the matter on what they call 'the interpretation route', that they achieve a similar object based primarily on the evidence of the surrounding circumstances as an aid to construction of the words used. Thirdly, alternatively, on what they call 'the implied term route' they say by necessary implication, in order to give business efficacy to the words actually used, we must infer some limitation on those words.

They only resort to the third of these lines if, by the interpretation route, it is not possible to give a secondary meaning to the actual words of the lease.

As to the first of their arguments—i.e. that the matter is decided by the words in brackets in paragraph (ii) of the proviso namely the words '(other than the amount of the rent)' as being sufficient to exclude the obligation to pay the 'extra reviewed rent'—I cannot accept this proposition. In my view, the words quoted are merely conveyancing over-caution. 'Amount', in my judgment, means what it says, i.e. initially £14,982 (the 'basic initial rent') and £1680 (the 'extra initial rent').

I propose to take the defendants' second and third points together because they turn, in one degree or another, on the extent to which I can properly take account of surrounding circumstances in construing this lease: before going to the facts I propose to touch briefly on the relevant principles which are sought to be applied as to which I think both parties are agreed. I start by reminding myself of the warning which appeared in *Norton on Deeds* and which was cited by Lord Simon of Glaisdale in *Wickman Machine Tools Ltd* v. *L Schuler AG* [1974] AC 235 at p 263, where he said this:

'There is one general principle of law which is relevant to both questions. This has been frequently stated, but it is most pungently expressed in *Norton on Deeds* (1906), p 43, though it applies to all written instruments:'

The quotation is here:

'"… the question to be answered always is, 'What is the meaning of what the parties have said?' not, 'What did the parties mean to say?' … it being a presumption *juris et de jure* … that the parties intended to say that which they have said".'

With that warning in mind, I now turn to two House of Lords decisions and to two opinions of Lord Wilberforce. The first is in *Prenn* v. *Simmonds* [1971] 1 WLR 1381, and I would emphasise that in the House of Lords this case was decided exclusively on the question of interpretation and not on rectification, although rectification has been widely argued in the Court of Appeal and at first instance, and, as Lord Wilberforce pointed out, that had let in a great deal of evidence which was not admissible on the construction point, but his opinion deals with the matter and decides the matter, as did the rest of their Lordships, purely on the basis of construction. The first passage I want to cite is from the bottom of p 1383 where Lord Wilberforce said this:

'In order for the agreement of July 6 1960 to be understood, it must be placed in its context. The time has long passed when agreements, even those under seal, were isolated from the matrix of facts in which they were set and interpreted purely on internal linguistic considerations. There is no need to appeal here to any modern, anti-literal, tendencies, for Lord Blackburn's well-known judgment in *River Wear Commissioners* v. *Adamson* (1877) 2 App Cas 743 at p 763 provides ample warrant for a liberal approach. We must, as he said, enquire beyond the language and see what the circumstances were with reference to which the words were used, and the object, appearing from those circumstances, which the person using them had in view. Moreover, at any rate since 1859 (*Macdonald* v. *Longbottom* 1 E & E 977) it has been clear enough that evidence of mutually known facts may be admitted to identify the meaning of a descriptive term.

I now pass to the second passage, which is on p 1384, where Lord Wilberforce said this:

'On principle, the matter is worth pursuing a little, because the present case illustrates very well the disadvantages and danger of departing from established doctrine and the virtue of the latter.'

That, I intervene to say, is the doctrine of restricting the extent to which surrounding circumstances can be brought in as an aid to intention. Lord Wilberforce continues:

'There were prolonged negotiations between solicitors, with exchanges of draft clauses, ultimately emerging in clause 2 of the agreement. The reason for not admitting evidence of these exchanges is not a technical one or even mainly one of convenience (although the attempt to admit it did greatly prolong the case and add to its expense). It is simply that such evidence is unhelpful. By the nature of things, where negotiations are difficult, the parties' positions, with each passing letter, are changing and until the final agreement, though converging, are still divergent. It is only the final document which records a consensus. If the previous documents use different expressions, how does construction of those expressions, itself a doubtful process, help on the construction of the contractual words? If the same expressions are used, nothing is gained by looking back; indeed, something may be lost since the relevant surrounding circumstances may be different. And at this stage there is no consensus of the parties to appeal to. It may be said that previous documents may be looked at to explain the aims of the parties. In a limited sense this is true; the commercial, or business object, of the transaction, objectively ascertained, may be a surrounding fact. Cardozo J thought so in the *Utica Bank* case ((1918) 118 NE 607). And if it can be shown that one interpretation completely frustrates that object, to the extent of rendering the contract futile, that may be a strong argument for an alternative interpretation, if that can reasonably be found. But beyond that it may be difficult to go.'

Before I deal with the third case I will just say this at this stage: when we look at the surrounding circumstances in the case before me, this is not as it seems to me, a case where such evidence of changing circumstances is unhelpful because there are continuing negotiations, and because you cannot say at what stage a consensus was reached. On the one vital point there is an exchange of letters which seems to me to set out a record in a convenient form of what ultimately found its way into the lease. I also bear in mind what Lord Wilberforce says about the commercial or business object of the transaction, because, as will be seen at the end of the day, one of the main reasons why I have come down in favour of the defendants in this case is because, as it seems to me, the plaintiffs' construction would largely make nonsense of a provision of the lease.

The third case to which I want to refer briefly is a passage in another opinion of Lord Wilberforce in *Reardon Smith Line Ltd* v. *Yngvar Hansen-Tangen* [1976] 1 WLR 989. The passage in question, which really re-emphasises what Lord Wilberforce said in the *Prenn* case, is at p 995. He says this: 'But it does not follow that, renouncing this evidence,' that was evidence said to show intention

'one must be confined within the four corners of the document. No contracts are made in a vacuum: there is always a setting in which they have to be placed. The nature of what is legitimate to have regard to is usually described as "the surrounding circumstances" but this phrase is imprecise: it can be illustrated but hardly defined. In a commercial contract it is certainly right that the court should know the commercial purpose of the contract and this in turn pre-supposes knowledge of the genesis of the transaction, the background, the context, the market in which the parties are operating.'

In order to apply those principles to the case before me, it is necessary to turn briefly to the facts of what I will still call the surrounding circumstances, though I accept readily Lord Wilberforce's statement that it is not a description of precision.

At the time of the negotiations in 1974 for the lease in the present case, the commercial development, of which plots 3 and 3a were to form part, was still in the planning stage. It followed therefore, that prospective tenants like Howard Rotavator were able to have special requirements of their own built into the basic plan. These included, in particular, additional office space, and the exchange between the parties which illustrates the background, which resulted in having a basic rent and an extra rent, is conveniently to be found in three letters to which I will now briefly refer ...

[The judge then went on to consider the correspondence and evidence before him relating to the facts of the case. He concluded:]

I simply do not begin to understand how a valuer, faced with a need to assess the fair market rent, is to take into account an obligation to pay the extra rent—I am not using the technical term—unless it be simply a question of subtraction. If there is some simple explanation of how this would be done, I would have been greatly helped if Mr Spettigue had said what it was, but on the state of the expert evidence as it stands, it does seem to me that the plaintiffs' construction of this lease must result, either in whole or in part—and, if in part, substantially in part—in taking away with one hand what is given with the other, because if the rent review of the basic rent is to take into account the obligation to pay the extra rent, that presumably must result in a reduction of the figure which would otherwise be obtained; but once that figure has been obtained, the formula for ascertaining the rent review of the extra rent requires that figure to be taken into account, and, as far as I can see, it virtually makes the rent review for the extra review of rent formula of little use. Certainly, when one sees the background against which this lease was entered into (which is not the subject of any doubt) and the purpose of the 'extra reviewed rent', it seems to me that if the fair rack rental value is to be ascertained on the basis of 'the covenants and conditions (other than the amount of the rent)' in this lease, it is right and proper, and indeed necessary, in order to give business efficacy to this lease, to add in the words—whether one does it by implying the term or by deriving it from the surrounding circumstances, in my judgment, matters not—which will exclude the extra rent review provision from the calculation of the fair rack rental value.

7.2 'Willing lessor' and 'willing lessee' as an abstract concept

Where a review clause refers to a willing lessor and a willing lessee it is important to distinguish between these abstract concepts and the actual parties concerned with their actual wishes and concerns etc.

F.R. EVANS (LEEDS) LTD v. ENGLISH ELECTRIC CO. LTD

Queen's Bench Division   (1978) 245 EG 657

The tenants occupied large factory premises under a 21-year lease. It gave both parties a right to require a review of the rent at the end of the third and twelfth years of the term. The tenant had the further right to determine the lease at the end of the fourteenth year of the term. An issue arose over the construction of the review clause at the first review date. The clause provided

'As from the end of the third year ... of the said term the yearly rental hereunder shall if either party so desires ... be revised so as to represent the full yearly market rental as hereinafter defined of the demised premises as they shall be at the end of the third ... year of the said term ... (assuming the premises to be fully maintained and repaired in accordance with the lessee's covenants in this lease contained).'

The full yearly market rental was defined as the rent at which the demised premises

'are worth to be let with vacant possession on the open market as a whole between a willing lessor and a willing lessee for the remainder of the said term outstanding at the end of the third or twelfth year of the said term ...'

The arbitrator made two alternative findings as to the level of rent, namely a maximum of £515,000 and a minimum of £290,000 p.a. Which, if either was appropriate depended on the assumptions which were to be made in assessing the full yearly market rental and in particular whether a 'willing lessor' and 'willing lessee' should be identified with the actual parties concerned.

Held: For the purposes of the review clause the 'willing lessor' and 'willing lessee' were abstractions. A willing lessor was an abstraction, a hypothetical person with the right to dispose of the premises on an 18-year lease. As such he was unaffected by cashflow problems or importunate mortgagees. Nor was he a person who could wait until the market improved before letting his premises. He was a lessor who wanted to let his premises at a rent appropriate to all market factors. Similarly, a willing lessee was a hypothetical person actively seeking premises to fulfil needs which the premises could satisfy. He would take account of market factors but be unaffected by liquidity problems, governmental or other pressures to boost or maintain employment in the area. This profile might or might not fit the tenant but it was not the actual tenant. It would be assumed that there was a hypothetical tenant bidding for the lease and the rent had to be determined at a figure which the hypothetical tenant—the willing lessee—would agree. However, the hypothetical negotiations were not to be conducted on the assumption that if the parties failed to reach agreement on the rent the hypothetical tenant would be free to occupy two or more smaller units as an alternative to the demise but the arbitrator should assess the reality of such an alternative option when fixing the rent. The appropriateness of the rent was to be judged in the light of all the circumstances of the case—other than those relating to the landlord and tenant as actual juridical persons—and that one of those circumstances was the rental values prevailing in the area. Any circumstances which affect the actual parties but which would not affect the hypothetical lessor and lessee were irrelevant. The possibility of the parties' failing to agree had to be disregarded. The decision supported the landlord's contentions more closely than the tenant's case.

On appeal, Donaldson J's decision and reasoning was upheld and approved by the Court of Appeal. The arbitrator made an award determining a rent of £515,000 p.a., following Donaldson J's decision.

DONALDSON J: Only a small part of the lease is relevant to a decision on this question of law. That part is as follows:

'4 (2) As from the end of the third year ... of the said term the yearly rental hereunder shall if either party so desires ... be revised so as to represent the full yearly market rental as hereinafter defined of the demised premises as they shall be at the end of the third ... year of the said term ... (assuming the demised premises to be fully maintained and repaired in accordance with the lessee's covenants in this lease contained).

4 (4) The full yearly market rental for the purpose of this lease shall mean the rent at which the demised premises are worth to be let with vacant possession on the open market as a whole between a willing Lessor and a willing Lessee for the remainder of the said term outstanding at the end of such third or twelfth year of the said term as the case may be upon the terms and conditions of this lease (excepting stipulations in this lease as to the amount of the rent but including like provisions as to rent revision from any later date herein specified) without any fine or premium being taken and there being disregarded:

(i) any effect on rent of any tenants or trade fixtures or fittings installed in the demised premises by the Lessee or any occupying tenant or of any improvement or additions carried out to the demised premises not more than twenty-one years before the First day of October one thousand nine hundred and seventy-six otherwise than in pursuance of any obligation under this lease.

(ii) any effect on rent of the fact that the Lessee or its tenant has been in occupation of the demised premises and

(iii) any goodwill attached to the demised premises by reason of the business carried on thereat.

The issue of law between the parties concerns the assumptions which are to be made in assessing this full yearly market rental as defined ...

Curiously there is no authority giving guidance upon how a rent review clause of this nature is intended to be operated. Despite the diligent research of counsel, all that has been discovered are authorities on rating valuation, compulsory purchase and taxation. These authorities are not irrelevant, but they apply only by analogy. In the circumstances, I propose to start by examining the instructions contained in the lease. The first, and most important, instruction is that the new rent is to be that which the premises are worth for letting on the open market with vacant possession on 1 October 1976. It is implicit in this instruction, and is expressed in the later part of clause 4 (4), that the tenants are to be deemed to have moved out or to have never occupied the premises. The second instruction is that the premises are being offered in their actual condition (subject to the assumption as to maintenance and repair) on an 18-year lease, having the same terms *mutatis mutandis* as the present lease. The third instruction is that there is in fact a rent upon which a willing lessor and a willing lessee could and would agree as being the rent which the premises were worth on 1 October 1976 for an 18-year term. This is implicit in the clause and is confirmed in fact by the arbitrator's alternative findings.

The first, and perhaps the most important, conflict between the parties is whether, in the application of the clause, the willing lessor is to be identified with the landlords and the willing lessee with the tenants. In a sense the willing lessor must be the landlords because only they can dispose of the premises, but for the purposes of the clause the landlord is an abstraction—a hypothetical person with the right to dispose of the premises on an 18-year lease. As such he is not afflicted by personal ills such as a cash flow crisis or importunate mortgagees. Nor is he in the happy position of someone to whom it is largely a matter of indifference whether he lets in October 1976 or whether he waits for the market to improve. He is, in a word, a willing lessor. He wants to let the premises at a rent which is appropriate to all the factors which affect marketability of those premises as industrial premises—for example, geographical location, the extent of the local labour market, the level of local rates, and the market rent of competitive premises, that is to say, premises which are directly comparable or which, if not directly comparable, would be considered as viable alternatives by a potential tenant.

Similarly, in my judgment, the willing lessee is an abstraction—a hypothetical person actively seeking premises to fulfil needs which these premises could fulfil. He will take account of similar factors, but he too will be unaffected by liquidity problems, governmental or other pressures to boost or maintain employment in the area and so on. In a word, his profile may or may not fit that of the English Electric Co. Ltd, but he is not that company.

Against this background I turn to the findings of fact in order to consider their relevance:

(a) The fact that there is no other property on the market which provides the accommodation and facilities provided by the Walton Works is certainly relevant. But its effect upon the negotiations has to be balanced by two other factors. First, while the hypothetical tenant is a willing lessee, he is not an importunate one. He wishes to take a lease of the premises, but he is operating in a commercial field and in deciding what to offer by way of rent, will take account, covertly or overtly, of the alternative of taking a lease of two or more other premises. This is not to say that he would prefer that solution. This will depend upon the level of rent which is under consideration. He is a willing lessee and is quite content to take the Walton Works at the right price. It is just that he is not considering the proposition or negotiating in a vacuum.

(b) The fact that the property could be subdivided and let in parts or sublet and the advantages and disadvantages of that approach are irrelevant. The clause contemplates a letting as a whole.

(c) The fact that it is very likely that English Electric Co. Ltd would have been the only potential lessee is relevant, but its relevance is indirect. It does not matter whether the only potential lessee was this company or the XYZ Co. Ltd. What matters is that in the state of the market there was not likely to be more than one willing lessee. But the effect of this fact is not decisive because this single potential lessee is to be assumed to be a willing lessee—neither reluctant nor importunate, but willing. Just as the hypothetical lessor cannot rely overmuch upon the fact that no property similar to Walton Works is available on the market, so the hypothetical lessee cannot rely too much upon the fact that he has no competitors—he is, and is known to be, a willing lessee. Furthermore, it is known that he will remain a willing lessee so long as the willing lessor does not press his demand for rent beyond the point at which he is ceasing to act as a willing lessor and at which a willing lessee would cease to be such.

If authority be required for the proposition that monopoly positions on either or both sides do not render hypothetical agreements impossible, it is to be found in *Tomlinson* v. *Plymouth Argyle Football Co. Ltd* [1960] EGD 330, a rating case, and in *IRC* v. *Clay* [1914] 3 KB 466, a taxation case.

(d) The fact that if the tenants had not been in occupation in October 1976 they would not have made any bid for the lease being offered is wholly irrelevant. I am quite prepared to accept that the tenants are most unwilling lessees. This does not matter. The arbitrator's concern is with the attitude of the hypothetical *willing* lessee, who is not in occupation of the premises. The clause assumes that there is such a person and it is nothing to the point to prove that there was not.

(e) The fact that the tenants in October 1976 could have split their operation into parts and could have moved those parts into smaller alternative premises in the United Kingdom is also quite irrelevant. It is irrelevant because it confuses the hypothetical lessee with the actual tenants. Certainly the hypothetical lessee would consider this alternative and it would affect the amount of the rent which he would be prepared to offer, but he would remain a willing lessee. The extent of the influence exerted by this alternative would depend upon the extent to which more than one lease and divided premises might be expected to increase his costs. And it is not English Electric's costs which come into the equation, but average and assumed costs of a hypothetical potential lessee.

I now turn to the respective contentions of the parties.

The tenant's contentions

(i) I accept that it is to be assumed that there is at least one hypothetical tenant bidding for the lease. Indeed I would go a little further than the tenants have gone. On the findings of fact, which were of course unknown to the tenants when their contention was formulated, the arbitrator would be justified in proceeding on the basis that, although there was one person who was willing to become lessee of the Walton Works, it was unlikely that there would be more than one.

I reject entirely the proposition that the potential lessee either is, or necessarily has any of the characteristics of, the English Electric Co. Ltd. He is a complete abstraction and, like the mule, has neither pride of ancestry nor hope of posterity. He is someone whose needs are such that, in relation to the Walton Works, he is a willing lessee.

(ii) I accept that the rent must be determined at an amount which the hypothetical tenant—the willing lessee—would agree. I do not accept that the person with whom he has to agree that rent is the landlord. Such a concept imports the personal circumstances of F R Evans (Leeds) Ltd. The willing lessee has to agree this rent with a hypothetical landlord—the willing lessor.

The negotiations are assumed to be friendly and fair, but, subject to that qualification, would be conducted in the light of all the bargaining advantages and disadvantages which existed on 1 October 1976. But these advantages and disadvantages are those which affected the property and any lessee of that property is merely one indication of the balance of advantage and disadvantage and by no means one which is necessarily decisive.

I do not agree that the hypothetical negotiations—or 'higgling of the market place' to use the delightfully archaic phrase which occurs in some of the authorities—are to be conducted on the assumption that if the parties failed to reach agreement on the rent, the hypothetical tenants will be free to occupy two or more smaller properties as an alternative to taking a lease of the Walton Works. The parties *will* reach agreement and the willing lessee will not take up any of the alternative options. However, in the course of the higgling, he will point out to the willing lessor, and the willing lessor will accept, that taking two or more alternative properties is a theoretically available alternative option, the relative advantage or disadvantage of which will be reflected in the rent which is ultimately agreed. In the absence of real higglers, it is for the arbitrator to assess the reality of such an alternative option, its relative advantage or disadvantage and the extent to which the new agreed rent would reflect those facts.

The landlord's contentions

(i) I accept that there is a person who is willing to take the Walton Works as a whole on the terms of the lease offered (other than rent), but I do not accept that that person may be the English Electric Co. Ltd. For the purposes of fixing the new rent, he is not.

I accept that this person is willing to enter into meaningful negotiations, much though I dislike the word 'meaningful', which in this context I take to mean neither more nor less than 'genuine'.

I accept that the negotiations are designed to arrive at the appropriate rent in all the circumstances which in fact affect the property and in theory affect the hypothetical lessor and lessee. I would not myself have used the expression 'fair rent' which, like 'meaningful', has in recent years been much bandied about in the political arena and may have become distorted in the process. However, I do accept that the appropriateness of the rent is to be judged in the light of all the circumstances of the case—other than those relating to the landlord and tenant as actual juridical persons—and that one of those circumstances is the rental values prevailing in the area. There are, of course, many others. The rent for which each is negotiating is that which is high enough to be acceptable to a willing lessor and low enough to be acceptable to a willing lessee. In the hypothetical life of hypothetical higglers, there is always one rent and never more than one rent which meets these criteria. If the arbitrator is heard to murmer 'Oh happy hypothetical higglers' this is only too understandable. He has my sympathy.

(ii) I do not agree that the rent is one which F R Evans (Leeds) Ltd would agree. The person who has notionally to agree the rent is the hypothetical willing lessor.

I accept that the rent has to be agreed in the light of all the circumstances which in fact affect the property and in theory affect the hypothetical lessor and lessee. Any circumstance which affects the actual landlord and the actual tenant, but which would not affect the hypothetical lessor and lessee is irrelevant. I agree that these circumstances include, but stress that they are not limited to, the fact that it is unlikely that there will be more than one willing lessee and that in October 1976, which was the relevant date, there was no other property on the market which provided the accommodation and facilities provided by the Walton Works.

I also agree that the possibility of the parties' failing to reach agreement is to be disregarded—to borrow and adapt an immortal phrase 'We are not interested in the possibilities of a failure to reach agreement. They do not exist.' But as the negotiations proceed each will be considering whether it would not be better at a given level of rent to break off the negotiations. True it is that they will resist these temptations, but the extent to which they operate upon their respective minds will be reflected in the rent which will, notionally, be agreed in the end.

My comments on the respective contentions of the parties have involved some degree of repetition because these contentions overlap in some respects. For this I apologise. It will be seen that I do not wholly agree with either party's contentions and in some ways my disagreement is as much or more with what is omitted than with what is included.

I have been much pressed to decide in favour of one or other contention as this would avoid a remission to the arbitrator with some degree of further delay and expense. However, what is at stake is £225,000 per annum for a period of nine years—over £2m. I am inclined to think that the views which I have expressed tend to support the landlord rather that the tenant, but I cannot be sure that the arbitrator would adhere to his provisional assessment of £515,000 per annum if he were to read and apply those views. Justice therefore requires that the award be remitted to him for the making of a final award. Let me stress that he is completely free to adhere to the figure which he previously thought was appropriate or to substitute any other figure. He has heard all the evidence and I do not contemplate that he will require further evidence or argument, although I do not wish to fetter his discretion in any respect.

I therefore answer the question of law by holding that it is not correct to adopt wholly the contentions of either party and that, within the scope of disagreement indicated by the special case, the assumptions which should be made are those set out in this judgment.

7.3 (a)   Narrow user clauses

Where the review clause requires the market rent to be fixed on the basis of open market rental with vacant possession, and the premises are, in fact, let to a particular tenant with a user clause which restricts use of the premises only to that named tenant's offices, the review clause has to be construed on the footing that the rent was to be the highest obtainable from any hypothetical lessee, and there would be no point in offering vacant possession to the hypothetical lessee if the premises could only be used for the named tenant's business. Therefore, the hypothetical lease necessarily had the name of the hypothetical lessee in blank as a party with the user's name equally blank.

THE LAW LAND COMPANY LTD v. CONSUMERS' ASSOCIATION LTD

Court of Appeal   (1980) 255 EG 617

The review provisions of a lease provided for the revision of the rent to a market rent on the hypothesis of a tenant offering the open market rental with vacant possession on the terms of the lease, including the user clause, which prohibited the use of the premises other than as the offices of the Consumers' Association. The appellant tenant argued that the review had to be carried out on the basis that the appellant, the Consumers' Association, was the only possible prospective tenant. The judge held that the hypothetical tenant was not restricted solely to the appellant.

Held: The appeal was dismissed. The identity of the tenant in the user clause could not be ascertained until the hypothetical new tenant was identified. Accordingly, the review should be on the basis that the premises could only be used by the hypothetical tenant, who could be anybody, and whose name could then be entered in the user clause. Applied in *Jefferies and Others* v. *O'Neill and Others* (see later, page 167) and *Sterling Law Office Ltd* v. *Lloyds Bank PLC* (1984) 271 EG 894 (page 170).

TEMPLEMAN LJ: The question is whether, in valuing the market rent as defined by the rent review clause, the valuer must assume that the demised premises may be let to anyone, or must assume that the demised premises can only be let to the present tenants, the Consumers' Association or their associated organisations. The statement of the question indicates the answer.

By the lease dated 10 December 1972, the respondent plaintiff landlord, the Law Land Co. Ltd, demised the premises 13-14 Buckingham Street, Strand, London, to the appellant defendants, Consumers' Association, from 25 March 1973 for a term of 15 years. Consumers' Association is a company limited by guarantee. The rent reserved by the lease was £55,400 per annum, subject to provisions for rent review. The lease referred to the parties to the lease as 'the Lessor' and 'the Lessees,' and by clause 3 (2) (a) those expressions, where the context so admits, are deemed to include the persons deriving title under them respectively. By clause 2 (11) (b) the tenants covenanted not, without the prior written consent of the landlord, to use or permit the demised premises or any part thereof to be used, other than as offices of the Consumers' Association and its associated organisations. Clause 3 (5) conferred on the landlord a power which was exercised and requires a revision of the rent from 25 March 1978, and provides a similar power of revision exercisable on 25 March 1983. The rent, from each revision date, shall be whichever is the greatest of (a) the rent payable immediately before the revision date; (b) a rent equal to the market rent; and (c) the initial rent of £55,400 per annum. By clause 3 (8) and in the events which have happened, the market rent falls to be determined by a surveyor who has been appointed for that purpose.

The object of a rent revision clause is to enable the landlord to obtain the market rent; that is to say, the highest rent anyone is willing to offer at the reversion date. I expect therefore to find that the market rent mentioned in clause 3 (5) is not greater or less than the landlord would have been able to obtain and would have been willing to accept on the relevant revision date from anybody who required the premises for his own use for office purposes.

Clause 3 (5), paragraph (a) (iii), defines the market rent; it means the yearly rent at which the demised premises, fully repaired in accordance with the provisions of the lease, might reasonably be expected to be let in the open market with vacant possession by a willing lessor for the then remainder of the term thereby granted without taking a premium, and subject to the provisions of the lease other than the rent thereby reserved, there being disregarded any of the tenants' goodwill and any of the tenants' improvements. That clause envisages the existence of an open market, an offer with vacant possession, a willing lessor and, by implication, a willing lessee. The rent review clause of the lease requires the tenants to pay from the reversion date a rent as high as the landlord could obtain from any hypothetical lessee on the reversion date, on the footing that the hypothetical lessee was competing in the open market and would be given vacant possession. There would be no market rent or open market if the premises could not be used by the hypothetical lessee, and there would be no point in offering vacant possession to the hypothetical lessee if the premises could only be occupied and used by the Consumers' Association and its associated organisations before and after the grant of the hypothetical lease to the hypothetical lessee.

[Counsel] on behalf of the tenants, submitted that the provisions of the hypothetical lease must be identical with the provisions of the actual lease and therefore that the hypothetical lessee will be subject to a covenant in the terms of clause 2 (11) (b) not, without the prior written consent of the landlord, to use the premises otherwise than as offices of the Consumers' Association and its associated organisations. [Counsel for the tenants] put his point forcefully and logically by saying that all one does is to copy out the whole words of the lease in a hypothetical form. But it is not possible to copy out the hypothetical lease until one knows the identity of the hypothetical lessee. In the same way as clause 2 (11) (b) could not have been completed originally until the name of the lessee was known, so in my judgment that clause cannot be completed in the hypothetical lease until the name of the hypothetical lessee is known. As [counsel] for the landlord, submitted, the hypothetical lease necessarily has the name of the hypothetical lessee in blank as a party, and clause 2 (11) (b) must likewise be in blank, just as the draft of the original lease was in blank in its inception. In my judgment the submission made by [counsel for the tenants] on behalf of the tenants is inconsistent with the references in the rent review clause to 'market rent', 'open market' and 'vacant possession', and produces results which are both incredible and unworkable. If the hypothetical lease contains a provision that the demised premises can only be used by Consumers' Association and its associated organisations, no hypothetical lessee could, or would, agree to take such a lease from the landlord without first procuring a binding agreement by the tenants to take an underlease for substantially the whole term at a rent higher than the rent payable by the hypothetical lessee to the landlord. But Consumers' Association would not be willing to pay an underlessee of the hypothetical lessee a higher rent than they would be willing to pay the landlords as hypothetical lessees themselves.

[Counsel for the tenants] was driven to concede that if the tenants' construction of the rent review clause were correct, the rent determined by the valuer is the rent which the landlord would be willing to accept and the tenants, Consumers' Association, would be willing to pay for the demised premises at the revision date. The surveyor is to determine what rent the landlords and the tenants would agree after negotiations between them and between them alone. I do not understand how the surveyor could arrive at a market rent, or any other rent, in these circumstances.

[Counsel for the tenants] suggested that the surveyor might first assess the rent which would be payable by a hypothetical lessee if he were permitted to use the premises for his own offices; in other words, a rent for a lease which was not on offer. But then [counsel for the tenants] submitted that the surveyor might, or would, or ought to make a discount from this rent, which to my mind is the market rent, in order to give effect to the fact that only Consumers' Association could use the premises. The discount, it was submitted, might take into account Consumers' Association's capacity to pay the true market rent according to its financial position; the surveyor might also take into account whether Consumers' Association required larger or smaller premises, or whether these premises were just right for them during the remainder of the term, and if he found that Consumers' Association might require larger or smaller premises, then in some way, and for some reason which I am quite unable to understand, the discount he would then make on the true market rent would be higher than it would be if the demised premises were exactly suitable in size and facilities for the business of Consumers' Association and so remained until the year 1985. [Counsel for the tenants] did not accept that the market rent payable by Consumers' Association should be the rent which Consumers' Association would have to pay on the open market in the neighbourhood to secure equal comparable premises on the revision date.

It is quite plain that neither the landlord nor the tenants could have intended that the rent should vary according to the capacity of the tenants to pay or according to the requirements of the tenants for accommodation; the language of the rent review clause is not apt to produce this result, and in my judgment any assessment of a rent which the landlord and the tenants would agree on the revision date must be hopeless speculation even though carried out by an experienced valuer grimly determined to do his best ...

[After considering some authorities, Templeman LJ continued:]

There is, moreover, this further objection: If [counsel for the tenants] is right, the whole of this rent review clause, with all its references to market rent, an open market and vacant possession, really only amount to this, that the parties have agreed that the revised rent should not be less than the rent which the landlord and the tenants would agree on the revision date, or the rent which the surveyor determines that they would have agreed. I find it impossible to construe clause 3 (5) as having that meaning, and I have no doubt that if the parties had been asked to sign a lease which plainly said that, each would have refused to do so.

[Counsel for the tenants] submits that the landlords are protected because they cannot receive less than the initial rent of £55,400, and thus if the surveyor determines that Consumers' Association would only be prepared to pay a peppercorn rent, the landlord is protected. But the rent review clause is designed to achieve a higher rent for the landlord; the existence of the guaranteed minimum rent of £55,400 cannot affect the true construction of the rent review clause itself and in my judgment this clause is designed to obtain for the landlord a higher rent, not in accordance with the subjective unknown bargaining between this particular landlord and these particular tenants, but by reference to comparable properties being let to anybody in the market-place. As I have indicated, the result of the tenants' construction is inconsistent with any rational intention on the part of the landlord and the tenants; it is inconsistent with the obvious object and intention of this common form rent revision clause; it is inconsistent with the language of the rent revision clause itself, and in particular with the reference to market rent and open market. On the other hand, the clause works perfectly well if the provisions which have to be included in the hypothetical lease are the provisions set forth in the original lease with the necessary modification that the name of the lessee will be different and therefore the name in clause 11 (b) will be different. Once that is accepted then it seems to me that the lease, including the rent review clause, makes good sense and there is no difficulty, either for the surveyor or for the court.

Whitford J held that clause 2 (11) (b) in any event allowed an assignee of the tenants to use the demised premises as offices for that assignee. [Counsel] who appeared for the landlord, sought to uphold this conclusion. He and the learned judge relied on the provisions of clause 2 (13), which contains complicated provisions regarding assignments and underlettings. He said, with force, that clause 2 (13) is only consistent with the possibility of assignments and underlettings to assignees and subtenants who are third parties; that is to say, persons who are not the Consumers' Association and are not associated organisations of Consumers' Association itself; and, as he says, clause 2 (13) points towards permitted assignments and underlettings which cannot be unreasonably refused by the landlord, and it must follow that clause 2 (11) (b) cannot have been intended to prevent assignees or subtenants who are third parties from using the demised premises as the offices of those third parties. I acknowledge the force of this submission and the incongruity of the fact that the combined effect of clause 2 (11) (b) and clause 2 (13) is that in effect the landlord can refuse consent to an assignment or underletting to a third party, whether reasonably or unreasonably, simply by making it clear that the landlord will not consent to any change of user. However, clause 2 (11) does not use the expression 'lessee' which the landlord deliberately defined to include the Consumers' Association and persons deriving title from the Consumers' Association, but with deliberation uses the words 'Consumers' Association and its associated organisations.' I find it impossible to construe this clause as though it applied to assignees and subtenants who are third parties, and if and so far as there is any incongruity and conflict between clause 2 (11) (b) and clause 2 (13), it must be the landlord who suffers for present purposes by drawing the confines of clause 2 (11) (b) so tightly that in effect he has destroyed the force of some of the provisions of clause 2 (13), but he has perfectly plainly said and stipulated that under this original lease there shall be user only by the Consumers' Association and its associated organisations. He has said that because they, the Consumers' Association, are the original lessees under the lease and, for the reasons I have already given, when it comes to a rent review the revision is in respect of a hypothetical lease in which the original hypothetical lessee will be subject to a covenant whereby the premises can only be used as offices for the purposes of that hypothetical lessee and its associated organisations, if any.

In these circumstances, being in favour of [counsel for the tenants] on the question of the construction of clause 11 (b), I need not consider the authorities which he cited and in which the courts have, for the most part, declined to allow the provisions of an assignment clause impliedly to revoke or modify the provisions of a user clause ...

The learned judge made a declaration in accordance with the submissions made to him regarding the construction of clause 2 (11) (b) on its own; he declared that the provisions of clause 2 (11) (b) were effective to restrict user of the demised premises by an assignee of the defendants to use as offices of such assignee. As I have already indicated, it seems to me that that would be to contradict the plain words of the clause, and in my judgment that declaration ought to be set aside and there should be substituted the declaration which the appellants tenants seek, namely, that the provisions of clause 2 (11) (b) are effective to restrict, without the prior written consent of the lessor to other user, the user of the demised premises, both by the defendants and by any assigns thereof, to use as offices of the Consumers' Association or its associated organisations.

The second declaration that the learned judge made, consistently with his first, was that the surveyor, in determining the market rent under the lease, was required to determine such rent at which the demised premises might reasonably expect to be let in the open market, subject *inter alia* to a provision that the premises could only be used as offices of the lessee. By the expression 'lessee', I understand that the learned judge intended to mean the lessee for the time being, as in the lease; but for the reasons I have indicated, and on the true construction of clause 2 (11) and the rent review clause, it seems to me that declaration ought to be varied, and that it should read:

'... surveyor should determine such rent at which the demised premises might reasonably expect to be let in the open market subject, *inter alia*, to the provision that the premises could only be used as offices of the original hypothetical lessee, but not by his assigns or any other persons other than his associated organisations if any.'

It may be that counsel will wish to address us on the exact wording which the revised declaration should bear, in the event of my Lords agreeing with my general conclusions, which in sum, for the reasons I have given, are that the rent review clause requires the surveyor to assume that the open market hypothetical lessee would become entitled to a lease in the form of the existing lease, save that his name would be substituted for the name of Consumers' Association in the opening words of the lease, and that his name would be substituted for the words 'Consumers' Association' in clause 2 (11) (b).

I would vary the order of the learned judge accordingly.

The order was varied as suggested. **BRIGHTMAN LJ** and **BUCKLEY LJ** agreed, adding: At one stage in the argument I was disposed to the view that what must be treated as offered on the open market under clause 3 (5) of the lease must be a lease subject to a restricted user clause in precisely the terms in which it is to be found in clause 2 (11) (b), restricting use of the premises or any part thereof to use as offices of the Consumers' Association and its associated organisations.

But that view must inevitably lead to the result, in the circumstances of this case, of there being effectually only one possible prospective hypothetical tenant, for the reference to 'associated organisations' does not, in my view, really affect that position, because organisations associated with the Consumers' Association would not be likely to be in competition with the Consumers' Association for a lease of these premises, and consequently they would not contribute to the making of a market in any real sense of the word.

The whole question really turns upon the meaning to be put upon the words 'subject to the provisions of this lease' in clause 5 (3) of the lease.

When one considers that the hypothesis upon which the clause is to operate is that the premises are vacant and that they are being offered on the market to a lessee who is prepared to accept them upon the terms of a lease tendered by the lessor, it is reasonable to suppose that the lease so hypothetically tendered will be a lease in which the name of the lessee will not be stated, because the assumption is that the lessee has not yet been identified. Also if the lease is to be a lease in the form of that with which we are concerned, clause 2 (11) (b) will necessarily be a clause in which the user covenant does not yet specify the name of the tenant which is to be inserted in that clause, although it will be drawn in such a way as to suggest that, when the identity of the hypothetical tenant has been identified, the name of that tenant will be inserted in the clause as the name of the Consumers' Association is inserted in the clause in the actual lease.

Construing the words 'subject to the provisions of this lease' in that way, it seems to me that a perfectly satisfactory method of operating the rent review clause in conjunction with the user clause is available, and I think so to construe the words 'subject to the provisions of this lease' is a perfectly legitimate way, in the circumstances, in which to read those words. It does have the remarkable consequence that the sub-clause which deals with, and controls, assignment of the lease is rendered really nonsensical, or practically so, for reasons which have already been indicated by Templeman LJ. But that, it seems to me, is the result of the lessor in the present case having used what appears to have been a common form lease, and using it in a way which has had that result. If the user clause confines use to use as offices of the Consumers' Association, it really is senseless to contemplate the Consumers' Association assigning to anyone other than perhaps an associated organisation while that restrictive clause is in operation, and there is no duty on the lessor to agree to any modification of the user clause to facilitate an assignment; so that the assignment clause is, to a very great extent, stultified by the user clause. But in my judgment that does not affect the appropriate way in which to construe the rent review clause.

7.3 (b)   Open market rent and implications necessary to give practical effect to bargain made by the parties

Where after prolonged negotiations a lease specified that the revised rent shall be at the open market rental the court must ignore the actual factual circumstances and the question of whether an open market valuation is in fact practicable, and make the necessary implications to give effect to the agreement.

JEFFERIES AND OTHERS v. O'NEILL AND OTHERS

Chancery Division   (1983) 46 P & CR 376

After detailed and lengthy negotiations the landlords granted the tenants, a firm of solicitors, a lease of first-floor premises adjoining the tenants' existing offices. While negotiations were on foot, the tenants had applied for planning permission, (available only for themselves), for the new premises. Access to the new premises was only at first floor level and through the solicitors' own freehold premises. There was no access to the demise save through the tenants' own building. The rent review clause, however, provided for the rent to be that at which the demised premises might reasonably be expected to be let on the open market by a willing lessor to a willing lessee. The tenants contended that the rent should be fixed on the basis that the premises could not be let to anyone else.

Held: Although the facts made the tenants special lessees, the lease, after detailed and lengthy negotiations had provided for an open market valuation, and the court would imply such terms as were necessary to give effect to the agreement made between the parties.

Law Land Co. Ltd v. *Consumers' Association Ltd* (1980) 255 EG 617 followed.

NOURSE J: For more than four years everything seems to have gone smoothly between the parties. However, on 11 July 1980, some nine months before the 1974 planning permission expired, the plaintiffs' firm applied with the knowledge and approval of the defendants for an unconditional extension of the existing permission. Possibly to the surprise of the plaintiffs' firm and the defendants, that application was granted on 24 September 1980. The result is that the permission to use the premises as offices is no longer personal to the plaintiffs' firm. The next material event was that on 4 November 1980 the defendants' agent wrote to the plaintiffs' side formally calling for a rent review as from 1 January 1981 in accordance with what the defendants then contended and now contend is the effect of the rent review provisions in the plaintiffs' lease. However, there soon emerged in correspondence between the two sides a fundamental dispute as to the construction and effect of those provisions. That dispute has now become the subject-matter of these proceedings ...

The lease provides that the rent for the second five years of the term shall be £2800 per annum or such greater yearly rent as shall become payable under the rent review provisions to which I have referred. Those are detailed provisions in a familiar form requiring the rent to be that at which the demised premises might reasonably be expected to be let in the open market by a willing lessor to a willing lessee with vacant possession and as a whole for the residue of the term outstanding at the commencement of the second five years, there being disregarded three matters which are also frequently disregarded on other exercises of that kind. Those provisions must be construed against the factual background known to the parties at or before the execution of the lease including first, the existing access through no. 753 alone; secondly, the removal of the staircase in no. 757 and the provisions of the staircase lease as to its reinstatement only if the plaintiffs' lease should for any reason come to an end other than upon terms for renewal in favour of the owners or occupiers of no. 753 incorporating terms for access to the upper floors through that opening; and, thirdly, the fact that the planning permission then in existence was personal to the plaintiffs' firm and might well have continued to be so.

Those three factors would seem to me to have invested the plaintiffs with the guise of very special purchasers, but none the less they and the defendants became parties to a lease containing elaborate provisions for the fixing of an open market rent as between a willing lessor and a willing lessee. It seems to me that, if the plaintiffs' contentions are correct, they will have the result of depriving those provisions of any practical effect. Indeed it is to be noted that the declaration they seek in terms requires the valuer to proceed on the basis that there is no open market at all. But, even if those words were to be struck out, the practical result would be the same. The lease might just as well have provided that the rent should be £2800 per annum or such higher rent, if any, at which the demised premises might reasonably be expected to be let by a willing lessor to a willing lessee who was already the occupant of no. 753. Even that might have been stating the area of choice too widely in view of the personal nature of the then planning permission. In any event, it would not to my mind have needed much imagination for the parties to conclude in 1976 that, if the defendants' only practical course in 1981 was to be taken to be to let the premises to the occupants of no. 753, whoever they might be, the rent then obtainable would be very much less than £2800. On that footing the lease could just as well have made provision for that rent to be payable throughout and it could just as well have omitted the rent review provisions altogether.

Is there any way in which such an apparently radical disregard of those elaborate provisions can be avoided and commercial efficacy given to the terms of the lease as they stand? [Counsel for the tenant] submits that there is. He says that the implication of terms into leases should be governed by precisely the same principles as the implication of terms into commercial documents of other kinds. It seems to me that on the authorities the law has certainly arrived at a position where that is so. On the other hand, [counsel for the landlord] submitted with some force that, in the case of leases, the approach should be somewhat cautious since, so far at any rate as knowledge of background facts is concerned, those are matters which can only be within the knowledge of the original parties to the lease and cannot be assumed to be within the knowledge of assignees of the term or the reversion respectively.

In the present case, [counsel for the tenant] submits that there is a simple and obvious implication to be made, namely that to the three matters which the valuer is to disregard there should be added a fourth. He says that there should be disregarded any effect upon rental value caused by the existing access via no. 753 at first-floor level and the absence of a staircase or any other means of access from the ground floor of nos 757 and 757A. In support of that contention, [counsel for the tenant] relies strongly on the fact that the correspondence shows that the original rent of £2800 was fully negotiated between agents on both sides and moreover without regard to the access from no. 753 and the lack of it from nos 757 and 757A. That submission is one which I find to have been made out on the fact. [Counsel for the tenant] then submits that, when the parties referred to an open market rent in the lease, they must have intended that it should be one arrived at by a similar hypothetical process of negotiation. I have not found this an entirely easy question to decide. Had it not been for the decision of the Court of Appeal in *The Law Land Co. Ltd* v. *Consumers' Association Ltd* (1980) 255 EG 617 I think I might have had some difficulty in acceding to [counsel for the tenant's] submissions. But in that case the court did, in order to give commercial efficacy to a very comparable rent review provision in a lease, make an implication of what seems to me to be the same character as that for which the defendants contend in the present case. It is true that in the *Law Land* case the implication was of a different kind. It required an extension of the user provision so as to incorporate the name of the intending hypothetical lessee for the purpose of the rent review provision as well as being a party to the hypothetical lease. In the present case, on the other hand, the implication sought would require an amendment and—let it be said—a substantial amendment to the rent review provision itself by adding an additional matter to be disregarded by the valuer.

[Counsel for the landlord] advanced an argument to the effect that for me to go in this case as far as the defendants ask me to go would involve going very much further than the Court of Appeal went in the *Law Land* case. I think it is possible that I am going further, but it seems to me that I am not going further than is permitted by the principle on which the Court of Appeal proceeded in that case. They thought that the important question was whether, as Brightman LJ put it at p 623, column 1: 'Some modification has to be made to the strict wording of the rent review clause if it is to work.' All three judgments, in particular perhaps that of Buckley LJ, make it clear that an implication can be made only if the rent review provision will not work without it. What [counsel for the tenant] is really saying in this case is not that the rent review provision will not work without his implication but that it will not have any practical effect without it. It seems to me, however, that that comes to the same thing as saying that the rent review provision will not work without it. I have already indicated why I think that, if the plaintiffs are right in this case, it will result in the rent review provision not having any practical effect. It seems to me that their contention would result in the whole of the rent review provisions, which occupy nearly two pages of the lease, being not much more than waste paper. Further, it seems to me clear on the facts and on the terms of the lease as a whole, and even with the caution which [counsel for the landlord] properly advocated, that the only implication which can and ought to make is that for which the defendants contend. On that ground I will make whatever counter-declaration is appropriate to reflect the view which I have expressed.

I should add that the originating summons seeks an alternative declaration that determination of the rental value as directed by the lease is impossible of performance. In order to obtain that declaration, the plaintiffs would have to show that the rent review provisions were void for uncertainty. That is an argument which appears to have been raised at an initial stage of some of the other cases to which I was referred, but in at least one of them the court pointed out that it would have to be a very strong case for it to arrive at such a conclusion. In the event, [counsel for the landlord]—very rightly, in my view—did not press that point.

7.3 (c) 'Market rent' synonymous with 'open market rent' in the context of review provisions

There is no difference between the meaning of 'open market rental' and 'market rental' in the context of rent review provisions

STERLING LAND OFFICE DEVELOPMENTS LTD v. LLOYDS BANK PLC

Chancery Division   (1984) 271 EG 894

A 42 year lease of business premises (drafted in a relatively unsophisticated form), provided that for the remaining 21 years of the term the rent should be *inter alia* 'equal to the market rental for the demised premises with vacant possession'. A covenant in the lease provided that the premises were not to be used for any purposes 'other than as a branch of Lloyds Bank Ltd.' The tenants submitted that for the purposes of the review the terms of the lease for the last 21 years would be in fact the terms on which the tenants, Lloyds Bank, would occupy the premises for that period.

Held: The tenant's submission would be rejected. The restriction on user should be construed as relating to the user of the hypothetical willing lessee so that the user covenant would be read as a blank to be filled in when the hypothetical lessee's business was known. *Law Land Co. Ltd* v. *Consumers' Association Ltd* followed.

HARMAN J: The underlease was made on 11 March 1962 between Ringway Properties South Ltd (described as 'the landlords') and the tenant (described as 'the lessees'). It has not been explained, nor is it necessary so to do, how the reversion comes to be now vested in the landlord, but that it is so vested is common ground. The descriptions of the parties in the underlease do not include any reference to successors or assigns, but clause 9 on p 16 of the underlease declares that those descriptions shall include successors and assigns unless the context requires a different construction. The underlease is for a term of 42 years from Christmas Day 1960, so it was, even in those days, for a long term. The rent reserved by the *reddendum* is, omitting irrelevant parts:

'YIELDING AND PAYING ... unto the Landlords during the first TWENTY ONE YEARS of the said term ... the yearly rent of ONE THOUSAND SEVEN HUNDRED AND SIXTY NINE POUNDS and thereafter and during the remainder of the said term ... the yearly rent as provided by Clause 7'

On turning to clause 7 on p 16 of the underlease, one finds the following terms, omitting irrelevant words:

'THE yearly rent to be paid by the Lessees during the last 21 years of the said term shall be the greater of (a) One thousand seven hundred and sixty nine pounds or

(b) an amount equal to the market rental for the demised premises with vacant possession'

Thus one sees that this is an early example of a rent review clause based upon market rental.

Nowadays, of course, rent review clauses are very familiar. They are drawn in elaborate terms, making provision for all sorts of possible questions. They are set out in the precedent books at great length and they are the subject of such litigation. This clause, by contrast, is in the very simplest terms, as was perhaps natural in those early days. The rent is to be 'an amount equal to the market rental for the demised premises with vacant possession'. Any person practising nowadays in the field of landlord and tenant will at once think of a number of questions as to the meaning of these artless phrases; for example: In what state are the premises assumed to stand—as they in fact are at the date of review, in proper repair or in some other, and what, state? For what term are the premises to be assumed to be available—for 21 years or some other term? On what conditions are the premises offered for letting—as [counsel for the plaintiff] expressed it in the originating motion on the 'usual' covenants, on the covenants in the underlease, or on some other, and, if so, what, covenants? The lease offers no express answer to any of these questions.

[Counsel for the plaintiff landlord] submitted that the court had to construe the words used in the context of this lease as a whole, but must not add words or imply terms unless it was *necessary* so to do. He referred me to the tenant's covenants in clause 4 (9) (a) of the underlease, whereby the user is defined as 'not ... for any purposes other than as a branch of Lloyds Bank Ltd'. He referred me also to clause 4 (22) (a) and (b), whereby the tenant covenanted (in fairly usual terms), firstly, not to underlet part of the premises at all, and, secondly, not to underlet the whole of the premises without consent which was not to be unreasonably withheld. These two covenants produce a familiar difficulty: if the tenant proposes a respectable and responsible assignee of the whole of the premises, the landlord cannot refuse consent to the assignment, but, since the assignee must, almost by definition, be some person other than Lloyds Bank, the landlord can object to the assignee using the premises for the purposes of its respectable business, thereby wholly frustrating the assignment. No other particular clauses were referred to by [counsel for the plaintiff landlord].

His argument as to the arbitrator's duty was that the arbitrator was required by the terms of clause 7 (b) to determine the market rental for the demised premises with vacant possession. That must mean, he said, that the arbitrator had to make an assessment of what a hypothetical tenant would pay for these premises standing vacant on the particular date. In such a case, since the tenant is hypothetical, his, her or its name is not known and its business is not known. Therefore clause 4 (9) (a) must contain a blank, and the user covenant can only be read as 'the demised premises shall not be used other than as ...', only to be completed when the hypothetical tenant's business or name (if that, as here, describes the business) is known. He submitted that the length and covenants of the hypothetical letting should be the same as in this lease but only so far as such could be known to the hypothetical landlord. [Counsel for the plaintiff landlord] conceded that, on that basis, the arbitrator would have to fix the market rent for the premises for a term of 21 years, which, although formally assignable, would leave the landlord in a position to control absolutely assignments by means of the user covenant which could not be varied save at the landlord's wish. But that, submitted [counsel for the plaintiff landlord], is a letting which could occur in the real market and the court should stick where possible to real events.

[Counsel for the plaintiff] referred to the Court of Appeal decision in *Law Land Co. Ltd* v. *Consumers' Association Ltd* (1980) 255 EG 617. That was a case on a lease containing a rent review clause, and the user clause restricted the user to that of the tenants, the Consumers' Association, or their associates. The rent review was to be to 'the greatest of (a) the rent payable immediately before the revision date; (b) a rent equal to the market rent; and (c) the initial rent ...': see at the foot of col 1, p 617. Templeman LJ accepted the submission that the hypothetical lessee must be an unknown person and that the user covenant could not be completed until the letting was agreed upon. The learned lord justice, about two-thirds of the way down the second column on p 617 equates 'market rent' and 'open market rent' and sees no difference between those phrases. So also does Buckley LJ (at p 623, the first column, the third para of the judgment) accept that a rent 'properly described as a market rent' is the same as a rent arrived at after the premises had been offered on the open market. Brightman LJ emphasised that 'The lease is a commercial document and we have to find a commercial solution to the problem posed': see at p 623, the first column. All these observations were relied on by [counsel for the plaintiff] as indicating how I should decide this case.

[Counsel for the plaintiff's] final submission was that, there being no reference to improvements made by the tenant nor to the state of repair, the duty of the arbitrator was to inspect the demised premises, value them *rebus sic stantibus* and determine what a prospective tenant would pay for those premises for a 21-year lease assignable but subject to a user covenant tying the user to the tenant's business.

[Counsel] for Lloyds Bank, submitted that no valuation could ever be made without knowing the terms on which the property to be valued was to be disposed, that is to say, freehold or leasehold, the length of term, user and others. There were here, he submitted, as [counsel for the plaintiff's] motion raised the question, three possible sets of terms: first, on the terms of this lease; second, on "the usual covenants"; third, the terms likely to be available at the time of the valuation in the open market. He urged that the first was the correct implication, and that that meant all the terms of this underlease, including the user covenant as presently standing. The terms of this underlease would, he said, in fact be the terms on which Lloyds Bank would occupy them for the next 21 years; thus it was fair to both parties that those terms should govern the rent payable. He submitted that both 'the usual covenants' and 'the terms available in the market' were inherently uncertain, likely to lead to lengthy argument and could not have been contemplated by the parties when they made this lease in 1962.

He referred to *Ponsford* v. *HMS Aerosols Ltd* [1979] AC 63, where Lord Dilhorne and Lord Fraser both referred to valuations of premises 'if let on the terms of this lease' although the rent review covenant in that case contained no such express words. It is plain that the point now before me was not argued in *Ponsford's* case but was assumed. It is none the less some guidance as to what is the natural meaning of words such as these.

As to the 'usual covenants' test, he referred to Foster J's decision in *Chester* v. *Buckingham Travel Ltd* [1981] 1 WLR 96 to show that some of the actual covenants in this lease are directly at variance with the covenants there held to be 'usual'. [Counsel for the defendant] also pointed out the undoubted fact that the terms of the 'usual covenants' vary according to the times, and to the length and difficulty of ascertaining them. On this point, I am wholly convinced by [counsel for the defendant] that any valuation should, if possible, not be on the terms of the 'usual covenants'. I am also content to accept that the valuer should not be asked to determine what covenants might be expected in the open market at the date of valuation.

[Counsel for the defendant] then turned to the *Law Land* case. He submitted that the absence in the present case of the word 'open' before the word 'market' makes a substantial distinction from the terms of the covenant in the *Law Land* case. In my judgment, that point is unsound. I do not believe there is any difference between an 'open market rent' and a 'market rent'. I am convinced that the words 'market rent' are not by themselves apt to refer to a rent fixed within a closed or circumscribed market to which only certain bidders are admitted.

[Counsel for the defendant] also referred to the user covenant. In the *Law Land* case the premises were to be let as offices. Here, if the letting is to a hypothetical tenant, there is, until the business is known, no definition whatever of the use to which the premises may be put. It could be used as a shop, a bank or an office; and the rents payable could vary substantially. This is a more impressive point, but in my judgment it does not change the nature of the construction to be put on the words in clause 7. The result of there being a lease of these premises on offer, with no defined user clause, is that any lawful user of the premises may be a bidder for them, and his offer would be relevant in arriving at the market price. It is possible that user as a bank branch would provide a narrower market and perhaps thereby a lower level of rental competition than a market open to all lawful users. To that extent Lloyds Bank may have to pay a higher rent than if the market were confined to bank branches. But since the premises are to be assumed to be let with vacant possession, it seems to me inevitable that the user can only be controlled by express words in the hypothetical lease or by the general law.

I was shown the decision in *F R Evans (Leeds) Ltd* v. *English Electric* (1977) 36 P & CR 185. That seems to be a very special case turning upon most unusual facts, and I get no guidance from it for the purposes of this case, any more than did the Court of Appeal get guidance from it in the *Law Land* case.

In my view, [counsel for the plaintiff's] contentions are correct. I find the analogy between this case and the *Law Land* case compelling ...

No order was made as to costs.

The effect of the court's order on the motion was that the underlessees' covenant in clause 4 (9) (a) of the underlease would be assumed, for the purpose of determining the market rental, to read 'That the demised premises shall not be used for any purposes other than as premises of the hypothetical willing lessee'.

7.4 (a) Imperfect drafting and problems of construction relating to narrow user clauses

Where the wording of a review clause is unclear or confused as to the assumptions which are to be made on what user is to be taken into account for valuation purposes, the court may construe and/or amend the wording so as not to impose on a tenant an obligation to pay for a user he does not have and cannot require the landlord to give him; that the rent must be assessed on the footing that, apart from matters specifically excepted, the rent should be revised to bring it up to date on the same basis as the rent was negotiated when the lease was granted. Where there was a restriction on user and written consent was required from the landlord to amend it, there was no implied term that the landlord's consent to change of use would not be unreasonably withheld.

PEARL ASSURANCE PLC v. SHAW

Chancery Division   (1985) 274 EG 492

A lease of business premises with a very restrictive user clause contained a rent review clause which provided that the rent was to be ascertained 'taking no account *inter alia* of any restriction on the user of the demised premises as the landlord may from time to time permit'. The provision on its face and in the context of the lease as a whole was absurd and some adjustment to the wording had to be made to make sense of the provision. The landlord contended that the rent had to be fixed disregarding the restrictive user, and on the basis that there was provision in the lease that the landlord would permit change, while the tenant submitted that it had to be fixed on the actual restricted user permitted under the lease.

Held: The tenant's submissions would succeed. The result that the draftsman of the lease had intended, (but failed to express), was that the expert should leave out of account restrictions on the user of the demised premises which had from time to time been modified by the landlord to the extent of permitting a previously impermissible user. To attribute that meaning to the material provision of the review clause involved doing considerable violence to the language. It involved substituting for the wording 'apart from' the words 'to the extent of', which amounted to substitution for 'apart from' by a phrase with opposite import. However, such radical surgery as this was needed to make sense of the relevant provision. This conclusion was supported for two reasons: (i) it had to be assumed that when the lease was negotiated the rent was negotiated in the light of, among other things, the use which the tenant was entitled to make of the demised premises. The purpose of a rent review was, generally speaking, to enable a landlord to bring the rent originally negotiated up to date and to substitute for it the rent that the parties might have been expected to agree if the rent had been negotiated on the same basis as before, but in the light of market conditions prevailing at the time of the review and, of course for the shorter term then unexpired. The court should thus lean against a construction which required the rent to be fixed on revision to be ascertained without regard to the use which, under the lease, the tenant is to be entitled to make of the demised premises, unless that intention was spelled out in reasonably clear terms. Failing to do so could impose on the tenant to pay a rent for a user he did not have and could not require the landlord to give him; (ii) the words of exception 'as the landlord may from time to time permit' pointed to a permission not given by, but given subsequently to the lease. It was more natural to relate them to a modification of restrictions on the lease agreed by the landlord subsequent to the grant of the lease.

There was no implication that the landlord could not unreasonably withhold his consent to a change of use in the circumstances. Dictum of Megaw LJ in *Guardian Assurance Co. Ltd* v. *Gants Hill Holdings Ltd* (1983) 267 EG 678 approved; *Bocardo S.A.* v. *S. & M. Hotels Ltd* [1980] 1 WLR 17, at p 22, doubted.

VINELOTT J: (a) By clause 2 the landlord demised the premises to the tenant for a term of 15 years from 28 March 1978 at the rent there specified up to 24 March 1979, and thereafter at the rent there specified 'or such other rent as may from time to time become payable under the provisions of the first schedule hereto'.

(b) By clause 3 (14) the tenant covenanted not to use the demised premises for any of a very large list of specified trades or activities, which I do not need to cite because the clause ends with the general words: 'nor to use or permit or suffer to be used the demised premises otherwise than as a Typing and/or Language School or professional or commercial offices or as a showroom'.

(c) Clause 3 (27) contains covenants by the tenant relating to the planning legislation. By subpara (a) the tenant agreed to comply in all respects with the Planning Acts. By subpara (b) the tenant covenanted to obtain all such licences and permissions as might be required for the carrying out of any operations on the demised premises or the institution or continuance

'of any use which may constitute development within the meaning of the Planning Acts, but so that the tenant shall not make any application for planning permission without the prior written consent of the Landlord'.

By subpara (d) the tenant covenanted:

Notwithstanding any consent which may be granted by the Landlord under these presents not to carry out or make any alterations or additions to the demised premises or any change of use (being an alteration or addition or use for which the consent of the Landlord is required to be obtained and for which planning permission needs to be obtained).

(d) Para 1 of the first schedule provides for the rent to be reviewed at the expiration of every fifth year of the term. The rent is to be the full rack rent that would be obtainable for the demised premises fully maintained in accordance with the tenant's repairing and other review as between willing lessee and willing lessor, with vacant possession:

'taking no account of (i) any goodwill attributable to the demised premises by reason of any trade or business carried on therein by the Tenant or any underlessees (ii) any restriction on the user of the demised premises apart from such user of the demised premises as the Landlord may from time to time permit (iii) any improvements to the demised premises lawfully carried out by the Tenant or any underlessees with the consent of the Landlord other than improvements effected at the expense of the Landlord or in pursuance of any obligation to the Landlord whether under the provisions of these presents or otherwise and in all respects on the terms and conditions of these presents including the provisions of this paragraph',

the rent to be referred in default of agreement for the decision of an expert nominated by the President of the Royal Institution of Chartered Surveyors.

What immediately strikes the mind of the reader is that although the language of subpara (ii) seems at first sight to make perfectly good grammatical sense, that is to say, it is not a mere meaningless jumble of words, it is none the less on the face of it, at least taken in the context of Schedule 1, an absurd provision, which cannot have been intended by the parties. They cannot have meant what they have apparently said. The first limb of subpara (ii) up to the words 'apart from' requires the expert to leave out of account any restriction on the user of the demised premises. The following words require some permitted users to be excepted from the unlimited category of users, restrictions on which are to be left out of account. But if all restrictions are to be left out of account, all possible uses, permitted or not, can be taken into account.

[Counsel] who appears for the landlord, accepts, and I think rightly accepts, that the second limb cannot be simply disregarded as a senseless addition to the first limb. Subpara (ii) must be construed as a whole, and if, taken as a whole, no intelligible sense can be attributed to it, it must fall as a whole, a consequence which, I should add, is not one which has been urged on me by [counsel] who appeared for the tenant.

[Counsel for the landlord's] explanation of subpara (ii) is shortly as follows. He draws a distinction between clause 3 (14), which in terms permits specified uses of the demised premises, and other provisions, in particular clause 3 (27), which expressly or impliedly restrict the user of the premises, and which do not in terms permit a specified use. The restriction in clause 3 (14) he described as a purely contractual restriction, the restrictions in, in particular, clause 3 (27) being related to non-contractual statutory restrictions.

The latter restrictions are restrictions which, under subpara (ii), are to be left out of account in ascertaining the rent. But the restriction in clause 3 (14) does fall to be taken into account, because it answers both limbs of subpara (ii), being a restriction on the user of the demised premises, but one under which the landlord permits a specified class of user. So, while the expert can take into account the restrictions in clause 3 (14), he must assume that within the range of permitted uses there would be no restriction in the planning legislation as applied by clause 3 (27) to a change of use within the permitted range. I should say at this stage that the permitted use of the demised premises under the planning legislation does not extend to use as showrooms, which I understand would be its most profitable use, at least as regards the ground floor.

The obvious difficulty which faces this interpretation is that if that were the result aimed at by the draftsman, it is surprising that he did not simply say 'apart from (or except) the restriction in clause 3 (14)', which is the only one which in terms contains a specific exception from a restriction on the user of the demised premises. Moreover, this distinction he draws between contractual and statutory restrictions seems to me an artificial one in the context of this lease. In particular the last part of clause 3 (27) (b) (following the words 'but so that') is a contractual restriction fettering the right of the tenant to apply for planning permission to a change of use.

[Counsel for the tenant] submitted that what the draftsman had in mind, and failed notably to express, was that the expert should leave out of account restrictions on the user of the demised premises which have from time to time been modified by the landlord to the extent of permitting a previously impermissible user. To attribute that meaning to subpara (ii) involves doing considerable violence to the language. It seems to me to involve substituting for the words 'apart from' the words 'to the extent of', though the same result could I think be achieved by other equally radical alterations, some suggested by [counsel for the tenant]. [Counsel for the landlord] objected that this involves rather more than an addition to subpara (ii) of words inadvertently omitted or the deletion of words inadvertently left in. It requires the substitution for the phrase 'apart from' of a phrase having precisely the opposite import. I have none the less come to the conclusion that this radical surgery is necessary if sense is to be made of subpara (ii). There are two reasons which in my judgment together support this conclusion.

First, it must be assumed that when the lease was negotiated the rent was negotiated in the light of, among other things, the use which the tenant would be entitled to make of the demised premises. The purpose of a rent-review clause in general is to enable a landlord to bring the rent originally negotiated up to date and to substitute for it the rent that the parties might have been expected to agree if the rent had been negotiated on the same basis as before, but in the light of market conditions prevailing at the time of the review and, of course, for the shorter term then unexpired.

Looked at in that light I think the court should lean against a construction which requires the rent fixed on revision to be ascertained without regard to the use which, under the lease, the tenant is to be entitled to make of the demised premises, unless, of course, that intention is spelled out in reasonably clear terms. Otherwise, the effect of the review might be to impose on a tenant an obligation to pay a rent appropriate to a very profitable use, but one very obnoxious to the landlord, and one which he had been careful to forbid in the strongest possible terms—the effect, that is, of making the tenant pay for something which he not only has not got, but which he cannot require the landlord to give him.

The second reason is that the words of exception 'may from time to time permit' seem to me to point to a permission not given by, but given subsequently to, the lease. On [counsel for the landlord]'s construction, the words of exception point unequivocally to clause 3 (14), where the user permitted is permitted for the term of the lease. It seems to me more natural to relate them to a modification of restrictions in the lease agreed by the landlord whether expressly or by acquiescence, subsequent to the grant of the lease. The draftsman may well have felt some doubt as to whether, for instance, if the landlord, by letter or perhaps by an informal oral consent, permitted the tenant to use the premises for some purpose not within the terms of clause 3 (14), that permitted user would or would not fall to be disregarded and may have thought that the rent might fall to be assessed on the footing that the permitted user had to be disregarded (in that under para 1 the rent is to be assessed on the assumption that the new lease is in all respects on the terms and conditions of the original lease).

[Counsel for the landlord] submitted that the rent should none the less be assessed on the footing that the landlord could not withhold his consent unreasonably to a request by the tenant that he give his consent to the making of a planning application for a change of use requiring planning consent. He made his submission on two grounds.

First, he submitted that in clause 3 (27) (b) the words 'such consent not to be unreasonably withheld' should be implied. He relied in support of this submission on an observation of Megaw LJ in *Bocardo S.A.* v. *S & M Hotels Ltd* [1980] 1 WLR 17, where the learned lord justice said at p 22:

'It follows that the deemed proviso "such consent is not to be unreasonably withheld" applies only if and to the extent that the covenant or agreement in the lease, by its terms, provides for assignment with consent. Such a provision would, in strict law, be meaningless or ineffective, unless it were to have implied in it some such term as "such ... consent is not to be unreasonably withheld". For if the landlord was entitled to refuse consent at his own entirely unrestricted discretion, the provision for assignment with consent would add nothing to, and subtract nothing from, the effect in law of the contract as it would be without those words being included. For a contracting party is entirely free to agree to a variation of the contract at the request of the other party. That applies equally well where, as here, the variation of the contract would constitute a novation. It seems to me to follow that the effect of section (19) (1) of the Act of 1927, on its true analysis, was merely to make statutory an implied term which must already have been implied, if the express words were to have any sensible purpose.'

Recently my brother Mervyn Davies J declined to follow and apply this observation in a case where, as in this case, the lease contained a covenant against alteration to the user of the premises without consent, and where it was similarly sought to import the words 'such consent not to be unreasonably withheld'. Having cited the passage I have cited, Mervyn Davies J said:

'So the learned judge took the view that a covenant to assign only with consent carries an implied term that such a consent is not to be unreasonably withheld. From that basis Mr Carnwath said that a covenant to change user only with consent must carry a similar implied term. It is my duty to be guided by the learned lord justice, but since his words were plainly *obiter* I may take his guidance only if I think it right to do so. Unfortunately I am not in that position. As I see it, if A and B choose in a lease to express what it is not necessary to express, one is not obliged to conclude that the expressed words bear not only the expressed meaning, but also some additional implied meaning.'

(See *Guardian Assurance Co. Ltd* v. *Gants Hill Holdings Ltd* (1983) 267 EG 678).

I respectfully agree with the reasoning and the conclusion of Mervyn Davies J. It is of course true that the words 'without the prior written consent of the landlord' in a sense add nothing to the bald prohibition on the making of planning applications by the tenant unless modified in the way suggested, but the clause would have read very oddly without the words requiring the consent of the landlord, since it would then on its face have contained both a covenant not to change the use of the premises without planning consent, so far as planning consent was required for the change of use, and a covenant not to apply for consent. Moreover, it is not uncommon to provide that a tenant is not to be permitted to do something under a lease without consent, and it seems to me no objection that, given consent, the parties could modify the restriction. What the words 'without consent' contemplate is that a consent may be given under the lease and without a variation of the terms of the lease.

What is striking in the case of this lease and, I think, in the case of the lease before Mervyn Davies J, is that in many other contexts the words 'without prior written consent' are qualified by 'such consent not to be unreasonably withheld'. Although in at least one respect this underlease is clumsily drawn, it is plainly professionally drawn, and the omission of those words in clause 3 (27) para (b) must, I think, be taken to be deliberate.

[Counsel for the landlord's] alternative submission is that the restriction in clause 3 (27) para (b) is overridden by the requirement in Schedule 1 that the rent is to be ascertained as that appropriate in a lease negotiated as between willing lessor and willing lessee.

It is said that if the lessee, assumed to be willing to take a lease for the then unexpired term, was only willing to take one on terms that the use was changed within the range permitted by clause 3 (14), but to a category of use for which planning consent was required, the requirement that the negotiation be taken to be between willing lessor and willing lessee imports that the landlord would give consent to the necessary application, at least to the extent that it was reasonable for the proposing tenant to seek to make that use of the premises.

The answer to that submission in my judgment is that the rent must be assessed on the footing that, apart from matters specifically excepted, the new lease is on the same terms and conditions as the original lease. If that assumption narrows the market of available tenants and so lowers the market rent, that is the consequence of restrictions within the lease which are there and which in fact bind the existing tenant.

7.4 (b) Landlord not entitled unilaterally to impose extended user on tenant to increase rent level on review

C. & A. PENSIONS TRUSTEES LTD v. BRITISH VITA INVESTMENTS LTD

Chancery Division   (1984) 272 EG 63

The tenant covenanted it would not, during the term of the lease, exercise or carry on or permit to be used, exercised or carried on in the demised premises any trade or business other than such as might be authorised in writing by the lessor and head lessor. The tenants did not request an extension of the user of the premises but the landlords nonetheless wrote to them purporting to give the tenants authorisation to use the premises for any trade or business within Use Classes III, IV and X of the Town and Country Planning (Use Classes) Order 1972. The landlords had granted the tenants the authorisation unilaterally for the purpose of extending user so as to justify an increase in rent on review. A dispute arose between the parties. Judge Thomas, (sitting as a High Court judge in the Chancery Division) held that it could not have been intended and should not be construed that the clause should entitle the landlords to impose upon the tenants an extended range of permitted uses which they did not ask for and did not want.

JUDGE THOMAS (sitting as a deputy High Court judge): The user clause in question, which is clause 4 (13), is in the form of a covenant by the underlessee (defined as 'the lessee' in the underlease) and is in the following terms:

'That the Lessee will not during the said term use exercise or carry on or permit to be used exercised or carried on in any part of the demised premises any trade or business whatsoever other than such as may be authorised in writing by the Lessor and Head Lessor.'

On 28 September 1970, that is shortly before the underlease was granted, a deed was entered into between the GLC (as successor to the LCC) and Daniel T Jackson Ltd, which authorised the granting of the underlease and the use of the demised premises for the trade or business of polyether foam conversion, textile laminating and fibres bonding for the furniture and automotive industry. The demised premises have, in fact, been used for those or similar purposes since the grant of the underlease,

178

although no written authorisation for such use has ever been given pursuant to clause 4 (13) itself. Nothing, however, seems to turn on that.

The term of the underlease became vested in the defendants on 26 September 1974. On 21 October 1971 the plaintiffs acquired the interest of Daniel T Jackson Ltd. On 20 September 1983 they acquired the freehold interest of the GLC and on that day they wrote a letter to the defendants irrevocably authorising them, 'pursuant to the provisions of clause 4 (13) of the said underlease', to use the demised premises 'for any trade or business whatsoever failing within Classes III, IV or X of the Town and Country Planning (Use Classes) Order 1972'. Those classes in fact are, respectively, use for light industry, general industry and warehousing, but I do not think that that fact matters for present purposes.

The defendants had not asked the plaintiffs for the authorisation contained in that letter. The plaintiffs gave it unilaterally in order to enlarge the authorised uses of the demised premises so that they would be in a position to argue in favour of a greater increase in rent under the current rent review.

On a literal reading of clause 4 (13), the authorisation contained in the letter seems to fall within its provisions, but I do not think that a strict literal interpretation of the clause leads to a sensible construction of what the parties must have intended.

Taken literally, the clause enables the lessor unilaterally and arbitrarily to impose upon the lessee a particular trade or business use which the lessee has not asked for, does not want, and is not able to carry on on the demised premises. This seems to me to lead to an absurdity, which the parties cannot have intended. One can think of many examples to illustrate the point.

In my view the parties must have intended, and, if asked, would have said so, that the lessor's authorisation required by clause 4 (13) is the authorisation (which, of course, may be granted or refused) of a trade or business sought by the lessee to be carried on upon the demised premises and a term to that effect should be implied in the clause. This can be achieved by inserting the words 'requested by the lessee' between the words 'may be' and 'authorised' in the clause.

The rent under the current rent review should, accordingly, be determined on that basis.

I will make a declaration that the assumption as to the permitted use on which the reviewed rent should be determined is that the use of the premises is for any trade or business whatsoever which may be requested by the lessee and authorised in writing by the lessor.

Chapter 8

The effect of statutory requirements on rent levels

8.1 (a) Interpretation of clauses requiring that statutory restrictions on rent levels be disregarded for valuation purposes

LANGHAM HOUSE DEVELOPMENTS LTD v. BROMPTON SECURITIES LTD AND ANOTHER

Chancery Division   (1980) 265 EG 719

An underlease for a term of 42 years was granted in 1977. It demised shop and showroom premises, which included residential flats on the upper floors. The tenant, *inter alia* covenanted to use the upper floors as high-class residential flats, each to be occupied by one family or household only, and not to underlet any part of the premises save for the underletting of the entirety of each flat at a full rack rent without taking any fine or premium. The tenant was required, on notification thereof, to give the landlord particulars of the registration under the Rent Act 1968 or any amendment or re-enactment thereof of any rent for any part of the premises. The rent review clause, (clause 4 (6) (a), provided that, in default of agreement, the revised rent should be determined by a chartered surveyor nominated by the president of the Royal Institution of Chartered Surveyors

> 'to be that at which having regard to the terms of this underlease (other than the amount of rent currently payable) the demised premises might reasonably be expected to be let in the open market by a willing lessor to a willing lessee there being ignored the matters set out in the Landlord and Tenant Act 1954 section 34 (1) (as amended by the Law of Property Act 1969) and any statutory restrictions on the amount of rentals.'

The clause was brought into operation and a dispute arose between the parties. The landlord sought a declaration that:
(1) it should not be assumed that any part of the demised premises is, will or may be sublet on a regulated tenancy within the meaning of section 18 (1) of the Rent Act 1977; (2) if it should be assumed that any part of the demised premises is, will or may be sublet on a regulated tenancy, there should be ignored the fact that the rent recoverable under such regulated tenancy is, will or may be registered and (3) that in determining such rent the chartered surveyor nominated by the President for the time being of the R.I.C.S. pursuant to the terms of the said clause 4 (6) (a) is acting as an expert and not as an arbitrator.

Held: The first two questions turned on the last eight words of clause 4 (6) (a) which did not require any assumptions to be made as to any flats being let or not let on regulated tenancies. The words meant what they said. The surveyor was to take the premises as he found them. On the evidence none of the flats had ever been let on a regulated tenancy, and each of them appeared to have been let from time to time on short lettings, (apparently to foreigners), which, whether by virtue of the Rent Act 1977 section 9 or otherwise, were not regulated tenancies. The surveyor was to take all this into account and also that the tenant might or might not always be able to let the flats in the same way in the future. The last eight words of the clause required the surveyor to ignore all statutory restrictions on the amount of any rent payable by any subtenant to the tenant, as well as on the amount of any rent payable by the tenant to the landlord. The choice of the mode of letting the flats lay with the tenant, and so far the tenant had been successful in letting the flats on terms not subject to any staututory restrictions. This could change in the future, but there was nothing so improbable in the tenant agreeing to accept the risk of such changes as to require the words of clause 4 (6) (a) to carry a strained and improbable meaning.

Clause 4 (6) (a) had to be compared with the earlier clause 4 (5) which allowed for arbitration in respect of insured damage to the premises. When this clause was read side by side with clause 4 (6) (a) it was clear that clause 4 (6) (a) did not, either in substance or form, point to arbitration rather than valuation. The rent review process therefore was one of valuation and not arbitration.

SIR ROBERT MEGARRY V-C: The first two questions turn on the last eight words of clause 4 (6) (a), and I shall deal with them together before turning to the third question.

It seems to me that clause 4 (6) (a) does not require any assumptions to be made. Certain matters must be ignored, but I do not think that assumptions as to any flats being let or not let on regulated tenancies are to be made. The surveyor is to take the premises as he finds them. On the evidence, none of the flats has ever been let on a regulated tenancy, and each of them appears to have been let from time to time on short lettings which, whether by virtue of the Rent Act 1977 section 9 or otherwise, are not regulated tenancies. Many of the lettings have been to people with names suggesting the Near East, and for a week or so at a time. The surveyor should take all this into account, and also the fact that the tenant may or may not always be able to let the flats in this way. In the end, the difference between [counsel for the landlord] and [counsel for the tenant] appeared to be not so much a difference on the first two questions in the originating summons as a difference on the meaning and effect of the last eight words of clause 4 (6) (a).

What [counsel for the landlord] said was that these words meant what they appeared to say. In determining the sum under the clause, the surveyor must ignore, *inter alia*, any statutory restrictions on the amounts of rentals that can be charged for any of the flats, whether in respect of regulated tenancies, restricted contracts, or anything else under the Rent Act 1977 or any other statute. On the other hand, [counsel for the tenant] said that this was an improbable meaning. Why should a tenant who might sublet flats at restricted rents agree to pay the landlord rent at a rate based on ignoring the restrictions on rent that bound him? With that in mind, the last eight words of the sub-clause should be read as merely relating to any restrictions on the rent which the tenant must pay to the landlord, and not as including any rent which the tenant would receive from the subtenants. Although [counsel for the tenant] did not suggest that there was at present any statutory restriction on the rent which the tenant had to pay, there might one day be another 'rent-freeze,' perhaps of the type that there was some six or seven years ago, and the eight words would apply to that. [Counsel for the tenant] said on such a construction the eight words would follow on naturally from the reference to the Landlord and Tenant Act 1954, section 34 (1), which plainly applied as between the landlord and tenant and related to matters such as improvements effected by the tenant.

I cannot accept [counsel for the tenants'] contentions. The choice of the mode of letting the flats lies with the tenant, and so far the tenant seems to have been successful in letting the flats on terms which are not subject to any statutory restrictions on rent. True, either economic conditions or the law, or both, may change, and make it more difficult, or, for that matter, easier, for the tenant to continue in this way. But I can see nothing so improbable in the tenant agreeing to accept the risk of such changes that one must put a strained meaning on the words of the subclause and give them a meaning which seems to me to be improbable. Further, [counsel for the landlord] emphasised that the last word of the subclause was 'rentals,' and that if all that was intended was to require any statutory restrictions on the amount of the tenant's rent to be ignored, it was odd that the draftsman used 'rentals' instead of 'rent.' I agree. The last eight words would be a remarkable way of conveying to the surveyor that in relation to statutory restrictions on rent, he must pay due regard to any that applied to the rent payable by all the subtenants to the tenant and ignore only those which related to the rent payable by the tenant to the landlord. I can see nothing to support the view that the words were intended to have this partial and selective effect. In my judgment, the last eight words of the subclause require the surveyor to ignore all statutory restrictions, whatever the statute, on the amount of any rent payable by any subtenant to the tenant, as well as on the amount of any rent payable by the tenant to the landlord.

I turn to the third question in the summons. Is the chartered surveyor nominated by the president for the time being of the Royal Institution of Chartered Surveyors to perform his task as an arbitrator or is he to do it as a valuer, without any process of arbitration? Looking at the subclause by itself, I can see some force both in [counsel for the tenants'] answer of 'arbitrator' and in [counsel for the landlords'] answer of 'valuer.' But the sub-clause does not stand by itself. The clause immediately preceding it, clause 4 (5) runs as follows:

'If the demised premises are damaged or destroyed by any of the insured risks and the insurance in respect thereof has not been vitiated by any act or omission of the tenant or of any person claiming title to any part of the demised premises through it then the rents hereby reserved or a proper proportion thereof according to the extent of the damage shall abate and in case of difference touching this proviso the same shall be referred to the award of a single arbitrator to be appointed by the President for the time being of the Royal Institution of Chartered Surveyors and in accordance with the provisions of the Arbitration Act 1950 or any statutory modification thereof for the time being in force.'

When one puts clause 4 (5) and clause 4 (6) (a) side by side, the contrast is striking. Clause 4 (5) reeks of arbitration. It uses language such as 'in case of difference,' 'award,' 'single arbitrator' and 'Arbitration Act 1950.' Clause 4 (6) (a) uses none of these words: there is merely a 'sum' to be 'determined' by a chartered surveyor on the basis stated. None of [counsel for the tenants'] ingenuities seem to me to come within striking distance of prevailing against this clear contrast. The lease was drafted by a draftsman (with the singular including the plural, and the masculine the feminine) who knew very well how to make it plain that there was to be an arbitration: and knowing this, clause 4 (6) (a) was drafted in terms which neither in substance nor in form pointed in any real way to an arbitration rather than a valuation. I accept, of course, and under clause 4 (6) (a) there might well be a default of agreement that arose from a positive disagreement rather than a mere failure to make or attempt to make an agreement: but in face of the contrast, that falls far short of anything that could establish clause 4 (6) (a) as containing an arbitration clause. The process under that clause is, in my judgment, one of valuation and not arbitration.

The Vice-Chancellor gave directions as to the form of the declarations and awarded the costs of the summons to the plaintiffs.

8.1 (b)   Effect on rent levels of tenant's statutory right to review under the Landlord and Tenant Act 1954

Where a lease provides that on review, rent is to be fixed at the open market rental, the court may, depending on the wording of the lease decide that both parties must have envisaged that at the review dates they would have to take into account accepted valuation methods which would include taking into account the rights of renewal given to tenants under Part II of the Landlord and Tenant Act 1954. (It is of course possible to contract out of the Landlord and Tenant Act provisions in which case such a situation would not arise.)

PIVOT PROPERTIES LTD v. SECRETARY OF STATE FOR THE ENVIRONMENT

Court of Appeal   (1980) 41 P & CR 248

The respondents, the Secretary of State for the Environment, occupied business premises for a term of 42 years from 24 June 1971 at a rent of £785,000 from 5 August 1971 to 5 August 1972, and thereafter at a yearly rent of £1,570,000. Under the rent review clause in the underlease, the lessors were entitled to call for review of the rent at certain specified dates. The rent was to be the rack market rental value, defined as 'the best rent at which the demised premises might reasonably be expected to be let in the open market ... for a term not exceeding five years and one half of another year.' The lessors called for a review of the rent as from 24 June 1978, in accordance with the rent review clause. The parties failed to agree on a new rent and an arbitrator was duly appointed. A dispute arose as to whether the rack rent of the premises which was to be assessed on the assumption that they were to be let as a whole for a term of five and a half years, was also to be assessed on the assumption that no account was to be taken of any possibility of the tenancy being continued or renewed under the provisions of the Landlord and Tenant Act.

Held: The court's task was to discover what the parties had intended when they had executed the underlease by considering the words that they had used, regard being had to the purpose of the underlease and the circumstances in which it had been made. Both parties must have envisaged that at the review date professional valuers would be engaged who would be likely to apply current valuation methods commonly accepted by valuers, and in 1978 valuers would have taken into account the effect on the rents of demised premises occupied for business premises of the rights given to tenants by Part II of the 1954 Act; this would mean assessing the rent for a term of five and a half years one of the potentialities of which was that it might be continued or renewed.

Lawton LJ gave the judgment of the court: The court's task has been to find out what the parties to the underlease intended when they executed it on 4 August 1971. This has to be done by considering the words that they used, regard being had to the purpose of the underlease and the circumstances in which it was made.

When making the underlease, both parties must have envisaged that, at the review dates, they would have to retain the services of professional valuers who would be likely to apply, when assessing the rack rental market value of the demised premises, such methods of valuation as were from time to time commonly accepted by valuers. Counsel for the lessee accepted that one method of valuation applied in 1978 was to take into account the rents of comparable properties, if there were any—and in this case there were none directly comparable. Another method was to assess the general level of rents for properties used for similar purposes in the neighbourhood. He conceded before Phillips J, and again before us, that in 1978 valuers could be expected to take into account in the ordinary way of their work, when assessing what rents should be paid, the effect on demised premises of any relevant legislation. In 1978, valuers would have taken into account the effect on the rents of demised premises occupied for business purposes of the rights given to tenants by Part II of the Landlord and Tenant Act 1954. Those rights included, subject to such right as the Act gives to landlords, the grant of a new tenancy comprising the property, or part of it, in the tenancy that had come to an end: see sections 29 and 30. The question asked by the arbitrator (which was drafted by counsel) is not accurately worded. The Act of 1954 does not continue, save in limited circumstances, or renew tenancies: it provides for the grant of new tenancies. Counsel's concession was stated by Phillips J in these terms [(1979) 39 P & CR 386, 389]:

> 'There is no doubt that the existence of the Act of 1954 has an effect on the level of rents of business premises. Thus, assuming business premises to be offered for a term of five years, a bidder in the market, bearing in mind the possibilities of a continuation or renewal of the tenancy, will tend to offer more than he would do if the Act did not exist and there was no such possibility. Mr Burke-Gaffney [counsel for the lessee] agreed that that was so.'

It is against a background provided by these considerations that clauses 7 (3) and (4) of the underlease have to be construed. Clause 7 itself must have been inserted to provide the lessors with some protection against inflation. The rent would have to be assessed at the specified intervals. Clause 7 (4) set out how the reassessment was to be done. The parties were to envisage the demised premises (that is, the buildings that were being occupied for business purposes) being put on the market as a whole for a term not exceeding five and a half years and then to decide what was the best rent at which such buildings could be expected to be let. A bidder would be likely to have in mind the possibility that a new tenancy might be granted under the Act of 1954 at the end of the term and increase his bid to take account of that possibility. Counsel for the lessee agreed that that was the ordinary way in which valuers worked. The rent that the bidder would offer to pay would be a rent for a term not exceeding five and a half years, not a rent for that term plus a further term that might be granted under the Act of 1954.

That was the way in which Phillips J dealt with the construction. He said [(1979) 39 P & CR 386 at pp 392-393]:

> 'To take account of the possibilities under the Act of 1954 is not to assess the rent for a term longer than five and a half years, as Mr Burke-Gaffney contended, but to assess it for a term of five and a half years, one of the potentialities of which is that it may be continued or renewed.'

In our judgment, that was the right construction. It disposes of this appeal. A negative answer to the question asked by the arbitrator is the result of applying the method assessment set out in clause 7 (4) of the underlease. This method may be difficult to apply. Mr Burke-Gaffney submitted that, if it were used, the parties' valuers would be given such a difficult task because of the speculative elements necessarily involved in assessing possibilities that clause 7 (4) should not be construed according to the literal meaning of the words used. The reasoning behind that submission was that the parties could not have intended to commit themselves to make or receive payments that had been fixed by guesswork. We do not agree. The valuers produced figures. The arbitrator accepted those of the lessee's valuer and marked down those of the lessors. The task was done— which is the best answer to the submission that it was too difficult to do.

Note: When drafting a review clause, it is important to consider whether what is to be reviewed is simply the residue of the term granted by the lease or whether any period of continuation by statute is to be included for review purposes. This should be made clear.

8.2 Rent freeze legislation and its effect on a 'fair rack rental' which is 'payable' on review

COMPTON GROUP LTD v. ESTATES GAZETTE LTD

Court of Appeal   (1978) 36 P & CR 148

Although the review provisions of an underlease were to be carried out at the review date in 1974, at which time counter-inflation legislation was in force with the intent to freeze rents, the provisions had to be construed in the light of circumstances existing at the date of the underlease, namely, October 1967, bearing in mind at that date there was no statutory restriction on business rents nor was there any reason to suppose that the parties had a possible restriction of that type in mind; accordingly, the outstanding question between the parties depended on the proper construction of the review provision and in particular the two closely linked expressions, 'fair rack rent' and 'payable' in that provision. The meaning of those words varied according to their context, and in the context of the underlease in question, they meant, respectively, the full annual value of the holding, and the rent 'reserved' or contracted to be paid by the terms of the lease; thus, although the surveyor reviewing the rent should take the counter-inflation into account he would not be prevented from increasing the rent by the legislation. He was further required to exclude from consideration the possibility of any future use of the premises in breach of planning control.

Rawlance v. *Croydon Corporation* [1952] 2 QB 803 and *Newman* v. *Dorrington Developments Ltd* [1975] 1 WLR 1642 distinguished.

SIR JOHN PENNYCUICK: The main question outstanding upon the summons turns upon the proper construction of the review provision in the underlease, and in particular two closely linked expressions, 'fair rack rent' and 'payable' in that provision. The review provision must be construed in the light of the circumstances existing at its date, namely 26 October 1967, although the review under the provision falls, of course, to be carried out in the light of the circumstances existing at the review date, 29 September 1974. It is important to bear in mind that in October 1967 there was no statutory restriction upon business rents; nor is there any reason to suppose that the parties had a possible restriction of that nature in mind.

Clause 1 of the underlease contains the common form words of reddendum, namely, 'yielding and paying therefor'; that is, for the premises demised. The rent expressed to be reserved by the *reddendum* is

'(a) during the first seven years ... the yearly rent of ... £5500; (b) during the next seven years ... the yearly rent of ... £5500 or if the lessors shall serve written notice [within the specified time], requiring the rent payable for the demised premises to be reviewed [then] such yearly rent as the respective surveyors of the lessors and lessees shall ... agree in writing as being a fair rack rent as between a willing landlord and a willing tenant which would be payable for the demised premises if the same were then to be let as a whole for a term of seven years with vacant possession upon the terms of this lease *mutatis mutandis* ...'

There follow certain qualifications which I need not refer to again and there are similar provisions for a rent review applicable for the remaining seven years; then there is the provision which I have already read as to valuation by surveyors.

The effect of the review provision is that, if the lessor requires a review, the surveyors must make an estimate of the fair rack rent which would be payable upon a hypothetical seven year lease negotiated between a willing landlord and a willing tenant at the review date, upon the same terms, *mutatis mutandis*, as those contained in the lease itself and the rent so estimated will be substituted for the initial rent of £5500. In this provision the two critical expressions for the present purpose are 'fair rack rent' and 'payable for the demised premises.' These expressions are closely interconnected and of course both must be construed in relation to each other and in the context of the provision as a whole, and indeed of the lease as a whole. Taken together the expressions must, I think, denote either market value reserved or restricted rent recoverable; together they have no other sensible meaning.

I mention at this stage that it is quite clear that the rack rent to be determined by the surveyors as at the review date must be a rent which will continue to be payable throughout the whole of the seven year term; there is no question of the rent going up or down after the first year during the remaining years of the term.

It is most unlikely that in the unrestricted market of 1966 the parties would have had the second alternative, that is to say, restricted rent recoverable in mind, but one must of course construe the provision as it is drawn. It seems to me that the general tenor of the provision indicates the first alternative; that is to say, market rent reserve.

Then one turns to examine more meticulously the precise words used in the provision. In my judgment, each of the two expressions is, according to its context, capable of two meanings. So far as now relevant, the words 'rack rent' may mean either (a) a rent which represents the full annual value of the holding; or (b) the maximum rent which is permitted by law. I think the former is the primary meaning of the word in legal language: see *Re C. R. Sawyer and Withall, Solicitors*, [(1919) 2 Ch 333, 336] in which Sargant J said:

'Rack rent has been defined in 2 Blackstone's Commentaries, p 43, as "only a rent of the full value of the tenement or near it"; and in a judgment of Holmes LJ in *Ex parte Connolly to Sheridan and Russell*, [(1900) 1 IR 6] it is defined thus: "a rack rent in legal language means a rent that represents the full annual value of the holding."'

Sargant J [(1919) 2 Ch 333, 338] in terms approved of Holmes LJ's definition.

However, the latter meaning has been adopted by the courts, including the Court of Appeal, in certain recent cases where the premises were subject to statutory control; see in particular *Rawlance* v. *Croydon Corporation* [(1952) 2 QB 803]—I shall turn to that case a little later.

So far as now relevant, the word 'payable' may mean either (a) 'reserved' or (b) 'recoverable'; that needs no elaboration.

In my judgment, the clue to the construction of the provision is to be found in the expression 'payable for the demised premises'; that expression occurs twice in the provision. It first occurs in the passage authorising the lessor to require a review of the rent payable for the demised premises. Those words indicate a review of the rent reserved by the formula 'yielding and paying,' the purpose being to substitute a revised rent for £5500 as the subject matter of the reservation: one has not yet reached the hypothetical lease. It seems to me that on that first occasion where the expression 'payable for the demised premises' occurs, it plainly means 'reserved.' Then the expression occurs again in the passage describing the hypothetical lease. It is accepted by [counsel] who appeared for the lessee, that the expression 'payable for the demised premises' must bear the same meaning in each of the two passages in which it is found, and so it seems to me that the word 'payable' must mean 'reserved' in the second passage, as it clearly does in the first. Once it is accepted that payable' in the description of the hypothetical lease means 'reserved' it is I think clear that the expression 'fair rack rent' in that description must mean rent representing full annual value. Indeed, almost by definition a willing landlord and a willing tenant could hardly be supposed to agree upon the reservation of a rack rent in an unrestricted market in any other sense. This conclusion is supported by the insertion of the word 'fair,' which itself suggests the upshot of free negotiation rather than an amount statutorily imposed ...

[The judge then went on to consider the cases of *Rawlance* v. *Croydon Corporation* and *Newman* v. *Dorrington Developments Ltd* and to distinguish them for the following reasons:]

I think I ought for completeness to mention *Newman* v. *Dorrington Developments Ltd* [(1975) 1 WLR 1642]. That case was cited at length by [counsel for the lessor]. The position there was that a three year lease dated 1970, when the rent control over dwelling-houses was in force, and had been in force for a long time and was likely to continue to be in force for a long time, contained an option for renewal for a further three years at a rent to be agreed or determined by an arbitrator as being the yearly commercial rack rent at which the premises might reasonably be expected to be let in the open market. Brightman J held that that expression denoted the full rent which the law permitted to be recoverable, and he relied on *Rawlance* v. *Croydon Corporation* [(1952) 2 QB 803]. That case is distinguishable on the very important ground that the lease which contained the renewal provision was made when the control under the Rent Act was in force. If Brightman J had intended to go beyond that particular case and lay down a general rule as to the construction of the expression rack rent, then I would not agree with him. But, I see no reason to suppose that he had such an intention.

The point of construction is a relatively short one, and I have endeavoured to analyse the construction of the provision to the best of my ability. I would add, upon this main point, that the conclusion which I have reached produces a fair result. It would be manifestly unfair that the lessor should be held to the 1974 rent for seven years by reason of a transient and unforseeable wage freeze. Indeed, I think [counsel for the lessee] very properly, did not suggest that the substantial merits of the case were on his side ...

I would add, in order to avoid any possible misunderstanding, that the surveyor, in making his valuation of rack rent, is of course entitled to take into account any effect which the existence of the freeze might have on the determination of that rent. It is for him to say what weight he would attach to it.

BROWNE LJ: In my view the word 'rack rent' is not a phrase which has a precise meaning which it always bears. Sir John Pennycuick has already referred to what Sargant J said in *Re C.R. Sawyer and Withall* [(1919) 2 Ch 333]. I shall not read again the passage which Sir John has already read [(1919) 2 Ch 333 at p 336], but I think it is also helpful to read a few words which Sargant J said [(1919) 2 Ch 333 at p 338]:

> '... I do not think that the phrase "rack rent" has any such absolutely definite and inflexible legal meaning as has been contended for. In my judgment the definition of rack rent by Holmes LJ in the case above referred to *Ex parte Connolly to Sheridan and Russell* [[1900] 1 IR 6], or indeed the looser definition of Blackstone, is sufficiently definite for the purposes of the order ...'

The meaning of 'rack rent' may I think vary according to the context in which it appears, in this case in the rent review clause in the lease. The authorities cited as to the meaning of 'rack rent' in various statutory provisions, to some of which Sir John Pennycuick has already referred, in which it is often the subject of a special statutory definition, seem to me irrelevant for the purposes of this appeal. Nor can I agree that it necessarily or always has the meaning which [counsel for the lessee] suggests; that is, the maximum amount of rent which a landlord could lawfully receive and which the tenant could be legally compelled to pay. I think that the word 'payable' is also a word of which the meaning may vary according to its context.

The words 'paying' and 'payable' are used three times in clause 1 of this lease, the rental clause:

'(1) Yielding and paying therefor—(that is, for the demised premises)—unto the lessors (a) during the first seven years of the said term the yearly rent of ... £5,500; (b) ... if the lessors shall serve written notice on the lessees ... requiring the rent payable for the demised premises to be reviewed; (and (c)) ... such yearly rent as the respective surveyors ... shall ... agree in writing as being the fair rack rent as between a willing landlord and a willing tenant which would be payable for the demised premises (on the assumptions specified.)'

[Counsel for the lessee] agreed that (a) is what he called 'the traditional reservation phrase,' but he says that this throws no light on the meaning of 'payable' in (b) and (c). The question is whether 'rent payable' in (b) and 'rent ... payable' in (c) mean the rent reserved—that is, the rent contracted to be paid—or the restricted rent which the landlord could in fact lawfully receive and the tenant could be compelled to pay at 29 September 1974, having regard to the freeze.

It seems to me plain that in (b) 'the rent payable' means the rent reserved; what is to be 'reviewed' is the yearly rent of £5500 for the first seven years, which is the rent reserved by the 'yielding and paying' formula.

I find it impossible to say that 'rent ... payable' in (c) has a different meaning from "rent payable" in (b), and indeed [counsel for the lessee] conceded that 'payable' had the same meaning in both places. Further, if the clause is read as a whole, it provides, leaving out the words which are immaterial for this purpose:

'Yielding and paying ... (a) during the first seven years ... the yearly rent of ... £5,500 ... (b) during the next seven years ... the yearly rent of ... £5,500 or if the lessors—(serve notice requiring review)—such yearly rent as the respective surveyors ... shall ... agree ... whichever shall be the greater.'

The phrase 'yielding and paying' governs the rent to be determined on the review as well as the £5500 for the first seven years, and the rent determined on the review, like the original £5500, is in my view clearly the rent reserved. In this context 'rack rent' means in my view the full annual value which the parties contract shall be paid—the rent reserved—even though temporarily the landlord cannot lawfully receive, or the tenant be compelled to pay, that amount in full. It is clear from article 14 of the 1973 Order that there is nothing unlawful or invalid about an agreement or determination fixing a rent above the limit laid down by the Order.

NEWMAN v. DORRINGTON DEVELOPMENTS LTD

Chancery Division   [1975] 1 WLR 1642

The tenant occupied premises under a protected tenancy whereby the rent was subject to rent control imposed by statute. The lease contained an option to renew the lease with the rent to be fixed at the commercial yearly rack rental at which the premises might reasonably be expected to be let in the open market. The tenant purported to exercise his option to renew but the landlord resisted the grant.

Held: An order for specific performance would be made. A landlord could agree to grant a lease at 'the commercial yearly rack rental at which premises might reasonably be expected to be let in the open market' notwithstanding that the rent was in fact controlled by statute; and this controlled rent would be the rack rent of the premises in the open market.

BRIGHTMAN J: The cases which I have read seem to come to this, that if a contract is made, whether by ordinary offer and acceptance or by the grant and exercise of an option for a sale or lease at a price or rent which is greater than that which can be lawfully recovered at the time when the contract is due to be performed, the court will not force the bargain upon the parties, because it is not a bargain which can lawfully be implemented according to its terms.

These authorities are not, in my view, decisive of the present case. Here, the option is not, in terms, an option for the grant of a lease at a rent which exceeds the permitted rent. It is an option for the grant of a lease at a rent which is determined to be 'the commercial yearly rack-rent at which the demised premises might reasonably be expected to be let in the open market.'

...

In the result, I do not think that there is any impossibility involved in an agreement by a landlord to grant a lease at 'the commercial yearly rack-rent at which the demised premises might reasonably be expected to be let in the open market' notwithstanding that the rent is controlled by statute. The case is not in essence different from any other case in which the quantum of rent is reduced by some form of legislative control. Take this example by way of illustration. A dwelling house may be lettable at a low rent because it lies in a district zoned for residential occupation, but if it were available for office use it might be let at a much higher rent. Nevertheless the lower rent is truly a rack-rent. No doubt there are other cases in which the hand of the legislature precludes the realisation of the highest rent potential of a property. Value, as Romer LJ said, can only be ascertained in the light of factors which affect or control its disposability.

In the result, I decide that the tenant, having exercised the option, is entitled to an order for specific performance.

Chapter 9

Restrictive user clauses and their effect on rent review provisions

9.1 Restrictive user clauses may seriously depress rent levels

PLINTH PROPERTY INVESTMENTS LTD v. MOTT, HAY AND ANDERSON

Court of Appeal   (1979) 249 EG 1167

An arbitrator raised the question of whether he was to determine the 'fair rack' rent payable under a review clause in strict accord with certain restrictions in the underlease as to user and assignment or whether he could take account of possible relaxations. The clause provided that the rent was to be fixed 'having regard to rental values of property then current and to the provisions of this Underlease'. The underlease contained a restriction on the tenants not to use the demised premises otherwise than as offices in connection with the lessee's business as consulting engineers. The restriction on user seriously lowered the rent below general market levels so that the arbitrator found that on the basis of a restricted user to civil engineer's business the yearly rent should be £89,200 whereas the full market rental would be £139,455 p.a. The arbitrator and the judge on appeal ruled in favour of the lower figure. The landlords appealed.

Held: The clause (restricting the user of the premises to the business of consulting engineers) obviously had a very depressing effect on the rent since no tenant would take them unless there was a considerable discount made on the rent. The arbitrator could not possibly assess the rent on the basis that a landlord will always relax or waive a clause of this kind wholly gratuitously. A landlord would never do that unless he was paid a considerable sum in return and this was all hypothetical and so intangible it could not be taken into account in determining the rent. The arbitrator was entitled to find that the restrictive user clause depressed the rent so as to produce a much lower annual figure since when a lease provided for rights and obligations on each of the parties to it, and the rent had to be assessed on the basis of those provisions, it had to be assumed that those rights would be enforced and the obligations would be performed.

LORD DENNING MR: The underlease says—and these are the important words—

'... the amount to be determined by the arbitrator shall be of such amount as shall in the opinion of the arbitrator represent the fair rack rental market value for the demised premises.'

Pausing there for a moment, the position is that, if there had been no special clauses in this underlease affecting the matter, at the present time the rent would have been fixed at a sum of over £130,000 a year for these premises, as against the figure in 1966 of £32,914 a year. The underlease goes on to say that the rent is to be fixed 'having regard to rental values of property then current and to the provisions of this

Underlease.' That is the crux of the case—'having regard to ... the provisions of this Underlease.'

One of the important provisions of the underlease is a restriction on the tenants

'not to use the demised premises or any part thereof or suffer the same to be used otherwise than as offices ... in connection with the Lessee's business of Consulting Engineers.'

It seems to me that that restriction would affect very seriously any rent which the lessee would pay for the premises. He would not pay anywhere near the full market rent if his use of the premises was restricted to the business of civil engineers. For instance, he could not underlet them to a chartered accountant or any other professional person or to a business firm.

I must also read two other clauses about assigning or underletting. Clause 18 (a) says:

'That there shall not be any assignment underletting or parting with possession of part only of the demised premises nor any underletting or parting with possession or control of the demised premises.'

That clause was concerned with assigning *part* of the premises. Then clause 18 (b) goes on to deal with the assignment of the *whole* of the premises. It says:

'That there shall not be any assignment of the whole of the demised premises without the previous written licence of the Lessors and the Superior Lessors such licence not to be unreasonably withheld in the case of a responsible assignee or underlessee.'

Although the underlessees could assign the premises with the written licence of the lessors, that did not affect the clause about user. If they assigned to anybody else, the assignee would still be subject to the clause that they were not to be used otherwise than as offices in connection with civil engineering business ...

Mr Godfrey submitted that it is wrong to take the restriction on user as having much effect on the rent because it was always open to the lessor to relax it or waive it; and no doubt he would relax it or waive it in his own interests so as to get a higher rent from time to time. Mr Godfrey said that he would relax it or waive it as a matter of business, and he would get a higher rent accordingly. Accordingly the rent should be fixed at the high sum. I will read the one important sentence in the case stated:

'... whether the arbitrator can take into account the fact that the landlord might consent to a change of user and/or to an underletting of the whole or part of the premises.'

As Brandon LJ pointed out in the course of the argument, it does not say 'with or without consideration.' Looking at it as a matter of practical business, one has to remember that, owing to this restrictive clause, if the lessees wanted to use the premises for any other purpose than the business of civil engineers they would have to get the landlord's agreement to do so. The landlord would immediately say,

'I'm not going to give my consent unless you make it worth my while. If you pay me a substantial sum, then I'll give my consent for these premises to be used for some other business, such as the business of a chartered accountant; but I am not going to give my consent unless it is made worth my while.'

That seems to me obvious as a matter of commercial practice. So this clause (restricting the user of the premises to the business of consulting civil engineers)

obviously must have a very depressing effect on the rent. No one is going to take premises of this kind with such a depressing restriction on them unless there is a considerable discount on the rent. That is the way in which the arbitrator viewed it. He could not possibly assess the rent on the basis that a landlord will always relax or waive a clause of this kind wholly gratuitously. A landlord would never do that unless he was paid a considerable sum—and how is one to work that sum out? It is all hypothetical. It is so intangible that, as a practical matter, it cannot be done. I think the arbitrator was quite entitled to say that this restrictive clause has such a depressing effect on the rent that the proper rental value of these premises under the review clause for the succeeding eight years should only be the figure of £89,200 and not the figure of £130,455.

SHAW LJ: ... The lease says what matters are to be taken into account in determining the fair rack rental. They do not include highly speculative factors, which are incapable of estimation on any basis such as the chance that the landlord might waive the restriction on user and, if he does, how much he would require to be paid for so doing.

Also agreeing, BRANDON LJ said: I am of the same opinion. It seems to me that when a lease provides that the arbitrator is to have regard to the provisions of the lease, it means the provisions that give rights and impose obligations on each of the parties to it. What the arbitrator has to consider is what those rights and obligations are on either side and assess the rent in the light of them. He is not to say to himself 'Those who have rights may not enforce them and those who have obligations may not be required to perform them.' He is to assume that the rights will be enforced and the obligations will be performed. He is to look at the legal position of the parties and nothing else.

Note: See also the earlier case of *Ratners (Jewellers) Ltd* v. *Lemnoll Ltd* (1980) 255 EG 987, where a restriction on user reduced the rent by 5%. Contrast these cases with the 'hypothetical' user cases (see earlier page 147), as in *Bovis Group Pension Fund* v. *G.C. Flooring and Furnishing Ltd* (1984) EG 1252, where the actual user of the premises is to be disregarded when fixing the rent.

9.2 Interpreting assumed user and its effect on rent levels

The review clause in a lease may provide that the rent be reviewed on the basis that the premises have a use for any purpose within a particular use class, or some other use class within which falls the use or uses of the demised premises permitted by the planning authority from time to time.

WOLFF AND ANOTHER v. LONDON BOROUGH OF ENFIELD

Chancery Division   (1984) 273 EG 1121

A rent review clause provided that the fair market rent for the premises was to be the best annual rent obtainable between a willing landlord and a willing tenant on a letting of the whole premises with vacant possession for use for any purpose within Class III of the Town and Country Planning (Use Classes) Order 1972 or any other class or classes of the order permitted by the planning authority from time to time. The former use for the building was light industrial. At the date of the existing lease they were vacant but planning permission had been given to allow a change of use to a non-teaching service unit for the Middlesex Polytechnic. The landlords submitted that in applying the review clause the reference to Middlesex Polytechnic should be ignored and the permission treated as extending to any non-teaching service unit without restriction.

Held: The permission had been specifically restricted to such use for the polytechnic and did not extend to any other organisation. Such a use, however, was not within any of the use classes in the order, and even if the user were without restriction to a specific organisation, it would not be within them. The rent should be reviewed on the basis of the fair value of the premises as a whole for light industrial use until such time as there was a change of permission. *Carpet Decor (Guildford) Ltd* v. *Secretary of State for the Environment* (1981) 261 EG 56 considered.

WHITFORD J: Effectively, the position so far as use as at the date of the lease was concerned was this. The premises were then standing vacant. They had in fact been previously occupied by an organisation that was using them for light industrial purposes. Prior to the date of the leases there had been an application for change of use. There had been in fact a permission granted. There can be no doubt from the documents in the case that at the time when the leases were drawn up Super Services (Holloway) Ltd would have been aware that there had been this application and would have been aware of the use that was in contemplation.

Against this background I come to that part of the first lease which says how you are to determine the fair market rent. It is clause 1 (2) and it runs, so far as is material, in these terms:

'The said fair market rent shall be the amount which shall be agreed between the Landlord and the Tenant to be the best annual rent for the time being obtainable as between a willing landlord and a willing tenant in respect of the demised premises on a letting thereof as a whole with vacant possession for use for any purpose within Class III of the Town and Country Planning (Use Classes) Order 1972 or any other class or classes of the said order within which falls the use or uses of the demised premises permitted by the planning authority from time to time.'

...

There was the application and, as I have indicated, it was, and must have been known to the original lessors to have been, successful, and the declarative permission was granted. The permission that was granted was a permission for change of use of the premises from light industry to a non-teaching service unit for the Middlesex Polytechnic.

If one now comes back to clause 1 (2) of the first lease, I have to approach it, as I see it, in this way. You have got to consider premises which are notionally vacant with no use of any sort of kind being carried on. As I have said, I do not really think what actually happened is of any moment at all, and you have got to consider the premises being let as a whole. Then you can proceed to determine what as between willing landlord and willing tenant would be a fair rent for those premises used for Class III purposes, and then you have got to see whether there could be a use for purposes within any other class or classes of the relevant order within which fall the use or uses of the demised premises permitted by the planning authority from time to time. Of course, it was quite sensibly contemplated that over the years—of course, there was going to be only one rent review on the first lease, but at five-year intervals there will be a number of possible rent reviews on the second lease—whatever might be the position in respect of the planning permission which had been granted at the time when these leases were entered into, there might be further applications for change of use. Whatever was permitted as at the date when the agreements were entered into, there was not necessarily going to be the permitted use at the first rent re-view date or indeed at any subsequent rent review date. The lessees might from time to time seek to secure permission for other uses which would be of service to them.

So the question arising is this. If one looks at what was permitted by the planning permission granted in July 1977, can it be said that the use permitted falls within any class or classes of the order, which of course necessarily carries with it the question—if it does, which class or classes are included within the permission granted? It was not, of course, suggested that there is a class of non-teaching service units, and even if there were it must to my mind be quite plain that there is no class of non-teaching service unit for the Middlesex Polytechnic. [Counsel] on behalf of the plaintiffs, says it would be quite wrong to pay any attention to the inclusion of the reference to the Middlesex Polytechnic in the permission granted. Provided the permission granted is used by somebody within the general ambit of the grant it does not matter who that person is, that is to say this permission was adequate to enable anybody to say that they ought to be allowed to operate a non-teaching service unit even though they were not going to do it for Middlesex Polytechnic. That, says [counsel for the plaintiffs] is because a case, *Carpet Decor (Guildford) Ltd* v. *Secretary of State for the Environment*, has so decided. It is reported in (1981) 261 EG 56. It was a case that was heard by Sir Douglas Frank, sitting as a deputy judge of the Queen's Bench Division. It was a case concerned with the use of vaults which had been used for a considerable period of years for the storage of documents. A point in time arrived at which the vaults ceased to be used for the storage of documents. They were in fact used for the storage of carpets. It was said: 'This is a repository use and the use for the storage of carpets as opposed to the storage of documents does not amount to a change of use.' It was held that this was right. The use for the storage of carpets was still a use within the same class and accordingly did not constitute development. The report of the case certainly makes it quite clear that what was applied for and in fact originally secured was a permission to use the vaults as a store for papers of National Provincial Bank Ltd and as residence for a caretaking employee of the said bank but for no other type of store or for any other person or corporation. We do not need to consider the question of residence of the caretaker. There was an application which in terms was seeking permission for the limited purpose of storage of papers for the National Provincial Bank and nobody else.

The report indicates that the application, which contained a question 'State whether the permission is desired as a permanent development or use for a limited period and if the latter for what period', resulted in an answer given on the application form 'during ownership by National Provincial Bank only'. I think [counsel for the plaintiffs] can rightly say that from the terms of the report it would appear that the permission that was granted was granted for the development described and the only condition that was recorded was that there should be no variation of the deposited plans and particulars without previous authorisation by the relevant council. There was an argument submitted that the planning permission was limited in time to the ownership of the premises by the National Provincial Bank. Sir Douglas Frank says this:

'I think that this case turns on the proper construction of the planning permission. As a general principle, where a local planning authority intend to exclude the operation of the Use Classes Order or the General Development Order, they should say so by the imposition of a condition in unequivocal terms, for in the absence of such a condition it must be assumed that those orders will have effect by operation of law. As I have said, the parts of the planning permission relied on here are in common form and printed on the documents. Their purpose is to ensure that the operations are carried out in accordance with the deposited plan and that the premises shall be used for the purpose described. I do not read this document as doing more than that, and certainly not as excluding the operation of the Use Classes Order.'

Referring to the argument based upon the reference to use for the storage of papers for the National Provincial Bank, Sir Douglas Frank said:

> 'Mr Harper argued that both the use and its duration were defined in the application and incorporated in the permission and therefore cut down the scope of the permission, thereby making it not open to the appellants to rely on the Use Classes Order'.

It does appear to me from the terms of the report that some question arose in that case on which from the report as cited I am not entirely sure that it emerges very clearly whether it was argued that the permission in relatively general terms could be cut down by referring back to the terms of the application. I am, however, entirely in agreement with the approach of Sir Douglas Frank, which as I see it is that you have got to look at the terms of the planning permission to decide what use has been permitted, and in this case it is a use of the premises as a non-teaching service unit for the Middlesex Polytechnic. That to my mind quite plainly is a limitation which must be taken on the words which we find and that this permission could not be used as a shield for the use of the premises in question as a non-teaching service unit for any other organisation. Even if this were wrong, as I think I have already indicated, it is plain that there is no class of non-teaching service unit as a whole. It is well established—*Wells* v. *Minister of Housing and Local Government* (1967) 18 P & CR 401 is a case in point—that permission may in fact be granted which extends to activities which do not fall within any of the use classes in the order. This was a case concerned with a builder's yard and the question was whether the erection of a plant making batches of concrete would involve change of use or not. The uses that were involved in the operation of the yard as a builder's yard were manifold and in his judgment Lord Denning points out in the plainest possible terms that there may well be permission granted for uses which cannot be brought within any particular class. It is, I think, the more likely to be the case where the activities in any particular building or area which are going to be carried on and for which permission has been granted are manifold in character, I think that the facilities that one would expect to find being operated in a non-teaching service unit for any organisation, whether for the Middlesex Polytechnic or not, are likely to be manifold. The permission that was granted was granted in respect of all or any facilities which might be appropriate to the activities of a non-teaching service.

It cannot to my mind be sensibly suggested that the permission that was granted in the circumstances of this particular case was a permission falling within any class or classes in the Use Classes Order and in the result, until there is a change of permission, the rent must be reviewed upon the basis of a fair value of the premises as a whole for light industrial use.

Judgment was given for the defendants with costs.

9.3 Taking trading results into account

The valuer may be able to take trading results into account in order to show that the area or site is not a good one for the business which occupies the premises on the basis of a restrictive user clause. However he should not base such a premise on the results of a single business, but on wider evidence, nor should he take into account the results of the tenant's business for the period subsequent to the review date for the purpose of discovering whether the tenant was justified in having had misgivings at the time of the review.

DUVAN ESTATES LTD v. ROSSETTE SUNSHINE SAVOURIES LTD

Queen's Bench Division   (1982) 261 EG 364

ROBERT GOFF LJ: Then I come to his new submission, which is based on paragraph 3 of the award. It appears that before the arbitrator reliance was placed upon *Plinth Property Investments Ltd* v. *Mott, Hay and Anderson* (1978) 249 EG 1167 for the proposition that there should be a rent reduction where there is a restrictive user clause, and it is plain that that authority does indeed support that proposition—the point being, quite simply, that where there is a restrictive user clause then the market would be reduced and that could have a depressing effect on the rent. But, as [counsel for the landlord] was constrained to admit, and I am sure he was right in this, what the arbitrator did was to accept that principle and to apply it, because when he refers to the case he says: 'I accept this principle'. Then it becomes plain frcm the figure which he chose, in paragraph 4, that he did indeed accept it and made a reduction in respect of it. Of course, the reduction which he made was a matter purely for his own judgment and one with which this court could not possibly interfere. So there is no error of law by the arbitrator in so far as he applied the principle.

But then another point was made by [counsel for the landlord] which he did pursue before me, and that was as follows. In paragraph 3 the arbitrator went on to say:

'However, I do not agree with the suggestion of Mr Staddon, the lessee's consultant, that the manufacture of meat pies and pasties and the like was not a viable operation.'

and then came the sentence of which [counsel for the landlord] complains:

'The 1978 results were not supported by those for 1979, which I am entitled to take into account to verify whether or not the misgivings expressed at the review date were justified.'

[Counsel for the landlord] said:

'There we have yet another example of the arbitrator taking into account events and facts after the review date and that he ought not to have done. Therefore he erred in law and the court should give leave to appeal and remit the matter to the arbitrator to reconsider his valuation.'

Now first of all, [counsel for the tenant] said that, in fact, the only basis upon which trading results could be relevant was simply and solely for the purpose of showing that the site or location was not a good place for the business in question. I have no doubt that there are cases, indeed one was cited to me, where this may be so, and evidence can be called to this effect:

'Now this is the way my business has gone over the last few years and that really shows that this is not a good spot for the business which is the subject of the restrictive user clause and, for that reason, the rent ought to be reduced.'

A case concerning hotels was cited to me which showed that this is so [*Harewood Hotels* v. *Harris* [1958] 1 WLR 108]. But I am bound to say that I do not accept [counsel for the tenant]'s submission that that is the only purpose for which you can look at trading results. It could be that, quite apart from the location of the business, the particular business which is the subject of the restrictive user clause could be so depressed that applicants for leases, under the lease containing that clause, would be less ready or willing to pay a high rent; and therefore a general depression in that business, or a general depression in that business in that area, might be relevant in a particular case as having a bearing upon the rent which is payable as at the review date.

Now it seems to me that this was basically the argument which was being advanced in this case. If one looks at the written submissions put in on behalf of the plaintiffs I find the sentence:

'We propose calling a director of our client company to give further evidence to the arbitration as to the nature of the user and his personal knowledge of competitors and the state of the industry as at July 1978.'

So this does seem to be the point being made on behalf of the tenants here. They are saying that the state of the industry as at the review date was very bad and that that must be taken into account in considering the rent as at the review date. It seems to me to be quite a legitimate argument to advance but, of course, it would have to be supported by evidence.

If one looks at the arbitrator's award and the sentence of which [counsel for the landlord] complains, what one finds is this. The arbitrator was saying:

'In the context of this argument being advanced by the tenant, the 1978 results (which I read to be the trading results for the tenant's business for the calendar year 1978 which are obviously being relied upon in support of this argument) were not supported by those for 1979, which I am entitled to take into account to verify whether or not the misgivings expressed at the review date were justified.'

As I read it, the tenants were saying to the arbitrator: 'Look at our 1978 results. They were bad. Therefore, as at the review date, we had misgivings as to the state of the pie and pasty manufacturing industry in this area.' Now it seems to me that in relation to that submission and in relation to the weight, if any, to be attached to the 1978 accounts, it was not right for the arbitrator to look at the 1979 results, because there he was doing what [counsel for the landlord] complains of, namely, he was looking at subsequent events to discover not whether it was justifiable to have misgivings as at 1978 but whether those misgivings were proved in the result to have had a sound basis, which, of course, was not the point that he had to consider. Therefore it can be said that the arbitrator did, on the basis of these reasons, err in law in having regard to 1979 accounts for that purpose.

But the question arises whether or not, in those circumstances, I should give leave to appeal on this particular point. I must have regard to the provisions of the 1979 Arbitration Act and it is, I think, clear under the Act that the applicant for leave has to point to, first, a question of law arising out of the award, and I think they have done that. But that is not enough. They have to go further, because section 1 (4) provides:

'The High Court shall not grant leave ... unless it considers that, having regard to all the circumstances, the determination of the question of law ... could substantially affect the rights of one or more of the parties to the arbitration agreement.'

and the question arises whether this particular point of law is one which could substantially affect the rights of the parties.

[Counsel for the landlord] says that I cannot tell, looking at this award, how far the 1979 results had an influence upon the arbitrator's conclusion as to the sum he should knock off the £7500 by virtue of the restrictive user clause. Now I look at the arbitrator's reasons and I see that the arbitrator rejected the submission being advanced by a consultant, Mr Staddon, on behalf of the lessee, that the manufacture of meat pies and pasties was not a viable operation. I look at it this way. If the 1978 trading results of one company were the only hard evidence placed before the arbitrator as to manufacturing meat pies generally, it seems to me that that was the most fragile basis upon which to advance a submission as to the general viability of manufacturing meat pies and pasties. By itself it could carry very little weight indeed. If, on the other hand, there was other evidence upon which the arbitrator could proceed, then he must look at the 1978 results in the context of the other evidence; but, once again, the 1978 results of one company must be of marginal importance to the wider question whether or not there was a general depression in the manufacturing industry in meat pies and pasties. It seems to me that given the nature of the submission being advanced and the particular item, namely the 1978 results of one company, in respect of which the arbitrator took a matter wrongly into account, it is impossible for me to say that taking into account an illegitimate matter as undermining this one particular factor—the 1978 results—is something that could substantially affect the rights of the parties. It seems to me that the 1978 results, taken by themselves, must be something of very minor importance indeed. The only way in which this arbitrator could have been persuaded that the whole manufacture of meat pies and pasties, even limiting it to the particular area in question, was not viable would be to look at a far wider range of evidence before he could reach any such conclusion.

For that reason I am not prepared to hold that this particular question of law, namely, a question of law relating to the taking into account of the 1979 accounts, is a question of law which could substantially affect the rights of one or more of the parties to this arbitration agreement. It seems to me, in truth, that the present case is precisely the sort of case which the Arbitration Act 1979 is designed to exclude from reconsideration by the courts. This is a marginal point in fact, and only a marginal point, and because it is marginal it is just the sort of question for which the court ought not to invoke the process of review. I therefore conclude that this is a case in v nich I should not grant leave to appeal for the reason I have given, namely, that I do not consider that, having regard to all the circumstances, the determination of the question of law could substantially affect the rights of one or more of the parties to the arbitration agreement. It follows that the application for leave to appeal is dismissed.

Note: The question of law in this case did not 'substantially affect the rights of one or more of the parties' to the arbitration agreement and leave to appeal under the Arbitration Act 1979 s 1 (4) was refused.

See also, *Harewood Hotels Ltd* v. *Harris* [1958] 1 WLR 108 and *W J Barton Ltd* v. *Long Acre Securities Ltd* [1982] 1 WLR 398; see pages 511-2.

Chapter 10

Imperfect drafting and some related problems

10.1 Deciding the date for assessing reviewed rent—whether the court should allow *ex post facto* valuation

Imperfect drafting can give rise to many different problems of construction. Although each case will turn on its own facts and particular wording, some guidance may be drawn from some of the individual cases cited below. When construing a clause to determine the date on which the rent payable on review should be assessed, the issue of whether there should be *ex post facto* valuation may arise.

WEBBER v. HALIFAX BUILDING SOCIETY

Chancery Division   (1985) 273 EG 297

The defendant tenant building society took a 42 year lease of business premises, which adjoined the society's existing premises, with a view to extending their premises. The demised premises were in poor condition. A rent-free period was given to the tenant during which time major works were carried out by the tenant. The lease provided for seven yearly reviews but it was, however, carelessly drafted. A dispute arose between the landlord and tenant with regard to how the rent should be determined on review, and, *inter alia*, the court was invited to decide whether the rent payable from the start of each review period should be assessed by reference to the market value at the date of actual determination of the review date or the value at the commencement of the review period which involved *ex post facto* valuation.

Held: The revised market rent should be determined with regard to the market values in existence at the beginning of the review period and not at the date at which the valuation was actually made, *London & Manchester Assurance Co. Ltd* v. *G.A. Dunn & Co.* (1981) 262 EG 143 and (1982) EG 39, CA considered.

JUDGE PAUL BAKER QC (sitting as a judge of the High Court): Moving on for the moment to clause 4, which is the review provision, the preliminary part says this:

> 'THE reviewed rent' [that is not an expression, I think, that has been defined anywhere in the lease] '(payable by the Society during the Review Periods as hereinbefore provided) shall be determined in manner following that is to say it shall be whichever shall be the higher of the first reserved rent of One Thousand Five Hundred Pounds and the open market rental value of the demised premises for the review period.'

So that preliminary part deals with what is a very common sort of provision—that the reviewed rent shall only take effect if greater than the subsisting rent.

199

It then goes on: 'provided that and it is hereby agreed as follows:—(i)' and this again is an important provision for the purposes of these issues

'The expression the open market rental value as aforesaid means the sum in relation to the review period determined in manner hereinafter provided as being at the time of such determination the annual rental value of the demised premises in the open market on a Lease for a term of Seven Years certain (consisting of the review period) with vacant possession at the commencement of the term but calculated on the basis of the rental value of the original premises as shown on the said plan and in the said photographs annexed hereto as if such building was a "developers shell" meaning to say that a tenant would be required to provide his own shop front and interior fixtures and fittings but at the same time having regard to the fact that the Landlord has contributed a sum of Two Thousand Two Hundred and Fifty Pounds by way of rent abatement for repairs to the demised premises at the commencement of this Lease And Also upon the supposition (if not a fact) that the Society has complied with the obligations as to repair and decoration herein imposed on the Society.

Well that concludes what there is of the review provisions. Then the lease goes on to clause 5 (or I should say the first of the clauses numbered 5 in the lease), which contains the tenants' covenants. These are in fairly standard form and there is not much of it which I need refer to. I should notice perhaps that in clause 5 (vi) there is a proviso. It was obviously contemplated that the society would expand in the manner I have described, but there was a proviso that at the end of the term the society would reinstate the interior walls dividing the demised premises from the society's adjoining premises at 59 Oxford Street.

The next clause I should notice in this connection is subclause (viii) of clause 5. That was the usual clause against alterations:

'Not without the written consent of the Landlord first obtained such consent not to be unreasonably withheld (and then only in accordance with plans previously approved by the Landlord): (a) to build or place at any time on the demised premises any buildings structure or erection (b) to make or suffer to be made to any buildings structure or erection forming part of the demised premises any alterations or additions either internally or externally or to cut or injure any of the outside or inside walls floors or joists or to carry out or suffer ...'

...

On the face of it the drafting of that lease leaves much to be desired. I do not think it would be too strong an expression to say that the drafting was slipshod: one sees that for a start in the actual numbering of the clauses. As I have already mentioned, there are two clause 5s; in both clauses 3 and 4 there are subclauses (i) but no subclauses (ii), and matters of that sort. Clause 4 comes from a standard form (what there is of it) of rent-review clauses in the well-known publication *The Encyclopaedia of Forms and Precedents*, 4th ed, in the standard form for office lettings. The material provision is at p 841, para 1, and it is quite plain that much of that wording, although not all of it, comes from that standard form. Para 2 (and we do not have this in the lease at all) deals with the manner of making a review, dealing with such points as the initiation of it and the times at which various steps are to be done and who is to do the valuation and matters of that sort. They are very common matters. Obviously none of that, it being omitted from the lease that I have got here, can be introduced as a matter of construction, and no one has suggested that it should be.

I think before parting with the standard form I should notice that in the standard form *reddendum* (which is 10 pages earlier in the form) there is a clause simply 'To pay during the term the reserved rents and the further or additional rents hereinafter mentioned at the times and in the manner herein provided. There is nothing in that clause, contrary to what we have in this lease which I have to consider, about determination of the rents. It is merely that they are to be paid at the times and in the manner hereinafter provided.

With that introduction I can come to the first issue, which is formulated in this way:

> 'IT IS ORDERED that the following issue be determined by the court, whether upon the true construction of the lease the rent payable thereunder with effect from the start of each review period as therein defined is to be calculated—and then I pass over the first issue which has been agreed now—(b) By reference to the market value of the premises and other comparable premises as at the date of the determination of the reviewed rent and not at any other date.'

I should say at one that the review has not yet taken place for the 1978 review—the period of seven years beginning at 1978.

The landlord's position is that, as and when that valuation is made, that is the date by reference to which the lease for the term of seven years referred to in clause 4 (i) is to be valued. So it is to be valued at current rates. The defendants' position is that, on the true construction of this lease the review date is to be at the beginning of the review period. This struck me at first as a difficult and obscure point, but I have heard some excellent argument from both counsel in this case and the result of that has enabled me to come to a clear conclusion in the matter, and perhaps I should say at once that I am with the defendants (tenants) on this matter.

I approach it in this way. Going back to clause 3 (i) we have this (I have read the clause out, but I must refer to it again): it does provide for the determination to some extent. It says: 'For the residue of the said term at a rent to be determined and when determined to be payable at the expiration.' By ordinary grammatical construction, 'at the expiration' refers to the rent to be payable. It is not entirely apt for that because the rent is not payable at the expiration; it is payable as from the expiration and it is paid throughout the whole period quarter by quarter as it falls due. But it is apt, as I see it (although not wholly practicable), as a matter of grammar and logic that it could refer to the determination of the rent, which is a once-and-for-all operation at that date, that is to say, at the expiration of the preceding seven-year period. The fact that it deals with both the determination and the payment of the rent is, I think, underlined by the concluding words of the paragraph—'and in accordance with the provisions hereinafter contained'. That obviously refers not to the payment but to the determination of the rent (that is what clause 4 is partially concerned with) and the fact that it is the word 'and' means that 'to be determined' is qualified in at least two ways. It is qualified 'to be determined ... at the expiration ... and in accordance with ...'. So basically on that ground I find that that is a clear guidance in this clause to the date of the expiration of the preceding period as being the date of the termination of the rent for the succeeding period.

As I say, it is not wholly practicable to require the determination to be done on that precise date, it might be, and I also notice as regards this that there is nothing about the manner of the determination provided there or anywhere else. The parties have agreed, in default of any other machinery provided in the lease that the court has to be appealed to to make the determination, but that is as a last resort. The lease does not expressly mention, nor in my judgment can it be contemplated that the court should be appealed to as the first resort, and the manner of determination could be either direct agreement (a very common provision) or some indirect agreement such as reference to a surveyor to work it out, or an arbitrator, or, as a last resort, the court but only *faute de mieux*. That is on clause 3 (i).

Now I must move to clause 4 and see what that can tell us about the matter. The linchpin of the landlord's position in this issue is the words: 'at the time of such determination' in 4 (i) as indicating that the expression 'open market rental' means the sum determined in manner hereinafter provided as being at the time of such determination the annual rental value'. The purpose of this clause is not *prima facie* to lay down when the determination is to take place: it is concerned to define the subject-matter of the determination—what it is that has to be determined. The timing and manner is to be provided elsewhere.

'Manner hereinafter provided as being at the time of such determination' refers to the determination provisions which are to be found elsewhere. As we have seen, the lease is defective and they are not 'hereinafter provided', but I am satisfied that the provisions are to be found elsewhere in the lease, namely in clause 3.

Dealing with the various supporting arguments put forward on both sides in relation to this clause, it was said that one of the difficulties is that what has to be valued in a lease for seven years certain consisting of the review period. That to my mind points very strongly in favour of the tenant's position in this matter—that that seven years is fixed at the beginning of the relevant review period. It is not a lease for seven years at the time of determination, but is a lease for a particular seven years fitted into there. As it happens, the seven years is almost up, and it was said:

'Well, it can still be valued at the present date, one year away from the next review period. It will only be one year to value, but of course it will be valued, not as a one-year lease, but as a one-year lease with the 1954 Act protection. That will not diminish it very much and, as for its being seven years, well, it is quite common to have a back-dated lease from the time it takes effect'

and indeed, of course, we have it in this very case, where the term starts in March and the lease is dated the following May. But that to my mind is not a proper way of looking at this, if only because it further contemplates not just a lease for seven years certain but a lease with vacant possession at the commencement of the term; that the lease to be valued is valued as if it was then in possession and the rent is to start running as from that date. It is contemplated that as from that date there will be a lease with a rent right from the time, and that to my mind, far from indicating that the date of determination is when the determining body (whether it be a surveyor or whether it be an official referee or a judge) gets around to it, points in exactly the opposite direction.

It was said then that there will be difficulties in *ex post facto* valuation. That of course is true. It is much easier to value at a current date with comparables, but there is nothing impossible about it. It is frequently done and there is some authority to indicate how that should be accommodated. Then it is said: 'Well, the lessee can initiate the procedure here,' and in some of the cases that is produced as an argument in favour of a later valuation, but there again, having regard to what I see as the clear words of the matter, that does not seem to me an argument of great substance.

So for those reasons I am clearly of the opinion that the determination is to be measured, and the valuation to be done, as from the beginning of each review period as it comes along.

My attention was drawn to a number of authorities, to most of which I shall make some brief reference, but of course, as was rightly said, these are of very limited value on points of construction and in none of them, I think it is right to say, was the present issue the matter for decision. The highest was that the date of determination was a matter of assumption against which the judges made their decision.

The first case was *Accuba Ltd* v. *Allied Shoe Repairs Ltd* [1975] 1 WLR 1559, but I do not propose to take up time with that case, because, as it happens, the assumption made there was perfectly consistent with the finding that I have made here. More important, in the present connection, is the case of *London and Manchester Assurance Co. Ltd* v. *G A Dunn & Co.* which was reported both before Peter Gibson J in (1981) 262 EG 143, and also on appeal in (1982) 265 EG, starting on p 39 and continuing on p 131, the Court of Appeal consisting of Lawton, Oliver and Slade LJJ. There were a number of points for decision. It was plain on the construction of the relevant review provision that there was an opening date for an initiating notice in that case. It was doubtful whether there was a closing date (that was one of the issues) and, if there was a closing date, time was of the essence, that closing date having been missed. Then there were issues of estoppel. That bare recital of the issues shows that there was considerable opportunity for differences of view, and, if I may say so with all due deference, the lords justices took very full advantage of those opportunities, but the point I am on that the moment is that the time of determination in that case was assumed to mean the time at which the determination was in fact made. All the judges assumed it, but I think it appears most clearly from Slade LJ's judgment at p 132 in the middle of the second column:

'It has, I think, been common ground throughout the argument in both courts that, in view of the wording of clause 5 (1), there is no question of the surveyor, if and when appointed, being required to make an *ex post facto* determination of the rent as at the commencement of the relevant review period. He is required to determine it in accordance with the clause 5 (1) formula, but otherwise in the light of market conditions prevailing when he makes his determination.'

There are passages in the other judgments which bear that out. So that was a matter of common ground: it certainly was not a matter of decision.

Going back to Peter Gibson J's judgment, where the clause is set out in full, one sees that the corresponding part is almost in identical wording and has evidently been taken from the same precedent as the one that I have referred to earlier, but of course it has the very elaborate provisions in it which are omitted from the lease before me. But what is more to the point for this purpose is that in the *reddendum* there is nothing at all comparable to clause 3 (i), giving some indication of the time for determination that we have here. The relevant provision is this: 'Yielding and paying' and so forth

'during the next five years of the term commencing on December 25 1977 (hereinafter called "the first review period") the rent payable by the lessee shall be whichever is the higher—£18,000 per annum and the open market rental of the demised premises for the review period'.

Then, 'Such reviewed rents to be determined in accordance with the provisions in that behalf.'

So there is nothing there comparable to a determination at a particular date or anything of that nature.

Touche Ross & Co. v. *Secretary of State for the Environment* (1982) 265 EG 982 is another case which I think I should notice. Again it is a decision of the Court of Appeal; in this case comprising Lawton, Griffiths and Dillon LJJ, and it proceeded on the same basis, that the time of determination was when actually the determining surveyor or arbitrator got round to determining it. What had happened was that there was a late reference to the surveyor (late in the sense that it was outside the time for reference to the surveyor that the clause had provided) and the issue was whether time was of the essence, which His Honour Judge Finlay, sitting in this court, I think, had said it was, but on which the Court of Appeal (in this instance unanimously) took a different view. As I say, the whole matter is one of assumption only (there is certainly no decision on the point), but we have here a different type of clause. What I note about it is that in the definition of market rack rental for the purposes of this clause it means the annual amount obtainable, at the date of agreement or determination as aforesaid, as between a willing landlord and a willing tenant. There seems to be a very strong context in that case for the assumption made, but here the context, there being clause 4 (i) referring to provisions elsewhere for the determination and linking them in, is that one is compelled to look elsewhere for it. Then one comes, as I have indicated already, to clause 3. I think that deals with the authorities.

10.2 (a) Omissions, mistakes and rectification

Where a document fails to set out the common intention of the parties, rectification of the document may be granted if all the conditions for rectification are met. However, in *Pugh* v. *Smiths Industries* (for facts and further extracts see above at page 127, 6.4), rectification was refused.

PUGH v. SMITHS INDUSTRIES LTD AND OTHERS
F.A. WELCH v. SMITHS INDUSTRIES LTD AND OTHERS
SMITHS INDUSTRIES LTD v. PUGH AND OTHERS

Chancery Division   (1982) 264 EG 823

GOULDING J: There is a common intention, it is submitted, to have a rent review clause. Nothing is said about any special or one-sided rent review clause, and it must have been in the minds of experienced estate agents on each side that rent review clauses just keep the market rent up to date in the way the House of Lords describes in the authorities. That continuing common intention was not carried into effect by the lease actually executed, [counsel for the tenant] submits, because what was put in it was a very extraordinary clause that would not be within the common professional understanding of 'rent review clause' without some special qualification. I am paraphrasing, but I hope not wholly misrepresenting, his argument. Therefore there was a slip or misunderstanding that on the lines of *Joscelyn* v. *Nissen* justified rectification by the court. All the more so because as [counsel for the tenant] says on instructions, though it is not actually in evidence, no one was conscious of this point when the rent review machinery was set in motion. It came as a surprise, he suggests—and I will assume for the moment that it is so—to both parties when [counsel for the landlord] raised the point and, although [counsel for the tenant] did not put it quite this way, Smiths Industries Ltd are simply seeking to take advantage of a verbal misfortune of the tenants and get something they were never meant to get.

I can see the force, in a broad way, of that argument, but it contains I think a fatal error of reasoning. For rectification it is necessary not only to see that something in the written document is not in accord with a common intention but to see what the common intention was. I do not know at all, and I should be merely guessing if I said I did know, that Smiths Industries Ltd would have been content with the rent review clause modified in the way that [counsel for the tenant] proposes. What does seem to be clear is that both sides were represented, when it came to drafting, by highly experienced solicitors who knew a good deal about leases and agreed, in great detail, the wording of the lease, and I think their clients, who, or, in the case of the company, whose officers, could not be expected consciously to have every detail in mind, really intended to have the benefit of and to be bound by whatever form of words should be agreed on their behalf between their respective solicitors. The correspondence that Young and Brown put in evidence does show indeed with what attention to the minutiae of detail their own solicitors saw to the business.

Accordingly I am forced to the conclusion that in spite of its superficial attraction the claim for rectification is not only brought forward at a very late date but does not really get off the ground.

A clause which provides that a reviewed rent shall, in default of agreement, be fixed by an arbitrator should be construed as an agreement to arbitrate and not as an agreement to abide by a valuation. The rent should be such as it would have been reasonable for these landlords and these tenants to have agreed under the lease. It would consequently be proper for the arbitrator to take into account all considerations which would affect the mind of either party in connection with the negotiation of such a rent, as for example, past expenditure on improvements.

THOMAS BATES AND SON LTD v. WYNDHAM'S LINGERIE LTD

Court of Appeal [1981] 1 WLR 505

A lease was granted pursuant to a renewal clause in an earlier lease. The earlier lease provided that the rent should be agreed between the parties or, in default of agreement, fixed by an arbitrator. The initial rent was agreed but the parties agreed that subsequently the rent should be reviewed on specified dates in the future. The new lease which was drawn up by the landlords provided for the reviewed rents to be such as shall have been agreed between the lessor and the lessee but made no provision in default of agreement. When the lease was executed, the tenants noticed the clause was defective but failed to bring this to the landlords' notice. At the next review date the parties could not agree a new rent and the landlords brought an action, *inter alia*, for rectification of the lease. The judge made an order declaring that the rent during the review periods should be the market rent for the premises and required the lease to be rectified to provide for the revised rents, in default of agreement, to be determined by an arbitrator. The tenants appealed.

Held: The judge's order regarding rectification would be affirmed but deleting the declaration, that where one party to a document was aware that it did not give effect to a common intention of the parties due to a mistake on the part of the other party and executed the document without telling the other party and where (*per* Buckley LJ) the mistake was one calculated to benefit him, or (*per* Eveleigh LJ) the mistake was detrimental to the other party, he was precluded from resisting rectification on the ground that the mistake was not, at the time of the execution of the document, mutual. Here on the evidence the judge was right to order rectification of the lease.

When the arbitrator fixed the revised rent pursuant to the rent review clause as rectified, he would have to assess what rent it would have been reasonable for the landlords and the tenants to have agreed under the lease having regard to all the circumstances relevant to any negotiations between the parties for a new rent from the review date. *Ponsford* v. *H.M.S. Aerosols Ltd* [1979] AC 63 distinguished. (Considered later in the judgment of Buckley LJ: see later for facts—page 237 under 'improvements'.) *Per* Buckley LJ: If the decision on the rectification point were wrong, then by a process of implication, the rent to be ascertained in default of agreement would be a fair rent as between the landlords and the tenants. It would be most unjust for the landlords to receive no rent because of the failure of the parties to agree.

BUCKLEY LJ: The landlords claim rectification in the present case on the basis of a principle enunciated by Pennycuick J in *A. Roberts & Co. Ltd* v. *Leicestershire County Council* [1961] Ch 555, 570 where he said:

'The second ground rests upon the principle that a party is entitled to rectification of a contract upon proof that he believed a particular term to be included in the contract, and that the other party concluded the contract with the omission or a variation of that term in the knowledge that the first party believed the term to be included ...'

'The principle is stated in *Snell on Equity*, 25th ed. (1960), p 569 as follows: "By what appears to be a species of equitable estoppel, if one party to a transaction knows that the instrument contains a mistake in his favour but does nothing to correct it, he (and those claiming under him) will be precluded from resisting rectification on the ground that the mistake is unilateral and not common."'

Of course if a document is executed in circumstances in which one party realises that in some respect it does not accurately reflect what down to that moment had been the common intention of the parties, it cannot be said that the document is executed under a common mistake, because the party who has realised the mistake is no longer labouring under the mistake. There may be cases in which the principle enunciated by Pennycuick J applies although there is no prior common intention, but we are not, I think, concerned with such a case here, for it seems to me, upon the facts that I have travelled through, that it is established that the parties had a common intention down to the time when Mr Avon realised the mistake in the terms of the lease, a common intention that the rent in respect of any period after the first five years should be agreed or, in default of agreement, fixed by an arbitrator.

The principle so enunciated by Pennycuick J was referred to, with approval, in this court in *Riverlate Properties Ltd* v. *Paul* [1975] Ch 133, where Russell LJ, reading the judgment of the court, said, at p 140:

'It may be that the original conception of reformation of an instrument by rectification was based solely upon common mistake: but certainly in these days rectification may be based upon such knowledge on the part of the lessee: see, for example, *A. Roberts & Co. Ltd* v. *Leicestershire County Council* [1961] Ch 555. Whether there was in any particular case knowledge of the intention and mistake of the other party must be a question of fact to be decided upon the evidence. Basically it appears to us that it must be such as to involve the lessee in a degree of sharp practice.'

In that case the lessee against whom the lessor sought to rectify a lease was held to have had no such knowledge as would have brought the doctrine into play. The reference to 'sharp practice' may thus be said to have been an *obiter dictum*. Undoubtedly I think in any such case the conduct of the defendant must be such as to make it inequitable that he should be allowed to object to the rectification of the document. If this necessarily implies some measure of 'sharp practice', so be it; but for my part I think that the doctrine is one which depends more upon the equity of the position. The graver the character of the conduct involved, no doubt the heavier the burden of proof may be; but, in my view, the conduct must be such as to affect the conscience of the party who has suppressed the fact that he has recognised the presence of a mistake.

For this doctrine—that is to say the doctrine of *A. Roberts & Co. Ltd* v. *Leicestershire County Council*—to apply I think it must be shown: first, that one party A erroneously believed that the document sought to be rectified contained a particular term or provision, or possibly did not contain a particular term or provision which, mistakenly, it did contain; secondly, that the other party B was aware of the omission or the inclusion and that it was due to a mistake on the part of A; thirdly, that B has omitted to draw the mistake to the notice of A. And I think there must be a fourth element involved, namely, that the mistake must be one calculated to benefit B. If these requirements are satisfied, the court may regard it as inequitable to allow B to resist rectification to give effect to A's intention on the ground that the mistake was not, at the time of execution of the document, a mutual mistake ...

It seems to me, as I have already said, that the omission from the review clause of any reference to arbitration was one which was clearly contrary to the landlords' interests, one which must have occurred as a result of a mistake, and one which Mr

Avon, on his own evidence, recognised, and must I think be taken to have recognised, as having been the result of a mistake on the part of Mr Bates ...

I agree that it is highly improbable that Mr Bates would have purposely adopted a form of clause which was so disadvantageous as the review clause is with the omission of any reference to arbitration ...

So far as rectification is concerned, the language which the judge has adopted follows the language used in the option clauses in this case, except that he used the word 'determined' instead of 'fixed,' and perhaps it would have been better if the word had been 'fixed'.

If the lease is so rectified the question arises: by what measure is an arbitrator to fix the rent if the parties do not agree? [Counsel for the landlords] initially contended that the arbitrator so-called would act not as an arbitrator but as a valuer. He based that argument upon the use of the words 'shall have agreed' and the word 'fixed' in the review clause. On that basis he submitted that the rent should be the market rent for the property, on the authority of a decision of the House of Lords in *Ponsford* v. *H.M.S. Aerosols Ltd* [1979] AC 63. Subsequently he conceded that the clause must be read as an agreement to arbitrate and not as an agreement to abide by a valuation. Upon that footing he agreed that, upon the true construction of the clause, the rent should be such as it would have been reasonable for these landlords and these tenants to have agreed under the lease. It would consequently be proper for the arbitrator to take into account all considerations which would affect the mind of either party in connection with the negotiation of such a rent, as, for example, past expenditure by the tenant on improvements ...

In my judgment, [counsel for the landlords] was right to make that concession and to have accepted that the present case falls within the reasoning of the minority of the House of Lords in *Ponsford* v. *H.M.S. Aerosols Ltd* and not within the reasoning of the majority in that case. The review clause which was there under consideration was a review clause in a lease which provided for a yearly rent of £9000:

> 'during the first seven years of the said term and during the second and third seven years of the term ... the sum of £9,000 aforesaid or such sum whichever be the higher as shall be assessed as a reasonable rent for the demised premises for the appropriate period such assessment to be made in the following manner that is to say: (a) Such assessment as shall be agreed between the parties hereto in writing'—and there were certain provisions as to the date by which that agreement should be reached—'(b) In the event of the parties hereto failing to reach such agreement as aforesaid on or before the date appointed ... then the reasonable rent for the second and third periods shall be fixed or assessed by an independent surveyor: ...' [see [1977] 1 WLR 1029, 1031].

That form of clause, as it seems to me, focuses attention upon what is there described as 'a reasonable rent for the demised premises' for the appropriate period, and that expression is first used without any reference to agreement between the parties to the lease at all. It then goes on to provide that such assessment—that is to say, the fixing of the amount of the rent so to be charged—shall be either agreed or, in default of agreement, arrived at by valuation by an independent surveyor. That form of wording, in my judgment, certainly affected the views of the majority in the House of Lords in that case. Viscount Dilhorne said, at p 77:

> 'The rent payable by the lessees will of course be rent for the demised premises but as I see it, the task of the surveyor is not to assess what would be a reasonable rent for the lessees to pay but what is a reasonable rent for the premises.'

Lord Fraser of Tullybelton said, at p 83:

'In my opinion the words point unambiguously to the result contended for by the landlords ... and they mean the reasonable rent assessed on an objective basis, without reference to the particular landlord or the particular tenant or to the history of how the premises came to be built or paid for.'

Lord Keith of Kinkel, at p 86:

'In my opinion the words "a reasonable rent for the demised premises" simply mean "the rent at which the demised premises might reasonably be expected to let."'

The other two Lords, Lord Wilberforce and Lord Salmon, took a contrary view. They thought that what had to be ascertained was what would be reasonable between the particular parties to the transaction. However, they were in the minority upon the construction of that particular rent review clause. But it appears to me that the terms of the clause there under consideration were noticeably different in important respects from the clause which we have, which refers to nothing other than such rent as the parties shall have agreed. Consequently I think that [counsel for the landlords] was well advised in making the concession which he made.

[Counsel for the tenants], on the other hand, who had argued in the earlier stages of the appeal that in default of agreement the rent should continue after the review date at the original rate of £2350 per annum, conceded that in the light of a decision of this court in *Beer* v. *Bowden (Note)*, post p 522, he could no longer support that argument. That again was a concession which I think he was constrained to make. *Beer* v. *Bowden* was only brought to the attention of counsel and, through counsel, to the attention of the court late in the course of the argument.

So the parties are now at one, that on the true construction of the clause as rectified, the rent is to be fixed by the arbitrator at such amount as it would be reasonable for the parties to agree having regard to all such considerations as I have mentioned. This was not the construction adopted by the judge, who, as appears from the terms of his order, implied a term that the rent to be agreed should be the market rent. His attention had not, of course, been drawn to the decision of this court in *Beer* v. *Bowden*. As I understand the position, neither party now contends that the judge's view in that respect is right, and I myself am satisfied that the market rent would not provide a proper standard to adopt in the present case. In my judgment, in default of agreement between the parties, the arbitrator would have to assess what rent it would have been reasonable for these landlords and these tenants to have under this lease having regard to all the circumstances relevant to any negotiations between them of a new rent from the review date.

If I were wrong on a point of rectification, then, on construction and by a process of implication, the rent to be ascertained in default of agreement must, I think, be a fair rent as between the landlords and the tenants. It would be most unjust that the landlords should receive no rent because of failure of the parties to agree. The landlords have granted a 14-year term and the court must endeavour to fill any gap in the terms of the lease by means of a fair and reasonable implication as to what the parties must have intended their bargain to be. See in this connection the decision of this court in *F. & G. Sykes (Wessex) Ltd* v. *Fine Fare Ltd* [1967] 1 Lloyd's Rep 53, which was a case very different on its facts from the present, but in which the court explained the function of any court of construction where parties have embarked upon any commercial relationship but under terms that are not altogether adequate to cover the eventualities. The court would ascertain by enquiry what rent the landlords and the tenants, as willing negotiators anxious to reach agreement, would arrive at for each of the two rent review periods. In short, the standard would be the same, as I see it, as would have to be adopted by an arbitrator under the clause if it is rectified in the way in which I consider that it should be rectified.

10.2 (b)   Correcting an omission and filling in the lacuna

WOLVERHAMPTON AND DUDLEY BREWERIES PLC v. TRUSTHOUSE FORTE CATERING LTD

Chancery Division   (1984) 272 EG 1073

A rent review clause was defective in that it contained a lacuna as a result of which the reviewed rent could not be fixed. The landlord submitted that an implication could be made with reasonable certainty which would fill the lacuna, so that the document would, with the addition of the appropriate words, contain the agreement that the parties had intended to express. The result of the landlord's submissions meant that if the landlord served a review notice which specified a sum for a revised rent, then unless there was either an agreement between the parties within three months after the date of posting that notice or there was an election by the tenant for an arbitration by an independent surveyor, then that sum became the rent payable on review. The tenant contended for more alterations so as to avoid the possibility of being burdened with the landlord's specified sum in the trigger notice in the event he was out of time for arbitration. Time was stated to be of the essence in the lease.

Held: This was a case where the court could collect 'from the four corners of the document' that something had been omitted and could further, with sufficient precision, identify the nature of the omission. This was notwithstanding the danger that under the provisions as construed, the landlord could specify any sum in his trigger notice, which, should the tenant fail to act promptly, could become binding on the tenant.

HARMAN J: The matter arises out of a lease dated 4 February 1974 between Wolverhampton and Dudley Breweries and Trusthouse Forte Catering. The lease, being for a term of 21 years, contains as do so many modern leases provisions for review of the rent at seven-year stages. The first seven years are taken up by express provisions with defined sums and nothing helpful or useful can be derived from (A) (B) and (C) of the *reddendum*.
   One comes then to (D) of the *reddendum* which is:

'for the next 7 years of the said term either the yearly rent of £6,000 or the open market rental value of the demised premises at the review date whichever is the higher ...'

When I first observed this subclause during [counsel for the landlord's] opening, it seemed to me that it might leave one with a lacuna such that it required one to know the one or the other of two figures and to take the higher and that if one did not know both the figures there was no way one could determine which was the higher. [Counsel for the tenant] has pointed out to me that within the context of this document as a whole the *reddendum*, which requires the rent to be paid during the said term, that is throughout the whole 21 years, coupled with the provision for review built in, does carry a necessary implication that if the figure which is uncertain in (D) (that is the open market rental value of the demised premises) remains uncertain, then the fixed sum of £6000 must continue, and it seems to me that that is a reason for coming to the conclusion that this is not one of those unhappy cases, sometimes called 'gap' cases, where no effective rent has been reserved. It has a material bearing on the matter, because if it were a 'gap' case the court would, I think, strive to fill the gaps if it possibly could and would be the more willing to read implications into the review machinery to make it work. However, I believe that my initial reaction was wrong and no such pressure is upon the court from this *reddendum*.

From the *reddendum* which I have read it will be obvious that there are terms there which are not defined at this stage of the matter. 'Open market rental value' and 'review date' are both matters which require definition. They are in fact defined in the second schedule to the document. That has a definition in (1) of the 'open market rental value', on which for this particular question's purposes nothing turns, and then has in (2) a definition of review date as being the expiration of the 7th and 14th years respectively of the said term, as the context requires, and then in (3) comes the words which have given rise to this summons. For this present purpose I had better read the whole down to the point at which it ceases to become controversial:

'The Lessors shall serve notice on the Lessees requiring a review of the rent not earlier than a clear two quarters of a year immediately preceding or later than two clear quarters of the year immediately following the review date ...'

Pausing for an instant as I read, it is odd that in the second line the reference is to 'a clear two quarters of a year', but in the third line only to 'two clear quarters', and one begins to wonder slightly about the drafting, or perhaps the typing, of the document and questions about 'attorneys' blundering clerks' begin to raise themselves in the back of the mind of the reader.

The clause goes on in line 5,

'... and the market rental shall be (a) such sum as shall be agreed between the parties before the expiration of 3 months immediately after the date of posting of such notice as aforesaid in substitution for the said sum ...'

I pause again to say that at that point quite evidently something is wrong. The phrase 'in substitution for the said sum' is meaningless because there is no 'sum' which is 'said' at that point. One therefore is clear that one is in difficulties with the document. I return to the reading:

'... or (b) determined at the election of the lessees, (to be made by counternotice in writing served by the lessees upon the lessors not later than the expiration of 3 months after the said 3 months) by an independent surveyor appointed for that purpose by the parties ...'

and so forth, with a machinery provision to make the Arbitration Act apply.

As will be apparent to anybody who has followed those recitals there is at once a lacuna. So much [counsel for the tenant] entirely accepted. That something is wrong can be gathered with certainty from the four corners of this clause.

One's first reaction, of course, was to refer to the counterpart to see whether the counterpart to the lease produced any better guide so that one might see in some way that there had been typing errors in the original which did not appear in the counterpart. Unfortunately, the counterpart is even worse than the original since it even omits the (a) before the provisions as to agreement between the parties of a sum, and one is left with no assistance whatever from the counterpart, and merely a certainty of blunder.

[Counsel for the tenant] also calls attention, and in my view this is material and falls to be borne in mind, that this particular lease contains in subclause (5) of the second schedule the express provision:

'All stipulations as to time in the foregoing subclauses numbered (1), (2), (3) and (4) shall be of the essence of the contract and shall not be capable of enlargement save as agreed in writing by the parties.'

Thus it is quite plain that this is a document which carries very serious (to describe them as penal is wrong) consequences in that the time limits must be observed, failing which the rights given have gone.

I return, then, to the subclause (3) to consider, having determined that there is something wrong, what one should do. I am guided in this by the words of Jenkins LJ in *Re Whitrick, decd* [1957] 1 WLR 884, for the citation of principle at p 887, where the lord justice said in the second paragraph on that page:

'The reading of words into a will as a matter of necessary implication is a measure which any court of construction should apply with the greatest caution. Many wills contain slips and omissions which fail to provide for contingencies which, to anyone reading the will, might appear contingencies for which any testator would obviously wish to provide. The court cannot rewrite the testamentary provisions in wills which come before it for construction. This type of treatment of an imperfect will is only legitimate where the court can collect from the four corners of the document that something has been omitted and, further, collect with sufficient precision the nature of the omission.'

Here, as I have said, the fact that the court can and must collect from the four corners of the document that something has been omitted is agreed. [Counsel for the tenant] does not contest it. But, the second part of the lord justice's principle is just as important: 'One must collect with sufficient precision the nature of the omission.'

There was also cited to me an earlier case upon a settlement, *Re Daniel's Settlement Trusts* [1875] 1 ChD 375, where a strong Court of Appeal overruled Sir George Jessel MR on a question of construction and made an implication. The facts of both *Re Daniel* and *Re Whitrick* are miles from this case and are of no help. The principle, however, enunciated by Jenkins LJ is of help, and is said by both sides to apply, not only to documents such as settlements and wills which are the unilateral act of the settlor or testator but also to bilateral or multilateral documents which are the result of consensual negotiation, such as leases or, indeed, such as commercial contracts, and for that *Chitty on Contracts* at para 765 is a guide and support by way of textbook authority.

[Counsel for the tenant]'s attack upon [counsel for the landlord]'s attempted implication here turns entirely on the question of whether there is reasonable certainty that the implication [counsel for the landlord] makes must be the correct implication. [Counsel for the landlord] submits that having gathered a blunder one should also gather with adequate clarity and certainty the proposition that one can read into this lease in the fifth line immediately before the little 'a' in brackets the words 'specified in such notice or' and then '(a) such sum as shall be agreed.' If that is done, he says that the matter is an implication, a correction by construction of a document which is obviously faulty and about which it is reasonably certain that that phrase must have been what the parties intended.

The result of it is that if the lessor serves a review notice which specifies a sum, then unless either there is an agreement between the parties within three months after the date of posting of that notice or there is an election by the lessee for an arbitration by an independent surveyor, then that sum bites. It operates entirely satisfactorily to make sense of the words 'in substitution for the said sum' at the end of (3) (a) because the said sum will then be the sum specified in such notice. It is plainly a possible implication in a document where there is a blunder, and it is a persuasive implication.

[Counsel for the tenant]'s attack on it runs as follows. He says, in my view correctly, that I must be reasonably certain that that is the right implication and that I cannot be so certain because there is another equally appropriate set of words that could be read into the doument, which if read into the document would deal with the difficulties as aptly as [counsel for the landlord], or reasonably aptly at least, and that if there are two reasonably apt implications I cannot with certainty say that one of them must apply.

[Counsel for the tenant]'s implication is to say that in (3) (b) the election for arbitration shall not be at the sole right of the lessee, but shall be at the mutual right, or alternative right, of the lessor and the lessee. He says that if one implies by way of construction into (3) (b) words such as the following, 'determined at the election of the'—I insert—'lessors or'—I go back to reading—'lessees to be made by counternotice in writing served by the'—I insert—'lessors or'—I go back to reading—'lessees upon the'—I insert—'lessees or'—I go back to reading—'lessors not later than 3 months ...' one can get an entirely businesslike, sensible and apt set of machinery. Further, he says that it must be remembered that this is a lease where time is expressly made of the essence of the operations by subclause (5) to which I have already referred. If that be not the way it should have been written out, one is construing the lease so as to leave the landlord with the right to plant what I described, and I think [counsel for the tenant] accepted, as a time bomb under the lessee; a delayed action bomb ticking away which, if the lessee does not remember the date accurately and allows the review date to go past, will land him (if I may be colloquial) with whatever sum the landlord has chosen to put into his review notice which starts the whole process of (3) running. In my view it is correct that the landlord can put any sum into his notice. He could put a million pounds a quarter into it. It is clear that if [counsel for the landlord]'s construction were right the result would be that if the tenant fails to exercise the election given by (3) (b) he would be landed with such an appalling burden.

[Counsel for the tenant] says that I have got to deal with the oddity of the phrase at the end of (a) in (3) 'in substitution for the said sum', because, said [counsel for the tenant], facing correctly and boldly his difficulties, if I do not I shall leave the lease with a plain nonsense verbally in it. He said that is quite easy. One can say, since we are plainly dealing with a lease which is deficient in some ways, that there is a deficiency here in that the word 'sum' is wrong and 'in substitution for the said rent' ought to have been used rather than 'in substitution for the said sum'.

I find [counsel for the tenant]'s argument impressive, particularly by reason of the danger to the tenant that arises on the fact that the landlord may specify any sum and if the tenant fails to act he may find himself paying a figure far beyond that which he should have done. None the less, as it seems to me, [counsel for the landlord]'s construction is right. [Counsel for the tenant]'s ingenious set of insertions involves alterations at, I think, four different places in the document. To my mind it is far more likely, when construing a matter by implying extra words, that one single phrase is what is to be implied rather than words dotted about up and down the document. In my view, I do reach reasonable certainty that the correct reading of this lease, which is agreed to be a document where there is a blunder, is to be modified by construction by adding in the words, 'specified in such notice or' before (a) (3).

Note: In *Amalgamated Estates Ltd* v. *Joystretch Manufacturing Ltd* (1980) 257 EG 489 (see earlier, page 87) it was held that there was no implied term that the rent specified in a landlord's review notice has to be a *bona fide* pre-estimate of the market rental of the premises.

10.2 (c) Rectification on the grounds of mutual mistake

An order for rectification on the grounds of mutual mistake was made in the case of *Equity & Law Life Assurance Society Ltd* v. *Coltness Group Ltd*, on an application by the landlord and was effective against the current lessee who had taken an assignment from the original tenant. The assignee was held not to have established that it was a purchaser for value without notice.

EQUITY & LAW LIFE ASSURANCE SOCIETY LTD v. COLTNESS GROUP LTD

Chancery Division   (1983) 267 EG 949

An underlease granted in 1965 for a term of 25 years provided for rent reviews at the end of the seventh and 14th years. The landlord and tenant agreed terms for the implementation of the first rent review which were recorded in a memorandum which was affixed to the original underlease and which stated:

> 'until the expiration of the within-written lease the rent payable thereunder [exclusive of the contributions to be paid by the tenant to the landlord under the provisions of clause 2 (2)] shall be £4900 a year.'

(The contributions were towards the landlord's costs and expenses.) Subsequently the tenant assigned its lease. When the second review period was due, however, a dispute arose between the landlord and the assignee, with the assignee contending that there could be no second review since there was an agreement under which the rent from December 1972 was fixed at the sum of £4900 per annum which agreement overrode the rent review clause in the lease. The landlord sought a declaration in his favour as to the true construction of the agreement affixed to the underlease or rectification.

Held: The landlord's case on construction failed but on the evidence it would be right to rectify the agreement since it was never intended between the parties that the agreement should override the second rent review provided for in the underlease. Mere undertakings of certain obligations under a lease without payment for value did not make the assignee a purchaser for value.

WHITFORD J: There are really only two questions to be decided. Firstly, the question of construction. One has to read the memorandum to decide what it means in the light of the document as a whole. If, as the plaintiffs contend, it amounts to no more than an agreement for payment of a rental of £4900 per annum from December 1972 until expiry, but subject to all the other provisions of the lease, that is to say, subject *inter alia* to the review in 1979, then that is an end of the matter. I may say at once that I have come to the conclusion that the plaintiffs' case on construction fails. If their case on construction fails, they have a second line of attack, because what they say is that if, contrary to their submission, on a true construction of the underlease, as amended by the memorandum endorsed, the rent payable is for a fixed sum from December 1972 to the expiry, then there should be rectification because this is a case of mutual mistake. It was never intended as between them and Associated Development Holdings (formerly Executive Business Services Ltd) that provision for a second review should be overridden. The negotiations leading up to the memorandum were concerned and concerned only with a first review of the rent payable. So they say that the memorandum should be rectified so as to include the proviso that the rent payable should be £4900 per annum subject to further review of rent pursuant to clause 5 of the lease.

That is a question of evidence and I may say at this stage that I have come to the conclusion that the plaintiffs have satisfactorily established their case on mutual mistake, so that really this is a case where there ought to be rectification, subject only to the third and last point, which is whether there should be rectification as against these defendants albeit they were *bona fide* purchasers for value without notice. I do not think that the defendants have succeeded in making out their case in this regard, and so the plaintiffs succeed on rectification as against the defendants.

Let me, however, go back. As I have said, in my view on construction the plaintiffs' case fails. It was submitted on behalf of the plaintiffs that to construe this memorandum in the sense contended for by the defendants would lead to absurd results, and hereunder particular reference was made to clause 4 (b), the terms of which I have already referred to. It is said that under the construction propounded by the defendants they themselves would lose the benefit of the provision that if there were a fire and they were to seek, as under clause 4 (b) of the lease they would be entitled to, to secure the suspension in respect of rent payable for some appropriate period. I think it was rightly said that the construction contended for by the defendants is, on the face of it, the meaning which the words must convey to any person reading the memorandum. And I think it is right further that if this memorandum be construed in the sense contended for, the provisions of clause 4 (b) would still continue to operate because they operate as against whatever rent may in fact have been reserved at any given time under the agreement. They would have operated against the original rent, a rent after a first review or a second review, or against any rent which was in fact negotiated for the remainder of the term so as to exclude further review. It is, I think, significant that there is an express saving of the additional contribution by way of rent provided for by clause 2 (2), but it is also significant that there was no express saving in respect of the rent review provision.

I do not think it can be suggested that one ought *prima facie* to come to some sort of contrary conclusion upon the basis that it would be absurd to imagine that a rent review provision would be forgone by a landlord. Evidence has been sworn by affidavit on both sides, in particular Mr Tooke, who was the partner in the firm of Godfrey Payton & Co. responsible for the review on the plaintiffs' side at the relevant time. In his experience of rent reviews, which goes back for a period of 30 years, he has come across occasions when, in addition to the rent at the time of the rent review, settlement has ben reached on other terms so as to vary the frequency of the rent review, or even to fix a final figure and to exclude all possibility of any further rent review.

One of the oddities of this case is that there was quite a correspondence at the time of the rent review and there was even correspondence about the memorandum, so that particular case was taken on the plaintiffs' side as regards the terms of the memorandum. Undoubtedly the language chosen by the plaintiffs was language from which the plaintiffs, or at least Mr Gunraj, who was in this regard the solicitor in the employment of the plaintiffs, was not happy to move. It is strange to observe that when he was seeking from another firm of solicitors, Titmuss, Sainer and Webb, their approval of the terms of this memorandum, apart from some alterations which the plaintiffs were not prepared to accept, which I think were intended to overcome stamp duty, Mr Gunraj on behalf of the plaintiffs also rejected a variation in the terms of the memorandum. This variation would have recorded the lease which was vested in Associated Development Holdings as having been varied pursuant to provisions of the rent review herein mentioned that is to say mentioned in the main agreement, which might have improved the plaintiffs' position on construction. Anyway this was rejected and I find myself unable to accept as a matter of construction that the language can be given anything other than its apparent meaning.

That brings me to mistake. As I have said, there has been evidence put in and I have, I think—at least it was not suggested to the contrary—the whole of the relevant correspondence. I have had the evidence of Mr Tooke, his affidavit and his evidence given orally because he was called for cross-examination. It was indeed in cross-examination that he told me, and he said it was a matter of experience, that he had had negotiations where not merely the rent had been reviewed but the actual terms, as to periods for review. Giving oral evidence he told me that there was never any question of anything having been discussed during the negotiations other than the amount of the rent, that there was never any question of changing the provisions with regard to review. This, I think, is amply borne out by the correspondence through which I have been taken in some detail.

I am aware, and I have already referred to it in another context, of the fact that the language here chosen is language chosen by the plaintiffs. I am aware, too, of the fact that under the basis of their claim in respect of rectification the language chosen could have been very much happier. I was referred to passages in a well-known textbook about the importance, where a plaintiff is claiming rectification, of his producing strong tangible evidence and so forth. I was reminded also of the observations of Lord Russell of Killowen that what is required in a case of rectification is convincing proof. I am quite convinced that the plaintiffs have proved their case in this regard. If there had been any question of excluding a review at the end of the 14th year this must have been a matter of discussion even if it were not dealt with in correspondence, and I cannot myself believe that it would even have been discussed without, if it were agreed, having been confirmed and referred to in the correspondence. The terms of the memorandum do not adequately represent the bargain that was struck, and the plaintiffs' case in this particular regard is made out.

As to the question of a defence by these defendants based on an assertion that they were bona fide purchasers for value—they were not. A Mr Gibbons has been much concerned, both at one time as a director of Executive Business Services but at a later stage as a director or chairman of the defendant company, in the business carried on at the premises in question. He in fact signed the underlease on behalf of Executive Business Services Ltd, and he also signed as guarantor. Interrogatories were put to him and he accepts that he was aware of the rent-review provisions, but he asserts, and he was not cross-examined about it, that he was not in any way aware of the details of the rent-review terms. He was not aware of what had been agreed and he had in fact relinquishd his directorship of what by now had become Associated Development Holdings at the end of 1972. Asked whether the underlease was purchased by the defendants from Associated Development Holdings he says quite uncompromisingly that it was not. There was no question here of the defendants having acquired their interest for value in terms of some sort of cash payment. What was advanced on their side was that they undertook certain obligations when they took the assignment of the underlease, and that no doubt is true. But it does not, in my judgment, make them a purchaser for value.

So far as the question of notice is concerned, had the defendants succeeded on the first half of this point they would have got home. I do not think it can be suggested, if one looks at the terms of the memorandum, that this is a case where it ought to be said that, merely from an inspection of the terms of the memorandum, the defendants should have been put on notice to make further inquiry. It is true enough that at a later stage a Mr O'Dell, who was advising some of the interests on the defendants' side, when he first saw this memorandum expressed amazement as to its terms and that he did not think they were clear enough, but this is not a case of the type of *Re Nisbet and Potts' Contract* [1906] 1 Ch 386. The latter was a case concerned with acceptance by a purchaser of a possessory or squatter's title acquired within 40 years prior to its purchase, where it was found by Farwell J and by the Court of Appeal that it was no good for the purchasers to assert that he had no notice of adverse title. He should have been put upon inquiry and reasonable care would have demanded that he should have made inquiry. I do not think the terms of the memorandum would put anybody on inquiry or make it reasonable that they should make inquiry.

Then it was contended that the knowledge of Mr Gibbons should be attributed to the defendants. I do not know that I would accept that that proposition could be said to be good, but what was his knowledge? On the face of it, he had no knowledge of the negotiations which had taken place. That is at any rate what he was sworn to in answer to interrogatories and he has not been cross-examined on it. On the question of notice, the defendants could have in fact succeeded, but in my judgment they have failed to establish that they were bona fide purchasers for value. The plaintiffs succeed and there will be an order for rectification as asked.

10.2 (d)   Accidental omission of a review clause and rectification

Where the omission of a rent review clause from a lease was accidental and the lessees knew before the lease was executed that the lessor believed that such a clause was included, the court may order rectification of the lease.

CENTRAL & METROPOLITAN ESTATES LTD v. COMPUSAVE AND OTHERS

Chancery Division   (1983) 266 EG 900

The landlord granted a 20-year lease at a rent of £3500 a year without providing for a rent review. Before the lease was granted negotiations between the parties had contemplated that the rent would be reviewed every five years. The landlord sought rectification.

Held: There were clear indications in the documentary evidence and the inherent probabilities of the circumstances that the tenant had executed the lease in the knowledge that the landlord had mistakenly thought it contained provision for rent reviews. The landlord was entitled to relief from the consequences of his unilateral mistake. The lease was rectified by the insertion after the figure of £3500 of the words, 'for the first five years of the term (such rent to be reviewed at the expiration of such period and of each subsequent period of five years)'. The tenant would, however, be allowed to surrender the lease at the end of the first five year period.

GERALD GODFREY QC (sitting as a High Court judge): But I accept (and it is not now suggested otherwise) that, unlike the plaintiff, Mr and Mrs Brennan were indeed aware on 28 May 1980 that the lease contained no rent review provision. If there was any mistake at all at this date, it was unilateral and not common; the plaintiff's mistake but not the defendants'. When a party to a deed insists that it accurately reflects his intention at the time he executed it, it is a strong thing to do to hold against him that, contrary to what he says, he was aware not only that the deed did not contain the provision sought to be inserted by rectification but also that he knew the other party believed that it did contain that provision. With this in mind, I address myself to the central question: have Central & Metropolitan satisfied me, on the evidence, that when Mrs Brennan executed the lease on 28 May 1980 on behalf of Compusave she must have been aware that Central & Metropolitan believed it to contain a rent review provision which it did not in fact contain?

In arriving at the conclusion to which I have come, I have taken into account what I have found to be the unsatisfactory nature of the evidence of Mr Brennan and Mrs Brennan, the correspondence to which I have referred, and what explanation of the facts is inherently most probable, as I conceive I am entitled to do: compare *Mortimore* v. *Shortall* (1842) 2 Dr & War 363. Against the assertions of Mr and Mrs Brennan that they believed the lease to be in accordance with the agreement they had reached with Central & Metropolitan (which they say they thought was an agreement for a lease of 20 years at a rent of £3500 per annum for the whole term) Central & Metropolitan was unable to offer any direct evidence of its own as to the defendants' state of mind. But this is not surprising. In any case in which the plaintiff seeks rectification of a document and the defendant denies that he was aware of a mistake made by the plaintiff but had suppressed that fact, the plaintiff is rarely going to be able to dispute this by direct evidence. I must attach considerable weight to the assertion of Mr and Mrs Brennan that the lease accorded with their understanding of Central & Metropolitan's intentions; but I am entitled, and I think

216

bound, to attach at least the same weight to what seems to me the tenor of all the documentary evidence and the inherent probabilities of the case. Even then, I would hesitate to come down in favour of the plaintiff in a case of this sort if, at the end of the day, I thought the evidence to be pretty evenly balanced. But in the present case I am convinced, after weighing in the scales, on the one side, the assertions of Mr and Mrs Brennan that they thought that the lease accorded with Central & Metropolitan's intentions in not containing a rent review provision against, on the other side, what seem to me to be the clear indications given by the documentary evidence and the inherent probabilities of the case, that, whatever they say now, Mr and Mrs Brennan must have realised on 28 May 1980 that Central & Metropolitan intended the lease to contain a rent review provision and that its failure to do so must be ascribed to Central & Metropolitan's unilateral mistake. In these circumstances it would be against conscience to allow Compusave, which on this analysis must be taken to have suppressed the fact that it had recognised the presence of a mistake, to take advantage of it.

Central & Metropolitan contends that accordingly the lease ought to be rectified by inserting therein an additional clause providing for the rent payable under the lease to be adjusted to a fair and reasonable rental at the expiry of every fifth year of the term. But, in my judgment, the court has no jurisdiction to go that far. Whenever the court is asked to rectify an instrument, it is essential that the extent of the rectification (though not necessarily the exact words) should be clearly ascertained and defined by evidence contemporaneous with or anterior to the instrument: see *Bradford (Earl)* v. *Romney (Earl)* (1862) 30 Beav 431. In my judgment, the lease here ought to be rectified, not as claimed by Central & Metropolitan, but by the insertion in the *reddendum*, after the figure of £3500, of the following words: 'for the first 5 years of the said term (such rent to be reviewed at the expiration of such period and of each subsequent period of 5 years)'. To insert anything more would be, in my opinion, not to rectify the instrument but to mend the bargain made by the parties; and that is not the function of a court of equity. It would of course be absurd to ascribe to the parties an intention to agree upon a rent review provision which is void for uncertainty; but this rent review provision is in my judgment free from that vice. It predicates a review to a 'fair and reasonable' rent. If an officious bystander, listening to the parties trying to agree a review of the rent in accordance with this provision, had suggested that their bargain was that the rent should be reviewed to a 'fair and reasonable' rent, I have no doubt that they would have suppressed him with a testy 'Oh, of course.' The implication is both necessary and obvious. If the parties are unable to agree for themselves what the 'fair and reasonable' rent from any review date is to be, the amount of the rent will have to be fixed by the court. And the court would direct an inquiry what rent it would be fair and reasonable for the landlord and the tenant to agree under the lease (regard being had to all the circumstances relevant to any negotiations between the parties for a new rent from the review date): compare the approach of the Court of Appeal in *Thomas Bates and Son Ltd* v. *Wyndham's (Lingerie) Ltd* [1981] 1 WLR 505 [, (1981) 257 EG 381] and of the majority of the House of Lords in the recent case of *Sudbrook Trading Estate Ltd* v. *Eggleton* [[1982] 3 WLR 315; 265 EG 215] to the problems, similar in some ways to ours, which arose in those cases.

I have, earlier in this judgment, described the failure of anyone on Central & Metropolitan's side to notice the omission of a rent review provision as remarkable; and so I think it is. How the three principal actors, Mr Parnes (the responsible director), Mr Simmonds (the estate agent) and Mr Lenga (the solicitor) came each of them to be so careless of the interests of Central & Metropolitan in this way is quite beyond me. But there it is; and the result is that those responsible for the conduct of the matter on behalf of Central & Metropolitan have been to a large extent the authors of its misfortune. In my judgment, I am entitled, remembering that rectification, like other equitable remedies, is a discretionary remedy, to take this into account; and I do not propose to exercise my discretion in favour of rectification except on terms which give Compusave (which, although it took advantage of these blunders, did not itself make them) an opportunity to throw up the lease. On any footing, Compusave was willing to pay a rent of £3500 per annum for these premises for a term of five years and Central & Metropolitan were prepared to accept such a rent for such a period. Justice will, in my judgment, be done if Compusave is given an opportunity to surrender the lease at the expiration of the fifth year of the term on giving not less than three months' notice in writing to Central & Metropolitan of its intention so to do. Accordingly, Central & Metropolitan will have the lease rectified in its favour only if it is prepared to submit to the lease being further rectified by the insertion in it of a break clause on the lines I have proposed. I shall invite counsel for Central & Metropolitan to sign and counsel for Compusave to approve a minute of the order required to give effect to this judgment, the case to be mentioned to me again if they fail to agree.

10.2 (e)   Mutual mistake and the frequency of the rent review periods

Where there has been a mutual mistake and the frequency of the rent review periods does not reflect the common intention of the parties, the Court will order rectification of the lease accordingly. The fact that the landlords are the successors in title to the grantors of the lease is no bar to rectification. Section 63 of the Law of Property Act 1925 provides authority, if required, to effect the transfer of the original landlords' right to have the lease rectified.

BOOTS THE CHEMIST LTD v. STREET

Chancery Division   (1983) 268 EG 817

A 25-year lease allowed for rent reviews at the end of the seventh and fourteenth years. The parties had intended to review every fifth year, however. The evidence showed that the travelling draft had been modelled on a precedent for a 21-year term with reviews at 7 and 14 years. This had been corrected to five years in one part of the clause but not in another.

Held: Rectification would be granted because all the condition were satisfied: (i) clear evidence of mistake, (ii) instrument failing to represent the parties' common intention, (iii) intention continuing to date of execution.

FALCONER J: The matter is a relatively simple one in that it concerns rectification of a lease and in particular a clause dealing with the interval of the rent review provisions to be found in the lease. I need refer only to the relevant clause, which is clause 8 (1). I should perhaps preface it by saying that the lease is for a term of 25 years and the relative provision in the operative part of the lease relating to the rent is: 'YIELDING AND PAYING THEREFOR during the said Term hereby granted ...'—and then some words not relevant—'for the first five years thereof the yearly rent of £2750 (subject to review as hereinafter mentioned) ...' That is all I need to read from that. The review clause is clause 8 (1), and that is in these terms:

> 'The Lessors shall be entitled by notice in writing given to the Lessee at any time during the first six months of every fifth year of the Term to call for a review of the yearly rent for the time being payable under this Lease and if upon such review it shall be found that the then current rack rent value of the premises is greater than

the rent then payable hereunder the yearly rent then payable shall be increased to the amount of current rent value as aforesaid as from the end of'

and I draw particular attention to these words, which are the words in question, which are said to be a mistake 'the seventh and fourteenth years of the Term as the case may be'. The plaintiffs' claim is that plainly there is a mistake, as indeed there plainly is in some way in that clause. The mistake, they say, is that the words: 'the seventh and fourteenth years of the Term as the case may be' should be amended to read: 'each fifth year of the Term'.

I have been satisfied on the evidence that the initial antecedent agreement prior to the execution of the lease, which came some considerable time after the initial antecedent agreement by which the terms were agreed because of the defendant's difficulties in obtaining finance and planning permission, quite clearly was upon the footing that there should be rent reviews every five years. It is sufficient for me to refer to the letter of 12 February 1974, which is the first in a bundle of correspondence from Mr Smith, who was called to give evidence before me, then the negotiator for the agents acting for the then landlords, who were the predecessors in title of the present plaintiffs. It is in these terms:

'Further to our meeting on Tuesday morning, I have advised my clients of your offer to rent the above premises at £2400 per annum, subject to contract for a term of 25 years with rent reviews at five-yearly intervals on a full repairing and insuring basis.'

There was a subsequent offer by the defendant which raised the rent but thereafter the question of the term of 25 years and of the rent reviews at five-yearly intervals did not arise. I have had it explained to me how the error appears to have arisen. The travelling copy draft of the lease which is before me shows clause 8 (1) and the clause as originally typed out. I have had evidence to show that it was taken from a corresponding lease in respect of shops in the premises below the offices, the subject of the lease in suit. The lease for the shops below was a 21-year term one with rent reviews at seven and 14 years of the term, and the evidence established that the rent review clause had been copied and taken out and placed in the draft for the lease in question.

At the first appearance of the words 'the seventh and fourteenth years' the travelling draft quite clearly has been typed out with crosses and replaced by 'every fifth year'. That is exactly as it appears in the executed lease but what had been overlooked was a similar correction towards the end of the clause, where the words in the original draft, as in the executed lease, are: 'as from the end of the seventh and fourteenth years of the Term as the case may be' and of course it is the plaintiffs' case that the words 'the seventh and fourteenth years of the Term' should be replaced by the words 'each fifth year of the Term' to make them correspond with the amendment in the initial part of the clause, where the words 'the seventh and fourteenth years' had been altered in the way I have indicated.

I am satisfied on the evidence that there was a mutual mistake. I have had the mistake explained to me and it is quite plain how the lease should be rectified, if it is to be rectified. I have been referred, very properly, by [counsel] on behalf of the plaintiffs, particularly in the absence of the defendant, his defence having been struck out, to para 56 of the section on Mistake in Vol 32 of the fourth edition of *Halsbury's Laws of England*, dealing with the question of rectification. I should read the first sentence of that paragraph: 'To justify the court in correcting a mistake in an instrument the evidence must be clear and unambiguous that a mistake has been made.' That of course is the first requirement and I am quite satisfied as to that. The sentence in the paragraph goes on. 'That the instrument does not represent the parties' common intention' and that is perfectly plain and I am quite satisfied as to that.

The next requirement is 'what that common intention was'. I am quite satisfied that the common intention was that there should be five-yearly reviews—the interval should be five years. The passage goes on:

'and that the alleged intention to which it is desired to make the agreement conformable continued concurrently in the parties' minds down to the time of the execution of the instrument.'

I have already indicated that it is clear from the evidence that there was never any discussion after the initial antecedent agreement as to the terms that were discussed in the letter, to which I have referred, of 12 February 1975. There was never any further negotiation of either the terms of the lease or the interval at which the rent review was to be operated, so that, subject to a point of law to which I shall refer in a moment, I am satisfied that all the requirements set out in that paragraph are met with here and that, subject to what I shall say in a moment, this is a proper case for making the order sought.

Very correctly, [counsel for the plaintiffs] has drawn my attention to this point, which is indeed a point of law that the counsel for the defendant, when he made an application that I should set aside, or rather vary, the order of the master striking out the defence, urged should be taken into account. It is this: the present plaintiffs are not the original landlords with whom the negotiations were conducted by the defendant and with whom the lease was made as landlords. The present plaintiffs are the successors in title of the original landlords. The question, shortly, is whether, as successors in title they are entitled to the benefit of such interest or equity to have the lease rectified in the way in which it is sought to be rectified that would have existed in their predecessors in title, the original landlords. [Counsel for the plaintiffs] deals with that shortly by drawing my attention to the wording of section 63 of the Law of Property Act 1925, subsection (1) of which reads:

'Every conveyance is effectual to pass all the estate right, title, interest, claim and demand which the conveying parties respectively have in, to, or on the property conveyed.'

I need not read any further. But he submits, I think rightly so, that under that provision the transfer, which was a transfer of the freehold reversion, subject, of course, to the lease, from the original landlords to the present plaintiffs, is effective to pass such interest as there may be or may have been in the original landlords to have the lease rectified in the manner now sought to have it rectified.

That being so, I am satified that this is a case in which I ought to make the order sought and I therefore order rectification of the lease in the way sought in the prayer of the statement of claim: that is to say, by deleting from clause 8 (1) of the lease the words: 'the seventh and fourteenth years of the Term as the case may be' and inserting in place thereof the words: 'each fifth year of the Term.'

It remains to deal with the question of costs. [Counsel for the plaintiffs] has asked for costs. He has pointed out that as is plainly the case from the correspondence, the mistake having been discovered some considerable time ago before the action was brought, the plaintiffs, through their solicitors, drew the attention of the defendant to the mistake and asked him to agree rectification. I should say that they asked him to agree rectification offering to pay all necessary expenses. There was no response and eventually the action had to be brought in order to secure the rectification sought. However, it is not to be overlooked that the whole question of the need for rectification, and I have held that there was a need for rectification, arose because of an error on the part of the solicitors of the plaintiffs' predecessors in title acting originally. I think it would not be a proper case in which I should grant costs to the plaintiffs and I make no order as to costs.

10.3 (a)   What terms the court may imply when the review clause provides no machinery for fixing rent in default of agreement

A review clause which provides no machinery for fixing a revised rent in default of agreement may be construed as having an implied term that the rent payable was the fair market rent, discounting any of the tenant's improvements.

BEER v. BOWDEN

Court of Appeal   [1981] 1 All ER 1070

Under the terms of a 14-year lease the rent was to be reviewed every five years. The rent payable for the first five years was £1250 per annum. On review the new rent was

> 'to be such rent as shall ... be agreed between the Landlords and Tenant but no account shall be taken of any improvements carried out by the Tenant in computing the amount of the increase, if any, and in any case (the rent shall be) not less than the yearly rental"

of £1250 payable under the lease. The parties did not agree on a new rent for the first review period and the landlord issued an originating summons asking whether on the true construction of the rent review clause, the rent payable was the proper and reasonable rental for the premises having regard to their market value on the first review date, 25 March 1973, and if so, whether the proper and reasonable rent was £2850. The judge held that the tenant was liable to pay a fair rent at the first review date excluding the tenant's improvements and that it was not to be less than £1250 a year, and the rent for the next review period should be determined on the same basis on the next review date, namely 25 March 1978. The tenant appealed contending that either on the true construction of the review clause or by an implied term of the lease the rent continued to be £1250 in default of agreement, and that a term for a fair rent could not be implied as there was no arbitration clause or other machinery for determining the rent in the absence of agreement in the lease.

Held: The appeal was dismissed. On a true construction of the rent review clause, 'the rent (to) be agreed' by the parties was a fair rent excluding the tenant's improvements, provided, however, that in the event of depreciation of value of the premises the rent was not to be reduced below £1250 p.a. The clause could not mean that in the absence of agreement the rent was to remain at £1250 p.a. because such an interpretation would render the clause inoperative since the tenant would never agree to pay a higher rent.

As there was a lease in being, and the tenant conceded that some rent was payable, the court could despite the absence of an arbitration clause imply a term to fill the gap in the lease if the parties could not agree a revised rent. Since the parties clearly intended that a fair rent should be fixed by agreement on the review dates, the court would imply a term that in the absence of agreement, the rent payable during the second five years should be the market rent excluding the tenant's improvements. *Foley* v. *Classique Coaches Ltd* [1934] 2 KB 1 applied.

GOFF LJ: ... The premises were demised for a term of ten years from 25 March 1968. The clause then reads—

> 'paying therefor as follows:—Until the 24th day of March 1973 (yearly and

proportionately for any fraction of a year) the rent of £1250 per annum and from the 25th day of March 1973 such rent as shall thereupon be agreed between the Landlords and the Tenant but no account shall be taken of any improvements carried out by the Tenant in computing the amount of increase, if any, and in any case not less than the yearly rental payable hereunder such rent to be paid in advance by four equal quarterly payments on the four usual quarter days.'

The term of ten years was increased in 1971 to fourteen years ...

Counsel for the tenant, who has taken every point here which could be taken on behalf of the tenant, has put forward as his first submission an argument that the words in clause 1, 'and in any case not less than the yearly rental payable hereunder', on their true construction, mean 'and in default of agreement the yearly rental payable hereunder', that is, £1250. He says that clause 1 is really in three parts: first, it reserves a rent of that amount for the first five years; second, it provides that the rent for the second five years shall be as the parties agree; and, third, so construing the words I have mentioned, he says it provides that in default of agreement the rent shall continue to be £1250. He treats the words, 'but no account shall be taken of any improvements carried out by the Tenant in computing the amount of increase, if any' as if they were in parenthesis, but he does not take into that parenthesis the further words, 'and in any case not less than the yearly rental payable hereunder'.

I think, for my part, that that is an impossible construction. It is not, on the scheme of the clause as a whole, in my view, the natural meaning of the words; and, if one is to treat any part of it as in parenthesis, I think the provision about rent is as much in the parenthesis as the provision about tenant's improvement. But, secondly, that construction would make the clause futile, because, if in default of agreement the rent was to continue to be £1250, obviously the tenant would never agree to pay more, however much the premises might appreciate in value, and conversely, in the unlikely event of them depreciating, the landlord clearly would not agree to accept less. All that that clause was doing, as it seems to me, was setting out the basis on which it was contemplated that the parties would seek to agree on the rent to become payable at the end of the first five years. I think 'such rent as shall thereupon be agreed' must be 'such fair rent'. It does not make sense otherwise. So the basis was that it was to be a fair rent, not taking into account improvements made by the tenant himself, and in the perhaps unlikely event of depreciation, the rent was not to be reduced below £1250. Accordingly, in my judgment, that submission fails.

Then counsel for the tenant seeks to obtain the same result by a different method, by implying a covenant that in the absence of an agreement the rent shall be £1250. In approaching that argument, it must be observed first, as I have said, that the tenant does not suggest that the lease ever was or has become void for uncertainty. If he had done so, I think he would have been in difficulties, but it is not necessary to pause to consider that further, because he has not done so, and the court has to approach this problem on the footing that there is a subsisting lease. Second, he concedes (and, in my judgment, rightly) that he cannot stay on there and pay no rent at all. Quite apart from the fact that one would naturally lean towards that conclusion, he has quite fairly indicated that there are provisions in the lease which support it and indeed render it ienvitable. He has referred us to the covenant for quiet enjoyment and the provision about cesser or suspension of rent in the event of damage to the premises by fire.

That being so, we have to imply some term defining what the rent is to be. He submits that there are two alternatives: one £1250; the other, a fair market rent for the premises; of course, subject to the qualification about tenant's improvements. Given, therefore, that some implication has to be made, I asked him on what in the lease he founded the implication that the rent should be £1250. His answer was: 'I say, look at the two alternatives, look at such authorities as there are, and where market rent is implied they show that there must be something in the nature of an arbitration clause to fix a rent. Here there is nothing to justify implication of market rent.' He said: 'If the landlord wants to get an increased rent, there must be something in the lease clearly giving him the right to that advantage.' Buckley LJ has suggested that that might be improved on in this way: clause 1 shows there must be at least £1250 and there is no clear machinery for imposing a higher rent. Whichever way you look at it, I can see no justification whatever for accepting the alternative implied term which crystallises and fixes the rent for the residue of the 14 years at the sum of £1250.

The second authority, *Foley* v. *Classique Coaches Ltd* [1934] 2 KB 1, [1934] All ER Rep 88 is relied on by both sides. The landlords in the court below relied on it in support of implying a fair rent by analogy with what was there implied, a reasonable price. But counsel for the tenant relies on it because he says it shows that one could only make an implication of that character if assisted by the presence of an arbitration clause. It is fair to say that if one looks only at the judgment of Maugham LJ he did appear to be relying substantially on the arbitration clause in arriving at his conclusion (see [1934] 2 KB 1 at 16, [934] All ER Rep 88 at 94). But I do not think that is the true ratio of the case. Where you have got an arbitration clause, then if you imply a term that there shall be a reasonable price (as it was in that case) or a fair rent (as it would be in this), any dispute as to what is reasonable or fair falls within the arbitration clause; and, if you have not got one, it falls to be resolved by the court. But, in my judgment, the presence or absence of an arbitration clause does not matter ...

Now, the court must imply a term in order to give business efficacy to the contract, and I ask myself: why should it choose the alternative which is inconsistent with the basis which the parties showed they contemplated, rather than the one that implements it? Really, counsel for the tenant is attempting by an implied term to get himself back into the first submission, that of an implied agreement fixing a rent in default of agreement, and his second argument produces the same futility. It is quite obvious from cl 1 that the parties intended that the rent should be increased if the premises appreciated in value, and none the less so although they used the words 'if any'. They clearly contemplated also, as it seems to me, that the rent should be increased to such amount as would be a fair rent for the premises excluding tenant's improvements. They failed to agree. There is a hiatus. As the judge rightly held, that hiatus has to be filled by an implied term, and it seems to me quite obvious that one must imply the alternative which gives effect to that clearly expressed intention of the parties.

In my judgment, therefore, the judge was right; and I would dismiss the appeal.

GEOFFREY LANE LJ: Counsel for the tenant submits that on the face of the agreement and on the true construction of it, the landlord has failed to stipulate for anything more than the original rent of £1250 per annum, and that therefore the court should fix that amount as the proper rent for the next period. Counsel concedes that if that is the case, then on the further review which is due to take place in 1978, exactly the same thing will happen and the tenant will be in the happy position of paying a rent for the whole of the rest of the term which is well below the market value. That is plainly a highly undesirable result on any view, because it would mean in effect that the court would be implying an unfair rent. But, for the reasons which have been set out by Goff LJ, that is not a tenable construction of the terms of the lease.

The court should, if it can, give effect to the intention of the parties as exhibited from the terms of the agreement itself. That intention was quite clearly to fix at these moments of review a fair rent by agreement between the parties, subject to the provisos which they set out.

Now, in the absence of such agreement, the court, as is made quite clear from the decision of this court in *Foley* v. *Classique Coaches* [1934] 2 KB 1, [1934] All ER Rep 88, must try to produce the same effect for the parties. It seems to me that the judge's order in this case produces precisely that desirable effect.

BUCKLEY LJ: I agree. It appears to me that the introduction by implication of a single word in the clause in the lease relating to the rent to be payable solves the problem of this case; that is, the insertion of the word 'fair' between the words 'such' and 'rent'. If some such implication is not made, it seems to me that this would be a completely inoperative rent review provision, because it is not to be expected that the tenant would agree to an increase in the rent if the rent to be agreed was absolutely at large. Clearly the parties contemplated that at the end of five years some adjustment might be necessary to make the position with regard to the rent a fair one, and the rent review provision with which we are concerned was inserted in the lease to enable such an adjustment to be made. The suggestion that on the true construction of the clause it provides that the rent shall continue to be at the rate of £1250 a year unless the parties otherwise agree would, in my opinion, render the provision entirely inoperative, because, as I say, one could not expect the tenant voluntarily to agree to pay a higher rent.

10.3 (b)   Fixing a fair rent on the basis of agreement between the parties

A clause which provides for a rent to be determined on the basis of agreement between the parties and in default of agreement by an arbitrator required the arbitrator to fix a fair rent as between the particular parties taking into account all the circumstances and considerations which would affect the minds of the parties. The test is a subjective one.

LEAR v. BLIZZARD

Queen's Bench Division   [1983] 3 All ER 662

Clause 3 (2) of a 21 year lease provided for a new 21 year lease to be granted at 'a rent to be agreed between the parties hereto or in default of agreement at a rent to be determined by a single arbitrator'. The parties could not agree the basis on which the arbitrator should determine the rent. The arbitrator applied to the court asking, *inter alia*, whether the rent should be assessed as an open market rent or a fair rent, and if a fair rent whether that meant a fair rent for this particular landlord and tenant had they both been willing negotiators anxious to agree, and whether all the circumstances should be taken into account which might affect the parties' minds.

Held: Clause 3 (2) had to be construed on a subjective basis. The emphasis in the clause was on what was to be agreed between the parties and the arbitrator was required to determine what it would be reasonable for these landlords and this tenant to agree in all the circumstances. *Thomas Bates* v. *Wyndham's (Lingerie) Ltd* [1981] 1 WLR 505 CA applied.

TUDOR EVANS J: Counsel for the tenant points out that the option in *Thomas Bates & Son Ltd* v. *Wyndham's (Lingerie) Ltd*, with immaterial differences, is indistinguishable from the language of the option clause in the present case. But it was the review clause which fell to be construed in that case. Even so, I can find no material difference in the language and its effect. The option clause is radically different from the clause which had to be construed in *Ponsford* v. *HMS Aerosols Ltd*. It seems to me that in the present case the emphasis in the clause is on what is to be agreed between the parties, and the arbitrator is required to determine what it would be reasonable for these landlords and this tenant to agree in all the circumstances of the case. I think that it was the intention of the parties to the lease that, in default of agreement between them, the arbitrator should determine a rent which it would have been reasonable for these landlords and this tenant to agree and to take into account

224

all the considerations which would affect the minds of the parties. In other words, the test to be applied is subjective and not objective. Counsel for the landlords accepted that the decision in *Thomas Bates & Son Ltd* v. *Wyndham's (Lingerie) Ltd* was against his submission but he contends that the decision was based on a concession by counsel for the landlords in that case and that the construction put on the clause was in default of argument to the contrary. That is not accurate. It is true that counsel for the landlords in that case ultimately conceded, in effect, that a subjective construction was the proper construction but the Court of Appeal examined whether the concession was well founded ...

Counsel for the landlords here made three further submissions with respect to the *Thomas Bates* case. Firstly, he pointed out that the clause in that case provided for 'such rents as shall have been agreed', which he contends is significantly different from 'a rent to be agreed', the words used in the present case. The former language is said to lay greater emphasis, as I understood the argument, on the word 'agreement' and that therefore the arbitrator was required to fix a rent such as these particular landlords and tenant would have agreed. But I do not follow why this should be so. Both clauses emphasise the fact of agreement between the parties. It seems to me that the arbitrator in the present case is to assess the rent which it would be reasonable for the parties to agree. Secondly, counsel for the landlords submitted that a clause, similar in language to the clause in the present case, had been construed in an objective sense in *Beer* v. *Bowden* [1981] 1 All ER 1070, [1981] 1 WLR 522 and that, since the decision in that case conflicts with the decision in *Thomas Bates & Son Ltd* v. *Wyndham's (Lingerie) Ltd*, I am free and I have to choose which to follow. In *Beer* v. *Bowden* the material clause provided, in language part of which was very similar to that in the present case, for a rent review of—

'such rent as shall thereupon be agreed between the Landlords and the Tenant but no account shall be taken of any improvement carried out by the Tenant in computing the amount of increase, if any ...'

The parties failed to agree a new rent. On the landlord's originating application, it was ordered that the tenant was to pay as rent 'what the ... premises are reasonably worth', which was taken in the Court of Appeal as meaning a fair rental value for the premises on the open market. The argument of the tenant before the Court of Appeal, on the basis that the court had to imply some term as to what the rent should be, was that it could only be either a fair market rent or the rent originally reserved in the lease (see [1981] 1 All ER 1070 at 1073, [1981] 1 WLR 522 at 525 per Goff LJ). The court implied the former term. As far as I can see, it was never argued that a subjective test should be applied in deciding what the rent should be, whereas in the *Thomas Bates* case the point was central to the whole case. In these circumstances, I do not think that it can be properly said that there is a conflict between the two cases, but if I am wrong I should follow the decision in the *Thomas Bates* case where the question whether the clause should be construed in an objective or subjective sense was directly considered and the relevant authorities were referred to. Thirdly, counsel for the landlords submitted that the clause in the present case contains the words 'the demised premises', indicating that the rent is to be determined in relation to their actual state at the time of assessment by the arbitrator, whereas those words were absent from the rent review clause in the *Thomas Bates* case. It is quite true that the clause in the latter case did not expressly contain the words, but for what was the new rent to be paid if it was not for the demised premises? I think that the presence of the words in the clause in the present case are superfluous to the question of the construction of the meaning of the words 'at a rent to be agreed between the parties'. It seems to me that they do not add anything to the meaning of the clause.

Chapter 11

Repairs and rent levels

11.1 A tenant's own failure to repair will not reduce the rent payable

Depending on the wording of the particular lease, when determining what rent should be payable under a rent review clause, a tenant may not argue that his own failure to repair should produce a lower rent on renewal.

HARMSWORTH PENSION FUNDS TRUSTEES LTD v. CHARRINGTONS INDUSTRIAL HOLDINGS LTD

Court of Appeal   [1985] 274 EG 588

Any diminishing effect on the reviewed rent caused by the tenant's own failure to repair the demised premises in breach of his obligations to do so, should be disregarded when determining the rent payable.

WARNER J: It seems to me that the real issue between [counsel for the landlord] and [counsel for the tenant] is in which of two fairly recent decisions of the Court of Appeal I should look for guidance. The first of those decisions in point of time was *Fawke* v. *Viscount Chelsea* [1980] QB 441, on which [counsel for the tenant] relies. The second was *Family Management* v. *Gray* (1979) 253 EG 369, on which [counsel for the landlord] relies.

[Counsel for the tenant] accepts that, as [counsel for the landlord] points out, *Fawke* v. *Viscount Chelsea* was a case that arose out of the failure of the landlord to carry out his obligations to repair the exterior of the property. It was held that, in determining an interim rent for the property under section 24A of the Landlord and Tenant Act 1954, it was proper to have regard to the actual condition of the premises at the date when the interim rent was assessed. That, of course, would diminish the rent receivable by the landlord. There was no question in that case of any breach by the tenant of his repairing obligations, so that no argument of the kind that has been addressed to me was addressed to the Court of Appeal on behalf of the landlord. However, it is fair to say that both Goff LJ and Brandon LJ expressed themselves in their judgments as if the consequences of a breach by the tenant of his repairing obligations would have been the same as the consequences of the breach by the landlord of his. Goff LJ said (at p 453):

'The next question is how the valuers should regard want of repair and breaches of covenant when assessing an interim rent, and it seems to me they should consider what would be a reasonable rent for the tenant to pay from the date for commencement of that rent as a yearly tenant, having regard to the actual condition and state of the premises at that date, and having regard to the terms of the contractual tenancy so far as applicable to a yearly tenancy. This will mean that the hypothetical tenant will have the benefit of any covenant to repair on the part of the landlord and the burden of any on the part of the tenant, or there may be no covenant to repair on either side.'

He then cited a passage in the judgment of the judge whose decision was under appeal and commented on that and (at p 454) he continued:

'The fixing of an interim rent will not, however, affect the right of either party to sue the other for any breach of the repairing covenants in the contractual tenancy, which may have already occurred or may subsequently occur, save that in assessing damages for diminution in value with respect to any period after the determination of the contractual tenancy, credit must be given for the amount by which the interim rent was reduced on account of the want of repair from what it would have been if the premises had been in the state of repair required by the covenants. This may be considerably less than the actual diminution in value during the period of breach, since the valuation postulates prompt repair. The fixing of an interim rent would also not affect a claim by the tenant for damages for extra disturbance on the ground that the landlord's failure to repair after notice had made more extensive repairs necessary.'

Brandon LJ said (at p 475):

'It is clear that the market rent of premises may in general be affected not only by the terms of the tenancy concerning the obligations of the lessor and lessee in relation to repair, but also by the actual state of repair of the premises at the commencement of the tenancy.'

Then he took an extreme example:

'Let it be supposed first, that, under the terms of the tenancy it is an obligation of the lessor to put the premises into repair;' and 'that the premises are, at the commencement of the tenancy, so seriously out of repair, by reason of previous fire or flood, that they are only of partial use to the lease.'

He then went on:

'Similar considerations would, as it seems to me, apply if the premises were seriously out of repair at the commencement of the tenancy, not by reason of previous fire or flood, but by reason of the failure of the lessor or the lessee or both to perform their previous obligations to repair. The cause or causes of the premises being out of repair are not, for this purpose, significant; the fact that they are out of repair, for whatever cause or causes, is so.'

With those two judgments Stephenson LJ agreed.

[Counsel for the landlord] concedes that, if his argument in the present case is right, those passages in the judgments of Goff LJ and Brandon LJ were, to say the least, inappropriately worded in so far as they did not differentiate between the consequences of a breach of an obligation to repair by the landlord and those of a similar breach by the tenant. [Counsel for the landlord] invites me to disregard those *dicta* not only because, in so far as they related to the consequences of a failure by the tenant to repair, they were plainly *obiter* (and uttered without the Court of Appeal having had the benefit of hearing the relevant argument) but also because they are inconsistent with the later decision of the Court of Appeal in *Family Management* v. *Gray*. It seems to me that [counsel for the landlord] is right in that *Family Management* v. *Gray* decides that on an application for a new lease under the Landlord and Tenant Act 1954 a tenant is not entitled to set up in reduction of the rent to be paid under the lease defects in the premises arising from his own breach of covenant to repair.

[Counsel for the tenant] submitted that the case really turned on the evidence, and in particular on the evidence of a Mr Winbourne, who had been called as an expert on behalf of the tenant. The Court of Appeal held that that evidence had been misunderstood by the judge in the court below. [Counsel for the tenant] submitted that the case decided little else and that certain dicta to which I shall refer and which are material to the present case were *obiter*.

It is in fact difficult to tell from the judgments precisely what evidence it was that Mr Winbourne gave and to what point it was directed. That is because the account of his evidence given by Shaw LJ at p 371 of the report differs from the account of it given by Waller LJ at p 372; and Megaw LJ agreed with both judgments. He did not deliver a judgment of his own.

What, however, seems to me perfectly plain from the report is that both Shaw LJ and Waller LJ decided the case as they did because they accepted an argument that had been put forward by Mr Stimpson on behalf of the appellant. That argument was summarised by Shaw LJ in this way. After referring to a hypothetical situation about which Mr Winbourne had been asked in cross-examination, Shaw LJ said:

'It was not the real situation because of the operation of section 34 of the Landlord and Tenant Act 1954, and because there were business tenants in occupation who obviously had an interest themselves to protect and of whom it might be said that the almost certainty was that they would claim new leases under the provisions of section 34 when the occasion arose. As Mr Stimpson has urged in this court, when the negotiation of the terms of those new leases came to be dealt with between the reversioners and the prospective lessees they could not, in diminution of what was the proper rent to be paid, urge their own default in having failed to comply with the repairing covenants under the lease as a justification reason for a lower rent, whether arrived at by negotiation or determined by the court.

That has been the crux and gravamen of Mr Stimpson's submissions in this court, and he has said that it is clear from a reading of the judgment in which section 34 of the 1954 Act is nowhere specifically referred to, that the learned judge had taken Mr Winbourne's evidence as if it were evidence relating to the actual facts of the case, instead of being evidence which related to a hypothetical situation which had been put to him by counsel for the landlord.'

Waller LJ put in this way:

'For the reasons which my Lord has already mentioned, citing the case of *Smiley* v. *Townshend*, the proper basis for the valuation of this reversion is based on the rent which it would be likely to produce immediately following the termination of the lease, there being disregarded—and I quote section 34 (1) (a)—"any effect on rent of the fact that the tenant has or his predecessors in title have been in occupation of the holding".

Mr Stimpson has submitted that if the tenants, who had in their lease a repairing covenant, were to get the benefit of the fact that no repairs had been done, they would be getting a double benefit. He submits that the effect of Mr Winbourne's evidence and the effect of that section really drives one to the conclusion that if the judge had applied the proper test, he would have come to the conclusion that the rent—and again I quote, "... the holding might reasonably be expected to be let in the open market by a willing lessor, there being disregarded ..." that factor and, indeed the factor of goodwill—would be the rent at which these premises were, in fact, let. Therefore, the value of the reversion as at Christmas 1974 would be that at which the premises were, in fact, let, it being almost certain that the tenants in occupation with a righ to renew the lease if the rent could be properly negotiated would remain in occupation at that rent.'

It seems to me plain from those passages that the proposition that the subtenants could not rely, in diminution of the rents that they were to pay under their new leases, on the want of repair of the premises attributable to their own breaches of covenant formed part of the *ratio decidendi* of the case. That is the view taken also by the learned editors of *Woodfall's Law of Landlord and Tenant*, 28th ed, vol 1. There is at p 637 of that work a footnote which says this about *Family Managment* v. *Gray*:

'The Court of Appeal held that the damage to the reversion arising from the breaches of the head lease was nil or *de minimis* because it was to be expected that the subtenants would apply to the court for the grant of a new tenancy and because, on that application, they could not, having regard to section 34 of the Act of 1954, in diminution of the market rent to be paid by them, urge their own default under their own repairing obligations.'

I was referred to a passage in Bernstein and Reynolds' *Handbook of Rent Review* (at p 408) where they say:

'The arguments relied upon by Shaw LJ in *Family Management* v. *Gray* (above) and by Caulfield J in the *Hibernian* case (above)' that 'the tenant will be gaining a benefit from his own breach of covenant are not necessarily valid, at least in the context of rent review. For in so far as the dilapidations result in the tenant paying a substantially lower rent on review, the value of the landlord's reversion will have been substantially prejudiced by the breaches and the landlord will be entitled to damages equal to the amount by which his reversion has been diminished in value.'

[Counsel for the landlord] points out, and I agree with him, that that is not a very satisfactory way of looking at things from the landlord's point of view because a landlord's right to sue his tenant for damages may be of little or no value if the tenant is in financial difficulties.

I therefore propose in answer to question 3 in the originating summons to declare that upon the true construction of the lease, in determining the fair market yearly rack rent for the purposes of the successive reviews provided for in clause 2 of the lease, there should be disregarded any diminishing effect on such rent of any failure by the tenant to repair the demised premises in breach of its obligations under clause 3 (e).

Note: For *Fawke* v. *Chelsea* and *Family Management* v. *Gray*, see later page 508, under 'Lease renewal'.

11.2 It is not normally possible to fix a differential rent during the review period of an existing lease or where the lease itself provides for renewal at the then prevailing rent

NATIONAL WESTMINSTER BANK LTD v. B.S.C. FOOTWEAR LTD

Court of Appeal   (1980) 42 P & CR 90

By a lease dated 5 June 1957, premises were demised for a 21-year term from 25 March 1957 at a peppercorn rent for two months and 'thereafter (at) the clear net rent of £1250 per annum ... payable in arrear'. Clause 4 (2) of the lease provided,

'If the lessee shall be desirous of taking a further lease of the demised premises for a further term of 21 years from the expiration of the term hereby created and shall

CASEBOOK ON RENT REVIEW AND LEASE RENEWAL

on or before 25 March 1977, give to the lessor a notice in writing of such its desire and shall pay the rents hereby reserved and subject to there being no substantial breach of the covenants on the part of the lessee and conditions herein contained which is incapable of remedy the lessor will subject to the lessee having remedied any breach of covenant notice whereof shall have been given to the lessee grant a new lease to the lessee for a further term of 21 years from March 25 1978, at the then prevailing market rent (to be determined in default of agreement by a single arbitrator pursuant to the Arbitration Act 1950 ...) and subject in all other respects to the same covenants provisos and conditions as are herein contained except this sub-clause for renewal.'

The tenants duly gave notice requiring renewal of the lease, but the plaintiff landlords failed to reach agreement on the rent. The landlords issued a summons seeking *inter alia*, a declaration that on the true construction of clause 4 (2) of the lease the arbitrator therein mentioned was entitled, if he thought fit having regard to the evidence adduced before him, to determine the rent which was to be subject to periodic rent reviews during the term of the new lease. The judge made the declaration.

Held: The appeal was allowed. On its true construction clause 4 (2) of the 1957 lease provided for a renewal of the lease on exactly the same terms except that the prevailing market rent in 1978 was to be substituted from the beginning of the new term to be payable throughout that term and, thus, in the absence of agreement between the parties, the arbitrator was only empowered to consider in 1978 the annual rent of £1250 in the 1957 lease and to insert for the whole of the new term the rent which on the evidence before him, he thought was proper in view of the prevailing market rents in 1978; he had no power to insert reviews if the original lease did not provide for them.

TEMPLEMAN LJ: The salient words are the requirement that the landlords, if the tenants wish, must grant a 21-year lease from 25 March 1978, 'at the then prevailing market rent' (namely, in 1978), to be determined by the arbitrator, and the lease must be subject, in all other respects, to the same covenants, provisos and conditions as are contained in the original lease, excluding the proviso for renewal.

In my judgment, the arbitrator has no power to introduce any variations between the original lease and the renewed lease. The arbitrator must determine the rent, and only the rent, and for this purpose he must determine the prevailing market rent.

It was argued, and the judge declared in his order, that upon the true construction of the clause which I have read, the arbitrator is entitled, if he thinks fit, having regard to the evidence adduced before him, to determine a rent which is to be subject to periodic rent reviews during the term of the new lease. The result of that declaration is to confer on the arbitrator a discretion to decline to determine the rent payable under the renewed lease for 21 years, but only to determine the rent for a period of three or five years, or some other period which he is free to choose, having heard indeterminate evidence; and then he has power to direct that subsequent rent for subsequent parts of the term of 21 years shall be determined by such persons, at such intervals and by such machinery, as the arbitrator may think fit to draft and award. Alternatively, [counsel], for the landlords, submitted, if the arbitrator does not see fit to lay down any machinery, then, instead of the arbitrator determining the rent for the whole of the term, he is allowed to determine the rent for the initial period which seems to him to be proper, say three or five years, and then (if you please) to leave it to the judges of the Chancery Division to do the arbitrator's work for him and to say what the rent ought to be for subsequent periods.

In deciding whether to redraft the 1957 lease, the arbitrator is apparently to be assisted by evidence, but we do not know on what basis he could possibly form his view as to how the lease ought to be redrafted, except, I understand, that he must look and see how most leases are drafted in present times and what kind of rent review clause was popular in the year 1978.

It is common ground that a rent review clause may take many forms. All rent review clauses enable the rent to be increased; some enable the rent to be reduced; some enable the tenant to surrender the lease if the rent review provides an amount of rent which his business cannot afford; some oblige the tenant, whether he likes the new rent or not, to keep the lease and pay up, so that he is at the mercy of galloping inflation instead of being, as the lessee of this 1957 lease was, and as we must assume he bargained to be, in receipt of the comfort of having a certain rent for a long period.

In my judgment, this lease, including clause 4 (2), is, in effect, a 42-year lease with one rent review after 21 years; and what the landlords are seeking to do now, for perfectly understandable reasons in the light of history, is to redraft so that, instead of having one rent review after 21 years, they will secure for themselves rent reviews after 26, 31, or whatever other years the arbitrator thinks fit.

I fail to find in clause 4 (2) anything which confers on the arbitrator the wide and discretionary powers which are claimed by the landlords. Nor, in my judgment, does the clause enable the arbitrator to decline to perform his duty, namely, to fix a rent for 21 years. He cannot say: 'I see my way clear for five years, but I am going to throw up my hands in horror and say it is quite impossible for me to fix the rent for the remaining 16 years.' No one has suggested that in practice any arbitrator worth his salt will be inclined to throw up his hands. What is said is that, if the arbitrator fixes the rent at the beginning of 21 years for the whole period, then the landlord is in danger of not getting the fruits of inflation which he might otherwise get if there were rent review clauses. But what the landlords' predecessors in title gave away these landlords cannot now take back.

The judge conjured the power to insert a rent review clause which he ascribed to the arbitrator out of the word 'prevailing.' He said in his judgment that the word 'prevailing' meant 'that which is in general use or practice,' but he omitted from that definition the fact that what has to be prevailing is the rent; it is the rent which is to be in general use or practice. It may be general use or practice to provide a rent review clause, but that is a different matter from the prevailing rent.

The judge appears himself to have recognised that if the arbitrator is authorised to order periodic reviews of rent, then the original lease, on this hypothesis, gave the arbitrator the power to redraft the new lease so that it does not correspond with the old lease. In his judgment the judge said:

'... I think the right view of clause 4 (2) is that there is implied in the words "at the then prevailing market rent" that the arbitrator is to determine the terms as to rent having regard to the prevailing market conditions, and if those market conditions involve a provision for reviews of the rent at stated intervals then his task is to determine what, according to the practice and usage of the market at the relevant time, is the appropriate kind of review formula ...'

Thus the judge opined that the task of the arbitrator is to determine a review formula, but in my judgment it is quite impossible to read that into clause 4 (2). All that the arbitrator is empowered to determine, and is bound to determine, is rent. He is not empowered to impose any formula and redraft the lease by virtue of his award. The arbitrator is concerned with an amount and not with a formula.

The alternative argument was put forward by [counsel] for the landlords. He relied, in his persuasive speech in support of the rent review clause which the judge had been persuaded to introduce, on what he said would be an unrealistic result. In 1978 no landlords, he said—and there was evidence for this—would dream of letting premises for 21 years at a fixed rent. Every landlord would insist on having a rent review clause and, therefore, when the arbitrator sets out to find the prevailing market rent for a 21-year lease—a fixed rent—he will find there is nothing prevailing and that there is no market.

It is common ground that does not make the task of the arbitrator impossible. Arbitrators are often faced with property which is of a peculiar nature and has, in practice, no market comparable, and yet they do not have the slightest difficulty in fulfilling the requirement that they shall fix the market rent then prevailing. In fact, although landlords may not let properties these days, voluntarily, for 21 years without rent review clauses, there is in the evidence example upon example of landlords who, like the present landlords, as a matter of history, are caught with obligations which they, or their predecessors in title, have entered into, and there are leases which require rent reviews after 10 years from now, 14 years from now, 21 years from now. The fact that a modern landlord, free from any obligations, would not enter into a lease of this nature is *nihil ad rem*. The fact is the tenants' predecessors in title were prudent and wise enough to extract in 1957 a lease which did permit and require them to stay there for 21 years and then permitted them to stay there for another 21 years if they wished to do so, at a rent which was to be fixed for that second period of 21 years by an arbitrator during the year before the first lease expired.

These landlords agreed to do that, which [counsel for the landlords] vigorously urged no landlord in 1978 would do. The answer is, this is not a 1978 lease, it is a 1957 lease. But the hypothesis which the arbitrator has to make is that this lease, with a 21-year term at a fixed rent, is on offer and he must decide the market price for a rent as between landlord and tenant if that lease came on to the market. I really think, with all respect to [counsel for the landlord] that was the strength of his submission, namely, that in 1978 landlords who are free from obligations would not enter into a lease of the sort which is envisaged. That does not affect the true construction of the lease made in 1957. It does not produce a terribly unrealistic result at all. It does not even produce a difficult result. What it does produce is a result which the landlords never realised might be disadvantageous, namely, the result that, whether inflation goes up or down within the next 21 years, both the landlords and the tenants will have to put up with the rent which is fixed by the arbitrator in 1978 at the beginning of the term.

As an alternative, [counsel for the landlord] argued that, if the arbitrator cannot incorporate a rent review clause, he can at least introduce a differential rent. He could, for example, provide that the rent shall be £2000 for the first three years, £3000 for the next three years, and so on, as his fancy dictates. Alternatively, said [counsel for the landlord] if he formed the view that annual inflation was inevitable at 10 per cent compound, then he could provide a rent of (say) £2000 in the first year increased every subsequent year by 10 per cent, and so on.

For that submission, he relied principally on the authority of *Fawke* v. *Viscount Chelsea* [[1980] QB 441], in particular on the judgment of Goff LJ, who came to the conclusion that section 34 (1) of the Landlord and Tenant Act 1954 authorised the court, in fixing the rent payable under a business lease, to fix a rent which, so far as the decision went, was a rent which could be kept at a lower figure until the premises had been put in repair and could then be increased, and, as far as *obiter dicta* is concerned, supported the view that, in any event, a judge, determining a rent for the purposes of the 1954 Act, could provide for a differential rent possibly similar to that which [counsel for the landlord] has urged.

To turn [counsel for the landlord's] own argument against him, it will be a remarkable lease, even for the year 1980, which contained any differential rents of the type which he prayed in aid. Whether the evidence as regards the market would support him in that regard, I doubt. In *Fawke* v. *Viscount Chelsea*, the courts were concerned with statute and with a tenant who had no right to a lease of any particular term. The court had power to grant to a tenant a lease of such period, not exceeding 14 years, as the court thought fit. In those circumstances, it seems to me that the court was faced with a different task. It could balance, on the one hand, the virtues of giving a long lease with differential rents against the alternative of giving a short lease so that the landlord could then come along and obtain the benefit of inflation, and I am not surprised that differential rents are possible under that statute.

But we are dealing here with a perfectly common form lease which deliberately set out, for the first 21 years, to have all the advantages and disadvantages of a fixed rent of £1250 per annum—a certainty which has its benefit for the landlord, in that he knows he is going to get that sum for 21 years, and which has benefits for the tenant in that he knows exactly what his obligations will be.

Against that background, when we find that the lease itself provides for a renewal and the renewal is to be on exactly the same terms as the old lease, except that there is to be substituted the prevailing market rent at the date of the beginning of the new lease, it seems to me that, on the true construction of that clause in that lease, what the arbitrator has to do is to reconsider the figure '£1250' in the original lease and to insert the figure which he thinks proper, having regard to 1978 prevailing market rents. Then what the landlords have to do is to engross the new lease in exactly the same terms as the old lease, but instead of the figure '£1250' there will appear the figure which the arbitrator thinks proper, payable from 25 March 1978. The two months' peppercorn rent does not apply.

Note: This situation must be compared with the statutory right to a new lease under the 1954 Act where the court may impose a differential rent, see *Fawke* v. *Chelsea* and *Family Management* v. *Gray* (later under Lease Renewal).

11.3 Breaches of a landlord's repairing covenants will not normally permit the fixing of a differential rent

Even where there are breaches of repairing covenants by the landlord it will not normally be possible to fix a differential rent on review.

CLARKE v. FINDON DEVELOPMENTS LTD

Chancery Division   (1983) 270 EG 426

The defendant landlord had failed to comply with his repairing covenant by the commencement of the review period under a lease. The parties had agreed that in fixing the reviewed rent the prospect of the landlord remedying the breaches of repair or, on the other hand, the prospect of the tenant obtaining damages for the breach of repair should be taken into account. The landlords asked the court:

'whether in determining the review rent payable for the premises under clause 3 the arbitrator has jurisdiction to determine a rent which varies from time to time during the review period according to the situation with regard to the state of the premises.'

The tenant contended that once the arbitrator had fixed the rent it remained fixed at that level, while the landlords argued that the arbitrator was entitled to impose a differential rent varying with the state of the premises.

Held: This was the continuation of the existing lease with only a new substituted rent, therefore the arbitrator had only to reconsider the amount of rent due at the review date in the original lease and to insert the figure which he considered proper in the prevailing market conditions at the time. *National Westminster Bank Ltd* v. *B.S.C. Footwear Ltd* (1980) 42 P & CR 90 applied. *Fawke* v. *Viscount Chelsea* [1980] QB 441 distinguished. Further, it had been agreed by both the landlord and the tenant that in determining the rent, the arbitrator should take into account the prospect either, on the one hand, of the landlord remedying the breaches, or on the other hand, of the tenant obtaining damages for their breach. Since the arbitrator had taken that prospect into consideration once under that heading, there was absolutely no room for the arbitrator to take the same matters into consideration by fixing a differential rent thereafter as this would give the landlords the benefit of the matter twice over.

WALTON J: The crucial clause is clause 3, which provides that:

'THE Tenant shall pay for each successive period of SEVEN years after the first Seven years of the term an annual rent which shall be determined in accordance with the following formula that is to say such rent shall be the rent (but not less than the rent firstly hereinbefore reserved) at which the demised premises might reasonably be expected to be let in the open market by a willing Landlord by a Lease for a term of years equivalent to the residue of the said term with vacant possession on the same terms and subject to the same incidents in all other respects as this present demise and upon the supposition (if not a fact) that the Tenant had complied with all the repairing covenants herein imposed on the Tenant—

but not a word is said about the compliance by the landlord with the landlord's covenant, and for obvious reasons. Then it goes on as usual, that:

'PROVIDED that if no agreement is reached between the parties by the penultimate quarter day prior to the commencement of each such period as aforesaid as to the rent at which the demised premises might reasonably be expected to be let in the open market on the basis herein before described then the question shall be referred to the decision of a single arbitrator to be appointed by the President for the time being of the Royal Institution of Chartered Surveyors ...

...

So that, in contradistinction to the case put forward by the tenant, who were simply saying 'When the arbitrator has fixed a rent, that is that and that finishes it', what the landlords have now been arguing for is that the arbitrator is empowered, of course if the evidence so justifies—and, as to that, I have no idea whatsoever—to impose a differential rent varying with the state of repair of the premises. I can see a recipe almost for disaster and bad landlord and tenant relations if anything like that is done, but what I have to determine is whether it can be done.

There are apparently two cases, and only two cases, which are said to bear on this point. The first is *Fawke* v. *Viscount Chelsea* [1980] QB 441, where the court decided that this could be done under the terms of section 34 of the Landlord and Tenant Act 1954, and that provides that:

'The rent payable under a tenancy granted by order of the court under this Part of this Act shall be such as may be agreed between the landlord and the tenant or as, in default of such agreement, may be determined by the court to be that at which, having regard to the terms of the tenancy (other than those relating to rent), the holding might reasonably be expected to be let in the open market by a willing lessor, there being disregarded—'

various matters which are not material for present purposes. The premises there were apparently largely out of repair, and the court found itself able and empowered under section 34 (1) to fix a differential rent depending upon the state of repair of the premises. The leading judgments were given by Goff and Brandon LJJ, but it does seem from the speeches of all three lords justices that this is an exceptional case and an exceptional remedy was required in relation thereto. I must of course loyally accept, as I do, that that is something which is properly permissible under the terms of that subsection. But in a case concerning a rent review clause, *National Westminster Bank Ltd* v. *BSC Footwear Ltd* (1981) 42 P & CR 90, the court held that, on the true construction of the rent review clause then in question, it provided for a renewal of the lease on exactly the same terms, except the substitution of the new prevailing market rent, and that the arbitrator would have no power to fix the kind of differential rent that was fixed in *Fawke* v. *Viscount Chelsea*. In the course of the leading judgment, which was delivered by Templeman LJ, he said that this was a totally different situation. He said, at p 95:

'In *Fawke* v. *Viscount Chelsea*, the courts were concerned with statute and with a tenant who had no right to a lease of any particular term. The court had power to grant to a tenant a lease of such period, not exceeding 14 years, as the court thought fit. In those circumstances, it seems to me that the court was faced with a different task. It could balance, on the one hand, the virtues of giving a long lease with differential rents against the alternative of giving a short lease so that the landlord could then come along and obtain the benefit of inflation'

and, pausing there, also the benefit of any repairs

'and I am not surprised that differential rents are possible under that statute.

But we are dealing here with a perfectly common form of lease which deliberately set out, for the first 21 years, to have all the advantages and disadvantages of a fixed rent ...—a certainty which has its benefit for the landlord, in that he knows he is going to get that sum for 21 years, and which has benefits for the tenant in that he knows exactly what his obligations will be.

Against that background, when we find that the lease itself provides for a renewal and the renewal is to be on exactly the same terms as the old lease, except that there is to be substituted the prevailing market rent at the date of the beginning of the new lease, it seems to me that, on the true construction of that clause in that lease, what the arbitrator has to do is to reconsider the figure'

for rent

'in the original lease and to insert the figure which he thinks proper, having regard to 1978 prevailing market rents.'

It seems to me that that passage applies with even greater force to the present case, where there is not even the question of the grant of a new lease but the continuation of the existing lease with merely a new substituted rent, and I do not at all accept [counsel for the landlord] submission that the terms of clause 3 of that lease are so closely analogous to that of section 34 of the 1954 Act that one reaches the position under that Act. It seems to me to be as plain as a pikestaff that all that the arbitrator was supposed to do under clause 3 was to come up with a new figure for the rent to be inserted in place of the original rent of £1250. So even if the matter had simply rested on that, I should have come tot he clear conclusion that this case was governed by the *National Westminster Bank* case and not by the *Fawke* case. But it seems to me that [counsel for the landlord]'s argument here is completely and utterly out of court by reason of the answer which both parties have agreed must be given to the first question. So here we start out with it being agreed by both the landlord and the tenant: 'Yes, of course one has got to take into account the prospect either, on the one hand, of the defendants remedying the breaches, or on the other hand of the tenant obtaining damages for their breach', and, having taken that prospect into consideration once under that heading, there just is not the faintest possible room for the arbitrator to take those same matters into consideration by fixing a differential rent thereafter. It would be a matter of taking precisely and exactly the same things

235

into consideration and dealing with them in one branch by adjusting the rent for the full seven-year period or whatever it is that he has to do, and in the other branch by taking it as an adjustment to be made at various times in the rent, ie a differential rent. That would be giving the landlords the benefit of the matter twice over, and that, on any footing, cannot be right.

Therefore, for those two quite separate reasons, I have come to the conclusion that in this particular case the second question must be answered firmly in the negative.

Chapter 12

Improvements made by the tenant

12.1 Improvements made by the tenant become part of the demised premises and may be assessed for review purposes

If the effect on the rent of the tenant's improvements is to be disregarded then an express provision is required to that effect (but see *Beer* v. *Bowden* earlier, 10.3 (a).

PONSFORD AND OTHERS v. H.M.S. AEROSOLS LTD

House of Lords   [1979] AC 63

The plaintiffs' predecessors in title granted the defendant tenants a lease of factory premises for 21 years from June 1968 at a yearly rent of £9000 p.a. for the first seven years. The rent review clause provided that for the second and third period of seven years the rent should be £9000 or such a sum, which ever would be the higher, as would be assessed as 'a reasonable rent for the demised premises'. It further provided that the assessment should be made by agreement of the parties or, in default of agreement, by an independent surveyor. In 1969 the premises were burnt down and rebuilt out of the insurance proceeds. At the same time, the defendants at their own expense and after obtaining the plaintiffs' licence to carry out the work, made extensive improvements, and alterations to the factory premises at a cost of nearly £32,000. It was common ground that the improvements, once made, became part of the demised premises. Further, by a term of the licence, all conditions of the lease were to apply to the premises 'when as altered and shall extend to all additions'. When the rent for the second seven-year period came to be assessed, the parties disagreed as to the level of a reasonable rent and a surveyor was appointed. The plaintiffs issued a summons to determine whether the proper basis for assessing a reasonable rent under the rent review clause should have regard to the premises in their existing state or whether the works of improvement made at the defendants' expense should not be taken into account. The judge held that a reasonable rent should be assessed without having regard to the improvements made by the defendants on the basis, *inter alia*, that it would be unreasonable for the plaintiffs to have both the benefit of the improvements to the property and an increased rent. The Court of Appeal reversed his decision.

Held: The appeal was dismissed with Lord Wilberforce and Lord Salmon dissenting.

On a true construction of the rent review clause, 'a reasonable rent for the demised premises' was that which was reasonable for the premises and not what would be reasonable for the tenant to pay; that the improvements became part of the demised premises to which the conditions of the lease applied and that, accordingly, a reasonable rent was to be assessed by having regard to their improved condition, without considering who had paid for the improvements. *Cuff* v. *J. and F. Stone Property Co. Ltd* [1979] AC 87 approved.

VISCOUNT DILHORNE: It is common ground that the improvements made by the lessees formed part of the demised premises and the question on which there has been and is much division of judicial opinion is whether, when assessing a reasonable rent for the demised premises, regard should be had to the fact that the improvements were paid for by the lessees. If in consequence of them, the rent was assessed at a higher figure than it would otherwise have been, the lessees say that is not fair. They should not, they say, be required to pay rent on account of expenditure they have made on their landlord's property. They point out that if the lease had been for only seven years and they had been granted a new tenancy by order of the court under Part II of the Landlord and Tenant Act 1954 as amended by the Law of Property Act 1969 and the rent for that tenancy fell to be determined by the court, the effect of the improvements on the rent for which the holding might reasonably be expected to be let in the open market by a willing lessor would have had to be disregarded by section 34. It would be highly anomalous that they should have to pay a higher rent on a review under the lease they had for the second and, it may be, for the third periods of seven years than that which they would have had to pay on the grant of a new lease under the Act. What, they say, has to be determined on a review of the rent is what is a reasonable rent for them to pay for the demised premises and they contend that it would not be reasonable to require them to pay anything on account of the improvements they have made.

Our task can indeed be simply stated. It is just to decide the meaning of the words 'assessed as a reasonable rent for the demised premises.' Their meaning is not altered or affected by the fact that in 1954 Parliament decided that in assessing the rent of a new tenancy granted under the Landlord and Tenant Act, the effect of improvements such as those made in this case was to be disregarded. Lessors and lessees are usually advised by lawyers on the terms of leases. If the parties to this lease had agreed that the effect of improvements was to be disregarded in assessing the rent, that could easily have been stated and if that had been agreed, I expect it would have been. A precedent which could be adapted is in section 34 of the Landlord and Tenant Act. In the absence of any such express provision as Parliament thought it necessary to include in section 34, I do not think that one is entitled to conclude that by the use of the words 'assessed as a reasonable rent for the demised premises' the parties were seeking to express their agreement that in assessing the rent, the effect of improvements made by the lessees was to be disregarded.

If it be thought to be unfair as Parliament clearly thought it unfair, that a tenant should pay a rent which reflected the value of the improvements made by him, that is no ground for interpreting the words in question as the appellants contend. It is not for us to re-write the lease. It may be that the parties in 1968 did not consider what was to be the effect on the assessment of the rent if the lessees made improvements. One does not know, but just as I see no grounds for supposing that they did consider it, I see no ground for concluding, if they did consider it, that the landlords agreed that the effect of improvements should be excluded.

Rent review provisions are now commonly included in leases at the instance of lessors to give them some protection against inflation. If they were not included, landlords might only be disposed to let for a shorter term. Their object is to secure that in real terms the rent payable does not fall below that initially agreed on. It was not disputed in this case that that is their main object. In the present case and in many others provision is made for the assessment to be made by an independent surveyor. What has he to do? Surely it is to assess what rent the demised premises would command if let on the terms of the lease and for the period the assessed rent is to cover at the time assessment falls to be made. That rent may depend to some extent on local factors such as deterioration of the neighbourhood. In assessing it, the surveyor will be assessing the reasonable rent that others, not just the sitting tenant, would be prepared to pay for the use and occupation of the premises. He will not consider the tenant's position separately.

It may be said that this is treating a reasonable rent for the demised premises as the rent obtainable on the open market and that the decision in *John Kay Ltd* v. *Kay* [1952] 2 QB 258 shows this to be wrong. That was a decision on section 12 of the Leasehold Property (Temporary Provisions) Act 1951 which gave the court power to grant a tenancy 'at such rent and on such terms and conditions as the court in all the circumstances thinks reasonable,' and it was held that that did not mean the rent which the property would fetch if offered in the open market as property to let. If the wording of this lease had been similar to that, the surveyor would in my opinion have been entitled, indeed would have been bound, to have regard to the particular circumstances of the tenant. I do not think that the decision in that case affords any support for the view that the task of the surveyor under the lease was not to assess what would be paid in rent for the use and occupation of the demised premises if offered to let on the open market. What significance then is to be attached to the word 'reasonable'? I think that it was included to give the surveyor some latitude. He might know that if the premises were to let, there was someone who would be prepared to offer an exceptionally high rent for their use. The use of the word 'reasonable' would enable him to disregard that.

The rent payable by the lessees will of course be rent for the demised premises but as I see it, the task of the surveyor is not to assess what would be a reasonable rent for the lessees to pay but what is a reasonable rent for the premises. That, when assessed, is payable by the lessees. If the effect of the improvements on the rent payable is to be disregarded, then the lessees will not be paying a reasonable rent for the demised premises but a reasonable rent for the demised premises less the improvements; but it is recognised that the improvements are part of the demised premises. If the effect on the rent of the improvements is to be disregarded then in my opinion an express provision is required to effect that as was necessary in the Landlord and Tenant Act.

In *Cuff* v. *J. & F. Stone Property Co. Ltd (Note)* [[1979] AC 87], Megarry J also had to consider a provision for the review of rent in a lease in all material respects similar to that under consideration in this case. He too had to consider the meaning of the words 'assessed as a reasonable rent for the demised premises.' In the course of his judgment which I found illuminating and with which I respectfully entirely agree he said, at p 90 D-F:

'There is nothing save the expression "reasonable rent" to give colour to the view that anything save pure matters of valuation are to be considered ... it seems to me to put an impossibly heavy burden on the word "reasonable" in this lease to say that it allows and requires the surveyor to explore questions of who paid for the improvements, and in appropriate cases to allow some discount for this, calculated on an unspecified basis.'

He held, at p 91 B, that 'the surveyor must take the premises as he finds them, and then determine what he considers to be a reasonable rent for those premises, regardless of who provided them or paid for them.'

Roskill LJ in his dissenting judgment in the present case attached great importance to the different factual background in that case. There the improvements had been made some 12 years before and so the phrase 'the demised premises' clearly included the improvements when the lease was executed. In the present case it is not disputed that 'demised premises' included the improvements made after the lease was executed and this being so, I do not myself see that the fact that in *Cuff* v. *J. & F. Stone Property Co. Ltd (Note)*, [[1979] AC 87] the improvements were made before the lease was entered into affords any ground for distinguishing that case from this. In that case there had been a lease to J. & F. Stone Lighting and Radio Ltd and on 3

March 1966, when the lease was expiring, the court made an order for the grant of a new lease. No doubt the rent fixed by the court disregarded the effect of the improvements but the defendants in the action tried by Megarry J were not the lessees in whose favour the court had made the order. It appears from Megarry J's judgment that the form of the lease they entered into was agreed between them and their landlords. Whether the rent review provision he had to consider was a term of the tenancy which the court ordered to be granted, the judgment does not reveal, but it would not affect the meaning of the provision in my opinion if it was.

Roskill LJ also wondered whether Megarry J would have reached the same conclusion if it had not been conceded for the lessees that the improvements were not simply to be disregarded but I do not see any reason to suppose that Megarry J would have come to a different conclusion if that concession had not been made.

Megarry J had to decide the meaning of the words used in the lease, as we have to do, and I do not see how the factual background or the concession to which I have referred can properly be considered as aids to the determination of the meaning of ordinary English words.

LORD KEITH OF KINKEL: agreed and said: ... At first impression the word 'reasonable rent for the demised premises' suggest that what has to be ascertained is simply the rent that is reasonable for the premises as such in their actual state, the situation being viewed entirely objectively. 'The demised premises' must mean the demised premises as improved, by virtue both of the ordinary law and of the passage I have quoted from the licence agreement. So upon this view any contribution the improvements might have made to rental value would have to enter into the assessment.

It was however argued for the tenants that to proceed in that way would involve assessment of the rent on the basis of market value, whereas the lease provided for a different basis, namely that of a 'reasonable' rent. It was not maintained that the assessment should be made upon the assumption that the improvements did not exist, but it was said that any assessment of a 'reasonable' rent could not ignore that the improvements had been paid for by the tenants. Otherwise an unreasonable result would be reached and one which was unfair to the tenants, considering that the landlords had not contributed to any increase of rental value resulting from the improvements and that their capital value would enure to the landlords' benefit at the expiry of the lease.

It must be recognised, in my view, that, if the approach is to be a purely objective one, it is difficult to perceive any difference in meaning between 'a reasonable rent' and 'the market rent,' and so there is force in the argument that if the parties had intended a purely objective assessment they would have used the latter expression, which is in common use in contexts such as this one. I am not impressed by the suggestion that the expression 'a reasonable rent' might have been used merely in order to exclude any freak or special rent that a prospective tenant might be prepared to pay, because I think that in estimating the market rent a valuer would proceed on the general level of rents for comparable premises without reference to any such freak or special rent. I regard it as a proper inference that when agreeing on the terms of the rent review clause the parties did not have present to their minds the situation which might arise by reason of the execution by the tenants of improvements, because I consider that if they had they would have made specific provision about the application of the clause to that situation, but whether or not that is correct the clause must have been envisaged as capable of operating in respect of the original unimproved premises. Would the surveyor then have reached any different result than if he had simply been instructed to ascertain the market rent? I would think not, because I am not able to envisage any circumstances which he would take into or leave out of account in one case but not in the other. It may be, of course, that in the surveying profession 'a reasonable rent' is well known to bear a particular meaning distinct from that of 'the market rent,' but there is no available material to indicate whether or not that is so. As it is, I consider that in either case the surveyor would have regard to the condition of the premises, the terms and provisions of the lease, and the general level of rent for comparable premises in the same locality or in similar localities, and I would not expect any difference in the resulting assessment. Even if the difference of wording were intended to lead to a different approach of the rent review, it is to be expected that the different approach would be capable of application where there had been no improvements.

That being so in the normal case, does the difference of wording lead to a different result when the tenant has carried out improvements at his own expense? I think it could do so only if there were grounds for inferring that the particular wording used here was used in contemplation of that particular situation, and, as I have already said, I do not consider that such grounds exist. Further, I do not think that parties can have had in view the additional factor that any licence agreement for improvements would fail to make provision for the manner in which the improvements were to be dealt with on a rent review.

In my opinion the words 'a reasonable rent for the demised premises' simply mean 'the rent at which the demised premises might reasonably be expected to let.' Considering that the demised premises necessarily include the improvements, to arrive at a lower rent by reason that the tenants paid for the latter would in substance mean that a rent for part only of the demised premises was being assessed. The fact that the assessed rent leads to an unreasonable result as between the particular tenant and the particular landlord does not mean that it is not a reasonable rent for the premises. The unreasonable result is due to circumstances which were not in contemplation when the terms of the rent review clause were agreed and which were therefore not expressly provided for. They might have been expressly provided for at the stage when the licence for the improvements came to be granted, but they were not. I consider that the construction which the tenants would place upon the review clause involves a severe straining of the language used and is not the correct one. I therefore reach the conclusion that the decision of the majority of the Court of Appeal was right.

Reference was made in the course of the argument to a number of statutory provisions regulating, in certain circumstances, the relationship of landlord and tenant of business premises, in particular section 34 of the Landlord and Tenant Act 1954. Section 34 is of some significance, in my view, as indicating the need, when it is desired that certain matters including improvements carried out by a tenant, should be disregarded in the assessment of a rent, to provide expressly for this. But apart from that I do not consider that any of the provisions referred to are of assistance in resolving the present problem of construction.

Reference was also made to the decision of Megarry J in *Cuff* v. *J. & F. Stone Property Co. Ltd (Note)*, [[1979] AC 87] finding in favour of the landlords in circumstances closely akin to those of the instant case. While I should not be disposed to adopt the whole of the reasoning of the learned judge in that case. I agree with him at pp 89, 90, 91, that the expression 'reasonable rent' is to be read in a valuation sense, and that 'the surveyor must take the premises as he finds them, and then determine what he considers to be a reasonable rent for those premises, regardless of who provided them or paid for them.'

My Lords, for these reasons I would dismiss the appeal.

A 'reasonable rent' is not the same as a rent which it is reasonable for the tenant to pay, thus a tenant's own improvements may be taken into account when the rent is reviewed even on a statutory renewal of the lease since it will have been renewed on the same terms as originally granted. However, the initial rent will exclude improvements if they fall within the purview of the statute.

CUFF v. J. & F. STONE PROPERTY CO. LTD

Chancery Division [1979] AC 87

On 21 November 1966, Mr Cuff, the landlord granted the tenants, J. & F. Stone Property Co. Ltd, a 14 year lease of premises. The lease provided, *inter alia* that

'the yearly rent payable by the lessee during the last seven years of the term hereby granted shall be the sum of £2400 ... or such sum as shall be assessed as a reasonable rent for the demised premises for the said period ...'

When the review clause came to be operated, the tenants contended that certain improvements made by them should be disregarded in the assessment. The landlord issued an originating summons to determine the issue.

Held: When the lease was executed, the improvements had already been made some 12 years earlier. The demise plainly included the improvements as part of the premises. There was nothing said about the improvements in the lease. The provision for assessing the rent was expressed purely in valuation terms, and there was nothing save the expression 'reasonable rent' to give colour to the view that anything save pure matters of valuation were to be considered. The ancient principle is that what the tenant makes part of the demise enures for the landlord's benefit, subject to rules relating to tenants' fixtures and to any statutory qualifications of principle. The limited qualification made by section 34 of the Landlord and Tenant Act 1954 (as amended by the 1969 Law of Property Act, see post) contributed nothing to determining the issue before the court. Though this qualification was relevant when the county court was determining the initial rent under a new tenancy granted under statute, the rent for the second seven years was purely a creature of the lease itself. The word 'reasonable' as used in the lease did not allow and require the surveyor to explore questions of who paid for improvements and to allow some discount for this calculated on an unspecified basis. The tenants' improvements could not be disregarded when the rent was reviewed under the terms of the lease which did not exclude them.

MEGARRY J: In 1966, when the lease was running to its end, there were proceedings in the Bow County Court in which the lighting company sought a new tenancy under the Landlord and Tenant Act 1954. On 3 March 1966, the court made an order for the grant of a new tenancy at a rent of

'£2400 per annum with rent review at the end of seventh year. New tenancy for 14 years to commence at termination of current tenancy. (Under section 64 of the Landlord and Tenant Act).'

The rent fixed by the court no doubt gave effect to section 34 of the Landlord and Tenant Act 1954, which included a provision for the disregarding of

(c) any effect on rent of any improvement carried out by the tenant or a predecessor in title of his otherwise than in pursuance of an obligation to his immediate landlord.'

Having obtained that order for a new tenancy, the lighting company requested the landlord to grant the lease not to it, but to another company named J. & F. Stone Property Co. Ltd, which I shall call the 'property company.' That company is the defendant in this summons. There is no evidence before me as to the relationship between these two companies, though one would infer from their names and the events that there is some connection.

A form of lease was duly agreed between the landlord and the property company, and a lease for 14 years was granted, bearing date 21 November 1966. This was a demise of

'All that messuage or dwelling house shop and premises known as Number 80 High Street North in the London Borough of Newham together with the yard or garden thereto.'

In accordance with the order of the county court, provision was made for rent review. The clause in question reads as follows:

'Provided also and it is hereby declared that the yearly rent payable by the lessee during the last seven years of the term hereby granted shall be the sum of £2,400 aforesaid or such sum as shall be assessed as a reasonable rent for the demised premises for the said period such assessment to be made in the following manner that is to say:—either (a) such assessment as shall be agreed between the parties hereto in writing before December 25 1972 (b) in the event of the parties hereto failing to reach such agreement as aforesaid on or before the date appointed (in respect of which time is to be deemed to be of the essence of the contract) then the reasonable rent for the last seven years of the term hereby granted shall be fixed or assessed by an independent surveyor appointed for that purpose by the parties hereto or failing agreement as to such appointment by 25 March 1973 (time in this respect to be deemed to be of the essence of the contract) then by an independent surveyor appointed for that purpose by the President for the time being of the Royal Institute of Chartered Surveyors. The assessment fixed by the independent surveyor shall be communicated to the parties hereto in writing and immediately upon such communication the rent so assessed as a reasonable rent for the last seven years of the term hereto granted shall be the rent payable for that period under the terms hereof.'

When the rent review clause fell to be operated, there were at first negotiations between the parties, but in the end a surveyor was appointed. The valuers of each party nevertheless continued their negotiations, and there is some evidence before me to the effect that if the improvements are to be disregarded, the rent will be something of the order of £3500, whereas if the improvements are to be taken into account, the rent will be of the order of £4600. A consequence of this difference was that the originating summons was issued; and before me Mr Prince has appeared for the landlord and Mr Priday for the property company.

What from the summons and the evidence initially appeared to be the question for decision was whether or not the surveyor was to have regard to the improvements. The summons sought a declaration that the rent was to be assessed 'without disregarding any improvements' to the demised premises effected by the property company or the lighting company. However, as the argument proceeded it became apparent that this was not the real question between the parties, for [counsel for the defendant] advanced no contention, whether based on section 34 or otherwise, that the improvements should be wholly disregarded. His case was that while he accepted that the improvements should not be wholly disregarded, he asserted that, to put it shortly, the surveyor should temper the effect to be given to the improvements by what he considered to be reasonable. This assertion [counsel for the plaintiff] rejected. Accordingly, if I were simply to answer the question asked by the summons in its original form, resolving the real issue merely by what I said in my judgment, it seemed to me that there might be difficulties if the unsuccessful party wished to appeal from my order; for an appeal lies against the order rather than the judge's reasons for the order, and an appeal against an order which, in effect, was supported by both parties would present obvious difficulties. The parties therefore agreed an amendment to the summons, so that the plaintiff is now seeking a declaration that the rent is to be assessed without any regard to the fact that the improvements to the premises have been effected by the property company or the lighting company.

[Counsel for the plaintiff's] case was of elemental simplicity. When the lease was granted in 1966 the improvements admittedly formed part of the demised premises. What is to be assessed is 'a reasonable rent for the demised premises.' In default of agreement, that assessment is to be made by an independent surveyor. Therefore the question is a pure matter of valuing the demised premises in their actual physical condition, disregarding the provenance of the improvements. The valuation is to be on the basis of what rent is reasonable for those premises. [Counsel for the defendant] on the other hand, stressed the distinction between the 'market rent' and a 'reasonable rent,' and pointed to *John Kay Ltd* v. *Kay* [1952] 2 QB 258, 267. There, Evershed MR said:

> 'The reasonable rent is arrived at by applying the subjective test of what the judge thinks is right and fair, as distinct, for example, from the objective test of what the evidence shows is the market value.'

The surveyor must therefore, said [counsel for the defendant], say what was the right and fair rent for the premises as they stood; but in doing that he must consider not only what was physically there, but also all matters put before him by the parties, including the circumstances in which the improvements were made. He must then duly reflect those circumstances in saying what was a right and fair rent. To the objection that it might be very difficult to say how much of a discount should be allowed for the fact that an improvement had been provided by the tenant or someone associated with him, [counsel for the defendant] answered that just as the question of the rent 'which it would be reasonable for the tenant to pay' as an interim rent under the Landlord and Tenant Act 1954, section 24A, might depend on the length of the judge's foot (see *English Exporters (London) Ltd* v. *Eldonwall Ltd* [1973] Ch 415, 433), so in this case the length of the surveyor's foot might be decisive.

I go back to the lease. When it was executed, the improvements had already been made some 12 years earlier. The demise plainly included the improvements as being part of the premises. Not a word is said in the lease about the improvements. The provision for assessing the rent is expressed solely in valuation terms. There is nothing save the expression 'reasonable rent' to give colour to the view that anything save pure matters of valuation are to be considered. The ancient principle is that what the tenant makes part of the demised premises enures for the landlord's benefit, subject to rules such as those relating to tenant's fixtures and to any statutory qualifications of the principle. The limited qualification made by section 34 (*c*) of the Landlord and Tenant Act 1954 (on which see *In re 'Wonderland,' Cleethorpes* [1965] AC 58) admittedly contributes nothing to the determination of this case. Though this qualification was relevant when the Bow County Court was determining the initial rent, the rent for the second seven years is purely a creature of the lease. In those circumstances, it seems to me to put an impossibly heavy burden on the word 'reasonable' in this lease to say that it allows and requires the surveyor to explore questions of who paid for the improvements, and in appropriate cases to allow some discount for this, calculated on an unspecified basis. What sort of deduction should be allowed if the improvements were paid for by the tenant itself, or partly by the tenant and partly by a subsidiary company, an associated company, or a related company, or wholly by such a company? If one accepts to the full that 'reasonable' means 'right and fair,' one may still say that it means 'right and fair' in a valuation sense, without extending it to the whole range of moral and ethical considerations. I say nothing of the improbable case of a reasonable rent which is to be assessed not by a surveyor but by a philosopher or theologian: but I do say that in the absence of provisions sufficiently indicating the contrary, a provision for a reasonable rent to be assessed by a surveyor to be appointed, in default of agreement, by the President of the Royal Institution of Chartered Surveyors will not cast the surveyor loose upon uncharted and perhaps unchartable ethical seas such as these. The word 'reasonable' no doubt requires the surveyor to reject a rent which, though obtainable in the open market by reason of special circumstances, appears to him to exceed the rent for the premises which is right and fair; but I do not think that it does more than that.

If the formula used in the lease had been the formula relating to interim rent that fell to be considered in the *Eldonwall* case [1973] Ch 415, namely the 'rent which it would be reasonable for the tenant to pay,' [counsel for the defendant]'s hand might perhaps have been strengthened; for such language more readily admits of a construction which allows regard to be paid to the individual circumstances of the particular tenant. But here there is the bare phrase 'reasonable rent,' used in relation to the demised premises: the question is not that of the rent 'which it would be reasonable for the tenant to pay,' but that of 'a reasonable rent for the demised premises,' and that, as it seems to me, is a matter not affected by who paid for the premises or any part of them. In my view the surveyor must take the premises as he finds them, and then determine what he considers to be a reasonable rent for those premises, regardless of who provided them or paid for them.

Note: Compare the effect of the phrase 'a rent which it is reasonable for the tenant to pay' as used in *English Exporters (London) Ltd* v. *Eldonwall Ltd* (1973) Ch 415 (see later page 291).

12.2 Statutory provisions and their effect on improvements made by the tenant in relation to rent levels on review

The court may be empowered to grant a new tenancy under the Landlord and Tenant Act 1954. Section 34 defines which of the tenant's improvements may be disregarded when the level of rent is fixed. However, following the House of Lords' decision in *East Coast Amusement Co. Ltd* v. *British Transport Board* [1965] AC 58, reported on appeal as *In re Wonderland* [1962] Ch 696 section 34 was amended by section 1 of the Law of Property Act 1969. In that case, improvements to the premises were made by the appellant tenant during a previous tenancy which expired prior to the grant of a new lease in 1938. The House of Lords held that para (c) of section 34 to be included. However, it seems that even where a lease was drafted was making the application for the new tenancy and which were effected during the term of the tenancy in existence when the application was made or by a predecessor in title of the tenant under the same tenancy, and that the improvements carried out by the appellant tenant under the original lease of the premises granted in 1926 should not be disregarded when determining the new rent.

The *Wonderland* decision was so unpopular that the 1954 Act was amended to avoid the tenant in effect being charged extra rent for previous voluntary improvements. Obviously, just what improvements will or will not be disregarded under the review provisions of a lease will depend on the terms and actual wording of the individual lease, and it is not unusual for the provisions of the 1954 Act under section 34 to be included. However, it seems that even where a lease was drafted many years after the enactment of section 1 of the 1969 Act with its amendment to section 34 (c) of the 1954 Act, if the 1969 amendment is not expressly referred to, the words of the 1954 Act section 34 are to be included unamended but they are to be construed as they appear in the lease in accordance with the matrix of facts. See further comment below.

Improvements made voluntarily by a tenant during a previous tenancy will not necessarily be disregarded for the purposes of fixing a revised rent even when the provisions of section 34 are expressly referred to in the rent review clause of the lease, since they may not be interpreted in the same way as if they were applied under statutory lease renewal under the 1954 Act.

BRETT v. BRETT ESSEX GOLF CLUB LTD

Chancery Division   (1985) 273 EG 507

The plaintiff landlord granted a lease over a piece of land for a term of 50 years from 9 July 1973. The lease contained a covenant by the defendant tenant to erect at its own expense a clubhouse for the use of members etc. A review clause provided for the yearly rent to be reviewed at intervals and said there should be disregarded, if applicable, those matters set out in section 34 (a), (b) and (c) of the Landlord and Tenant Act 1954. Between 1973 and 1977 the golf course was laid out and in 1975 the clubhouse was built. From 1978 the lease was superseded by a new 50 year lease which, by clause 4, provided that the reviewed rent should be fixed, *inter alia*, disregarding, if applicable, those matters set out in paras (a), (b) and (c) of section 34 of the 1954 Act. The landlord claimed that when the reviewed rent was determined the improvements to the land made by the tenant (i.e. the clubhouse and golf course) had to be taken into account under the 1978 lease. The tenant contended that any reviewed rent had to ignore the existence of the clubhouse and golf course because the obligation to lay out the golf course under the 1973 lease had been discharged and the clubhouse had not been built pursuant to any obligation imposed by the landlord as the 1973 lease had only granted permission to erect a clubhouse without imposing an obligation on the tenant to do so. Section 34 (c) of the 1954 Act said that there was to be disregarded

'any effect on rent of any improvement carried out by the tenant or a predecessor in title of his otherwise than in pursuance of an obligation to his immediate landlord.'

The question the court had to determine was whether the provisions in the 1978 lease referred to this paragraph as originally enacted or as it was amended by section 1 of the Law of Property Act 1969, which provided that the rent payable under section 34 (1) was to be that which the premises might reasonably be expected to be let in the open market by a willing lessor, there being disregarded '(c) any effect on rent of an improvement to which this paragraph applies', and then the following was added

'(2) Paragraph (e) ... applies to any improvement carried out by a person who at the time it was carried out was the tenant, but only if it was carried out otherwise than in pursuance of an obligation to his immediate landlord and either it was carried out during the current tenancy or the following conditions are satisfied ...'

Held: The reference to the 1954 Act in the words of the 1978 lease was a reference to that Act as originally enacted and not as later amended by the 1969 Act. However, when the words of the relevant paragraph (c) of the 1954 Act were incorporated into the 1978 lease they did not necessarily have the same significance as they had when forming part of the statute. In the 1954 Act they appeared in a provision concerned with applications for a new tenancy whereas in the 1978 lease they appeared in the context of rent review provisions. On this basis and having regard to the 'matrix of facts', the words 'carried out by the tenant' in that paragraph were apt to cover an improvement carried out by the tenant at any time, including the period when the tenant occupied the premises under an earlier lease. Accordingly the erection of the clubhouse and the golfcourse should be disregarded when fixing the reviewed rent under the 1978 lease.

JUDGE FINLAY QC (sitting as a judge of the High Court): The provisions for review of the rent contained a provision in similar terms to that in the 1973 lease, provided, that is, that on the ascertainment of the open market rent in accordance with the provisions of the lease there should be disregarded, if applicable, those matters set out in paras (a), (b) and (c) of section 34 of the Landlord and Tenant Act 1954.

The question that arises in these circumstances is whether that reference to the Landlord and Tenant Act 1954 is a reference to that Act as originally enacted or a reference to that Act as amended by the Law of Property Act 1969. The relevant paragraph that gives rise to the difficulty is para (c). I will read the relevant section of the 1954 Act as unamended, having regard in particular to para (c) which gives rise to this difficulty. The section provides that—

'The rent payable under a tenancy granted by order of the court under this Part of this Act shall be such as may be agreed between the landlord and the tenant or as, in default of such agreement, may be determined by the court to be that at which, having regard to the terms of the tenancy (other than those relating to rent) the holding might reasonably be expected to be let in the open market by a willing lessor, there being disregarded—
'(a) any effect on rent of the fact that the tenant has or his predecessors in title have been in occupation of the holding,
'(b) any goodwill attaching to the holding by reason of the carrying on thereat of the business of the tenant (whether by him or by a predecessor of his in that business),
'(c) any effect on rent of any improvement carried out by the tenant or a predecessor in title of his otherwise than in pursuance of an obligation to his immediate landlord ...'

The Act as amended provides in section 34 (a)—'the rent payable under the tenancy granted by order of the court under this Part of this Act ...'—It then contains the same provisions for agreement in default of agreement, and continues with a reference to the rent—'at which the holding might reasonably be expected to be let in the open market by a willing lessor, there being disregarded ... (c) any effect on rent of an improvement to which this paragraph applies'. And in order to determine to what para (c) in section 34 (1) of the amended Act applies, one has to look at sub-section (2). That provides that:

'Paragraph (c) of the foregoing subsection applies to any improvement carried out by a person who at the time it was carried out was the tenant, but only if it was carried out otherwise than in pursuance of an obligation to his immediate landlord, and either it was carried out during the current tenancy or the following conditions are satisfied—
'(a) that it was completed not more than 21 years before the application for the new tenancy was made,
'(b) that the holding or any part of it affected by the improvement has at all times since the completion of the improvement been comprised in tenancies of the description specified in section 23 (1) of this Act,
'(c) that at the termination of each of those tenancies the tenant did not quit.'

The amendment appears to have been enacted in the light of the decision of the House of Lords in 1965 in *East Coast Amusement Co. Ltd* v. *British Transport Board*, on appeal in a case reported as *In re 'Wonderland', Cleethorpes* (1965) AC 58. There improvements had been effected by the Appellant company prior to the lease in relation to which the tenants had served notice under section 26 of the Landlord and Tenant Act 1954 requesting a new tenancy. The lease which was current at the time of their request was one granted in 1938 and the structural works which affected the development and improvement had been carried out in 1926. It was held by the House of Lords that on its true construction para (c) of section 34 referred only to improvements carried out by the tenant who was making the application for a new tenancy and effected during the term of the tenancy current

247

when the application was made or by a predecessor entitled to the same tenancy, since in the context of section 34 'the tenant' was limited to the person who under the current tenancy was making application to the court for the renewal of such tenancy. In consequence the work carried out by the company, the tenant at all material times, but carried out in 1926, should not be disregarded. Viscount Simmonds said at p 70 at F:

'For me the critical question is—What is meant by "the tenant?" and I reject the premise upon which the Appellants must rely that it includes the individual tenant in any other capacity than that in which he makes his application to the court, i.e. as tenant under the current tenancy which he seeks to have renewed. Part II of the Act (within which section 34 falls) begins and ends with the tenancy then current which is to be extended or renewed. When that tenancy was created, a new relation was established between landlord and tenant. It is to be assumed that, when it was established and the old chapter, if there was one, was closed, the parties took into account what were then their respective rights and liabilities and founded on them accordingly. A new chapter then began and it is only with what thereafter happened that the court is concerned. This is perhaps only another way of saying that in the context the words "carried out by the tenant" import carried out during the current tenancy, and I arrive at that conclusion upon a consideration of the meaning which must be given to "the tenants".'

In consequence of that decision I am told, and it seems a reasonable proposition, the 1969 Act made the amendments which I have already indicated when reading the relevant provisions of that section. There appears to be no direct authority on the question which now arises as to whether a reference in a lease granted after the passing of the amending Act, the Law of Property Act 1969, to section 34 of the Landlord and Tenant Act 1954 or the provisions contained in that section is to be construed as a reference to the provisions contained in the 1954 Act as originally passed or to the Act as amended by the Act of 1969. But in *Euston Centre Properties Ltd* v. *H. J. Wilson Ltd* [1982] 262 EG 1079, Cantley J was concerned with a question which arose under a lease granted in 1975, that is after the amending Act, which contained a provision dealing with the revision of rent that there should be disregarded any of the matters referred to in section 34 (a), (b) and (c) of the Landlord and Tenant Act 1954. It was assumed by Cantley J and counsel that that reference was a reference to the 1954 Act as amended in 1969. Nothing appears to have turned upon that assumption because the question which arose in the case whether improvements effected prior to the grant of the relevant lease and at a time when the company which later became the tenants were licensees of the ground on which the improvements were erected should or should not be disregarded by the reason of the provisions contained in the lease. Had the reference not been assumed to be to the Act as amended but to the original Act the very same result would have followed, because in any event the tenants, the parties to the litigation, had not been tenants at the relevant time ...

[Having considered the cases, Judge Finlay said he approached the point without any guiding authority:]

The decision of the House of Lords on the construction of para (c) was a decision made in relation to an application for a new tenancy. It was, therefore, a decision dealing with the true construction of the section in relation to a matter to which the statute was applicable. That is not the case here. I have come to the conclusion that [counsel for the tenant]'s submission is well founded and that the proper approach here is to look at the lease and see what words are incorporated in it and, having done that, to construe the words so incorporated in accordance with the ordinary canons of construction. That does not mean, of course, that a judicial interpretation of those very words in a different context might not in certain circumstances throw the clearest light upon that meaning, but it does mean, in my judgment, that the decision of the House of Lords as to what is meant by section 34 of the original 1954 Act is not decisive of the question—what is meant by words taken from section 34 and incorporated in this lease by the reference made in the manner that I have already several times indicated.

What then is the true construction of the wording of para (c) when it is incorporated in this lease? I have come to the conclusion that the words in referring to an improvement carried out by the tenant refer to and are apt to include an improvement carried out by the tenant at any time. It might well be that in certain circumstances the matrix of fact would clearly indicate that that was a construction which was entirely unacceptable; e.g. suppose there had been an improvement effected by this tenant some 15 years before, that other lessees had in the meantime occupied the premises and the tenant who in the distant past had made the improvement then became tenant again, it would be contrary to reason and common sense to construe the words 'an improvement carried out by the tenant' is attributable to such a matter. But here the matrix of fact, far from contradicting the conclusion which one reaches on mere consideration of the literal meaning of the words, reinforces that conclusion. Here the improvement was carried out by the tenant holding the premises of the same landlord; it was carried out during the currency of a term which at the time when the improvements were effected had some 48 years to run. That term was within a few years surrendered by operation of law when the same landlord granted to the same tenant a new lease at a different rent and with some slight changes of the terms of the lease particularly as to rent review for another term of 50 years, thus extending the original term; in effect for a further five years. In the matrix of fact I find support for and nothing repugnant to the adoption of the construction which I place upon para (c) as incorporated in the lease that it is apt to refer to this particular improvement, the erection by the present tenant of the clubhouse that was erected in about 1975. Accordingly, I come to the conclusion that that improvement falls to be disregarded under the conditions of the lease.

Note: The effect of this decision is that unless a lease which refers specifically to section 34 of the Landlord and Tenant Act 1954 also specifically refers to the amendment made by the 1969 Act, then the amendment is excluded and the interpretation put on the words in the lease must depend on the whole context of the lease and the 'matrix of facts'.

Since the 1969 amendment was enacted in order to avoid the consequences of the decision in *In re Wonderland* [1965] AC 58 considered above in Judge Finlay's judgment. This decision in *Brett* clearly fails to implement Parliament's intention. It is notable that in *Euston Centre Properties* v. *H. & J. Wilson Ltd* [1982] 262 EG 1079 (also referred to by Judge Finlay) both counsel and the judge assumed that the relevant provision in the lease referred to the 1954 Act as amended, but in the event, since the tenant was only a licensee at the material time, nothing turned on the point.

For a general survey of valuation methods where improvements on rental value fall to be disregarded, see *GREA Real Property Investments Ltd* v. *Williams* (1979) 250 EG 651 and *Estates Projects Ltd* v. *Greenwich Borough Council* (1979) 251 EG 851, both decisions of Forbes J. The facts and an extract from the judgment of the *Estates Project* case are to be found at Chapter 15, page 309, later.

12.3 Voluntary improvements made by the tenant pursuant to landlord's licence

Improvements made voluntarily by the tenant at his own request and for which purpose the landlord granted a licence giving him permission may not as a rule be taken into account in fixing the rent under a rent review clause in the lease unless the covenants imposed by licence included a positive obligation on the tenant to carry out the works (but see *Selous Street Properties Ltd* v. *Oronel Fabrics Ltd and Others* (1984) 270 EG 643 where the landlord's licence imposed extra charges on the tenant). In the case below, the lease specifically referred to section 34 of the 1954 Act as amended by section 1 of the Law of Property Act 1969. (Compare *Brett* v. *Brett Essex Golf Club Ltd* at 5 (b) above, where the amendment was not specifically included.) Section 34 of the 1954 Act as amended by section 1 of the 1969 Act provides that a tenant's voluntary improvements during the current tenancy should be disregarded and it also applies to improvements made by the tenant's predecessor in title made within the previous 21 years of the application, that there had been a business tenancy ever since and that at the termination of any prior tenancy the tenant did not quit.

GOLDBOLD v. MARTIN THE NEWSAGENTS LTD

Chancery Division   (1983) 268 EG 1202

The tenant occupied business premises for a term of 20 years which provided for a rent review every five years. Under the previous 21-year lease the landlords had from time to time granted three licences for the tenant to carry out improvements to the premises. The review clause provided that

'any effect on rent of any improvement of the demised premises or any part thereof carried out by the Tenant at the Tenant's expense otherwise than in pursuance of any obligation to the Landlord and carried out during the current tenancy or'

in respect of which

'the conditions as contained in section 34 of the Landlord and Tenant Act 1954 as amended by section 1 of the Law of Property Act 1969 are satisfied.'

The question before the court was whether the value of those improvements was or was not to be taken into account in the fixing of the new rent and whether the improvements were made pursuant to an obligation to the landlord.

Held: This would depend on whether the various covenants by the tenant to do the various works were such that they were carried out pursuant to an obligation to the immediate landlord, or not. This would depend on the construction to be placed on the tenant's covenants and in particular as to whether they should be construed as imposing a positive obligation on the tenant to carry out the works; or whether simply they imposed an obligation on the tenant if he decided to take advantage of the licence, then to carry out the works properly. Here the wording of the licences was such that in each case the effect was that the improvements authorised were not to be taken into account in fixing the rent under the review. *Ridley* v. *Taylor* [1965] 1 WLR 611 considered.

JUDGE BLACKETT-ORD (sitting as a deputy High Court judge): It will be seen that the wording of the Act, to a large extent, overlaps the express provisions of clause 2 (1) (b) but goes further in applying to improvements made by a tenant's predecessors within the previous 21 years.

I refer to the licences in question. They are similar in substance, though they vary in detail. The first, dated 22 December 1964, was granted by the original landlord under the then subsisting lease of 21 December 1956 to the original tenant. It recites clause 2 (12) of the lease whereby the tenant covenanted not to make any structural alterations. It recites:

'the Tenant being desirous of executing in and upon the premises ... works of alteration and addition detailed on the specification plan annexed hereto ... has requested the Landlords to grant to it licence to execute such works in conformity with the said plan subject to the approval of the Landlords' surveyor and the Landlords have agreed to grant such licence upon the terms and subject to the conditions hereinafter expressed'

Clause 1 provides:

'In pursuance of the said agreement and in consideration of the premises the Landlords hereby grant licence and authority to the Tenant to execute in and upon the demised premises the several works of alteration ... on condition that the said works of alteration shall be completed or carried out in all respects to the reasonable satisfaction of the Landlords' surveyor.'

In clause 2 there are a number of covenants by the tenant, upon two of which the landlord relies:

'(a) to carry out the said works of alteration in a proper and workmanlike manner using the best obtainable materials and to comply with the provisions of all Acts of Parliament ... and to make good any damage to the demised premises or any part thereof as a result of the works of alteration aforesaid—(c) To do all things necessary and make all payments necessary for obtaining the consent so far as requisite of any statutory or local authority or owners of adjoining properties and obtain any necessary licence for commencing the aforesaid works of alteration and at his own cost and expense to make good all damage caused through the carrying out of the said works.'

The works authorised were the erection of a concrete garage and the construction of two bedrooms in the roof space. I should have said that the premises comprised in the lease consist of a newsagent's shop at Bedfont, Middlesex, with living accommodation over.

The 1968 lease related to a new shop front and extensive refitting of the shop. It was made by the new landlords, Philtown Properties Ltd, to the original tenants and recites:

'(3) The Lease contains covenants on the part of the Tenant (inter alia) not at any time during the said term without the Licence in writing of the Landlord first obtained erect or place any new or additional new building or erection on any part of the demised premises or make any alteration or addition whatsoever in or to the premises thereby demised ...
(4) The Tenant has requested the Landlord to grant to the Tenant a Licence to carry out the several alterations and works ["the said Works"] ... referred to in the Schedule, hereto which the Landlord has agreed to grant upon the terms and subject to the conditions hereinafter contained.'

Paragraph 1 provides:

'The Landlord as requested ... HEREBY GRANTS unto the Tenant LICENCE AND CONSENT to carry out in and upon the demised premises not later than the 17th day of July One Thousand nine hundred and sixty eight the said Works in conformity with the said drawings and in accordance with the covenants by the Tenant hereinafter contained and the terms covenants and provisions of the Lease as varied by this Deed and in all respects to the satisfaction of the Landlord's Surveyor.'

Clause 2 contains a provision for increasing the rent which was then £270 a year, by £15 a year. Clauses 2, 3 and 4 are directed to endeavouring to be sure that this additional annual payment was rent in the technical sense, although clause 4, out of context, could perhaps be construed more widely because it is in these terms:

'4. THE right of re-entry reserved to the Landlord by the Lease shall be EXERCISABLE by the Landlord as well in case of the non-payment of the additional rent hereby covenanted to be paid or of the breach of any of the covenants on the part of the Tenant herein contained as in case of the non-payment of the rent reserved by the Lease or of a breach of any of the covenants as amended by this Deed on the part of the Tenant therein contained.'

So there is a general reference to the tenant's covenant in the deed, which includes those which are then inserted as clause 5 which deal with the question of alterations. In 5 (1) there is a covenant very similar to 2 (a) in the 1964 licence, in these terms:

'5 (1) At its own expense to carry out and complete the said Works in conformity with the said drawings and the provisions of the Lease in a good and substantial and workmanlike manner with new good and sound materials within the period and in the manner hereinbefore specified.
(2) Before commencement of the said Works to produce to the Landlord for its approval copies of all necessary permissions ...'

It is unnecessary to read the rest. It requires the tenant to give the landlord 10 days' notice of starting the works and allows the landlords' surveyor to enter and inspect.

The final licence is dated 19 March 1971 by Philtown Properties to the present tenant, who by then had acquired the 1956 lease. That licence again recites the covenant against alteration and in recital (4) says:

'(4) The Tenant has requested the Landlord to grant to the Tenant a Licence to carry out the several alterations and works (such alterations and works being hereinafter referred to as "the said Works") ... which the Landlord has agreed to grant upon the terms and subject to the conditions hereinafter contained.'

This time it was a substantial extension to the rear of the shop. In the operative part:

'1. THE Landlord as requested as aforesaid hereby grants unto the Tenant LICENCE AND CONSENT to carry out in and upon the demised premises not later than the 18th day of September One thousand nine hundred and seventy-one' [six months ahead] the said Works in conformity with the said drawings and in accordance with the covenants by the Tenant hereinafter contained and in all respects to the satisfaction of the Landlord's Surveyor—
2. In consideration of this Licence the Tenant hereby covenants with the Landlord as follows—
(1) At its own expense to complete the said Works in conformity with the said drawings ... and in a good and substantial and workmanlike manner with new good and sound materials within the period and in the manner hereinbefore specified.
(2) Before commencement of the said Works to produce to the Landlord for its approval copies of all necessary permissions ... and to comply with the terms and conditions of any such permissions or consent.
(3) To give the Landlord not less than ten days' notice in writing ...' [of commencement] '(4) To permit the Landlord's Surveyor'

substantially in the same terms as the 1968 licence.
In 3 there is a slight change:

'3. IT IS HEREBY AGREED AND DECLARED between the parties hereto—

(1) That the covenants on the part of the Tenant herein contained shall be deemed to be incorporated in the Lease and the terms and conditions of the Lease shall apply to the demised premises as altered in pursuance of this Licence and that the power of re-entry contained in the Lease shall be construed and have effect accordingly—

(2) If the said Works are not completed in the time limit hereinbefore specified or in the event of any breach before the completion of the said Works of the covenants on the part of the Tenant herein contained this Licence shall become null and void.

The question is whether the various covenants by the tenants to do the various works are such as to make them such that they were carried out pursuant to an obligation to the immediate landlord, or not. That depends upon the construction of the respective tenant's covenants and in particular as to whether they are to be construed as imposing a positive obligation on the tenant to carry out the works, or whether simply they impose an obligation on the tenant if he decides to take advantage of the licence, then to carry out the works properly.

Surprisingly, I have not been referred to any authority, so I must consider within the wording of the Act, section 34 (2) which, in its tortuous language, applies to any improvement, but only if it was carried out otherwise than in pursuance of an obligation to the tenant's immediate landlord. My impression is that the draftsman had in mind, primarily, an obligation imposed by the lease. But, of course, the provision can also apply to an obligation imposed in some other contractual document. But looking at the licences it is clear that they were all granted at the request of the tenant and the language of clause (1) in each case is the language of permission. Those claims do not say that it has been agreed that the tenant shall carry out; he is simply granted permission. In my judgment the following clauses are in each case subsidiary to that. Although the wording is different in each case the effect is that the improvements authorised are not to be taken into account in fixing the rent under the present review. I am fortified in that view by the opinions expressed by Harman LJ and Russell LJ in the case of *Ridley* v. *Taylor* [1965] 1 WLR 611, where their lordships took the view that covenants of the nature of which I have been considering are not generally to be construed as imposing positive obligations.

12.4 Tenant's improvements consistent with the terms of the lease and their effect on rent review

Where premises are taken as a 'shell', the valuation for review purposes will depend on the terms of the lease. If it is open to the tenant to fit out the 'shell' in a manner consistent with the covenants in the lease, valuation of the rental of the premises should take into account the possibility of amalgamating the demise with the adjoining premises, which was permitted by a landlord's licence under the terms of the lease.

WEBBER v. HALIFAX BUILDING SOCIETY

Chancery Division   (1985) 273 EG 297

The lease of premises granted to the tenant for a 42-year term contained a covenant against alteration without the landlord's consent such consent not to be unreasonably withheld by the landlord. The tenant subsequently joined the demise up with his adjacent freehold premises pursuant to a licence from the landlord which provided that the tenant would reinstate the premises at the end of the 42-year term. The lease provided for seven yearly reviews on the basis of

'the annual rental value of the demised premises in the open market for a lease for a term of seven years certain (consisting of the review period) ... calculated ... as if such building was a "developer's shell", meaning to say that a tenant would be required to provide his own shop front and interior fixtures and fittings ...'

Held: The valuation of the premises as a 'developer's shell' had to be on the terms of the lease, namely, on the basis that it was open to the tenant to fit out the 'shell' consistently with the covenants in the lease. Therefore, such a valuation should take regard of the possibility of amalgamating the premises with the premises next door.

JUDGE PAUL BAKER QC (sitting as a High Court judge): I am asked to rule on whether the rent is to be calculated

'on the basis that the hypothetical lease whereunder the rent is to be determined is assumed to be subject to the same terms and conditions (save as to rent) as the terms and conditions of the lease'.

That general question in fact boiled down during the course of the hearing to a very narrow point. It is common ground that one approaches a rent-review clause of this sort, which talks of a hypothetical lease (the lease for seven years but which does not mention terms) which is on the same terms as the existing lease, save as to rent, and of course save as to any provision which is necessarily excluded by the hypothesis and by the matters referred to in the review provision. That seems to emerge from the decision of the House of Lords in *Ponsford* v. *HMS Aerosols Ltd* [1979] AC 63, but I do not think I need refer to it in any particularity because, as I have said, it is common ground between counsel in this case that that is the proper approach to the matter.

The argument has turned again on a point of construction. I think this is the way it is put: the terms of the review provision (clause 4 (i)) leads one to the proposition that the covenant against alterations (which I have read out already) should be modified so as to prohibit absolutely amalgamation with the adjoining premises. It is said: 'Well, the relevance of that is that if you could have that amalgamation, then the next-door people might pay a special rent, and that is what the valuers have to disregard.' With the covenant as it is, of course it prohibits alterations, but it is qualified not to be unreasonably withheld and there is authority that that does not prevent an amalgamation with adjoining premises as a matter of principle; it may on the particular facts of the case, but not automatically as a matter of general principle. The landlord is normally protected in those circumstances by a covenant as we have here to reinstate and separate out the premises at the end of the term.

I think the argument was this. [Counsel] for the tenants argued this and he put it this way. It is clear from clause 4 that the parties, by importing a developer's shell, which I mentioned, intended the premises to be valued as a separate unit. I can accept that part of the submission, but then at (e) he submitted that 'it was wrong to import into the terms of the lease any provision which destroys its separateness'. So that what one fastens on to is the fact that it has to be valued as a developer's shell, the argument, as I understand it, meaning that therefore it has to be valued as a developer's shell ignoring any possibility of amalgamation, and that must be prohibited. I am quite unable to accept that view of the matter. As it seems to me, the purpose of the developer's shell, and the £2250 with which it is linked, is simply that the valuers are not to value any improvements carried out by the tenants, save in so far as the landlord has contributed to them. I am putting it very broadly and I am not concerned to determine exactly how it operates, but that is what it is for and it is limited to that. When they value it as a shell they value it without the fixtures and fittings which the tenant has put in there at his expense. They ignore all that, except in so far as the landlord has enabled that to be done by waiving his rent for a period, and that sort of thing. They value that, but of course they value it on the terms of the lease—that, having got the shell, it is then open to the tenant obviously to fit it out in one way or another, and fit it out in a manner which is consistent with the covenants in the lease. It certainly does not mean that it is to remain as a shell throughout the period; nor can I see any ground for saying that it is to remain as a separate but fitted premises, and therefore on that point I am in favour of the landlord and I will declare accordingly on that issue.

12.5   Effect of reinstatement clause on rent review

A tenant's obligation to reinstate the premises to their former condition may or may not be disregarded for the purposes of determining the rent if there is no express provision on the point. Where the tenant pays for the alterations himself and the landlord takes no extra rent or premium in return for his permission for the alterations, there is no reason why the tenant's obligation to reinstate should be taken into account and reduce the rent payable on review.

PLEASURAMA PROPERTIES LTD v. LEISURE INVESTMENTS (WEST END) LTD

Chancery Division   (1985) 273 EG 67

The tenant under an underlease was granted a licence by the landlord to convert retail shop premises into a dolphinarium, with a dolphin pool and auditorium. The licence contained a covenant by the tenant to reinstate the premises for normal shopping use at the termination of the underlease. The licence did not provide for the payment of extra rent or a premium for the privilege of alteration. The underlease contained a rent review clause which provided for the appointment of an independent surveyor if the parties were unable to agree the revised rent. The parties could not agree as to whether the tenant's obligation to reinstate should be taken into account when the valuer fixed the revised rent.

Held: As the licence did not expressly make provision on the issue, the court had to decide what the probable intention of the parties had been in the light of the licence and the underlease read together, and the nature of the transaction. Where the tenant had been granted a licence to convert business premises at his own expense with no financial benefit being taken by the landlord and where the licence obliged the tenant to reinstate the premises at the expiration of the underlease, there was no reason why, in the absence of any express provision, the costs of the reinstatement should be taken into account when assessing the revised rent at a future rent review.

NOURSE J: It is to be noted that the licence made no provision for any monetary consideration to change hands, either by way of an increased rent or by way of premium. The head landlord and the sublessor appear to have been content with provisions which would procure the reinstatement of the premises on the determination of the underlease, while putting them to no additional expense in the meantime.

The present position is that the first additional rent, if there is to be one, became payable as from 1 March 1983. However, the plaintiff and the defendant have been unable to agree a rent between themselves and, moreover, have been unable to agree whether the independent valuer, who must now decide the matter, should be instructed to take into account the plaintiff's obligation to reinstate the premises or to leave it out of account. It is the interest of the plaintiff as the present sublessee under the underlease to contend that the obligation ought to be taken into account, because an obligation of that kind will doubtless reduce the yearly rent which ought reasonably to be expected to be obtainable for the demised premises in the open market. Conversely, it is the interest of the defendant as the present sublessor under the underlease to contend to the contrary effect.

As earlier stated, the question depends on the true construction and effect of the underlease and licence when read together. [Counsel] for the plaintiff submits that the licence had a permanent effect on the interests of both grantor and grantee so as to bind any successor to either interest, with the result, among other things, that the grantee's interest in the premises as offered on the open market would have to be valued by taking the obligation to reinstate into account. Alternatively (it may be a different way of expressing his first submission), [counsel for the plaintiff] says that the licence operated as a variation of the essential terms of the underlease so that the matter had thenceforth to be read and construed with reference to the variations so effected.

There is to some extent no divergence between the submissions of [counsel for the plaintiff] and those of [counsel] for the defendant. It is obvious that some at least of the terms of the underlease were permanently varied by the licence. It is also obvious that, as a matter of contract, it was open to the parties to vary any of the terms of the underlease in any manner and to any extent which they might mutually agree. If you look only at clause 2 (3) of the underlease, the obligation to reinstate must be left out of account because the covenant by which the plaintiff is committed to that obligation is not a covenant 'on the part of the tenant ... similar to those herein contained'. The question which I have to decide is whether, by the licence, the parties have evinced a mutual intention that the covenant to reinstate contained in that document should be treated as if it was a covenant on the part of the tenant contained in the underlease.

It is agreed between [counsel for the defendant] and [counsel for the plaintiff] that there is no specific provision to that effect. The first way in which [counsel for the plaintiff] seeks to achieve it is by a method which he claims, perhaps correctly, does not involve any process of implication. He says that it is simply a question of reading the two documents together in a fair way and deciding what is their combined effect. He says that, if you do that, clause 2 (vi) of the licence is found to be an express provision which, although not specifically achieving the desired effect, does nevertheless achieve it mainly by construing the two documents together. Alternatively, he submits that if it is necessary for him to rely on a process of implication then the plaintiff still passes the necessary test.

In relation to implication [counsel for the plaintiff] has referred me to a valuable passage in the speech of Lord Wilberforce in *Liverpool City Council* v. *Irwin* [1977] AC 239 at p 253 E–F. There Lord Wilberforce states that there are varieties of implications which the court thinks fit to make and that they do not necessarily all involve the same process. His lordship identifies four different categories of implication, or rather four shades on a continuous spectrum. However, it appears from a later passage in his speech at p 254 F, to which [counsel for the defendant] referred me, that Lord Wilberforce was of the view that an implication could only be made in that case if there was a necessity for it. In my view, that is the basic requirement of any species of implication, whether under the doctrine of *The Moorcock* (1889) 14 PD 64 or otherwise.

At the end of the day, whichever way it is put, I have to be satisfied that, by the licence read in the light of the underlease, the parties to the licence intended that the obligation to reinstate was to be taken into account for the purpose of fixing the additional rent. There is certainly no necessity for that. I am bound to say that [counsel for the plaintiff] has failed to satisfy me that that was their intention.

Indeed, I have been satisfied by the argument of [counsel for the defendant] that their intention must be taken to have been to the contrary effect.

[Counsel for the defendant] submitted that it was obvious that the parties intended, first, that the sublessee should have all the benefits to be derived from the alterations, in exchange for which it should bear the burden of having to reinstate the premises on the determination of the underlease, and, secondly, that while the sublessor should not receive any benefit from the alterations it was not to suffer any burden or detriment from them either. Clearly the sublessee would never have requested permission to make the alterations if it had not thought that they would render the premises more profitable to it. If that be right, the sublessor was doing it a favour by allowing it to make them. Why should the parties be taken to have intended that the sublessor should not only do the sublessee a favour without charging it any premium or additional rent, but should also itself suffer a detriment by exposing itself to the probability of receiving less rent than it would otherwise receive on subsequent reviews of the existing rent?

While [counsel for the plaintiff]'s first argument has an intellectual attraction, it does not stand up to the test of commonsense. His second argument fails for lack of necessity. It seems to me that [counsel for the defendant's] approach is the only one which the court can adopt. To do otherwise would be to fly in the face of ordinary commercial commonsense.

I do not propose to go into any of the other arguments, none of which appear to me to be decisive, except to say this. It seems to me that if there was any lingering doubt at the end of the day it would be resolved in favour of the defendant by the provisions of subclause 2 (3) (c) of the underlease. That provision—which requires that there should be disregarded any effect on rent by reason of any improvements carried out by the tenant in order to put the demised premises in any better condition—is simply not reconcilable with the notion that regard should be had to an obligation to eliminate such improvements and reinstate the premises to their former condition. I find it very hard to see how that result could have been achieved by the licence without some specific provision which made it clear that that was what the parties intended.

12.6 Status of improvements carried out in anticipation of grant of lease with encouragement of landlord

There may be circumstances where a tenant's improvements carried out before the lease is granted may be disregarded for rent review purposes.

HAMBROS BANK EXECUTOR AND TRUSTEE CO. v. SUPERDRUG STORES

Chancery Division   (1985) 274 EG 588

The tenant, with the encouragement of the landlord, went into possession of premises and carried out substantial improvements and alterations in anticipation of taking a lease of them while negotiations were in progress. The rent review clause provided that when assessing the revised rent the tenant's improvements should not be taken into account when fixing the rent on review. The alterations included removal of a lift hoist and surrounding walls and enlargement of the ground floor and its shop window and extension of the basement area. On review the landlord contended that the tenant's improvements should not be disregarded since they had not been executed by the tenant when he was in fact a tenant as defined by the review clause.

Held: When the contents of the lease were read literally, the provision in the rent review clause required to be disregarded any effect on rent of any improvement carried out by Superdrug Stores Ltd who was the tenant under the lease. Since all the improvements were carried out by Superdrug the landlord's case failed. The factual matrix left no room for doubt but that both parties to the lease regarded the shopfitting works as works which would constitute an improvement carried out by the tenant for the purposes of rent review provision in the lease and required to be disregarded on any rent review.

The facts came near to being an attempt by a landlord to take advantage of a situation which it had itself encouraged by consenting to its tenant going into possession and commencing the shop fitting works in advance of the lease.

Scott J: Accordingly, the lift hoist and its surrounding walls had been removed before the commencement of the lease on 15 September. The floor area of the ground floor had been increased by that removal before the commencement of the lease. The reinforced steel joist had not been put in, but that was a small and relatively trivial job. Thereapart, nothing else needed to be done to make the extra floor area usable for shop purposes.

Counsel has told me, and I think it is accepted, that the removal of the lift hoist and surrounding walls has added some 70 sq. ft of usable floor-space to the ground floor. I take it there has been the same addition of usable floor-space to the basement. The effect of this, if it represents an improvement which may be taken into account on the rent review, would be to add to the rent to be paid under the lease as from 29 September 1981 a sum of some £3000 per annum. There would also, of course, be an effect on subsequent rent reviews.

The question, therefore, is whether or not under the rent-review provisions of the lease the works relating to the removal of the lift hoist and surrounding walls fall to be disregarded. [Counsel] for the plaintiffs, submits that they do not fall to be disregarded. He directed my attention particularly to the wording of the rent-review clause. What is to be disregarded is 'any effect on rent of any improvement carried out by the tenant'. 'The tenant' in that context, he submitted, meant the person who, at the time the works were carried out, was the tenant under the current tenancy. Since the lease was not granted until 15 September the defendants were not, he argued, when the relevant improvements were carried out, 'the tenant' for the purposes of this provision. It would follow that the improvements were not improvements carried out by 'the tenant' and did not fall to be disregarded.

In my view, for a number of reasons, this argument cannot be accepted. First, I will consider how the matter stands on a literal reading of the lease without recourse to any factual matrix to assist construction. The original tenants were the defendants. The defendants are named in the lease, Superdrug Stores Ltd. The defendants are not called 'Superdrug Stores Ltd' throughout the lease; they are defined as 'the tenant'. 'The tenant', therefore, becomes the expression which when used in the lease means Superdrug Stores Ltd. True it is that the expression 'the tenant' includes, under clause 4 (9), the successors and assigns of Superdrug Stores Ltd. But Superdrug Stores Ltd has no successors or assigns as yet and the primary meaning of 'the tenant' remains Superdrug Stores Ltd.

So, if the contents of the lease are read literally, the provision in the rent-review clause requires to be disregarded any effect on rent of any improvement carried out by Superdrug Stores Ltd. The removal of the lift hoist and the surrounding walls, the increase of the ground-floor area and the extra length given to the shopfront represent improvements which, it is common ground, were carried out by Superdrug Stores Ltd. So far as the literal meaning of the lease is concerned, therefore, in my judgment, the plaintiffs' case fails.

[Counsel for the plaintiffs] submitted that the factual matrix of the lease was neutral. It gave no indication, he submitted, whether the parties would have regarded the improvements in question carried out by Superdrug Stores Ltd before the actual date of the lease as appropriate to be disregarded on a rent review or appropriate to be taken into account on a rent review. That submission I regard as flying in the face of the facts. The correspondence put before me shows that the original rent of £19,000 per annum was asked for by Kenfield Properties Ltd for the premises as they then stood. The improvements, the shopfitting works, were undertaken by Superdrug Stores Ltd for their own purposes with a view to becoming tenants of the premises under the lease eventually granted on 15 September 1976 and with no other view whatever. Consent to those shopfitting works being carried out was granted by Kenfield Properties Ltd on the footing that Superdrug Stores Ltd would become tenants of the premises under that lease. At the relevant time all the terms of the lease had been agreed. The factual matrix to the lease suggests that both parties thought that the defendants would be doing the shopfitting works as tenants under the prospective lease.

I do not think that the factual matrix leaves any room for doubt but that both parties to the lease regarded the shopfitting works as works which would constitute an improvement carried out by the tenant for the purposes of the rent-review provision in the lease and required to be disregarded on any rent review.

[Counsel for the plaintiffs] referred me to certain authorities which I should mention. The first was a decision of Cantley J in *Euston Centre Properties* v. *H. & J. Wilson Ltd* reported at (1981) 262 EG 1079. In that case there was a rent-review clause in the lease which required to be disregarded 'the matters referred to in section 34 (a), (b) and (c) of the Landlord and Tenant Act 1954'. The learned judge construed that provision as referring to the 1954 Act as amended. Paragraph (c) of section 34 as amended requires to be disregarded 'any improvement carried out by a person who at the time it was carried out was the tenant'. That statutory provision is clear and unambiguous. It requires the person to be the tenant at the time the improvement is carried out. Cantley J so held. His decision does not seem to me to be relevant to the construction of the rent-review provision with which I am concerned.

The second rent-review case referred to by [counsel for the plaintiffs] was *Brett* v. *Brett Essex Golf Club Ltd* reported at (1984) 273 EG 507. That, too, was a case where a rent-review clause in a lease incorporated by reference the provisions of section 34 of the 1954 Act. His Honour Judge Finlay, sitting as a judge of the High Court, came to the conclusion that the reference in the lease was to the 1954 Act as originally enacted and not as amended. He concluded that the relevant provisions of section 34 as originally enacted meant that an improvement was to be disregarded if it was an improvement made by the tenant at any time, whether or not made by him in his capacity as tenant of the current tenancy. I do not regard that decision either as of any real relevance for the purposes of the present case; but, if it has any weight at all, it is against the submissions made by [counsel for the plaintiffs].

The third case was a case in the House of Lords, *Re 'Wonderland', Cleethorpes* [1965] AC 58. That was a case where a tenant had made an application for a new lease and the provisions of section 34 of the 1954 Act came directly into play. That was a case before the 1969 amendment was enacted. It was held by Viscount Simonds that the provision in paragraph (c) of section 34 requiring improvements carried out by a tenant to be disregarded for the purposes of assessing the rent of the new tenancy, was a provision which related only to improvements carried out by the tenant during the current tenancy. The point in issue in that case, however, was whether various works carried out many years previously by the person who in fact was the tenant under the current tenancy fell to be disregarded by reason of the statutory provision. The House of Lords concluded that they did not.

I am not clear that the dicta and principles expressed by their lordships in that case indicate what their view would have been had the improvements been carried out shortly before the current tenancy by the person shortly to become the current tenant and with a view to the grant of the current tenancy. The example I am contemplating is that of a tenant who negotiates a tenancy with a landlord and is allowed into possession before the grant of the lease in order to carry out various improvements to adapt the premises for his use as tenant. Let it be supposed that the term originally granted expires, that there is no provision in the lease for renewal or rent review and that the tenant, relying on his statutory rights, applies for a new tenancy. I do not take the *Wonderland* case as any authority for the proposition that in assessing the rent for the new tenancy the improvements made by the tenant in those circumstances fall to be taken into account on the ground that they were improvements carried out before the grant of the lease. That was not the factual situation with which the House of Lords in the *Wonderland* case was concerned. It is a factual situation which raises, to my mind, quite different considerations from those with which the House of Lords was concerned. I do not regard the dicta by Viscount Simonds and Lord Morris to which [counsel for the plaintiffs] referred me as having any bearing on the facts in the present case.

I return briefly then to those facts. Kenfield Properties Ltd agreed, albeit, perhaps, subject to contract, to grant to the defendants a lease containing the rent-review provision I have read and allowed the defendants into possession in advance of the final grant of the lease to enable the defendants to carry out shopfitting works in anticipation of their use of the premises after the grant of the lease. The lease was then granted. The proposition that the landlord can then turn round and say 'Now I am entitled to take advantage of all the improvements you have done before we actually got around to executing the lease because those improvements do not fall to be disregarded on the rent review' is one which I find quite unacceptable. It is near to being, in my view, an unconscionable attempt by a landlord to take advantage of a situation which it has itself encouraged by consenting to its tenant going into possession and commencing the shopfitting works in advance of the lease.

I am satisfied, however, that under the lease of 15 September 1976, whether read literally or construed in the light of its factual matrix, the removal of the lift hoist and the surrounding walls represents an improvement which under the terms of the lease falls to be disregarded on the rent review.

The plaintiffs' claim was dismissed with costs.

Chapter 13

The continuing liability of the original lessee for rent after rent review

13.1 The original lessee may remain liable for a higher rent fixed on review by the assignee or a subsequent assignee as the tenant for the time being if he is liable by privity of contract

Where the original lessee is bound by privity of contract he will remain liable for the rent even after assignment. This liability will extend to the higher rent agreed by an assignee after review or by agreement with the landlord, even though the original lessee knew nothing about it. A tenant should consider whether he would be wise to sublet rather than assign since if he sublets and the sub-tenant fails to pay rent he can at least dispose of the premises himself, possibly re-occupy them and take prompt steps not to let arrears continue to mount before taking action.

CENTROVINCIAL ESTATES PLC v. BULK STORAGE LTD

Chancery Division   (1983) 268 EG 59

The defendant was the original lessee of premises held under a 21-year lease granted in 1964. The rent was £17,000 a year with a review after 14 years. In July 1978 the defendant tenant assigned the residue of its term to Airfix Products Ltd, and Airfix as assignee of the term agreed a revised rent of £40,000 a year with the landlord. Airfix failed to pay rent on Michaelmas Day 1981 and, following the issue of a writ, a further gale of rent remained unpaid in April 1982. The landlord sued the defendant for unpaid rent owed by Airfix claiming that as the defendant was the original tenant under the lease it remained liable to the landlord for the acts done by the tenant's assignee. The tenant contended that it was not bound by acts done which were prejudicial to it by an assignee of the term, and/or alternatively the terms of the lease precluded its being held liable for the acts of an assignee.

Held:
(1) An assignee is the owner of the whole estate granted to him and can deal with it so as to alter it or its terms. The estate so altered then binds the original tenant, because the assignee has been put into the shoes of the original tenant and can do all such acts as the original tenant could have done. A surrender of part of the term does not determine the lease. *Haslemere Estates Ltd* v. *British Olivetti Ltd*, (McNeil QC, unreported) followed.
(2) The basic principle of liability was not excluded by the terms of the lease.

HARMAN J: These two actions each claim £10,000, being a quarter's rent due respectively on Michaelmas Day 1981 and on Christmas Day that year. The problem

261

raised in both actions is, however, by no means limited to a question of money unpaid. The real question is a point of law of some interest and general application.

In broad terms it may be stated as being whether an original tenant under a lease containing a rent review clause is bound by privity of contract to pay the landlord for the time being of the premises a rent agreed or otherwise determined with a subsequent assignee of the term. That obligation, it was contended, arose although the original tenant never authorised, or knew of, or had any connection whatever with, the agreement or other process whereby the amount of the new rent was determined. No suggestion was made during argument that the landlord's position could be different depending upon whether it was the original landlord or, as here, a successor in title to the reversion. I have therefore not attempted to consider that point, but have assumed it for the purposes of this judgment.

On the pleadings the matter stands as follows. The statement of claim alleges that premises were let by a predecessor in title of the plaintiff to the defendant by an underlease dated 2 July 1965 for a term of 21 years from Christmas Day 1964. The rent reserved was £17,000 per annum, payable quarterly in advance on the usual quarter days. The rent was to be reviewed with effect from the expiry of the first 14 years of the term, either by agreement in writing or by a surveyor acting as an expert.

In July 1978 the defendant assigned the residue of its term to Airfix Products Ltd. At that date the first 14 years of the term had not expired.

By a document dated 17 January 1979 the plaintiff, which had acquired the reversion, and Airfix Products Ltd, which was then the assignee of the term, agreed a revised rent at a figure of £40,000 per annum. On Michaelmas Day 1981, a usual quarter day, Airfix Products Ltd failed to pay the gale of rent then falling due, and it remained unpaid at the date of issue of the writ on 23 February 1982. A further gale of rent fell due on the next due quarter day, Christmas Day 1981, which was not paid then and remained unpaid at the date of issue of the second writ on 8 April 1982.

The defence make proper admissions as to the underlease, subject to detailed reference to its terms, and admit the devolution of the term and of the reversion. The agreement allegedly recorded in the memorandum of 17 January 1979 is put to strict proof. The real thrust of the defence in the second part of para 5, which alleges that that agreement, if made, was *res inter alios acta*. Further, in para 6, it is contended that the rent, if any, payable by the defendant is limited to the original rent of £17,000 per annum.

Other points were raised, such as that Airfix Products Ltd was firstly liable for the rent and that the plaintiff had a duty to mitigate its loss and had failed to try to do so. A reply was served and further and better particulars given, but at the hearing before me [counsel] for the plaintiff very sensibly limited his argument to the points adumbrated above, thus saving what, in my present view, would have been a fruitless inquiry into those matters. Further, at an early stage of the opening, [counsel for the defendant] abandoned the contention that there was a duty to mitigate, and no time was therefore taken up by (and I do not have to consider) that issue.

The first issue raised is one of fact. Did the plaintiff and Airfix Products Ltd make an effective agreement, recorded in the memoranda attached to the underlease and counterpart, both of which were proved in evidence before me? I hold on the evidence adduced that they did. [Counsel], who conducted the defendant's case with skill and responsibility, did not feel able to argue to the contrary at the conclusion of the evidence.

The matter thus becomes an issue of law. Is the defendant, who had no knowledge of or connection with the agreement made, bound to pay rent at the rate fixed by that agreement? It appeared to me that clause 5 (i) of the underlease which referred to rent in an 'amount ... fixed by agreement in writing ... at least six calendar months before December 25 1978' might have meant that only an agreement made before the specified date was effective, and here the agreement was made after the specified date. However, [counsel for the defendant] at an early stage of the hearing conceded expressly that, on the basis of the decision in the House of Lords in *United Scientific Holdings Limited* v. *Burnley Borough Council* [1978] AC 904, the agreement was effective within the terms of clause 5 (i).

The issue of law divides, as [counsel for the defendant] submitted, into two parts. Firstly, he contended that in general terms an original tenant is not bound by acts prejudicial to him done by an assignee of the term. Secondly, he contended that even if an original tenant can, in law, be bound by acts done by an assignee, yet upon the true construction of this particular lease and the terms of clause 5 (i) itself the defendant here was not bound by the agreement of January 1979.

Upon the first part of the issue there is, to my mind surprisingly, little or no authority. As a matter of principle [counsel for the plaintiff] submitted that each and every assignee of a term—though it might be at three or four removes from, and never in any contractual relationship with, the original tenant—was the agent of and had authority to bind the original tenant to the assignee's bargain. I do not find the concept of agency apt for this relationship. Express agency is a matter of contract; ostensible agency, of holding out. The idea of agency for an undisclosed principal seems remote from any possible fact in a matter involving original tenant and assignee. Further, when an assignee makes some arrangement with the holder of the reversion, the assignee is almost always dealing on his or its own behalf. The idea that the assignee is both principal and agent for another principal involves difficulties which in my judgment point to the relationship normally called agency being an inappropriate one by which to classify the relationship of assignee and original tenant. In truth I believe that the relationship is *sui generis* to the law of landlord and tenant. There are many special features about the relationships arising in that field of law not to be found in other branches of the law. The running of covenants with land and the ancient origin of this branch of the law make it in my judgment natural that the relationship does not fall easily into other categories.

But if there is, as I hold, no agency enabling an assignee to bind the original tenant, what is the position? In my judgment the basic answer which any real property lawyer would give to a question about an assignee's power to deal with a tenancy interest is that each assignee is the owner of the whole estate and can deal with it so as to alter it or its terms. The estate as so altered then binds the original tenant, because the assignee has been put into the shoes of the original tenant and can do all such acts as the original tenant could have done.

That basic answer is supported by the decision of the Court of Appeal in *Baynton* v. *Morgan* (1888) 22 QBD 74. The first point decided by Lord Esher MR is that a covenant by an original tenant in a lease is not a contract of guarantee. No question of suretyship arises. The liability is a primary liability of the original tenant (see pp 77-78). Fry LJ at pp 80-81 and Lopes LJ at p 83 arrive at the same conclusion.

The other point in the case was whether the liability of the original tenant to pay rent ceased because of a surrender by the assignee of part of the demised premises. It was argued that the covenant to pay rent was one entire obligation; it could not be apportioned. And part of the demised premises having been surrendered, it was said that the whole rent was not payable, and indeed was not claimed; and since there could be no apportionment, no rent was payable by the original tenant.

All three members of the Court of Appeal rejected this argument. Lord Esher at the foot of p 78 and the top of p 79 held that the covenant is to pay the rent on the specified quarter day in the term. He went on to hold that an assignee is given power by an assignment to do anything which the original lessee could have done. It follows, he held, that since the surrender of part of the premises by the original lessee does not determine the term, no more does a surrender of part by the assignee determine the term. Consequently the term remains and the covenant is enforceable. Fry LJ was to a similar effect. Lopes LJ at p 82 stated:

'The rule of law is that a lessee remains liable upon his express covenants, notwithstanding an assignment and acceptance by the landlord of rent from the assignee ...'

He continued:

> 'Then how can the liability under the express covenant be got rid of? It may cease by reason of a surrender of the term, a surrender of all the premises demised by the lease, an eviction, or a release.'

He goes on to hold that none of those conditions applied and consequently the original tenant's covenant remained enforceable. That decision on principle, in my judgment, governs this case.

I also had cited to me an unreported decision of Mr David McNeill QC, as he then was, sitting as a deputy judge of the Queen's Bench. The case was entitled *Haslemere Estates Ltd* v. *British Olivetti Ltd.* The claim by a landlord was to recover from an original tenant a rent increased by a rent review, agreed with a second assignee of the term. As in the present case the original tenant knew nothing of the rent review or of the agreement. In the *Haslemere Estates* case, in addition, the first assignee was not concerned with the rent review. Mr McNeill QC held, at p 12 of the transcript, B to G, that the original tenant was bound by the second assignee's agreement. He cited *Baynton* v. *Morgan* and held that the original tenant is, in law, a party to the agreement for a review of rent because the assignee 'stands in his shoes'. I am not bound by that decision but I entirely agree with it. I reach the same conclusion myself in this case.

I now turn to the distinctions alleged to exist in the particular terms of this underlease and clause 5. The terms are naturally different from those in the *Haslemere Estates* case. [Counsel for the defendant] argued valiantly that the differences were such as to overcome the basic principle which I have held to exist, that an assignee stands in the shoes of an original tenant and can alter the obligations affecting the original tenant. He pointed out that the terms in the lease defining the parties, which in the *Haslemere Estates* case included a reference to assigns of the lessee as well as to successors in title, in this present case include only a reference to successors in title; he referred to a difference in the reddendum and other details, all of which [counsel for the defendant] most helpfully set out in a typescript document comparing the two clauses. Clause 2, which contains the vital covenant in this case, was in the *Haslemere Estates* case a great deal more elaborate than in the *Centrovincial* case, this present case, and the reference in clause 5 (i) itself to an agreement in writing between the parties all went to make the obligations here different from those in the *Haslemere Estates* lease. In my judgment the differences are semantic rather than substantial.

[Counsel for the defendant] suggested that the provisions of clause 5 (i) referring to an 'agreement in writing between the parties' required the agreement of those who executed the underlease, they being in truth the parties to it, as well as the agreement of the landlord for the time being and the tenant for the time being. In contrast, he said, a rent fixed under clause 5 (i) by a surveyor acting as an expert was imposed on the lease itself. [Counsel for the defendant] pointed to other oddities of wording, notably clause 2 (xvi) where the tenant's covenants are modified to show that a covenant not to compete is limited to competition with the original landlord. This showed, said [counsel for the defendant], that when the draftsman wished he knew how to make obligations apply to particular estate-holders; he had not done so in clause 5 (i).

Hard though [counsel for the defendant] tried and elegantly as he put his points, I found them unconvincing. In my judgment the basic principle to which I have referred is not excluded by any term of this particular lease, and accordingly the plaintiff succeeds.

Further, the result I have reached seems to me to accord with practical dealings between landlords and tenants and their respective assigns. If an original tenant wishes to ensure that no rent review is made without his or its consent the machinery to secure that result is, as [counsel for the plaintiff] submitted, easily to hand. The original tenant instead of assigning the residue of the term can simply grant an underlease upon identical terms but for the same period less two or three days. The difference in value between the residue of the term and a subterm of almost the same duration would be very small, if any. The distinction between assigning and subletting for a very slightly shorter period, and the consequences in law on the relationships between the various parties are, in my judgment, well known to all concerned in the real property market.

Note: See also *Torminster Properties Ltd* v. *Green and another* [1983] 2 All ER 457 (ante, page 97 Effect of surrender on rent review), where the lessee and thus his sureties were held liable to pay the reviewed rent from the date of the review under a lease which had been surrendered before the arbitrator had fixed the revised rent but after review provisions had been set in motion. The revised rent was payable from the date of review until the date of surrender.

13.2 Position of original lessee, successive assignees and sureties

There are mutual obligations owed to the landlord by the original lessee, assignees and guarantors for payment of revised rents. Where the payments are in arrears, all may be liable to the landlord, but as between the original tenant and an assignee, the original tenant will have priority and may claim an indemnity as against the assignees and their guarantors. Further, on payment, he could be subrogated to the landlord's rights against the surety of the assignees. See *Selous Street Properties Ltd* v. *Oronel Fabrics Ltd and Others* (1984) 270 EG 643.

13.3 A revised rent may be fixed in advance of an assignment

The parties may determine and agree a rent payable on review in advance of an assignment which becomes the rent payable on review. Obviously the facts must support such an agreement being alleged, which may be rectified in appropriate circumstances. See *Equity & Law Life Assurance Society Ltd* v. *Coltness Group Ltd*, at 10.2 (c) earlier under 'Rectification on the grounds of mutual mistake, at page 212.

Chapter 14

Submitting to arbitration or valuation by an expert

Arbitration is a specialised subject which is heavily governed by the Arbitration Acts 1950 and 1979. The cases which have been included illustrate some of the basic and most important issues which can arise in the field of rent review. They do not provide a full and exhaustive guide to the subject, for which readers are recommended to consult the recognised specialist works on arbitration (such as Mustill and Boyd's *Commercial Arbitration, Russell on Arbitration* and John Parris' *Arbitration: Principles and Practice*). With regard to the arbitrator's power to award costs, it should be noted that a *prior* agreement between the parties, e.g. in the terms of the lease, will be of no effect when the matter falls to be determined by arbitration. However, once arbitration has begun the parties may agree the costs. 'Section 18 (1) of the Arbitration Act 1950 gives the arbitrator complete discretion, and thereafter, natural justice takes over.' (See 'Award of Costs in rent review arbitrations and in disputes as to rent under the Landlord and Tenant Act 1954, Part II–2' by Graham Plumbe (1985) 275 EG 1202.)

14.1 Determining points of law on review

The parties may wish the court to define the basis on which the arbitrator is to review the rent if a point of law arises. Section 2 of the Arbitration Act 1979 provides for the determination of a preliminary point of law by the court but this does not exclude the ordinary jurisdiction of the court which is regulated by the Arbitration Act 1950, section 4.

   The position was considered by Judge Paul Baker QC (sitting as a High Court judge) in **Scottish and Newcastle Breweries PLC v. Sir Richard Sutton's Settled Estates** (1985) 276 EG 77. (For full facts and decision see earlier, 6.2, page 108.)

JUDGE PAUL BAKER QC: A d: , ute has arisen between the plaintiff and the defendant as to the true construction of the lease and it has been agreed between the plaintiff and defendant that the arbitration will not be proceeded with until the question posed in the originating summons herein has been answered.

   So arbitration is under way and the purpose of these proceedings is to clarify and limit the areas of dispute in the arbitration. In those circumstances, [counsel for the tenants] very rightly, called my attention to the provisions of the Arbitration Act 1979, section 2 (1), which is set out conveniently on p 1463 of the current *Supreme Court Practice*. That specifically deals with the question of a determination of a preliminary point of law by the court, and section 2 (1) says:

'Subject to subsection (2) and section 3 below, on an application to the High Court made by any of the parties to a reference—

...

(b) with the consent of all the other parties, the High Court shall have jurisdiction to determine any question of law arising in the course of the reference.'

Certainly that is one means of determining a preliminary point which may arise in an arbitration, but it does not exclude, in my judgment, the ordinary jurisdiction of the court. That position is regulated by the Arbitration Act 1950, section 4, conveniently set out at p 1411 of this work. That is a well-known provision in arbitration proceeding, to the effect that:

'If any party to an arbitration agreement, or any person claiming through or under him, commences any legal proceedings in any court against any other party to the agreement, or any person claiming through or under him, in respect of any matter agreed to be referred, any party to those legal proceedings may at any time after appearance, and before delivering any pleadings or taking any other steps in the proceedings, apply to that court to stay the proceedings, and that court or a judge thereof, if satisfied that there is no sufficient reason why the matter should not be referred in accordance with the agreement, and that the applicant was, at the time when the proceedings were commenced, and still remains, ready and willing to do all things necessary to the proper conduct of the arbitration, may make an order staying the proceedings.'

It is clear that the defendants do in fact consent and have obviously taken steps in these proceedings, so there is no question of any stay being given and, of course, it is not desired.

The effect of that provision is, as I see it, that the ordinary jurisdiction of the court is not ousted and can be appealed to at any stage, and so I have here, as I see it, an originating summons under Order 7 under the general inherent jurisdiction of the court to make declarations as to the construction of documents, among other things. That is how I propose to proceed. I do not see myself as proceeding under section 2 of the Arbitration Act 1979.

14.2 (a) The test to determine whether a surveyor is to act as an expert or an arbitrator

Where a lease provides for an independent surveyor to be appointed to determine the revised rent, the ultimate test of whether he is to act as an expert or an arbitrator or quasi-arbitrator will depend on whether the surveyor was appointed to fix the rent wholly or in part on the evidence and submissions of the parties or whether he was entitled to act solely on his own expert opinion. If he acts as an expert he will owe a duty of care to the parties and may be sued in negligence.

PALACATH LTD v. FLANAGAN

Queen's Bench Division   (1985) 1 ETLR 85

The rent review provisions in a lease provided for an independent surveyor to be appointed to determine the revised rent. The lease stated that the surveyor was to act as an expert and not as an arbitrator, and that he should consider any statement of reasons or valuation or report submitted to him but that these submissions should not limit or fetter him and that he was entitled to rely on his own judgment and opinion. A surveyor was appointed and duly determined the revised rent.

The landlords were dissatisfied with the rent fixed and issued proceedings claiming the surveyor was negligent. The defendant surveyor's defence was that he was required to determine the revised rent as an arbitrator, or alternatively as a quasi-arbitrator, and that accordingly at all material times he was immune from suit. The matter came before the court as a preliminary issue.

Held:

(1) Public policy demanded that where there was a duty to act with care with regard to another person, (here there was such a duty), and if there was a breach of the duty of care which caused the other person damage, such damage should be made good, *dictum* of Lord Salmon in *Arenson* v. *Arenson* [1977] AC 405 at 419 applied.

Here the surveyor had acted as an expert. The onus was on the defendant to establish he was a quasi-arbitrator. The parties had expressly stipulated that the surveyor appointed was to act as an expert and not as an arbitrator, and although the provisions in the lease were not conclusive of the matter they were a very potent factor.

The question was whether the surveyor had exercised a judicial function in determining the revised rent; although the surveyor had followed some procedures which were typical of the judicial process, the ultimate test was how he was to arrive at his decision. Was he obliged to act wholly or in part on the evidence and submissions of the parties, or was he entitled to act solely on his own expert opinion?

If he was entitled to act solely on his own expert opinion then he could not be exercising a judicial function or quasi-judicial function. In the light of the express provisions of the lease it was clear that the parties did not intend that the surveyor should act as an arbitrator. The object of the lease was to enable the surveyor to inform himself of the matters which the parties considered relevant to the issue. He was not obliged to make any findings accepting or rejecting the opposing contentions. Nor did he have to accept as binding any matters agreed between the parties.

He was appointed to give his own independent judgment as an expert, after reading the representations and valuations of the parties (if any) and giving them such weight as he thought proper (if any). That being so there was no basis for conferring immunity on the surveyor in respect of a claim for damages for negligence in and about giving that independent advice, *dictum* of Lord Wheatley in *Arenson* v. *Arenson* [1977] AC 405 at 428 applied. *Sutcliffe* v. *Thrackrah* [1974] ACT 727 considered.

MARS-JONES J: By a lease dated 28 June 1977, made between the plaintiffs as landlord and OHS Transport Ltd as tenant, the premises were demised for a term of 25 years from 24 June, 1977. The rent reserved by the lease was as follows:

'(i) for the first 5 years of the said term the yearly rent of £16,000;

(ii) for the next 5 years of the said term and for each successive period of 5 years thereafter the relevant yearly rent ascertained in accordance with the Second Schedule of the Lease.'

The second schedule to the lease provided that the yearly rent from 24 June 1982, until June 1987 should be ascertained as follows:

'(i) if the Landlord and the Tenant should not have agreed the amount thereof in writing the Landlord might by notice given to the Tenant require the amount of the said yearly rent should be determined by an independent surveyor.

(ii) The said independent surveyor should be appointed by the Landlord and

Tenant jointly, or in default of agreement between them by the President ... for the time being of the Royal Institution of Chartered Surveyors on the application of the Landlord.'

The parties were not able to agree an independent surveyor so to act, and the plaintiff requested the President of the Royal Institution of Chartered Surveyors to appoint an independent surveyor to act in this case ...

Happily, I do not have to rule on this point, because [counsel for the defendant] has conceded from the outset that apart from the immunity which he claims for the defendant he would owe a duty of care in tort to the plaintiff in respect of his determination. Furthermore, it is common ground that the obligations imposed upon the defendant in tort would be in no way different from those which would arise by reason of a contractual relationship.

Before I proceed to consider the submissions of counsel, it is necessary to recite in detail the relevant provisions of the lease. These appear in the second schedule, D2 p 21, para 4:

'At any time before (but not more than six months before) or more than six months after the beginning of any review period (if there has been no such agreement about the firstly reserved rent for that review period) the Landlord may by notice to the Tenant require the firstly reserved rent for that review period to be determined by an independent surveyor (hereinafter called "the surveyor").

'5. The surveyor shall be appointed:

'(1) by the Landlord and Tenant jointly OR in default of agreement between them.

'(2) by the President (or either the chief officer or acting chief officer) for the time being of the Royal Institution of Chartered Surveyors on the written application of the Landlord ...

'6. The surveyor shall give to the Landlord and to the Tenant notice in writing of his appointment and shall in that notice invite each of them to submit to the surveyor within a specified period not exceeding four weeks its (that is to say the Landlord's or the Tenant's as the case may be) proposal for the yearly amount of the rent supported (if so desired) by either or both of: (i) a statement of resons and (ii) a professional valuation or report.

'7. The firstly reserved rent for any review as so determined by the surveyor shall be the yearly rent at which in his opinion the demised premises if fully repaired maintained and decorated in accordance with the provisions of this Lease might at the date of the surveyor's determination or at the beginning of the review period (whichever is the earlier) reasonably be expected to be let in the open market (with vacant possession) by a willing lessor to a willing lessee for a term equal to the then unexpired residue of the term hereby granted and otherwise in accordance with all the provisions of this Lease ...

'8. For this purpose the surveyor:

'(1) will act as an expert and not as an arbitrator

'(2) will consider any statement of reasons or valuation or report submitted to him as aforesaid but will not be in any way limited or fettered thereby

'(3) will be entitled to rely on his own judgment and opinion

'(4) will within two months after his appointment or within such extended period as the Landlord and the Tenant may agree give to the Landlord and to the Tenant written notice of the amount of the rent as determined by him and his determination will be final and binding on the Landlord and on the Tenant.'

Having regard to the express terms of clause 8 of the second schedule, that the surveyor will act as an expert and not as an arbitrator, [counsel for the defendant] has put forward his case on the basis that on a proper interpretation of the Second

Schedule the defendant was appointed as a quasi-arbitrator. A detailed review of the authorities shows that since at the latest the 19th century the status and immunity of a quasi-arbitrator has been recognised by our laws: see *Pappa* v. *Rose* [1871] LR 7 CP at pp 32 and 525; *Tharsis Sulphur and Copper Co.* v. *Loftus* [1872] LR 8 CP and *Finnegan* v. *Allen* [1943] KB 425. However, the House of Lords has reviewed those and many other authorities on these issues in *Sutcliffe* v. *Thackrah* [1974] AC 727 and in *Arenson* v. *Arenson* [1977] AC 405.

Counsel are agreed that the wide dicta in the earlier cases can only be adopted in so far as they are consistent with the general principles enunciated by the Law Lords in these two cases, which were intended to provide authoritative guidance for the future: see the observations of Lord Wheatley in *Arenson* v. *Arenson* at p 429.

Not surprisingly, much of my time has been taken up considering the speeches in those two leading cases. Counsel for the plaintiff and counsel for the defendant have found support for their respective contentions in those speeches. [Counsel for the defendant] submits that all five law lords in *Sutcliffe* v. *Thrackrah* appear to have recognised the status and immunity of the quasi-arbitrator, and the majority of the House of Lords appear to have done to in *Arenson* v. *Arenson*.

[Counsel for the plaintiff], on the other hand, contends that whether there is such a thing as a quasi-arbitrator remains open to doubt, having regard to the observations of Lord Salmon in *Sutcliffe* v. *Thackrah* and Lord Kilbrandon in *Arenson* v. *Arenson*.

The description 'quasi-arbitrator' was defined by Lord Morris in *Sutcliffe* v. *Thackrah* at p 752 of that report in these terms:

'There may be circumstances in which what is in effect an arbitration is not one that is within the provisions of the Arbitration Act. The expression "quasi-arbitrator" should only be used in that connection. A person will only be an arbitrator or quasi-arbitrator if there is a submission to him either of a specific dispute, or are present points of difference, or of defined differences that may in the future arise, and if there is agreement that his decision will be binding.'

That is the only assistance I have been able to obtain from the speeches of the Law Lords in these two cases by way of definition of the function 'quasi-arbitrator'.

[Counsel for the plaintiff] placed at the forefront of his submissions 'the starting point' enunciated by Lord Simon of Glaisdale in *Arenson* v. *Arenson*, p 419 at C:

'Skilfully though this argument was deployed, I find it less than compelling. My main objections are that the journey starts at the wrong place, and arrives at the wrong place. It starts with the immunity conferred on the arbitrator for reasons of public policy, but in my judgment this is a secondary and subordinate consideration of public policy. There is a primary and anterior consideration of public policy which should be the starting point.

'That is that, where there is a duty to act with care with regard to another person, and there is a breach of such duty causing damage to the other person, public policy in general demands that such damage should be made good to the party to whom the duty is owed by the person owing the duty. There may be a supervening and secondary public policy which demands, nevertheless, immunity from suit in the particular circumstances.

'But that the former public policy is primary can be seen from the jealousy with which the law allows any derogation from it. Thus a barrister enjoys immunity, but only in respect of his forensic conduct; since his duty to the court may conflict with and transcend his duty to his client: *Rondel* v. *Worsley* [1969] 1 AC 191. And a diplomatic envoy enjoys immunity, but only so long as he is in post, plus a reasonable time thereafter for him to wind up his official affairs: *Musurus Bey* v. *Gadban* [1894] 1 QB 533.'

Words to the like effect are to be found at p 436 F-H. I respectfully agree with the submissions made by [counsel for the plaintiff], and feel I am obliged to make that my starting point.

The onus is upon the defendant to establish that he was a quasi-arbitrator, namely a person who is in much the same position as an arbitrator or judge, as Lord Wheatley put it in *Arenson* v. *Arenson* at p 428. A person to whom a dispute or difference has been remitted by the parties to resolve in such a manner that he is called upon to exercise the judicial function, as [counsel for the plaintiff] put it.

The parties expressly stipulated in para 8 of the second schedule that the surveyor appointed 'will act as an expert and not as an arbitrator'. He submitted that those words demonstrated that (1) the parties were aware of the difference between an arbitrator and an expert; (2) that they did not want to appoint an arbitrator; and (3) they did want him to act as an expert. I must confess that I, too, consider it would be fanciful to imagine the parties intended the surveyor to act as an arbitrator or quasi-arbitrator despite such a clear and unambiguous stipulation to the contrary.

[Counsel for the defendant] on the other hand has contended and countered that argument by submitting that these words alone are not conclusive of the matter, as Greer J stated in *Taylor* v. *Yielding* [1912] SJ Reports 253: 'You cannot make a valuer an arbitrator by calling him so, or vice versa.' Para 8 is not conclusive of the matter. However, it is a matter which I must take into account, and it is in my judgment a very potent one.

It is common ground between counsel that it is for the defendant to prove that he is entitled to immunity for negligence in the discharge of his duty, and that in deciding that matter I must have regard primarily to the terms of the second schedule, which defined his functions and how he was to discharge them. The most helpful definition of the essential distinguishing features of a judge or arbitrator are to be found in the speech of Lord Wheatley in *Arenson* v. *Arenson* at p 428:

'The indicia are as follows:
'(a) there is a dispute or a difference between the parties which has been formulated in some way or another;
'(b) the dispute or difference has been remitted by the parties to the person to resolve in such a manner that he is called upon to exercise a judicial function;
'(c) where appropriate the parties must have been provided with an opportunity to present evidence and/or submissions in support of their respective claims in the dispute; and
'(d) the parties have agreed to accept this decision.'

At one time I was inclined to think that all these elements were present in the instant case. In my judgment, there was a dispute or difference between the parties to this lease as to what the revised yearly rent should have been as from 24 June 1982, calculated on the basis set out in clause 7 of the second schedule of the lease, and the dispute or difference had been reduced into precise figures.

Secondly, the dispute had been remitted by the parties to the defendant. Thirdly, the parties were invited to submit to the defendant within a specific period their proposals for the yearly amount of the rent, supported by either or both of (a) a statement of reasons and (b) a professional valuation or report. This provision was mandatory so far as the defendant was concerned. He had to issue those invitations to the parties. Whether they accepted or not was entirely up to them, but counsel agree that this requirement in a lease is exceptional.

Fourthly, the parties had agreed to accept the defendant's determination as final and binding. The only element which is open to argument is whether the defendant was to exercise a judicial function in making his determination. Did the parties intend that this was to be a judicial enquiry to be conducted upon the ordinary principles upon which judicial enquiries are conducted, by hearing the parties and evidence of witnesses, and was the defendant to arrive at a decision upon that evidence? See the observations of Cockburn CJ in *In re Hopper* [1867] LR 2 QB 367 at pp 372-373.

As I understand it in the instant case, no oral hearing was contemplated at which the parties could put their respective cases through the mouths of witnesses, or to challenge each other's witnesses by cross-examination. Although there was no express provision for the disclosure of any matters or reasons or valuation to the opposite party, this was in fact done in this case; and the parties made counter-submissions based thereon.

The defendant carried out an inspection of the premises without any representative of the parties being present, but in his letter of 29 December 1982, the defendant indicated that he would not have been averse to a representative of the parties accompanying him.

However, although the defendant acting under the terms of the second schedule followed some procedures which are typical of the judicial process, the ultimate test is how was he to arrive at his decision? Was he obliged to act wholly or in part of the evidence and submisions made by the parties? Or was he entitled to act solely on his own expert opinion? If the answer to the question is the latter, then the defendant could not be exercising a judicial function or a quasi-judicial function—if there is any such distinction.

In the instant case the defendant was specifically enjoined in clause 8 of the second schedule to act as an expert, and was not to be limited or fettered in any way by the statement of reasons or valuations submitted by the parties, but was entitled to rely on his own judgment and opinion. In the light of those express provisions it is impossible for me to hold that the parties intended that the defendant should act as an arbitrator or quasi-arbitrator in determining the revised rent.

I am satisfied that the provisions of clause 8 were not intended to set up a judicial or quasi-judicial machinery for the resolution of this dispute or difference about the amount of revised rent. Its object was to enable the defendant to inform himself of the matters which the parties considered were relevant to the issue. He was not obliged to make any finding or findings accepting or rejecting the opposing contentions. Nor, indeed, as I see it was he obliged to accept as valid and binding upon him matters upon which the parties were agreed. He was not appointed to adjudicate on the cases put forward on behalf of the landlord and the tenant.

He was appointed to give his own independent judgment as an expert, after reading the representations and valuations of the parties (if any) and giving them such weight as he thought proper (if any). That being so, there can be no basis for conferring immunity upon the defendant in respect of a claim for damages for negligence in and about giving that independent expert view.

As [counsel for the plaintiff] put the matter at the conclusion of his submissions, the court is being asked to afford the defendant immunity by designating him an arbitrator or quasi-arbitrator (1) when that is the opposite of what the parties had expressly stipulated; (2) when the effect of such a ruling would be to prevent the plaintiff recovering the loss which it alleges it had suffered with no other right of appeal, challenge or remedy; (3) in circumstances which go beyond the principles enunciated by the House of Lords in *Sutcliffe* v. *Thackrah* and *Arenson* v. *Arenson*, and which goes against the primary public policy expressed in them.

Accordingly, the preliminary issue must be resolved in favour of the plaintiff and the question addressed to the court answered in the negative.

Factors to be taken into account when deciding whether the 'umpire' in rent review valuation is to act as an expert rather than an arbitrator.

SAFEWAY FOOD STORES LTD v. BANDERWAY LTD

Chancery Division   (1983) 267 EG 850

(For facts see earlier, page 124.)

GOULDING J: The other point is not directly related to the question I have just decided. It arises on that part of the rent review clause which I have not yet read. That provides alternative machinery if the two valuers cannot, as they are directed to do, reach agreement as to the fair market rent at the time of review. The passage is as follows:

'In the event of such valuers not having reached such agreement by the expiry of a period of four weeks next following the date of the service of the said notice they shall agree upon an umpire to settle the question whose decision shall be final and binding upon both parties and if within the before mentioned period of ten days either party shall not have appointed a valuer as aforesaid or if within the said period of one week next following the said period of four weeks the said two valuers shall not have agreed upon such umpire or such an umpire shall not have been appointed then in the first contingency the other party and in the second contingency either party may request the President for the time being of the Royal Institution of Chartered Surveyors to appoint a member of that Body (but not the valuer appointed as aforesaid by either party) to settle the question and the parties hereto shall be bound as aforesaid by the decision of the person so appointed.'

The question that I am asked to decide is whether, as the tenant contends, an umpire so appointed must act as an arbitrator in accordance with the Arbitration Acts 1950 and 1979 or whether, as the landlord suggests, the umpire is to act as an expert making a valuation. I have some doubt as to the propriety of deciding that question, because it is not yet in evidence that the valuers have disagreed, and I presume they would hardly know that until they knew the construction of the clause on the first point. However, it is a comparatively small matter to decide this question and I think that, as both sides apparently want it decided at this point and I cannot prejudice any third party, I will do so, though pointing out that it is an indulgence and contrary to the usual practice of the court.

It is not suggested by [counsel for the plaintiffs] that the two primary valuers to be appointed one by each party are arbitrators, but, he says, when they disagree and an umpire is appointed, either by the valuers themselves or by the president of the Royal Institution of Chartered Surveyors, the very word 'umpire' and the direction that he is to settle the question suggest not so much a valuation as a quasi-judicial proceeding, and accordingly the umpire, in [counsel for the plaintiffs'] contention, ought to act as an arbitrator in accordance with the statutory provisions governing English arbitration.

To my mind, once it is accepted that the primary process intended is one of valuation and not of arbitration, the mere word 'umpire', attached to the individual who is to make the determination should the valuers fail to agree, is quite neutral and does not cast any real light on the matter in dispute; nor do I get much help from the phrase 'to settle the question'. Moreover, the definitions of the word 'umpire' in dictionaries that have been cited are not to my mind of any material assistance.

A useful summary of the differences between the functions of an arbitrator on the one hand and an independent valuer on the other was referred to by [counsel for the plaintiffs]. It is contained in a volume called *A Handbook of Rent Review* by Mr Ronald Bernstein QC and Mr Kirk Reynolds and it is at p 906 in the edition that I have. It lists seven points of difference, of which numbers 1 and 2 seem to me of great materiality for present purposes. Point 1 is this:

'The Arbitrator acts (as does a judge) only on evidence and arguments submitted to him and bases his decision thereon. His award must lie between the extremes contended for by the parties.'

Whereas 'The Independent Valuer has the duty of investigating to discover the evidence (though he may receive evidence from the parties).' Secondly, 'The Arbitrator cannot decide without receiving evidence from the parties or (when proceeding *ex parte*) one of the parties.' Whereas,

'The Independent Valuer must decide upon his own knowledge and investigations, but he may be required by the instrument under which he is appointed to receive submissions from the parties.'

In the context in which it occurs I think it is pretty plain that this umpire, as he is called, was intended to be a valuer who was to use his own knowledge and make such investigations as he, a qualified surveyor, would think fit, not to act as a quasi-judge upon evidence and arguments of the parties or their representatives. I say that for four reasons, none of which is conclusive in itself but which, taken together, seem to me to be a clear pointer.

First of all, the whole question is one of expertise in arriving at a fair market rack rent at a particular date. It is in its essential nature one of valuation rather than a question with two clearly defined sides to be argued and decided. Secondly, as [counsel for the defendants] pointed out in his submissions, the umpire is to be appointed and to operate under the same machinery not only in the case where the two original valuers disagree but also in the case where either party has not appointed a valuer within the stipulated time, so that in part at least he is intended to supply the place of a valuer, who, it is conceded, is not an arbitrator but an expert. Thirdly, the umpire is not merely in default of agreement to be appointed by the president of the Royal Institution of Chartered Surveyors but is expressly to be a member of that body. Thus it is contemplated that he will need expertise in the field of a surveyor.

Finally, again as was pointed out by [counsel for the defendants], there is in a quite different part of the lease a covenant on the part of the tenant in these terms:

'To pay to the Lessor on demand a fair proportion of the expense of cleansing lighting repairing and maintaining all things used or enjoyed by the Lessee in common with any other person and of all party and other walls ... and in the event of any dispute arising under the provisions of this Clause the matter shall be referred to a single arbitrator in accordance with and subject to the provisions of the Arbitration Act 1950 or any statutory modification or re-enactment thereof for the time being in force.'

Accordingly, it is argued, one must conclude that the draftsman of this document, when he wanted to provide for an arbitrator, did so in express terms.

As I have said, I do not find any of those points conclusive on its own, but taken together they appear to me clearly to point to the conclusion that the umpire is to act as an expert and not as an arbitrator. Accordingly, on the second question also the defendant must succeed, and the result, I suppose, is that the originating summons, which seeks two declarations in the sense contended for by the plaintiff, must be dismissed.

Note: See also, earlier, page 180, *Langham House Developments Ltd* v. *Brompton Securities Ltd and Another* (1980) 256 EG 719.

14.2 (b)   An arbitrator must act judicially and may not take his personal knowledge of the facts into account

The arbitrator acts in a judicial capacity and his function is to decide the issues on the evidence put before him. If he takes into account his own knowledge of the facts of the case without the consent of the parties and without disclosing the extent of his knowledge and affording the parties the opportunity to adduce evidence in this regard or make submissions on it, his decision is liable to be quashed.

TOP SHOP ESTATES LTD v. C. DANINO
TOP SHOP ESTATES LTD v. TANDY CORPORATION

Chancery Division   (1985) 273 EG 197

LEGGATT J: The motions are for an order under section 23 of the Arbitration Act 1950 that the arbitrator in each case, Mr R M McKenzie FRICS, be removed and that his award dated 1 December 1983 be set aside on the grounds that the arbitrator misconducted himself in certain respects which are set out in the notices of motion. In particular it is said that in making his award he took account of his own knowledge without the consent of the parties and without disclosing the extent of his knowledge and affording to the parties the opportunity to adduce evidence or make submissions in relation to it. Then it is said that, as is apparent from his award, he initiated what are in the awards described as 'a series of pedestrian counts', again without the consent or knowledge of the parties and without their agreeing with the manner in which it was proposed that pedestrian counts should be conducted and, indeed, without their being afforded an opportunity to make submissions about how those pedestrian counts should be interpreted. The arbitrator is further criticised for having taken account of studies of pedestrian flow at busy periods with the like criticisms made of the use that he sought without the parties' consent to make of that material. Finally, it is said in relation to the Danino arbitration that since the arbitrator, as he put it, 'validated from another direction' inadmissible evidence put forward by the respondent's surveyor without disclosing such validated evidence or affording to the applicant the opportunity of dealing with it, once more he must be regarded as having, as it says in the notices of motion, misconducted himself, or, as it might have been said, misconducted the proceedings, in a way which would render him amenable to an order under section 23. It was made plain by counsel for the claimants that while the notices of motion speak of the arbitrator being removed, the intention of that part of the order sought is to secure that, if the matter is to be remitted to an arbitrator, it should be remitted to an arbitrator other than the arbitrator who sat in each of the relevant arbitrations.

The arbitrator was served with notice of these proceedings and he has elected, as he was entitled to do, to put in an affidavit in relation to each matter in which he seeks to explain his conduct of the arbitration. It will be necessary to look in a little more detail at the affidavits, but suffice to say that both affidavits go beyond a mere statement of what happened at the arbitration and purport to set out the reasoning which the arbitrator followed in arriving at each of the conclusions criticised in the notices of motion. Not only is that criticism of his affidavits made by counsel for the claimants but counsel for Tandy has not sought to uphold those parts of either affidavit which are concerned with the arbitrator's mental processes. The arbitrator has had the advantage of being represented before me by Mr Kirk Reynolds. He has not sought to suggest that any of the passages criticised could be upheld in relation to the substantive matters with which the notices of motion are concerned. Rather, he says, one should look at them as explaining what in fact motivated the arbitrator in order that he should be saved from any more serious criticism that the court might feel constrained to make of his conduct.

The arbitrations concerned arose out of two leases. The lease now vested in Tandy and formerly in the claimants was made in 1978 in relation to premises called 8 The Broadway, at Crawley in Sussex. The lease relating to Danino, which also was vested formerly in the claimants, was made in 1979 and related to 30 The Boulevard, Crawley. Disputes having arisen between the parties, the president of the Royal Institution of Chartered Surveyors appointed Mr McKenzie as arbitrator. In each case what he was concerned with was the rent review due at the Christmas quarter day of 1982 and the amount to be appointed in respect of each of the premises. In September 1983 the arbitrator made directions. On 15 November he conducted what appears to have been the first of more than one inspection of the premises, the subject of the arbitrations. On 18 November, though this does not appear on the face of either of the awards, it seems from the affidavits since made by the arbitrator that he had a qualified assistant conduct the pedestrian count of which complaint is made. It may be assumed, since the arbitrator says he acted on it, that some form of report, though what form is not specified, was made by the anonymous assistant to the arbitrator. On 1 December 1983, as he had said he would at the time when he made his directions, the arbitrator published his awards. As soon after that as 16 December 1983 affidavits were sworn in support of the present notices of motion, which were themselves issued a few days later. The arbitrator remained mute in response to these criticisms until 19 June when he swore the affidavits to which I have already referred.

In support of the notices of motion there are sworn affidavits, each in similar form, by the surveyor acting for the claimants, Mr Warren Thomas. He explains by reference to the awards, which he exhibits, what the more detailed matters of criticism are of the respective awards. He exhibits also the directions which, as I have indicated, were made on 29 September 1983. In those directions the arbitrator provides that the matter shall be dealt with by written representation. He calls for submissions from the parties dealing with specified matters. He says in para 4: 'Facts relating to the comparable transaction shall be validated unless both parties agree otherwise.' He makes provision for exchange of submissions and for counter-submissions to be made though not exchanged. At para 6 in each case, he says: 'I will then inspect the property and present my award by 1 December 1983.' Those words are particularly relied upon for the actual language which the arbitrator has chosen to use omitting any mention, notwithstanding the guidance afforded by the guidance notes issue by the Royal Institution of Chartered Surveyors, of any intention to inspect comparable properties that might be referred to by either surveyor.

The award itself must be looked at in the light of the criticisms made. The particular award to which I shall for present purposes refer is that made in the Tandy arbitration although the like considerations apply, of course, to the Danino arbitration. At p 2 of the award in the Tandy arbitration, the arbitrator says: 'I have also inspected, or pavement inspected, the comparisons referred to by the parties.' In his general observations, part of his paragraph numbered 1, the arbitrator said:

'I therefore propose to examine each comparable in the light of respective submissions and my own knowledge and observation. The day of my inspection was dry and reasonably sunny though cold. The centre was busy enough to confirm my personal assessment of relative positional qualities, these views being since confirmed by a series of pedestrian counts taken between 11 am and 3.30 pm on Friday, 18 November 1983, also a dry and reasonably sunny day.'

In his second numbered paragraph dealing with comparison evidence, the arbitrator mentioned that:

'Respective surveyors' interpretation on positional quality conflicts and my own view is that it is difficult to distinguish between the two locations that are both, in comparative terms, secondary and both lacking a consistently heavyweight pedestrian flow.'

Later, in relation to one of the landlord's comparisons, the arbitrator said: 'The position enjoys a strongly biased pedestrian flow to the south side of the broad walk because the bulk of the old town shopping is to the south.' Then, in relation to another of the landlord's comparisons, also in the broad walk, the arbitrator said in conclusion on that score:

'I disagree with the landlord's surveyor's assessment of positional quality, however, and, from my own knowledge and observed pedestrian flow, the broad walk is quite considerably busier than the west side of The Broadway.'

Later in his award, in referring to one of the tenant's comparisons the arbitrator said:

'There is little to choose in pedestrian flow between The Broadway and Haslett Avenue, frontages of this unit and the pedestrian flow in both cases being relatively light.'

Then, again in relation to another of the tenant's comparisons, he said:

'The positional difference between the subject property and the entire block nos 20 to 76 The Boulevard are not greatly different in terms of pedestrian flow, although the subject property appears marginally superior in general character.'

Finally, in relation to assessment of award, the arbitrator said:

'The most direct and appropriate physical comparison to the subject property is that offered by 11 The Broadway which is of similar size and in a superior location. It lacks the disadvantages suffered by the subject property where I incline towards the tenant's surveyor's assessment that the location is secondary, tends to be obscured by bus queues and is generally less busy in terms of passing flow than its visual prominence would suggest. It is noticeable that many people cross The Broadway diagonally to the disadvantage of no 8,'

and the arbitrator refers first to physical and positional comparison offered by 11 The Broadway and then to inferences that may be drawn from others of the comparables mentioned. He says that he took account of: '3. My own knowledge, taken together with studies of pedestrian flow at busy periods,' and he mentions also the arguments adduced by the parties.

That reference appears to me to constitute the plainest possible statement that one of the four matters of which the arbitrator took account in reaching his conclusion as to the appropriate annual rent was his own knowledge taken together with studies of pedestrian flow at busy periods. To the same effect, as I have already remarked, is the arbitration relating to Danino where the similar matter which he said he had taken into account was: 'My own knowledge, together with studies of pedestrian flow at busy periods.' In that case there were four rather than three other matters of which he said he took account. The Danino arbitration was the one in which, at an earlier point in his award, the arbitrator said:

'The lessee's surveyor has relied upon a rent review transaction where he himself was acting for the lessee and refers also to a neighbouring property where his unsupported figures are accepted, as I have validated evidence from another direction.'

In his affidavits the arbitrator explained that the other direction was another of several arbitrations in some if not all, of which the claimants were also claimants but which were decided quite separately from the arbitrations now before the court.

On behalf of the arbitrator, [counsel] refers to a passage in *Russell on Arbitration*, 20th ed, p 444, in which there are cited comments by Donaldson J in the case of *Port Sudan* v. *Chettiar & Sons* [1977] 1 Lloyd's Rep 166, at pp 178, 179. The learned judge explained the modern practice as being for the notice of motion in these circumstances to be served upon the arbitrator, and said that he then has a choice whether to participate fully in the proceedings as an active party, to content himself with filing an affidavit setting out any facts which he considers may be of assistance to the court, or to take no action. In this case it is the first of those three alternatives which the arbitrator regards himself as having selected.

It being acknowledged on the arbitrator's behalf that what he says in the passages from his affidavits which are objected to is not material to whether his award should be set aside or not, I do not consider that it would be profitable for me to recite the explanations that the arbitrator gives for how he came to make the award in the form in which he did. He is anxious, for example, to point out that in relation to the inspection of comparables, although he admittedly should have said when he gave directions that it was his intention to inspect them, the parties might be thought, upon one construction of the submissions made by the landlord's surveyor, to have contemplated that he would. So he contends that, it being a common practice, unsurprisingly, for an expert arbitrator to inspect comparables, he should be forgiven for assuming that both parties intended him to do so. I think in the circumstances it would suffice if I say that the court will always take, unless there be cogent reasons to the contrary why it should not, a charitable view of what motivated an arbitrator in coming to particular conclusions or conducting an arbitration in a particular fashion even if, having reviewed the arbitration and the award following it, the court takes the view that the arbitrator has indeed (whether one describes it as 'technically' or not) misconducted either himself or the proceedings. It might be said, as [counsel] on behalf of the arbitrator submits, that in arranging upon his own initiative for a pedestrian count to be taken, the arbitrator was acting over-zealously. It does not seem to me to be profitable to seek to select epithets appropriate to describe the conduct of the arbitrator in such circumstances. If he was acting over-zealously, than more relevantly, he was, in my judgment, also acting under a misapprehension of his function as an arbitrator, which is not to play the part of Perry Mason where he feels that the submissions or evidence of the parties might usefully be supplemented.

In reply upon these matters, [counsel] for the claimants, remarks, as he was entitled to, that the claimants at all events (and it may be also counsel for Tandy) had assumed on reading the affidavits lately sworn by the arbitrator that he wished to be heard on the substantive matter and that the affidavits were being proffered in some way in support of submissions that he would wish to make on such issues. It would, as [counsel for the claimants] suggests, have been simpler, since the arbitrator wished to do no more than to explain why he had behaved as he did, had he written a letter to the parties and, if need be, invited them to put it or its contents before the court so that the course which he had taken should not be misunderstood. [Counsel for the claimants] submits, and in my judgment is entitled to submit, that Donaldson J cannot have intended in the dictum which I have cited from *Russell on Arbitration* to suggest that arbitrators should put in affidavits not complying with the rules of evidence for the purpose of explaining what their reasoning was, notwithstanding that the court is not entitled, as the authorities show, to pay regard to such reasoning in reaching a conclusion whether what the arbitrator did is properly characterised as misconduct. [Counsel for the claimants] submits that an arbitrator must not receive evidence in the absence of the parties, nor may he use any factual knowledge acquired in other proceedings. He next submits that an expert arbitrator may use his expert knowledge for the purpose of understanding and evaluating evidence but not so as to supply it. In aid of that submission he relies in particular upon the case of

Fox v. *P G Wellfair Ltd* (1981) 2 Lloyd's Rep 514 [also reported at (1981) 263 EG 589, 657]. That was a case which for present purposes is of no consequence in relation to its facts but rather for the general observations made by the Court of Appeal upon issues relevant to these motions. At p 522 the Master of the Rolls, Lord Denning, said about the arbitrator's function:

'He can and should use his special knowledge so as to understand the evidence that is given—the letters that have passed—the usage of the trade—the dealings in the market—and to appreciate the worth of all that he sees upon a view. But he cannot use his special knowledge—or at any rate he should not use it—so as to provide evidence on behalf of the defendants which they have not chosen to provide for themselves, for then he would be discarding the role of an impartial arbitrator and assuming the role of advocate for the defaulting side.'

Dunn LJ, at p 528, said this:

'It is well established that where an arbitrator hears evidence in the absence of either or both parties, his award will be set aside on the ground of misconduct, unless perhaps it can be shown that evidence would not have affected the award,'

and the learned lord justice cites, among other authorities, *Walker* v. *Frobisher* (1801) 2 Ves Jun 69a, also cited by [counsel] on behalf of the claimants in the present case. The learned lord justice remarked that in that and another case: '... where it was held that the principle applied to mercantile as well as legal arbitration'. The authorities cited for that proposition include two further authorities relied on by [counsel for the claimants] *Royal Commission on the Sugar Supply* v. *Trading Society Kwik-Hoo-Tong* (1922) 38 TLR 684 and *Eastcheap Dried Fruit Co.* v. *N V Gebroeders Catz Handelsvereeniging* (1962) 1 Lloyd's Rep 283. Dunn LJ then said:

'On the analogy of those cases, it seems to me that an expert arbitrator should not in effect give evidence to himself without disclosing the evidence on which he relies to the parties, or if only one to that party. He should not act on his private opinion without disclosing it. It is undoubtedly true that an expert arbitrator can use his own expert knowledge. But a distinction is made in the cases between general expert knowledge and knowledge of special facts relevant to the particular case.'

The learned lord justice proceeded a little later in his judgment:

'So if the arbitrator is relying on general expert knowledge there is no need to disclose it. O'Connor LJ gave a good example in argument. An arbitrator is required to value a bull killed by the negligence of one of the parties. If the expert arbitrator relies on his general knowledge of the value of bulls, including fluctuations in the market known to anyone who studies the market, there is no need to disclose it. But if he has recently sold an identical bull for a certain sum, it is necessary to disclose that to the parties. Of if the dead bull is found by the arbitrator, unknown to the parties, to be suffering from some disease or injury which reduces its value, it is necessary to disclose that fact to the parties. So in assessing rents an expert arbitrator can rely on his general knowledge of comparable rents in the district. But if he knows of a particular comparable case, then he should disclose details of it before relying on it for his award.'

The last citation from that case useful for present purposes is to be found towards the end of Dunn LJ's judgment at p 532 where he said in relation to an ancillary arbitration which was the subject of the appeal in that case:

'The same considerations apply to a lesser extent to Mr Fisher's arbitration. In any event, in view of the misconduct in relation to the main arbitration, I do not think that the award in Mr Fisher's arbitration can stand either. Mr Fisher must have lost confidence in the arbitrator by reason of his conduct of the main arbitration.'

For the claimants, [counsel] also submits that if an arbitrator does use evidence of his own, the award will be set aside unless the party opposing the grant of relief can affirmatively establish that no other award would reasonably have been possible if that evidence had not been given. That reproduces the language in the *Eastcheap* v. *Gebroeders* case cited by Dunn LJ in *Fox* v. *Wellfair*. Finally, on the law, [counsel for the claimants] submits that evidence is not admissible from the arbitrator of his process of reasoning either to construe his award or to spell out the weight given by him to any consideration. In aid of that submission the principal authority is *Duke of Buccleuch and Queensberry* v. *Metropolitan Board of Works* (1872) LR 5 HL 418. It is spelt out in some detail by Cleasby B when giving his opinion. That view of the law, to the effect that the court cannot investigate the secret thoughts and intentions of an arbitrator, was specifically approved in the speeches of their lordships and in particular in the speech of Lord Cairns at p 462.

The submissions which [counsel for the claimants] makes are in effect not controverted either by the arbitrator or on behalf of Tandy. The only room for dispute, it is said, is upon the facts. The claimants rely on the clear indications in the awards that the arbitrator has used his personal knowledge as well as the pedestrian counts. These, it is said, are matters which he was not entitled to take into account and when one finds reference to personal knowledge one is entitled to assume that it means what it appears in its context to mean, that is to say, knowledge of a specific character acquired by him and peculiar to him rather than such as may be known to experts generally practising in Crawley or, alternatively, in the South of England. It is indisputable that the arbitrator did inspect the comparable properties without having contemplated expressly in the terms of his directions that he would do so. It is indisputable also, as is obvious from the conclusion of each of the awards, that he relied upon the pedestrian counts. It also appears that part of his personal knowledge was derived not merely from that but also from matters which he had gleaned in the conduct of other arbitrations.

To meet these criticisms, [counsel for Tandy Corporation] submits, first, that the arbitrator has not in fact been guilty of misconduct. When one looks at what is said about pedestrian counts, it appears that the parties were in conflict about how well placed the premises were and they always envisaged that what [counsel for Tandy Corporation] terms 'a view' would be held by the arbitrator, meaning an inspection, as it would appear, not merely of each of the properties, not merely of the immediate locality in which each of the properties was, but in a wider context of The Broadway generally and extending even to the comparable premises. [Counsel for Tandy Corporation] argued that because the landlords knew that the same arbitrator was acting in other arbitrations, it would have been unrealistic for them to assume that the arbitrator would act as though he had not seen any other relevant premises than the one the subject of the arbitration in question. The inspection, it is said, was intended to be conducted by the arbitrator with his eyes open and it was further intended that the product of his inspection should constitute part of the evidence. He could not but note what he saw and he plainly was not limited upon any inspection to a mere assessment of room configurations and matters within the premises concerned but was entitled to look wider afield. So in this fashion it is sought to suggest that not only the position of the premises but the pedestrian flow as it passed them were matters of which the arbitrator was entitled to take cognisance and where necessary, apparently, to supplement what he might observe for himself by experiments conducted on his behalf by his qualified assistant.

It seems to me that that view of pedestrian counts conducted by or under the auspices of an arbitrator in aid of an inspection of premises, or as a check or confirmation of an impression which he otherwise gained or which he thought was established or suggested elsehow, is wholly illegitimate. There can be no warrant for it and, while, of course, I accept that the arbitrator was motivated by the most worthy intentions and did not think for a moment to do anything which could possibly be regarded as unjust to either of the parties, none the less a moment's reflection will make plain that if either of the parties objected to the amount in which he assessed the rent, they were quite entitled to assume, and, indeed, bound to assume, in my judgment, having regard to the way in which the award and the conclusions of it were expressed, that the pedestrian count had played a part in the conclusion to which the arbitrator came. It is rightly said in this context by [counsel for the claimants] that one is not merely dealing with a 'Yes' or 'No' answer by an arbitrator; one is dealing with the assessment of a rent, which may well, therefore, be based at any given point on the scale constituted by the difference between the amounts contended for by the respective surveyors. In those circumstances, even confirmation of a conclusion provisionally reached, or reached without recourse to pedestrian counts, might well be affected in some amount by pedestrian counts conducted in the way that the arbitrator now says they were.

The court must pay regard in this context not merely to any actual effect that there can be shown to have been upon the arbitrator's conclusion but to the risk that anyone reading his awards might suppose that he had been influenced by these considerations; and anyone reading the awards would have to do so without paying regard to the contents of the arbitrator's affidavits. In so saying, I do not intend any criticism of the arbitrator, still less to suggest that he should be disbelieved when he says that he was motivated as he says he was, but it is important that an award should be construed by reference to that which it says and not by reference to afterthoughts of the person making it.

[Counsel for Tandy Corporation] also submits that if he were wrong in his primary submission, still there was no misconduct because here it is affirmatively shown that the matters complained of, and in particular the pedestrian counts, could not have affected the award. I have already made comments about that and in this context would merely stress the circumstance that it is for the person seeking to uphold the award to establish that but for the matters wrongfully introduced the result would have remained the same. For the reasons I have indicated, it seems to me that [counsel for Tandy Corporation]'s valiant attempts to establish that the references to the pedestrian counts suggest that they were to constitute no more than a check on a check do not provide a sufficient answer; still less do they establish that which it is necessary for him to establish affirmatively if the award is to be allowed to stand.

Finally, it is said on behalf of Tandy that it is not enough that the matters of which complaint is made might have affected the award. If they raise no more than the mere possibility that the answer would have been otherwise if regard had not been paid to the matters complained of, the court should not interfere. That is, of course, a well-known principle recently approbated in this court by Lloyd J, but in my judgment of no relevance whatever in the present context.

In relation to personal knowledge, [counsel for Tandy Corporation] submits, with somewhat more support from the language of the awards, that the arbitrator cannot be unequivocally shown to have taken account of specific matters known to him rather than to more general matters. He suggests that because the landlords must have known that the arbitrator would look, for example, at the premises which were the subject of the other arbitrations with which he was concerned, they cannot but have recognised that the results of those inspections were matters which he would or might take into account in dealing with the present references. I have tried hard to understand the logical force of that submission, but, although I, of course, am sympathetic with a layman who is required to disregard particular inspections that he may have made for totally different purposes, it appears to me that it is quite illegitimate for an arbitrator not to have indicated an intention in the context of the relevant arbitrations that he will take into account other inspections that he may

CASEBOOK ON RENT REVIEW AND LEASE RENEWAL

make and, indeed, which either or both of the parties may know that he is to make. The mere fact that he is to view other premises constitutes no warrant for his taking the result of those inspections into account in connection with the arbitrations concerned unless he has made plain that that is what he intends to do and afforded the parties the opportunity of making their submissions or their comments about those other premises. Upon that basis also, therefore, it appears to me that the awards of the arbitrator are exceptionable.

The reference to validation of a comparable in the Danino award really falls within the same principle as I have last referred to in relation to both.

For these reasons, therefore, I must hold, without there being implicit in my so holding any imputation upon the personal conduct of the arbitrator or his sense of fairness, that he has misconducted the proceedings in such manner as makes it necessary that the proceedings the subject-matter of each of the awards in the Tandy and Danino cases should be set aside, and I so order.

The arbitrator's award was set aside and an order made for his removal and the appointment of a new arbitrator. The respondents, Tandy Corporation, were ordered to pay costs, but an order against the arbitrator personally to pay costs was refused.

Note: If an arbitrator does take his own knowledge of the facts into account when making his award, the award may be set aside unless the party opposing the grant of relief can establish that no other award would have reasonably have been possible if that evidence had not been used, see *Fox* v. *P G Wellfair Ltd* (1981) 2 Lloyd's Rep 514.

14.3 Factors to be taken into account when deciding whether time should be extended for arbitration of a rent review provision

CHARTERED TRUST PLC v. MARYLANDS GREEN ESTATE CO. LTD

Chancery Division   (1984) 270 EG 845

A lease of commercial premises contained provision for a rent review to be triggered by a landlord's notice to which the tenant was entitled to serve a counter notice within three months, (time to be of the essence), referring the matter to arbitration. The landlord served a notice on the tenant, but the tenant did not respond with his counter notice. The tenant later began negligence proceedings against his professional advisers and joined the landlords as defendants. He sought a declaration that the trigger notice was ineffective. The landlord responded by serving a new trigger notice to which the tenant again failed to respond (owing to confusion between the tenant's advisers). The tenant applied under section 27 of the Arbitration Act 1950 for an extension of time for referring both the landlord's trigger notices to arbitration.

Held: As a result of the tenant's delay time would not be extended in relation to the first notice; but time would be extended to the second notice on terms that interest would run on the arrears of reviewed rent as ultimately assessed. Consideration of whether there was prejudice to the lessor and/or hardship to the tenant and/or hardship and possibility of negligence claims against the tenant's professional advisers were taken into account. *Per curiam*: There is no analogy between an application to strike out a claim for want of prosecution and an application under section 27.

VINELOTT J: Despite the failure of the tenant or its advisers to serve a counternotice negotiations continued in an endeavour to agree the new rents. Mr Stewart met Mr O C Smith on July 7. There was some correspondence between the surveyors between then and 24 September 1982 when the negotiations were broken off. The difference between the surveyors apparently turned on the effect on the rental value of the user provision in clause 2 (15) of the lease, Hilbery Chaplin & Co. apparently taking the view that the premises could be valued as a banking hall and that regard ought to be paid to retail shop values, while Mr Stewart, relying on a decision of the Court of Appeal in *Plinth Property Investments Ltd* v. *Mott, Hay and Anderson* (1978) 249 EG 1167, claimed that the only permitted use was as offices in connection with the business of commercial bankers. The terms of the covenant in clause 2 (15) are in fact indistinguishable from the terms of the covenant considered by the Court of Appeal in the *Plinth Property* case, save only that the covenant there related to user as offices in connection with the tenant's business of consulting civil engineers. Mr Stewart assessed the rent at an aggregate sum of £22,500 per annum. It appears from the pleadings in the other action that Donaldsons assessed them at an aggregate of £28,000 per annum.

There followed some without prejudice negotiations between Mr Vokes and the lessor's solicitors and Donaldsons' solicitors with a view to the settlement of all the outstanding issues. Those negotiations came to an end in early 1982. The application that is now before me, seeking an extension of time pursuant to section 27 of the Arbitration Act 1950 in relation both to the first notice and to the second set of notices, was issued on 26 November 1982.

Section 27 reads as follows:

'Where the terms of an agreement to refer future disputes to arbitration provide that any claims to which the agreement applies shall be barred unless notice to appoint an arbitrator is given or an arbitrator is appointed or some other step to commence arbitration proceedings is taken within a time fixed by the agreement, and a dispute arises to which the agreement applies, the High Court, if it is of opinion that in the circumstances of the case undue hardship would otherwise be caused, and notwithstanding that the time so fixed has expired, may, on such terms, if any, as the justice of the case may require, but without prejudice to the provision of any enactment limiting the time for the commencement of arbitration proceedings, extend the time for such period as it thinks proper.'

In *SI Pension Trustees Ltd* v. *William Hudson Ltd* (1977) 35 P & CR 54 an underlease provided for the review of the rent payable from a specified review date and that the new rent unless agreed before the review date should be determined by an arbitrator appointed on the application of the lessor before the review date. The lessor allowed the review date to pass without making an application for the appointment of an arbitrator. An application was made in the Queen's Bench Division pursuant to section 27 for an extension of the time within which the lessor could apply for the appointment of an arbitrator. At the time when the application came before the Court of Appeal the case of *United Scientific Holdings Ltd* v. *Burnley Borough Council* had been decided by the Court of Appeal, but the appeal to the House of Lords had not been heard. The landlord had started an action in the Chancery Division claiming that time was not of the essence of the provision for the determination of the rent by an arbitrator or that alternatively the tenant by entering into and continuing negotiations for a new rent had led the landlord to believe that strict adherence to the timetable would not be insisted on and was accordingly barred from relying on it. However, the application in the Queen's Bench Division proceeded on the footing that,

'subject to any argument in the Chancery proceedings failure to apply for the appointment before the review date effectively prevents an arbitrator determining a revised rent and therefore prevents the landlord from claiming one.'

On that footing Forbes J held that the effect of the clause was to bar a claim by the landlord and that the case accordingly fell within the terms of section 27. That decision was referred to without disapproval by Lord Denning MR in *Sioux Inc.* v. *China Salvage Co.* [1980] 1 WLR 996 where he reviewed the cases decided since *Liberian Shipping Corporation 'Pegasus' Ltd* v. *A King & Son Ltd* [1967] 2 QB 86 on the construction of section 27 and in particular the meaning of the words 'undue hardship'. It is clear from the decision of the Court of Appeal in that case that if section 27 applies where a landlord fails to trigger a provision for an upward review of rent to be determined by arbitration it must also apply where a tenant fails to trigger a provision under which if a rent review is initiated by an assessment or claim by the lessor which is disputed by the tenant the tenant has the right to have the new rent determined by arbitration. (See in particular the judgment of Sir David Cairns at p 1002.)

In *Amalgamated Estates Ltd* v. *Joystretch Ltd* (1980) 257 EG 489 it was also assumed by the Court of Appeal that section 27 applies to a provision in a rent review clause under which on the application of the lessor or tenant the rent falls to be determined by arbitration. (See per Lawton LJ at p 491, second column, and per Templeman LJ at p 493 though the actual point did not fall to be decided in that case.) [Counsel] who appeared for the lessor, does not contend, and in the light of these authorities could not I think contend in this court, that section 27 has no application to a provision for the appointment of an arbitrator under a rent review clause in a lease, albeit that time is made of the essence of the right of either party to have the determination of the rent reviewed by arbitration ...

[After reviewing further authorities, Vinelott J continued:] With these considerations in mind I turn to the question whether the time for giving notice requiring the appointment of an arbitrator should be extended in relation to the lessor's first notice. [Counsel for the lessee] submitted that there would be no relevant hardship to the lessor in allowing a counternotice to be served. Of course the lessor will not be entitled to rely upon the failure of the tenant to serve a counternotice within due time as barring his right to have the rent determined by arbitration. But that is not a hardship to the lessor to be weighed against the tenant in considering whether to grant relief under section 27. The arbitration provisions in the lease must be read subject to section 27. The lessor accordingly did not acquire any vested right to the higher rent fixed in his notice when the period for serving the counternotice expired. The delay has not otherwise prejudiced the lessor. In particular the delay will not give rise to any difficulty in the conduct of the arbitration. Valuers were instructed before the period for serving the counternotice expired, and it can be assumed that all relevant information as to comparable rents and the like was obtained. The main issue to be determined in the arbitration will be one of law, namely the effect on the rental value of clause 2 (15) of the lease.

[Counsel for the lessee] submitted that the loss to the tenant, if it is compelled to pay rent at the higher figure, will be out of proportion to any fault on its part. He submitted in the light of the issues raised in the claim against the tenant's surveyor in the pleadings that, even assuming that the first notice was valid, the action is by no means certain to succeed and if it does the payment of a lump sum discounted over the period during which the higher rent is payable will not put the tenant in the position which in fairness it ought to be put, namely of paying a fair rent ascertained by arbitration. These are powerful arguments and if the application had been made promptly the tenant would, I think, have been entitled to relief. The difficulty which confronts the tenant is that it elected to pursue its remedy against its surveyor. In those proceedings the lessor has now been joined as defendant. The facts that the tenant has instituted proceedings against its surveyor and that in those proceedings the lessor has been joined so as to be bound by a decision as to the validity of the first notice would not in themselves I think be an automatic bar to an application for relief under section 27. There is no reason in principle why a tenant should not in these circumstances commence proceedings for damages for negligence so as to keep the claim alive. Equally there is no reason why a tenant in these circumstances should not in the same or separate proceedings challenge the validity of the notice (in *SI Pensions Ltd* v. *William Hudson Ltd* there were concurrent proceedings in the Chancery Division raising the question whether time was of the essence of the rent review clause and whether if it was the tenant was estopped from relying on the landlord's failure to serve the notice in due time). But the conduct of the tenant in commencing these proceedings must be looked at in the light of the very considerable period that has passed since it became plain that the lessor would rely on the failure of the tenant to serve a counternotice in due time. The proceedings against Donaldsons were commenced some 18 months and the pleadings in the action were closed some six months before the originating summons which is now before me was taken out. In the light of the delay and of the prosecution of the other proceedings the tenant must I think be taken to have waived its right to seek relief under section 27. I should add for completeness that the submission that the claim for damages in the action against Donaldsons, if the action succeeds, will not put the tenant in the position which it ought to occupy carries little weight on the facts of this case. By the time that the proceedings against Donaldsons are heard and damages are assessed the first review period will be near its end if it has not expired.

I turn therefore to the second notices. The question whether the time for serving counternotices in answer to the second set of notices would be extended is, of course, hypothetical in that the lessor will not have to rely on the second set of notices unless the tenant succeeds in establishing that the first notice was invalid. But it is I think right that the point should be decided now. [Counsel for the lessor] submitted that the tenant similarly has a plain claim against Bairstow Eves or its solicitors and will not suffer undue hardship if relief is refused. That I think considerably overstates the position. As regards Bairstow Eves, their liability will clearly turn on the terms of their instructions. They were instructed at a late stage and instructions were given orally. It is apparent from the terms of the letter of 26 May as summarised in Mr Vokes' affidavit (though I should observe in passing that the letter itself is not exhibited) that Mr Stewart did not appreciate that Bairstow Eves were instructed to take any steps necessary to keep alive the tenant's right to have the rent determined by arbitration. [Counsel for the lessor]'s main submission was that the tenant's solicitors could not escape liability. He submitted that it was *prima facie* their responsibility to see that any necessary counternotice was served in good time. But again the facts of its case so far as they appear from the affidavit evidence are very unusual. On both occasions when surveyors were instructed they were instructed by the tenant without the intervention of their solicitors. Phillips and Buck were instructed to seek advice from counsel following service of the second set of notices, but I do not know what the term of their instructions were and I cannot on the evidence before me safely assume that the tenant did look to its solicitors to take any steps necessary to protect the right to arbitration by serving counternotices in good time. It is noteworthy that on the earlier occasions where proceedings were commenced against Donaldsons claiming that they were under a duty to the tenant to ensure that all necessary steps were taken to keep alive the tenant's right to have the rent determined by arbitration no claim was made against Phillips and Buck and it is not suggested in Donaldsons' defence that the responsibility was theirs. On the evidence before me I cannot rule out the possibility that Phillips and Buck if sued would be able to establish that the tenant's property department took responsibility for ensuring that all the necessary steps were taken. [Counsel for the lessor] submitted that that is an unlikely outcome. I do not think that the court is in a position to speculate as to the likelihood or otherwise that a claim against one or other of the surveyors or the solicitors would succeed. By contrast, in *Adams* and in *Thompson* v. *Bowen* it was apparent from the explanation for the delay given by the solicitors that there was negligence on their part. The explanation amounted to a virtual admission of negligence.

The other factors that must be weighed are first, any prejudice to the lessor if the period for serving a counternotice is extended, and also the delay from 26 June 1980 to 26 November in making this application. Subject to one matter which I will turn to later I do not think that the lessor has established that it will suffer any hardship if the period for serving a counternotice is extended. The lessor will be deprived of a lucky windfall resulting from confusion as to the person responsible for serving counternotices and of which it has had possession for a comparatively brief period. [Counsel for the lessor] submitted that the delay in making this application was excessive having regard to the very short period fixed by the rent review clause for the service of a counternotice and bearing in mind that the tenant had been given a second opportunity of serving notice in good time. However the delay after 26 June is more apparent than real. It is clear and it is not disputed that negotiations continued between the surveyors until September and between solicitors until October. When the fact that a counternotice had not been served became apparent in July the tenant in my judgment did not act unreasonably in deferring the issue of this application while negotiations were proceeding. When the negotiations came to an end it acted promptly.

Under the terms of the lease no interest is payable on arrears of rent. The prejudice to the lessor is being kept out of any higher rent between the time when arbitration takes place and the time when it might have been expected to have taken place if a counternotice had been served in good time will not be fully made good by the payment of arrears at the rate ultimately fixed. In these circumstances relief should I think only be granted on terms that interest will be payable on any arrears of rent payable when the arbitration is concluded during that period. I will leave it to counsel to formulate the precise terms of that condition.

14.4 An essential element in an arbitration agreement may be the existence of bilateral rights of reference by the landlord and the tenant

According to the case cited below, an essential element in an arbitration agreement is the existence of bilateral rights of reference by the landlord and the tenant; therefore, if only one party to the agreement has the right to elect to appoint an independent surveyor to fix the revised rent, then there would be a lack of mutuality which would prevent that party from invoking section 27 of the Arbitration Act 1950.

However, since two cases, *Ronaasen* v. *Metsanomistajain* 40 Lloyds List Reps 267 and *Barni* v. *London General Insurance* 45 Lloyds List Reps 68 were not cited (in which experienced commercial judges rejected the contention that there could only be a binding arbitration agreement if there was mutuality), the authority of this recent case appears doubtful.

TOTE BOOKMAKERS LTD v. THE DEVELOPMENT AND PROPERTY HOLDING CO. LTD

Chancery Division   [1985] 2 WLR 605

A lease of business premises contained a rent review clause which provided that the rent should be the open market rental as (a) specified in a notice in writing from the lessor to the lessee, or (b) agreed between the parties before the expiration of three months immediately after the date of such notice, or (c)

> 'determined by the election of the lessee by counternotice in writing to the lessor not later than three months after the lessor's said notice time to be of the essence hereof by an independent surveyor ... and every such determination shall be made in accordance so far as not inconsistent herewith with the provisions of the Arbitration Act 1950 ...'

The lessor served a notice in writing specifying a new rent payable. The lessee's agent queried the lessor's figure and suggested an alternative rent which was not accepted. After the three months' period for service of the lessee's counternotice had expired, the lessee purported to serve a counternotice out of time and commenced proceedings seeking an extension of time under section 27 of the Arbitration Act 1950 and claiming that unless extension of time was granted the lessee would suffer undue hardship in that the rent specified by the lessor exceeded the open market rent by £1825 p.a.

Held: The clause conferred the right of election only on the tenant so that the essential element of mutuality which was necessary for an arbitration agreement was lacking. Accordingly, the lessee could not invoke section 27 of the Arbitration Act 1950. *Baron* v. *Sunderland Corporation* [1966] 2 QB 56 followed.
Per curiam:
Undue hardship: Hardship was caused when a justifiable claim which may succeed is barred by a time limit. Undue hardship is caused when that hardship is not warranted by the circumstances. Subject to evidence being produced that the rent was excessive, a finding of undue hardship would have been made in the present case. The cashflow of a trading applicant was not a decisive matter in relation to the exercise of discretion. It was permissible to take account of the probability of an applicant recovering damages from a third party in negligence. Had there been an arbitration agreement contained in the review clause the application for an extension of time would have been granted.

PETER GIBSON J: By virtue of the provisions of clause 2 and clause 5 of the lease the rent payable for the period of five years commencing from 25 December 1984 was to be the open market rental value of the property, which should be (a) as specified in a notice in writing from the lessor to the lessee, or (b) agreed between the parties before the expiration of three months immediately after the date of such notice, or (c):

'determined at the election of the lessee by counternotice in writing to the lessor not later than three months after the lessor's said notice time to be of the essence hereof by an independent surveyor appointed for that purpose by the parties jointly in writing or upon the failure to agree upon such appointment within one month after the date of the said counternotice then by an independent surveyor appointed for that purpose by the President for the time being of the Royal Institution of Chartered Surveyors and every such determination shall be made in accordance so far as not inconsistent herewith with the provisions of the Arbitration Act 1950 or any statutory modification or re-enactment thereof for the time being in force'

...

I must now read section 27 of the Arbitration Act. That provides:

'Where the terms of an agreement to refer future disputes to arbitration provide that any claims to which the agreement applies shall be barred unless notice to appoint an arbitrator is given or an arbitrator is appointed or some other step to commence arbitration proceedings is taken within a time fixed by the agreement, and a dispute arises to which the agreement applies, the High Court, if it is of opinion that in the circumstances of the case undue hardship would otherwise be caused, and notwithstanding that the time so fixed is expired, may on such terms, if any, as the justice of the case may require, but without prejudice to the provisions of any enactment limiting the time for the commencement of arbitration proceedings, extend the time for such period as it thinks proper.

It is common ground between the parties that the agreement to which section 27 refers is an arbitration agreement as defined by section 32 of the Act, and that definition is that it 'means a written agreement to submit present or future differences to arbitration, whether an arbitrator is named therein or not' ...

[Counsel] for the defendant, takes two points against the lease being an arbitration agreement. First, unless and until the plaintiff elected for arbitration by serving a counternotice, there was no arbitration agreement and the plaintiff merely had an unexercised option. Second, an essential element of an arbitration agreement is the existence of bilateral rights of reference, and such rights were plainly not present in clause 5 (ii) (c), conferring as it did the right of election on the plaintiff alone. [Counsel for the defendant] also submitted that there was no evidence of undue hardship.

As it seems to me clear beyond question that there is authority binding on this court which makes good [counsel for the defendant's] second submission, I shall go straight to the question raised by that submission. For that submission [counsel for the defendant] relies on the decision of the Court of Appeal in *Baron* v. *Sunderland Corporation* [1966] 2 QB 56. In that case the schoolteacher plaintiff employed by the defendant, the local education authority, sued the defendant for additional salary, which he claimed was due to him in accordance with the provisions of the Burnham Report. The defendant applied for a stay on the basis of a clause in the Burnham Report which established a committee of reference for the determination of any question relating to the interpretation of the Burnham Report brought forward by a local education authority acting through the authority's panel or by any association of teachers acting through the teachers' panel. There was thus no right in the plaintiff himself to refer any question to the committee. At first instance the county court judge granted a stay under section 4 of the Arbitration Act which allowed a stay against any party to an arbitration agreement commencing legal proceedings in the circumstances there specified. The Court of Appeal, in what appears to have been an unreserved judgment, not surprisingly allowed the appeal. Davies LJ said this at p 64:

'It seems to me that this is about as unlike an arbitration clause as anything one could imagine. It is necessary in an arbitration clause that each party shall agree to refer disputes to arbitration; and it is an essential ingredient of an arbitration clause that either party may, in the event of a dispute arising, refer it, in the provided manner, to arbitration. In other words, the clause must give bilateral rights of reference. The present clause, as I see it, does nothing of the kind. It provides that the local education authority, acting through the authorities' panel, may "bring forward" (to use the words in the report) the question, or the Association of Teachers, acting through the teachers' panel, may do so, or, alternatively, by consent of the chairman, someone else may do so. In the present case we do not know whether the teacher is a member of the union or whether the teachers' panel would be prepared to bring forward his contention. We do not know whether the chairman would consent to the matter being brought forward. As I say, there is a complete lack of mutuality in this matter. Quite apart from that, I cannot, for myself, see that this committee of 22 really resembles anything like an arbitrator or arbitrators plus an umpire. I think, therefore, that on the ground on which he decided this case the judge was wrong.'

Davies LJ then went on to deal with another point.

Russell LJ, in his brief judgment, agreed but did not refer to the grounds which I have cited from Davies LJ's judgment.

Salmon LJ also agreed, and said this at p 65:

'The judge approached this case as if section V of the Burnham Report were an arbitration clause which is written into the contract of service between the teacher and the local authority by the relevant statutory instrument. For my part, in spite of the valiant attempts of Mr Percy [who was counsel for the defendant] to persuade us to the contrary, I think that this is the wrong approach, and I agree entirely with the reasons given by Davies LJ for concluding that the judge's view is not tenable.'

There is, therefore, in that case clearly a *ratio decidendi* (though there are others too) that 'it is an essential ingredient of an arbitration clause that either party may refer [a dispute arising] to arbitration, and that the clause must give bilateral rights of reference'; and all this was said in the context of what was meant by an arbitration agreement for the purposes of the Arbitration Act.

There are powerful criticisms of the relevant part of the decision of the Court of appeal in *Russell on Arbitration* 20th ed pp 38 and following, and *Mustill and Boyd's Commercial Arbitration* (1982) p 52. But unless it can be shown that this part of the *ratio decidendi* of the Court of Appeal has been overruled or there are other inconsistent decisions of the Court of Appeal which permit me to prefer the *ratio decidendi* in such other decisions of equal authority, then, whatever my personal views on the matter, I must loyally accept the ratio of *Baron* ...

It may, however, assist, if I were to express my views briefly on the question of undue hardship, if I had been able to reach a conclusion other than the one to which I have said I have compelled on the arbitration agreement point. Subject to the evidential point, I would not have had any hesitation whatever in saying that undue hardship had been shown in the present case. Hardship is caused when a justifiable claim which may succeed is barred by a time-limit. Undue hardship is caused when that hardship is not warranted by the circumstances. I cannot see that the cashflow of a trading applicant, which can never be a safe guide to the means of the applicant or otherwise to his prosperity, is a decisive matter in relation to the consideration of the exercise of discretion. Otherwise, every large company or wealthy individual would be unable to invoke section 27, however monstrous the circumstances. In my judgment, it is permissible to take account of the probability of an applicant recovering from a third party in negligence, but in the present case I do not see how the learned master was able to reach the conclusion that he did in relation to a possible claim against Mr Woolf. I have already referred to the limits on the instructions to Mr Woolf that he was instructed merely to negotiate, and it seems to me I would be speculating to say that there was a probability of any recovery from Mr Woolf, particularly in the circumstances which I have already rehearsed as to the course of the negotiations. I have in mind especially the failure by the defendant's agents to honour their promise on 9 August to place their rental evidence before Mr Woolf. For my part, I would have thought there was ground for excusing the failure to serve a notice within the time-limit in view of the course of those negotiations. Further, the delay was slight, a matter of less than two months, and no hardship whatever has been shown to have been suffered by the defendant. Accordingly, subject only to the evidential point, and subject also to a possible term in relation to interest, so as to compensate the defendant for being out of pocket for the rent to which he would otherwise be entitled as a result of the delay in going to arbitration, I would have granted the application if I had held that there was an arbitration agreement.

14.5 The revised rent which has been determined by arbitration is payable from the quarter day following the publication of the arbitrator's award

SOUTH TOTTENHAM LAND SECURITIES LTD v. R. and A. MILLETT (SHOPS) LTD AND OTHERS

Court of Appeal   [1984] 1 WLR 710

A lease provided for a specified annual rent to be paid until 25 March 1980 and thereafter, until 25 March 2001, if the parties failed to agree a revised rent then the sum determined by an arbitrator. The lease entitled the landlords to re-enter the premises if the rent was in arrear for 21 days. The rent was payable quarterly in arrear. The parties did not agree a rent and the matter went to arbitration. The arbitrator was appointed to determine a revised rent which would take effect retrospectively from 25 March 1980 in accordance with the review provisions. On 31 October 1980 the landlords were notified that the arbitrator had made his award which was available from him on request. On 6 November 1980 the landlords informed the lessee of the contents of the award. By 26 November 1980 the landlords had received the original rent but not the increased rent for the two quarters 25 March to 29 September 1980 and they re-entered the premises in purported exercise of their rights of forfeiture. The landlords issued proceedings claiming *inter alia* arrears of rent. Woolf J held that the increased rent did not become payable until the quarter day following the publication of the arbitrator's award on 31 October 1980. Accordingly, the landlords re-entry had been wrongful and that they were not entitled to recover rent for the period 29 September to 26 November 1980. The landlords appealed.

Held: The appeal would be dismissed. Although an arbitration award was published when the arbitrator notified the parties that he had reached a decision, the contents of the award were not known until the award was taken up and the arbitrator's fees paid; thus, to hold a tenant liable to pay rent from the date of publication of the award was unworkable, and that since the lease provided for rent to be paid quarterly, arrears in respect of the period pending the arbitrator's determination were payable on the quarter day following the ascertainment of the new rent.

O'CONNOR LJ: It seems to me that it is much better, in cases such as this, that there should be no doubt about when the rent is due. If the parties choose to put into a lease that rent is due on quarter days, then there are good grounds for saying, where arrears arise in this fashion, that they should not be due until the next following quarter day. In my judgment, the judge came to a correct decision on this point.

It is to some extent a choice between two periods, because, of course, I appreciate the submissions [counsel for the landlords] has made that as soon as the award is published, or the rent agreed, one has got a date which is certain. The argument which took place in the court below is no longer relevant here as to the date of publication, but I must say something about it. The law is that an award is published when the arbitrator notifies the parties that he has made his award, but they do not know the contents of it until it is taken up and his fee paid. So that in the present case the parties were notified by letter of 30 October that the award was ready, they received the letter on 31 October—that is how the date of publication was fixed—but of course they did not know the contents of it until the award was taken up. The tenant cannot be expected to pay rent the amount of which he does not know. So, therefore, the publication of the award as a fixed day for discharging the obligation is, in my judgment, quite unworkable. One has to allow some reasonable period of time in individual cases as to when it can be said that the tenant has ascertained how much is due. In the nature of things it is very unlikely to be the day when the award is published. That seems to me to be an objection which points strongly to some other date as being a suitable certain date when the rent is due. As I have said, in the present case it does not seem to be possible to say that it was 31 October. We do not know when the actual details of the award reached the landlords. They wrote off on 31 October enclosing the arbitrator's fee. I do not know what the days of the week were in 1980 but they are unlikely to have received it back before 2 November. Therefore, would it be 2 November from which the 21 days ran or would it be 3 November? Or some later date? There are postal delays, there are weekends to be considered. This kind of uncertainty points strongly to looking for some more certain date from which the arrears of rent are to begin. It is, as I have said, sufficiently found, in my judgment, in the lease. I am confident that the judge came to a correct decision and that where you have got a clause such as this then the arrears of rent do not become due and payable until the quarter day next following the ascertainment of the new rent.

Lastly, modern rent review clauses deal with this problem, so that it does not arise: see, for example, the clause in *Torminster Properties Ltd* v. *Green* [1983] 1 WLR 676. It is desirable that rent review clauses in leases should deal specifically with what is to happen where there is delay in arriving at the new rent beyond the review date.

14.6 Evidence which is admissible before an arbitrator to establish the market rent

The general position in relation to admissibility of evidence of market rent was succinctly stated by Megarry J in **English Exporters (London) Ltd v. Eldonwall Ltd** [1973] 1 Ch 415 at 423.

MEGARRY J: Putting matters shortly, and leaving on one side the matters that I have mentioned, such as the Civil Evidence Act 1968 and anything made admissible by questions in cross-examination, in my judgment a valuer giving expert evidence in chief (or in re-examination): (a) may express the opinions that he has formed as to values even though substantial contributions to the formation of those opinions have been made by matters of which he has no first-hand knowledge; (b) may give evidence as to the details of any transactions within his personal knowledge, in order to establish them as matters of fact; and (c) may express his opinion as to the significance of any transactions which are or will be proved by admissible evidence (whether or not given by him) in relation to the valuation with which he is concerned; but (d) may not give hearsay evidence stating the details of any transactions not within his personal knowledge in order to establish them as matters of fact. To those propositions I would add that for counsel to put in a list of comparables ought to amount to a warranty by him of his intention to tender admissible evidence of all that is shown on the list.

I have spent some little time in dealing with this matter of evidence as it appears to be the subject of no direct modern authority, and experience suggests that it is a matter upon which there is considerable misunderstanding. When a list of comparables is being prepared for the trial, as is usual and convenient, it is all too common to include in the list transactions upon which there will be no admissible evidence but only hearsay of a greater or lesser degree of reliability. If the parties exchange lists of comparables at an early date, often much time and money can be saved by the experts on each side agreeing such of the transactions in each list as, after any necessary inquiry, they feel they can accept as being reliably summarised; and in this way the additional expense of proving a favourable comparable not within an expert's own knowledge can be avoided. But if the other side will not accept the facts, then either the transaction must be proved by admissible evidence or it must be omitted as a comparable.

It is clear that the parties may agree to submit hearsay evidence of comparables which would not otherwise be admissible before the arbitrator. *Henry Bath and Sons Ltd* v. *Birgby Products* (1962) 1 Lloyd's Rep 389.

If a party does not agree to submission of such hearsay evidence he must object during the tendering of such evidence, as the case cannot then be re-opened at a later date by one of the parties.

TOWN CENTRE SECURITIES LTD v. WM MORRISON SUPERMARKETS LTD

Queen's Bench Division   (1982) 263 EG 437

The court was asked to consider *inter alia*:
1.(a) Whether the evidence as to comparables by the landlord's valuer was hearsay.
1.(b) Whether the evidence as to comparables by the tenant's valuer was hearsay.
2. If the answers to 1 (a) and 1 (b) were yes, whether such evidence was admissible, nevertheless.
3. If the answer to 2 was no, whether (a) it was too late for either the tenant or the landlord to object to the admission of the evidence after the conclusion of the case, if no objection was taken to its admission during the course of the evidence, or,
(b) the arbitrator had a discretion to admit such evidence;
(c) in the circumstances the arbitrator had a discretion to allow the landlord to re-open the case and to grant an adjournment for it to call further evidence.

Held:
1.(a) Yes.
1.(b) Yes. Much of the valuers' evidence was based on hearsay or depended on secondary evidence of documents.
2. Yes. Hearsay evidence may be admissible in civil proceedings if no objection is taken to it at the time it is tendered, see s 1 of the Civil Evidence Act 1968 and s 6 (3) of the Civil Evidence Act 1972 which extended the provisions of Part I of the 1968 Act to statements of opinion.
3. Did not arise.

Had the issue of evidence still been a live issue the arbitrator would have had no discretion to re-open the hearing after it was over. This case was 'a special case stated' by the arbitrator under section 21 (1) (a) of the Arbitration Act 1950. However, this section was repealed by the Arbitration Act 1979. The arbitration proceedings in the present case were begun before the 1979 Act came into operation on 1 August 1979. The 1979 Act abolished the powers to state a special case on a question of law arising in the course of the reference and to state an award in the form of a special case.

MICHAEL TURNER QC (sitting as a deputy High Court judge): It is common ground between the parties that the arbitrator properly entered upon the arbitration and heard evidence on 31 July and 3 and 6 August 1979; such evidence consisted in the main (if not entirely) of expert evidence by qualified and experienced valuers led by each of the parties, which was in its turn subject to cross-examination by the opposing party. Paragraphs 5 and 6 of the special case conveniently summarise the nature of some of the evidence that was led. Paragraph 5 provides:

'Valuations were exchanged on 21 June 1979. There was no indication in the particulars of the transaction submitted by Mr Buckle that he did not have personal knowledge of the transactions or that the Landlord would not adduce such evidence.'

Paragraph 6 provides:

'By a letter dated 5 July 1979 the Landlord gave notice to the Tenant of Mr Hepper's intention to rely on the two transactions referred to in paragraph 7 below in terms which indicated that the basis of his knowledge might be information given to him by others. By a letter dated 6 July 1979 the Tenant notified the Landlord that it would not object to late delivery of these particulars, assuming that they were to be proved by properly admissible evidence.'

It is to be inferred that whereas the valuation prepared by Mr Hepper expressly indicated that he either had or had not direct knowledge of the matters referred to in his valuation, there was nothing in Mr Buckle's valuation to indicate either way. From the facts recited in paragraphs 7 and 14 of the case, the true inference in regard to Mr Hepper's valuation is probably that he did indicate that he had first hand knowledge of the relevant comparables.

When the landlords gave notice to the tenants on 5 July that it was Mr Hepper's intention to rely upon two additional transactions, the tenants responded to the effect that they would raise no objection to late delivery of the particulars relating to those transactions if properly proved. One of the principal reasons for exchanging valuations prior to a hearing is that each party has the opportunity of inquiring into the transactions affecting the properties referred to therein, with a view to obtaining confirmatory evidence, evidence which may show that it is not a comparable at all or that the weight to be attached to that comparable for various reasons is less than the other party suggests.

When Mr Hepper came to give evidence-in-chief it became apparent that in so far as his evidence affected those last two properties it was based upon hearsay, but it was directed nevertheless to establishing those properties as comparables. When Mr Buckle came to give his evidence-in-chief it was given in proof form to which was annexed a bundle of documents ('AJB'), which was placed before me, and again it became apparent that in respect of every property which he sought to establish as a comparable, the evidence upon which he relied was hearsay; further, the nature of that evidence was itself, in some cases at least, based upon hearsay. At no stage during the course of the evidence of either of these witnesses was objection taken to any of it on the grounds that it was inadmissible. As the economical and helpful summary of the cross-examination of both these witnesses in paragraphs 7 and 10 (b) of the case demonstrates, it was directed not to the hearsay point because that had already been established by their evidence-in-chief, rather was it directed to matters concerned with the weight which should attach to their evidence. It is unnecessary to burden this judgment with examples from the case for they speak for themselves.

As can be seen from the case the tenants were ultimately to take the point that all the evidence, save possibly for that dealt with in Mr Hepper's valuation, led on behalf of the landlords—what I may call 'comparable fact' evidence—was hearsay and therefore inadmissible, and they supported that submission by reference to the judgment of Megarry J (as he then was) in the case of *English Exporters (London) Ltd* v. *Eldonwall Ltd* [1973] Ch 415. Both parties have referred to, and sought to rely upon, passages from the judgment in that case during the course of the argument before me. It may be helpful at this stage if I endeavour to summarise the arguments, as they have finally emerged, on the main points for determination on this special case.

For the landlords it was submitted that (1) the evidence to which the objection refers was hearsay. (2) Comparable fact evidence was not admissible in chief, unless it was evidence of fact of which the witness knew at first hand. (3) Hearsay evidence of comparables was inadmissible in chief even if sought to be given in support of an opinion on values. (4) The tenants' solicitor not having objected to the admission of hearsay evidence at the proper time, *videlicet*, at the stage at which it was tendered, could not or ought not to be allowed to raise it after both parties had closed their case.

For the tenants it was submitted that (1) the decision in the *Eldonwall* case was well known to all practising in this field. (2) There is a clear distinction between expert evidence of opinion on the one hand, and expert evidence of comparable fact on the other. In regard to both categories of evidence it is permissible to lead evidence-in-chief of particular transactions. (3) The failure of the tenants to object to the hearsay evidence was justified because it was admissible in support of opinion evidence although not on comparable fact evidence. (4) Consequently, the failure to take the objection when the evidence was tendered cannot be construed as consent to the admission of hearsay as comparable fact evidence. (5) If inadmissible evidence is nevertheless allowed in, it remains inadmissible and therefore of no probative effect.

Before expressing my conclusions it is helpful to refer to certain passages in the judgment in the *Eldonwall* case. Although both parties in that case adduced evidence from experts, only the expert called by the landlords sought to give evidence of comparables. At p 419 G of the judgment Megarry J said:

'As is also far from unknown, some of the comparables were less comparable than others, and some turned out to be supported only by hearsay evidence, or by evidence that was in other respects less than cogent. There was no formal process of a ruling being made to exclude those comparables which are supported only by hearsay evidence; but I was discouraging, and in the event Mr Ibbotson, though rueful, did not seriously argue the point, or press it?

From which it would appear that counsel for the tenant in that case had taken the objection in regard to inadmissibility of hearsay evidence as supporting comparables, although the judge made no ruling on that objection when it was taken.

At p 420 A of the judgment the learned judge continued:

'For all I know, that misunderstanding may in recent years have been fostered by a passage in *Woodfall's Landlord and Tenant* 27th Ed (1968) p 1350 to which Mr Lightman very properly referred me. There, the editors take the view that when a valuer is giving his opinion on rental value under the Act of 1954: "... he should state his reasons for holding that opinion even if this involves reference to comparisons of which he only knows at second-hand, that surely going to weight rather than admissibility." There are further passages amplifying that view, but I think that this is a sufficient indication of the general import of a paragraph which seems to contend that valuers are entitled to give hearsay evidence of comparables.

The learned judge continued:

'In such circumstances, two of the heads under which the valuers' evidence may be ranged are opinion evidence and factual evidence. As an expert witness, the valuer is entitled to express his opinion about matters within his sphere of competence. In building up his opinions about values, he will no doubt have learned much from transactions in which he has himself been engaged, and of which he could give first-hand evidence. But he will also have learned much from many other sources, including much of which he could give no first-hand evidence.

At p 421 A the learned judge continued:

'On the other hand, quite apart from merely expressing his opinion, the expert often is able to give factual evidence as well. If he has first-hand knowledge of a transaction, he can speak of that. He may himself have measured the premises and conducted the negotiations which led to a letting of them at £X, which comes to £Y per square foot; and he himself may have read the lease and seen that it contains no provisions, other than some particular clause, which would have any material effect on the valuation; and then he may express his opinion on the value. So far as the expert gives factual evidence, he is doing what any other witness of fact may do, namely, speaking of that which he has perceived for himself.'

Lower down the page at letter D the learned judge continued:

'But basically, the expert's factual evidence on matters of fact is in the same position as the factual evidence of any other witness. Further factual evidence that he cannot give himself is sometimes adduced in some other way, as by the testimony of some other witness who was himself concerned in the transaction in question, or by proving some document which carried the transaction through, or recorded it; and to the transaction thus established, like the transactions which the expert himself has proved, the expert may apply his experience and opinions, as tending to support or qualify his views.

That being so, it seems to me quite another matter when it is asserted that a valuer may give factual evidence of transactions of which he has no direct knowledge, whether *per se* or whether in the guise of giving reasons for his opinion as to value.'

At p 442 B the learned judge continued:

'It therefore seems to me that details of comparable transactions upon which a valuer intends to rely in his evidence must, if they are to be put before the court, be confined to those details which have been, or will be, proved by admissible evidence, given either by the valuer himself or in some other way.'

Then at letter E the learned judge continued:

'On principle, therefore, I would not accept the proposition in *Woodfall*, p 1350 and in this I do not think I would be alone. To the end of the passage in question, *Woodfall* very properly appends a footnote which reads: "See, however, *Wright* v. *Sydney Municipal Council* ..." The case cited seems to me to provide much support for the views that I have expressed; and *Woodfall* does not attempt to discuss or refute the decision. In *Wright* v. *Sydney Municipal Council* much the same sort of point came before Sly J, Gordon J and Ferguson J. The case concerned a sale and not a tenancy, but that seems immaterial. It was contended ... that an expert valuer "was entitled to state what sales he had knowledge of, even from hearsay and to give the details of such sales, including price, etc, in evidence ..." but this contention was rejected. Sly J said that the expert could, in addition to giving direct evidence of sales of other comparable land, provided there was legal evidence of these, testify that, *inter alia*, he had kept in touch with sales not made by himself in the district, to show that he was competent to give evidence of values in the district. Sly J added ...: "But he has no privilege beyond any other witness to speak in detail of the prices realised for other lands unless he can give legal evidence of such sales, or that evidence has already been given by the witnesses. It would be a most dangerous thing to allow an expert to speak of the details of sales of which he really knows nothing, and see the difficulty a plaintiff in a case like this would be in if he had to answer such evidence not knowing whether the sales were really existent or not. I think the same principle applies whether the evidence is given in chief or in reply." At p 365 Gordon J took a similar view, and at p 366 Ferguson J rejected the contention that the witness could "give hearsay evidence of the particulars of the transactions in question": see also *Phipson* ... Bramwell B, I may say, apparently would have put matters on an even narrower basis, saying that a valuer may state his opinion of the value of land, but that he must not in chief add that he says this because some other land sold for such-and-such a price, although he may say this in cross-examination: see *Sheen* v. *Bumpstead* ... However, this, I think, was an obiter remark in a dissenting judgment (although *Phipson* ... does not reveal this), and for many years now such evidence has not been rejected in chief when the witness has been speaking from his first-hand knowledge.

Putting matters shortly, and leaving on one side the matters that I have mentioned, such as the Civil Evidence Act 1968 and anything made admissible by questions in cross-examination, in my judgment a valuer giving expert evidence-in-chief (or in re-examination): (a) may express the opinions that he has formed as to values even though substantial contributions to the formation of those opinions have been made by matters of which he has no first-hand knowledge; (b) may give evidence as to the details of any transactions within his personal knowledge, in order to establish them as matters of fact; and (c) may express his opinion as to the significance of any transactions which are or will be proved by admissible evidence (whether or not given by him) in relation to the valuation with which he is concerned; but (d) may not give hearsay evidence stating the details of any transactions not within his personal knowledge in order to establish them as matters of fact. To those propositions I would add that for counsel to put in a list of comparables ought to amount to a warranty by him of his intention to tender admissible evidence of all that is shown on the list.

What these passages clearly establish, in my judgment, is that at common law it is not permissible in evidence-in-chief to adduce in support of opinion evidence particular examples. It follows, therefore, that I am unable to accept [counsel for the tenant]'s primary submissions as to the admissibility of such evidence as affording any justification for the failure to take the objection at the time such evidence was tendered. But I have still to deal with his final submission on this aspect of the case, that even though no objection was taken, that which was and, arguably, remained inadmissible was of no probative effect. It is here not merely permissible but relevant to have regard to the provisions of section 1 of the Civil Evidence Act 1968, subsection (1) of which provides:

'In any civil proceedings a statement other than one made by a person while giving oral evidence in those proceedings shall be admissible as evidence of any fact stated therein to the extent that it is so admissible by virtue of any provision of this Part of the Act or by virtue of any other statutory provision or by agreement of the parties, but not otherwise.'

From the fact that parties may agree to the admissibility of hearsay evidence, which had long been the practice in many civil cases, it follows that such a statement, subject to the provisions of section 6 (3), is admissible as evidence of the facts contained in it. It may be noticed in passing that the Civil Evidence Act 1972 extended the provisions of Part I of the 1968 Act to statements of opinion. It may be deduced that whatever may have been the jurisprudential arguments in the past seeking to rationalise the basis for the rejection of hearsay evidence, now that its admission depends on procedure and discretion on the one hand or agreement of the parties on the other, it is difficult to accept this part of [counsel for the tenant]'s argument in the bald terms in which it is couched.

So I remind myself of what transpired in the *Eldonwall* case (see the judgment at p 419 H) and the reference by [counsel for the tenant] to two further cases, namely, *Gilbey* v. *Great Western Railway* (1910) 102 LT 202 and *Beare* v. *Garrod* (1915) 113 LT 673. In all three cases it is apparent that objection to the admissibility of the relevant hearsay statement was, or must have been, taken during the course of the hearing; albeit in *Garrod*'s case that it may not have been taken until the witness giving that evidence had concluded it. These cases were cited in support of [counsel for the tenant]'s submission, but in my judgment they do not help his case, for either by implied agreement or waiver, by not taking the objection when the evidence was tendered, and bearing in mind [counsel for the tenant]'s statement that the *Eldonwall* case was well known in this class of litigation, the tenants in the present case gave up their right to insist upon compliance with the strict rules of evidence. I am fortified in this conclusion in that under the provisions of the Civil Evidence Act the admissibility of such evidence is, as I have stated, now a matter of procedural, rather than substantive, law. In the event, such evidence became admissible and it is for the arbitrator to assess its weight in accordance with the provisions of section 6 (3) of the Act.

After the tenants had taken the point on the admissibility of the evidence of both Mr Hepper and Mr Buckle (as appears from the case), the landlords in their turn sought to take similar objection to the evidence of the tenants' valuer, Mr Lund. The landlords' solicitor had not availed himself of the opportunity to do so as the evidence was tendered. [Counsel for the landlord] sought to persuade me that Mr Lund's evidence was not in any material respect based on hearsay. From the summary of the evidence of this witness in the case, the inference is that much of it was based on hearsay and what could not be deduced as inference (for example, the purported executed leases) manifestly was not the best evidence. Further, if in truth Mr Lund did have personal knowledge of the various comparables produced by him as evidence, the terms in which the summary of his evidence in the case are cast tend strongly to the contrary effect, for if it were otherwise it was an elliptical way of giving evidence of facts of which the witness did have first-hand knowledge. As summarised in the case there is no obviously sound reason for supposing that Mr Lund's evidence stood on a significantly different footing from the evidence of Mr Hepper and Mr Buckle discussed above. It, too, was hearsay or depended on secondary evidence of documents. The landlords by their conduct are to be taken as either having agreed to the admissibility of hearsay evidence or, alternatively, to have waived their right to object to it.

Except in regard to matters of formality the courts do not encourage a party to reopen its case after it has been closed. The classic statement on this topic is to be found in *Phipson on Evidence*, 12th ed, para 1616, which reads:

'Evidence in reply, whether oral or by affidavit, must, as a general rule, be strictly confined to rebutting the defendant's case, and must not merely confirm that of the plaintiff. Thus, where the latter had closed his case without calling a defendant who did not appear, the plaintiff was not allowed to call him in reply.'

Having regard to the view expressed above in regard to the hearsay question, no detailed consideration of this topic is now called for; were it still to have been a live issue I would have held that the arbitrator had no discretion on the facts of this case to permit the landlords to reopen their case.

14.7 An arbitrator has no power to insert rent reviews in a lease where none is provided

In *Bracknell Development Corporation* v. *Greenlees Wennards* (1981) 260 EG 500, Falconer J held that where an arbitrator had to determine a 'full and fair market rent' for a 21 year lease which was granted to the tenant under an option to renew, the arbitrator had no power to insert rent reviews but had to fix a single rent for the whole 21 year term. See also page 230 earlier.

Chapter 15

Arbitration and rent reviews

15.1 Post review comparables—whether acceptable as evidence

When fixing a revised rent under a review clause, the arbitrator may, it seems, take into account rents of comparable properties which were fixed after the review date specified, see Staughton J in *Segama* v. *Penny Le Roy Ltd* below. Staughton J distinguished the earlier decisions of Whitford J in *Ponsford* v. *HMS Aerosols Ltd* (1976) recorded in the *Handbook of Rent Review* at page 1769 (the point was not argued on appeal, apparently), and Robert Goff J's decision in *Duvan Estates* v. *Rossette Sunshine Savouries Ltd* (1982) 261 EG 364, (see below at page 305) where he held the point to be *obiter* (the arbitrator had there not relied on the post comparable evidence to fix the rent). However, the position may be resolved in future on appeal since, as Staughton J himself recognised, different judges may take different views on the point. However, on the basis that his was the later decision in which earlier decisions were considered, it may be taken to reflect the current position. In terms of common sense it has much to recommend it.

SEGAMA N.V. v. PENNY LE ROY LTD

Commercial Court (1984) 269 EG 322

A dispute arose between the landlord and the tenant as to whether the arbitrator in fixing a reviewed 'market' rent on the basis of vacant possession, was entitled:
(i) to have regard to available rents of comparable properties which had been settled after the review date;
(ii) to include for his consideration any rents agreed for a similar property between an existing landlord and an existing tenant, or whether such evidence should be excluded.

Held:
(1) What the arbitrator had to have regard to was the worth of the property. The arbitrator was entitled to hold that the evidence as to rents agreed after the review date was admissible. If a rent of comparable premises had been agreed on the day after the relevant date, such a rent was relevant in determining the market rent on the review date. As the lapse of time before the relevant date became greater then the evidence would become progressively unreliable as evidence of rental values at the relevant date. The same would be true of rents agreed *before* the relevant date, but it was never argued that they should be excluded.
(2) The arbitrator first had to have regard to the *worth* of the property in terms of rent, of similar property let with vacant possession at the relevant time. In

ascertaining that worth, he could have regard to the rents agreed at a different time, for similar property not let with vacant possession. But the arbitrator had to consider how far the evidence of rents so agreed helped him to determine the answer to the actual question which was before him. Even if such evidence was not within the category which the arbitrator was required to take into account it was not expressly or by implication, excluded from his consideration for the reasons stated above.

STAUGHTON J: In clause 5 (3) of the lease ... it was provided that the market rent should be deemed to mean 'the yearly rental value of the demised premises having regard to rental values current at the relevant time for similar property ... let with vacant possession'. It was agreed, before me at any rate, that 'the relevant time' means in this instance 1 October 1982. The parties, as is customary, referred the arbitrator to rents agreed for comparable properties on or before that date. But by the time that the matter came to be argued before him, there were also available rents agreed for comparable properties after 1 October 1982. Paragraph 1 of the arbitrator's award reads as follows:

'The only issue of law which arose in this reference was the admissibility of post-review date comparables, that is to say rents of comparable properties agreed after the review date for the subject premises.'

That is the first and main question of law which I have to consider on this application. It is plain to me that the point is of general importance to landlords and tenants. No doubt there are a great many leases containing similar clauses and raising the same problem. In the *Handbook of Rent Review* by Bernstein and Reynolds there is this passage at p 941: 'Whether evidence of transactions occurring after the review date is admissible, and, if so, for what purpose and to what extent, is controversial.' It is certainly not a one-off case.

The second question raised by the landlords before me is whether evidence was properly considered by the arbitrator as to rents of comparable premises agreed between existing landlords and existing tenants, or whether the evidence should have been confined to rents agreed by tenants who had not previously occupied the premises in question. Evidence of the former class was put before the arbitrator, and he clearly attached importance to it. I cannot detect in the award any suggestion that the relevance of that evidence depended on any question of law. But there are indications in it that the arbitrator had in mind that there might be a distinction between evidence of agreements with existing tenants and evidence of agreements with new tenants. Accordingly, I am prepared to assume that the landlords argued for such a distinction at the arbitration.

This second question is also, I think, one of some general importance. If indeed it is a question of law (which was not apparent to the arbitrator) it will probably affect a good many cases besides that presently before me.

I shall consider each of the two questions that I have mentioned in turn; and then a third point, that is whether the determination of either or both of them could, in terms of section 1 (4), 'substantially affect the right of one or more of the parties to the arbitration agreement'.

(1) Evidence of rents agreed after the review date

The arbitrator has set out the contentions of the parties and his own conclusions with care, clarity and concision (in the second sense of that word). He held that the evidence was admissible; and he added (in para 17):

'I accept that the further away from the review date one progresses then the rental evidence will become progressively unreliable as evidence of rental values at that date. This is, however, a question of weight and not admissibility and is a matter for me to consider when reviewing the evidence.'

I wholly agree with his conclusions. But the point is one of law; it was argued at some length before me; and it is of general importance. So I must state my own reasons.

Essentially the question is one of construction and divides into two parts. First, what is meant by 'rental values current at the relevant time'? Does that phrase mean only rents actually agreed or does it mean the current worth of premises in terms of rent? No customary or technical meaning was proposed, save in so far as one may appear from the authorities. I shall consider the cases later. As a matter of ordinary English, the word 'value' is more consistent with the notion of worth than with the narrower concept of rents actually agreed. Since it is the worth of the demised premises at the relevant date that has to be ascertained, in terms of market rent, it seems to me entirely plausible that the arbitrator should be enjoined to have regard to the worth of similar property—whether demonstrated by evidence of agreements reached before or after the relevant date. When the clause speaks of the 'rental value of the demised premises', it evidently refers to worth rather than to an agreed rent. Why should the words 'rental values', later in the same sentence, have a different meaning?

The second part of the question is whether, even if the arbitrator is directed by the clause to have regard to rents agreed for similar property on or before the relevant date, he is thereby precluded from having regard to any rents agreed subsequently. The rule that the expression of one or two things is the exclusion of the other might suggest that he is. But it requires more than such *prima facie* inference as that rule provides to exclude evidence which is otherwise relevant and admissible. See *W N Lindsay & Co. Ltd* v. *European Grain and Shipping Agency Ltd* [1963] 1 Lloyd's Rep 437, per Diplock LJ at p 445: 'Any clause in a contract relied upon as excluding evidence which would ordinarily be admissible is to be strictly construed.'

There are six cases which are said to be in some degree relevant to this point. The first is *Bwllfa and Merthyr Dare Steam Collieries (1891) Ltd* v. *Pontypridd Waterworks Co.* [1903] AC 426. At any rate the arbitrator thought the case relevant, although, [counsel] for the tenants, expressly disclaimed its aid before me. There a dispute arose as to the statutory compensation payable to the owners of a mine, because the undertakers of a waterworks served them with a notice requiring them not to work coal under a certain parcel of land. Evidence was tendered that the value of coal rose after the date of the notice. It was held by the House of Lords that the evidence was admissible. The principle behind the decision is said to be found in the speech of Lord Macnaghten at p 431:

'If the question goes to arbitration, the arbitrator's duty is to determine the amount of compensation payable. In order to enable him to come to a just conclusion it is his duty, I think, to avail himself of all the information at hand at the time of making his award which may be laid before him. Why should he listen to conjecture on a matter which has become an accomplished fact? Why should he guess if he can calculate? With the light before him, why should he shut his eyes and grope in the dark.'

I agree with both counsel that the decision is not relevant to the present case. The task of the arbitrator in that case was to assess, at the date of the notice, a fact which at the time lay in the future; he had to discover what profit the owners of the mine would have made by working the coal in question. The headnote itself says so. If new material was available by the time of the hearing to answer that question with greater certainty, he should have had regard to it. Similar problems arise when a tribunal is required to forecast, as at a given date, how likely it is that some future event will occur. Such a determination is often required in the law of contract. In connection with the doctrine of frustration, Lord Sumner said, in *Bank Line Ltd* v. *Arthur Capel & Co.* [1919] AC 435 at p 454: 'What happens afterwards may assist in showing what the probabilities really were, if they had been reasonably forecast'. In each of those two situations, when the task is to make a finding as to some fact which lies in the future, or to assess the probability of some future event occurring, the *Bwllfa* case is powerful authority that evidence of later facts will be relevant. But I do not, with respect, see that it touches, one way or the other, on the question whether later events are relevant to the determination of the existing market rent on a given date.

In *Melwood Units Pty Ltd* v. *Commissioners of Main Roads* [1979] AC 426 it was necessary to assess compensation for the compulsory acquisition by the respondent of land for the purposes of an expressway. Compensation had to be assessed as at September 1965. At that date there had already been a grant of planning permission, in principle, for development of adjacent land as a drive-in shopping centre. After September 1965 two further events occurred. Definitive planning permission was granted; and a purchaser agreed to buy the adjacent land at $40,000 per acre. It was held that those events had been wrongly rejected as irrelevant to the assessment of compensation. Lord Russell of Killowen, delivering the advice of the Judicial Committee, said (at p 436):

'Now it is plain that in assessing values for the purpose of compensation for resumption on compulsory acquisition a tribunal is not required to shut its mind to transactions subsequent to the date of resumption. They may well be relevant or of assistance to a greater or lesser degree, and in the instant case the figure paid by David Jones Ltd was the only figure available at the date of assessment of the value of adjacent land to a person wishing to develop the land for its "highest and best use".'

[Counsel for the applicants] sought to distinguish that case on the ground that it was concerned with compensation, which must be fair, as opposed to a market rent which is what tenants are prepared to pay and landlords to accept. For my part, I do not at first sight find the distinction very compelling.

The case of *Ponsford* v. *HMS Aerosols Ltd* (1976), decided by Whitford J, is recorded by a brief note in the *Handbook of Rent Review* at p 1769. It was likewise a rent review case. The learned judge said this:

'Now an assertion has been made on the defendants' side that in coming to a conclusion as to what would be the appropriate rent for the period starting on 25 June 1975 the person making the assessment is entitled to consider not only the state of the market up to that date but also the way in which the market has subsequently moved ... I think that the only sensible way to give effect to what was agreed between the parties is to hold, as the plaintiffs have suggested that I should hold, that the assessment should be made in the light of the assessor's knowledge as to the state of the market up to the period when the new rent was due to come into effect, but that there should be omitted from consideration any developments that may have taken place subsequent to that date.'

So far as I can tell from that meagre evidence, the case was concerned with movement of the market, or with 'developments', after the relevant date. I can readily understand why those should be left out of account: the issue was about the market rent on the relevant date, and not what it became thereafter in consequence of change, or movement, or developments. If the landlord or the tenant submitted that in fairness those factors should be taken into account, one can see why that contention failed.

Industrial Properties (Barton Hill) Ltd v. *Associated Electrical Industries Ltd*, undated and unreported but also recorded in the Handbook of Rent Review (p 1749) was decided by Judge Fay QC. The learned judge said this:

'Clearly the major problem I have to solve in arriving at a decision on value is the yield properly to be taken into account as at 25 December 1973. About this I have a good deal of evidence ... I accept that at Christmas 1973 there were virtually no property sales being effected, and when later in 1974 the market redeveloped, it was at values considerably lower and yields considerably higher than prior to December 1973.'

His Honour then referred to *Curling* v. *Jones* [1963] 1 WLR 748; *Bwllfa & Merthyr Dare Steam Collieries* v. *Pontypridd Waterworks Co.* [1903] AC 426; *Re Bradberry* [1943] 1 Ch 5, and continued:

'If I were dealing with quoted shares instead of land the position would be clear enough. If shares had to be valued as at a certain day, for example for estate duty purposes, the value is the mid-market price on that day and it would be idle to urge that six months later that price was halved, or that on the day of valuation they were on a downward trend because of apprehensions which later were found to be well-founded. No, I must ask myself what a skilled valuer would have done at Christmas 1973 knowing all that had happened up to then but denied full knowledge of the catastrophes of 1974.'

Again it appears to me that the judge was considering changes which occurred in the market after the relevant date, and not later evidence as a guide to what the market rent on the relevant date had been.

Duvan Estates Ltd v. *Rossette Sunshine Savouries Ltd* (1982) 261 EG 364 was an application for leave to appeal under the Arbitration Act 1979, decided by Robert Goff J. The learned judge said this (at p 365):

'The point in broad terms ... is that in considering a valuation of this kind it is proper to have regard to the relevant facts existing as at the review date, which is 17 July 1978, and not to have regard to facts and events existing after that date. In support of that proposition he relied upon a passage at the end of the judgment of Whitford J in *Ponsford* v. *HMS Aerosols Ltd*, a case which went on appeal [1979] AC 63; (1978) 247 EG 171. But I was provided with a transcript of Whitford J's judgment because on this point, apparently, the appeal was not pursued.

As a general principle I entirely accept that; indeed, I do not understand that Mr Cohen on behalf of the landlord contested the principle as such.'

However, he went on to hold that the arbitrator had not relied upon the disputed evidence in reaching his conclusion. 'In those circumstances', the judge continued, 'I do not think, on a bare reading of the reasons of the award, that the arbitrator was infringing the principle which both parties accept should be applicable'. The material which the judge was referring to in those passages was indeed evidence of rents agreed after the review date. Thereafter he went on to consider other evidence subsequent to the review date, of a different nature. In relation to that evidence he did find an error of law on the part of the arbitrator. But as it was not one which could substantially affect the rights of the parties, he refused leave to appeal.

It can, I think, be said of the learned judge's conclusion, which is relevant to the present case, first that it was *obiter*; secondly, that the point was apparently conceded; and, thirdly, that the *Melwood* case was not cited.

Finally, there is the decision of Judge Finlay QC, sitting as a judge of the Chancery Division, in *Gaze* v. *Holden* (1983) 266 EG 998. There a testator had by will granted an option to purchase a farm at a fair market value, 'such value to be ascertained by a valuation in the usual way'. At the date when the option was exercised the farm had been subject to a subsisting lease. The question was whether the arbitrator would be entitled to take into account the fact that the lease had been surrendered, if that should occur before the arbitrator made his determination. The learned judge said this (at p 1004):

'Mr Wood, as I understand it, was disposed to accept that the prices obtained, for example, on subsequent sales could be looked at as they furnished evidence of what the state of the market was at the date when the property fell to be valued. He instanced the case where the prices obtained on a subsequent sale might indicate whether the hypothesis that the market trend was a rising one or a falling one was well or ill-founded. But subject to that exception that subsequent events may furnish evidence of what the value was at the relevant date, his submission was that you were not entitled to look at subsequent events for the purpose of determining what weight should be given to contingencies which at the relevant date, for the purposes of the valuation, remained unresolved.'

So the point in issue here was again conceded, but the concession was the opposite to that made in the *Duvan Estates* case. The judge continued:

'I have come to the conclusion that "valuation in the usual way" means taking into account events which have happened at the date when the property falls to be valued—in this case 8 February 1980—and taking into account not only the actualities at that date but the possibilities in relation to all the circumstances; and that the valuer has, as best he can, to form his own judgment as to how these possibilities and various prospects that are inherent in the then existing situation affect the value of the property as at that date; but he is not entitled to take into account events which happened subsequently and which resolve how these various possibilities and prospects in fact turn out. To do so would be to introduce into the valuation a species of foreknowledge which would not be available to any willing buyer or willing seller entering into a contract as at the date on which the property falls to be valued.

The real exercise which the valuer is carrying out in making a valuation in accordance with the principles laid down by the testator in the first schedule of his will is the exercise of determining, applying to the problem all the skill and experience which he has, what a willing seller would be prepared to accept as a price and what a willing buyer would be prepared to pay. To endow either buyer or seller, or both of them, with foreknowledge of how events were going to turn out would make that exercise one which was entirely different in character to that which the testator had indicated as the appropriate method of valuation.

In reaching that conclusion I am fortified, on reconsidering the authorities to which I have referred,by the fact that in the very first of them (the *Bwllfa* case) it is made clear that the House of Lords was not dealing with the matter as a case of valuation but as a case of determination of compensation. I have come to the conclusion (fortified, as I say, in that way) that the *Bwllfa* principle does not apply to the valuation that has to be effected for the purposes of administering the testator's estate in relation to this option.'

It is apparent that the judge was considering the same type of problem as arose in the *Bwllfa* case and not the problem that arises in this case. He was considering whether later evidence could be taken into account in assessing, at the date of the valuation, how likely it was that some future event would occur. This is not the problem which arises here—since otherwise the case could have been decided on counsel's concession—and I say no more about it. I do not regard *Gaze's* case as having any direct bearing on the present case.

In that state of the authorities the arbitrator was, in my judgment, entitled to hold that the evidence as to rents agreed after the relevant date was admissible, and I consider that he was right to reach that conclusion. If rent of comparable premises had been agreed on the day after the relevant date, I cannot see that such an agreement would be of no relevance whatever to what the market rent was at the relevant date itself. If the lapse of time before the agreement for comparable premises becomes greater then, as the arbitrator said, the evidence will become progressively unreliable as evidence of rental values at the relevant date. The same is no doubt true of rents agreed some time *before* the relevant date; but nobody suggested to me that those should be excluded. So, too, political or economic events may have caused a change in market rents, either before or after the relevant date. All those factors must be considered by the arbitrator in assessing the weight to be attached to a rent agreed for similar premises, whether before or after the relevant date. It may happen that no rents of comparable premises that were agreed on the relevant date, or for months beforehand, can be found, but a great number very shortly thereafter. It does not seem right to me that the arbitrator should be bound to disregard them.

I recognise that different judges may take different views on this issue; but, for my part, I feel bound to say that I consider that the arbitrator's conclusion was right.

(2) Evidence of rents agreed between existing tenants and landlords

The question of law here is, according to [counsel for the applicants] whether 'market rent' means open market rent, or whether it includes a rent agreed between a landlord and a sitting tenant. He points to the words in the lease: '... having regard to rental values current at the relevant time for similar property ... let with vacant possession.' In my judgment, that is not the right question. I suspect that the market rent, to be ascertained for the demised premises, must be a rent which would be paid in the market for those premises with vacant possession. But even if that is right, it does not follow that the arbitrator must exclude from consideration any rents agreed for similar property between an existing landlord and an existing tenant. He may think it right, as one of the steps in his determination, to adjust any such rent to what it would have been for vacant possession; whether the adjustment would be up or down, or none at all, I do not know, and [counsel for the applicants] put nothing before me to suggest an answer. I can see that an adjustment may be required. But I do not consider that such evidence must as a matter of law be altogether excluded.

My reasons for reaching that conclusion are essentially the same as I have already set out in connection with the construction of clause 5 (3) under the first issue. First, what the arbitrator must have regard to is the *worth*, in terms of rent, of similar property let with vacant possession at the relevant time. In ascertaining that worth, he can have regard to the rents agreed at a different time, for similar property not let with vacant possession. But he must consider how far evidence of rents so agreed helps him to determine the answer to the actual question which is before him.

Secondly, even if such evidence were not within the category which the arbitrator is required to take into account, it is not expressly or by implication excluded from his consideration, for the reasons which I have already given. Accordingly I consider that the arbitrator was right on this issue also. Furthermore, it is not an issue upon which, as far as I am aware, different judges are likely to take different views.

(3) 'Substantially affect the rights of one or more of the parties to the arbitration agreement'

This arises under section 1 (4) of the Arbitration Act 1979. Issue (1), on the findings of the arbitrator, made a difference only to the extent that the rent would have been £19,250 per annum instead of £18,250 if he had decided it in a different sense. The arbitrator does not expressly say how different his award would have been if he had decided issue (2) otherwise than he did; but it is clear that the difference could well have been substantial.

The landlords say in their notice of motion that they are also landlords of 44 and 45 Sloane Street, where rent review is pending before the same arbitrator. That the case is of some importance to the landlords can be inferred from the fact that they appeared before me by leading counsel. But should I take their other rights and interests into account in deciding whether to grant leave to appeal in this case? [Counsel for the applicants] points out that section 1 (4) refers to 'the rights of *one or more* of the parties to the arbitration agreement'. He argues that if the rights of one party only are substantially affected the question of law qualifies under section 1 (4).

If the other two properties are taken into account, I have no means of knowing how substantially the rights of the landlord will be affected. Issue (1) makes a difference of £1000 a year for five years in relation to 43 Sloane Street. In the context of a rent of £18,250 a year that is not substantial. In the absence of any other information, I suppose that I must assume figures of a similar order for 44 and 45. The total amount in issue would then be £15,000 instead of £5000. That is bordering on substantial in the context of this case. But I do not accept that it is right to take the other two properties into account. That a point of law is of general public importance has to be considered in deciding whether the discretion should be exercised in favour of granting leave to appeal. I do not consider that the general importance of the point to one of the parties is also relevant under section 1 (4). The subsection provides that leave shall not be granted unless 'the determination of the question of law concerned could substantially affect the rights of one or more of the parties to the arbitration agreement.' This is an important protection to the party who has succeeded in the arbitration (in this case the tenants). He is not to be harried further upon insubstantial matters. I think that the subsection refers to a question the determination of which on appeal will directly affect the rights of one or more of the parties, and not one which will indirectly affect one of the parties if the determination is used as a precedent.

Conclusion

Both the issues in this case are of some general importance. The appropriate guideline is, accordingly, that provided by Lord Diplock in *Pioneer Shipping Ltd* v. *BTP Tioxide Ltd (The Nema)* [1982] AC 724 at p 743: 'Leave should not be given ... unless the judge considered that a strong *prima facie* case had been made out that the arbitrator had been wrong in his conclusion.' ... But the same wisdom applies, not merely to commercial contracts but to an agreement such as the present where landlords and tenants of premises in Sloane Street agreed that the rents payable on a review should be determined by the arbitrator.

Note: In *National Westminster Bank plc* v. *Arthur Young McClelland Moores & Co.* (see earlier page 128), Walton J refused to grant a certificate under s. 1(7) of the Arbitration Act 1979 as he considered that his decision (that the reviewed rent should be fixed disregarding the existence of the review clause in the lease) was a point of construction and not a point of law of general public importance. The Court of Appeal said it had no jurisdiction to hear an appeal from this decision (see Practice Note, *National Westminster Bank plc* v. *Arthur Young McClelland Moores & Co.* [1985] 1 WLR 1123).

But on the question of post-review comparables, compare carefully Robert Goff J's judgment below.

DUVAN ESTATES LTD v. ROSSETTE SUNSHINE SAVOURIES LTD

Queen's Bench Division   (1982) 261 EG 364

ROBERT GOFF J: Today, [counsel] on behalf of the tenants, asks for leave to appeal from this award. He does so on the basis that the arbitrator erred in two respects in his award. At one time he advanced three arguments, but one of those arguments he, in my judgment quite rightly, did not pursue. The point, in broad terms, [counsel for the tenants] says, is that in considering a valuation of this kind it is proper to have regard to the relevant facts existing as at the review date, which is 17 July 1978, and not to have regard to facts and events existing after that date. In support of that proposition he relied upon a passage at the end of the judgment of Whitford J in *Ponsford* v. *HMS Aerosols Ltd*, a case which went on appeal [1979] AC 63; (1978) 247 EG 1171; but I was provided with a transcript of Whitford J's judgment because on this point apparently the appeal was not pursued. As a general principle, I entirely accept that. Indeed, I do not understand that [counsel], on behalf of the landlords, contested the principle as such. Now [counsel for the tenants] said, first of all, that the arbitrator erred in reaching a figure of £1.25 per sq ft. He referred me to a passage in paragraph 2 of the arbitrator's reasons where, at the end of that paragraph, he said:

'It is evident to me that a rate of £1.25 per square foot has been established for the standard 6,000 square foot unit and generally applied for the rent reviews from September 1978-February 1979, and which confirms the valuation basis adopted at the July 1978 review date. On the evidence presented the rental value, as at 17 July 1978 and in accordance with the terms of the Lease but without a very restrictive user clause, would be £1.25 per square foot, i.e. £7500.'

There, said [counsel for the tenants], was the arbitrator doing the very thing which he ought not to be doing; because what he was doing was looking at figures resulting from rent reviews after the review date. [Counsel for the landlords] was able to rebut [counsel for the tenant]'s assertion to some extent on this point; but it turned out that the evidence placed by both parties before the arbitrator did in part infringe this particular principle. However, I put that on one side. I have to ask myself the simple question: did the arbitrator err in law having regard to these figures in respect of reviews made between September 1978 and February 1979? In considering that question, I have to consider what the arbitrator was doing in the light of the evidence before him and also consider the way he expressed his reasons in his award.

It appears that what happened was this. The landlords called evidence relating to premises let on this particular estate. They called evidence of a particular arbitrator's award in respect of a review as at a review date in July 1978. The figure which that particular award produced was indeed the figure of £1.25 per sq ft. They also produced a schedule showing other figures (I think largely settlements) which had been fixed in respect of reviews of rent in the succeeding nine months or so after that date. This showed a consistent picture of £1.25 per sq ft except in the case of one set of premises which was considerably smaller in size and, not surprisingly, the figure was somewhat larger, namely, £1.50 per sq ft.

The tenants, on the other hand, called evidence of premises not on this particular estate, but I assume not far away, where the premises were put on the market in July 1978 but as to which agreement was not reached on the rent until December 1978. In the light of that evidence the arbitrator was plainly entitled to hold, as indeed he did hold, that the evidence as at July 1978 pointed to a rental of £1.25. But he went on to say that that was, in effect, the evidence before him of the particular letting as at July 1978, but so as to put beyond doubt any question as to his conclusion he recorded the fact that he was comforted to find that subsequent lettings in the succeeding few months confirmed that figure. I do not think that the arbitrator was relying upon this latter evidence to reach his conclusion. He was simply saying: 'I am thankful to see this evidence does not cause me to depart from the conclusion which I have formed on the basis of the relevant evidence, as at the review date.' In those circumstances I do not think the arbitrator, although one quite understands why he referred to this particular schedule which the landlord placed before him, was basing his conclusion upon evidence other than evidence as to the position as at the review date. In those circumstances, I do not think, on a fair reading of the reasons of the award, that the arbitrator was infringing the principle which both parties accept should be applicable. Therefore, I reject [counsel for the tenants'] first submission.

15.2 The arbitrator's power to make an interim award

The arbitration agreement should be construed as a whole, and if that leads to the conclusion on the true construction of the *express* terms of the agreement that it did not intend to provide for the inclusion of the right to make an interim award then there is no such power; see section 14 of the Arbitration Act 1950.

TOWN CENTRE SECURITIES LTD v. WM MORRISON SUPERMARKETS LTD

Queen's Bench Division   (1982) 263 EG 435

MICHAEL TURNER QC (sitting as a deputy High Court judge): The arbitration agreement was contained in a clause of an underlease dated 10 April 1972 whereby the plaintiffs (hereafter called the landlords) subdemised premises known as unit 43, The Merrion Centre, Leeds, to the defendants (hereafter called the tenants) for a term of 42 years from 10 April 1972. So far as material the lease provided for a peppercorn rent until 9 October 1972 and thereafter a yearly rent of £77,402.48 and any increased rent as thereinafter provided. The underlease also provided for rent reviews to take place at intervals, the first of which was after the expiration of the sixth year and before the expiration of the seventh year of the term, provided that the appropriate notice was served. If, after service of such a notice, no agreement was reached in regard to the rent proposed by the landlords, the underlease made provision for the assessment of the amount of the rent to be determined by arbitration. Clause 6 (c) (ii) of the underlease provided:

> 'Unless the market rent has been agreed or determined before the expiration of the Notice referred to in subclause (a) hereof the existing rent then payable shall continue to be payable until the market rent has been agreed or determined and the amount of any difference between the existing rent and the market rent calculated from the expiration of the said Notice shall be added to the next instalment of rent due after the market rent has been agreed or determined.'

The final point to call for consideration is whether or not the arbitrator had any discretion or power to make an interim award. The arbitration agreement does not expressly confer any such power. Section 14 of the Arbitration Act 1950 reads as follows:

> 'Unless a contrary intention is expressed therein, every arbitration agreement shall, where such a provision is applicable to the reference, be deemed to contain a provision that the arbitrator or umpire may, if he thinks fit, make an interim award, and any reference in this Part of this Act to an award includes a reference to an interim award.'

[Counsel for landlord]'s primary submission was that the word 'expressed' in this section meant just that, and that it was not enough that the proper construction of the arbitration agreement should lead to that result unless it expressly so stated. I am quite unable to accept this submission. In its context the section requires that the arbitration agreement should be construed as a whole, and if that leads to the conclusion that it did not intend to provide for the inclusion of the right to make an interim award then there is no such power.
[Counsel for the tenant] drew attention to the phrase 'where such a provision is applicable to the reference', and submitted that under the arbitration agreement embodied in clause 6 (c) (ii) of the underlease the arbitrator's sole function was to

determine the market rent for the premises. That power expressly did not empower him to determine anything but the market rent, so that any determination other than that of the market rent would constitute an assumption of powers not contained in the agreement. Moreover, as can be seen, this clause in the underlease provides machinery for what is to happen in regard to the back payment of the difference between the rent provided for by the underlease and the market rent when it has been determined or agreed. Although not decisive of the point, there are obvious difficulties in the way of applying this machinery, first, to an interim award and, subsequently, to a final award. In my judgment the language of clause 6 (c) (ii) points strongly to the conclusion that the arbitrator has, and is intended to have only, the power to determine what is the market rent once and for all, and that the suggested provision that the arbitrator has any power to make an interim award is inconsistent with the language of this clause.

In coming to this conclusion I have regard to the judgment of Lord Denning MR in *Fidelitas Shipping Co. Ltd* v. *V/O Exportchleb* [1966] QB 630 at p 638 E, where he said:

'A special case can now be stated with respect to an interim award, just as with a final award: see sections 7 (4) and 9 (2) of the Arbitration Act, 1934, now replaced by sections 14 and 21 (2) of the Arbitration Act, 1950. Nowhere is an "interim award" defined. But it seems to me that an interim award may be of two kinds. It may be an interim order made pending the final determination of the case; such as an award that an instalment under a building contract be paid pending final determination of the amount due. Or it may be an interim decision given on a particular issue or issues between the parties, pending final determination of the whole case; such as a decision that a contract was concluded, but leaving over the question of damages. Such an award is not a final award because the arbitrator has not exhausted his duties. It is, however, an award because it is an order or decision on an issue calling for determination. It is, therefore, an interim award: and it can be stated in the form of a special case for the decision of the High Court.'

and also to the judgment of Goff J in *SL Sethia Liners Ltd* v. *Naviagro Maritime Corporation* [1981] 1 Lloyd's Rep 18 at 25, col 2, where the learned judge said:

'There are however two aspects of this power to which I must refer.
  'First, since the jurisdiction of an arbitrator is a jurisdiction to decide disputes, it follows that the power to make an award is a power to decide matters in dispute between the parties. An award, interim or final, can only be an award in respect of matters referred to the arbitrators for decision. It follows, therefore, that (in the absence of some special agreement between the parties) a submission of disputes to arbitration will not generally give the arbitrators the power to order that one party shall pay a sum to the other, unless the arbitrators decide that that sum is due and owing. Arbitrators can decide, by way of interim award, that a minimum sum is payable by one party to the other, if they decide that that sum at least is due and owing; but they cannot generally order that one party should pay a minimum to another on account of claims, simply because on a rough look at the case it looks as though such a sum at least will prove to be payable, without actually deciding that that sum is due and owing. So to order would result in a change in the parties' respective economic positions, without deciding any matter in dispute; generally speaking, arbitrators have no power to order such a change. The second point is this. An interim award can relate to any issue in the matters in dispute referred to the arbitrators; it may relate to an issue affecting the whole claim (eg the issue of liability, reserving the issue of quantum for a final award), or may relate to a part only of the claims or cross-claims submitted to them for decision. It follows that arbitrators, when making an interim award, must specify the issue, or the claim or part of a claim, which is the subject matter of the interim award.

15.3 Appealing against an arbitration award of rent; setting the award aside

Section 1 of the Arbitration Act 1979 provides that leave to appeal against an award shall not be granted by the court unless the determination of the question of law concerned could substantially affect the rights of one or more of the parties to the arbitration agreement. Leave should not be given unless the judge considers that a strong *prima facie* case has been made out that the arbitrator has been wrong in his conclusion. See, *Segama N.V.* v. *Penny Le Roy Ltd* earlier page 298 and later, page 318. An arbitration may be set aside if the arbitrator has relied on research which he has carried out without the parties' knowledge, see *Top Shop Estates Ltd* v. *C. Danino* and *Top Shop Estates Ltd* v. *Tandy Ltd and Another*, page 275 earlier, in 14.1 (c).

15.3 (a)   Fraud, mistake or miscarriage and a wrong method of valuation: errors on the face of the record

The valuation can be impeached not only for fraud, but also on the grounds of mistake or miscarriage. Although the court is not a valuer, it can say whether a method of valuation is wrong, and where the arbitrator adopts the wrong method of valuation which is not in accordance with the terms of the lease, the court may hold there is an error on the face of the record and remit the award to the arbitrator.

ESTATES PROJECTS LTD v. GREENWICH LONDON BOROUGH

Queen's Bench Division   (1979) 251 EG 851

FORBES J: There are only three provisions in the lease that I think are relevant. The first is the length of the term, for 53 years from 25 December 1972; the second is the *reddendum*—the rent should be for the first five years of the said term a rent of £5500 per annum; and for the successive periods of five years and a final period of three years of the said term, the review periods, the rent to be determined in accordance with the provisions contained in clause 2 (1) (b).

Turning to 2 (1) (b):

'The rent payable during the continuance of the review periods shall be the open market value of the demised premises at the appropriate review dates but in any event during the first review period not less than £5500 per annum and in each of the subsequent review periods not less than the rent which shall have been payable during the immediately preceding review period AND it is hereby agreed that the following definition and provisions shall apply:

(i) The expression open market rental value means the rental value of the demised premises in the open market which might reasonably be payable between a willing landlord and a willing tenant on a lease for a term of years equivalent in length to the residue unexpired at the appropriate review dates of the term of years hereby granted with vacant possession at the commencement of the term ... and there being disregarded any effect on rent of all work carried out by the council in fitting out the demised premises suitable for use as offices and (if applicable) those matters set out in paragraphs (a) (b) and (c) of subsection (1) of section 34 of the Landlord and Tenant Act 1954 and there being disregarded (so far as may be permitted by law) all restrictions whatsoever relating to rent or security of tenure contained in any statute or order rules and regulations thereunder and any directions thereby given relating to any method of

determination of rent such lease being on the same terms and conditions (other than as to the amount of rent and length of term) as this present demise without the payment of any fine or premium.
and:

(iii) The open market rental value shall be determined in manner following that is to say it shall be such annual sum as shall be:

(a) Specified in a notice in writing signed by or on behalf of the landlord and posted by recorded delivery post in a pre-paid envelope addressed to the tenant at its registered office at any time before the beginning of a clear period of two quarters (but not greater than four quarters) of a year immediately preceding the appropriate review date

(b) Agreed between the parties before the expiration of three months immediately after the date of receipt by the tenant of such notice as aforesaid in substitution for the sum specified in the landlord's notice under (a) above or

(c) Determined at the election of the tenant (to be made by counter notice in writing served by the tenant upon the landlord not later than the expiration of the said three months) by an independent surveyor appointed for that purpose by the parties jointly in writing or upon their failure to agree upon such appointment within one month immediately after the date of service of the said counter notice then by an independent surveyor appointed for that purpose on the application of either party alone to the President for the time being of the Royal Institution of Chartered Surveyors and in either case in accordance with the provisions of the Arbitration Act 1950.

And there is one other subclause I should read, which is subclause (16) of clause 2, and it is in these terms. The tenant covenants: 'Not to use the demised premises or any part thereof otherwise than as offices or as to the ground floor as offices or shops.'

There was, in fact, no provision requiring the tenant to carry out the works referred to.

The premises are a terrace of four elderly properties, originally, no doubt, houses but, at the time of the lease, shops with upper parts. It appears that all the improvement works, or the overwhelming proportion of them, were required to bring the upper parts of the premises into a state which would comply with the provisions of the Offices, Shops and Railway Premises Act 1963, and the appropriate fire regulations, and thus permit their use as offices. At the first review the parties could not agree about the rent and an arbitrator was appointed under the terms of the rent review clause. The landlord is dissatisfied with his award and therefore applies to set it aside.

I shall deal at once with one of the main points made by [counsel] for the tenant. He says, quite rightly, that an arbitrator's award is normally to be regarded as final and cannot be set aside except for misconduct or where the award is bad on its face. But an award is bad on its face if the arbitrator has misconstrued or misinterpreted the contract, and that is the landlord's argument in this case. In any case there is a wider discretion to remit, rather than set aside, if that is the appropriate course to adopt.

This case began at a time at which I was considering a reserved judgment in another rent review case, *GREA Real Property Investments Ltd* v. *Williams* [(1979) 250 EG 651]. In view of some similarities both in the facts and in the arguments addressed to me in that case and this one, I invited counsel in this case to return after considering anything I had said in the *GREA* case to address me with any further argument they might deem appropriate, and they have both done so.

Before me the contentions have now, I think, been reduced to these: [Counsel] says, for the applicants, the arbitrator's approach does not properly reflect the intention of the parties. [Counsel for the applicants] maintains that the division into ground and upper floors was not warranted. Now here I disagree with [counsel for the applicants] and agree with the arbitrator. The lease clearly, in my view, envisages the possibility of the user of the premises as ground-floor shops and upper-floor offices, and in arriving at an open market value, if there is a difference between the value of the premises for use for one purpose or for another, it is obviously right to take the higher value in those circumstances because that is what a market is about. As I say, I accept the approach on this of the arbitrator. I think he was clearly entitled to look at the rental value of the ground floor for use as a shop, or shops, and I do not think the fact that that, as it were, divides the premises matters, because it is a division in accordance, it seems to me, with the user clause in the lease; precisely the way in which the arbitrator approaches it.

Where there are premises properly comparable with the subject premises in an unimproved state, it seems to me, as I said in the *GREA* case, that it is sensible to use such comparables to arrive directly at a rent for the premises which disregards the effect on rent of improvements; it does not seem to me that it is necessary to start off by finding what is the improved rent and then deducting something to arrive at the unimproved rent if you have unimpeachable comparables which you can use to arrive at the unimproved rent direct. Clearly, the arbitrator in this case thought that the comparables put forward by Mr Jones, the tenant's valuer, were satisfactory, and he accepted them; and I think he was entitled to do so. But the same approach cannot be adopted for the upper floors, because, as I understand it, there are no directly comparable or analogous cases available. None, that is, of upper parts in use as offices without improvements of this kind. Of course, the tenant's valuer maintained that without the improvements the upper floors could not be used as offices at all, because it would have been illegal to do so, and it was for that reason that he only gave them a nominal value, and, as I have indicated, the only permissible use for these floors under the lease was as offices. In the absence of comparables for the upper floors as offices the arbitrator resorted to a devaluation of the capital cost, adjusted to take account of inflation, in order to arrive at a rental equivalent.

As I sought to explain in the *GREA* case, I do not think this method is necessarily a valid one. What must be observed is the intention of the parties, and that, in cases such as this, is primarily twofold. First, the parties realise that in an inflationary period the rent at the beginning of the lease would almost certainly not represent a fair rent as between the parties at the end. They therefore make an estimate at the beginning of the lease for a short period only and put in review clauses to take care of the incidence of inflation thereafter; the, rejected, alternative would be to seek to find some figure which would be fair between the parties over the entire length of the lease—in this case 53 years—a very considerable distance to peer into the future. And secondly, I think the parties realise that because the tenant is paying for works which will eventually inure to the benefit of the landlord, it is only fair that the landlord, during the currency of the lease, should not get the benefit, in rental terms, of those works and the tenant should. I emphasise that that is because the works, as both parties would know full well, would in the end inure to the benefit of the landlord. To adopt any capital revaluation method to arrive at a rental value in those circumstances seems to me to be probably not in accordance with those intentions in at least two respects. First, it is the value of the tenant's works, in rental terms, which has to be eliminated and cost is not necessarily an index of value, though, of course, it may sometimes be so. Certainly, the historic cost of building improvements brought up to date by a kind of percentage increase, to take account of the inflation of cost, does not necessarily amount to the same thing as the value of the improvement in an inflationary period. And secondly, there is involved the assumption that the cost of the improvements will be incurred by the tenant at each review date, whereas the intention of the parties was that the improvements, being already done, the landlord should not benefit from their rental value during the whole of the lease although, of course, the value of them would fall into his pocket, as it were, at the determination of the lease. Parenthetically, my view is that this fact precludes, in these cases, the assumption of a sinking fund.

Now this court is not a valuer. All I can do is to say whether there is an error on the face of the award, and there will be such an error if a method of valuation is adopted which clearly does not follow the intention of the parties. I can say, therefore, whether a method of valuation is wrong, but not necessarily what method of valuation is right. It may be that a method of valuation is put forward which stands the test of the intention of the parties; but if it is not, the court cannot substitute its own views about valuation methods for those of the experts in this field. All the court can say is, 'No. These methods do not properly reflect the intention of the parties. [Counsel for the landlord] has, however, suggested that the method put forward by the landlords in the *GREA* case may well be the right method of valuation; it is worth, perhaps, just looking at that for a moment. That was to take the rent agreed at the time of the demise as representing the assessment by the parties of what was in truth the value of the premises disregarding the effect on rent of the tenant's improvements. That would, of course, have been the value at the time of the demise. To find the amount of the discount, which represents the tenant's improvements in rental terms, you must then find the value of the premises as at the time of the demise on the basis that the improvements had been carried out. Those two figures, if you can find them, will provide, so the argument runs, an indication of the proportion of the whole improved rent which is properly the landlord's share on the one hand and the tenant's on the other. So far, it seems to me that that is admirably logical and in many cases may be comparatively easy to assess. The argument then goes on: 'You can then apply the proportion so found in the agreed improved rent at the review date.'

Now, as I indicated in the *GREA* case, this method has considerable attraction, but I had at that stage some doubt about the validity of assuming that the proportion was always constant; a doubt which I expressed, in that judgment, in this way (if I may quote a passage):

'While the calculation for 1969 [that was the time of the demise] would seem to rest on a firm base in relation both to the intention of the parties and to the dictates of commonsense, I am not so sure about the 1976 calculation [that was the first review date]. This assumes that the proportion which the value of the tenant's works bears to the whole will remain constant whatever happens. It may be, however, that inflation has had, or would have in the future, different effects on site values, major construction works and works of improvement such as the tenant's here. These are the three components which make up the total value of the building [(1979) 250 EG at p 655].

[Counsel for the applicants] says that the doubt I had in that case is unnecessary because once the improvements are completed they become part of the realty so that there is no necessity to divide the value of the premises into its component parts. I find that an attractive argument, but again, as in the *GREA* case, I have no valuation evidence upon that point and although such a method may have been adumbrated by the landlord before the arbitrator, it was certainly not pursued in any depth.

Now, I put it in that way because, as I sought to say in the *GREA* case, that method of valuation in cases such as this seems to me to have a great many attractions. I am not sure that the assumption that the proportion always remains constant is necessarily valid in every circumstance and before being satisfied about that one will, it seems to me, require some valuation evidence on that point. It may be that my doubts about it are fanciful and that valuers could indicate that one need not bother one's head about that sort of thing. It may be, on the other hand, that evidence would show that, in fact, there are differences. I do not know, and as I have indicated, this court, not being a valuer, cannot supply its own view about these matters for expert valuation evidence.

For the reasons I have given I think that while the method adopted by the arbitrator in valuing the ground floors can be seen as validly carrying out the intention of the parties, I do not think the valuation adopted for the upper floors accords with that intention. That, if I am right, is a misconstruction of the provisions of the lease and, therefore, an error on the face of the award and, as such, the court has a discretion to set the award aside. However, and I have not, I think, heard argument from counsel on this, I see no reason to set the award aside and I would rather remit it to the arbitrator, who is fully conversant with this matter, which is of some complexity, and I think that that would be the best way of dealing with it. The parties would then be given an opportunity of leading further evidence on the question of the proper valuation method for the upper floors and of adducing any further argument that was desirable. I can see no objection to that taking place before the arbitrator who signed this award. It may be, of course, that he does not want to take it up again, but that is a different matter.

After some discussion with counsel on both sides the judge made an order that the award should be remitted to the arbitrator for reconsideration in the light of his lordship's judgment. It was also ordered that the applicants should have their costs in any event.

15.3 (b)   Technical misconduct and procedural mishaps: sense of grievance of one party

Though an arbitrator is not even guilty of technical misconduct and it is unlikely that his award has been influenced, where there has been a procedural mishap or error which would justify one party to the award in feeling a sense of prejudice, the award should be remitted to the arbitrator for his further consideration.

SHIELD PROPERTIES AND INVESTMENTS LTD v. ANGLO-OVERSEAS TRANSPORT CO. LTD

Commercial Court of the Queen's Bench   (1985) 273 EG 69

Following the processes required under a rent review clause of commercial premises, an arbitration took place. The tenants were dissatisfied with the award and sought to have it set aside under sections 22 and 23 of the Arbitration Act 1950, on the grounds (1) that the arbitrator had wrongly admitted in evidence details of discussions which were allegedly 'without prejudice'; (2) that he had wrongly admitted hearsay evidence in the form of a list of unverified comparables which were provided by the landlord; (3) there had been a wrongful failure by the arbitrator to disclose to the tenants a letter written to the arbitrator on behalf of the landlords, where the landlords offered to sent written confirmation of that evidence.

Held:
(1) The tenants had lost the right to complain of the arbitrator's hearing of the allegedly 'without prejudice' discussions, because they had merely protested and then allowed the arbitration to continue;
(2) Although the arbitrator's receipt of an offer of evidence from one party, which in the event he neither took up (because he found them little help), nor communicated to the other party, could not be described as even 'technical misconduct', it did amount to a procedural irregularity, in that he should have copied the landlord's letter and sent it to the tenants. Even in the absence of misconduct, the court had to consider whether there had been any mishap or misunderstanding or error in procedure in the course of the arbitration which could lead, or might have

led to an unjust result, which included the possibility that the same result had been achieved but nevertheless one party had a justified sense that he might have been prejudiced by the procedural course of the arbitration. Accordingly, although the arbitrator had apparently acted with scrupulous regard for the interests of each party and had paid very little attention to the landlord's comparables, the case would, under the circumstances, be remitted to the arbitrator for reconsideration and such further action as he considered appropriate. (The tenants were awarded half the costs of the hearing.)

BINGHAM J: Having been appointed, he issued written directions for the conduct of the arbitration following a meeting with the surveyors for the two parties on 24 February 1983. In the course of those directions, in accordance with the parties' wish, he directed that the matter should be dealt with by way of written submissions rather than an oral hearing although he reserved the right to call for a hearing if he considered it necessary. He requested the parties by a specified date to agree facts relating to the premises and to list matters on which they were unable to agree. He undertook to make a preliminary inspection of the premises having received the agreed statement of facts. Then, in para 4, he directed as follows:

'I request the parties to deliver to me at 4.00 pm on 31 March 1983 their submissions in duplicate and these will be exchanged before me a that time. I would remind both parties that any "without prejudice" negotiations or offers, whether oral or written, should not be referred to in any way in the submissions. Details of any comparable transactions should whenever possible be agreed by the parties. Those in which the parties were not personally involved should be supported by written confirmation from agents who were concerned.'

That was para 4. He then made provision for cross-representations to be delivered by each party, if they wished, for further inspection and for the giving of a reasoned award which the parties had requested.

Following those directions both parties submitted their representations. The tenants submitted a case, which runs from p 76 to p 116 of the bundle of documents helpfully prepared for this hearing, and in the upshot the tenants contended for a total rental of £97,500. It is to be noted that they submitted a list of comparable transactions on which they relied to support their assessment and they enclosed confirmatory letters from the agents who had direct knowledge of those transactions. That was clearly in accordance with the arbitrator's direction in para 4. Furthermore, it is to be noted that the tenants said nothing at all of anything that had passed between them and the landlords in the course of any negotiations or discussion. The landlords also submitted representations, which appear at p 24 of the bundle before me, and they, more modestly in this document, contended for a total net rental of £320,000, that figure appearing on p 35.

There are two matters to be noted in the course of this submission. The first is that the landlords do refer to discussions with the tenants. On p 25, in the course of para 2.1, they say:

'Messrs D J Freeman & Co., Solicitors to Shield Properties Investments Ltd, served notice on the undertenant on 28 May 1982 quoting a new rent of £400,000 per annum, with effect from 25 December 1982.'

This is slightly inaccurate in that the notice was not by D J Freeman & Co. and was in the sum of £475,000 and not £400,000. Para 2.1 continues:

'In response, Mr Richards has indicated that he would only be prepared to settle at a figure equating to about half of the quoted rent and, consequently, the differences were too great to reach agreement and the matter is to be determined by arbitration.'

It is also apparent from the submissions that the landlord enclosed a list of comparables but did not enclose any substantiation of those comparable transactions from the agents who had personally dealt with them, in accordance with the directions of the arbitrator. Instead the landlords did send a covering letter to the arbitrator, dated 30 March 1983, in which, in the third paragraph, they said: 'I, therefore, now attach our proof of evidence referring to the case

'together with our valuation and would confirm that with regard to all comparables, we have obtained written confirmation from representatives of the parties involved and most of the information has been provided on a confidential basis for the purpose only of this arbitration. We will, of course, let you have copies of this correspondence should you so require.'

When the tenants saw the reference to the negotiations with the landlords, they complained, in para 2.1 of their counter-submission which appears on p 171 of the bundle. Mr Richards there said, on behalf of the tenants:

'I am surprised, especially in the light of your specific written instructions of 25 February 1983, para 4, that Mr Toye has referred to our previous discussions. These discussions with Mr Toye prior to arbitration were on a strictly without prejudice basis and in order to correct any impression created in Mr Toye's submission, I indicated that I would only be able to recommend my clients to consider a figure substantially less than half the quoted rent. I stated that all discussions were strictly without prejudice, because given the rent quoted in the rent notice of £475,000, it was evident from the outset that arbitration was probable.'

It is to be noted that, although the counter-submission contained that paragraph, the tenants did not seek to halt the proceedings; they did not seek any investigation or decision by the arbitrator as to whether the discussions had been without prejudice; they did not seek any undertaking that the matter would be entirely disregarded, and that that reference would be ignored; and they did not make any move whatever to challenge the continuance of the arbitration or to change the arbitrator. Subject to that protest they allowed the matter to proceed. The tenants also protested about the landlords' conduct in respect of the comparable transactions on which they relied. In para 12 of their counter-submission, on p 194, Mr Richards, on behalf of the tenants, said this:

'I refer to your written directions to the parties of 25 February 1983, and particularly to direction 4. From the copy of Mr Toye's submission passed to me and subsequent enquiries regarding his comparables, it would appear that Mr Toye was neither personally involved in the transactions to which he refers, nor has he provided supporting written confirmation from the agents who were concerned. Strictly without prejudice to the above and despite inadequate information being provided in order to respond fully to Mr Toye's comparables, I wish to make the following observations:'

He then details in turn the comments which he makes on each of the comparable transactions on which the landlords had relied.

Mr Richards, on behalf of the tenants, did not make reference to Mr Toye's letter of 30 March 1983, for the very good reason that he had not had a copy of that letter and did not know of its existence. He says, in his third affidavit filed in support of this application, in para 2, that had he seen the letter he would have asked for production of the written evidence which Mr Toye told the arbitrator that he had. He continues:

'Had I seen that evidence, it may well be—in the circumstances, it would not be proper for me to put it higher than that—that I would have wished to make points in respect of the copies of the correspondence Mr Toye had, in my evidence in reply.'

It seems to me that there is no reason whatever to doubt what he says there and that had he known that such documents existed and were being proffered to the arbitrator he would almost certainly have asked for the information to be produced to him. He did not do so, as I say, because he did not know of the letter. It is fair also to point out that the arbitrator himself did not ask the landlords for their supporting correspondence.

On 4 March 1983 the arbitrator made his award and gave reasons for the conclusion to which he had come. He fixed the rent at a total figure of £251,000 and reached that figure by treating the office and storage space separately and taking, for the office space, a basic rent per sq ft to which he added a percentage uplift to reflect the tenant's limited repairing liability and a further uplift to reflect the value of the long period without a rent review. So far as the non-office space was concerned he took two rates and added an addition to reflect the limited repairing liaiblity. So far as the comparable transactions are concerned he said, in 2 (i) of his reasons: 'I did not find the comparables of much help as the transactions cited related mostly to small areas of space or to properties too remote from New Street.'

Counsel now applies that the award should be set aside and the arbitrator removed, alternatively that the award should be remitted on the grounds of misconduct on three grounds. First, that there was a wrongful reception by the arbitrator of evidence of without prejudice discussions. Second, on the grounds that there was improper admission of hearsay evidence from the landlords on the subject of comparables and, third, on the basis that there was a wrongful failure by the arbitrator to disclose to the tenants the letter of 30 March 1983.

So far as the without prejudice point is concerned, there is a challenge on the affidavit evidence before me as to whether the discussions which took place between the landlords and the tenants were conducted on a without prejudice basis or not. That is an issue which I quite clearly cannot resolve on a conflict of affidavit evidence and I approach the question on the basis that, whether or not anything was expressly said, these discussions may very well have been on a without prejudice basis. I have no doubt that Mr Richards genuinely believes that they were and I have no reason whatever to doubt that Mr Toye genuinely believed that they were not. But I think it only right and fair to proceed on the basis that Mr Richards may be right and Mr Toye wrong.

That being so, as it seems to me, the tenants had a clear option as to how they proceeded. They could, as I have indicated, have sought a ruling from the arbitrator as to whether the material was covered by privilege or not. They could have sought to halt the proceedings. They could have sought a change of arbitrator. They could have sought a clear understanding on the record that all that evidence would be entirely ignored. In fact, as I have indicated, they adopted none of those courses. Mr Richards made the protest which I have read but, subject to that, proceeded with the arbitration.

It seems to me that the situation was clearly one in which the tenants had an election. Either they made a bold and unequivocal protest and raised the matter, either seeking a determination or seeking to halt the proceedings entirely on the basis that the arbitrator could no longer fairly dispose of the matter or they could allow the matter to continue. It seems to me plain on the information before me that they adopted that latter course and I bear in mind that even if the material was brought to his attention, and should not have been, he had a discretion to continue if satisfied that no injustice would be done by doing so. Had the matter been explored I have no doubt that he would have indicated that he paid no attention to that evidence at all and I very strongly suspect that the matter would have proceeded on that understanding. But, be that as it may, it was, I think, up to the tenants to make their position plain, to make a stand if they wished to insist on this point and not to allow the arbitration to proceed, reserving their right to challenge the result on this ground if it proved to be unattractive to them. Accordingly, as it seems to me, this ground of challenge fails.

When I turn to the question of the comparables it seems plain that there was, as indeed [counsel] for the landlords has been constrained to acknowledge, an irregularity in the way that this matter was handled. The arbitrator's direction was that any transaction relied upon should be vouched in effect by some person having first-hand knowledge. The landlords did not adopt that procedure, at any rate to the extent that they did not submit the verification by the agents. But the tenants were not entirely disabled from dealing with these transactions and in fact to some extent did so. It is argued by [counsel for the tenants] that the two transactions to which it appears that the arbitrator may have paid some attention are nos 7 and 11, one relating to Cutlers Gardens and the other relating to another property in New Street. The tenants did make submissions on those properties. They made representations on the Cutlers Gardens development, although making the point, quite clearly and strongly, that certain of the factual material relevant to the letting was not available and could not be considered in the absence of direct evidence. The same point is made in respect of the New Street property, although, again, Mr Richards did make a comment on various aspects relating to it.

What then, in the upshot, is the proper approach to these irregular features of this hearing? Mr Collier submits that the procedure was irregular both because the agreed procedure for handling the evidence was not adhered to and also because the letter written by the landlords to the arbitrator was not copied by him. In the event, as I have indicated, the arbitrator did not pursue the offer made to him by the landlords and did not call for that correspondence. In theory there may be two reasons for his failing to do so. One, which I have no doubt the landlords infer was the true reason, was that he regarded the comparable transactions as giving him so little assistance as to make further inquiry unnecessary and unhelpful. There is, however, another possible reason, which is no doubt the one which the tenants would incline to, that the arbitrator felt that if a respected surveyor such as Mr Toye said that he had confirmation of what he was saying in his submission then that could be relied upon.

The question which I have immediately to consider is whether this failure by the arbitrator both to follow the agreed procedure and to copy the letter to the tenants is one that can, within the limits of previous authority as to its meaning, be characterised as misconduct. There is, of course, no doubt about the rule that natural justice must be observed in the conduct of arbitrations and I say, in parenthesis, that that rule is no less cardinal in a case where lawyers are not involved, in a rather more informal arbitration run between surveyors; indeed it may very well be that the need for strict adherence to the customary safeguards is more necessary where the eagle eye of lawyers on each side is absent. It is further, of course, quite clear that arbitrators must not communicate with one party unknown to the other, must not receive evidence from one party unknown to the other and must not pay attention to evidence from one party which the other party has not had the opportunity to meet.

However, in my judgment, the facts of the present case fall into a slightly different category. The arbitrator did not in any real sense receive evidence, he merely received an offer from one party of evidence which, in the event, he did not take up and did not communicate to the other party. Even allowing for the fact that misconduct denotes no more than procedural irregularity, none the less it seems to me that it would be stretching even the watered down interpretation of that language to describe what happened here as misconduct because, of course, it is an inescapable fact that misconduct, however technical, does reflect on the way in which an arbitrator has conducted an arbitration. None the less that does not on current authority conclude the matter and it is necessary to consider whether, even in the absence of misconduct, there has been any mishap or misunderstanding or error in procedure in the course of this arbitration which could lead, or might have led, to an unjust result. By an unjust result, of course, one must include the possibility that the same result has been achieved as would have been achieved but none the less in circumstances in which one party has a justified sense that he may have been prejudiced by the procedural course which the arbitration took.

This seems to me such a case. As I have indicated I do not think that it would be in any way appropriate to stigmatise the conduct of this arbitrator as misconduct. I have no doubt that he acted throughout with a scrupulous regard for the interests of each party and his award strongly suggests to me that he set out to do the very best he could to achieve the correct rental for these premises. It also seems likely to me that he paid very little attention to any of the comparable transactions to which the landlords drew his attention. None the less, the fact is that a letter was sent which the tenants never saw and one can very well understand the tenants' feeling that it may have been read by the arbitrator as giving some confirmation to the comparables which they had advanced and may even perhaps subconsciously have affected the arbitrator's mind. I have no doubt that when the matter is drawn to his attention he will be able to approach the matter on an entirely scrupulous basis, putting out of his mind anything which should properly not be within it. Whether he orders that the material proffered by Mr Toye be produced to him and copied by the other party or whether he approaches the matter on the basis of ignoring completely the comparable transactions for which no adequate verification has been produced is, I think, a matter very much for his judgment in the light of any representations made by one party or the other. His overall obligation is to be scrupulously fair in dealing with this matter and no suggestion has been made that anything in his conduct disables him from acting in that way.

Accordingly, and bearing in mind the principles laid down in a number of cases, most notably perhaps *The Aros* [1978] 1 Lloyd's Rep 456, this seems to me a case in which there has been a procedural mishap and in which, in all the circumstances, it would be right that the matter should be remitted to the arbitrator for his further consideration having regard to the terms in which I have given judgment.

I make it clear, although I hope it is entirely clear already, that I am not making a finding of misconduct against him and I am certainly not, as indeed the tenants themselves are not, criticising in any way his fairness of objectivity or personal conduct in this matter.

15.4 Appeals from points of law arising in rent review arbitrations

Even though a point of general public importance may arise during arbitration, if the judge in the High Court considers the arbitrator has decided the issue correctly and/or that no *prima facie* case has been made out that the arbitrator was wrong, or there is no issue which could substantially affect the rights of one or more of the parties, leave to appeal against the awards will be refused under section 1 of the Arbitration Act 1979.

SEGAMA N.V. v. PENNY LE ROY LTD

Commercial Court (1984) 269 EG 322

(For facts and further extracts see earlier at page 298.)
The landlords claimed the right to appeal against Staughton J's High Court decision on points of law arising in the arbitration. These were whether post review comparables could be taken into account when fixing a reviewed rent and whether,

though the basis for the revised rent was to be that the premises were let with vacant possession, the arbitrator did not have to exclude evidence of rents fixed for similar properties where there was an existing landlord and an existing tenant. The question of whether the judge should exercise his discretion and grant leave to appeal was argued, the landlord contending that there should be a right to appeal against the arbitrator's award and that the judge should exercise his discretion and grant leave on the grounds: (i) that the issues substantially affected the rights of one of the parties, under section 1 (4) of the Arbitration Act 1979, in that the landlord owned several other similar properties which were occupied by different tenants, on which similar points would be decided by the same arbitrator; (ii) that the other rents to be fixed on the other properties by the same arbitrator should be taken into account in deciding whether there was an issue which substantially affected the rights of one or more of the parties; and (iii) that a point of law of general importance to the landlord, who was one of the parties, should be considered by the judge when exercising his discretion in deciding whether or not leave to appeal should be granted from the arbitrator's award.

Held: Leave to appeal was refused. The landlord's other properties should not be taken into account. The general importance of a point of law to one party was not relevant under section 1 (4) of the Arbitration Act 1979.

STAUGHTON J: *'Substantially affect the rights of one or more of the parties to the arbitration agreement'*

This arises under section 1 (4) of the Arbitration Act 1979. Issue (1), on the findings of the arbitrator, made a difference only to the extent that the rent would have been £19,250 per annum instead of £18,250 if he had decided it in a different sense. The arbitrator does not expressly say how different his award would have been if he had decided issue (2) otherwise than he did; but it is clear that the difference could well have been substantial.

The landlords say in their notice of motion that they are also landlords of 44 and 45 Sloane Street, where rent review is pending before the same arbitrator. That the case is of some importance to the landlords can be inferred from the fact that they appeared before me by leading counsel. But should I take their other rights and interests into account in deciding whether to grant leave to appeal in this case? [Counsel for the landlord] points out that section 1 (4) refers to 'the rights of *one or more* of the parties to the arbitration agreement'. He argues that if the rights of one party only are substantially affected, the question of law qualifies under section 1 (4).

If the other two properties are taken into account, I have no means of knowing how substantially the rights of the landlord will be affected. Issue (1) makes a difference of £1000 a year for five years in relation to 43 Sloane Street. In the context of a rent of £18,250 a year that is not substantial. In the absence of any other information, I suppose that I must assume figures of a similar order for 44 and 45. The total amount in issue would then be £15,000 instead of £5000. That is bordering on substantial in the context of this case. But I do not accept that it is right to take the other two properties into account. That a point of law is of general public importance has to be considered in deciding whether the discretion should be exercised in favour of granting leave to appeal. I do not consider that the general importance of the point to one of the parties is also relevant under section 1 (4). The subsection provides that leave shall not be granted unless 'the determination of the question of law concerned could substantially affect the rights of one or more of the parties to the arbitration agreement.' This is an important protection to the party who has succeeded in the arbitration (in this case the tenants). He is not to be harried further upon insubstantial matters. I think that the subsection refers to a question the determination of which on appeal will directly affect the rights of one or more of the parties, and not one which will indirectly affect one of the parties if the determination is used as a precedent.

Conclusion

Both the issues in this case are of some general importance. The appropriate guideline is, accordingly, that provided by Lord Diplock in *Pioneer Shipping Ltd* v. *BTP Tioxide Ltd (The Nema)* [1982] AC 724 at p 743:

'Leave should not be given ... unless the judge considered that a strong *prima facie* case had been made out that the arbitrator had been wrong in his conclusion.'

That was said in the context of a commercial contract where it could be assumed that the parties had decided, for good or evil, to make the arbitrator the final judge of fact and law in their dispute, subject only to the rights which are conferred by the Arbitration Act 1979. But the same wisdom applies, not merely to commercial contracts but to an agreement such as the present where landlords and tenants of premises in Sloane Street agreed that the rents payable on a review should be determined by the arbitrator.

Lord Diplock's guideline has recently been interpreted by the Master of the Rolls, Sir John Donaldson, in *Antaios Compania Naviera SA* v. *Salen Redienna AB* (1983) unreported, at p 3 of the transcript:

'I am, of course, construing Lord Diplock's speech as if it had read "But leave should not be given, even in such a case, unless the judge considered that a strong prima facie case had been made out that the arbitrator might well have been wrong in his construction" rather than "the arbitrator had been wrong in his construction". I think that this must have been his intention as otherwise where there are known to be differences of judicial opinion on a matter such as this, whether leave to appeal was granted or refused would depend upon the accident of whether the judge hearing the application did or did not take the same view as the particular arbitrator. This cannot have been the intention of Parliament. If I am wrong in so construing Lord Diplock's speech, then I think that this is one of those cases in which it is permissible to remind oneself that the speeches in *The Nema* were intended to provide guidelines rather than to remove the discretion granted to the judge hearing the application, and that guidelines, by definition, permit of exceptions, albeit great care must be exercised to ensure that the exceptions do not become so numerous as to blur the edges of the guidelines or even render them invisible.'

Later the learned Master of the Rolls said this, at p 9:

'It is quite different if there are known to be differing schools of thought each claiming their adherents among the judiciary, and the Court of Appeal, given the chance, might support either the school of thought to which the judge belongs or another school of thought. In such a case leave to appeal to the High Court should be given provided that the resolution of the issue would substantially affect the rights of the parties (section 1 (4) of the 1979 Act) and the case qualified for leave to appeal to the Court of Appeal under section 1 (7) of the 1979 Act, as no doubt it usually would.

Ackner LJ at pp 21-22 and Fox LJ at p 24 made observations to the same effect.

On issue (1) in this case, the relevance of rents agreed after the review date, so far from considering there to be a strong *prima facie* case that the arbitrator was wrong, I consider that he was right. But this is a point upon which there may well be different schools of thought among the judiciary. It is also a point of general importance. So it qualifies in that respect as a question of law for which leave to appeal should be granted. The problem is that it does not, in this case, affect the rights of one or more of the parties substantially. So it is caught by what Lord

Diplock called 'the ban imposed by the first part of section 1 (4)', which exists, as I have said, for the benefit of the successful party in the arbitration. Much as I might consider it advantageous to the public if the issue were settled by the decision of the Court of Appeal, I cannot grant leave.

Issue (2), the relevance of rents agreed between existing landlords and tenants, does affect the rights of the parties substantially, or at any rate, may well do so. It is also a point of general importance. But again I do not consider there to be a strong prima facie case that the arbitrator was wrong, and I do consider that he was right.

And in this instance there is no material to suggest that different schools of thought exist among the judiciary. (It might be argument that this issue is infected with doubt, because I decided it by a similar process of reasoning to that which I adopted on issue (1), where there are or may be different schools of thought. I do not find such an argument convincing.) Accordingly, whether I follow the precise words of Lord Diplock in *The Nema* or the explanation of the Court of Appeal in the *Antaios* case, I ought not to grant leave to appeal on issue (2).

The application is dismissed.

The landlords' application was dismissed with costs. Leave to appeal was refused.

Note: See also *Duvan Estates Ltd* v. *Rossette Sunshine Savouries Ltd* (1982) 261 EG 364 at page 305 earlier.

PART II

LEASE RENEWAL
(Part II of the Landlord and Tenant Act 1954)

Chapter 16

The applicability of Part II

16.1 The requirements of section 23 of the 1954 Act

16.1 (a) Tenancy

Whether a tenancy or a licence has been created depends on the intention of the parties to be derived from the whole of the document.

ADDISCOMBE GARDEN ESTATES LTD v. CRABBE

Court of Appeal   [1958] 1 QB 513

The trustees of a member's law tennis club entered into an agreement with the owners of tennis courts whereby the owners purported to license and authorise the trustees to use and enjoy the premises for two years from 1 May 1954, in consideration of monthly payments of 'court fees'. The agreement contained a number of clauses including that the trustees should repair and maintain the premises 'in good tenantable repair and condition' and render them up at the expiry of the 'licence' in such condition; permit the 'grantors' and their agents 'at all reasonable times to enter the premises to inspect their condition and for all other reasonable purposes'. The owners agreed *inter alia* that the 'grantees' should 'quietly enjoy' the premises without interruption. The agreement also contained a provision that the 'grantors' might 're-enter and determine the licence in the event of non-payment of any of the said payments of court fees ... or on any breach of the grantees' stipulations'.

The agreement expired on 1 May 1956 but, thereafter, the trustees continued to occupy the premises claiming that the agreement granted them a tenancy which was protected by Part II of the 1954 Act.

Held: The agreement taken as a whole, although described as a licence, on its true construction created the relationship of landlord and tenant and not that of licensor and licensee, for the relationship was determined by the law and not by the label which the parties chose to put on it.

JENKINS LJ: As to the first question—whether the so-called licence of 12 April 1954, in fact amounted to a tenancy agreement under which the premises were let to the trustees—the principles applicable in resolving a question of this sort are, I apprehend, these. It does not necessarily follow that a document described as a licence is, merely on that account, to be regarded as amounting only to a licence in law. The whole of the document must be looked at; and if, after it has been examined, the right conclusion appears to be that, whatever label may have been attached to it, it in fact conferred and imposed on the grantee in substance the rights and obligations of a tenant, and on the grantor in substance the rights and obligations of a landlord, then it must be given the appropriate effect, that is to say,

325

it must be treated as a tenancy agreement as distinct from a mere licence.

First, one must observe that the document is described by the parties as a licence. Secondly, one must observe that the draftsman has studiously and successfully avoided the use either of the word 'landlord' or the word 'tenant' throughout the document. The nearest to the use of the word 'tenant' is the reference to 'tenantable repair' in clause 4, subclause (iii); so that if the question depended on the label attached to the document, one would be constrained to say that this, in accordance with its label, was a licence. But if it is right (as I have no doubt it is) to look at the substance of the matter, I think that a different conclusion inevitably ensues.

I might mention, as regards the character of the premises, that we have been supplied with an agreed plan which shows that, although the whole of the premises are not completely enclosed, as it were, in a ring fence, the greater part of them appear to occupy a particular enclave in the extensive grounds of the Shirley Park Hotel, though there are two outlying rectangular portions, one, I think, consisting of tennis courts, and the other containing some other appurtenances. There is nothing in the character of the premises as shown on the plan to make them an unfit subject of a tenancy agreement as distinct from a licence.

Looking at the substance of the matter, what do the grantees get? By clause 1 they are licensed and authorized 'to enter upon use and enjoy' the items mentioned; and it seems to me that those words, taken together, are apt to give to the tenant something in the nature of an interest in the land. I would next observe that in clause 2 provision is made for the licence, as it is called, extending for the fixed period of two years from 1 May 1954. There is thus a term certain which would be appropriate to the grant of a tenancy. Then in clause 3 it is provided that: 'The grantees shall have the use and enjoyment of the premises in consideration' of a payment. The payment is described as a payment of 'court fees'; it is fixed at the sum of £37 10s. per month, and it has to be paid in advance on the first day of each month. In all but name, that appears to me to be a rent or *reddendum* in consideration of the right to 'enter upon use and enjoy' the premises which is granted by clause 1.

So far, it seems to me that the rights expressed to be conferred on the grantees are, in substance, the rights of a tenant as distinct from the rights of a mere licensee; and, as I have said, there is the correlative obligation of making monthly payments which, although not so called, are in fact, as it seems to me, in the nature of rent. Then there are the various agreements by the grantees with the grantors in clause 4, beginning with the agreement to make the monthly payment of the court fees very much like the agreement to pay the rent which is always to be found in a tenancy agreement. There is a significant provision in sub-clause (iii) under which the grantees agree 'to repair and maintain the club house.' It seems inappropriate that a mere licensee should be saddled with an obligation to repair. Then one finds as to repairs that the items mentioned are to be maintained 'in good tenantable repair,' an expression to which I have already called attention. That, one cannot help thinking, to some extent supports the view that the grantees are tenants, although I do not attach very much weight to it, as I am impressed by the argument of [counsel for the plaintiffs] that 'good tenantable repair' is a phrase which might have been adopted as giving a standard of repair to serve as the measure of the grantees' repairing obligation. But, for what it is worth, that is, I think, if anything, an indication in favour of tenancy rather than licence.

Then under subclause (iv) there is the obligation to maintain the tennis courts. In subclause (v) there is a provision which, I think, is not without significance. That is the provision under which the grantees shall not

'without the grantors' previously written consent cut down or injure any plants trees bushes or hedges or remove from the said property any soil clay sand or other materials and not make any excavations thereon except for the purpose of maintaining the [tennis courts] in accordance with the agreement and conditions hereinbefore contained.'

The significance of that is that it should have been thought necessary expressly to prohibit the grantees from doing certain things which quite plainly, if they were mere licensees, they would have no right or power to do. What business could a licensee have to cut down or injure plants, trees, bushes or hedges, or to do any other of these things, including the removal of 'soil clay sand or other materials'? In a similar sense one may note the provision in subclause (vi): 'not to erect any building or other structures upon the said property except such as shall be approved by the grantors.'

Then there is the provision which [counsel for the plaintiffs] called in aid, which is the restrictive provision in subclause (vii):

'to use the said premises as a private lawn tennis club and club house for the convenience of members of the club their guests and their staff only,' and so on; and in subclause (viii): 'not to allow any persons except members guests and servants of the club to use the said premises for any purpose but this clause shall not prevent the club inviting or allowing a reasonable number of members of the general public to enter thereon for the purpose of attending functions specially organized for those interested in the game of lawn tennis.'

In my view, those provisions afford no real asistance to [counsel for the plaintiffs], for they are just what one would expect to find in a tenancy agreement of premises intended for use as a lawn tennis club. I do not think that anything turns on subclause (ix), which is the one by which the grantees were to 'cause the chairman for the time being of the grantors or his nominee to be an *ex-officio* member of the general committee.' That does not seem to me to carry the matter further one way or the other, though it appears to be a provision to which it was difficult to give effect having regard to the rules of the incorporated body. Shirley Park Lawn Tennis Club Ltd. Subclause (x), under which residents of the hotel who should make application were to be elected honorary members of the club, in my view, is simply a privilege reserved to the grantors, and I do not think that it really throws any light on the character of the grantees' interest.

The next provision of importance is the agreement to permit 'the grantors and their agents at all reasonable times to enter the said premises to inspect the condition thereof and for all other reasonable purposes.' The importance of that is that it shows that the right to occupy the premises conferred on the grantees was intended as an exclusive right of occupation, in that it was thought necessary to give a special and express power to the grantors to enter. The exclusive character of the occupation granted by a document such as this has always been regarded, if not as a decisive indication, at all events as a very important indication to the effect that a tenancy, as distinct from a licence, is the real subject-matter of a document such as this.

In subclause (xii) there is provision 'to deliver up the said premises at the termination of this licence in a condition consistent with the foregoing provisions.' 'To deliver up' seems to me to be an expression more appropriate to a tenant with an interest in the land than to a person who has a mere contractual right to be on the land; it is an expression universally used, I think, in all tenancy agreements and leases. The provision as to insurance points in the same direction; it would, I think, be curious if a mere licensee, with no interest in the premises, was made liable for insurance. Then in clause 5, sub-clause (ii), there is what is practically a common form covenant for quiet enjoyment such as is found in every tenancy agreement or lease; and it seems to me that this clause points strongly in the direction of a tenancy agreement here. In clause 6, sub-clause (i), there is the provision:

'that the grantors may re-enter and determine the licence in the event of non-payment of any of the said payments of court fees for fourteen days (whether formally demanded or not) or on breach of any of the grantees' stipulations.'

Those references to re-entry and 'non-payment of any of the said payments of court fees for fourteen days (whether formally demanded or not)' are provisions wholly appropriate to a tenancy agreement; and I should have thought that a reference to re-entry was really inappropriate to the case of a licence; the conception of re-entry is the resumption of possession by the landlord, and the determination of the interest of the tenant.

This decision was applied in:

SHELL-MEX AND B.P. LTD v. MANCHESTER GARAGES LTD

Court of Appeal   [1971] 1 WLR 612

The owners of a petrol filling station allowed a garage company to go into occupation of the premises pursuant to an agreement called a licence under which the garage company agreed to do all they could to foster the sale of the owners' products and not to impede their rights of possession and control of the premises. On the expiry of the agreement the garage company contended that it constituted a tenancy to which Part II of the 1954 Act applied.

Held: The terms of the agreement showed that the transaction constituted a licence and not a tenancy. In particular, the owners retained rights of possession and control over the premises which were inconsistent with the grant of a tenancy and the agreement was personal in its nature as the purpose was to promote the sale of the owners' products and it depended on the personal capabilities of the garage company.

LORD DENNING MR: I turn, therefore, to the point: was this transaction a licence or a tenancy? This does not depend on the label which is put on it. It depends on the nature of the transaction itself: see *Addiscombe Garden Estates Ltd* v. *Crabbe* [1958] 1 QB 513. Broadly speaking, we have to see whether it is a personal privilege given to a person (in which case it is a licence), or whether it grants an interest in land (in which case it is a tenancy). At one time it used to be thought that exclusive possession was a decisive factor. But that is not so. It depends on broader considerations altogether. Primarily on whether it is personal in its nature or not: see *Errington* v. *Errington and Woods* [1952] 1 KB 290.
    Applying this principle, I turn first to the document itself. It is called a licence. By the first clause the Shell-Mex company

'grants to the licensee licence and permission to use upon the terms and conditions and solely for the purpose hereinafter specified the land and buildings situate at and known as Greyhound Filling Station ...'

By the second clause:

'The purposes for which this licence is granted are to enable the licensee to carry on upon the premises: (1) the business of selling ... such grades of the brand or brands of motor fuel as the company may from time to time nominate ...'

and also rendering such services as are commonly supplied at service stations. By the conditions the licensee agrees

'to use every endeavour and due diligence to sell and foster the sale of the company's motor fuel ... and other petroleum products in such manner as the company may from time to time direct.'

328

And the company agree

'... to supply or cause to be supplied to the licensee at the premises such quantities of the company's motor fuel ... and other petroleum products as the licensee may from time to time reasonably require and order from the company at the wholesale schedule price ruling at the date and place of delivery ...'

The provisions seem to me to be personal in their nature. There is a personal tie between the parties whereby the licensees are to deal in Shell petrol only and are to take all their supplies from Shell, who are to supply them.

It is noticed also that there is no proviso for a right to re-enter. There is a special stipulation which seems to me to connote that the Shell-Mex company remain in possession themselves. It is clause 19 of the first schedule under which Manchester Garages agree:

'Not to impede in any way the officers servants or agents of the company in the exercise by them of the company's rights of possession and control of the premises and in particular to give all reasonable assistance and facilities to such officers servants or agents for the alteration at any time of the layout decorations or equipment of the premises.'

That shows that the Shell-Mex company's men can go and visit the premises whenever they like. The Manchester Garages Ltd are not to impede them in any way, but are to give them assistance.

Those provisions point to a licence and not a tenancy. But [counsel for the defendants] says that Manchester Garages Ltd have exclusive possession, and that that carries with it a tenancy. That is old law which is now gone. As I have said many times, exclusive possession is no longer decisive. We have to look at the nature of the transaction to see whether it is a personal privilege, or not.

Next [counsel for the defendants] says that all these clauses are just what you would find in an ordinary tenancy of a filling station. He suggests that, if this case were to go for trial and he was to have discovery, he would find many a tenancy agreement of a filling station in which there were parallel clauses. He refers to *Little Park Service Station Ltd* v. *Regent Oil Co. Ltd* [1967] 2 QB 655, where there was a tenancy of a filling station and not a licence.

It seems to me that when the parties are making arrangements for a filling station, they can agree either on a licence or a tenancy. If they agree on a licence, it is easy enough for their agreement to be put into writing, in which case the licensee has no protection under the Landlord and Tenant Act 1954. But, if they agree upon a tenancy, and so express it, he is protected. I realise that this means that the parties can, by agreement on a licence, get out of the Act. But so be it. It may be no bad thing. Especially as I see that the parties can now, with the authority of the court, contract out of the Act, even in regard to tenancies: see section 5 of the Law of Property Act 1969.

BUCKLEY LJ: I agree. It is clear on authority that in considering whether a transaction such as we have before us in this case constitutes a licence or a tenancy the court is not to have regard to the label which the parties give to the document or to the formal language of the document, but to the substance of the transaction. During the course of his argument [counsel for the defendants] has taken us through the detailed provisions of the document with which we are here concerned and has pointed out that many of the clauses in it are clauses which could appropriately find their place in a tenancy agreement. That I think is perfectly true; but it is not to say that they do not equally appropriately find their place in a licence. One must look at the transaction as a whole and at any indications that one finds in the terms of the contract between the two parties to find whether in fact it is intended to create a relationship of landlord and tenant or that of licensor and licensee. There are in this case none of those features present which in *Addiscombe Garden Estates Ltd* v. *Crabbe* [1958] 1 QB 513 led the court there to conclude that the intention of the parties was to create a tenancy. They are referred to succinctly by Parker LJ in his judgment, at p 529. In that case there was a clause expressly permitting the grantors to enter on the premises to inspect the plant, which would have been unnecessary had they had a right to enter on the premises apart from the agreement. There was a covenant for quiet and uninterrupted enjoyment by the grantee—a covenant appropriate to a lease but inappropriate, I think, to a licence where the licensor had a right of possession in respect of the subject-matter; and, perhaps most cogent of all, there was a term for re-entry upon breach of covenant, which is a term of a kind quite inappropriate, in my judgment, to a licence. Nothing of that kind is to be found in the present case. The only clause which points one way or the other, I think, is clause 19 in the first schedule which Lord Denning MR has already read and clearly recognises that and notwithstanding the bargain between the parties, the plaintiff company retained rights of possession and control over the property in question. That seems to me to be consistent only with the fact that this transaction was in truth a licence transaction and not a tenancy under which the grantee would obtain an exclusive right to possession of the property during the term of the tenancy, subject, of course, to any rights reserved by the grantors. But the way in which this document is framed is not such as to contain any reservation of rights by the grantors to enter on the property or to exercise any rights over it: it is assumed that they retain the right to possess and enter on the property notwithstanding the transaction; and that is a state of affairs which, in my judgment, clearly indicates that this should be regarded as a licence and not a transaction giving rise to the relationship of landlord and tenant. It may be that this is a device which has been adopted by the plaintiff company to avoid possible consequences of the Landlord and Tenant Act 1954, which would have affected a transaction being one of landlord and tenant; but, in my judgment, one cannot take that into account in the process of construing such a document to find out what the true nature of the transaction is. One has first to find out what is the true nature of the transaction and then see how the Act operates upon that state of affairs, if it bites at all. One should not approach the problem with a tendency to attempt to find a tenancy because unless there is a tenancy the case will escape the effects of the statute.

In **Matchams Park (Holdings) Ltd v. Dommett** (1984) 272 EG 549, the plaintiff permitted the defendant to occupy a stadium under what the parties agreed was a licence, pending execution of a formal agreement. No such agreement was ever signed but the defendant was permitted to continue in occupation and subsequently claimed he had become a tenant under Part II of the 1954 Act.

Held: The relevant provisions, whilst consistent with a tenancy, were not decisive and were capable in law of giving rise to a licence only. Throughout the negotiations, the plaintiff had made it clear that they were only willing to grant a licence and the intentions of the parties were clearly to that effect.

SLADE LJ: It is common ground that the mere fact that the draft agreements which were circulated between the parties described the arrangement as a 'licence' rather than a lease does not determine this question. The decision of this court in *Addiscombe Garden Estates Ltd* v. *Crabbe* [1958] 1 QB 513 shows that the nature of the relationship between the parties to an arrangement such as this is to be determined by law, by reference to the substance of the matter rather than by reference to the description which the parties have chosen to give to their agreement.

The recorder, in analysing the substance of the relationship between the parties, clearly attached great weight to the fact that, as from May 1981, the defendant, according to his findings of fact, was intending to obtain, and did obtain, exclusive occupation of the premises. This, as [counsel] submitted on behalf of the defendant, is indeed a strong pointer towards the existence of a tenancy when one is inferring the intention of the parties.

However, the decision of this court in *Cobb* v. *Lane* [1952] 1 All ER 1199 shows that the mere fact of exclusive possession being enjoyed by the grantee is by no means conclusive. The purport of this decision is, I think, adequately summarised in the headnote, which I will read:

'The fact of the exclusive occupation of property for an indefinite period is no longer inconsistent with the occupier being a licensee and not a tenant at will. Whether or not a relationship of landlord and tenant has been created depends on the intention of the parties, and in ascertaining that intention the court must consider the circumstances in which the person claiming to be a tenant at will went into occupation and whether the conduct of the parties shows that the occupier was intended to have an interest in the land or merely a personal privilege without any such interest.'

We were also referred to the decision of this court in *Shell-Mex and BP* v. *Manchester Garages Ltd* [1971] 1 All ER 841. Lord Denning MR summarised the relevant test succinctly in the following words, at p 843:

'I turn, therefore, to the point: was this transaction a licence or a tenancy? This does not depend on the label which is put on it. It depends on the nature of the transaction itself: see *Addiscombe Garden Estates Ltd* v. *Crabbe*. Broadly speaking, we have to see whether it is a personal privilege given to a person, in which case it is a licence, or whether it grants an interest in land, in which case it is a tenancy. At one time it used to be thought that exclusive possession was a decisive factor, but that is not so. It depends on broader considerations altogether. Primarily on whether it is personal in its nature or not.'

In the light of what Lord Denning has said, [counsel for the defendant], in argument, placed some reliance on the fact that the relationship between the parties in the present case was of a purely commercial nature and was not in any way founded on ties of family or friendship.

Nevertheless, I think that the judgment of this court in *Somma* v. *Hazlehurst* [1978] 2 All ER 1011 well indicates that a mere licence may exist in law, even though the relationship between the parties is of a purely commercial nature and exclusive occupation of the relevant property is given. Cumming-Bruce LJ, at p 1020, delivering the judgment of the court, said this:

'Counsel for the respondents, basing himself on the judgment of Denning LJ in *Facchini* v. *Bryson* and the reasoning in *Marchant* v. *Charters*, submits that in a 'Rent Act' situation any permission to occupy residential premises exclusively must be a tenancy and not a licence, unless it comes into the category of hotels, hostels, family arrangements or service occupancy or a similar undefined special category. We can see no reason why an ordinary landlord not in any of these special categories should not be able to grant a licence to occupy an ordinary house.'

The learned recorder also attached great weight to the fact that the draft licence in the present case had given the defendant powers to grant sublicences. Such a provision is perfectly consistent with a tenancy, but in my view by no means inconsistent with the existence of a mere licence granting exclusive possession. The same comment may be made in relation to the right of re-entry given to the plaintiffs under the draft licence, on which [counsel for the defendant] placed some reliance, and also the right given to the defendant to receive the payments from Mr Slack. All these factors, coupled especially, of course, with the grant of exclusive possession, are certainly pointers in the direction of a tenancy and could well have led the court properly to infer an agreement for the grant of a tenancy if there was no evidence as to the parties' actual intentions. But the fact remains that it is the parties' intentions which are paramount. The observations of Buckley LJ in *Shell-Mex* v. *Manchester Garages* (at p 845 of the report) are, in my opinion, apposite in the present case, where he said this:

'During the course of his argument counsel for the defendants has taken us through the detailed provisions of the document with which we are here concerned and has pointed out that many of the clauses in it are clauses which could appropriately find their place in a tenancy agreement. That I think is perfectly true; but it is not to say that they do not equally appropriately find their place in a licence. One must look at the transaction as a whole and at any indications that one finds in the terms of the contract between the two parties to find whether in fact it is intended to create a relationship of landlord and tenant or that of licensor and licensee.'

With all respect to the recorder's judgment and to [counsel for the defendant's] powerful argument, both seem to me to have overlooked the fact that the plaintiffs have, from the very beginning in the present case, made it crystal clear that they did not wish to intend to create a tenancy. Furthermore, the defendant, who, it is worthy to note, is obviously an experienced businessman and throughout had the benefit of solicitors' advice, must, in my opinion, at all material times, have been well aware that this was their intention. It is common ground that no tenancy came into existence during the period of 26 May 1980 to 25 May 1981. The plaintiffs had made it quite clear that though they were willing to grant him a licence in respect of the period after 25 May 1981 they were not willing to grant him a tenancy: I refer, for example, to their letters of 18 May 1980 and 15 December 1980, from which I have already quoted. Furthermore, the defendant's solicitors had unequivocally accepted that position. I refer to their letter of 12 November 1980, from which I have also already quoted.

[Counsel for the defendant] has naturally submitted that the recorder who had seen the witnesses, had drawn his inference as to the parties' intentions and that this court should be very slow to interfere with the inference which he had drawn. But in my judgment, with all respect to the recorder, the only proper inference is that, in advance of the execution of a formal agreement, the defendant was to occupy the stadium as licensee and not as tenant, whether or not, as a matter of fact, he enjoyed exclusive possession of the premises. The recorder, in my view, clearly drew the wrong inference. I think ground 1 of the plaintiffs' notice of appeal really puts the matter in a nutshell, where it is submitted, in my opinion correctly:

'the learned judge failed to apply the paramount test in deciding whether the defendant had a licence or a tenancy. He ought to have asked: "What was the intention of the parties?" Instead he asked only: "Did the defendant have exclusive possession and was this a personal transaction?"'

Accordingly, despite [counsel for the defendant's] persuasive submissions, I, for my part, would allow this appeal.

The grant of exclusive possession at a rent for a term is decisive of a tenancy.

STREET v. MOUNTFORD

House of Lords   [1985] 2 WLR 877

The landlord, Mr Street, granted Mrs Mountford the right to occupy furnished rooms at Nos 5 and 6, St Clements Gardens, Boscombe, at £37 per week subject to conditions set forth in an agreement which was entitled 'licence agreement' and which contained a declaration signed by Mrs Mountford to the effect that she understood that the agreement did not give her a tenancy protected under the Rent Act 1977. Mrs Mountford and her husband moved into the rooms of which they had exclusive occupation. Subsequently, Mr Street sought an order in the county court declaring whether the occupancy under the agreement was a licence or a protected tenancy under the Rent Act 1977.

Held: Where an occupier was granted (1) exclusive possession for (2) a term (3) at a rent, then subject to certain well established exceptions created by service occupancy or where there was no intention to create legal relations or where there was no intention to grant a tenancy and all the circumstances and conduct of the parties showed that all was intended was that the occupier should be granted a personal privilege with no interest in the land, a tenancy would be created. On the facts, Mrs Mountford was a tenant.

LORD TEMPLEMAN: My Lords, the only intention which is relevant is the intention demonstrated by the agreement to grant exclusive possession for a term at a rent. Sometimes it may be difficult to discover whether, on the true construction of an agreement, exclusive possession is conferred. Sometimes it may appear from the surrounding circumstances that there was no intention to create legal relationships. Sometimes it may appear from the surrounding circumstances that the right to exclusive possession is referable to a legal relationship other than a tenancy. Legal relationships to which the grant of exclusive possession might be referable and which would or might negative the grant of an estate or interest in the land include occupancy under a contract for the sale of the land, occupancy pursuant to a contract of employment or occupancy referable to the holding of an office. But where as in the present case the only circumstances are that residential accommodation is offered and accepted with exclusive possession for a term at a rent, the result is a tenancy.

The position was well summarised by Windeyer J sitting in the High Court of Australia in *Radaich* v. *Smith* (1959) 101 CLR 209, 222, where he said:

'What then is the fundamental right which a tenant has that distinguishes his position from that of a licensee? It is an interest in land as distinct from a personal permission to enter the land and use it for some stipulated purpose or purposes. And how is it to be ascertained whether such an interest in land has been given? By seeing whether the grantee was given a legal right of exclusive possession of the land for a term or from year to year or for a life or lives. If he was, he is a tenant. And he cannot be other than a tenant, because a legal right of exclusive possession is a tenancy and the creation of such a right is a demise. To say that a man who has, by agreement with a landlord, a right of exclusive possession of land for a term is not a tenant is simply to contradict the first proposition by the second. A right of exclusive possession is secured by the right of a lessee to maintain ejectment and, after his entry, trespass. A reservation to the landlord, either by contract or statute, of a limited right of entry, as for example to view or repair, is, of course, not inconsistent with the grant of exclusive possession. Subject to such reservations, a tenant for a term or from year to year or for a life or lives can exclude his landlord as well as strangers from the demised premises. All this is long established law: see *Cole on Ejectment* (1857) pp 72, 73, 287, 458.'

My Lords, I gratefully adopt the logic and the language of Windeyer J.

Note: This decision was concerned with residential accommodation, but it is submitted that the fundamental propositions as to what constitutes a tenancy apply in the field of business tenancies as well. In his review of the authorities, Lord Templeman considered *inter alia Shell Mex and B.P. Ltd* v. *Manchester Garages Ltd* [1971] 1 WLR 612 (earlier, p. 328) emphasising that the agreement there could only be regarded as a licence if it did not confer the right of exclusive possession and that no other test for distinguishing between a tenancy and a licence appeared understandable or workable.

In *Manchester City Council* v. *National Car Parks* (1982) 262 EG 1297, an agreement for the use of land in the centre of Manchester as a car park between the hours of 12.01 a.m.–2 a.m. and 7 a.m.–12 p.m. was held to be a licence and not a tenancy within the 1954 Act. The fact that the Council had not enforced the restriction on the hours of use did not affect this conclusion based on the terms of the agreement and the surrounding circumstances.

In *Wang* v. *Wei* (1975) 119 SJ 492, a management agreement relating to a restaurant business was held to be a sham and was treated as conferring a tenancy of the premises upon the manager.

In *Clore* v. *Theatrical Properties Ltd* [1936] 3 All ER 483, an agreement which provided that: 'the lessor doth hereby demise and grant unto the lessee the free and exclusive use of all the refreshment rooms ... of the theatre ... for the purpose only of the supply to and the accommodation of the visitors to the theatre ...' was held to be a licence and not a tenancy. The case illustrates that it is possible to grant a business concession without creating a tenancy within Part II of the 1954 Act.

16.1 (b)   Premises

The letting of incorporeal hereditaments together with land may constitute premises.

STUMBLES v. WHITLEY

House of Lords   [1930] AC 544

An hotel was let under a lease which also included the fishing rights in a water known as the Lower Ley. The tenant sought the grant of a new lease and the question was whether the new lease should include the fishing rights.

Held: Where an incorporeal right, such as a right of fishing, is demised along with corporeal hereditaments by the same lease and the lessee uses both for the purpose of his trade or business, the incorporeal right is part of the 'premises' within Part II of the 1954 Act.

VISCOUNT HAILSHAM: When we look at section 17, the definition section, and we find the reference to 'any premises held under a lease,' I see no sufficient reason for supposing that the Legislature did not there include not merely the actual buildings in which a trade is carried on, but also the land surrounding them, the easements granted as appurtenant to them, and any other incorporeal hereditaments which may form part of the premises in the strict legal sense of the term which are the subject-matter of the *habendum*. Any other construction would, it seems to me, defeat the plain purpose of the Act, which obviously was to provide that in the circumstances defined in the Act the tenant should have a right to continue to carry on his trade or business in the premises in the legal sense in which he was carrying them on under the lease for which he seeks that renewal.

In **Bracey v. Read** [1963] Ch 88, the plaintiff agreed to let to the defendant for three years 'the right to train and exercise racehorses on the gallops at his farm with rights of access thereto'.

Held: The word 'premises' in Section 23 (1) of the 1954 Act was not confined to buildings but included the land on which the buildings were erected and the land immediately surrounding them and such incorporeal hereditaments as easements, and such other things which were properly described as premises in the strict legal sense when the context so required. Accordingly, the letting of the gallops was within Part II of the 1954 Act.

In **Land Reclamation Ltd v. Basildon District Council** (1979) 250 EG 549, the Court of Appeal held that a right of way, which stood by itself and was not the subject of a more comprehensive demise including a corporeal hereditament, fell outside Part II of the 1954 Act.

16.1 (c)   Occupied by the tenant ... for the purposes of a business

A tenant occupying a building for the sole purpose of subletting parts thereof falls outside section 23 (1).

BAGETTES LTD v. G.P. ESTATES LTD

Chancery Division   [1956] Ch 290

The defendants took an assignment of a leasehold interest in premises comprising 13 self-contained flats, 10 of which were sub-let at the material time.

Held: Such an occupation, although for a 'business' was not one to which Part II of the 1954 Act applied since it involved the progressive elimination of the holding.

JENKINS LJ: A building wholly sublet in flats from top to bottom could not qualify for protection under Part I of the Act of 1927 because such subletting would not be a use of the premises for carrying on a trade or business within the meaning of the Act, by reason of its exclusion by section 17 (3). A building similarly dealt with could not qualify for protection under Part II of the Act of 1954, not because the subletting of the premises in flats would not be a business within the meaning of section 23 of that Act, but because the tenant would *ex hypothesi* not be in occupation of any part of the premises. In a case in which the tenant of premises sublet part of them in flats and retained the remainder in his own occupation for the purpose of providing services for the tenants of the part comprised in the sublettings (which is, in effect, this case) the tenant could not have claimed protection under Part I of the Act of 1927 because of the exclusion of the subletting of flats from the definition of use for carrying on a trade or business in section 17. In a like case under the Act of 1954 the tenant can claim, rightly as I think, that the subletting of the flats is a business within the meaning of section 23 and can also claim, again rightly as I think, that the purposes for which he occupies the remainder of the premises, that is to say, the provision of services for the tenants of the flats sublet, are purposes of a business carried on by him within the meaning of the same section. So far, then, he satisfies section 23 both as regards the occupation of part of the premises by him, and as regards the purposes of such occupation, which are purposes of his business of subletting the flats into which the part of the premises not in his occupation is divided. But these claims can surely be maintained only so long as the tenant continues as tenant of the entirety of the premises, whether occupied by him or sublet. Once the flats which it is his business to sublet are excluded from his tenancy the remaining parts of the premises, though still in his occupation, are no longer occupied by him for the purposes of any business. Once the flats are gone the business for the purposes of which he formerly occupied the remainder of the premises, that is to say, the provision of services for the tenants of the flats sublet, as part of the entire business of letting and managing those flats, is gone also, and is incapable of continuance or revival.

What is the bearing of Part II of the Act of 1954 on such a case? I repeat that its manifest intention is (to quote once more the language of the long title appropriate to this case) 'to enable tenants occupying property for business ... purposes to obtain new tenancies in certain cases.' That intention is, as I think, faithfully carried out by the provisions of Part II of the Act upon a fair and reasonable construction of those provisions. I think it is implicit in those provisions, and in particular sections 23 and 32, that the business for the purposes of which a tenant occupies premises of which he claims a new tenancy must not be of such a character that it is necessarily brought to an end by the very process of the ascertainment of the holding and the ordering and granting of a new tenancy of the holding as ascertained, with the result that the tenant is presented with a holding which, though occupied by him, is not so occupied for the purposes of any business whatever.

A tenant of an apartment building may occupy the whole building for the purposes of a business even though the individual residents have the exclusive occupation of their flats as a residence for the purposes of the Rent Act 1977.

LEE-VERHULST (INVESTMENTS) v. HARWOOD TRUST

Court of Appeal   [1973] QB 204

The tenant company had a tenancy of premises comprising a number of fully furnished flats, each separately occupied. The tenant company had the right of access to all parts of the building to provide services.

Held: Having regard to the degree of control and extent of the services provided to each flat, the tenant company 'occupied' the entire premises for the purposes of its business.

STAMP LJ: The question then to be asked is whether it can be correctly stated of any part of 11, Courtfield Gardens that it is not occupied by the tenant or by Mr or Mrs Lee for the purposes of the business. Can it be said that the tenant of the house who carried on there the business described and conducted the activities enumerated by Sachs LJ, including, to mention only some of them, the supply of furniture, blankets, bed linen and towels to the rooms where the occupants reside, the cleaning of the rooms and, when required, the provision of light meals to those rooms, was not occupying them for the purposes of the business?

As Sachs LJ has pointed out and as a glance at *Stroud's Judicial Dictionary* will show, the words 'occupation' and 'occupier' are not words of art having an ascertained legal meaning applicable, or prima facie applicable, wherever you find them in a statute, but take their colour from the context of the statute in which they are found; and I am not prepared to give the word 'occupied' where it appears in section 23 (3) a construction which would exclude from 'the holding' part of a house *in which* the business is carried on day by day, and the whole of which is used by the tenant for the purposes of his business. The situation is very different to that in *Bagettes Ltd* v. *G.P. Estates Ltd* [1956] Ch 290, where the tenant did not by his servants enter the flats which had been let to carry on the business which one finds here of providing services to the residents.

In the context of statutory provisions to give security of tenure to business tenants the occupation referred to in section 23 (3) must as a matter of construction be given the same meaning as the occupation referred to in subsection (1), and what in my judgment is contemplated by both sub-sections is occupation 'for the purposes of' the business carried on by the tenant; and if you find the business—here that part of the business which consists of what can conveniently be summarised as 'room service'—being carried on in each room in the way this tenant carries it on in this case, I conclude that the whole house and each room in it is within the meaning of the section 'occupied' by the tenant 'for the purposes of' its business and that no part is excluded from 'the holding' by the effect of subsection (3).

But the point remains that the residents of 11, Courtfield Gardens have had granted to them within the meaning of section 70 of the Rent Act 1968 'the right to occupy' their respective rooms 'as a residence'. Is it then right to say that the two types of occupation of a single room, one for the purposes of a business and the other 'as a residence,' one an occupation within the meaning of section 23 of the Landlord and Tenant Act 1954 for the purposes of a business and the other within the meaning of section 70 of the Rent Act 1968 'as a residence,' cannot co-exist? In my judgment the submission to that effect is not well founded.

Occupation by servants of the tenant may be sufficient.

CHAPMAN v. FREEMAN

Court of Appeal   [1978] 1 WLR 1298

The tenant of a cottage used it to provide accommodation for staff employed at his nearby hotel. In proceedings by the landlord for possession of the cottage on the ground that it was a dwelling-house not occupied by the tenant, the tenant claimed that the tenancy was subject to Part II of the 1954 Act as the cottage was occupied for the purposes of his hotel business.

Held: To be 'occupied for the purposes of a business' within the meaning of section 23 (1) premises had to be occupied for a purpose necessary to the furtherance of the business and not, as was the occupation of the cottage for the purpose of housing hotel staff, merely for the convenience of the business.

LORD DENNING MR: This raises a very nice question. Illustrations were canvassed in the course of the argument. One of the most interesting was of a barrister who has his business chambers in the Temple but has his residential flat a block or two away. Is he occupying the flat for the purposes of his profession which he carries on in his chambers? The answer is No. He occupies his flat for his convenience in connection with his profession, but he does not occupy it for the purposes of his profession. Another illustration was where a company sets up a new factory in a town and finds houses for its staff in the neighbourhood. They are not occupied for the purposes of the business which the company is running. They are used for housing purposes.

Those illustrations remind one of the cases we used to have in the old days about service occupations. Such as the toll-keeper who had to live in a cottage next to the toll-bridge, or the stockman who has to live in the centre of the stockyard so as to carry out his duties. Those servants occupied for the purposes of the business: see *Ramsbottom* v. *Snelson* [1948] 1 KB 473.

Speaking generally, the test is whether it is *necessary* for the individual to live in the house in order to perform his own particular duties properly; or whether it is just for *convenience* that he should live there in connection with his duties.

Coming back to our present case, it seems to me that there is no evidence, and was no evidence before the judge, to show that it was necessary for any of the staff to live in the cottage for the better performance of their duties. It is no doubt highly convenient that they should live there, but that is not enough. It would be extending the Act far too widely if it were held that every dwelling house which the owner of a business took in order to house his staff was held on a business tenancy. The truth is that it is a dwelling house simply for the convenience of the person carrying on the business. It is not a business tenancy.

The last two foregoing cases were considered in:

GROVESIDE PROPERTIES LTD v. WESTMINSTER MEDICAL SCHOOL

Court of Appeal (1983) 267 EG 593

A medical school sought a new tenancy of a flat, consisting of four study rooms, kitchen, sitting-room, bathroom and lavatories and used for residential accommodation of its medical students, on the grounds that it occupied the flat for the purposes of its business, namely, running the medical school.

Held: The school did occupy the flat as was evidenced by the substantial degree of control which it exercised and the furniture and equipment which it provided. Furthermore, it occupied it for the purposes of a business in the wide sense of an 'activity', namely, running a major medical school since the occupation of the flat by the students was not merely to provide a residence but to foster a corporate or collegiate spirit in furtherance of their medical education.

Fox LJ: In section 23 (1) of the Landlord and Tenant Act 1954, Parliament draws a distinction, as a matter of language, between two requirements: first, that the premises should be occupied by the tenants and, secondly, that the premises should be so occupied for the purposes of a business carried on by them. There is, I think, a substantial degree of relationship between the two but I will deal with them separately as did counsel for the appellant plaintiffs.

The first question, then, is whether the medical school occupied the flat. The word 'occupied' is not a term of art and has no precise legal meaning; nor, as it seems to me, can one determine whether somebody is an occupier by itemising the circumstances found to be present in individual cases where a person was held in fact to be an occupier, and then determining how many or how few of those are present in the case to be decided.

In *Lee-Verhulst (Investments) Ltd* v. *Harwood Trust* [1973] QB 204, the applicant carried on in one building the business of letting furnished apartments. Mr Lee, who controlled the applicant company, exercised a virtually complete control of the apartments; he was present there most of his time; he lived on the premises and kept a close watch on everything; he had no other occupation. In concluding that the company did occupy the whole of the premises, Sachs LJ said this at p 213:

'For reaching that conclusion it is neither necessary nor desirable to provide a definition of that word which would deal with all the greatly varying sets of circumstances that can exist. As a number of elements have been taken into account, each of a physical nature and each involving a degree of presence on the part of the tenant personally or by goods under his ownership, it is however well to observe that it could be proper in some other case to reach the same conclusion even if one or more of those elements were subtracted.'

As was recognised in that case, one must look at the substance of the whole matter and take a commonsense approach. Without attempting a definition, control must, I think, be an important element. I am left with the strong impression in this case of the existence of a substantial degree of control by the medical school. It was very restrained and very sensibly exercised, but I think it was of dominant importance. The students were only there at all because they were students of the medical school; it was not an ordinary relationship between persons letting and persons taking the accommodation. Of course, the students did pay, but the relationship, I think, was simply part of the general relationship between the medical school and a member of the student body.

Coming to more detailed matters, I mention the following:

(1) All the furniture and equipment was provided by the medical school, which was also responsible for the decoration;

(2) Mr Forest selected the students who lived in the flat and he said that he did that on the basis of 'will they fit in?'

(3) The medical school kept keys to the flat;

(4) There is no written agreement, but Mr Forest said that the students knew what was expected of them and would, for example, ask permission if they wanted to have a party;

(5) Mr Forest visits the flat about once a month and spends half an hour to an hour there. He says he does that to see what is going on and to 'get the feel' of the place. There is, I think, no reason why he should go there every day; it is only a single flat.

It seems to me that the only sensible conclusion from all this is that the medical school does occupy the premises; it is simply part of the school, and Mr Forest says as much in his evidence. 'I do not', he said 'distinguish the flat from the rest of the school'; in my opinion that represents the reality of the matter ...

I come then to the second question: Were the premises occupied by the medical school for the purposes of a business carried on by it within the meaning of section 23 (2)? That includes any activity carried on by a body of persons, whether corporate or unincorporate. The word 'activity' in the definition in section 23 (2) must, in my opinion, extend the scope of what goes before it (see per Parker LJ in *Addiscombe Garden Estates Ltd* v. *Crabbe* [1958] 1 QB 513 at p 530). Precisely what limits one must put on the word, I need not consider. It seems to me that the running of a major medical school must be an 'activity' within section 23 (2).

Was then a flat occupied for the purposes of that activity? On the evidence I can only conclude that it was. The activity is medical education. If, as the evidence establishes, the fostering of a corporate spirit among the students is an important part of their educational process, and the achievement of such a spirit is materially assisted by the provision of accommodation in the flat, I think it follows that the occupation of the flat is for the purposes of the activity carried on by the school. The occupation of the flat was solely designed to promote the orderly and contented residence of the students.

[Counsel] for the plaintiffs has referred us to the case of *Chapman* v. *Freeman* [1978] 1 WLR 1298, which was concerned with a residential hotel and restaurant in a village in Cornwall. Near the hotel there was a cottage. The proprietor of the hotel took a yearly tenancy of the cottage and used it to house some of the hotel staff. Then, after some years, the owner of the cottage died, and her personal representatives sought to determine the tenancy and get possession. The owner of the hotel relied on section 23 of the Landlord and Tenant Act 1954. At the time of the hearing the cottage was used to house the hotel barman and his family. It was conceded that the owner of the hotel occupied the cottage, but it was held by the Court of Appeal that he did not occupy it for the purpose of the hotel business. Lord Denning MR, at p 1300, said that it was not necessary for the barman to live in the cottage in order to perform his duties; it was merely convenient. Geoffrey Lane LJ at p 1301 said:

'The tenant must go beyond mere convenience and show that the occupation was in furtherance of his business activities—in other words, that it was for business reasons that he was occupying the cottage and not merely for reasons of convenience.'

Eveleigh LJ at p 1302 said:

'The servant is not occupying for the purpose of the hotel business but simply as a resident.'

That decision does not lead me to any different view of the present case. The use by the students is not simply for convenience and it is not simply as a residence; it is to achieve an educational purpose for the advancement of their medical training, and it is to assist the achievement of the same purpose, and to the same end, that the medical school occupies the flat.

The *Lee-Verhulst* case (earlier, page 336) was applied in:

WILLIAM BOYER & SONS LTD v. ADAMS

Chancery Division   (1976) 32 P & CR 89

TEMPLEMAN LJ: In the present case, the defendant claims that he occupies the whole of the premises including the units for the purpose of carrying on the buiness of subletting and providing facilities and services to enable his sub-tenants to engage in light industry. The defendant does not devote the whole of his time to the business. Indeed he works elsewhere three days in the week but he is always on the premises between 10 and 11 in the morning, his wife is generally there when he is not, and when they both go away on holiday they arrange for someone to take their place. The services claimed by the defendant to be provided include the provision and maintenance of the central heating system, keeping the oil tanks supplied, servicing the boilers, keeping the heating equipment in repair and fighting running battles with the workmen in the units over the adjustment of the thermostat temperature controls and the time clocks. The defendant maintains the electric system supplying power, light and in some cases heat for the units. He is responsible for seeing that electric faults are remedied and the supply of electricity maintained. For all these purposes he requires to enter and does enter the units; the fixtures which constitute the central heating system in the units belong to him. He lights the courtyard. He provides a workman to clean the common toilets, the courtyard and the car park. He supplied towels until they disappeared. He sees to the emptying of the cesspit. He sorts out obstruction in the car park and the courtyard. He or his wife are available for messages and deliveries out of business hours though this service is seldom required. Finally on most evenings, the defendant makes a tour of and enters the units mainly to see that the heating and electrical fittings he supplies are safe, that electricity and heat for which he pays are not wasted, that there are no fire hazards and that the units are secure against intruders. The only control exercised by the defendant over the tenants of the units is to be found in provisions of the tenancy agreements which are designed to prevent the overloading of the electricity supply, to restrict types of work prohibited by the insurers and to prohibit work after 10 o'clock at night.
In the *Lee-Verhulst* case the time devoted by the landlord to the acivities of the business, the services rendered and the control exercised were extensive; the landlord's presence in the flats was marked by his chattels. In the present case all these factors are only present on a reduced scale or are missing. But in my judgment the activities of the defendant are sufficient to show that he is not so much acting as a landlord passively receiving rent but as the manager of a business actively earning profits by providing accommodation, facilities and services and by devoting time for this purpose.
Viewing the activities as a whole and applying, as best I may, the principle of and observations in the *Lee-Verhulst* case I conclude that the defendant is in occupation and was in September 1973 in occupation of premises including the units for the purpose of his business of providing accommodation, power, facilities and services

for the carrying on of light industries and that the defendant is entitled to the protection afforded by Part II of the Landlord and Tenant Act 1954.

In **Ross Autowash Ltd v. Herbert** (1979) 250 EG 971, the tenant's business at a shopping precinct was carried on by an associated company of the tenant although the tenant retained possession and control thereof and carried on the business of granting licences to stall-holders and providing a variety of services to them.

Held: The tenant occupied the premises for the purpose of a business carried on by it within the meaning of section 23.

In **Cristina v. Seear** (1985) 275 EG 898, premises had been occupied and the business had been carried on there since 1983 by limited companies, all of which had gone into liquidation and had been succeeded by another. The tenants owned all the shares in the latter company and therefore controlled it. They argued that the premises were occupied by them for the purpose of a business carried on by them within section 23 (1) in that the company, which they controlled, was a mere vehicle or *alter ego* through which the business was carried on by them.

Held: The tenants did not bring themselves within section 23 (1) of the 1954 Act.

PURCHAS LJ: Summarised, [counsel for the tenants'] submissions were as follows. The two tenants (Mr and Mrs Cristina) owned all the shares of the company and had the control which would result from that position. Therefore, said [counsel for the tenants] the basis of the decision in *Tunstall* v. *Steigmann* [1962] 2 QB 593 did not affect this case, because the reality of the position was that the business was in fact the business of the tenants, who were using a vehicle in the form of a company to carry on their business, and the fact that the company had been formed really was neither here nor there. Whether one uses the expression *alter ego*, which, with respect to some previous judgments, I find some difficulty in doing, or whether one says that in reality the company was merely the agent or manager of the tenants matters not. One cannot ignore the fact that when the creditor's petition was filed, albeit some months after the end of the tenancy but during the continued occupation by the tenants, the liquidation so far as one knows pursued a normal course. Such a process, with respect to the able arguments of [counsel for the tenants], seems in my judgment to be quite alien to the concept that the companies were mere managers of the business for which in fact the tenants held themselves immediately, and not merely vicariously, liable. However, that is merely dealing with the attack made by [counsel for the tenants] on the finding of the learned judge which, as I have already said, I find it difficult to criticise.

The second point upon which [counsel for the tenants] relies is related to the amendments to the Landlord and Tenant Act 1954 effected by section 6 of the Law of Property Act 1969. That section added a further subsection to section 30 of the Act of 1954, which itself detailed specific circumstances under which a landlord could oppose a tenant's application for a new lease. It is not necessary in this judgment to go into the details of that section. The basis of the submission is as follows. In *Tunstall* v. *Steigmann* the court was dealing with an objection by the landlord to an application for a new tenancy. Put very shortly, the landlord intended to use the premises for business to be conducted by a limited company of which he was a controlling shareholder. The court held that, notwithstanding the fact that he had a controlling interest in the company and effectively controlled it, the company was still a separate legal entity and that therefore the landlord could not say under the terms of section 30, as it then existed, that he required the premises for a business to be carried on by him. The argument was put forward by counsel for the landlord, along very much the same lines as those proposed *mutatis mutandis* on behalf of the tenant in this case by [counsel], and I read only two passages from the judgment of Willmer LJ. He said at p 603:

'Mr Bramall, in an attractive and forceful argument, has sought to support the judge's view on a number of grounds. First, he says that construing the language of the subsection in accordance with the ordinary meaning of the words used, the landlord here did intend to occupy the holding for the purposes of a business to be carried on by her. The business was in substance her business, the company being a mere piece of mechanism to enable the landlord's business to be carried on. This, it is said, was the reality; and we were invited to look at the reality and substance of the proposed occupation rather than at its form.'

Willmer LJ disposes of this argument at the bottom of p 604 and the top of p 605:

'I have certainly felt the force of the argument on behalf of the landlord; but in the end I am satisfied that it cannot prevail. There is no escape from the fact that a company is a legal entity entirely separate from its corporators—see *Salomon* v. *Salomon & Co.* [1897] AC 22. Here the landlord and her company are entirely separate entities. This is no matter of form; it is a matter of substance and reality. Each can sue and be sued in its own right; indeed, there is nothing to prevent the one from suing the other.'

[Counsel for the tenants] has said that, as a result of that decision and particularly with some comments made in the judgments as to what was described as 'the bizarre results', which are mentioned towards the end of Willmer LJ's judgment, Parliament enacted the provisions included in section 6 of the Law of Property Act 1969. [Counsel for the tenants] attempts to deduce from that that the intention of Parliament should be that the tenant should be treated in the like manner.

I regret that I am unable to accede to that submission. If anything was to be inferred from the enactment in 1969, it must in my judgment militate to the contrary, that if Parliament had intended to equate the position of the tenant with the landlord in this respect then one is entitled to consider that it would probably have taken some express step to achieve that. In the end, we are forced back on the construction of the Act and the authority of *Tunstall* v. *Steigmann* in so far as it deals with the question of the position of a tenant in occupation for the purposes of his business, and that authority remains unaffected by any subsequent legislation.

Occupation connotes an element of control and user.

HANCOCK AND WILLIS v. G.M.S. SYNDICATE LTD

Court of Appeal   (1982) 265 EG 473

The tenants, a firm of solicitors, took an assignment of a lease of premises for the purpose of additional accommodation and applied for the grant of a new tenancy. Subsequently, they granted an exclusive six–month licence to a printing company to occupy the premises but arranged to retain the use of a wine cellar and to be allowed to hold bi–monthly staff lunches in a back room. They left some furniture which was included in the licence and some files but without any arrangement for access to inspect them. Upon the expiry of the licence, the tenants resumed occupation.

Held: The tenants had ceased to occupy the premises for the purpose of a business carried on by them and were consequently not entitled to the grant of a new tenancy.

EVELEIGH LJ: The phrase 'occupied for the purposes of a business carried on by him' in my opinion is not used in the Act as one with any technical meaning. Furthermore, its meaning is not to be ascertained by breaking it down into various parts and analysing each word in those parts. It is a phrase which has to be construed as a whole and in a popular sense.

The words with which we are concerned import, in my judgment, an element of control and user and they involve the notion of physical occupation. That does not mean physical occupation every minute of the day, provided the right to occupy continues. But it is necessary for the judge trying the case to assess the whole situation where the element of control and use may exist in variable degrees. At the end of the day it is a question of fact for the tribunal to decide, treating the words as ordinary words in the way in which I have referred to them.

CUMMING-BRUCE LJ: In that situation, construing, as my Lord has said, the words of the section in a commonsense and ordinary way, without importing into the construction any technical or special meaning, how can it be said that, during the six months' period of the licence, the tenants were still occupying the office premises for the purpose of their business as solicitors? It is perfectly obvious that they were not: it is perfectly obvious that, for a consideration at the rate of £1000 a year, they had parted with their right to use the offices and transferred that right to the licensee, the printing firm. The edifice sought to be constructed below and here by [counsel for the appellants] on the presence of the vault and a few bottles, the right of the licensor to enter on the premises and use a back room for the purpose of staff lunches twice a month, the presence of some mouldering files and some drawers and cupboards which were left behind during the period of the licence by the licensor, the licensor retaining no right to have access thereto, or the fact that the licensee took as the perquisite of his licence the right to use the furniture left in the offices, cannot be constructed into any form of constructive occupation by the licensor of the parcels, the use whereof having been effectively transferred to the licensee.

In **Artemiou v. Procopiou** [1966] 1 QB 878 Salmon LJ said:

'It seems to me clear that anyone who goes into occupation of premises in which a seasonal business is carried on is occupying them all the year round for the purposes of the business; if not, it is difficult to see for what other purpose he would be occupying them during the out-of-season months.'

In **Teasdale v. Walker** [1958] 1 WLR 1076, business premises were near the front of a seaside resort and were used for mock auctions, being open only at Easter, Whitsun and from July to the end of September. The tenant made an agreement with one Glassman to the effect that the tenant would for one year employ Glassman as a manager to conduct the business as he thought fit and without interference from the tenant. He also received an option to renew the agreement for the next year. Glassman conducted the business in accordance with the agreement and at the end of the season vacated the premises, which thereafter as usual remained closed. The tenant applied for a new tenancy and the question arose whether the tenant was in occupation of the premises for the purpose of a business carried on by her. The Court of Appeal held that the tenant had ceased to occupy the premises.

PEARCE LJ: Where premises are only occupied during seasonal periods, that question has additional difficulties. It must, we think, be a question of fact and degree whether premises that, for instance, are used only for summer purposes can be said to be so occupied during the winter months. The answer to the question will no doubt depend partly on the length of the gap between the intermittent activities, especially in view of the past history of the occupation. If the tenant in this case has been in occupation for the purposes of a business carried on by her during the summer season of 1957, as well as those of 1955 and 1956, she would clearly, we think, be held to be in such occupation in the inactive months in the winter and spring of 1957–8. But in 1957 she had by the agreement with Glassman ceased her occupation for the purposes of a business carried on by her and broken the thread of her business.

The inference of continuous occupation, that during the vacant months of winter she could formerly successfully ask the court to draw in her favour from her summer occupation for the purposes of her business, is no longer available to her. We are asked to draw that inference from her answer given in evidence: 'If I get tenancy and Glassman does not exercise option Arnold will carry on' (presumably she meant as her agent). 'I have the keys.' In our view, particularly in view of the sham agreement with Glassman, that evidence is not sufficient to support the inference. She can hardly complain if her more recent activities are taken as a better guide than her earlier ones, especially since there is no evidence that she was going to give up living at Derby. Once the premises have ceased, as did these, to be premises to which the Act applies, some clearer indication is needed to bring them again within the Act. Indeed, we doubt if a mere intention to restart such a business in the coming season (*a fortiori* if it were only a conditional intention) would be enough to bring the premises again within the Act when once the thread of continuity has been broken and the premises have ceased to be within it. They were not then occupied by her for the purposes of any business carried on by her and they had not been so occupied during the preceding season. In our view, notwithstanding [counsel for the tenant's] able and forceful argument, the premises are not shown to be within the Act either on 17 December 1957 or on 21 February 1958, or on 2 March 1958, and the tenant's application was, therefore, ill founded.

(See further under the heading 'Tenancy ceasing to be one to which the Act applies' at page 364, and see *Linden* v. *Secretary of State for Social Services*, The Times, 21 November 1985, on occupation by a government department under section 56(3) of the 1984 Act.

It is possible for the character of a tenancy to change from protected under the Rent Act 1977 to business under Part II of the 1954 Act. A tenancy of residential premises will be a business tenancy if the tenant's business activity is a significant purpose of the occupation and is not merely incidental to the residential occupation.

CHERYL INVESTMENTS LTD v. SALDANHA
ROYAL LIFE SAVING SOCIETY v. PAGE

Court of Appeal   (1978) 248 EG 591

LORD DENNING MR: There was much discussion before us as to the meaning of the Business Tenancy Act 1954 (I use those words because I think 'Landlord and Tenant Act 1954' is a little confusing): especially the word 'purposes' in section 23 (1); the time or times at which those 'purposes' had to exist; and the effect of a change by the tenant in the use to which he put the property. Could he take himself in or out of the Act at his option? I found all these matters so confusing that I do not propose to attempt a solution today. I am only going to take four simple illustrations to show how the statute works: for they will suffice for our present cases.

First, take the case where a professional man is the tenant of two premises: one his office where he works, the other his flat, conveniently near, where he has his home. He has then a 'business tenancy' of his office, and a 'regulated tenancy' of his home. This remains the situation even though he takes papers home and works on them at evenings or weekends and occasionally sees a client at home. He cannot in such a case be said to be occupying his flat 'for the purpose of' his profession. He is occupying it for the purpose of his home, even though he incidentally does some work there, see *Sweet* v. *Parsley* [1970] AC 132 at p 155 by Lord Morris of Borth-y-Gest.

Second, take the case where a professional man takes a tenancy of one house for the very purpose of carrying on his profession in one room and of residing in the rest of the house with his family. Like the doctor who has a consulting room in his house. He has not then a 'regulated tenancy' at all. His tenancy is a 'business tenancy' and nothing else. He is clearly occupying part of the house 'for the purpose of' his profession, as *one* purpose; and the other part for the purpose of his dwelling as *another* purpose. Each purpose is significant. Neither is merely incidental to the other.

Third, suppose now that the first man decides to give up his office and to do all his work from his home, there being nothing in the tenancy of his home to prevent his doing it. In that case he becomes in the same position as the second man. He ceases to have a 'regulated tenancy' of his home. He has only a 'business tenancy' of it.

Fourth, suppose now that the second man decides to give up his office at home and to take a tenancy of an office elsewhere so as to carry on his profession elsewhere. He then has a 'business tenancy' of his new premises. But he does not get a 'regulated tenancy' of his original home, even though he occupies it now only as his home, because it was never let to him as a separate dwelling, unless the landlord agrees to the change.

Those illustrations point to the solution of the present two cases.

The Royal Life Saving Society v. Ernest Donald Page

In 1963 the tenant, Mr Gut, made arrangements to assign the lease to Dr Ernest Donald Page. He was a medical practitioner who had his consulting rooms at 52 Harley Street. His major appointment was medical adviser to Selfridges and he did clinics there five days a week. He took his maisonette in Devonshire Street so that he could live there as his home. But he thought that in the future he might possibly want to use it occasionally so as to see patients there. So, when he took the assignment, he asked for consent to do so. Such consent was readily given by the Royal Life Saving Society (his immediate landlords) and by the Howard de Walden Estate (the head landlords). It was a consent to carry on his profession in the maisonette. After the assignment he moved in and occupied it as his home. He put both addresses (Harley Street and Devonshire Street) in the Medical Directory. He had separate notepaper for each address and put both telephone numbers on each. This was, of course, so that anyone who wished to telephone him could get him at one or the other place. But he did very little professional work at the maisonette. Over the whole period of the tenancy, he had only seen about one patient a year there. The last patient was in distress 18 months ago. He summarised the position in one sentence: 'Harley Street is my professional address, and the other is my home.'

On those facts it is quite clear that 14 Devonshire Street was let as a separate dwelling and occupied by Dr Page as a separate dwelling. There was only one significant purpose for which he occupied it. It was for his home. He carried on his profession elsewhere in Harley Street. His purpose is evidenced by his actual use of it. Such user as he made in Devonshire Street for his profession was not a significant user. It was only incidental to his use of it as his home. He comes within my first illustration.

Cheryl Investments Ltd v. Ronald Saldanha

Now on this point the evidence was this: Mr Saldanha is an accountant by profession. He is a partner in a firm called 'Best Marine Enterprises.' They carry on the business of importing sea foods from India and processing them in Scotland. The firm has no trade premises. The two partners carry on the business from their own homes. The other partner works at his home at Basildon. Mr Saldanha works at the flat in Beaufort Gardens and goes from there out to visit clients. When he went into the flat he had a telephone specially installed for his own use, with the number 589 0232. He put a table in the hall. He had a typewriter there, files and lots of paper. 'The usual office equipment,' said the manageress. He had frequent visitors carrying brief cases. He had notepaper printed: 'Best Marine Enterprises. Importers of Quality Sea-foods. Telephone 589 0232. PO Box 211, Knightsbridge, London SW3.' He issued business statements on that very notepaper. A copy of one was found by the maid in a wastepaper basket showing that the firm had imported goods at a total cost of £49,903.30 and sold them for £58,152.35. The maid (whose evidence the judge explicitly accepted in preference to his) said: 'I presumed Mr Saldanha conducted business there.'

On that evidence I should have thought it plain that Mr Saldanha was occupying this flat, not only as his dwelling, but also for the purposes of a business carried on by him in partnership with another. When he took the flat it was, no doubt, let to him as a separate dwelling. It was obviously a residential flat with just one large room with twin beds in it. No one can doubt that it was constructed for use as a dwelling and let to him as such within *Wolfe* v. *Hogan* [1949] 2 KB 194 at p 204. But as soon as he equipped it for the purposes of his business of importing sea foods—with telephone, table and printed notepaper—and afterwards used it by receiving business calls there, seeing customers there and issuing business statements from there—it is plain that he was occupying it 'for the purposes of a business carried on by him.' This was a significant purpose for which he was occupying the flat, as well as a dwelling. It was his only home, and he was carrying on his business from it. It comes within my second illustration.

16.1 (d) Business

Where bodies of persons are concerned, 'any activity' suffices.

ADDISCOMBE GARDEN ESTATES v. CRABBE

Court of Appeal   [1958] 1 QB 513

(For the facts of this case see page 325, earlier.)

JENKINS LJ: I read again sub-section (2) of section 23: 'In this Part of this Act the expression "business" includes a trade, profession or employment and includes any activity carried on by a body of persons, whether corporate or unincorporate.' Here the premises were used for the activities of a body of persons called the Shirley Park Lawn Tennis Club, and activities were there carried on, whether one should look at the individual members, or at the incorporated body. 'A body of persons, whether corporate or unincorporate'—it matters not which—was carrying on on the premises an activity in the shape of a lawn tennis club. The premises were, therefore, in my judgment, the subject of a tenancy to which the Act applies.

Note: See also *Groveside Properties* v. *Westminster Medical School* (1983) 267 EG 593, earlier.

In *Hillil Property & Investment Co. Ltd* v. *Naraine Pharmacy Ltd* (1979) 252 EG 1013, Megaw LJ said:

'The cases in which the word "activity" in section 23 (2) have been considered appear to have been cases where that which has been recognised as being an "activity" is such a thing as a lawn tennis club, occupying for the purpose of its activities as a members' club; and other similar instances. Though the activity in something which is not strictly a trade, a profession, or an employment, nevertheless, being an "activity" for this purpose it must be something which is correlative to the conceptions involved in those words.'

In that case, a company tenant who used premises simply for dumping waste building materials from another property was held not to be indulging in an 'activity' within section 23 (2).

Where individuals are concerned, they must be engaged in a 'trade profession or employment.'

ABERNETHIE v. A.M. AND J. KLEIMAN LTD

Court of Appeal   [1970] 1 QB 10

The tenant was granted a lease of a shop and rooms over it together with a garage and loft. He carried on a greengrocer's business in the shop and lived in the rooms over it. He regularly taught scripture on Sundays to some 30 children for about one hour in the loft. He received no payment but there was a subscription box into which donations could be made for a scripture mission. After a time, he closed the shop and from then on he held his scripture lessons on Sundays in the shop in summer and in his private sitting-room in winter.

Held: Since the Sunday school was carried on by the tenant alone and not by a body of persons, the question whether it constituted the carrying on of a business within section 23 of the 1954 Act depended on whether it was a 'trade profession or employment' and that the pursuit by a person gratuitously of a spare time activity in his own home did not qualify.

HARMAN LJ: Is it a trade, profession or employment? It is clearly not a 'trade'—clearly, I should have thought, not a 'profession.' It is not carried on professionally: it is carried on amateurishly, just the opposite to 'professionally.' So far as payment is concerned, it is without reward and for the satisfaction, I take it, of the conscience of the person who carries it on: he feels morally obliged to do so.

Is it, then, an 'employment'? True, the tenant does 'employ' himself once a week for an hour in teaching children the scriptures. Is that an 'employment'? In my judgment, it clearly is not. 'Employment' in that sense must mean something much more regular than that. It means, I should have thought, either employing somebody else or being employed by somebody else. However that may be, I cannot think that teaching scripture for one hour a week, done voluntarily, even with a serious sense of social obligation, is a 'business'; and I am rather at a loss to find out how the judge came to such a conclusion.

This case was considered in:

LEWIS v. WELDCREST LTD

Court of Appeal   [1978] 1 WLR 1107

Mrs Lewis was the tenant of a house. She occupied one room of the house and shared the kitchen, bathroom and one other room with her five lodgers, who occupied the remaining three usable rooms. The rooms were let furnished and the tenant paid for gas and electricity and she provided some food. Her weekly income of £26.81 was made up of £14.50 from the lodgers, supplemented by social security.

Held: Although the tenant's only gainful occupation was the taking in of lodgers, in view of that activity and the lack of commercial advantage it could not be regarded as an occupation within the description of a 'trade profession or employment' within section 23 of the 1954 Act.

Stephenson LJ: The purpose of that Act was primarily to give security for tenure to people who would be said, in the ordinary use of language, to be using the premises for a business, even if they were living there as well, using part as a dwelling and part as a business. When I look at the words of the definition in section 23 (2), I see nothing which extends that purpose to cover such activity in providing accommodation for boarders as the applicant provided in this house.

It seems to me that there is nothing in the Act, in its wording or in my understanding of its purpose, to put this lady in the category of a trader or a person carrying on business at those premises. It is no one factor; it is all the factors—the number of lodgers, the size of the place, the sort of sums and services which were involved. I am unconvinced by [counsel for the respondents'] attempts, without having challenged her evidence, to show that this lady was really reaping any commercial advantage out of this activity of taking in lodgers. She was, as it seems to me, doing it probably because she liked it and they help her to pay her way. As [counsel for the respondents] says, it was her only occupation. I have no doubt that she was good at it. She was rendering a service to the lodgers and, indeed, to the public, and sometimes to the welfare authorities, and she was rendering a service to the taxpayer in reducing the amount of social security which had to be paid her. But the one thing that she was not doing, in my judgment, was carrying on a business or trade, whether 'business' is limited to trade or whether it can have any wider connotation.

Part II does not apply where the tenant is carrying on a business use in breach of covenant unless the immediate landlord or his predecessor in title has consented thereto or the immediate landlord has acquiesced therein—section 23 (4).

BELL v. ALFRED FRANKS AND BARTLETT CO. LTD

Court of Appeal [1980] 1 WLR 340

The landlord's predecessor in title sub-let a garage to the defendant in 1964. The agreement was to use the premises for two standing private cars only. The defendant used the garage for a number of years partially for storage of business samples and the two cars for business purposes. The landlord's predecessor in title observed that use but did not object to it. In 1975, the head lease was assigned to the plaintiff who did not know of the business use. In 1977, the plaintiff gave notice to quit in terms of a residential tenancy and the defendant contended that the premises were used for business purposes and that the notice to quit was ineffective.

Held: 'Private' car meant a car both constructed and used for private purposes and the garage had been used for business purposes. Consequently, there was an infringement of the covenant. However, the immediate landlord (the plaintiff) had neither consented nor acquiesced therein and his predecessor in title had merely acquiesced rather than consented. 'Consent' in section 23 (4) of the 1954 Act was used in antithesis to 'acquiescence.'

Shaw LJ: That leaves for decision only the question whether there had been at some stage in the history a consent to the use of the garage against the prohibition contained in the agreement. This is a semantic and philosophical question which requires definition of the distinction between acquiescence and consent. It is quite clear that what section 23 (4) of the Act of 1954 intended was to ensure that the immediate landlord should not be bound by mere—and I use that word deliberately—acquiescence on the part of the immediate predecessor in title, because that goes far to giving to the tenant a protection and exposing the immediate landlord to an undue risk to which he ought not to be exposed. What is meant by acquiescence? It may involve no more than a merely passive attitude, doing nothing at all. It requires as an essential factor that there was knowledge of what was acquiesced in. In this case it is not in controversy that there was such knowledge on the part of the plaintiff's predecessor in title that the garage was used in the way in which it was.

If acquiescence is something passive in the face of knowledge, what does 'consent' mean? In the context of the contrast implicit in sub-section (4), the only practical and sensible distinction that can be drawn is that if acquiescence can arise out of passive failure to do anything, consent must involve a positive demonstrative act, something of an affirmative kind. It is not to be implied, because the resort of implication betokens an absence of express affirmation. The only sense in which there can be implied consent is where a consent is demonstrated, not by language but by some positive act other than words which amounts to an affirmation of what is being done and goes beyond mere acquiescence in it. It may lead, in this context, to a false conclusion to speak of 'implied consent,' which is what the judge said was the proper inference to be drawn from the long history of acquiescence. I would prefer for myself to say 'consent' involves something which is of a positive affirmative kind and that is what is required by section 23 (4) if the immediate landlord is to be deprived of the opportunity of taking advantage of a breach of a prohibition contained in the terms of the tenancy.

In my view, what is decisive of the appeal is that there was no acquiescence on the part of the plaintiff and no consent by Mr Allen. Accordingly, the requirements of the Act of 1954 were not called into play. The notice to quit was effective to terminate the tenancy and the plaintiff was entitled to an order for possession of the garage premises.

16.2   The exclusions contained in section 43 of the 1954 Act

A mining lease is not protected by Part II of the 1954 Act by reason of section 43 (1) (b).

O'CALLAGHAN v. ELLIOTT

Court of Appeal   [1966] 1 QB 601

LORD DENNING MR: The only real point in the case is whether or no, in the circumstances, this was a 'mining lease.' Under the Landlord and Tenant Act, 1954, there is an express exception in section 43 saying it does not apply to a tenancy created by a mining lease. To find the meaning of 'mining lease' we have, according to section 46 of that Act, to refer back to the Landlord and Tenant Act, 1927. Under that Act we find in section 25:

'The expression "mining lease" means a lease for any mining purpose or purposes connected therewith, and "mining purposes" include the sinking and searching for, winning, working, getting, making merchantable, smelting or otherwise converting or working for the purposes of any manufacture, carrying away, and disposing of mines and minerals, in or under land.'

In applying that definition, the question is what 'mines and minerals' there mean? 'Mines and minerals' are not defined in the Act of 1927: and so we have had cited to us many cases and many other statutes in which these words 'mines and minerals' have been used.

In this particular statute, I think that the words 'mines and minerals' are used in the wide sense which was given to them by Lord Romilly MR in *Midland Railway Co.* v. *Checkley*, and by Mellish LJ in *Hext* v. *Gill*. The words 'mines and minerals' include every substance which can be got from underneath the surface of the earth for the purpose of profit.

In this statute, there are no such circumstances to cut down the meaning of the words 'mines and minerals.' I think they include all substances capable of being worked for profit below the top surface of the land. They include sand and gravel and clay but not, I think, peat.

This view is borne out by the object the legislature had in mind in giving a right to a new lease. An ordinary tenant who builds up his own business and creates a goodwill in it should be entitled to a new lease. But a mining tenant does not do this. He is not creating a new capital asset adherent to the land. Quite the reverse. He is taking away part of the landlord's capital assets. He should not be entitled to a new lease, no matter whether it is coal, clay, sand or gravel.

In my opinion, therefore, this was a mining lease within the statute. The tenant has no right to a new lease. The landlords are entitled to possession.

Part II does not apply to a tenancy of (1) licensed premises for consumption on the premises unless the premises are structurally adapted for the reception of guests and travellers desiring to sleep on the premises or (2) the carrying on of a restaurant where the sale of intoxicating liquor does not form a substantial proportion of the business.

GRANT v. GRESHAM

Court of Appeal   (1979) 252 EG 55

The tenant of a public house sought to renew her lease under the 1954 Act on the basis that her business involved the provision of overnight accommodation and meals to a substantial extent other than the sale of alcohol. At its highest, her non-alcoholic proportion of sales was only 16–18 per cent. of the total takings.

Held: The proportion of non-alcoholic business was not substantial and the tenant was unprotected.

ROSKILL LJ: I ask myself—can it be said on the facts of this case, having regard to the nature of this business as a whole, which was primarily at any rate the running of a public house, that the transactions relating to non-alcoholic sale represented a substantial proportion of the total? That of course depends on what one means by the word 'substantial.' In recent legislation one finds the word 'substantial' used in many different contexts. We were referred to a number of cases upon the Rent Acts. One finds the same adjective or adverb used in other statutes; one finds it, for example, in the Homicide Act 1957 in connection with diminished responsibility. there can be no one meaning of the word, whether it appears as an adjective or adverb, which is applicable in all circumstances. One has to look at the context of the statute in which the wording is used and then look at the facts of the particular case. Now if one thing emerges with a reasonable degree of certainty in this case it is that so far as night lettings and night visitors were concerned the business was a comparatively small part of the whole. One finds in the learned judge's findings that in relation to those who were recorded in the visitors' book there were only 41 customer nights; and one finds that there were periods of time when there were no visitors there at all. At other times, perhaps in the summer, it would have been rather more, because no doubt this is an attractive place to stay. But I find myself unable to lay down any precise figure beyond which something is substantial or below which it is not substantial. I do not believe that is the right approach at all. I think that one has to look at this on the basis of fact most favourable to Mrs Gresham and then say—can it be fairly said that on those figures the non-alcoholic sales figures represented a substantial proportion of the business? And asking myself that question I have come to the conclusion, like the learned deputy judge, that I cannot do so.

In **Lansley v. Adda Properties** (1982) CLY 284, the tenant of premises under a 21 year lease applied for a new tenancy under Part II. The occupants were a registered members club of which the tenant was secretary and which supplied alcohol to its members under its registration certificate not requiring a justices' on-licence. The landlord took the point that the tenant was not entitled to the protection of Part II since section 43 (1) (d) excludes a tenancy of premises licensed for the sale of intoxicating liquor on the premises.

Held: 'licensed' in section 43 means holding a justices' licence under the Licensing Act 1964 and, consequently, a registered club did not fall within the exclusion and was protected.

See also: *J.G. Swales & Co.* v. *H.S. Mosley* (1968) CLY 2187.

A tenant at will by implication of law is not entitled to protection under Part II of the 1954 Act.

WHEELER v. MERCER

House of Lords   [1957] AC 416

LORD COHEN: It was common ground between the parties that there were two questions which your Lordships had to decide: (1) When the present proceedings were commenced, was the relationship between the parties that of a tenancy at will? Unless it was, it was common ground that the appellant was entitled to succeed. But if it was, then the second question arises. (2) Is a tenancy at will a tenancy within the meaning of the Act?

My Lords, on the first question I find myself in complete agreement with the county court judge when he says:

'In my opinion the defendant was a typical tenant at will, conforming to all the classical definitions of such a tenant. I refer to Woodfall's Law of Landlord and Tenant, 23rd ed., pp 283, 284; Foa, 7th ed., p 3, and Hill and Redman, 10th ed., pp 16 and 17, and the cases cited by those authorities. She was not in my view a mere licensee because she was in exclusive possession with the consent of the owner; nor was she a tenant at sufferance because I think the landlord's positive assent must be implied from the circumstances.'

I would, therefore, answer the first question in the affirmative, and I turn to the second question.

[Counsel], for the respondent, says that a tenancy at will is 'a tenancy agreement' within the meaning of section 69 (1), since a tenancy at will is a tenancy and agreement is of the essence of a tenancy at will; it is indeed the feature which distinguishes a tenancy at will from a tenancy at sufferance. I am prepared to accept that the expression 'a tenancy agreement' may comprise a tenancy at will, but I think that it might also be the apt language to use where the draftsman had in mind only a tenancy for a fixed term and a periodical tenancy. The question of the sense in which it is used in a particular statute must be answered by construing the statute as a whole, and, in my opinion, the language of section 25 is consistent only with the adoption of the narrower construction I have indicated. It is, I think, clear, reading subsections (2), (3) and (4) together, that subsections (3) and (4) are intended to comprise all the tenancies to which the Act applies. Subsection (3) deals only with tenancies which could be determined by notice to quit, and it was common ground between the parties that a tenancy at will is not such a tenancy, since a tenancy at will is determined, not by a notice to quit, but, for example, by death, bankruptcy or a demand for possession. Subsection (4) is to apply 'in the case of any other tenancy.' This is an omnibus phrase covering all tenancies to which the Act applies except such as are determinable by a notice to quit. It is clear, however, from the language of the subsection that it cannot comprise a tenancy at will because such a tenancy could never come to an end by effluxion of time.

A tenancy at will created by express agreement also falls outside the scope of Part II.

HAGEE (LONDON) LTD v. A.B. ERIKSON AND LARSON

Court of Appeal [1976] QB 209

LORD DENNING MR: In *Wheeler* v. *Mercer* [1957] AC 416, a tenant held over after his lease expired. He became a tenant at will by operation of law. He was held not to be entitled under the Act of 1954. That decision does not govern this case. Viscount Simonds left open the case of a tenancy at will created by express agreement. He said, at p 427:

'I do not exclude the possibility of such a contract being a "tenancy agreement" even if a tenancy at will arising by implication of law is not.'

On studying the provisions of the Act of 1954, I think that tenancies at will are not contemplated at all, no matter whether created by operation of law or by express agreement. Section 25 (3) and (4) show that the only tenancies contemplated as being within the Act are those which are brought to an end by notice to quit and those which are brought to an end by effluxion of time. Section 69 defines 'notice to quit' as meaning:

'a notice to terminate a tenancy (whether a periodical tenancy or a tenancy for a term of years certain) given in accordance with the provisions (whether express or implied) of that tenancy.'

There is no room there for a tenancy at will. It may be an oversight, but those sections do not contemplate a tenancy at will at all.

It is obvious, however, that if parties, by agreeing on a tenancy at will, can escape the provisions of the Act, it means that there is readily to hand a way of contracting out of the Act. This would be contrary to the intention of the Act of 1954, as it originally stood: because section 38 forbad contracting out, save in the case of tenancies for less than three months or at most six months: see section 43 (3). But in 1969 the legislature changed its mind on contracting out. By section 5 of the Law of Property Act 1969 it amended section 38 so as to permit a landlord and tenant to agree together that the Act shall not apply and that the tenant will not have a right to a new lease. Such an agreement is good and binding provided always that it is approved by the court and duly endorsed. We are told that the court invariably approves such an agreement when it is made by business people, properly advised by their lawyers. The court has no materials on which to refuse it.

Seeing that the legislature has opened up this new way of contracting out of the Act of 1954, I feel no hesitation in approving the alternative way which was opened by Cooke J in *Manfield & Sons Ltd* v. *Botchin* [1970] 2 QB 612, namely, that an express contract for a tenancy at will is not within the Act of 1954. Such a tenant has no right to a new lease when his tenancy at will is determined.

If the tenant takes such a tenancy at will, he runs the risk of being turned out; but so long as he does it on proper advice with his eyes open, he is bound by it. I would only add that a tenancy at will of this kind is very rare. The court will look into it very closely to see whether or not it really is a tenancy at will, or whether it is a cloak for a periodic tenancy. But once it is decided to be a tenancy at will, the tenant has no right to a new lease.

A prospective landlord and tenant in relation to a 'term of years certain' may apply jointly to court for approval of an agreement excluding the principal provisions of Part II of the 1954 Act.

IN RE LAND AND PREMISES AT LISS, HANTS

Chancery Division   [1971] Ch 986

A Lease was proposed to be granted for six months from 27 April 1971. The proposed tenancy agreement was expressed to be made under the authority of an order of the court pursuant to section 38 (4) (a) of the 1954 Act and included a provision excluding the provisions of sections 24 to 28 of the Act.

The parties applied for an order pursuant to section 38 of the Act authorising the inclusion in the proposed tenancy agreement of a provision excluding the provisions of sections 24 to 28 of the Act.

Held: The expression 'terms of years certain' in section 38 (4) of the 1954 Act could not be taken as extending to the proposed tenancy for six months unless it was possible to find some context to give it such an extended meaning and such a context was to be found in sections 24 and 26, so that the proposed agreement was one which the court could properly approve.

GOULDING J: The effect of the authorities and statutes to which I have referred is that in the Act of 1969 I cannot take the expression 'term of years certain' as extending to the proposed tenancy for six months unless I can find some context which will enable me to give the expression a more extended meaning than that which the words strictly bear.

On the whole, weighing up all those indications and relying most strongly on [counsel for the Crown's] observations about section 24 of the Act of 1954, I feel that there is enough context to justify me in giving an extended meaning to the words in the new subsection, section 38 (4), and, in my judgment, in that subsection the phrase 'a term of years certain' includes not only a term of one year or more but also a term for a period certain less than one year.

Chapter 17

Automatic continuance

A notice to quit served under the terms of a tenancy, though incapable of effecting a termination, may accelerate the landlord's right to terminate in accordance with Part II of the 1954 Act.

WEINBERGS WEATHERPROOFS LTD v. RADCLIFFE PAPER MILL CO. LTD

Chancery Division   [1958] Ch 437

Certain rooms in a building were demised to the plaintiffs for a term of 20 years from 29 September 1950. Clause 5 of the lease provided that if either the landlords or the tenants were desirous of determining the lease on the expiration of the first seven or fourteen years of the term they should give six months' notice in writing to the other side. The building was sold to the defendants who then served on the plaintiffs a notice of their intention to determine the lease on 29 September 1957.

Held: The notice was effective to cut down the term demised by the lease and the plaintiffs were holding over merely by virtue of Part II of the 1954 Act. However, the defendants could at any time serve a statutory notice under section 25 of the Act and the plaintiffs could at any time apply for a new tenancy under section 26.

HARMAN LJ: In my judgment the notice has the limited effect for which the defendants contend. Having regard to section 24 of the Act of 1954 it is not effective to put an end to the tenancies, but I do not see why it should be of no effect at all. What were the terms of years created by the leases?—not 20 years and 18 years certain, but 20 and 18 years determinable by notice at Michaelmas, 1957. This was the bargain made between the plaintiffs as parties to the leases, and the rights and obligations under them have devolved on the parties to this suit. It does not seem to me to be necessary, in order to give to the Act that effect which the statute intended, to deprive the landlords of the right to shorten the term in this way. The Act still leaves the tenants with the right of occupation which they would have had if the terms had originally been of seven and five years respectively, and the right to claim a new tenancy whether the landlords serve a statutory notice to determine under section 25 or not. The tenants have therefore got the right to obtain a new tenancy which they are promised in the long title to the Act and I do not see why they should have something more which the instruments of lease under which they held did not give them. The principle must be that the bargain should not be altered by the statute more than is necessary to give the statute its proper effect and I hold, accordingly, that though section 24 operated to prevent the notice from causing the terms to come to an end it was effective to break the terms as the instruments of lease provided that it should do. There is still time for the tenants to exercise their rights under section 26 (2) if no statutory notice be served by the landlords, or under section 29 (2) and (3) if such a notice shall be served.

A sub–tenancy continued by Part II of the 1954 Act beyond the term date of a superior tenancy does not operate as an assignment and survives the expiry of the superior tenancy. This can defeat an outgoing tenant's right to remove fixtures.

POSTER v. SLOUGH ESTATES LTD

Chancery Division   [1969] 1 Ch 495

The first defendant demised land to a tenant for a term of 21 years. A note at the end of the first schedule to the lease stated that the mill buildings on the land were tenants' fixtures and could be removed by the tenant at the end or sooner determination of the term. The tenant sublet part of the land to the second defendants. Subsequently, the tenant assigned all the land contained in the lease to the plaintiffs. By a further assignment, the tenant assigned to the plaintiffs the right to remove the buildings on the demised land. The second defendants' sub-tenancy continued by operation of the 1954 Act and when the plaintiffs' lease came to an end, the first defendants became the second defendants' landlords. The plaintiffs claimed that they were entitled to remove the mill buildings on the land.

Held: The second defendants were entitled to continue to enjoy the same rights as those which they had enjoyed during the contractual term and that one of those rights was to have the use of the mill buildings free from the plaintiffs' right to remove them.

CROSS J: The relevant sections of the Act are as follows. [His Lordship read sections 23 (1) (3), 24 (1), 29 (1) and 32 (1) and continued:]
 The effect of these provisions is, I think, that the tenant is *prima facie* at least entitled to go on occupying during the continuation of his tenancy and to have included in a new lease, if one is granted, the same business premises as were included in his original tenancy. Counsel for the plaintiffs submitted, and I agree, that the Act cannot operate to confer on the tenant higher rights with reference to the property included in his extended tenancy than he had under the unextended tenancy. If his lessor or a third party had a right exercisable during the unextended tenancy to remove some building on the demised property with or without an adjustment of rent, that right would, I think, continue to be exercisable during the continuation of the tenancy. If it was exercised, the 'holding,' for the purpose of the Act, would be to that extent diminished. But the difficulty in the way of the plaintiffs is that they had no right to remove these buildings during the currency of the subtenancy granted by their predecessors in title on 7 September 1955. The rent payable under that sub-tenancy was fixed on the footing that the tenant had the use of these buildings, and the plaintiffs' counsel was, I think, disposed to admit that the plaintiffs could not have removed the buildings during the short period from 15 March to 25 March, during which they remained the second defendants' landlord. He argued, however, that this position changed radically on 25 March when the plaintiffs ceased to have the reversion on the tenancy and became entitled as against the first defendants to remove the buildings by reason of the express terms of the headlease. But as I see it the effect of the Act is to allow the tenant to continue to enjoy the same rights as he enjoyed during the contractual period, and in this case one of these rights was to have the use of these buildings free from any right of the plaintiffs or anyone else to remove them. I appreciate that to reject the plaintiffs' argument gives an uncovenanted benefit to the first defendants. If the draftsman of the Act had foreseen such a case he would no doubt have provided for an apportionment of rent. But as it is I cannot prevent the first defendants getting this

benefit at the expense of the plaintiffs without depriving the second defendants of the rights which, as I read the Act, it gives them.

A headlease continued indefinitely by Part II is capable of supporting a sublease granted for a term longer than the unexpired residue of the headlease so that the latter does not operate as an assignment.

WILLIAM SKELTON & SON LTD v. HARRISON AND PINDER LTD

Judge Edgar Fay, QC   [1975] QB 361

In 1949, Mr Skelton granted the plaintiff company a lease of factory premises for a term of 21 years expiring on 26 April 1970. In 1962, Mr Skelton and the plaintiff company agreed to grant the defendants a 21 year underlease of the ground floor of the premises expiring (inadvertently) 3 days before the 26 May 1970. Mr Skelton also agreed to grant the defendants a reversionary lease of the ground floor from the date of the expiry of the headlease (expressed to be 26 May 1970) to 29 September 1983. In October 1969, the plaintiff company served a notice under section 25 of the 1954 Act purporting to terminate the defendant's tenancy in June 1970 and the defendants served a counter-notice stating that they were unwilling to give up possession.

Relying on the rights under the reversionary lease, the defendants, as landlords under that lease, served on the plaintiff company a notice under section 24 (3) (a) of the 1954 Act in March 1972 terminating the plaintiff company's tenancy of the ground floor on the ground that, since the plaintiff company was no longer in occupation, the tenancy of that part of the premises had ceased.

Held: At the time of the underlease, the plaintiff company had a term which, although expressed as a term certain in the headlease, would by operation of Part II of the 1954 Act continue indefinitely until terminated by notice in accordance with the Act so that even though the underlease was for a longer term than the headlease it did not operate as an assignment.

JUDGE EDGAR FAY QC: The defendants, on the other hand, advanced two separate lines of argument. The first is that since the underlease was for a longer term than the headlease, owing to the error of a month, it operated as an assignment; that in consequence the defendants were from the outset tenants of Mr Skelton, and that the plaintiffs had no right to give the section 25 notice. The plaintiffs meet this argument by claiming rectification; alternatively, that, as a matter of interpretation, the word 'May' be read as 'April' in the underlease; alternatively, by asserting that the effect of Part II of the Act is to give a sufficient reversion to the plaintiffs to support the underlease so that it does not have effect as an assignment.

At the time of the underlease in *Oxley* v. *James*, 13 M & W 209, the underlessor had a term which would continue indefinitely, defeasible by notice given by either landlord or tenant. At the time of the underlease in the present case the plaintiffs had a term which, although expressed as a term certain in the instrument, would by operation of Part II of the Act continue indefinitely, defeasible by notice under Part II. It is to be observed that, even if events occurred which caused the tenancy to cease to be protected by that Act, it would continue until terminated by notice: see section 24 (3) of the Act of 1954, which I shall have to consider later.

I can see no difference, in principle, between this kind of indefinite but defeasible reversion, and that in *Oxley* v. *James*, 13 M & W 209. It is not as though the contractual tenancy ceases and is replaced by a new statutory tenancy. The Court of Appeal has decided that under Part II of the Act the common law tenancy subsists, with a statutory variation as to mode of determination: see *H. L. Bolton (Engineering) Co. Ltd* v. *T. J. Graham & Sons Ltd* [1957] 1 QB 159, 168 and

Cornish v. *Brook Green Laundry Ltd* [1959] 1 QB 394, 409. For these reasons I hold that the unrectified underlease does not have effect as an assignment, and for this reason the defendants' first line of argument fails. In these circumstances it would be idle to consider rectification, and I shall not grant that remedy.

In the absence of express words to the contrary, a guarantee that a tenant will pay rent does not extend to any default after the fixed period of the lease expires although the tenancy continues by virtue of Part II of the 1954 Act.

JUNCTION ESTATES LTD v. COPE

Queen's Bench Division   (1974) 27 P & CR 482

The plaintiffs granted a lease of business premises to Swift–Planned Developments Ltd for seven years. The defendants joined in the lease as guarantors of the tenants, covenanting in clause 3 in the following terms:

> 'The guarantors ... hereby jointly and severally covenant ... that the tenant will pay the rent hereby reserved on the days and in the manner aforesaid and will perform all the tenant's covenants hereinbefore contained and that in case of default in such payment of rent ... the guarantors will pay and make good to the landlord on demand all losses damage costs expenses thereby arising or incurred by the landlord.'

Swift–Planned Developments Ltd subsequently assigned their tenancy to Gravsport Hire Limited, who continued in possession of the premises after the expiry of the lease under Part II of the 1954 Act. They failed to pay rent due and the plaintiffs brought an action against the defendants claiming that they were liable as guarantors for the unpaid rent.

Held: On its true construction, clause 3 of the lease did not cover any obligation of the tenant to pay his rent during any statutory extension of the term.

MACKENNA J: In my opinion the question between the plaintiffs and the defendants depends on the true construction of clause 3. I construe it as guaranteeing the performance of the obligation created by clauses 1 and 2 of the lease, namely, in the case of rent, the payment of the rent reserved by the lease during its seven years' term. I do not read clause 3 as covering any obligation of the tenant to pay his rent during any statutory extension of the term. If the plaintiffs had wanted a guarantee which would impose that indefinite liability on the defendants, that is, a liability continuing until either the plaintiffs had served a notice of termination, or the tenants had served a notice to quit, or a new tenancy had been applied for by the tenant and granted by the court, or the landlord had forfeited the tenancy, they should have made that intention clear in the language of the guarantee. They have not done so. I think that the language of clause 3 makes it clear that the guarantors are to be liable only for the seven years' rent if any part of that should be unpaid. If clause 3 is ambiguous about the guarantors' obligation, it should, on well-established principles, be construed against the plaintiffs, and I would so construe it.

Chapter 18

Non–statutory methods of termination

18.1 Surrender

A business tenancy can be brought to an end by surrender provided that the instrument of surrender is not executed before, or is not executed in pursuance of any agreement to surrender made before, the tenant had been in occupation for one month.

WATNEY v. BOARDLEY

Chancery Division [1975] 1 WLR 857

A lease gave the tenant the option to purchase the reversion in fee simple by serving notice not less than three months prior to the determination of the lease. The tenant exercised the option but was unable to complete the purchase. The landlords demanded possession of the premises and the tenant claimed that he was entitled to the benefit of section 24 of the 1954 Act.

The question in issue was whether the tenancy had been brought to an end by an 'instrument of surrender' (i.e. the notice exercising the option) within the meaning of section 24 (2) as amended by section 4 (1) of the Law of Property Act 1969.

Held: The notice exercising the option was a surrender which was not invalidated by section 24 (2) as amended since the exercise of the option was not an 'instrument of surrender' pursuant to the agreement contained in the lease as the surrender arose by operation of law.

GOULDING J: The relevant section of the Landlord and Tenant Act 1954 is section 24 and I will read the first subsection, premising that it is clear that the tenancy under the lease of 1967 was itself a tenancy to which Part II of the Act of 1954 applied. Section 24 (1) provides:

> 'A tenancy to which this Part of this Act applies shall not come to an end unless terminated in accordance with the provisions of this Part of this Act; and, subject to the provisions of section 29 of this Act, the tenant under such a tenancy may apply to the court for a new tenancy—(a) if the landlord has given notice under the next following section to terminate the tenancy, or (b) if the tenant has made a request for a new tenancy in accordance with section 26 of this Act.'

However, that subsection was qualified by subsection (2) as follows:

> 'The last foregoing subsection shall not prevent the coming to an end of a tenancy by notice to quit given by the tenant, by surrender or forfeiture, or by the forfeiture of a superior tenancy.'

That is how the Act of 1954 stood when originally enacted and in that form section 24 (2) would be a complete answer to the suggestion made in correspondence on behalf of the defendant, for I am satisfied that the effect of clause 5 of the lease followed by the notice exercising the option was to bring about a surrender of the tenancy on 6 July 1973. The difficulty arises because of amending legislation contained in the Law of Property Act 1969 which was passed, as I understand it, to make it more difficult to avoid by agreement the protection given to tenants of business premises by the Act of 1954. The Act of 1969 by section 4 (1) added the following words at the end of section 24 (2) (which I have read) of the Act of 1954:

'unless—(a) in the case of a notice to quit, the notice was given before the tenant had been in occupation in right of the tenancy for one month; or (b) in the case of an instrument of surrender, the instrument was executed before, or was executed in pursuance of an agreement made before, the tenant had been in occupation in right of the tenancy for one month.'

In other words the present law, so far as relevant, is that one cannot bring a protected tenancy to an end by an instrument of surrender if that instrument was executed in pursuance of an agreement made before the tenant had been in occupation in right of the tenancy for at least one month.

A possible answer to the plaintiffs' claim for possession is thus that (apart from statute) the tenancy under the lease was brought to an end by an instrument of surrender (namely the notice exercising the option) executed in pursuance of an agreement contained in the original lease and therefore made before the first month of occupation under the lease had elapsed. Three alternative replies have been made by counsel for the plaintiffs to that argument: first it is said that there is here no instrument of surrender; true it is that by the effect of the notice the term came to be surrendered three months later but the notice itself is not a surrender and on the face of it, is wholly different from anything that any ordinary layman or lawyer would describe as an instrument of surrender. Therefore it is submitted there is no instrument of surrender and the qualifications imposed on section 24 (2) of the Act of 1954 by the Act of 1969 have no relevance.

The second argument is that the lease or the option clause in the lease cannot fairly be described as an agreement in pursuance of which the purchase or exercise of the option took place. Reliance is placed on the familiar analysis of an option as being an irrevocable offer: that offer was accepted, it is said, by notice exercising the option. Then and then only did any agreement for surrender come into existence.

The third argument of the plaintiffs is that the agreement, if any, in pursuance of which notice was given to exercise the option was constituted not by the lease but by the agreement of 1970, which I have recited, incorporating and as it were re-publishing the relevant terms of the lease. That agreement was of course made long after the expiration of the first month of the tenancy.

I do not propose to say anything about the second or the third point: the second point in particular is of considerable difficulty having regard to the purpose of the amending legislation and the lack of precision in the words, 'in pursuance of,' and I ought to avoid any discussion of it unless necessary to my decision. It is not necessary because in my view the plaintiffs succeed on their first contention.

In the older language of the law of landlord and tenant the surrender in consequence of the exercise of the option to purchase would properly I think be described as a surrender by operation of law. The law operates because the relation of vendor and purchaser paying interest on the purchase money is inconsistent with the continuance of a tenancy under which rent is payable. If that is not the right way of looking at the matter it may be that the surrender should be considered as taking place by virtue of clause 5 of the lease operating after service of a notice exercising the option. On neither analysis would it be right, in my judgment, to describe the notice exercising the option as 'an instrument of surrender': it was not directed to surrender as such, but to purchase of the reversion. It did not at the date when it was served as a notice bring about a surrender; all it did was to produce such a state of affairs that the tenancy could not continue after the contractual completion date. Accordingly, to my mind, it would be an unjustified and strange interpretation of the term 'instrument of surrender' to describe the notice as such an instrument in the present case. Accordingly I hold that the Law of Property Act 1969 does not, in the circumstances of this case, deprive the landlord of the benefit of section 24 (2) of the Landlord and Tenant Act 1954 whereby that Act does not prevent the coming to the end of a tenancy by surrender.

Any agreement purporting to preclude the tenant from making an application or request under Part II of the Act or providing for the termination or the surrender of the tenancy in the event of his making such an application or request is void under section 38 (1).

TARJOMANI v. PANTHER SECURITIES LTD

Chancery Division   (1982) 46 P & CR 32

The tenant of a lease of business premises fell into arrears of rent and rates. He made an arrangement with the landlord and both parties put it in the form of a letter which stated that the tenant would be released from all outstanding rent and other arrears 'in consideration of the surrender of [the lease] taking place today ...' The tenant claimed that the agreement arising from the letter had the effect of precluding him from making an application or request under Part II of the 1954 Act and was void under section 38 of that Act.

Held: The letter fell within section 38 (1) and was unenforceable.

PETER GIBSON J: I turn next to the Landlord and Tenant Act 1954, as amended by the Law of Property Act 1969. It is common ground that the plaintiff had a business tenancy to which Part II of the 1954 Act applies. Section 24 (1) provides, so far as material:

'A tenancy to which this part of this Act applies shall not come to an end unless terminated in accordance with the provisions of this Part of this Act; and ... the tenant under such a tenancy may apply to the court for a new tenancy ...
    (b) if the tenant has made a request for a new tenancy in accordance with section 26 of this Act.'

The subsection (2):

'The last foregoing subsection shall not prevent the coming to an end of a tenancy by notice to quit given by the tenant, by surrender or forfeiture, or by the forfeiture of a superior tenancy unless ...
    (b) in the case of an instrument of surrender, the instrument was executed before, or was executed in pursuance of an agreement made before, the tenant had been in occupation in right of the tenancy for one month.'

The words in subsection (2) commencing with the word 'unless' were added by section 4 of the 1969 Act.
    Section 38 (1) of the 1954 Act reads, so far as material:

'Any agreement relating to a tenancy to which this Part of this Act applies (whether contained in the instrument creating the tenancy or not) shall be void (except as provided by subsection (4) of this section) in so far as it purports to preclude the tenant from making an application or request under this Part of this Act or provides for the termination or the surrender of the tenancy in the event of his making such an application or request or for the imposition of any penalty or disability on the tenant in that event.'

The words '(except as provided by subsection (4) of this section)' were added by section 5 of the 1969 Act. Then subsection (4), so far as material, provides:

'The court may ...
   (b) on the joint application of the persons who are the landlord and the tenant in relation to a tenancy to which this Part of this Act applies, authorise an agreement for the surrender of the tenancy on such date or in such circumstances as may be specified in the agreement and on such terms (if any) as may be so specified;
   if the agreement is contained in or endorsed on the instrument creating the tenancy or such other instrument as the court may specify; and an agreement contained in or endorsed on an instrument in pursuance of an authorisation given under this subsection shall be valid notwithstanding anything in the preceding provisions of this section.'

The whole of subsection (4) is an amendment inserted by section 5 of the 1969 Act. In section 69 (1) of the 1954 Act 'tenancy' is defined as including an agreement for a lease and a tenancy agreement. The term 'surrender' is not defined and therefore, on its face, it does not extend to include an agreement to surrender.

[Counsel for the plaintiffs] submits that the letter of 12 July 1982, did not constitute an effective express surrender because of section 52 (1) of the 1925 Act in that it was not under seal. However, he accepts that it operated in equity as an agreement to surrender. As it was not an actual surrender, section 24 (2) of the 1954 Act, he submits, does not apply. The letter of 12 July did, however, constitute an agreement relating to a business tenancy which purported to preclude the tenant from making an application under Part II of the Act in the sense that it had the effect of precluding the tenant from making such an application. Accordingly, he says, the agreement was void to that extent and not enforceable.

[Counsel for the defendants] accepts that the letter of 12 July was not effective to surrender the legal estate, but he submits that it was fully effective in equity as an immediate surrender of the beneficial interest of the plaintiff and thus had immediate effect as an equitable surrender. He relies on the doctrine of *Walsh* v. *Lonsdale* in support of this proposition. He says that it was a surrender for the purpose of section 24 (2) of the 1954 Act and accordingly section 38 (1) has no application. But in any event, he says, section 38 (1) only applies to agreements to surrender *in futuro* and not to agreements effecting immediate surrenders. Accordingly, he submits that there was an express surrender on 12 July and no statutory provision avoids it.

In my judgment, the express surrender of a lease such as that which the plaintiff held required a deed but, being in writing and supported by consideration in the form of the release by the defendant of the plaintiff's arrears of rent, it is effective in equity as a contract to surrender. But not being an actual surrender effective immediately to bring the tenancy to an end, in my judgment, it cannot be a surrender for the purpose of section 24 (2) of the 1954 Act. It may be that where a tenant holds under an agreement for a tenancy and does not have a legal estate, a surrender in writing but not under seal is effective as a surrender of his entire equitable interest, which is all that the tenant holds, and so comes within section 24 (2) of the 1954 Act, but that is not this case.

The agreements to which section 38 (1) of the 1954 Act apply are expressed in very wide terms. I see no difficulty concerning the letter of 12 July as coming within the very wide words 'any agreement relating to a tenancy to which this part of this

Act applies.' It is established by the decision of the Court of Appeal in *Joseph* v. *Joseph* that the word 'purports' in section 38 (1) means 'has the effect of.' If the tenant enters into agreement to surrender his business tenancy, that agreement has the effect of precluding the tenant from making an application under Part II of the Act. Accordingly, on the plain wording of section 38 (1) the letter agreement of 12 July would be avoided to that extent. However, [counsel for the defendants] submits that the agreement referred to in section 38 (1) must be construed as limited to an agreement to surrender *in futuro* and that as section 38 (1) is an anti-avoidance provision to prevent the landlord evading the provisions of Part II of the 1954 Act, it should not be construed in such a way as to cover the facts of the present case.

I accept that if there had been an immediate surrender, then section 38 (1) would have no application, but I have difficulty in accepting that the wide language of the section should be limited in the manner that [counsel for the defendants] suggested.

I therefore accept [counsel for the plaintiff's] submission on this point.

The phrase 'purports to preclude the tenant from making an application or request under this Part of this Act' in section 38 (1) of the 1954 Act means 'has the effect of precluding the tenant'. Thus, an agreement made by a tenant for the giving up of possession and surrender of his tenancy at a future date is void under the Act and cannot be enforced.

ALLNATT LONDON PROPERTIES LTD v. NEWTON

Court of Appeal   (1983) 45 P & CR 94

DILLON LJ: This is an appeal from the decision of Sir Robert Megarry V-C given on 20 November 1980. The appellants, who were the plaintiffs in the action, are the landlords, and the respondent, who is the sole defendant, is the tenant of certain business premises known as Building 665, Pulborough Way, Green Lane, Hounslow, held under a lease of 20 April 1972, for a term of 21 years from 25 March 1972.

Clause 3 (21) (b) of the lease contained a covenant by the tenant:

'Not, (subject to the proviso to this clause) to assign underlet part with the possession of occupation of the demised premises as a whole provided always that if at any time and so often as the tenant shall desire to assign or underlet the demised premises as a whole the tenant shall make to the landlords an offer in writing in the terms hereinafter mentioned ...'

The terms of the offer in writing were to be this:

'... shall be in the terms following namely the tenant shall offer to surrender the lease with vacant possession and otherwise free from encumbrances on a date three months from the date of the said written offer in consideration of the payment by the landlords to the tenant of a sum representing the net premium value (if any) of this lease for the unexpired residue of the term ...'

such value to be agreed or determined as provided in the clause.

On 6 December 1979, the tenant's solicitors wrote to the landlords asking for consent to an assignment of the lease to certain gentlemen, enclosing references. The landlords replied saying that they would not consider any application to assign until they had first been offered a surrender as required by the lease. On 20 December 1979, the tenant made the formal offer to surrender the lease in accordance with the terms of the lease. On 9 January 1980, the landlords by their solicitors stated that they were prepared to accept the tenant's offer of surrender in accordance with the terms of the lease. They suggested that the surrender date be 25 March 1980, provided vacant possession could be given by that date and they also made reference to surveyors inspecting the premises and the payment of some rent which had either by then been paid or was shortly thereafter paid.

After certain further correspondence which does not matter, on 6 March 1980, the tenant's solicitors wrote, and on behalf of their client they withdrew, or purported to withdraw, the offer to surrender. The tenant has, we are told, remained in occupation of the premises for business purposes ever since.

The proceedings were brought by the landlords claiming as the primary relief; 'A declaration that there exists an enforceable contract for the surrender by the [tenant] to the [landlords] of the lease'—and specific performance of that contract.

Sir Robert Megarry V-C rejected that claim because he held that the contract relied on—the offer of surrender and the acceptance of that offer—fell foul (as these were business premises) of section 38 (1) of the Landlord and Tenant Act 1954. That section [as amended by section 5 of the Law of Property Act 1969] reads:

'Any agreement relating to a tenancy to which this Part of this Act applies (whether contained in the instrument creating the tenancy or not) shall be void (except as provided by subsection (4) of this section) in so far as it purports to preclude the tenant from making an application or request under this Part of this Act or provides for the termination or the surrender of the tenancy in the event of his making such an application or request or for the imposition of any penalty or disability on the tenant in that event.'

Subsection (4) does not matter for present purposes because the parties did not so arrange their affairs as to fall within it.

In *Joseph* v. *Joseph* the Court of Appeal held that in section 38 (1) the expression 'purports to preclude the tenant from making an application or request under this Part of this Act' means 'has the effect of precluding the tenant.' Therefore, an agreement made in *Joseph* v. *Joseph* by tenants for the giving up of possession and surrender of their tenancy at a future date was void and ineffective under the Act and could not be enforced.

The Vice-Chancellor held that *Joseph* v. *Joseph* entirely covered the present case and precluded specific performance of the agreement relied on by the landlords. In my judgment he was entirely right in that conclusion; *Joseph* v. *Joseph* also binds us with the same result.

18.2 Forfeiture

Where there is a judgment for forfeiture and a subsisting application for relief against forfeiture, the tenancy does not 'come to an end by forfeiture' for the purposes of section 24 (2) of the 1954 Act.

MEADOWS v. CLERICAL, MEDICAL AND GENERAL LIFE ASSURANCE SOCIETY

Chancery Division   [1981] Ch 70

SIR ROBERT MEGARRY V-C: I turn to the language of the subsections mainly in point. By section 24 (1):

'A tenancy to which this Part of this Act applies shall not come to an end unless terminated in accordance with the provisions of this Part of this Act ...'

and the subsection then authorises 'the tenant under such a tenancy' to 'apply to the court for a new tenancy.' Pausing there, but for the forfeiture the tenancy in issue in this case would have expired at common law on 21 June 1979, but would then have been continued under section 24 (1). There is then section 24 (2), and it is on this, rather than on section 24 (1), that I think the case in the main turns. Section 24 (2) provides:

'The last foregoing subsection shall not prevent the coming to an end of a tenancy by notice to quit given by the tenant, by surrender or forfeiture, or by the forfeiture of a superior tenancy ...'

and then there are some exceptions which I need not read. It will be observed that mere forfeiture is not enough: there must be 'the coming to an end' of the tenancy 'by forfeiture.' Furthermore, the phrase 'the coming to an end' of the tenancy is shared by a 'notice to quit given by the tenant' and by 'surrender.' Is a forfeited tenancy which is the subject of a subsisting application for relief, which may restore the tenancy as if it had never been forfeited, a tenancy which has come to an end for these purposes, at any rate in the sense in which a tenancy which has been surrendered has come to an end?

The point is not easy, but in my judgment the answer is 'No.' I think that such a tenancy is a tenancy which may or may not have truly come to an end, and that the subsection is contemplating a tenancy which has in fact come to an end. The right of a tenant to apply for relief is part of the process of forfeiture, and until that process is complete, I do not think that the tenancy has come to an end within the meaning of section 24 (2) of the Landlord and Tenant Act 1954. The plaintiff's tenancy in this case had accordingly not been taken out of the operation of section 24 (1), and it continued under it, thus enabling the plaintiff to apply for a new tenancy.

18.3   Tenancy ceasing to be one to which Part II applies

If a business tenant temporarily vacates the demised premises while they are being repaired or following a fire, he will not lose his protection under Part II provided that he has the intention to return as soon as the premises are fit for occupation.

MORRISONS HOLDINGS LTD v. MANDERS PROPERTY (WOLVERHAMPTON) LTD

Court of Appeal   [1976] 1 WLR 533

A fire caused considerable damage to the roof and upper storeys of a building as a result of which the tenants' premises therein became unfit for occupation for the purposes of their business. They wrote to the landlords suggesting that the premises be made weatherproof and suitable for their occupation and generally expressing their desire to resume trading there. They kept the keys to the premises and left some fixtures and fittings after salvaging their stock. Subsequently, the landlords demolished the premises to which the tenants had not returned. The question at issue was whether the tenants had ceased to occupy the premises for the purpose of their business so as to preclude them from applying for a new tenancy under the 1954 Act.

Held: In order to have *locus standi* to apply for a new tenancy, the tenants had to show either that they were in physical occupation of the premises for the purpose of a business carried on by them or, if events beyond their control had led to their absence from the premises, that they continued to assert their right to occupancy. On the facts, the tenants had remained in occupation by maintaining their intention and right to occupy.

SIR GORDON WILLMER: So far as the law is concerned, I think it can be taken as axiomatic that in order to be in occupation one does not have to be physically present every second of every minute of every hour of every day. All of us remain in occupation, for instance, of our houses even while we are away doing our day's work. It follows, therefore, that occupation necessarily must include an element of intention as well as a physical element. If I leave my premises and emigrate to the United States of America with no intention of returning, it can well be said that I no longer remain in occupation. But if as a shopkeeper I close my shop for a fortnight in the summer to enable my staff to have a holiday, I apprehend that no one would contend that during that fortnight I ceased to be in occupation of my shop.

It is in the light of those considerations that I think one must look at the facts of this particular case. After the fire the tenants, as tenants, enjoyed the same right to occupy the premises as they enjoyed before. The premises, although damaged, were still in existence, and, as I understand the evidence, the tenants exercised during the first day or two following the fire their rights by going into the premises in order to save such stores and equipment as they could. If the tenants did not remain in occupation, then one might well ask the question: who did? The answer, I think, having regard to the argument in this case, would have to be that immediately following the fire the tenants ceased to be in occupation and the landlords themselves resumed occupation. But the landlords would be faced with the same difficult question as the tenants are faced with here, that they were not physically on the premises. For my part, I cannot accept that view of the case. It seems to me that the tenants, who had been in continuous occupation up to the fire and immediately after the fire, and who retained the intention to occupy, remained both in fact and in law the occupiers of the premises at the relevant time. They are consequently entitled to prosecute whatever remedy they may have in pursuance of the Landlord and Tenant Act 1954.

I omitted to observe, although Scarman LJ mentioned it, that the tenants retained the keys of the premises. They were thus in a position to exclude the public from the premises, or to open the door and invite the public to come in. If some person was invited to come in, I apprehend that the tenants would have had some difficulty in escaping their liabilities under the Occupiers Liability Act 1957.

However one looks at it, it seems to me that one cannot disregard the tenants' continuing occupation of these premises, notwithstanding the somewhat devastating effects of the fire that took place.

It only remains to add that, assuming I am right so far, I do not see how the subsequent demolition of the building at the instance of the landlords, which took place on 17 June can possibly have affected one way or the other such rights as the tenants had.

My conclusion, therefore, in agreement with Scarman LJ is that these tenants do have a perfectly good locus standi to pursue their remedy under the Act of 1954.

In **I. and H. Caplan Ltd v. Caplan (No. 2)** [1963] 1 WLR 1247, Cross J held that a tenant who had ceased to trade and had left the premises almost empty while awaiting the outcome of proceedings under the Act remained within the Act as his measures were purely precautionary. At page 1260 he said:

'I think it is quite clear that a tenant does not lose the protection of this Act simply by ceasing physically to occupy the premises. They may well continue to be occupied for the purposes of the business although they are *de facto* empty for some period of time. One rather obvious example would be if there was a need for urgent structural repairs and the tenant had to go out of physical occupation in order to enable them to be effected. Another example would be that which the

365

Court of Appeal had to deal with in *Teasdale* v. *Walker*. That was a case where premises were only occupied during the seasonal periods: they were closed and empty in the winter and only used in the summer. On the other hand, as the Court of Appeal pointed out in *Teasdale* v. *Walker*, a mere intention to resume occupation if you get a new tenancy will not preserve the continuity of business user if the thread has once been definitely broken. I think one must observe, however, that in *Teasdale* v. *Walker* the discontinuance of business occupation was before the tenant applied to the court for a new tenancy. She had let someone else occupy it for business purposes. He had gone out of occupation and given her back the key and the premises were empty when the summons was issued. In those circumstances the Court of Appeal considered that her expressed intention to start again herself, if and when she got a new tenancy, was not enough.

But, as it seems to me, the position may very well be quite different if the tenant is using the premises for business purposes at the date of the issue of the summons and subsequently goes out of physical occupation during the proceedings. Take this example: Suppose that a tenant in occupation for business purposes applies for a new tenancy. The landlords oppose the application and succeed in the court of first instance. The tenant then lodges a notice of appeal but his solicitors tell him that his chances are not very rosy and it is extremely likely that the landlords will be upheld in their objection and he will at long last have to give up possession. It seems to me to be not unreasonable for a tenant in those circumstances to say:

'Well, I must secure my way of retreat. I must make sure: I must preserve the goodwill of these premises and I must give continuity of employment to my staff. I cannot risk staying on here and being suddenly turned out. I am going to take some other premises to which I will transfer temporarily—possibly for ever, but possibly only temporarily—my staff and my stock. Those premises are admittedly not as nice as the ones from which I am being turned out. If I succeed, as I hope, in this appeal, I will go back. Of course, if I fail, I cannot go back and I must go on in the new premises.'

I think that on those facts I would be very loth to hold that the physical arrangement of occupation disentitled or deprived the tenant of his rights under the Act and, *a fortiori*, I think that would be so if he left a quantity of stock on the premises.

The landlords here may very well say that that example which I have taken is much more favourable to the tenants than the facts here because, as I have said, I think that the business which they hoped to set up if they succeeded in the appeal was not precisely the same business as they had discontinued although it was allied to it. The ladies' garment trade is obviously allied to the business that they had carried on before, although it is not exactly the same. Secondly, it may be said, very fairly, that the stock which they left behind, though it was physically left on the company's premises, was really dedicated to the purposes of the H.C.C. company and would not have been retailed on the company's premises if matters had panned out as the company thought that they would.

I appreciate the force of those arguments but all these cases, of course, are cases of degrees depending on their own particular facts. The facts here are most unusual and I think that this is distinctly a border-line case, but on the whole I have come to the conclusion that the thread of continuity, to use the words of the Court of Appeal in the case of *Teasdale* v. *Walker*, was not broken in this case.

In **Domer v. Gulf Oil Ltd** (1975), The Times, 4 March, Megarry J held that where there is no doubt that the tenant has ceased to occupy premises for business purposes, the landlord may apply to have the tenant's application for a new tenancy struck out as being an abuse of the process of the court.

See also *Hancock & Willis* v. *G.M.S. Syndicate Ltd* (1982) 265 EG 473 at page 342, earlier.

In **Aireps Ltd v. City of Bradford Metropolitan Council** (1985) 276 EG 1067, the Court of Appeal held that the court could not grant a new tenancy of premises which had ceased to exist (because they were demolished), which could not be reinstated and *ex hypothesi* could never again be occupied by the tenant for the purpose of his business. Nor could the court grant a new tenancy of premises which the landlord had agreed to let in substitution for the original premises even if they could be identified because they were not premises which were occupied by the tenant at the date of the application or at any material date.

If a tenancy ceases to be one to which Part II applies after the expiry of a fixed term, the tenancy does not end for that reason alone but the landlord may terminate by giving notice in writing under section 24 (3) (a).

WILLIAM SKELTON & SON LTD v. HARRISON & PINDER LTD

Judge Edgar Fay, QC   [1975] QB 361

(For the facts of this case see page 356, earlier.)

JUDGE EDGAR FAY QC: The defendants' other argument is that the reversionary lease, when it came into force, severed the reversion expectant on the plaintiffs' tenancy so that from that date the plaintiffs held the part of the factory they occupied from Mr Skelton, and the defendants' part from the defendants. This, say the defendants, takes the plaintiffs' tenancy of the defendants' part out of the protection of the Act, and opens the way for service of a notice under section 24 (3) (*a*).

I now come to the nub of [counsel for the defendants'] argument on this second branch of his case. He says that the severance of the reversion as governed by section 140 of the Law of Property Act 1925 has put an end to the application of Part II of the Act of 1954 to this part of the tenancy, and that this fact brings into play section 24 (3) (*a*) of that Act, under which effective notice to quit may be given. This is the notice which the defendants gave to expire on 1 July 1972. As from that date, he says, the plaintiffs' interest is gone, and the defendants' occupation is an occupation under what I have called the reversionary lease, but which, as from that date, ceased to be reversionary.

In order to deal with these submissions I must look, first, at the statutory provisions. Section 140 of the Act of 1925 reads as follows:

'(1) Notwithstanding the severance by conveyance, surrender, or otherwise of the reversionary estate in any land comprised in a lease, and notwithstanding the avoidance or cesser in any other manner of the term granted by a lease as to part only of the land comprised therein, every condition or right of re-entry, and every other condition contained in the lease, shall be apportioned, and shall remain annexed to the severed parts of the reversionary estate as severed, and shall be in force with respect to the term whereon each severed part is reversionary, or the term in the part of the land as to which the term has not been surrendered, or has not been avoided or has not otherwise ceased, in like manner as if the land comprised in each severed part, or the land as to which the term remains subsisting, as the case may be, had alone originally been comprised in the lease. (2) In this section "right of re-entry" includes a right to determine the lease by notice to quit or otherwise; but where the notice is served by a person entitled to a severed part of the reversion so that it extends to part only of the land demised, the lessee may within one month determine the lease in regard to the rest of the land by giving to the owner of the reversionary estate therein a counter notice expiring at the same time as the original notice.'

I need not read subsection (3).

The effect of the first two subsections is to provide that the right to determine the lease by a notice to quit remains annexed to the severed part of the reversionary estate, that is the defendants' interest, in like manner as if the defendants' part of the factory had alone originally been comprised in the lease. So the defendants are entitled to give to the plaintiffs, in respect of the defendants' portion of the factory, whatever notice the lease—that is, the headlease as modified by Part II of the Act of 1954—permits.

Section 24 (3) of the Act of 1954 provides:

'Notwithstanding anything in subsection (1) of this section,—(a) where a tenancy to which this Part of this Act applies ceases to be such a tenancy, it shall not come to an end by reason only of the cesser, but if it was granted for a term of years certain and has been continued by subsection (1) of this section then (without prejudice to the termination thereof in accordance with any terms of the tenancy) it may be terminated by not less than three nor more than six months' notice in writing given by the landlord to the tenant;'

I need not read paragraph (b). The notice given in this case complied as to length with this provision. The crux of the matter is whether the head tenancy, which was one to which Part II of the Act of 1954 applied, has ceased, quoad the defendants' part of the factory, to be such a tenancy. [Counsel for the defendants] says that the severance of the reversion has effected that cesser of protection. He says that because by section 23 (1) a tenancy to which Part II applies—which I shall call a protected tenancy—is one:

'... where the property comprised in the tenancy is or includes premises which are occupied by the tenant and are so occupied for the purposes of a business carried on by him or for those and other purposes.'

By virtue of the two words 'or includes' the plaintiffs initially enjoyed protection as regards the whole factory, because they occupied a part. But now they have a separate landlord of the severed part, and of that part they occupy none. So, says counsel, they have lost protection and the way is open for the section 24 (3) (a) notice.

[Counsel for the plaintiffs'] rejoinder is to cite the recent case in the Court of Appeal, *Jelley* v. *Buckman* [1974] QB 488. This was a case under the Rent Acts where land had been let together with a dwelling house. The reversion to the land had become severed from the reversion to the dwelling house. The Court of Appeal rejected the argument that, by reason of the severance, the land had ceased to be land let together with the dwelling house, and held that the whole still enjoyed the protection of the Rent Acts. Stamp LJ, giving the judgment of the court, said, at p 496: 'In our judgment, however, a severance of the lessor's reversion by conveyance does not bring two separate tenancies into being ...' and, after dealing with section 140 of the Law of Property Act 125, he said, at p 498:

'But it is one thing to say that each reversioner has rights and remedies similar to or even indistinguishable from the rights and remedies which he would have had if there had been two separate tenancies and quite another thing to say that this operates against the tenant and that he therefore has two tenancies; and we cannot read section 140 as producing the latter result. We can find nothing in the section to suggest for a moment that the legislature intended that following a severance to which the lessee was not a party he should find himself holding part of his land under one tenancy and part under another.'

Now I see the force of [counsel for the plaintiffs'] contention that, just as the severed land in *Jelley* v. *Buckman* [1974] QB 488 was still let together with the remainder, so here, in the words of section 23 (1), the tenancy is still, notwithstanding the severance, one which includes premises occupied for business purposes. If the question I had to decide was whether the two parts of the tenancy are let together with one another, the matter would be concluded in the plaintiffs' favour. But that is not what I have to decide. The question here is whether or not the defendants may serve a section 24 (3) (*a*) notice. There are words in section 140 of the Law of Property Act 1925 which govern notices. It may be significant that the Act of 1954, although it contains detailed provisions covering some specific situations such as sections 28 and 44 as to future tenancies and reversionary leases, has no specific provision as to the problem of the severed reversion. In passing the Act of 1954 Parliament must be taken to have had the provisions of the earlier Act in mind; and it may well be that the Act of 1954 contains no special provision because the matter is adequately covered by section 140 of the Act of 1925.

In any event section 140 clearly applies, and I must examine what it says about terminating a tenancy. Subsection (2) defines a 'right of re-entry' to include a right to determine a lease by notice to quit or otherwise. Subsection (1) provides, among other things, that every right of 're-entry' shall be in force 'in like manner as if the land comprised in each severed part, ... had alone originally been comprised in the lease.' Some meaning has to be given to these words. In the light of the Act of 1954 there are three situations affecting method of terminating the tenancy. First, it may never have been protected; in which case the rights of re-entry are those to be found in the relevant lease. Secondly, it may have been protected, and may have lost protection; in which case the right of re-entry is that provided by section 24 (3) (*a*) of the Act of 1954. Thirdly, it may continue to be protected; in which case the right of re-entry is that provided by section 25 of the Act of 1954.

Now, this cannot be the first case, since the plaintiffs enjoyed protection at one time because the relevant part of the factory was let together with the part they occupied. This may also be so because they may have, themselves, occupied this part before the underlease to the defendants. Whether or not they did so was not stated in evidence. Can this be the last case of the three, as [counsel for the plaintiffs] claims? If this is right the defendants can only terminate by a section 25 notice, and this contemplates a counter notice, and an application by the tenant for a new tenancy. But he cannot get a new tenancy because the court, unless the landlord agrees otherwise, can only grant a new lease of the holding—section 32 (1)—and the holding is defined in section 23 (3) as excluding any property not occupied by the tenant. The plaintiffs do not occupy, and thus cannot obtain a new lease. While it is true that a section 25 notice would then effectually bring the tenancy to an end it is a clumsy method and does not seem to me to be what the Act intends section 25 to be used for. Its true use is as the opening move towards the grant of a new tenancy. But if this is the second case these difficulties disappear. And it is the second case, in my judgment, if full effect is allowed to be given to the words in section 140, 'in like manner as if the land comprised in each severed part, ... had alone originally been comprised in the lease.'

This is a deeming provision; one must assume a hypothetical lease of the relevant land alone. But this is not occupied by the plaintiffs, and is not protected. But it once was, before the coming into force of the reversionary lease, and it seems to me that I here find the cesser of which section 24 (3) (*a*) speaks. For purposes other than this deeming no doubt the fact that there is but one tenancy means that the two parts of the land are still let together. But for the purposes of rights of re-entry the deeming provision is required to be applied. And it seems to me that I could not adopt [counsel for the plaintiffs'] submission without ignoring that deeming provision. This, in my judgment, is what distinguishes the present case from *Jelley* v. *Buckman* [1974] QB 488. Moreover it explains why there is no special provision in the Act of 1954 as to severed reversion.

The decision in the *William Skelton* case was considered in:

NEVILL LONG & CO. (BOARDS) LTD v. FIRMENICH & CO.

Court of Appeal   (1983) 268 EG 572

The reversions on two leases of adjoining properties used for business purposes and the ownership of a piece of land over which both lessees were given a right of way, were vested originally in the same owner. Subsequently, both reversions were sold to a third party and the piece of land subject to the rights of way became vested in Firmenich & Co., the appellants. A dispute arose between the lessees under the two leases, the respondents, and the appellants as to the application of the 1954 Act. The appellants argued that the reversion on the leases was severed by the transfers to the third party and that the appellants became entitled to a severed part of the reversion expectant on the termination of the tenancies in the rights of way. Accordingly, they argued, section 140 (1) of the Law of Property Act 1925 applied and that, so far as the appellants were concerned, the matter must be considered as if the only property originally comprised in the leases was the rights of way. On that hypothesis, the rights of way were not within Part II of the 1954 Act at all because they were not property capable of being occupied within section 23 of the Act. Hence, the terms of the leases having expired, the appellants claimed that they were entitled to their piece of land free of the rights of way.

Held: Notwithstanding the severance of the reversions, there continued in existence under each of the leases a single tenancy of the property thereby demised including the rights of way.

Fox LJ: The argument of the defendant is, broadly, as follows:

'The reversion expectant upon the determination of the leases became severed by the transfer of the freeholds to Meek and the defendants. The defendants are entitled to a severed part of the reversion expectant upon the termination of the tenancies in the rights of way.

Under the provisions of section 140 (1) of the Law of Property Act 1925 a reversioner may exercise his rights of re-entry or to quit in respect of his severed part as if the land comprised in the severed part had alone originally been comprised in the lease. Accordingly the matter must be approached, so far as the defendants are concerned, as if the only property originally comprised in the leases were the rights of way. On that hypothesis the rights of way are not within Part II of the Landlord and Tenant Act 1954 at all because they are not property which is capable of being "occupied" within section 23: see *Land Reclamation Co. Ltd* v. *Basildon District Council* [1979] 1 WLR 767.

The Act does not apply to a tenancy of a right of way only (*Land Reclamation Co.* case). Accordingly the 21-year periods for which the leases were granted having expired, the defendant is entitled to plot 3 free of the rights of way and can exercise, unhindered by the 1954 Act, all rights of re-entry to which they are entitled under the leases.'

We do not feel able to accept that argument.

By section 23 (1) the provisions of Part II of the 1954 Act apply to 'any tenancy where the property comprised in the tenancy is or includes premises which are occupied by the tenant and are so occupied for the purposes of a business carried on by him ...' That is an exact description of the tenancies created by the leases. It is quite true that, as decided in *Land Reclamation Co. Ltd* v. *Basildon Council (supra)*, a right of way is not property which can be described as 'occupied' by the tenant and if it is the only property comprised in the tenancy is outside the Act. But nevertheless Part II applies to the whole of the property comprised in the leases because, in each case, that property 'includes' property which *is* occupied by the tenant for the purposes of his business. The position is as stated by Buckley LJ in the *Land Reclamation* case at p 774 where he says:

'So it [ie the 1954 Act] will apply when part only of the whole property comprised in the lease is occupied by the tenant for business purposes. This may occur where the tenant uses some part of the property comprised in the lease for purposes other than business purposes; or it might occur where some part of the property comprised in the lease was, by its incorporeal nature, incapable of occupation.'

The latter example is this case. We should refer also to the judgment of Shaw LJ at p 782.

Thus far, therefore, the tenancies created by the leases will continue until determined in accordance with the Act. Further a new tenancy granted under the Act will be a new tenancy of the holding (section 32 (1)). There is excluded from the definition of the holding (section 23 (3)) property which is not occupied by the tenant. Section 32 (3), however, provides that 'rights' enjoyed by the tenant in connection with the holding shall be included in the new tenancy. The rights of way must, we think, come within that provision.

There remains the question what is the relevant tenancy for the purposes of section 23 (1)? Originally, in the case of each lease, it was the tenancy thereby created. Since then there has been a severance of the reversions. Does that create a separate tenancy in respect of each severed part of the reversion in consequence of the provisions of section 140 (1) of the Law of Property Act 1925? In our view it does not. The position was dealt with by the Court of Appeal in *Jelley* v. *Buckman* [1974] QB 488 at p 497. Stamp LJ, giving the judgment of the court, after referring to section 140 of the Law of Property Act 1925, said this:

'Now it is no doubt correct that the effect of the legislation is that each reversioner has rights and remedies similar to those which he would have had if he had granted a separate tenancy of the land in respect of which he is owner. But it is one thing to say that each reversioner has rights and remedies similar to or even indistinguishable from the rights and remedies which he would have had if there had been two separate tenancies and quite another thing to say that this operates against the tenant and that he therefore has two tenancies; and we cannot read section 140 as producing the latter result. We can find nothing in the section to suggest for a moment that the legislature intended that following a severance to which the lessee was not a party he should find himself holding part of his land under one tenancy and part under another. In relation to a lease for years as opposed to a weekly tenancy the change in the law would be dramatic and had the legislature intended to create that result one would expect to find some clear expression of that intention.'

In our opinion, it must follow that, notwithstanding the severance of the reversions, there continued in existence under each of the leases a single tenancy of the property thereby demised including the right of way. Further since, in the case of each lease, the actual land was occupied for the purpose of the lessee's business, each such tenancy must be within section 23 of the 1954 Act.

If there was a tenancy to which the 1954 Act applies, the tenancy continues in existence until determined in accordance with the provisions of the Act. There has been no determination. The expiration of the 21 years of the terms cannot itself have caused it; a purpose of the 1954 Act is to prevent that. It is said, however, that this fails to take account of the operation of section 140 of the Law of Property Act 1925.

Thus, it is argued that where the land comprised in the severed part of a reversion is or includes premises to which section 23 applies, the Act of 1954 modifies the mode of determination so that a notice is required to be served under section 24 (3) or section 25. But where the land comprised in the severed part is not such that the Act of 1954 modifies the mode of termination, then the mode of termination provided by the lease (and the remedies consequent upon that) remain in force. This, it is said, is the position here because the statutory fiction in section 140 (1) removes the right of way from the scope of the 1954 Act. We do not accept that. The position in our view is as follows. There is, for the reasons which we have indicated, a subsisting single tenancy under each lease which continues notwithstanding the severance. That tenancy will not come to an end unless terminated in accordance with the provisions of the Act (section 24 (1)). Now the landlord can indeed terminate the tenancy (section 25 (1)). The expression 'the landlord' is defined by section 44 (1) as follows:

'... the expression "the landlord", in relation to a tenancy (in this section referred to as "the relevant tenancy"), means the person (whether or not he is the immediate landlord) who is the owner of that interest in the property comprised in the relevant tenancy which for the time being fulfils the following conditions, that is to say—
(a) that it is an interest in reversion expectant (whether immediately or not) on the termination of the relevant tenancy, and
*(b) that it is either the fee simple or a tenancy which will not come to an end within fourteen months or less by effluxion of time or by virtue of a notice to quit already given by the landlord ...'

The defendants cannot, in relation to either of the single tenancies, be 'the landlord' within that definition (because they own plot 3 only) and cannot, therefore, serve notice under section 25 in relation to the single tenancies.

We think that for the defendants to determine the tenancy by means of a notice by them alone does not fit the statutory provisions and would indeed cut right across the protection given by the 1954 Act. Thus, section 25 contemplates a notice in respect of the whole of the property comprised in the tenancy. And the machinery set in motion by the notice is dealing, so far as the present case is concerned, with the whole also. Once an application for a new tenancy has been duly made, the Act directs that a new tenancy of the holding and of the rights contained in the current tenancy shall be granted unless one of the grounds of opposition in section 30 is established. All but one of those grounds refer to 'the holding', which does not suggest that a person having no interest in the holding could by himself constitute 'the landlord' in respect of the tenancy.

We should add that it seems to us that the defendants and Meek together could constitute 'the landlord' for the purposes of section 25 (either by serving a single notice or separate notices operating at the same time), since together they are entitled to the entirety of the land comprisd in the relevant reversion. In that connection it seems to us that the wide meaning of reversion adopted by the court in *Martyn* v. *Williams* 1857 1 H & No 817 in relation to incorporeal hereditaments would be appropriate here in relation to the right of way. But if the tenancy were so brought to an end, it is clear that a new tenancy could be granted including in each case the right of way (section 32).

But there is a wider aspect of the whole matter.

The defendants' argument, it seems to us, places too much weight upon the statutory fiction in section 140 (1). What we are primarily concerned with in the present case are the provisions of Part II of the 1954 Act. They are designed to protect business tenancies. That protection is a matter of much importance to the business community and we think that the proposition that there has been removed from the protection of the Act property which *prima facie* is within it needs to be approached with some caution. For the reasons which we have indicated, it seems to us clear that, despite the severance, a single tenancy remained in existence in respect of each lease. Prior to the severance, that tenancy was, in each case, plainly within the protection of the 1954 Act. We find it impossible to suppose that Parliament can have intended that the severance of the reversion could remove from the protection of the Act rights of access which might be of vital consequence to the business user of the demised property which itself at all times remained within the protection of the Act. The purpose of section 140 is to apportion conditions and rights of re-entry on severance and not to create new rights. It is not a general deeming provision that, where there has been a severance of the reversion, the severed part was the only property originally comprised in the lease. We see no reason to suppose that it was intended to have the effect of removing protective statutory rights of the tenant who would not normally even be a party to the severance. Whether there are circumstances in which a person can in relation to a tenancy within Part II of the Landlord and Tenant Act 1954 (and contrary to the decision in *Dodson Bull Carpet Co. Ltd* v. *City of London Corporation* [1975] 1 WLR 781) serve a notice under section 25 in respect of part only of the premises comprised in the tenancy (being a severed part of the reversion) we need not decide. But if he can, we think that for the reasons which we have indicated in relation to the intendment of the 1954 Act, that would in no way justify the conclusion that the rights of way in the present case are removed from the ambit of the 1954 Act by the severance of the reversion.

We were referred to *William Skelton & Son Ltd* v. *Harrison & Pinder Ltd* [1975] QB 361. That case was different from the present in this respect, that the plaintiffs there could not have obtained a new tenancy of the premises (the first floor) because they were not in fact in occupation.

Judge Fay in the *Wiliam Skelton* case said that, in the light of the 1954 Act, there were three possible situations. First, the property may never have been protected. Secondly, it may have been protected and lost protection. Thirdly, it may continue to be protected. 'Can this', said the judge at p 372, 'be the last case of the three, as Mr Finlay claims? If this is right the defendants can only terminate by a section 25 notice, and this contemplates a counternotice and an application by the tenant for a new tenancy. But he cannot get a new tenancy because the court, unless the landlord agrees otherwise, can only grant a new lease of the holding—section 32 (1)—and the holding is defined in section 23 (3) as excluding any property not occupied by the tenant. The plaintiffs do not occupy, and thus cannot obtain a new lease.' The judge concluded that the case came within the second of his three classes.

Thus, in *William Skelton* the plaintiff could not have obtained a new lease of the first floor at all—quite apart from any question of the operation of section 140 of the Law of Property Act 1925. But in the present case, in our view the plaintiffs could obtain new leases of the rights of way because of the provisions of section 32. The present case, therefore, falls within the third of the three classes. In our view the plaintiffs are entitled to the declarations sought and we would dismiss the appeal.

18.4 Agreement for a new tenancy

Where the landlord and tenant enter into a written agreement for a new tenancy of the holding, the current tenancy will cease to be subject to the 1954 Act on the date agreed for the new tenancy by virtue of the operation of section 28 of the Act: see *R. J. Stratton Ltd* v. *Wallis Tomlin & Co. Ltd* (1986) 277 EG 409, where letters passing between the parties were held to constitute an agreement for a new tenancy within the meaning of sections 28 and 69(2) of the 1954 Act.

Chapter 19

Statutory machinery for termination

19.1 The landlord's section 25 notice of termination

In the case of fixed term tenancies, the specified termination date must not be earlier than the date the tenancy would have come to an end by effluxion of time.

IN RE CROWHURST PARK

Chancery Division   [1974] 1 WLR 583

GOULDING J: The attack which is made on the notice is quite a short one and it arises under subsection (4), although to decide it it is necessary to bear in mind the rest of the provisions of the section. What is said is that the notice offends subsection (4) in that it specifies a date of termination earlier than the date on which, apart from the Act, the tenancy would have come to an end by effluxion of time. I therefore have to look at the instruments by which the respective tenancies were granted to see what the last mentioned date would have been.

The principal lease of 1958 demised the property comprised therein for the term of 16 years from 25 December 1956. The second instrument provided that the tenancy was granted for the period of the first lease; the third instrument was also made by reference, namely, for the duration of the lease on the mansion house. Accordingly, I am concerned in each case with a term of 16 years from Christmas Day 1956. It is agreed, having regard to the use of the proposition 'from,' that the first day of that term was St Stephen's Day, commonly called Boxing Day, 26 December 1956, and accordingly the last day of the term is Christmas Day, 25 December 1972. The tenant or his successor in title was entitled to remain in possession until the very last moment of Christmas Day 1972. In other words, the moment of termination of the contractual tenancy by effluxion of time would have been that point of time, that instant of midnight which divided Christmas Day from Boxing Day. Which then is the date on which, in the language of subsection (4), the tenancy would have come to an end? I have considered that question with helpful arguments from counsel in the light of all the other language of section 25, but in the end it seems to me that the words of subsection (4) are themselves sufficiently clear.

[Counsel] for the defendant, puts this question: 'On which day of the calendar does the year come to an end by effluxion of time?' The natural answer, in his submission, is 'On 31 December,' not on 1 January. I accept that submission. I think the natural usage is that for which [counsel for the defendant] contends. Further, there is sufficient authority to show that it is proper so to use language in relation to tenancies. I refer to *Sidebotham* v. *Holland* [1895] 1 QB 378. That was a decision of the Court of Appeal on a yearly tenancy, but the language and the reasoning used, in my judgment, can fairly be extended to the case of a fixed term. Accordingly, when in paragraph 1 of the notice the defendant gave notice to the plaintiff terminating each tenancy on Christmas Day 1972 he did, in my judgment, refer to the date on which, apart from the Act, the tenancies would have come to an end by effluxion of time and did not offend section 25 (4). Paragraph 2 of the notice was relied on by [counsel], for the plaintiff, because it requires the person receiving the notice to state whether she will be willing to give up possession of the premises on that date. [Counsel for the plaintiff] says that that points to giving up possession *before* the last moment of Christmas Day and therefore the construction I have put on paragraph 1 must be wrong. I do not think so. It would be an affirmative answer to paragraph 2 to state the occupier's willingness to give up possession at the last moment of Christmas Day and that would make the paragraph harmonise with the Act and with paragraph 1 of the notice, both interpreted in what I have held to be the ordinary use of language. Accordingly the claim made by the plaintiff in paragraph 1B of the originating summons must fail.

(See also *Ladyman* v. *Wirral Estates Ltd* [1968] 2 All ER 197.)

In **Lewis v. M.T.C. (Cars) Ltd** [1975] 1 WLR 457, the Court of Appeal held that the 'not earlier than' rule was irrelevant where a fixed term had expired and the tenancy continued under the 1954 Act.

RUSSELL LJ: Section 25 (3) and (4) are, in my view, the statutory provisions, and the only statutory provisions, which govern or control, in the case of all tenancies, what termination date may be specified in a section 25 notice. Section 25 (3) is in these terms:

'In the case of a tenancy which apart from this Act could have been brought to an end by notice to quit given by the landlord—(*a*) the date of termination specified in a notice under this section shall not be earlier than the earliest date on which apart from this Part of this Act the tenancy could have been brought to an end by notice to quit given by the landlord on the date of the giving of the notice under this section; ...'

Section 25 (3) (*b*) is not here material. Section 25 (3) (*a*), in my view, deals with any case in whch there is a contractual periodic tenancy for a fixed term with a special power to determine it prematurely. It is of course to be observed that in the case of a periodic tenancy, that tenancy would continue to exist as a common law contractual tenancy, because the statute prevented its termination by ordinary notice to quit.

Section 25 (4) is in these terms:

'In the case of any other tenancy, a notice under this section shall not specify a date of termination earlier than the date on which apart from this Part of this Act the tenancy would have come to an end by effluxion of time.'

That subsection controls the date of termination that may be specified in the section 25 notice in the case of any tenancy other than that which I have conveniently labelled as a periodic tenancy; that is to say, every case in which there is a contractual tenancy not within subsection (3), that is to say, a tenancy for a term certain. If at the date of the section 25 notice the contractual tenancy is still in existence, then the date of termination to be specified must not be earlier than the end of that term. But what of a case in which the fixed term of the tenancy has expired and the tenancy only continues by force of the statute? It seems to me really quite plain that neither subsection (3) nor subsection (4) of section 25 directly contains any provision controlling the date of termination that may be specified in the section 25 notice. Those subsections appear to me to be designed to recognise and prevent the overriding of contractual rights in the tenant in occupation and are not directed to the situation where those contractual rights have come to an end and only the artificial continuation of the tenancy exists under the statute. In my view, in such a case the statute imposes no fetter on the date of termination to be specified in the notice. It only requires, under section 25 (2), that the date of the notice be appropriately related in point of time with the selected termination date.

In **Westbury Property and Investment Co. Ltd v. Carpenter** [1961] 1 WLR 272, the Court of Appeal held that a landlord who had given his tenant notice under section 25 terminating his tenancy was not entitled to give notice terminating subtenancies until after the expiration of the tenancy as until then the tenant remained the 'landlord' in relation to the sub-tenancy.

In the case of tenancies which apart from Part II could be brought to an end by notice to quit, the specified termination date must not be earlier than the earliest date on which the tenancy could be so terminated. This category includes not only periodic tenancies but also tenancies containing a break clause.

SCHOLL MANUFACTURING CO. LTD v. CLIFTON (SLIM-LINE) LTD

Court of Appeal   [1967] Ch 41

A lease of business premises contained a break clause permitting either party to terminate the term by giving notice on or before a specified date. The landlord sent the tenant a notice to quit in a form prescribed under section 25 of the 1954 Act together with a covering letter stating such a notice was enclosed. The tenant contended that the notice was of no effect because it did not operate the break clause contained in the lease.

Held: The single notice terminated the term under both the break clause and the 1954 Act, thereby setting the statutory machinery in motion.

HARMAN LJ: It is objected by the tenants that this notice is of no effect. They say that, there having been no exercise of the break clause, it was not open to the landlords, by a mere notice in the prescribed form, under section 25, to put an end to a term of years which, as matters stood between the parties, went on until 1973.

In a decision of my own, in 1958, in *Weinbergs Weatherproofs Ltd* v. *Radcliffe Paper Mill Co. Ltd*, I had occasion to deal with the converse of this situation, as indeed the judge below pointed out. In that case there was a lease with a break clause in it and the landlords served a notice to quit to operate the break clause, but not in accordance with the form prescribed by section 25 of the Act. I held that, contrary to the tenants' contention, the notice was good to curtail the term under the break clause, although having regard to section 24 of the Act it did not bring the lease to an end. This part of the decision appears to be accepted by both sides, but I added some obiter dicta in the form of a suggestion that, if that view were not right, it would never be possible to bring a break clause into operation.

The judge below in this case, as he was well entitled to do, ignored that observation, which I think on reflection was wrong. In the present case, however, the question is whether, having regard to section 25 of the Act, the landlords may determine a lease having a break clause such as the present one under that section provided only that the termination date is not earlier than the date on which the break clause could operate. The judge held that the landlords could do this without first going through the formality of serving a notice to bring the break clause into operation. In my opinion the judge was right and, in fact, I think that section 25 so provides in express terms.

A second point was taken, namely, on the footing that the judge so far was wrong, yet the statutory notice, combined with the covering letter sent with it, was itself a sufficient notice to terminate the break clause. The objection made by the tenants was that on the face of it the notice referred merely to the statute and did not mention the break clause from beginning to end. It was said that the tenants had two rights, their contractual rights under the lease and their statutory right, and that each of these had to be brought to an end separately. The judge rejected this view, and so do I, and I hold with him that the notice and covering letter were quite sufficient to bring to the mind of the tenants the landlords' desire to put an end to the lease at the date which the break clause allowed, and that this was quite enough, so that if necessary the judge would have decided in favour of the landlords on that ground also. In this too I agree with him, and I would dismiss the appeal on both points.

DIPLOCK LJ: We are not here concerned with the grant of new tenancies under the Act but with the statutory modification of terms of tenancies relating to their coming to an end. Under the common law, apart from surrender or forfeiture, a tenancy may come to an end by effluxion of time, if for a term of years certain, or by notice given by the tenant to the landlord or by the landlord to the tenant, if a periodic tenancy, or a tenancy for a term of years certain subject to a break clause. The latter kind of notice given under a break clause, as well as the former given under a periodic tenancy, is in the statute called a 'notice to quit': see the definition section 69 (1); and, in this judgment, I shall use that phrase in its extended statutory meaning. The Act does not modify the terms of tenancies relating to surrender, forfeiture or notices to quit given by the tenant to the landlord (section 24 (2)). It does modify terms of tenancies relating to their coming to an end by effluxion of time or by notice to quit given by the landlord to the tenant. These terms in the lease or tenancy agreement no longer operate to bring the tenancy to an end: see section 24 (1). The Act substitutes for such terms statutory provisions. As regards a tenancy which would, apart from the Act, come to an end by effluxion of time, the substituted statutory provision is that it may be terminated either by the landlord giving to the tenant notice in the prescribed form at the time laid down in the Act, and specifying the date on which the tenancy is to come to an end (see section 25 (1)), or by the tenant giving notice to the landlord that he does not wish the tenancy to continue after the date on which, apart from the Act, it would come to an end by effluxion of time: section 27 (1). Where the tenant gives no such notice and the landlord does not give a prescribed notice which specifies the same date as that on which, apart from the Act, the tenancy would come to an end by effluxion of time, the Act prolongs a tenancy on the old terms, save that the landlord can give six to twelve months' notice to quit in the prescribed form, and the tenant can give three months' notice to quit in the prescribed form. As regards a tenancy which would, apart from the Act, come to an end by notice to quit given by the landlord in accordance with the terms of the lease or tenancy agreement, the provision substituted by the Act is that such tenancies may be terminated by the landlord by giving notice to quit in the prescribed form. The statutory provisions to which I have referred are not in addition to but in substitution for those terms contained in the lease or tenancy agreement which relate to tenancies coming to an end by effluxion of time or by notice to quit given by the landlord to the tenant.

To bring to an end a tenancy which by its terms is terminable on notice to quit given by the landlord to the tenant there is no need for the landlord under the Act to serve notice in accordance with those terms. The terms contained in the lease or tenancy agreement relating to its termination are relevant for two purposes only: First and always, to determine what date may be specified in the prescribed notice as the date on which the tenancy may come to an end and, secondly and sometimes, to determine at what date the notice must be given in order that it may be effective. Where the tenancy is for a term of years certain, the date to be specified in the prescribed notice on which it is to come to an end must not be earlier than the date on which, but for the Act, it would come to an end by effluxion of time—see section

25 (4)—and, in the case of notice by the tenant, it must be not other than that date. In the case of a tenancy terminable by notice to quit, the date specified in the prescribed notice must be not earlier than that on which the tenancy could, apart from the Act, be brought to an end by notice given by the landlord—see section 25 (3) (*a*)—and it may by paragraph (*b*) of the subsection have to be served earlier than it otherwise would.

Accordingly where, as here, the question is, has the tenancy of business premises come to an end when there has been no surrender, forfeiture or notice to quit served by the tenant and time for him to apply to the court for the grant of a new tenancy, under section 29, has expired (see section 64), the only questions that the court has to ask itself are: Have the landlords given to the tenant in due time a notice in the prescribed form, and has the date of termination specified in the notice expired? Those were the questions which the judge rightly asked himself, and the questions which, in my view, he answered rightly. The tenancy came within section 25 (3), for it was a tenancy which, apart from the Act, could have been brought to an end on 25 March 1966, by a notice to quit (in the extended meaning of the Act) given by the landlords. Therefore the termination date specified in the prescribed form of notice could be not earlier than 25 March 1966. The date so specified was 25 March 1966, and so complied with the requirements of the Act. The notice was served within the period limited by section 25 (3) that is to say, it was given not more than twelve nor less than six months before 25 March 1966. The notice, therefore, was a good notice and, since the tenants gave no counter-notice under section 29 (2) and made no request for a new tenancy under section 26, it was effective to bring the tenancy to an end on the date so specified, 25 March 1966. I therefore agree with the judge in the construction that he put upon the Act.

A periodic tenancy can be effectively terminated by a section 25 notice even though the specified termination date does not fall on the first or last day of a period as would be required at common law.

COMMERCIAL PROPERTIES LTD v. WOOD

Court of Appeal [1968] 1 QB 15

The tenant of business premises had a monthly tenancy at a monthly rent payable in advance on the first of each month. The landlords served a notice, pursuant to section 25 of the 1954 Act, to terminate the tenancy in the prescribed form on the tenant on 4 October 1965 to expire on 11 April 1966.

Held: Since the 1954 Act had substituted a statutory mode of termination of business tenancies, any contractual method of termination was irrelevant and there being nothing in sections 24 or 25 of the 1954 Act requiring a statutory notice of termination to expire on the anniversary of the tenancy, the landlord's notice was valid.

HARMAN LJ: In my view the Act of 1954 itself provides the answer quite clearly to the tenant's contention. Section 23, with which Part II begins, says that that Part applies to any tenancy where the property comprises premises occupied for the purpose of a business. Section 24 says in terms:

'(1) A tenancy to which this Part of this Act applies shall not come to an end unless terminated in accordance with the provisions of this Part of this Act; ...'

That is quite categorical. It is in clear terms stated that in the case of any tenancy to which this Part of this Act applies the tenancy shall not come to an end unless there is a statutory termination of it, and it is a statutory termination alone, so far as the landlord is concerned, which can bring the tenancy to an end. There is a saving for the tenant's right, but none for the landlord's.

When you come to section 25 you find out how this statutory right of the landlord to terminate the tenancy is to operate. That may be done '... by a notice given to the tenant in the prescribed form'—that prescribed form was employed here—'specifying the date at which the tenancy is to come to an end'; and then that is defined.

If that were all, any kind of notice would apparently do. All the landlord has to do is to serve a notice in the prescribed form stating his date and there is an end. When you look at section 25 (2) you find that the notice has to be between six and 12 months in duration. So that shows that, whatever else there may be in the contract, a notice of between six and 12 months must be given.

Subsections (3) and (4) seem to me to clinch the matter, because they go on to give protection which otherwise would not be given to a tenant. Subsection (3) says that where the contract provides for more than a six-monthly notice you prolong the statutory length of notice pro tanto; and subsection (4) says:

'In the case of any other tenancy'—that is, a periodic tenancy—'a notice ... shall not specify a date of termination earlier than the date on which ... the tenancy would have come to an end by effluxion of time ...'

Both those subsections seem to me to postulate that a notice under the Act of 1954 is the only way of bringing a tenancy to which Part II of the Act of 1954 applies to an end. I think that the judge dealt with this matter admirably in his judgment. He said:

'Was the effect of the section 25 notice of [4 October 1965] that it terminated the tenancy for all purposes or only for the purposes of the Landlord and Tenant Act? In my opinion, it terminated it for all purposes.'

He also said:

'Where a valid statutory notice under section 25 has been given, that, in my view, determines the tenancy just as effectively as a contractual notice would have done but for the Act.'

In both those statements I concur, and I think that the judge was perfectly right.

There was a further point taken, I think not earlier than in this court, which had to do with the fact that rent under this particular tenancy was payable in advance. It was payable monthly in advance on the first of each month. It is said that giving a notice for a day other than the first of the month disturbs without warranty the contractual obligation on the parties to pay and receive respectively rent at that date and no other, and that, therefore, that shows that at any rate where rent is payable in advance you must choose a date to make your six months' notice coincide with the date when the rent would become payable—the principle suggested being that no more disturbance of the contractual relations of the parties is to be assumed than is necessary to give validity to the statute.

I cannot take that as a serious point. It is quite true that it would be tidier, where the rent is payable in advance on the first of each month, if the landlords made their notice coincide with the date when rent became due; but that so slender an inconvenience should cut down the plain words of the statute is a thing I cannot accept at all.

A court will excuse minor slips in the landlord's notice provided that the tenant has fair warning of the case he has to answer.

BARCLAYS BANK LTD v. ASCOTT

Queen's Bench Division   [1961] 1 WLR 717

The landlords served on the tenant a notice of termination under section 25 of the 1954 Act. The notice stated that the landlords would not oppose the tenant's application to the court for a new tenancy provided that the tenant found a guarantor for the payment of rent and observance of the tenant's covenants in relation to any such new tenancy.

Held: The notice was invalid as no specified grounds for opposition under the 1954 Act had been stated.

BARRY J: A number of very useful authorities have been cited to me, but as I see it, none of them are directly in point, and I do not think any useful purpose would be served if I referred to them in detail. It appears to me that the real gist of these decisions was summarised by Hodson LJ in *Bolton's (House Furnishers) Ltd* v. *Oppenheim*. As I understand Hodson LJ's judgment, the question which the court really has to consider is whether the statement or notice given by the landlord has given the proper information to the tenant which will enable the tenant to deal in a proper way with the situation, whatever it may be, referred to in the statement of notice. It is clear from the authorities which have been cited to me that the construction of this notice should be a liberal one, and provided that the notice gives the real substance of the information required, then the mere omission of certain details or the failure to embody in the notice the full provisions of the section of the Act referred to will not in fact invalidate the notice.

In **Carradine Properties Ltd v. Aslam** [1976] 1 WLR 442, a lease for a 21 year term from 27 September 1968 provided for its earlier determination by either party at the end of the first 7 or 14 years on 12 months' previous notice in writing. A notice by the landlords dated 6 September 1974 served on the tenant gave notice to determine the term on 27 September 1973. The date stated in the notice should have been 27 September 1975.

Held: Adopting a benevolent approach, the court would treat the giving of a date past for termination of the lease as a slip which would be obvious to a reasonable tenant reading the notice and knowing the terms of the lease. Accordingly, the notice would be interpreted as an intention to determine the lease on 27 September 1975 and, therefore, the notice was valid.

The test established in the *Carradine* case was applied in **Safeway Food Stores Ltd v. Morris** (1980) 254 EG 1091, where a landlord's notice was held to be valid despite absence of reference to a garage included in the demise.

WALTON J: In the present case on that basis I think the question is first of all—is this curious building, the site of the former garage and now a frontless and backless wonder, pointing to the supermarket and nothing else, so closely connected with the supermarket that anybody would think that it was part of that supermarket known as the ground floor and basement of the numbers I have already read out? And it would seem to me that one has only to postulate that question to get the answer that of course it has no real connection with anything else and could not be used as part of anything else at all. It might have been much more difficult if it had remained as an actual garage which could have had some independent use and validity. At the moment the building has no independent use or validity whatsoever except as a way through from the other side of the road across the service road into the supermarket.

The matter does not rest there, because there is a reported case, *Germax Securities*

Ltd v. *Spiegal* in the Court of Appeal reported in (1978) 37 P & CR 204 in which the Court of Appeal approved the following formulation by Goulding J in *Carradine Properties Ltd* v. *Aslam* [1976] 1 WLR 442 of a test to decide whether a notice was valid:

'I would put the test generally applicable as being this. Is the notice quite clear to a reasonable tenant reading it? Is it plain that he cannot be misled by it? Applying that test as applicable to the present case I think the notice would be so, because the tenant receiving that notice and knowing the terms of the lease must have seen there was a mistake as it would not say 1973 in 1974. Once that is accepted it is obvious the notice is for 1975 and not 1973.'

That test was blessed by Buckley LJ in that case, Roskill LJ entirely agreeing with Buckley LJ, as also did Goff LJ. I was cited, of course, the case of very great weight and standing, *Hankey* v. *Clavering* [1942] 2 KB 326, where there was a notice to determine a lease on 21 December 1941 when it should have been in fact 25 December 1941. But that was a prospective notice, and the tenant would undoubtedly have been in reasonable doubt as to whether the landlord had made a mistake or whether the landlord was not really trying to bring the lease to an end on a date on which he had no right to bring it to an end at all.

So I return to the section 25 notice in the present case and it appears to me quite clear that no tenant of the supermarket, for such the premises are in fact, would have the slightest hesitation in knowing that the notice which he had received was a notice to terminate the whole of his tenancy. Indeed, as [counsel] for the defendant pointed out, it is not really anywhere suggested that the lessees were in any doubt, and the nearest that one gets to it is a solicitors' letter of 15 May 1979 in which it is said, 'Our clients expressly reserve their right as to the validity and effect of the two notices given by you and dated 19 March 1979,' which being interpreted is 'We think we have found a jolly good technical point which we hope to be able to run later,' and it certainly does not mean, 'We are in any real genuine doubt' whatsoever.

In **Philipson–Stow v. Trevor Square** (1981) 257 EG 1262, the landlord served a section 25 notice on the tenant stating its intention to carry out substantial works of redecoration on the holding and thus opposing the grant of a new tenancy. The tenant argued that no ground within section 30 (1) had been specified in the notice and asked for a declaration that the notice was bad.

Held: The notice was obviously intended to cite the ground in section 30 (1) (f) as to demolition or reconstruction although the word 'redecoration' did not appear in the statute. The notice was, therefore, good.

GOULDING J: Then there was another case in the Court of Appeal, *Marks (Morris)* v. *British Waterways Board* [1963] 1 WLR 1008. I think it is helpful if I read some short extracts from the judgment in that case. It should be borne in mind that the court there was considering not a landlord's notice under subsection (6) of section 25 of the Act but a landlord's counternotice under subsection (6) of section 26 thereof, which has to be served if the landlord desires to oppose a tenant's request for a new tenancy under section 26. Subsection (6) in section 26, like that in section 25, requires the counternotice to state on which of the grounds mentioned in section 30 of the Act the landlord will oppose the application. Accordingly, in my view, *Mark's* case is *in pari materia* with the cases on landlord's notices under section 25 although referring to the following section. Lord Denning MR at p 1015, having referred to an argument that the notice in that case was bad because it did not correctly represent the landlord's intention at the time, said:

'I think the correct answer is that the notice opposing the new tenancy—a landlord's notice—is to be regarded as in the nature of a pleading. It is a pleading which comes for proof at the date of the hearing. It is sufficient as long as it gives notice to the tenant of the case he has to meet. So long as it is not deceptive or misleading it avails the subsequent owner of the property who is the landlord at the date of the hearing.'

Harman LJ at p 1018 said:

'The only object, as Lord Simonds said in the *Betty's Cafés* case, of a counternotice is to inform the tenant of the case which will be made against him when the hearing comes on and provided it does that it is, I think, a good counternotice ...'

And, omitting two or three sentences, he continued:

'You must not mislead the tenant. You must not say anything which is fraudulent but if your notice is given in good faith and the fact about reconstruction can be substantiated by the person who is the landlord when the hearing comes on, I think the counternotice really has served the purpose which the legislature can be said to have required of it.'

And he finished that paragraph of his judgment by saying:

'It is true the notice is in a most unhappy form. It was not candid as it should have been. If I had thought it could have misled Marks I should be inclined to say it was a bad notice, but I do not think it did, having regard to the prior notice served and the knowledge of the facts which he had. Therefore, although I think we do perhaps rather stretch the section in doing so, I agree with the county court judge that this counternotice was a valid counternotice.'

And, at the very end of the report, at p 1021, Pearson LJ says of the counternotice:

'It gave him [that is the tenant] adequate warning of what was the contention on the other side which he would have to meet at the hearing and, therefore, it performed its function adequately.'

It will be observed, I remark in passing, from Harman LJ's judgment in the passage which I have cited, that in the *Marks* case there was some extrinsic evidence of the tenant's knowledge of material facts at the time of service of the notice. Nothing of that sort is before the court here and I have to construe the notice simply as a self-contained document, without reference to prior knowledge of either party.

Then there is another case in the Court of Appeal *Housleys Ltd* v. *Bloomer-Holt Ltd* [1966] 1 WLR 1244 and I cite from that a very compendious and generally expressed observation by Diplock LJ (as he then was). He said at p 1251:

'First as regards the technical point that the notice by the landlords given under section 25 (6) of the Act did not follow precisely the wording of paragraph (f) of section 30 (1) of the Act. This is a highly technical point. It is not, in my view, in any event an attractive one nor do I find it well founded. It is sufficient if a notice under section 25 (6) makes it clear to the tenant which of the seven separate grounds specified in section 30 (1) the landlord is relying on. The purpose of the notice under section 25 (6) is to let the tenant know on what grounds his request for a new tenancy, if made, will be resisted, so that he may make up his mind whether to exercise his rights and bring the matter eventually before a court for a decision.'

Other cases cited were *Lewis* v. *MTC (Cars) Ltd* [1974] 1 WLR 1499, a decision of Templeman J, another decision at first instance of *Carradine Properties* v. *Aslam* [1976] 1 WLR 442, a recent case, unreported, in the Court of Appeal of *Jomac Securities* v. *Spiegal* whereof I have seen a transcript of the court's judgment dated June 14 1978, and a still more recent case at first instance of *Safeway Food Stores Ltd* v. *Morris* (1980) 254 EG 1091.

Having gone through those authorities, from which I have cited one or two passages, I ask myself these questions about the notice dated 8 March 1979. Did it give notice to the tenant of the case she had to meet? Was it deceptive or misleading? Did it make clear which of the seven separate grounds specified in section 30 the landlord was relying on? It is all-important, I think, in looking at the notice, to observe that the notes on the back are part of the statutory form; that the body of the notice expressly calls the tenant's attention to those endorsed notes and that the statement of the landlord's ground of opposition is qualified by a parenthesis referring in particular to note 4 where the alternatives (a) to (g) are set out. If the tenant compared the language in paragraph 3 of the notice with that of the subparagraphs of note 4, she could, in my view, have no doubt that the landlord was aiming at subparagraph (f). There is a close resemblance between the language actually used and part of that in subparagraph (f) and there is not the slightest resemblance to or close relation with any of the other subparagraphs. A reasonable tenant, reading this notice, would I think conclude that the landlord was seeking to rely on subparagraph (f), but the same hypothetical reasonable tenant would also conclude that there was considerable doubt whether the landlord could make its case good, because it would be indeed strange if a substantial work of redecoration could be shown to be, in the statutory language, a substantial work of construction. Therefore, I answer my questions by saying: 'Yes, on a fair and not too technical construction the notice does give notice to the tenant of the case she had to meet'; and I would say 'No, it is not deceptive or misleading, although it is inaccurately expressed. And then I would say 'Yes, it does make it clear which of the seven separate grounds the landlord is relying on'.

In **Germax Securities Ltd v. Spiegal** (1979) 37 P & CR 204, the Court of Appeal held valid a landlord's section 25 notice giving the year of termination as 1976 instead of 1977, on the basis that no reasonably minded tenant would in the circumstances have been misled.

See also: *Tegerdine* v. *Brooks* (1978) 36 P & CR 261, (CA); *Sevenarts* v. *Busvine* [1968] 1 WLR 1929, (CA); *Housleys Ltd* v. *Bloomer-Holt Ltd* [1966] 1 WLR 1244; *Sunrose* v. *Gould* [1962] 1 WLR 20; *McMullen* v. *Great Southern Cemetery & Crematorium Co.* (1958) 172 EG 855; *Biles* v. *Caesar* [1957] 1 WLR 156.

In **Stidolph v. American School in London Educational Trust** (1969) 20 P & CR 802, solicitors for the landlord sent a section 25 notice by post to the tenant but they failed to sign the notice as required. However, they did sign an accompanying letter.

Held: The defect in the notice was cured by the accompanying letter.

A notice pursuant to section 25 of the 1954 Act will be valid although in an out–dated form provided it is 'substantially to the like effect' as the form currently prescribed.

SUN ALLIANCE AND LONDON ASSURANCE CO. LTD v. HAYMAN

Court of Appeal   [1975] 1 WLR 177

The landlord served a section 25 notice of termination on the tenant in the form prescribed by the 1954 regulations instead of the then current 1969 regulations. The material difference between the forms was that the time allowed the tenant for giving notice and applying for a new tenancy ran, in the old form, from the date of *receiving* the notice and in the new, from *the giving of* the notice.

Held: The notice was valid since there was no material difference between the two forms of notice as the times of giving and of receipt of such notices were the same, namely, the time of service.

STEPHENSON LJ: In my judgment, the effect of section 66 (4) of the Act of 1954 is that a notice under the provisions of the Act is both given and received when it is served in accordance with section 23 of the Act of 1927, and to anyone who knows the law, the time when it is given and the time when it is received are one and the same, namely, the time of service when the giving of the notice is in law complete. There is therefore on a true construction of the old form no material departure from the statute and no material difference from the new form. It is a distinction without a difference. It describes the same act from the landlords' and tenants' points of view. The giving and receiving of the notice are two aspects of the same action and are simultaneous, like 'the giving and receiving of a ring' in the Form of Solemnization of Matrimony in the Book of Common Prayer. The one gives, the other receives. The tenant takes what the landlord gives when he gives it, and he need not be there to take it from the landlord. The time when this two-sided act is done is the time when it is deemed to be done by the statutory provisions as to service. The tenant cannot say that he has not received it when the Act says that it has been served on him. The effect which a court of law must give to the different words in order to see whether their effect is substantially like is their true effect in the context of landlord and tenant.

These doubts, which the 1967 amendments sought to remove with 'an explanation of the relevant provisions of the Act' which I regard as inadequate, would never have existed if Parliament had spoken plainly of 'service' and 'served' in relation to notices instead of 'giving' and 'given' in section 25 and the regulations. Why not a plain statement that all notices referred to in this Act are given and received when served in accordance with section 23 of the Landlord and Tenant Act 1927, if it is too much trouble to repeat the words of that section, instead of resorting to the cryptic cross-reference in section 66 (4) of the Act of 1954? But the effect is, I think, the same, and the effect of using the words 'giving' and 'receiving' in reference to notices is substantially the same.

Note: This decision was followed in *British Railways Board* v. *A.J.A. Smith Transport Ltd (No 2)* (1981) 259 EG 766, where His Honour Judge Fitzhugh QC (sitting as a Judge of the High Court in the Chancery Division in Manchester) upheld the validity of a section 25 notice, which was in an out of date 1957 form containing only one material difference from the new form as to the county court jursidiction, as being 'substantially to the like effect' as the 'prescribed form'.

See also: *Bond* v. *Graham* (1975) 236 EG 563; *Snook* v. *Schofield* (1975) 234 EG 197, CA.

Since there is no provision for amendment, a landlord cannot depart from the grounds stated in his notice.

HUTCHINSON v. LAMBERTH

Court of Appeal   (1984) 270 EG 545

The landlord opposed the tenant's application for a new tenancy on two grounds, namely, arrears of rent and breach of user covenant. The evidence against the tenant on these grounds was unanswerable but the trial judge irregularly allowed the landlord to amend her grounds contained in her section 25 notice to rely additionally upon nuisance caused by the tenant. The tenant sought a new trial on the grounds *inter alia* that the trial judge should have heard no evidence on the issue of nuisance.

Held: Although the judge had no jurisdiction to deal with nuisance as such since the amendment to the grounds of opposition was irregular, the evidence was relevant to the exercise of the judge's discretion.

O'CONNOR LJ: The learned trial judge had directed herself absolutely correctly because it was for the landlord to make out one of the grounds of opposition; she considered two and she considered that both were made out. Secondly, she had to exercise her discretion as to whether she should refuse the application for a new tenancy against the tenants, which she did.

There are two grounds of appeal. First of all, let me deal with the straightforward one. A complaint is made that she should have entertained no evidence on the issue of nuisance, because, as I have already said, there is no power to amend the section 25 notice. Therefore that issue as a ground of opposition was before her quite wrongly: she had no jurisdiction to deal with it as such. There is no dispute about that.

[Counsel], who has said everything possible for the tenants, has submitted that the mere fact that the learned judge thought that it was a further ground of opposition which she could take into account may have influenced her in the exercise of her discretion and that therefore at the very least we should order a new trial. In my judgment that submission is not well founded, for this reason: if the case had been before the court solely on the ground of persistent delay in paying rent, it would have been open to the landlord to lead evidence of all collateral matters affecting the occupancy of the premises by the tenants, and they would have been permitted to give evidence in order to help the learned judge exercise her discretion as to what had been going on. Therefore it cannot be said that the evidence about nuisance was wrongly before her. In my judgment there is no basis under that complaint for saying that there should be a new trial.

Where two premies are demised to a single lessee and, as a matter of construction, the lease creates a single tenancy and not two tenancies, separate notices under section 25 in respect of each premises are invalid.

DODSON BULL CARPET CO. LTD v. CITY OF LONDON

Chancery Division   [1975] 1 WLR 781

GOFF J: In my judgment, looking at the document as a whole, as a matter of construction, this is clearly a single tenancy of nos 5 and 6, and not two tenancies. Defendants' counsel sought to escape these difficulties by saying the draftsman had intended to create two separate tenancies but had used and very imperfectly adapted a form appropriate to a single one. That is far too speculative, and in my view I cannot on any such ground violate what appears to me to be the plain meaning of what he has said. Alternatively, defendants' counsel submitted there might be a case for rectification, but nobody has ever asked for that, nor is there any evidence to establish a case for it. I therefore hold that there is but one tenancy.

The plaintiffs submit that there is nothing in the Landlord and Tenant Act 1954 to authorise a landlord to serve a notice of determination under section 25 as to part only of the premises comprised in the relevant tenancy, and indeed, quite the reverse, to allow him to do so would cut across and jeopardise the protection afforded by the Act. Defendants' counsel states that he cannot dispute that proposition and in my judgment he is plainly right in so doing. *Prima facie* therefore the no. 5 notice was invalid.

The conclusion that the Act of 1954 does not allow service of a notice under section 25 as to part only of the premises may give rise to difficulties where there has been a severance of the reversion and each reversioner is the landlord of his part within the definition in section 44 of the Act of 1954. It may be that the two can combine to give a notice, or it may be that no notice at all can be given until there is again a single landlord within the meaning of section 44. That problem can be dealt with when it arises. It cannot produce the result that the landlord whether of the whole or part can give a notice as to part, even the whole of his part. I understand it to be agreed that having reached the conclusion that the no. 5 notice was void it follows that the no. 6 notice was also void, but that the no. 5 and 6 combined notice was good and I so answer the question raised by each of the three summonses.

The foregoing case was applied in:

SOUTHPORT OLD LINKS LIMITED v. NAYLOR

Court of Appeal   (1985) 273 EG 767

Premises consisting of a golf links and a club house were demised by the landlords to the tenants for a period of 21 years at a single rent of £500 per annum. The lease contained an exception and reservation entitling the landlords to determine the lease as to the golf links only by twelve months notice. The landlords gave such a notice and at the same time gave notice under section 25 of the 1954 Act to determine that part of the lease.

Held:
(1) The lease did not create two separate tenancies so that the section 25 notice could be regarded as applying to the golf links to the exclusion of the club house. Furthermore, the exercise of the notice under the lease could not have the effect of creating two separate tenancies for the purpose of the 1954 Act;
(2) A section 25 notice must relate to the whole of the land comprised in the tenancy and since the notice related only to part, it was ineffective with the result that the tenancy of the whole premises continued under the 1954 Act.

OLIVER LJ: I have already referred to the statutory provisions, and it is accepted by [counsel for the respondents] that a section 25 notice must, if it is to be effective, relate to the whole of the land in whatever is the relevant tenancy. It cannot relate to part only of that land—and this emerges, in fact, from a number of authorities, in particular the decision of Goff J (as he then was) in *Dodson Bull Carpet Co. Ltd* v. *City of London Corporation* [1975] 1 WLR 781, and at p 785 letters G to H the learned judge said:

'The plaintiffs submit that there is nothing in the Landlord and Tenant Act 1954 to authorise a landlord to serve a notice of determination under section 25 as to part only of the premises comprised in the relevant tenancy, and indeed, quite the reverse, to allow him to do so would cut across and jeopardise the protection afforded by the Act. Defendant's counsel states that he cannot dispute that proposition and in my judgment he is plainly right in so doing.'

This was also treated, I think, as beyond serious argument in this court in *Kaiser Engineers & Constructors Inc.* v. *E R Squibb & Sons Ltd* and I need only refer to a very brief passage from the judgment of Russell LJ (as he then was) where he said:

'It is common ground that for the notice to be effective to operate the break clause in the 1965 lease it must on its true construction be a determination of the whole relationship of landlord and tenant under that lease. Equally if the notice is to be effective as a notice of determination under section 25 of the 1954 Act it must on its true construction be a determination of the whole of such relationship under that lease.'

Since the section 25 notice in this case relates, and could only relate, to the red land, the argument before the learned judge was based, as it had to be, on the contention that it was possible to spell out of the demise two separate and distinct tenancies—one of the blue land and one of the red land, and thus to validate the notice given only in relation to the red land as a notice given in respect of the whole of the land comprised in a relevant tenancy.

In **Tropis Shipping Co. Ltd v. Ibex Property Corporation Ltd** (1967) EGD 433, business tenants under three separate demises of premises at Ibex House, London, E.C., claimed a declaration that a single notice to terminate served on them by the landlords in respect of all three demises was invalid and of no effect.

Held: The notice was valid.

STAMP J: It was true that the terms of section 25 must be strictly complied with, and otherwise the leases would continue to subsist pursuant to section 24 of the Act. The tenants in support of their contention said first that in Part II of the Act 'tenancy' was spoken of in the singular and that in respect of several tenancies the machinery did not work; under section 25, therefore, a notice must be given in respect of each of several tenancies. Counsel for the tenants did however concede that such notices could be given on a single sheet of paper. In this case the notice described the three properties at the head of the form and went on to say that the landlords of those premises 'Hereby give notice determining the tenancy on 1 May 1967.' Attention had been directed to the use of the word 'tenancy' in the singular. No one, however, who knew that these properties were comprised in three separate leases and were subject to three separate tenancies could, on reading the notice, doubt that it could constitute a notice to determine each of the three tenancies on the date specified. The notice was intended to operate on the three tenancies, and he (his Lordship) would follow Barry J, in *Barclays Bank* v. *Ascott*, [1961] 1 WLR 717 at 722, quoted with approval by Pearce LJ, in *Sunrose, Ltd* v. *Gould*, [1972] 1 WLR 20 at 24, in holding that if a notice gave the proper information to the tenant enabling the tenant to deal in a proper way with the situation, the construction of such a notice should be liberal. Provided that the notice gave the substance and the real information required, then the omission of certain details or failure to embody in the notice the full provisions of the section of the Act would not invalidate the notice. The present notice described the premises and the date by which the tenancies were to be determined, lacked nothing, and gave the proper information to the tenants which would enable them to deal in a proper way with the situation. A report of the case of *Southern Corporation* v. *Airport Restaurant, Ltd,* in The Estates Gazette for 15 April 1961, at p 127, in which Wilberforce J, dealt with a question of notices under the Landlord and Tenant Act, 1954, had been referred to, but he (his Lordship) saw nothing there to suggest that Wilberforce J, thought that a single notice to determine two tenancies was necessarily invalid.

19.2 The tenant's counter-notice stating whether or not he is willing to give up possession

A course of conduct can, in certain circumstances, amount to an effective counter-notice under section 29 (2) of the Act.

LEWINGTON v. TRUSTEES FOR THE PROTECTION OF ANCIENT BUILDINGS

Court of Appeal   (1983) 266 EG 997

The tenant did not give a notice stating her unwillingness to give up possession but her solicitors and the landlords' solicitors had for several months been in correspondence about the sale to her of the freehold of the property. A draft contract and conveyance had been approved by the tenant's solicitors and her signed part of the contract and a cheque for the deposit had been sent to the landlords' solicitors to be held to the former's order.

Held: The correspondence made it clear that the tenant was unwilling to give up possession.

WALLER LJ: The question which the learned judge had to decide was whether or not written notice, albeit informal notice, has been given of the tenant's intention not to give up possession. It seems to me that even looking only at the letters after notice was given, namely the letters of 2 April, 26 April, 18 May and 27 May, those letters make it absolutely clear that the tenant had no intention of giving up possession of the property. It is true that the tenant was considering purchase of the property, but it is implicit, as I see it, that she did not intend to leave the property.

In the course of argument before us, Watkins LJ posed the question: Can it be fairly said that after the tenant received notice it was her continuation of negotiations which was sufficient indication of her intention not to leave? I should have thought the answer to that question was 'yes'.

When one takes into account the correspondence before the actual notice was given, here were the landlords who had agreed, orally—and I suppose agreed in writing but that it was not a written contract because it was subject to contract—that they would allow the tenant to purchase this property and the tenant had indicated that she would purchase the property for the sum mentioned, it was clear at that stage that she had no intention of giving up possession of the property; and when, during the period of two months, further letters were written saying that she had no such intention—albeit she was intending and the landlords' solicitors were negotiating on the basis that she would be purchasing the property—it seems to me clear (although it is not a simple notice) that she was evidencing her intention that she did not intend to give up possession of the property.

This particular section, unlike other sections of the Landlord and Tenant Act 1954, does not require a particular form of notice. Some of the provisions of the Act require strict compliance with form, but in this particular case the only thing which is required is that the tenant should, in writing, notify the landlords whether or not she is willing or unwilling to give up possession.

This case was distinguished in:

MEHMET v. DAWSON

Court of Appeal   (1984) 270 EG 139

The tenant wrote a letter to the landlord indicating his willingness to discuss with the landlord the purchase of the freehold of the demised premises. Subsequently, during a discussion between the parties, the landlord mentioned a price for the freehold and the tenant said it was too much.

Held: The letter did not constitute a valid counter-notice since it was consistent with the tenant's wishing to retain possession only if he could do so as freeholder. As to the subsequent discussion between the parties, this could not be construed as a waiver by the landlord of the notice since he had made it clear that he wanted the procedure under the 1954 Act to go ahead before discussing the purchase of the freehold.

EVELEIGH LJ: As to waiver and estoppel I propose to take them together. I cannot see that the facts of this case come anywhere near supporting an argument under either of those two heads. The view of the facts which seems to me to be the correct one was that, far from making any representation and far from inducing the applicant (the tenant) to proceed upon the basis that the landlord would not insist upon a written notice and that the landlord would not set in motion the procedure under the Landlord and Tenant Act, the position is quite the contrary. The landlord was saying to the tenant:

'I hear you when you say that you wish to buy the freehold, but let us first get on with the Landlord and Tenant Act procedure and I will serve the notice, and thereafter we can discuss the question of the purchase of the freehold.'

Once it is put that way, it seems to me that any argument in any greater detail on this point is quite out of the question.

The learned deputy judge went into the matter in rather more detail than I have done. I would adopt everything he says in respect of those two arguments. So one is then left with the argument that has perhaps occupied most time in this court, which was the subject of an amended notice of appeal, namely, that the letter of 23 November in the circumstances of the case did constitute written notice. In support of that argument [counsel for the appellants] submitted as indeed I would accept, that no formal notice is prescribed in order to comply with section 29 (2) of the Act. It is sufficient that there is some writing which conveys to the landlord the information that the tenant is unwilling to give up possession at the end of the tenancy. The question is whether or not this letter did so.

We have been referred to a case of *Lewington* v. *The Trustees of the Society for the Protection of Ancient Buildings* reported in *The Times* on 12 February 1983. In that case the landlord and the tenant had not only discussed the sale of the property but had agreed upon the price, namely £46,500 subject to contract. There was correspondence about the proposed sale and the landlord's solicitors sent a draft contract to the tenant for her approval. About a month later, the landlord's solicitors wrote to the tenant's solicitors enclosing a section 25 notice terminating the tenancy. They also referred to the draft contract and the tenant's solicitors replied acknowledging the notice and accepting service. Subsequently they wrote to the landlord's solicitors returning the draft contract and saying that they were enclosing the tenant's part of the agreement, duly signed, together with a cheque representing 10% deposit. The landlords then wrote to confirm that they were holding the tenant's part of the contract and the deposit cheque. In that case this court came to the conclusion that the correspondence in the case made it absolutely clear that the tenant had no intention of giving up possession. It made it clear that she was considering the purchase of the property and that continuance of the negotiations was sufficient evidence that she did not intend to leave it.

Each case must of course depend upon its own facts. In that case the parties had gone to great lengths in their negotiations and indeed had reached a position where it was being agreed between them that the tenant would be retaining the property. This case is far removed on the facts from that case. The question we have to consider is whether this letter of 23 November constitutes in all the circumstances of the case notice in writing of the intention not to give up possession. I, for myself, cannot see that it does constitute such notice.

The position as to the purchase or the proposed purchase was rather vague. It was quite consistent with the tenant taking the view that he only wanted to retain possession of the property if he could do so as the freeholder. There is nothing in the letter or the other attendant circumstances of the case to say that that is the wrong view to take of the position. At the very highest it could be put in the appellant's favour, it seems to me that this letter gives no indication one way or the other.

In **Taylor v. Michel** (1960) CLY 1739, the landlords served on the tenant a section 25 notice of termination in January 1960, which was formally acknowledged in writing. There was no further correspondence until March 1960 when the tenant's solicitor wrote to the landlord's solicitors informing them that his client 'would like if possible to negotiate for a lease on the following terms ...' and that 'she would, if possible, like to settle this matter to avoid any further worry.'

Held: the letter of March was not a sufficiently certain notification of the tenant's unwillingness to give up possession to satisfy the requirements of the 1954 Act.

Service of a counter-notice must be made within two months of the landlord giving notice as a condition precedent to an application for a new tenancy under section 24 of the Act.

CHISWELL v. GRIFFON LAND AND ESTATES LTD

Court of Appeal   [1975] 1 WLR 1181

The landlord of business premises served a section 25 notice of termination on the tenant. By a letter, the tenant notified the landlord that he was not willing to give up possession and that he intended to apply for a new tenancy. The letter was sent by ordinary post and was not received by the landlord. Subsequently, after the expiry of the 2 month time period for the service of a counter-notice, the tenant sent the landlord a copy of the letter.

Held: Since the tenant had not served his counter-notice within two months after service of the landlord's notice, the court had no power to entertain his application for a new tenancy.

ROSKILL LJ: I therefore go back, as my Lord has done, to section 25 (5) and I see:

'A notice under this section shall not have effect unless it requires the tenant, within two months after the giving of the notice, to notify the landlord in writing whether or not, at the date of termination, the tenant will be willing to give up possession of the property comprised in the tenancy.'

It seems to me, therefore, that it is quite plain that within two months from the date when the landlord gives his original notice the tenant must give his counter-notice; and unless he does so the provisions of section 29 (2), which require the tenant to have 'duly notified' the landlord of his unwillingness to surrender his tenancy at the date of termination, have not been complied with.

A counter-notice that expresses willingness to give up possession once served is irrevocable.

IN RE 14 GRAFTON STREET, LONDON W.1

Chancery Division   [1971] Ch 935

BRIGHTMAN J: The landlords' section 25 notice had been sent with a letter dated 26 September 1969, and it is common ground that this notice should be treated as 'given' on 27 September. The position therefore, on that day, was that 26 or 27 November (I assume 27 November, without so deciding) was the last day available to the tenants for serving a negative counter notice as a prelude to an application by the tenants to the court for an order for the grant of a new tenancy. In fact, as I have mentioned, the tenants' solicitors on 13 October had written a letter which the landlords accepted as, and which I hold to have been, a notification by the tenants within the meaning of section 25 (5) of the Act of 1954 that, on 1 April 1970, they would be willing to give up possession of the property. There was some discussion, unsupported by authority as I was told none existed, as to whether the tenants could, on or before 27 November, have revoked their positive counter notice and given the negative counter notice required by section 29 (2) to enable proceedings to be taken. In my view the purpose of section 25 (5) is to introduce an element of certainty into the relationship between the landlord and the tenant. A tenant is not bound to serve a negative counter notice before the end of the two month period allowed to him. He may pause for that period of time while he makes up his mind. If however he does serve a positive counter notice during the two month period, I think that he must abide by what he has done. If that were not the case, the positive counter notice would serve no purpose whatever compared with complete inaction, for in either case the landlord would not know where he stood until the end of the two month period. If a positive counter notice is revocable the tenant serving the same would be able to serve a negative counter notice right up to the end of the two month period. If on the other hand the tenant does nothing, he may likewise serve a negative counter notice right up to the end of the two month period. It follows that a positive counter notice would be wholly devoid of any function, even that of courtesy, if it were revocable at the will of the tenant. I, therefore, conclude that a positive counter notice is irrevocable; and that in this case the tenants ceased to be able to serve a negative counter notice after 13 October 1969, and that they then lost their right to apply to the court for an order for the grant of a new tenancy.

The court has jurisdiction to make an order compelling a co-trustee to sign a counter-notice and apply for a new lease, but the matter is one for the discretion of the court.

HARRIS v. BLACK

Court of Appeal   (1983) 46 P & CR 366

The plaintiff, the defendant and a Mr Chambers were joint tenants of business premises. Mr Chambers died and the legal estate vested in the plaintiff and defendant as trustees and beneficiaries for themselves. The parties carried on business in partnership together but due to a dispute dissolved the partnership. The landlord served a section 25 notice of termination on both parties and the plaintiff wished to serve a counter-notice but the defendant refused to assist him.

Held: Though the court had jurisdiction to make an order compelling a co-tenant to serve a counter-notice and join in an application for a new tenancy, it would be wrong to do so in the present case where the trustees were also beneficiaries and were at loggerheads.

Slade LJ: I would myself accept that there is jurisdiction in the court at the suit of one trustee to make an order compelling his co-trustee to join him both in signing a counter-notice of this nature and in applying to the court for a new lease. Nevertheless, I do not accept that there is any principle that, in *every* case where a lease of business premises exists, it is the duty of one trustee to co-operate with his co-trustee in this manner. I am sure that Buckley J would not have intended to lay down such a principle, even if the relevant landlord and tenant legislation had been in existence in 1902 when the case was heard.

The matter is, I think, one for the discretion of the court in the exercise of its equitable jurisdiction. Everything must depend on the particular circumstances of the particular case.

In the present case, I ask myself this question: Suppose that this were the trial of the action, would the plaintiff on the basis of the evidence now placed by him before the court—and the court can act on no other basis—have a realistic prospect of persuading it to order the defendant to join with him in signing the counter-notice and making the proposed application? On the basis of this evidence, my answer to this question is a clear 'No.' I emphasise that this is not a case where the two trustees are holding a business lease on trust for other beneficiaries. So far as the evidence shows, it is a case where they are holding the lease merely for themselves. Furthermore, it would appear, although we know very little indeed about the situation, that the defendant has a larger beneficial interest in the lease than the plaintiffs. At least, this is the inference I draw from the fact that he has been paying a larger share of the rent.

As things stand, unfortunately, these two gentlemen appear to be at loggerheads. They have been occupying separate parts of the premises for some time under some arrangement as to which the court has been given no information whatsoever beyond what I have already mentioned. If a new lease were to be taken up, it would subject the defendant, as well as the plaintiffs, to substantial new financial and other commitments. The defendant has made it quite plain that because of his relationship with the plaintiff he is unwilling to join with him in incurring these further commitments. In these circumstances the court would in principle, I think, be very unlikely indeed to compel the defendant to join with his former partner in taking up a new lease which he did not want. Conceivably, if there were special circumstances, for example relating to the particular terms on which the partnership was dissolved or other matters not now known to the court, different considerations might apply. But the plaintiff, in his very scanty evidence, has shown nothing which convinces me that he would have any realistic hope of persuading the judge at the trial to make either of the two orders which he seeks.

Note: See also *Jacobs* v. *Chaudhuri* [1968] 2 QB 470, at p 412, later.

19.3   The tenant's section 26 request for a new tenancy

A tenant's request for a new tenancy must include a proposal as to the duration for the new tenancy asked for.

SIDNEY BOLSOM INVESTMENT TRUST LTD v. E. KARMIOS & CO. (LONDON) LTD

Court of Appeal   [1956] 1 QB 529

Tenants of shop premises held on a seven year lease served on the landlords a notice under section 26 (3) of the 1954 Act in the prescribed form requesting a new tenancy as from the date of expiry of their existing lease at a new stated rent and 'as to the other terms of the new tenancy ... upon the terms of the current tenancy as set out' in the original lease. Subsequently, the tenants informed the landlords by letter that they had not stated in the request the length of term for which a new lease was sought and that the term sought was 14 years. The landlords opposed an application for a new tenancy on the ground that no valid request for a new tenancy had been served.

Held: The request was valid since it asked by implication for a new seven-year tenancy.

DENNING LJ: We are here concerned with a tenant's request for a new tenancy. On 7 December 1954, when the lease had just over six and a half months to go, the tenants made a request for a new tenancy which they asked should commence on 25 June 1955. If that request was a valid request, it operated to terminate the tenant's interest on the day 'immediately before the date specified in the request for the beginning of the new tenancy': see section 26 (5) of the Act. It would therefore bring the tenant's interest to an end on 24 June 1955, the very day on which the contractual lease expired. It would thus stop the statutory extension from arising at all.

The tenants, having thus themselves brought their existing tenancy to an end, should have followed up their request with an application to the court for a new tenancy. They had four months in which to do it under the provisions of section 29 (3) of the Act; but they did not do it within the permitted time or, indeed, at all. The result is that their interest came to an end on 24 June 1955, and they must quit unless they can in some way avoid the result.

The way they seek to do it is by throwing over their own request. They say that it was not a valid request because it did not comply with section 26 (3) of the Act, which provides that

'A tenant's request for a new tenancy shall not have effect unless it is made by notice in the prescribed form given to the landlord and sets out the tenant's proposals as to the property to be comprised in the new tenancy (being either the whole or part of the property comprised in the current tenancy), as to the rent to be payable under the new tenancy and as to the other terms of the new tenancy.'

In this case the request of 7 December 1954, was made by notice in the prescribed form. The tenants got a printed form which was an exact copy of the statutory prescribed form, and they filled it in. They gave first the time when they wanted the new tenancy to begin, 25 June 1955. They said secondly: 'We propose that the property to be comprised in the new tenancy should be the whole of the property comprised in the current tenancy.' And then thirdly—the important part for our purposes:

'Our proposals as to the rent to be payable under the new tenancy and as to the other terms of the new tenancy are an annual rent of £200 per annum upon the terms of the current tenancy as set out in the lease dated the 27th day of September, 1948.'

[Counsel] for the tenants, says that the request, in order to be valid, ought to state the *duration* proposed for the new tenancy. It is to be noticed that section 26 (3) does not expressly require the tenant to set out his proposals as to the duration of the new tenancy. He has only to set out the rent and 'the other terms of the new tenancy.' But I think that, in this context, the 'other terms' include the duration of the tenancy. That is seen by looking at section 35, from which it appears that 'terms' in this Act includes not only terms like the covenant to repair but also the term as to the duration of the tenancy. In addition, it is obvious that the proposed duration of the new tenancy is one of the most important matters which the landlords would want to know. The question whether they should accept the proposed rent will often depend very much on the proposed duration of the tenancy. The tenant should, therefore, state his proposal for duration, but it can, I think, be done sufficiently by implication.

The first question in this case is: does the proposal in the request sufficiently set out the duration of the new tenancy? I think that it does. The proposal is for 'an annual rent of £200 upon the terms of the current tenancy dated the 27th day of September 1948.' The word 'terms' in that proposal must have the same meaning as the word 'terms' in the earlier part of the same sentence, and that in turn as the same meaning as the word 'terms' in section 26 (3) of the Act. It includes, therefore, all the terms in the current lease, that is, not only the covenants to repair and so forth but also the term as to duration, namely, seven years, and the other term as to an option and so forth. The proposal therefore complied sufficiently with the Act in that it impliedly proposed a duration of seven years for the new tenancy.

Once a tenant has made a valid request for a new tenancy specifying the commencement date of the new tenancy, he cannot withdraw it and serve a fresh request.

POLYVIOU v. SEELEY

Court of Appeal   [1980] 1 WLR 55

A tenant of business premises under a lease for three years from the 16 July 1976 made a request for a new tenancy for three years commencing on 16 July 1979. The landlord served a notice of opposition on the tenant stating that he would oppose any application to the court for the grant of a new tenancy and giving his grounds. The tenant made no application to court within the time limited by the 1954 Act but instead made a further request for a new tenancy again for a term of three years commencing on 16 July 1979. He then applied to the court for a new tenancy relying on the second request.

Held: If a tenant who made a request for a new tenancy did not make an application to the court within the time specified by section 29 (3), by virtue of section 26 (5) his existing tenancy automatically came to an end on the date specified in his request as being the date for the commencement of the proposed new tenancy and he could not withdraw the request and make another.

BROWNE LJ: The judge based his decision on the view that this case was indistinguishable from an earlier decision of this court in *Stile Hall Properties Ltd* v. *Gooch (Note)*, post, p 62. That case apparently is only reported in the Estates Gazette (1968) 207 EG 715, but the judge was supplied, and we have been supplied, with a transcript of the judgment of this court, which consisted of Danckwerts LJ, Davies LJ and Edmund Davies LJ. The facts in that case, as they appear from the judgment, were these. The appellant, Mrs Gooch, was the tenant of property in Brentford under a lease dated 21 March 1960, for seven years from 7 January 1960, so that that lease would have expired on 6 January 1967. The tenant first gave a notice on 9 September 1966, but that notice was invalid because the date specified for the commencement of the new lease was more than 12 months after the date of the notice and was therefore invalid under the provisions of the Act that I have read. Then a second notice was served, dated 20 March 1967. That proposed that the date of commencement of the new tenancy should be 29 September 1967, and that the lease should be for 14 years. Nothing was done under that notice by way of making an application to the court. On 8 September 1967, the landlords wrote: 'As proceedings have not been commenced within the statutory four months, we therefore assume that your client will be vacating on the due date ...' As a result of that, on 26 September 1967, that being only two or three days before the termination of the tenancy by virtue of the previous notice, the tenant's solicitors wrote to the landlord's solicitors:

'We enclose tenant's request for a new tenancy of the above property. This is in place of our client's earlier request dated 20 March 1967, which was withdrawn by our letter ... dated 21 April 1967.'

That enclosed a notice which was in the statutory form and which specified 24 June 1968, as the date for the commencement of the new tenancy, that being, of course, about nine months later than the date that had been specified in the previous request for a new tenancy.

Danckwerts LJ said, later, p 63 E:

'Therefore there was an attempt by the tenant to withdraw her second notice, which was perfectly valid, and substitute a fresh one after the period of four months mentioned in section 29 had expired.'

He then went through the relevant provisions of the Act of 1954 and said, later, p 64 C-F:

'The only other thing to which I need refer is the passage in *Woodfall on Landlord and Tenant*, 26th ed. (1960), vol. 1, p 1410, in which it is observed: "It is important to observe that if the tenant fails to make this application to the court, irrespective of whether the landlord has served a notice of intention to oppose, the current tenancy ends immediately before the date specified by the tenant in his request for the commencement of the new tenancy and the tenant loses his right to a new tenancy and indeed all his rights under the Act." Apparently there is no case which deals with the observations in *Woodfall*, and so far as we have been informed no text-book or other book of that kind has commented on it in any way. It seems to me that the observations are plainly right. The effect of what the tenant did was that, by her request, she fixed the date of the termination of the continued tenancy that the Act conferred upon her by section 24 by reference to the date when she was asking for a new lease, and accordingly automatically under the provisions of section 26 the continued tenancy came to an end. That was the end of the matter, unless she had followed it up within two or four months as required by section 29 by an application to the appropriate court. She made no such application and accordingly the tenancy determined on 28 September 1967, and that is the end of the matter.'

Davies LJ referred to the request of 20 March 1967, and said, later, pp 64 G-65 B:

'The effect of that request would be, under section 26 (5) of the Act of 1954, to terminate the current tenancy on 28 September 1967. Of course, if the tenant had applied within the statutory period of four months the interim provisions for the continuation of the tenancy would have come into effect. But she did not. And therefore once the four months had expired the tenancy was due to come to an end on 28 September. Speaking for myself, I agree with the observations by the editor of *Woodfall on Landlord and Tenant*, 26th ed., vol. 1, p 1410, which have been read by Danckwerts LJ. It would seem to me, as [counsel for the landlords] suggests, to cut right across the intent of the Act if a tenant, such as the present defendant, having given a perfectly valid notice and having failed to take the necessary follow-up step to apply to the court for a new lease, could a couple of days before the statutory expiration of the tenancy serve (as was attempted to be done in the present case) another notice for 24 June 1968, which would, under the statute, continue the tenancy to 23 June 1968, and then, I suppose, on 21 June serve another one, and so on and on and on *ad infinitum.*'

[Counsel for the tenants] in this court has sought valiantly to distinguish *Stile Hall Properties Ltd* v. *Gooch (Note)*, later, p 62, on the same ground as that on which he relied before the judge: that is, that the ground of the decision in the *Stile Hall* case was that the second request specified a date for the commencement of the new tenancy which was different from and later than that specified in the first request, whereas here the second request specified the same date.

It seems to me that the ratio of the *Stile Hall* case was this. By virtue of section 26 (5) the existing tenancy terminates immediately before the date specified in the request for a new tenancy, unless the tenant within the time specified by section 29 (3) makes an application to the court. If he does make an application, the tenancy continues till three months after the final disposal of the proceedings: see section 64. If, however, the tenant does not make such an application, the tenancy automatically comes to an end on that date. If the tenant fails to make an application within the proper time, he cannot withdraw the first request and make another. In the *Stile Hall* case the court was obviously impressed by the hardship to the landlord if the tenant could go on serving successive notices and so continuing the tenancy *ad infinitum*. Here, of course, the tenant is not trying to do any such thing. It is true that the particular hardship to the landlord that impressed this court in the *Stile Hall* case would not arise in this case, but I find it impossible to distinguish this case from the *Stile Hall* case on the ground put forward by [counsel for the tenants].

19.4 Service of notices

The phrase 'place of abode' in section 23 of the Landlord and Tenant Act 1927 is not confined to the residence of the person concerned but includes his business address.

PRICE v. WEST LONDON INVESTMENT BUILDING SOCIETY LTD

Court of Appeal   [1964] 1 WLR 616

A tenant occupied business premises under a lease due to expire on the 1 August 1963. He also had other business premises and resided there. The landlords sent him by registered post a section 25 notice to terminate his tenancy to the business premises which was received and signed for by an employee of the tenant on 23 March 1963. The tenant did not receive the notice himself until the 29 March 1963. On the 28 May 1963, he served a counter-notice on the landlords and thereafter applied to the county court for a new tenancy. The question was whether the counter-notice had been served out of time. The tenant argued (i) that the business premises were not his 'place of abode' within the meaning of the Act (ii) that they were not in any event his 'last known' place of abode and (iii) that the landlord's notice had not in any event been validly served until it had been 'received' by him within the meaning of the form prescribed by the Landlord and Tenant (Notices) Regulations.

Held: 'Place of abode' was not confined to the tenant's personal residence but included business premises and the relevant form could not alter the provisions of the 1954 Act which referred not to 'receive' but to 'given'.

DANCKWERTS LJ: It was contended on behalf of the appellant that the meaning of the phrase 'place of abode' in the present case must be confined to his personal residence—using that phrase in the way in which I have used it, that is to say, as meaning the place where the person concerned lives and sleeps—because section 23 of the Landlord and Tenant Act 1927, was incorporated into the Landlord and Tenant Act 1954, for the purposes not only of Part II of that Act, which deals with business premises, but also for the purpose of Part I, which is plainly concerned with residential property, and it was said that, under the rules of construction, a phrase used in an Act must bear the same meaning throughout. I do not think that that principle is necessarily conclusive, however. In the present case the phrase must be construed with reference to the subject-matter with which in the particular case it is concerned. In a case of residential premises, it will mean residence in the narrow sense, but it seems to me that for the purposes of Part II of the Act, which is concerned purely with business premises, it must have a meaning wider than that, and the most sensible and natural meaning is not the residence of the person concerned, of which the landlords may very well be entirely ignorant, but the business address, which the landlords are much more likely to know and where for the purposes of the provisions of the Act the tenant is much more likely to be found. On the authorities which I have mentioned it is plainly the intention of the Act to include a business address which is not confined to personal residence.

Another argument was based upon the form and notes issued under the provisions of section 66 of the Landlord and Tenant Act 1954. [His Lordship read the second paragraph of form 7 and note 2 (supra) and continued:] The word 'received' is used. There is plainly, however, a reference intended to section 29 of the Landlord and Tenant Act 1954, in which the word is not 'received,' but 'giving.' It seems to me to be quite plain that neither the form nor the notes can alter the provisions of the Act in so far as they attempt to provide for a different situation from that contained in the sections of the Act to which I have referred, which use the word 'give,' 'giving' or 'given.' The form and notes would be *ultra vires* because the regulations in which they are contained could not enlarge the jurisdiction of the court as conferred by the provisions of the Landlord and Tenant Act 1954.

It seems to me, therefore, that the giving of the notice was complete when the registered letter was taken in and signed for on 23 March 1963, and, consequently, that the counter-notice sent by the tenant's solicitors was out of time, and that the judge reached the right conclusion and was correct in dismissing the application. The appeal must be dismissed.

DIPLOCK LJ: [Counsel for the tenants] did address to us an argument based on the contention that 'last known place of abode in England and Wales' meant the last place which the tenant had notified to his landlord as being the appropriate address to which notices should be sent. I mention that argument because I do not want [counsel for the tenants] to think that I have overlooked it, but it does not seem to me to be an argument which will really bear serious examination. The reference to 'last known place of abode' was in my view plainly put in to deal with the case where the landlord is unaware of a change of abode on the part of the tenant; in such a case a notice will be properly served if it is sent to the last place of which the landlord knew as a place of abode of the tenant. In this case, of course, it was sent, I agree with my Lord, to the place which was actually his place of abode at the time of the service of the notice within the meaning of the Act.

The foregoing decision was applied in:

ITALICA HOLDINGS SA v. BAYADEA

Queen's Bench Division   (1985) 273 EG 888

The defendant was the assignee of the residue of a 21 year lease of hotel premises of which the plaintiffs were the landlords. The landlords sent a notice determining the lease under section 25 of the 1954 Act by recorded delivery post to the hotel premises. The tenant failed to serve a counter-notice under the Act and the landlords brought proceedings for possession. The tenant claimed that he never received the section 25 notice and that it had not been sent to his 'last known place of abode' within the meaning of section 23 of the Landlord and Tenant Act 1927.

Held:
(1) The evidence showed that a section 25 notice in the correct form had been served by recorded delivery addressed to the tenant at the hotel premises which were the subject of the action and which were the tenant's only territorial link with England and Wales. Accordingly, although not received by the tenant, the notice had been left at his last known place of abode within the meaning of section 23 of the 1927 Act;
(2) The phrase 'place of abode' could include a business address and service in accordance with section 23 of the 1927 Act was good even though the notice was never received.

FRENCH LJ: In common parlance one does not equate a place of business with a place of abode or residence, or at least one does not by any means necessarily so equate. However, it is clear that there is a considerable number of decisions to the effect that in appropriate cases and in appropriate circumstances a place of business may be a place of abode, and a good number of those authorities are referred to in the case of *Price* v. *West London Investment Building Society* [1964] 2 All ER 318. In that case at p 321 Danckwerts LJ said the following:

'The argument on behalf of the tenant is largely based on the provision of section 23 of the Landlord and Tenant Act 1927 and in particular on the words "last known place of abode in England and Wales". It is contended that "place of abode" in that phrase means the place where the tenant dwelt—his residence in the sense of the place where he slept at night, if nothing more. However, a large number of authorities show that, at any rate for certain purposes, "residence" or "place of abode" may include a place where the person in question works and has his business. The reason why those results have been reached in those cases really depends on the purposes for which the statutory provisions are intended, and if they are intended to make sure that proceedings or notice of proceedings and the like shall come to the knowledge of a certain person (as has been pointed out in these cases) it often may be far more likely that a person will receive due notice of the matters in question if the notice is sent to him at his usual place of business rather than the place where he happens to go home and sleep at night.'

The question then arises whether 161 Praed Street within the authority of *Price* v. *West London Building Society* ought properly to be regarded as the defendant's last known place of abode in England or Wales at 30 December 1980, he by then being resident in Malta, having regard to the other hotel businesses to which I have referred. He had sold 24 Russell Street four years earlier. According to Mr Bayadea he had instructed all the persons with whom he carried on business not to write to him there. As to the Gresham and Welcome Hotels, there is no evidence as to what interest, if any, he had by then in those premises. The only evidence before me is that his son Emanuel, or maybe some other member of his family, managed two premises. The only connection which, according to the evidence, Mr Charles Bayadea retained with this country, apart from his family links, was his tenancy of 161 Praed Street. Accordingly, so far as the plaintiffs were concerned, 161 Praed Street is the only possible candidate as being first of all the place at which the defendant carried on business; secondly it was in the nature of things the place at which the relevant business was carried on, namely the business which attracted the protection of Part II of the 1954 Act; thirdly, as I have said, it was the only territorial link which Mr Charles Bayadea, the defendant, retained in England and Wales, and accordingly I come to the conclusion that 161 Praed Street was, properly speaking and within the meaning of section 23 of the 1927 Act, the defendant's last known place of abode in England and Wales. The fact that the section 25 notice may not have reached the defendant or some duly authorised agent of his does not detract from the efficacy of the service on the defendant at his last known place of abode. As a matter of construction section 23 in prescribing that notice may be served by sending it through the post in a registered letter addressed to him there makes it irrelevant for the purposes of the Act whether notice ever reached the premises, or whether, having reached the premises, it ever actually reached the tenant. *Dicta* to that effect by Megaw LJ in *Chiswell* v. *Griffon Land & Estates Ltd* [1975] 1 WLR 1181 at p 1188 express in more elegant language than mine the conclusion to which I have just referred on that construction.

Accordingly, in my judgment this notice was duly served in one of the manners prescribed by section 23 of the 1927 Act.

In **Stylo Shoes Ltd v. Prices Tailors Ltd** [1960] Ch 396, the tenants of business premises notified the landlords that their registered office and principal place of business had been transferred from Huddersfield to Leeds. Subsequently, the landlords served a section 25 notice on the tenants by sending it registered post to the tenant's former address in Huddersfield. The letter was redirected to Leeds and there received by the tenants.

Held: There had been a valid service of the notice since the requirements of the Act were satisfied if a letter containing the notice was delivered to and in fact received by the person to whom the notice was given.

In **Hogg Bullimore & Co. Ltd v. Co–Operative Insurance Society** (1985) 50 P & CR 105, the landlord served a section 25 notice on the tenant on 2 April 1984 and purported to terminate the tenant's tenancy on 2 October 1984. The tenant claimed a declaration that the notice was invalid as there were not six clear months between the date of service of the notice and the date of its expiry.

Held: Section 25 (2) required that the notice should be given not less than six months before the date of termination specified therein. The notice was not required to be of a clear six months length and the notice served by the landlord was valid.

19.5   Waiver of validity of notices

A party may be estopped from denying the validity of a notice.

BRISTOL CARS LTD v. R.K.H. (HOTELS) LTD

Court of Appeal   (1979) 38 P & CR 411

The tenant gave a notice requesting a new tenancy under section 26 of the 1954 Act but the notice was defective because the date of commencement was too early to be capable of inclusion in the notice. Neither party noticed the mistake. The landlords indicated that they would not oppose the new tenancy and they gave no notice that they would oppose the grant of a new tenancy. They then applied for an interim rent but did not pursue that application. Later, the landlords were advised that the tenant's request was bad and applied for the tenant's application to be struck out.

Held: The landlords were estopped by their conduct from denying the validity of the tenant's request and, alternatively, their application for an interim rent amounted to a waiver of any defect in the tenant's notice.

TEMPLEMAN LJ: So far as the first point is concerned, it seems quite plain that, on principle and authority, this is a defect in a document that is capable of being waived. So far as principle is concerned, in *Tennant* v. *London County Council*, the landlords served a notice under section 25 of the Act of 1954 determining the tenancy and objecting to the grant of a new tenancy. The tenant served a counter-notice, and applied under the Act for a new tenancy. He was held to have waived any objection to the validity of the landlords' notice. His point there was that the notice had not been signed by the correct person and therefore was not binding on him and was a defective notice. Jenkins LJ found—I think, as an alternative ground for his decision—that the tenant had waived objection. It never seems to have occurred to him or to the other members of the court, or to counsel, that waiver was not possible.

In my judgment, it is quite clear that the defect in the present case could be waived. It remains to consider whether the landlords did waive the requirements.

On the question whether, in the present case, the landlords have waived the defect in the request, the argument for the landlords is beguilingly simple. [Counsel for the landlords] put it in a variety of ways, but, at the end of the day, I think that it comes down to this. He says that there can be no waiver or acquiescence without knowledge: that the landlords did not know that the tenants' request dated 4 February 1976 was invalid until April 1977, and that, as soon as they found that it was, they took the point and objected to the grant of a new tenancy. If knowledge is requisite, as it is in some cases of waiver and acquiescence, then it is quite clear that the landlords did not have that knowledge.

In my judgment, however, this is a case of estoppel rather than waiver. The landlords innocently led the tenants to believe that they would not, and, after a certain period, could not, oppose the grant of a new tenancy. By the time that the landlords sought to assert the contrary, the position of the tenants had so altered that it would be unfair to allow the landlords now to contest the validity of the request and then to oppose the grant of a new tenancy. When the tenants served their request on the landlords, they were seeking, as is plain from the Act and the form, to ascertain whether the landlords would oppose the grant of a new tenancy—and, of course, a tenant does need to know that when he is contemplating how he is to conduct his business in the future. The landlords, on receiving that request, could have challenged it. They could have opposed the grant of a new tenancy, or they could have said nothing. If the validity of the request had been challenged, or if the grant of a new tenancy had been opposed, or if the landlords had remained silent, the tenants would at any rate have been on their guard. They might have reconsidered the request and served another notice. They might have looked elsewhere for premises. At any rate, they would not necessarily have spent the next year blissfully in the illusion that they were bound to obtain a new tenancy—a belief that, no doubt, affected their business administration and planning throughout the year.

The time came, *viz.* 4 April 1976 when the tenants, having received the letter from the receiver and knowing that the surveyors were in negotiation, were entitled, because of those events, and because the time for delivering a counter-notice had expired, to assume thereafter that the landlords not only were not going to oppose the grant of a new tenancy, but could not successfully do so. On that hypothesis, so far as they were concerned, time was irrelevant. No matter how long the negotiations took, no matter what changes of landlord there were, everything could be governed by an application to the court, and, so long as that was kept alive, they were bound to end with a new tenancy in the long run.

The lapse of time between February 1976, when the tenants served their request, and April 1977, when the landlords sought to assert the invalidity of the request, is a long time in the life of businessmen. The tenants were faced with an entirely new situation—the danger of losing their premises in 1977 at a time when, possibly, the property market had altered or the position as to alternative accommodation had altered: any plans that they had made during that year, on the assumption that they were going to stay, would be frustrated. Worse than that, however, the position was that, whereas, as I have indicated, it seems highly likely, to put it at its lowest, that the landlords and their predecessors in title had had no grounds on which to oppose the grant of a new tenancy, by April 1977, as a result of the passage of time, and (I suppose) the landlords getting themselves organised, the landlords were in a position at least to allege that they had the intention at that time of reconstructing the premises, so that this delay that took place because the tenants were blissfully thinking that they were bound to get a lease and that time was of no importance radically changed the position of the landlords and faced the tenants with an entirely new situation that meant that, if they had known of it originally, they might have taken a very different course of action.

It seems to me that, in those circumstances, the landlords were estopped from denying the validity of the notice [*sic*] because they had, innocently, led the tenants to believe that they would not oppose the grant of a new tenancy. Of course, not every delay or every representation will support an estoppel. In the present case, [counsel for the landlords] has pointed out that the landlords did nothing—that they knew nothing—and he said that there was very great difficulty in assessing the particular date on which, on this analysis, they became estopped from disputing the validity of the request. In my judgment, however, there is no doubt or difficulty in the present case. The inevitable conclusion from the facts that I have outlined is that the date when the landlords became estopped occurred before April 1977—certainly not later than 2 March 1977, when they applied for their interim rent. Accordingly, for my part I would hold that the landlords are estopped from disputing the validity of the tenants' request.

It was urged that the circumstances in the present case are not different from the circumstances in the *Kammins* case, in which, as I have said, the House of Lords, by a majority, held that the landlords had not been guilty of waiver. There are, however, striking differences between the *Kammins* case and the present. In the first place, the time-span was shorter. Secondly, the time-span was not such, and the circumstances were not such, that it could be seen quite plainly that the tenants would be in a position, when faced with an allegation of the invalidity of the request, different from that in which they would have been a year earlier. Thirdly, in *Kammins* the landlords had persistently opposed the grant of a new tenancy. They had given grounds for opposition, and the invalidity of the application was a second or alternative ground that came into operation admittedly at the last minute. The complaint of the tenants in the present case, however, is that the inevitable assumption that they would have made from the landlords' actions in the negotiations between February 1976 and April 1977 would have been that they need not bother to do anything but negotiate for the terms, and, if necessary, ask the court to decide the terms, of the lease that they were bound to get, whereas in *Kammins'* case the landlords made it clear that they would, if possible, resist the grant of a new lease. Accordingly, I do not find that the circumstances in *Kammins'* case, to which [counsel for the landlords] pointed, govern the present.

As an alternative ground, it seems to me that the action of the landlords in the present case in asking the court to grant an interim rent was an action that plainly waived any defect. On this head of the case, Lord Diplock in the *Kammins* case, as I have said, analysed the various grounds on which waiver could be put forward, and one ground to which he referred, but which did not apply in the *Kammins* case, was that of waiver that arose:

'... in a situation where a person is entitled to alternative rights inconsistent with one another. If he has knowledge of the facts which give rise in law to these alternative rights and acts in a manner which is consistent only with his having chosen to rely on one of them, the law holds him to his choice even though he was unaware that this would be the legal consequence of what he did. He is sometimes said to have "waived" the alternative right, as for instance a right to forfeit a lease or to rescind a contract of sale for wrongful repudiation or breach of condition; but this is better categorised as "election" rather than as "waiver." It was this type of "waiver" that Parker J was discussing in *Matthews* v. *Smallwood*.'

It seems to me that those words describe what happened in the present case. Although the landlords did not know it, they had the choice of affirming the request and application and applying for an interim rent on the basis that that was the course that they elected to take, or, alternatively, arguing that the application was invalid, in which case, of course, they could not apply for an interim rent. The action of applying for an interim rent was, in the words of Lord Diplock, an act inconsistent with their relying on their other choice, *viz.* to contend that the request was invalid.

Accordingly, on each of those two alternative grounds, I would dismiss the appeal.

Note: For the House of Lords' decision in *Kammins Ballrooms Co. Ltd* v. *Zenith Investments (Torquay) Ltd* see page 409, later. The decision in the *Bristol Cars* case was followed in *British Railways Board* v. *A.J.A. Smith (No. 2)* (1981) 259 EG 766, where a tenant was held to be estopped from disputing the validity of a landlord's section 25 notice which was defective in point of form. His Honour Judge Fitzhugh (sitting as a judge of the High Court) said:

'I prefer to base my judgment on the *Bristol* case and I hold that whatever may have been the position before the claim for a new tenancy was taken to the hearing before the learned Vice-Chancellor—I do not decide what any earlier position or positions was or were—on that date the tenant must have lost any right it might have had to dispute the validity of the notice, but, if that were not so, then at any rate it must have lost it at the hearing before the Court of Appeal on 25 November 1980 when the tenant knew all the material facts and knew also that a new tenancy could be claimed only if there had been a valid notice of termination and he elected to pursue that claim. That conduct was inconsistent with any right it may have had to dispute the validity of the notice. The tenant elected not to take the point and is now estopped from doing so. The fact that [counsel for the defendants] then declared that he proposed to reserve the point was of no effect. It is rather like the case of a landlord who had a right to forfeit a lease accepting rent arrears due after the right to forfeit had occurred on the basis that he accepted it only without prejudice to this right still to claim forfeiture of the lease.'

Chapter 20

Tenant's application for a new tenancy

20.1 Time limits

A business tenant who having requested a new tenancy under section 26 of the 1954 Act fails to apply to the court for such new tenancy within the time limits provided by the Act cannot later make such an application.

MEAH v. SECTOR PROPERTIES LTD

Court of Appeal   [1974] 1 WLR 547

A lease of business premises was demised to the tenant for 14 years from 24 June 1957 at a rent of £850 per annum. On the 21 December 1970, the tenant made a request for a new tenancy under section 26 for 21 years beginning on the 24 June 1971. On the 19 March 1973, he applied to the county court for a new tenancy whereupon the landlords applied to court to strike out his application on the ground that it was out of time.

Held: Under section 26 (5) of the Act, the effect of the tenant's request had been to terminate his existing tenancy on 24 June 1971 and that, accordingly, he had ceased to be a tenant on that date. He no longer had any rights under the 1954 Act and, therefore, his application would be struck out.

EDMUND DAVIES LJ: It is to be observed that whether the tenant has given notice under section 26, or whether there has been a termination by the landlord in accordance with section 25, it is the tenant, and only the tenant, who can make application to the county court. Section 26 provides:

'(2) A tenant's request for a new tenancy shall be for a tenancy beginning with such date, not more than 12 nor less than six months after the making of the request, as may be specified therein: Provided that the said date shall not be earlier than the date on which apart from this Act the current tenancy would come to an end by effluxion of time or could be brought to an end by notice to quit given by the tenant.'

Section 29 (3) provides:

'No application under subsection (1) of section 24 of this Act shall be entertained unless it is made not less than two nor more than four months ... after the making of the tenant's request for a new tenancy.'

Section 64 deals with the interim continuation of tenancies pending the determination of the court. Reverting to section 26, subsection (5) thereof provides:

'Where the tenant makes a request for a new tenancy in accordance with the foregoing provisions of this section, the current tenancy shall ... terminate immediately before the date specified in the request for the beginning of the new tenancy.'

What is said on behalf of the landlords is that the date designated in the tenant's request under section 26 for the beginning of the new tenancy sought being 24 June 1971, the existing tenancy accordingly came to an end either on 23 June or at the latest on 24 June 1971. They therefore asked the county court judge to strike out the tenant's application on the ground that any interest he had as tenant in 32, Old Compton Street had terminated in June 1971, yet here he was on 19 March 1973, making an application which, so it was submitted, was (a) not only hopelessly outside the time permitted by section 29 (3), but was also (b) an application in relation to a non-existent right.

The narrative of events which I have related serves to show, as I think, not only that the tenant is greatly out of time in making his application, but also that his request for a new tenancy beginning on 24 June 1971, meant that, having regard to section 26 (5), his existing tenancy terminated on that date. In the result, nearly two years before he made his section 24 (1) application to the court on 19 March 1973, he had ceased to be clothed with the garment of a tenant. By that date he had no more a tenant's right in respect of 32, Old Compton Street than a complete stranger had, and accordingly his application was not sustainable.

The court may enlarge the time available for service of a tenant's application.

ALI v. KNIGHT

Court of Appeal   (1984) 272 EG 1165

The tenant had failed to serve his application for a new tenancy within the time limit prescribed by the 1954 Act and the deputy registrar of the county court granted an extension of time so to do. There had been an agreement between the parties to waive the time-limit while negotiations continued. At one point the landlords purported to end the agreement as to the time-limit but nevertheless negotiations continued and an order for interim rent was made.

Held: The court had power to extend the time for service of a tenant's originating application for a new tenancy under Order 7 rule 20 (2) of the County Court Rules 1981 and it did not have to consider whether the tenant's failure to comply with the original time limit was due to any exceptional circumstances.

EVELEIGH LJ: The extension of time was granted under Order 7, rule 20, of the County Court Rules. By the County Court Rules it is provided that service of an originating summons shall be made within two months of its issue in cases coming under the Landlord and Tenant Act. Order 7, rule 20, subrule (2) reads:
'The court may extend the period for service of a summons from time to time for such period'
I leave out the intervening words
'as the court may specify, if an application for extension is made before that day or such later day (if any) as the court may allow.'

Before this court it is contended that the learned judge either had no discretion or wrongly exercised his discretion in granting an extension of time. The court has been referred to the case of *Robert Baxendale Ltd* v. *Davstone Holdings Ltd* [1982] 1 WLR 1385. There the court emphasised that the Act was taking away from a landlord rights that he otherwise had and that an exceptional case had to be made out for a tenant to be granted an extension of time under the rules. Counsel has said that in this case the principles enunciated in *Robert Baxendale Ltd* should be applied and this court should insist upon strict compliance with the rules, because no exceptional case had been made out. Whether or not the rigidity of the case of *Robert Baxendale Ltd* is still to be adhered to, I do not seek to discover. That case was decided when the rules of the county court were differently worded, and it may be that the difference in wording will be material in considering whether or not the court should treat a case today with that same strictness.

The appropriate order then was Order 8, rule 5. That rule contained in paragraph (2) the following words:

'Where reasonable efforts have been made to serve the summons within the said period and service has not been effected, the registrar may, on application, order that the time be extended for a further period not exceeding 12 months or for successive periods not exceeding 12 months each. Provided that the time shall not be extended for any period unless the application is made within the currency of the last preceding period.'

I do not read the whole of that order, but those words do not now appear in the current rules. Be that as it may, this case in my judgment is not a *Baxendale* situation at all. A particular situation has arisen; in other words, a special reason exists in the present case, namely, that the parties themselves agreed, to use their own words, to uplift the rules. Consequently, as by mutual consent the time envisaged by the rules has passed, there is no possible way in which the rules can be strictly adhered to. Consequently, the matter is opened up for the decision of the judge with a discretion, as I see it, unfettered by authority.

On behalf of the landlords it has been submitted that the learned judge should act by analogy with the rules and apply a two months' time-limit rigidly from the date of the receipt of the landlords' solicitors' letter abrogating the agreement between the parties. For myself, I can see that in many cases such a course may be considered appropriate by the learned judge, but I see no obligation upon him to follow such a course rigidly and to act by analogy with the decision in *Robert Baxendale Ltd.*

The court was also referred to the case of *Kammins Ballrooms Co. Ltd* v. *Zenith Investments (Torquay) Ltd* [1971] AC 850. Relying upon that case, counsel for the landlords has submitted that it is necessary at least for the tenant to show that there has been by the landlords a waiver or an election or that the landlord is estopped from taking the point that the tenant is out of time. But that case was concerned with the application of strict statutory provisions. It was held that those provisions, being for the benefit of the tenant, could be waived and that the tenant might be able to establish an election made by the landlord in his favour or show estoppel, but that those legal considerations would have to be established. That case, as I say, was dealing with strict rules or strict provisions of the statute. There was no provision in the statute for an exercise of discretion. In the present case the rules of the county court specifically make provision for the exercise of discretion in granting an extension, and the limit sought to be placed upon the exercise of that discretion on the basis of *Robert Baxendale Ltd* does not, as I have said, apply in this case because the parties had taken the case by agreement out of the application of the strict rules.

So therefore one has to ask whether or not the learned judge improperly exercised his discretion. I am not concerned to determine what order I would have made in this case. The material then before the judge was that, while the solicitors had indicated that they no longer would abide by the agreement to uplift the time or the procedure rules, they had not replied in contentious terms to the letter of 8 October which objected to the abrogation of the agreement, and they continued to negotiate; they fixed the rent, dating back as it did to March 1982; and they envisaged it running forward to such period as remained by virtue of section 64 of the Act to the tenant.

In all those circumstances it seems to me that the landlords' objection before the county court judge was a formality in the extreme. If, as my lord, O'Connor LJ, has suggested in the course of this hearing, the originating summons had been served in time and the parties had then agreed not to proceed with the hearing pending negotiations, the position would really not be substantially different from what it is today. As [counsel] for the tenant pointed out, the landlords' application for interim rent was made on the strength of the proceedings already started in the court by the tenant. The landlords did not take out an independent summons for that purpose. None of those points is conclusive, but they are all relevant matters in the case for the exercise of his discretion by the county court judge. I in those circumstances am quite unable to say that he acted improperly, and I would dismiss this appeal.

Note: The decision in *Robert Baxendale Ltd* v. *Davstone (Holdings) Ltd* [1982] 1 WLR 1385 to the effect that a business tenant had to adhere strictly to the timetable prescribed by the 1954 Act was based on the provisions of County Court Order 8 rule 5 (2) of the 1936 Rules which have since been replaced. The current provisions are contained in Order 7 rule 20 (2) of the County Court Rules 1981 upon which the decision in *Ali* v. *Knight* (above) is based.

In **Joan Barrie v. G.U.S. Property Management** (1981) 259 EG 628, the tenants had issued originating summonses in the High Court for new tenancies of premises in Liverpool. Service was not effected within the two-month time limit as required by Order 97 rule 6 of the Supreme Court Rules. The judge had a discretion to enlarge the time limits under RSC Order 6 rule 8 but refused to do so.

Held: The discretion should only be used in exceptional circumstances.

WALLER LJ: In my opinion, the principles applying to extensions of time are similar, whether it is a writ which requires renewal after 12 months, or an originating summons with the same time-limit, or an originating summons under the Landlord and Tenant Act 1954, with a time-limit of two months. There will, of course, be differences of detail, because of the different factual background; but whether it be a writ or an originating summons, the circumstances must be exceptional, or 'special' as is said in one of the cases, to justify an extension. The personal injury authorities show examples of circumstances which might be exceptional, and in relation to the Landlord and Tenant Act, the case of *Lewis* v. *Wolking Properties Ltd* [1978] 1 All ER 427 is an indication of the kind of exceptional circumstances which might apply in a landlord and tenant case.

It is unclear to what extent the decision in *Ali* v. *Knight* (earlier) has affected the foregoing decision which was concerned with the procedure in the High Court.

An application for a new tenancy which is made out of time is nevertheless 'an application' within the meaning of the 1954 Act so that the tenancy continues until three months after proceedings on it are disposed of.

ZENITH INVESTMENTS (TORQUAY) LTD v. KAMMINS BALLROOMS CO. LTD (NO. 2)

Court of Appeal   [1971] 1 WLR 1751

The tenant's application for a new tenancy was made less than two months after the request contrary to section 29 (3) of the 1954 Act. In the House of Lords it was held that the tenant's application failed because the landlords had not disentitled themselves by estoppel or waiver from relying on the irregularity. Subsequently, the tenant surrendered possession of the premises. The question in issue in the present action was the date when the tenancy terminated.

Held: The words 'an application made under the said Part II' in section 64 (1) of the 1954 Act covered the tenant's application and, accordingly, the tenancy continued until three months after the decision of the House of Lords and terminated when the tenants surrendered possession.

RUSSELL LJ: The House of Lords has explained the nature of section 29 (3) as being a procedural time requirement only, one which, if not fulfilled, affords a defence to the landlord, which he may or may not put forward, and which he may in any given case debar himself from putting forward by agreement or waiver. Section 29 (3) therefore is the equivalent of a provision saying: 'It shall be a ground upon which the landlord may resist or defend an application under section 24 (1) that it was made less than two months or more than four months after the making of the tenant's request.' If that be the true effect of section 29 (3), why is the application not an application made under Part II, and why are proceedings to determine whether the defence to the application is on the facts available to the landlords not 'proceedings on the application'? Stress was laid for the landlords on the fact that the right to apply under section 24 (1) was in terms subject to the provisions of section 29: but on the House of Lords' explanation of the scope and effect of section 29 (3), section 24 (1) means no more than that an application made otherwise than within the stated periods is vulnerable to defence on that ground. It seems to me that this approach, derived from the views on section 29 of the House of Lords, leads to the conclusion that it is not correct to speak of a 'valid application' or an 'invalid application' in discussing section 64. Section 64 speaks of an application under Part II and proceedings thereon, which ordinarily read would cover an application, albeit vulnerable to a particular defence (if asserted) which the other party can by conduct (waiver) render invulnerable to that particular defence.

It was however argued for the landlords that a construction which gives to a tenant who has failed to comply with a statutory timetable a long extra period of tenancy is unfair and open to abuse: and that particularly this is so in a case such as the present before the amendment of the Act of 1954 permitting some interim adjustment of the original rent. Suppose, it was said, a landlord to give notice of determination on a date, or a tenant to make a request for a new lease on a date, and five months to elapse with no further step by the tenant: the landlord should (it was said) surely be entitled to feel himself free to make his arrangements on the footing that his right to possession will be unassailable on that date. But, if after the four months the tenant may make an application and assert that under section 64 the tenancy will continue until three months after that application is finally disposed of, the landlord's arrangements will be in disarray. I fully appreciate this and the possibility of abuse: though the detriment to the landlord can at least be mitigated, where no shadow or a case of waiver or estoppel can be made out, by a prompt application to strike out the application as totally vulnerable, or an appeal as groundless. Whether in any given case an attempt to attract the benefits of section 64 by an application not made bona fide could be frustrated by the court, I do not pursue.

The correct answer in this case is that the proceedings up to and including the House of Lords are correctly described as proceedings on an application under Part II. True the application was, as it turned out, vulnerable to a defence because its making was by section 24 (1) subjected to the provisions of section 29 (3): but it was nevertheless such an application.

Note: For the House of Lords' decision see *Kammins Ballrooms Co. Ltd* v. *Zenith Investments (Torquay) Ltd* [1971] AC 850 at page 409, later.

The word 'month' in the 1954 Act means calendar month so that the period of a month or months ends upon the corresponding date in the appropriate subsequent month.

DODDS v. WALKER

House of Lords   [1981] 1 WLR 1027

On the 30 September 1978, the landlord gave notice to the tenant to determine his tenancy of business premises. Under section 29 (3) of the 1954 Act, the tenant had 'four months after the giving of the landlord's notice' to apply to the county court for a new tenancy. The tenant applied on the 31 January 1979 and the question in issue was whether the application was made one day too late.

Held: The 'corresponding date' rule applied so that in calculating the period which had elapsed after the giving of the landlord's notice and excluding that day, the relevant period was the specified number of months thereafter which ended on the corresponding day of the appropriate subsequent month. Accordingly the tenant had made his application out of time.

LORD DIPLOCK: My Lords, reference to a 'month' in a statute is to be understood as a calendar month. The Interpretation Act 1889 says so. It is also clear under a rule that has been consistently applied by the courts since *Lester* v. *Garland* (1808) 15 VesJun 248, that in calculating the period that has elapsed after the occurrence of the specified event such as the giving of a notice, the day on which the event occurs is excluded from the reckoning. It is equally well established, and is not disputed by counsel for the tenant, that when the relevant period is a month or specified number of months after the giving of a notice, the general rule is that the period ends upon the corresponding date in the appropriate subsequent month, i.e. the day of that month that bears the same number as the day of the earlier month on which the notice was given.

The corresponding date rule is simple. It is easy of application. Except in a small minority of cases, of which the instant case is not an example, all that the calculator has to do is to mark in his diary the corresponding date in the appropriate subsequent month. Because the number of days in five months of the year is less than in the seven others the inevitable consequence of the corresponding date rule is that one month's notice given in a 30 day month is one day shorter than one month's notice given in a 31 day month and is three days shorter if it is given in February. Corresponding variations in the length of notice reckoned in days occur where the required notice is a plurality of months.

This simple general rule which Cockburn CJ in *Freeman* v. *Read* (1863) 4 B & S 174, 184 described as being 'in accordance with common usage ... and with the sense of mankind,' works perfectly well without need for any modification so long as there is in the month in which the notice expires a day which bears the same number as the day of the month on which the notice was given. Such was the instant case and such will be every other case except for notices given on the 31st of a 31 day month and expiring in a 30 day month or in February, and notices expiring in February and given on the 30th or the 29th (except in leap year) of any other month of the year. In these exceptional cases, the modification of the corresponding date rule that is called for is also well established: the period given by the notice ends upon the last day of the month in which the notice expires.

The phrase 'not less than two months' in section 29 (3) of the 1954 Act is not to be construed as meaning 'more than two months'.

E.J. RILEY INVESTMENTS LTD v. EUROSTILE HOLDINGS LTD

Court of Appeal   (1985) 275 EG 716

On 23 March 1983 the landlord gave notice under section 25 of the Landlord and Tenant Act 1954. By a notice dated 22 May but served on the landlord on 23 May 1983, the tenant applied for a new tenancy under the provisions of section 24 (1) of the Act. The landlord contended that the tenant's notice was invalid and premature as under section 29 (3) of the Act the tenant had to serve his application for a new tenancy 'not less than two months nor more than four months after the giving of the landlord's notice'.

Held: The tenant had made his application exactly two months after the service of the landlord's notice. Since the phrase 'not less than two months' should not be construed as meaning 'more than two months', a date which was simply two months exactly could not be said to be more than two months and, therefore, the tenant's application was not premature and was valid.

Fox LJ: The landlord's case is that dates before the 24 May are less than 2 months from the 23 March. But that is construing the words 'not less than 2 months' as meaning 'more than 2 months.' I see no reason why the Court should do that. It does not give effect to the differing language which the draftsman has used in relation to the 2 and the 4 month periods. He has not said 'unless it is made more than 2 and not more than 4 months after the giving of the landlord's notice'. He has said 'not less than 2 months and not more than 4 months'. In my opinion just as there are dates which are less than 2 months after the 23 March and dates which are more than 2 months after the 23 March there must be a date which is simply 2 months, no more and no less, after the 23 March. That in my view, is the 23 May. In short, you apply the corresponding date rule (which gets you to the 23 May) and ask 'Was the application made before that?' If the application is made on the corresponding date, it cannot be said to be either before or after the corresponding date.

In **Hodgson v. Armstrong** [1967] 2 QB 299, the Court of Appeal held that the making of an application for a new tenancy is a procedural matter so that if the last day for an application falls on a day when the county court office is closed, the County Court Rules (see CCR 1984, Order 1 rule 9) will, if the application is made by post, have the effect of permitting it to be made on the next day the office is open.

A landlord who files a reply to a premature application does not thereby waive his right to invoke the time limit imposed by section 29 of the 1954 Act.

KAMMINS BALLROOMS CO. LTD v. ZENITH INVESTMENTS (TORQUAY) LTD

House of Lords   [1971] AC 850

The tenants of business premises made a request for a new tenancy and the landlords served a counter-notice indicating that they would oppose an application to the court for a new tenancy. The tenants filed an application for a grant of a new tenancy to which the landlords filed an answer taking no objection to the application being premature. Subsequently, the landlords claimed that the tenant's application was invalid since it had been made less than two months after the request for a new tenancy contrary to section 29 (3) of the 1954 Act.

Held: The landlords had not waived their right to object that the application was bad.

LORD MORRIS: The effect of section 24 of the Act is that a tenancy to which Part II applies does not come to an end unless terminated as provided by the Act. A tenant may apply for a new tenancy if the landlord has given a notice under section 25 to terminate the tenancy or if he (the tenant) has made a request for a new tenancy under section 26. On the making of an application the court must make an order for the grant of a new tenancy (see section 29 (1)) unless the landlord successfully opposes the application on grounds on which in accordance with section 30 the landlord is entitled to oppose. In that event the court must not make an order: see section 31 (1). The application of the tenant is made under section 24 but it is 'subject to the provisions' of section 29. In this way the time limits set out in section 29 are introduced. In my view they are time limits which regulate procedure. They provide for an orderly sequence of procedural steps. A tenant who fails to keep within the prescribed time limits will fail at his peril. He may find that his landlord will insist, as insist he may, upon strict observance. But if a landlord agrees to waive the strict observance of a time stipulation I do not consider that the language of section 29 makes it obligatory upon the court to hold that in spite of the landlord's agreement the court cannot and must not proceed.

If someone has an existing claim for money due or for damages he may be met by a plea that some statute has enacted that an action to enforce his claim must be brought within a certain period. Yet it has always been recognised that words such as 'no action shall be brought' are generally speaking not words which compel the court to hold that it lacks jurisdiction even if the party sued does not wish to rely on the statutory defence. The position is in my view similar in the case of a tenant who makes an application to the court for a new tenancy. He may be defeated if he has not applied within the statutory time limits. But if the landlord chooses not to insist upon a strict compliance with those limits I do not consider that the court is devoid of jurisdiction.

LORD DIPLOCK: So it becomes necessary to consider whether the respondents did waive this requirement. 'Waiver' is a word which is sometimes used loosely to describe a number of different legal grounds on which a person may be debarred from asserting a substantive right which he once possessed or from raising a particular defence to a claim against him which would otherwise be available to him. We are not concerned in the instant appeal with the first type of waiver. This arises in a situation where a person is entitled to alternative rights inconsistent with one another. If he has knowledge of the facts which give rise in law to these alternative rights and acts in a manner which is consistent only with his having chosen to rely on one of them, the law holds him to his choice even though he was unaware that this would be the legal consequence of what he did. He is sometimes said to have 'waived' the alternative right, as for instance a right to forfeit a lease or to rescind a contract of sale for wrongful repudiation or breach of condition; but this is better categorised as 'election' rather than as 'waiver.' It was this type of 'waiver' that Parker J was discussing in *Matthews* v. *Smallwood* [1910] 1 Ch 777.

The second type of waiver which debars a person from raising a particular defence to a claim against him, arises when he either agrees with the claimant not to raise that particular defence or so conducts himself as to be estopped from raising it. This is the type of waiver which constitutes the exception to a prohibition such as that imposed by section 29 (3) of the Landlord and Tenant Act 1954, and other statutes of limitation. The ordinary principles of estoppel apply to it.

My Lords, I think that the only kinds of 'waiver' that could avail the appellants in the instant case are either an estoppel in the strict sense of the term or a quasi-estoppel arising under the doctrine of promissory estoppel laid down in the *High Trees* case (*Central London Property Trust Ltd* v. *High Trees House Ltd*) [1947] KB

130 and *Combe* v. *Combe* [1951] 2 KB 215 or under the older doctrine of 'acquiescence' expounded by Fry J in *Willmott* v. *Barber* (1880) 15 ChD 96. I should be only too glad if I could find in the evidence before the county court judge material which would justify a finding of estoppel or quasi-estoppel on any of these grounds, but as to each of them it seems to me that the appellants have failed to establish at least one essential element.

As respects estoppel in the strict sense it is difficult to find in the conduct of the landlords in the proceedings or in the letters which their solicitors wrote any representation of an existing fact. Their answer to the tenants' application and their letters prior to 5 December 1968, fairly bear the inference, as was the fact, that the only defence on which they then intended to rely was that arising under section 30 (1) of the Act. But no inference can be drawn from this that they would not change their minds before the hearing and even if it could this would only operate as a promise which might possibly give rise to a promissory estoppel but not to an estoppel in the strict sense. Treated as a mere statement of the landlords' present intention it would operate to estop them from denying that they had that intention at the time the letters were written; but that does not help the tenants on this appeal.

Whatever may be the other limits of a *High Trees* promissory estoppel it cannot arise unless there is a promise intended by the promisor to affect his existing legal relationship with the promisee upon the faith of which the promisee has acted. I cannot spell out of the conduct and correspondence of the parties any promise by the landlords that they would never take the point that the tenants' application was out of time, nor can I infer from what they did or said any intention on their part to affect their existing legal relationship with the tenants as lessors and lessee. Furthermore the tenants called no evidence to suggest that they themselves thought that the landlords were making any promise of this kind on which the tenants acted. So the appellants, in my view, also fail to establish the essential elements of any promissory estoppel.

Finally, as to 'acquiescence' it was as a result of agreement between the parties that the hearing of the tenants' application was postponed until a date in December when it would be too late for the tenants to correct their error by making a fresh application. If the landlords had known of their own right to raise the objection that the application was out of time when they agreed to the December date of the hearing they would have been debarred by 'acquiescence' from relying upon that right. The essential elements of quasi-estoppel by acquiescence are stated in *Willmott* v. *Barber*, 15 ChD 96. As respects the party relying on the acquiescence he must be mistaken as to his legal rights and must have done some act on the faith of his mistaken belief. These conditions are satisfied by the tenants, who agreed to the postponement of the hearing in the mistaken belief that they had a legal right to proceed to an adjudication upon the application they had already made. One of the essential elements as respects the quasi-estoppel by acquiescence is that he must have encouraged the other party to act as he did; and this encouragement may be active, as in the instant case by agreeing to the postponed date, or passive by refraining from asserting his own inconsistent legal right. But in contrast to estoppel in the strict sense of the term the party estopped by acquiescence must, at the time of his active or passive encouragement, know of the existence of his legal right and of the other party's mistaken belief in his own inconsistent legal right. It is not enough that he should know of the facts which give rise to his legal right. He must also know that he is entitled to the legal right to which those facts give rise.

My Lords, the only evidence as to the landlords' knowledge of the existence of their own legal right to object to the application as being out of time is that they knew of it at the time they wrote their letter of 5 December 1968, by which date the tenants had already lost their own right to make a fresh application. Had there been evidence that the landlords acquired the knowledge of their right to take the objection, at some time before 2 December 1968, which was the last day upon which the tenants could have made a fresh application, the question would have arisen whether their failure to inform the tenants of this constituted such passive encouragement of the tenants' mistaken reliance on the validity of their existing application as would amount to 'acquiescence' in its validity. In view of the active part which the landlords had played in arranging for the date of the hearing to be postponed until after 2 December 1968, I have no doubt that their failure to inform the tenants with reasonable promptitude that their existing application was invalid would constitute passive encouragement of the tenants' reliance on its validity and provide the necessary element for the quasi-estoppel of acquiescence.

So the date upon which the landlords acquired that knowledge is crucial. If, as we have been informed and the letter itself suggests, the point was first appreciated by the landlords' counsel, the landlords would be prevented from relying on the point unless they drew the attention of the tenants to it as soon as reasonably possible after their solicitors had received counsel's opinion and had a reasonable opportunity to obtain the landlords' instructions. But the onus lay upon the tenants to establish acquiescence and to prove facts upon which this defence to the preliminary point could be founded. They made no attempt to do so and the county court judge was left in the dark as to the date at which the landlords first became aware of their legal right to rely upon the preliminary point.

Your Lordships must, I think, resist the temptation to fill this fatal gap in the appellants' evidence by speculation. Though I do so with reluctance, I for my part feel compelled to dismiss this appeal.

Note: See also under the heading 'Waiver of validity of notices' at page 399, earlier.

20.2   Joint tenants

The general rule is that all the tenants must be parties to the application and notice must be served by them jointly.

JACOBS v. CHAUDHURI

Court of Appeal   [1968] 2 QB 470

The landlord demised business premises to the applicant and his partner as joint tenants. Subsequently, the applicant and the partner fell out and the partner left, handing over the premises and the business to the applicant who carried it on thereafter. The partnership was later dissolved and the applicant alone had the sole beneficial interest in the business carried on in the premises. The landlord served a section 25 notice of termination and the applicant served on the landlord a counter-notice as one of the tenants stating that he was unwilling to give up possession and applied to the court for a new tenancy.

Held: One of two or more joint tenants was not 'the tenant' within the meaning of section 24 (1) and, therefore, there was no jurisdiction to entertain an application by one of two or more joint tenants for a new tenancy of business premises.

HARMAN LJ: The question is whether the applicant as one of the two joint tenants to whom the lease was granted in 1965 is a person entitled within the Act of 1954 to apply for and obtain a new tenancy.

The landlord objects to the grant of a new tenancy to the applicant, according to his answer, on the ground that the court has no jurisdiction to entertain the application because it is not made by the tenants under the lease, but by only one of them.

The applicant bases his case on the fact that he, and he alone, is the beneficial owner of what was formerly the partnership property and that Wootton has no beneficial interest at all, and is merely a bare trustee of the lease which would have been assigned to the applicant but for the prohibition against assignment contained in it. Under these circumstances, says the applicant, he does or should be held to come within section 23 (1) as being 'the tenant' occupying the premises for the purposes of a business carried on by him. He also says that he satisfies section 24 (1) as being 'the tenant under such a tenancy,' that is to say a tenancy within Part II of the Act of 1954.

The landlord, on the other hand, argued that the tenant must be the person or persons to whom the lease was granted or their successors in title. The landlord admits that the applicant is beneficially the sole owner of the business and all its assets, including the lease, but he says that this is irrelevant as Part II of the Act of 1954 is dealing with the legal estate and not the equities behind it. The Act of 1954 made an inroad, so to speak, on the common law rights of landlords to resume possession of their property when a lease expired, and this ought not to be stretched. The landlord knew when he made the demise that the persons to whom it was made might acquire statutory rights of renewal, but not that one of them severally might have such a right. The landlord points out that the wide definition of the word 'tenant' contained by reference in section 50 of the Act of 1954 does not apply to Part II, but only to Part III, and argues from this that only a person who can legally be described as tenant and not 'any person entitled in possession to the holding under any contract of tenancy' under the extended definition applying to Part III can be entitled. In my view, it is significant that this wide definition is not imported into Part II of the Act of 1954.

On the whole, I conclude that the landlord's argument must prevail. It is to my mind supported when one considers the option clause. It is admitted that one of the two joint tenants could not alone exercise that option, and if the word 'tenants' there means both the joint tenants in connection with the granting of a new lease, it is illogical that one of them should be entitled to exercise a statutory right likewise given to 'the tenant,' which word, of course, includes the plural. I would, therefore, dismiss the appeal.

Note: Section 41A of the 1954 Act (added by the Law of Property Act 1969) makes an exception where at some time the business was carried on in partnership by all the joint tenants and (1) the tenancy was then partnership property (2) the business is being carried on by one or some of the joint tenants and (3) none of the former partner–tenants is occupying some part of the property for business purposes in rights of the tenancy.

In cases outside section 41A where one joint tenant declines to join there may be a remedy under section 41 of the Trustee Act 1925 (power of court to appoint new trustees) or section 30 of the Law of Property Act 1925 (powers of court where trustees for sale refuse to exercise their powers). See also *Harris* v. *Black* (1983) 46 P & CR 366 (page 391, earlier) where the Court of Appeal held that the court had jurisdiction to make an order compelling a co–tenant to serve a counter-notice and join in an application for a new tenancy.

20.3 Procedure

A mistake in the name of the landlord in a tenant's application for a new tenancy may be corrected under the Rules of the Supreme Court Order 20 rule 5 where the mistake has not been misleading or caused injustice.

EVANS CONSTRUCTIONS CO. LTD v. CHARRINGTON & CO. LTD

Court of Appeal   [1983] QB 810

The tenant mistakenly named as landlord Charrington & Co. Ltd which had assigned the reversion under the lease in question to Bass Holdings Ltd, a company within the same group.

Held: Order 20 rule 5 of the Rules of the Supreme Court could not be applied to correct a mistake as to the actual identity of a party sought to be sued but it could be applied to correct a mistake made in describing or naming a party providing the identity of the party was known to the person making the mistake and the mistake was not misleading. Since it was clear that the tenant had intended to serve the notice on its landlord but had made a genuine mistake in naming it, Order 20 rule 5 could apply to amend the name to that of Bass Holdings Ltd.

DONALDSON LJ: In my judgment, the only question is whether it is possible and right to substitute the name 'Bass Holdings Ltd.' for 'Charrington & Co. Ltd.' A simpler solution would be to make a new application naming Bass as respondent, but this cannot be done as any such application would be out of time under section 29 (3) of the Landlord and Tenant Act 1954. The only possible basis for so amending the name of the respondent is under RSC Order 20, rule 5. This, so far as material, provides:

'(1) Subject to Order 15, rules 6, 7 and 8 and the following provisions of this rule, the court may at any stage of the proceedings allow the plaintiff to amend his writ, or any party to amend his pleading, on such terms as to costs or otherwise as may be just and in such manner (if any) as it may direct. (2) Where an application to the court for leave to make the amendment mentioned in paragraph (3), (4) or (5) is made after any relevant period of limitation current at the date of issue of the writ has expired, the court may nevertheless grant such leave in the circumstances mentioned in that paragraph if it thinks it just to do so. (3) An amendment to correct the name of a party may be allowed under paragraph (2) notwithstanding that it is alleged that the effect of the amendment will be to substitute a new party if the court is satisfied that the mistake sought to be corrected was a genuine mistake and was not misleading or such as to cause any reasonable doubt as to the identity of the person intending to sue or, as case may be, intended to be sued.'

A somewhat similar problem arose in *Beardmore Motors Ltd* v. *Birch Bros (Properties) Ltd* [1959] Ch 298 when the original landlord, Birch Bros Ltd, assigned its reversionary interest to Birch Bros (Properties) Ltd and the lessee applied for a new tenancy under the Landlord and Tenant Act 1954 naming Birch Bros Ltd as respondent. By the time that the error was discovered it was too late to issue a new summons against Birch Bros (Properties) Ltd. Harman J reluctantly refused to allow any amendment in the name of the respondent. The basis of his decision was that the difference in names reflected the different identities of two different parties, that the applicant had served Birch Bros Ltd and to allow the amendment would be to substitute a different legal entity as respondent and to deprive that entity of a vested right not to have to resist an application for a new lease after the expiration of the time limit prescribed in the Act of 1954. This was not, in his judgment, a case of misnomer or misdescription. Whether that decision was right or wrong is immaterial since Order 20, rule 5 did not exist at the time. However, it may well have prompted the making of Order 20, rule 5 (3).

In applying Order 20, rule 5 (3) it is, in my judgment, important to bear in mind that there is a real distinction between suing A in the mistaken belief that A is the party who is responsible for the matters complained of and seeking to sue B, but mistakenly describing or naming him as A and thereby ending up suing A instead of B. The rule is designed to correct the latter and not the former category of mistake. Which category is involved in any particular case depends upon the intentions of the person making the mistake and they have to be determined on the evidence in the light of all the surrounding circumstances. In the instant case I have not the slightest difficulty in accepting [Evans' solicitor's] assertion that he intended to sue the relevant landlord under the Act. After all, he was responding on behalf of his lessee client to a notice to quit given on behalf of the landlord and it would have been surprising, to say the least, if he had thought that it was appropriate to respond by claiming a new lease from the managing agent or any other stranger to the landlord and tenant relationship. Accordingly I would conclude that he made a genuine mistake of a character to which Order 20, rule 5 (3) can apply.

However, the matter does not stop there, because it is not every mistake of this character which can be corrected under the rules. The applicant for leave to amend has to satisfy the court that the mistake was not misleading or such as to cause any reasonable doubt as to the identity of the person intended to be sued. On the facts of the present case, I do not see how Charringtons or Bass or anyone else familiar with the surrounding circumstances, could have been misled or could have had any real doubt as to the identity of the person intended to be sued. The notice to quit had been given by Charringtons as managing agent for Bass and the application in reply was intended for Bass albeit addressed to Charringtons.

In the instant case all the criteria of RSC Order 20, rule 5 (3) are met. The mistake was genuine. Charringtons, as the managing agent of Bass could not have been misled and either they informed Bass of the originating application or they should have done so. Bass could not have been misled. Neither Charringtons nor Bass could have had any doubt that Evans was intending to name the landlord, i.e. Bass, as respondent. There can be no injustice in requiring Bass to make good its claim to possession on its merits. I would order that Charringtons' name be deleted as respondent, leaving only that of Bass and I would extend the time for service on Bass until the expiration of 14 days from today.

The court has jurisdiction to allow a tenant to amend, after the expiry of the four month period, the proposals contained in his application for a new tenancy made within that period.

G. ORLIK (MEAT PRODUCTS) LTD v. HASTINGS AND THANET BUILDING SOCIETY

Court of Appeal   (1974) 29 P & CR 126

STAMP LJ: In all other repects, in contrast with what is all too frequently found in cases under Part II of the Act of 1954, all the time provisions of the Act for the giving of notices and the initiation of proceedings were adhered to on both sides. In one respect, however, according to the landlords, the tenants failed, and the failure, it is contended, was fatal to their success on—or indeed to their being heard by the county court on—the only matter now in issue, that is, their claim for the vehicle parking terms to be included in the new lease. The original application of the tenants to the court under section 24 (1) (a) of the Act was made within the time limits prescribed by section 29 (3). It was in the form (Form 335) prescribed by Order 40, rule 8 (1), of the County Court Rules 1936. As originally submitted, however, the proposals included in paragraph 3 of the form obtained no reference to any term relating to the parking of vehicles whether on the landlords' land or otherwise. The proposals put forward were confined to rent. When the application came on for hearing before the judge, the tenants sought to claim rectification of the pre-existing lease so that it should be altered in such a way as to provide for the parking rights. It was pointed out that the court did not have jurisdiction to entertain such a claim. The tenants then, it would seem, abandoned any suggestion of rectification of the lease, but sought instead leave to amend the proposals contained in their application so as to include amongst them a term relating to the parking of their vehicles on, in part, the landlords' adjacent land. The application to amend was opposed by the landlords, one ground being the ground urged in this Court, namely, that because of the time limits in section 29 (3) of the Act, which had by then expired, there was no jurisdiction to give leave to amend. It does not appear to have been suggested that the landlords were taken by surprise, but, of course, if there were lack of jurisdiction the absence of any prejudice created by the granting of leave would not be relevant.

In our judgment, no ground has been shown for holding that there is no jurisdiction to allow an applicant to amend, after the four months period, the proposals contained in an application to the court made within that period. Counsel for the landlords is right in saying that the Act is strict, and uses strict language, in its time provisions. We are, however, unable to see anything in the Act which deprives the court of jurisdiction to grant leave to the applicant to amend the detail of his proposals after the expiration of the four months limit. The decision of this Court in *Williams* v. *Hillcroft Garage Ltd*, if not a direct authority for that proposition, provides, at the least, most persuasive indication that it is correct. Accordingly, we reject this second ground put forward in support of the appeal.

In **Williams v. Hillcroft Garage** (1971) 22 P & CR 402, the tenant made an application to the court for a new tenancy in Form 335 but failed to state specifically the rent, length of terms and other conditions proposed.

Held: The defect was formal only and did not render the application a nullity. The landlord's proper course would have been to ask for the particulars and then apply for the tenant's application to be struck out in default.

In **Morgan v. Jones** [1960] 1 WLR 1220, the Court of Appeal held that a landlord who opposes the grant of a new tenancy is bound to state whether or not he objects to the terms proposed by the tenant in accordance with the form prescribed by the County Court Rules. However, even if he does not so state, he is not bound by the terms proposed by the tenant nor debarred from giving evidence as to what the terms of a new tenancy should be at the hearing.

One tenant's application may be made for two or more tenancies provided that the application is clearly framed in respect of each of its parts.

CURTIS v. CALGARY INVESTMENTS LTD

Court of Appeal   (1983) 268 EG 1199

The tenant leased the ground floors and basement of two adjoining premises for business purposes from the landlord. One business was carried on there. The two leases were identical and the two premises were rated as one hereditament. The landlord served two notices determining the tenancies and the tenant served two counter–notices. However, he made only one application to renew both tenancies.

Held: There was nothing in the 1954 Act nor in the County Court Rules to prohibit a tenant's application from containing applications in respect of more than one separate tenant and in cases like the present there would be positive advantages.

CUMMING-BRUCE LJ: There being nothing in the Act to prohibit an application for two new tenancies in one application, the next question is: is there anything in the rules which prohibit making two applications under cover of a single originating application? I am unable to find anything express on the face of the County Court Rules which has that effect. But the learned judge took the view that, when the rules were considered in the context of the Act in which the procedure was prescribed, there was no reason for construing the singular in the County Court Rules, Order 40 rule 8, as including the plural; and the learned judge was moved to that conclusion by consideration of the factors that he described in the second paragraph of the brief note of his judgment.

Whatever might be the situation in other cases—as to which I say nothing—there seems to me no possible inconvenience to the landlord or to the court if this originating application is treated, as on its face by clause 9 it seeks to do, as bringing to the court applications for grants of new tenancies, one relating to no. 3 and one relating to no. 4. On the contrary, I can see that there may be positive advantages in the court dealing with both of these applications at the same hearing.

Two considerations move me to that thought. The first ground of the landlord's opposition to the grant of either of the new tenancies was a failure of the tenant to comply with his obligations under the repairing leases. But the landlord himself, in support of that allegation, has filed in court a schedule of dilapidations purporting to describe the tenant's failures to repair and, though parts of that schedule of dilapidations do identify want of repair specifically in no. 3 or specifically in no. 4, a great number of them are not identified as relating to one set of parcels as compared with the other set of parcels. So that the landlord, when presenting the description of his case in so far as it was founded on want of repair, himself by this document appeared to be treating, as was the reality of the situation, the two premises as a single hereditament.

Secondly, if the landlord succeeds in the proceedings on the second ground that he relies upon, the tenant may well be entitled to claim compensation and, if he does, the compensation is by statute or the rules to be related to the rateable value. Since 1976 there has only been one rateable value: the rateable value described as relating to no. 3/no. 4 Bouverie Place. So, if in the proceedings it turns out that the judge has to assess on the compensation in favour of the tenant, at first sight it seems as a matter of commonsense that the sensible thing to do is to assess compensation in one sum in respect of the two premises, and the landlord's schedule of dilapidations rather suggests that that is the way that the landlord expected the court to proceed.

Of course, if there had been two originating applications, it would have been open to the court, or might have been open to the court, to make an order that the two should be heard together or that one should immediately follow the other or something of that sort in the way that courts do in order to dispose economically of the business where there are common issues. The question is whether the Act and the rules, properly construed, force the court to conclude that the Act and rules either prohibit the inclusion of two matters in one originating application under Order 40, rule 8 or, alternatively, in the absence of prohibition, whether it is clear as a matter of construction that, where subrule (1) of rule 8 provides for an application for a new tenancy to be made by originating application, there is a clear intention that only one matter may be included in the originating application. That was the view of the judge.

With respect to him, I cannot accept his view. There is no prohibition either in the Act or the rules and I am unable to discern on my scrutiny of the proceedings any reason for thinking that the draftsman was expressing an intention in subrule (1) to restrict the subject-matter of an originating application to a single matter as compared with more than one matter.

The tenant must commence his application against the person who is the 'competent landlord' within the meaning of section 44 of the 1954 Act.

CORNISH v. BROOK GREEN LAUNDRY LTD

Court of Appeal   [1959] 1 QB 394

In this case, the Court of Appeal held that a business tenant whose tenancy is statutorily continuing under Part II of the 1954 Act may be 'the competent landlord' *vis à vis* his sub–tenant.

ROMER LJ: By reason of section 24 (1) of the Act of 1954, both Brook Green's tenancy from the trustees and Mrs Cornish's subtenancy from Brook Green continued in operation notwithstanding that, as a matter of contract, they both expired in September 1956; and as neither tenancy was terminated subsequently in any manner authorised by the Act, the continuation of both tenancies was still effective when in September 1957, Brook Green gave notice of their intention to oppose Mrs Cornish's application for a new lease. In *H. L. Bolton (Engineering) Co. Ltd* v. *T. J. Graham & Sons Ltd.* Denning LJ considered the position which arises from the continuation of a tenancy under the Act of 1954, and said that in his opinion the right view was that the common law tenancy subsisted with a statutory variation as to the mode of determination. In *Weinbergs Weatherproofs Ltd* v. *Radcliffe Paper Mill Co. Ltd* Harman J adopted the view of Denning LJ and said that 'having regard to the language used in the Act of 1954 the term must be thought of as continuing by way of a statutory extension.' Accordingly, in the present case, the rights and obligations created by the lease of 1949 from the trustees to Brook Green were still in force (subject to the variations effected by the Act) when Mrs Cornish's request to the trustees was rejected by them, as also were her own rights and obligations under her sublease of 1950. In these circumstances it would seem *prima facie* that Brook Green continued to be Mrs Cornish's landlord and entitled as such to oppose her application for a new tenancy. Nor can we find anything in the Act to displace the *prima facie* view. [His Lordship read section 44 (1) and continued:]

There is nothing in that subsection which militates against the view that Brook Green continued to be Mrs Cornish's landlord after September 1956, for all purposes, including the purposes of Part II of the Act of 1954; and, if they were, then they were her 'competent landlord' for the purposes of the Sixth Schedule to the Act if and so far as that Schedule has any relevance.

Note: This decision was applied in *Bowes-Lyon* v. *Green* [1963] AC 420.

If the respondent to the tenant's application ceases to be the competent landlord after proceedings are commenced the new competent landlord must be joined.

RENE CLARO (HAUTE COIFFURE) LTD v. HALLE CONCERTS SOCIETY

Court of Appeal   [1969] 1 WLR 909

The head landlords granted a lease of business premises to the tenant, who sublet a part of the premises to a sub–tenant for business purposes. The head landlords served on the tenant a notice to quit pursuant to the lease. The tenant in turn served a notice to quit on the sub–tenant and both applied to the county court for new tenancies. Subsequently, the tenant agreed to a consent order to vacate the premises.

The sub–tenant contended that the competent landlord for the purposes of section 44 (1) of the 1954 Act was the tenant and not the head landlords so that it was unnecessary to join the latter in the proceedings.

Held: At the date of the hearing of the sub–tenant's application, the tenant had ceased to be their landlord and, accordingly, the head landlords had become the competent landlord for the purposes of the 1954 Act. As that landlord had not been joined as respondent, the application for a new tenancy must fail.

LORD DENNING MR: The case depends on this: Who was the 'landlord' at the material time, namely, at the time when the application of the subtenants was heard by the county court judge?: for, if the head landlords were the 'landlord,' they ought to have been joined. The meaning of 'landlord' is given by section 44 (1) of the Landlord and Tenant Act, 1954, which says:

'... the expression "the landlord", in relation to a tenancy (in this section referred to as "the relevant tenancy"), means the person (whether or not he is the immediate landlord) who is the owner of that interest in the property comprised in the relevant tenancy which for the time being fulfils the following conditions, that is to say—(*a*) that it is an interest in reversion expectant (whether immediately or not) on the termination of the relevant tenancy, and (*b* that it is either the fee simple or a tenancy which will not come to an end within 14 months or less by effluxion of time or by virtue of a notice to quit already given by the landlord.'

In other words, you have to see whether, at the material time, the head tenancy had less than 14 months to go. If it had less than 14 months to go, the head tenant drops out and the head landlord comes into direct contact with the subtenant. The head landlord is to be treated as the 'landlord' for the purpose of section 44.

The question, therefore, is whether on 25 March 1968, Hallé Concerts Society had a tenancy which would come to an end within 14 months or less by effluxion of time or by virtue of a notice to quit already given by the landlord.

I will consider whether a 'notice to quit' had already been given by the head landlords. 'Notice to quit' is defined by section 69 to mean

'a notice to terminate a tenancy (whether a periodical tenancy or a tenancy for a term of years certain) given in accordance with the provisions (whether express or implied) of that tenancy;'

Now in this case the head landlords had only given one notice. It was a six months' notice to terminate, given in accordance with section 25 of the Act. But, besides being in accordance with section 25, it was also in accordance with the provisions of the tenancy: because it was in accordance with the notice required by the break clause, in that it gave the full time required by the contract of tenancy. In my opinion, that was sufficient to make it a 'notice to quit' within section 69. I see no good reason why a notice to terminate under section 25 should not also be a notice to quit within section 69: at any rate when it makes it clear that the landlord is going to oppose any application for a new lease and states the ground of it. That shows that the landlord means what he says, that the tenancy is to terminate and that the tenant is to go. That is a 'notice to quit.' I realise that in *Westerbury Property and Investment Co. Ltd* v. *Carpenter* [1961] 1 WLR 272, Danckwerts J took the contrary view. But I am afraid I do not agree with him. Nor do I think that *Green* v. *Bowes-Lyon* [1963] AC 420, affords much assistance. The House did not there consider the import of section 69. I am of opinion, therefore, that in this case the head tenancy would come to an end on 25 March 1968, by virtue of a notice to quit already given by the head landlords, so that at the material time the head landlords were the competent 'landlord.'

Next I will consider whether the new tenancy, at the material time, would come to an end by 'effluxion of time.' At the time when the case of the subtenants was called on for hearing, a consent order had been made in the previous case by which the head tenants were to give up possession on 30 April 1968. It seems to me plain that it would then come to an end 'by effluxion of time.' Once the month of April had passed, the head tenancy would clearly be at an end by the lapse of time.

It seems to me, therefore, that, on one ground or the other, the head tenants, the Hallé Concerts Society, had less than 14 months to go, either by effluxion of time or by virtue of a notice to quit. So they drop out. At the material time, the date of the hearing, the competent 'landlord' was Central and District Properties. The action was not properly constituted at that time without their being joined. They certainly should have been joined.

If the head landlords had been joined, the consequence is obvious. They would have proved that they intended to demolish and reconstruct: and the sub-tenants could have no possible claim to a new tenancy. The subtenants knew that would be their fate. That is why they did not join them. They knew they would be defeated. I think the judge was quite right in holding that the action was not properly constituted, and the claim for a new tenancy by the subtenants should be dismissed. I would, accordingly, dismiss the appeal.

In **Meah v. Mouskos** [1964] 2 QB 23, the Court of Appeal held that if a mortgagee of premises whose tenant has applied to the court for a new tenancy, puts in a receiver of the rent or goes into possession, the mortgagee thereby becomes 'the landlord' for the purpose of the proceedings and should be constituted a respondent for the purpose of the hearing.

The validity of the landlord's grounds of opposition to a new tenancy may be determined as a preliminary issue in order to save expense.

DUTCH OVEN LTD v. EGHAM ESTATE AND INVESTMENT CO. LTD

Chancery Division   [1968] 1 WLR 1483

A landlord gave a notice under the 1954 Act to terminate a tenancy stating that any application for a new tenancy would be opposed on the ground that it was intended to demolish or reconstruct the premises. The tenant stated that he would be unwilling to give up possession and he took out an originating summons seeking an order for the grant of a new tenancy on proposed terms. The landlord later took out a summons asking for an order that the question whether the landlord had the necessary intention to be determined first as a preliminary issue before any question as to the terms of a new tenancy.

Held: The court would direct that the issue of intention be determined before any other issue in the proceedings.

MEGARRY J: The convenience and economy of the course proposed by [counsel for the landlords] is plain. The cost and expenditure of labour involved in preparing to adduce valuation evidence is often far from inconsiderable. If the landlord succeeds on the issue under paragraph (f), none of that evidence will be required, and the waste on each side will be substantial. If, on the other hand, the landlord fails under paragraph (f), then during an adjournment each side can prepare for the conflict on the second limb: and in such cases, even if the parties agree no matter of substance between them, often they can at least during the adjournment agree where their differences lie.

Under RSC, Order 33 rule 3, to which [counsel for the landlords] referred me, the court has wide powers of ordering 'any question or issue arising in a cause or matter,' whether of fact, law, or law and fact mixed, to be tried 'before, at or after the trial of the cause or matter'; and by RSC, Order 33 rule 3, if such a trial substantially disposes of the cause or matter the court may dismiss that cause or matter. It may be that as a matter of wording RSC, Order 33, rule 3, can be said to assist [counsel for the tenants'] argument by distinguishing between the determination of the 'question or issue' and the 'trial of the cause or matter.' But I do not think that a 'question or issue' which arises in a 'cause or matter' ceases to be part of that 'cause or matter' merely because it is tried separately. The 'cause or matter' is still before the court, whether all of it or only part of it is to be heard on a particular occasion: and if the so-called 'preliminary issue' is brought before the court as [counsel for the landlords] seeks, I think the proceedings on that issue are nevertheless part of the proceedings on the originating summons. An alternative way of dealing with the matter would be to direct that the originating summons should be adjourned into court, but that until the issue on paragraph (f) had been resolved, no other proceedings in court should be taken under the originating summons until a date to be fixed by the court.

However it is put, it seems to me plain that the practice of conducting these proceedings in two stages is usually beneficial to all concerned. It also seems clear to me that it is equally beneficial that all parties should know at the outset that there will be these two stages. There may be exceptional cases; the differences between the parties as to the terms of the tenancy may be so small, or so little dependent on evidence that is expensive to adduce, that it is desirable that the whole case should be heard at one time. But where it is clear that there are substantial differences which can be resolved only by adducing evidence which is likely to be expensive or burdensome, then it seems to me that the normal course should be to direct a hearing in two stages. In this case I have heard nothing to make me think this is not a normal case in which it would be advantageous to defer resolving any other issues until the question under paragraph (f) has been determined.

In **In Re 20 Exchange Street, Manchester** [1956] 1 WLR 765, the tenants of business premises served a notice on the landlords stating that they were not willing to give up possession of the premises on the date specified in the landlords' notice. The tenants took out a summons applying for the grant of a new tenancy which was refused whereupon the landlords applied for an order abridging the time in which the tenants were allowed to appeal from six weeks to one week. Danckwerts J held that the court had no power to reduce the time in which a party may appeal to any shorter period.

20.4   Costs

On an application for a new tenancy under the 1954 Act, the county court judge has a discretion to make such order as to costs as he thinks just.

DECCA NAVIGATOR CO. LTD v. GREATER LONDON COUNCIL

Court of Appeal   [1974] 1 WLR 748

LORD DENNING MR: There is only one further matter which [counsel for the tenants] raised before us. It is as to the question of costs. The judge dismissed the application with costs on Scale 4. [Counsel for the tenants] does not challenge that order. But he draws attention to a note in the County Court Practice 1973, at pp 885-886, where it says:

'The administration of [the Landlord and Tenant Act 1954] by the courts often gives rise to special problems as to costs, but it seems that frequently each side is left to bear its own costs of an application to the court for the grant of a new lease. Thus, where both parties negotiated, but were unable to agree the terms on which a new lease should be granted, and an application was made to the court under the provisions of the Act, an order was made for the grant of a new lease but no order was made as to costs, leaving each side to bear its own costs.'

That was the usual practice which was noted in *Willis* v. *Association of Universities of the British Commonwealth (No. 2)* [1965] 1 WLR 836. But since that case, there have been amendments made by the Law of Property Act 1969. So much so that the former practice should no longer be allowed. The costs should be in the discretion of the county court judge to do as he thinks just.

Note: In *Demag Industrial Equipment Ltd* v. *Canada Dry (U.K.) Ltd* [1969] 1 WLR 985. Pennycuick J held that a landlord who withdraws opposition to a new tenancy of business premises after the tenant's application must pay the costs of the tenant.

A covenant in a business tenancy for the tenant to pay the landlord's legal costs and expenses on an application by the tenant for a new tenancy is void as being the imposition of a penalty under section 38 (1) of the 1954 Act.

STEVENSON & RUSH (HOLDINGS) LTD v. LANGDON

Court of Appeal (1979) 38 P & CR 208

BROWNE LJ: Section 38 (1) of the Act of 1954 is dealing with three types of provision contained in agreements relating to tenancies. The first type is provisions purporting to preclude the tenant from making an application or request under that Part of the Act. The second type is provisions for the termination or surrender of the tenancy in the event of the tenant making such an application or request. The third type is provisions for the imposition of any penalty or disability on the tenant in that event, that is, in the event of his making application for a new tenancy under that Part of the Act. It seems to me clear that the object of the subsection is to prevent contracting out of the provisions of the Act that entitle a tenant to apply for a new tenancy. The first and second limbs of the section are dealing with attempts by what I may call direct means to prevent a tenant from applying for or getting a new tenancy. The intention of the third limb, it seems to me, is to exclude attempts to prevent such an application by indirect means. I should, therefore, expect 'penalty' or 'disability' in the last limb to include any provision that would have the effect of deterring a tenant from exercising what would otherwise be his right under his Part of the Act. The effect of clause 3 (17) (c) is to impose on a tenant, if he makes an application, an obligation to pay what may be a very substantial sum in respect of costs. It seems to me clear that such a provision will or may deter a tenant from making such an application. Whatever the word 'penalty' may mean in some other contexts (and we have been helpfully shown the *Oxford English Dictionary* definitions), it is my view that, in the context of this provision, clause 3 (17) (c) does constitute the imposition of a penalty. I agree with Megaw LJ that, in the ordinary use of English, it may well constitute a penalty, and, having regard to what seems to me to be the plain object of section 38 (1), I have no doubt that it is within the meaning of the word in this context. It is not necessary to consider whether it could also be described as a 'disability,' nor is it necessary to consider the scope of that word. It may well be, as Waller LJ said in the course of the argument, that there is an overlap between the two words in this context.

Chapter 21

The landlord's opposition to a tenant's application

21.1 Failure to repair—section 30 (1) (a)

The court has a discretion under section 30 (1) (a) of the 1954 Act whether or not to grant a new tenancy.

LYONS v. CENTRAL COMMERCIAL PROPERTIES LONDON LTD

Court of Appeal [1958] 1 WLR 869

ORMEROD LJ: The applicant in this case applied to the court for the grant of a new lease under the Landlord and Tenant Act 1954. The landlords, in view of section 30 (1) (a) of the Act, opposed the grant on the ground that the tenant had been guilty of a breach of his covenant to repair, and the county court judge has upheld the objection, and refused to make an order for a new lease. The question at issue in the appeal is whether the judge has taken into account extraneous matters in coming to his decision; and it is necessary to consider what, if any, discretion is vested in the judge in considering objections which fall within section 30 (1) (a). The first three paragraphs of section 30 (1) have already been read, and I do not propose to repeat them here.

It is clear from the words of the section that there is a measure of discretion as regards the state of disrepair. The words are 'ought not to be granted a new tenancy in view of the state of repair of the holding.' Paragraphs (b) and (c) respectively refer to the 'persistent delay' of the tenant in paying rent, and 'other substantial breaches' by the tenant of his contractual obligations. These provisions seem to indicate that the neglect to repair to which the section refers should be substantial. But the word 'ought' in the section in my judgment implies that the discretion of the judge is not confined to the consideration of the state of repair. Without attempting to define the precise limits of that discretion, the judge, as I see it, may have regard to the conduct of the tenant in relation to his obligations, and the reasons for any breach of the covenant to repair which has arisen.

For example, in the present case there were negotiations proceeding at one time for the sale of the premises to Littlewoods, which if successful would have resulted in the premises being demolished. It might well be regarded as unreasonable to expect the tenant to expend money on repairs during such negotiations. On the other hand, there would appear to be no reason for failing to carry out the repairs after the negotiations were terminated. The object of paragraphs (a), (b) and (c) of section 30, as I see it, is to enable the judge to refuse to grant a new lease to a tenant who has shown himself to be unsatisfactory in the performance of his obligations under the contract of tenancy.

It is clear from his judgment that the judge considered the lack of repair to be serious, but he took into consideration the fact that the tenant had contracted to assign his interests in the premises to Littlewoods. He said: 'I have come to conclusion that this action is brought not to secure the sitting tenant but to secure the premises for Littlewoods.' It was argued that in spite of this passage in his judgment, the facts as found by him were such that there could be no proper exercise of his discretion other than to refuse to make an order for a new lease.

The contract with Littlewoods had, in my view, no bearing on the case. The question was one to be tried between the landlords and the existing tenant, and it was his breaches and his conduct which were material. It remains to be decided whether the case should be sent back for reconsideration by the judge, or whether on the material before this court an order should be made. It is true that the judge said: 'If this were a case of a small man who would lose his livelihood, I would have said despite the breaches I would grant a new lease.' It may be said that this is an indication that he might, if the case were sent back to him, exercise his discretion in favour of the tenant, although it may very well be that in saying this the judge was regarding himself, as he indicated early in his judgment, as having an overall discretion similar to that given by the Rent Acts. On the other hand, he found that there were severe breaches of covenant; that although the tenant had had nearly a year to remedy the breaches, he did not do so, and his final observation was: 'The applicant is not the sort of person who is likely to be a tenant to whom I should give relief.'

In these circumstances, in my judgment, this court can and should deal with the application and confirm the judge's refusal to make an order for a new lease.

21.2   Persistent delay in paying rent—section 30 (1) (b)

HOPCUTT v. CARVER

Court of Appeal   (1969) 209 EG 1069

A tenant of business premises applied for a new lease which his landlord refused. He had been a tenant for 20 years but over the last two years had been constantly late in payments of rent, which was due monthly, at one time delaying for five months. The county court judge refused a new lease.

Held: There was no ground for interfering with the judge's exercise of his discretion. No offer was made by the tenant for payment in advance in future nor was any security offered.

DANCKWERTS LJ: The landlord had resisted the tenant's application for a new lease because of his persistent delay in paying the rent when it became due. The court had a discretion in deciding whether to grant or refuse a tenancy in a case of that kind. The tenant had occupied the premises for 20 years, but there was evidence that over a period of two years he had constantly been in arrear with rent. There was ample evidence and grounds upon which the judge could reach the conclusion that he did.

SACHS LJ: There was no ground for suggesting that the judge was under any misapprehension as to any factor relating to the exercise of discretion. He (Judge Harington) had had before him a carefully prepared table relating to the past payments of rent. Up to the time the tenant realised the landlord might not be willing to grant him a new tenancy, there had been persistent delays in paying the rent, which was due monthly in arrear. Once five months went by with no payment of rent. It had been said on the tenant's behalf that his payments had lately become more punctual, but it was to be observed that that was while proceedings were pending. What would happen after a new tenancy was granted was uncertain. No offer was made for payment of the rent in advance in future, and there was no security offered for such payments. The county court judge had had evidence on which to arrive at his conclusions, and no ground could be shown for interfering with his exercise of his discretion to refuse a new lease.

21.3   Substantial breaches of obligations under the tenancy—section 30 (1) (c)

In exercising its discretion under section 30 (1) (c) of the 1954 Act, the court is entitled to consider the whole of a tenant's conduct and not merely matters specified in a notice of opposition.

EICHNER v. MIDLAND BANK EXECUTOR AND TRUSTEE CO. LTD

Court of Appeal   [1970] 1 WLR 1120

LORD DENNING MR: The tenant applied for a new lease, and the landlords opposed it on those grounds which they had put in their notice of opposition. The county court judge found that the dilapidation had been remedied. He said that the parting of possession to a subtenant was not serious, and that the manufacturing of plastic foam was not serious enough for the court to refuse a new lease. But the thing which he did find was a substantial breach was this:

'The Interlingua Translation organisation was set up without telling the landlord, which I consider is an extraordinary user of a landlord by a tenant and goes far beyond the normal limits of a landlord and tenant relationship.'

If the judge had refused a new lease on that ground, there could be no possible ground of appeal to this court. But [counsel for the applicant] says that the judge did not put it only on that ground. He put *other grounds* into the scale. The judge said:

'What I do consider very important is the relationship between the landlord and the tenant. This has been very unhappy for at least 11 years, and this is admitted by Eichner. This unhappy relationship has therefore existed since 1958. There is evidence of a great deal of litigation in the past, in 1958, 1959, 1961, 1965 and the present year ... It must be considered very carefully whether it is fair to saddle the landlord with a tenant with whom he is in constant litigation.'

The judge also referred to the payment of rent. He said: 'In considering the picture as a whole, I must consider Mr Eichner's history of paying rent and ability to pay the rent in the future.'

[Counsel for the applicant] submits that the judge ought not to have taken those other grounds into consideration, because they were not stated in the notice. He refers to section 30 (1) of the Act of 1954 which says that the landlord may oppose the new tenancy on the grounds stated in the notice: and, inferentially, *not* on any other grounds. If the landlord had wished to include those other grounds he should have specified them in his notice as 'any other reasons connected with the tenant's use or management of the holding' under section 30 (1) (*c*). The landlord not having put them in the notice, [counsel for the applicant] submitted that they should not be taken into account. For this he relied on a sentence of Harman J in *Lyons* v. *Central Commercial Properties Ltd* [1958] 1 WLR 869, 880, in which he said:

'In my judgment, the discretion vested in the court under section 30 (1) (*a*), (*b*) and (*c*) is a narrow one; it is limited to the question whether, having regard *only* to the grounds set out, a new tenancy "ought not" to be granted.'

But Ormerod LJ did not restrict the discretion so narrowly. He said, at p 878:

'Without attempting to define the precise limits of that discretion, the judge, as I see it, may have regard to the conduct of the tenant in relation to his obligations.'

I prefer the view of Ormerod LJ. I think the judge here was not confined to the breach of the tenant in carrying on the translation business of the Interlingua organisation. It was, I think, open to him to look at all the circumstances in connection with that breach: also, I may add, to look at the conduct of the tenant as a whole in regard to his obligations under the tenancy. The judge was not limited to the various grounds stated in the notice.

In any case, it seems to me that, if the judge had limited himself to this one substantial breach in connection with Interlingua Translations, he would have held that the tenant ought not to be granted a new tenancy.

I see no reason for interfering with the judgment of the county court judge, and I would dismiss the appeal.

For the decision in *Lyons* v. *Central Commercial Properties London Ltd* [1958] 1 WLR 869, see page 423, earlier.

21.4 Intention to demolish or reconstruct or effect substantial work of construction—section 30 (1) (f)

21.4 (a) Proof of intention

The intention must exist at the time of the hearing but it is immaterial that the landlord's notice was served by a predecessor who had no such intention himself.

MORRIS MARKS v. BRITISH WATERWAYS BOARD

Court of Appeal   [1963] 1 WLR 1008

The sub–tenant of business premises served a section 26 request on his immediate landlords who served on the sub–tenant a counter–notice opposing the application for a new tenancy on the ground specified in section 30 (1) (f) of the 1954 Act. The sub–tenant's landlords subsequently surrendered their lease to the freeholders and the freeholders' successors passed a resolution that all buildings on the site should be demolished and the site redeveloped.

Held: The counter–notice could avail a subsequent landlord who was the landlord at the date of the hearing if he could at that date prove that he had the requisite intention to demolish or reconstruct. Moreover, it did not matter that the landlord who had served it did not himself at that or any time have any such intention.

LORD DENNING MR: It is quite clear that if there is a landlord who, giving his notice of opposition to a new tenancy, has *at that time* the intent to demolish or reconstruct; and then afterwards he sells the property to a new landlord, that new landlord can take over the benefit of the notice and if the new landlord *at the date of the hearing* has himself the same intention, he can avail himself of the intention which his predecessor had expressed.

But the problem in this case is different. It is said that Ingram Perkins, at the time when they gave their notice of opposition to a new tenancy, had no intention to demolish or reconstruct. How then, it is said, can the notice be good? It is not accurate. It is not true. It is therefore bad. I think the correct answer is that the notice opposing the new tenancy, a landlord's notice, is to be regarded as in the nature of a pleading. It is a pleading which comes for proof at the date of the hearing. It is sufficient as long as it gives notice to the tenant of the case he has to meet. So long as it is not deceptive or misleading, it avails the subsequent owner of the property who is the landlord at the date of the hearing. If the subsequent landlord can prove that at the date of the hearing he has the requisite intention, the new lease must be refused. That, I think, follows from *Betty's Cafés Ltd* v. *Phillips Furnishing Stores Ltd* in the House of Lords, and I think that Plowman J correctly applied it in the recent case of *Wimbush (A. D.) & Son Ltd* v. *Franmills Properties Ltd*. For instance, I think it would have been quite legitimate for Ingram Perkins to have stated in their landlord's counter-notice that the landlords, that is, the people who *will be* the landlords at the relevant time, that is, at the date of the hearing, will oppose the application on the ground that the landlords at that time intend to demolish or reconstruct the premises and that they could not reasonably do so without obtaining possession of the holding. Such a pleading, it seems to me, would give full notice to the tenant of the case he had to meet. It would fall to be decided at the date of the hearing whether the landlord at that time had the relevant intention.

Now does this notice do any more than such a notice as I have described? I do not think it does. Although it says 'We oppose your application for a new tenancy' and 'We could not reasonably demolish the premises without obtaining possession of the holding,' nevertheless it refers to 'the landlords'' intention to demolish. I have no doubt that the tenant knew perfectly well that it was the British Transport Commission who were intending to demolish or reconstruct; and that this notice gave him perfectly fair warning of what was to take place, namely, that it was anticipated that by the date of the hearing the British Transport Commission or its successors, the British Waterways Board, would have taken it over; and that the contest at the date of the hearing would be whether they intended to demolish or reconstruct the premises. There was nothing deceptive or misleading about the notice. I hold, therefore, that the notice was good.

In **XL Fisheries v. Leeds Corporation** [1955] 2 QB 636, tenants of business premises applied to the landlord for the grant of a new tenancy. The landlord at the time of that application contracted to sell his reversionary interest in the premises to a local authority. Following completion of the sale, the local authority (within 2 months of the tenant's request for a new tenancy) gave notice to the tenants that they had bought the premises and that they would object to the grant of a new tenancy. In the course of his judgment **LORD EVERSHED MR** said:

The question is whether those sections contemplate or require that the landlord, throughout the whole period after the machinery of the Act has been set in motion, should be the same person, whether an individual person or a *persona ficta*. I think that the answer to that question is inevitably in the negative. I can find nothing in the sections or the language used therein which would require the continuity throughout of the same person as landlord; and, indeed, it would be a strange thing if the Act did so require, because, though Parliament may do many things, it cannot insist that a particular person shall live a particular length of time. It is, in other words, I think quite plain that when the landlord comes to put in his notice of opposition, it is sufficient if at the time he puts it in he is in fact the landlord. It is, therefore, sufficient if he, having acquired the premises or the reversion since the date of the request, is able to say when he puts in his notice of opposition before the two months' period expires that he is the landlord and (to take the example that I chose from section 30) that on the termination of the current tenancy he intends to reconstruct.

During the course of the argument this further question was somewhat debated, and I will say at once that, finding it unnecessary to give an answer to it, I prefer to leave it until it actually arises for determination. The question is this: suppose that landlord A had within the two months given notice of opposition based on intention to reconstruct, under section 30 (1) (*f*), and then, still within the two months, sold the premises to landlord B—what is B's position until the two months have expired? Is he (so to speak) limited and bound by the objections that landlord A has intimated? Is he free to abandon them and substitute new ones? Or is he left without any effective opposition at all? As I have said, I do not find it necessary to answer that somewhat difficult question, and I, therefore, pass it by, saying only this, that the presence of that possible difficulty does not seem to me to qualify the conclusion I have already expressed, that so far, in the ordinary case contemplated by Part II, I find nothing which could sensibly produce the result that the landlord must continue the same landlord throughout the whole period of the operation of the scheme of this part of the Act.

The observations of Lord Evershed MR were applied by Plowman J in *A.D. Wimbush & Son Ltd* v. *Franmills Properties Ltd* [1961] Ch 419.

Bare assertions of intention are not enough and the landlord will fail if serious difficulties lie ahead.

BETTY'S CAFES LTD v. PHILLIPS FURNISHING STORES LTD

House of Lords   [1959] AC 20

The tenants of business premises served a section 26 request for a new tenancy and the landlord company's secretary gave notice to the tenants that they would oppose the grant of a new tenancy under section 30 (1) (f) of the 1954 Act, stating that they intended to reconstruct the premises. At the time no resolution to that effect had been passed by the board. During the course of the hearing of the tenants' application, the board of the landlord company passed a resolution that, in the event of possession being obtained, a scheme prepared that year should be carried out and that expenditure up to £20,000 on the works should be approved.

Held: The landlord company had proved the necessary intention at the date of the hearing.

VISCOUNT SIMONDS: My Lords, as a preliminary to determining the date when the requisite intention must be proved to have been formed, there was much discussion upon the meaning of the word 'intends' in section 30 (1) (f). It might be regarded as somewhat academic in this case: for it is conceded that, whatever the meaning of the word, an intention had not been formed at the date of notice of opposition but had been formed on 23 April 1956. But the question has this degree of relevance, that the greater the fixity of intention and the less the mental reservation, the greater the difficulty in supposing that the landlord is to form that intention within two months of receiving the tenant's request or for ever hold his peace. In this context your Lordships have the advantage of a judgment delivered by Lord Asquith (then Asquith LJ), than whom there have been few greater masters of the English language in judicial interpretation or exposition, in *Cunliffe* v. *Goodman*. I will content myself with a single short passage, though much more might be usefully cited: 'An "intention," ' said the learned Lord Justice,

'to my mind connotes a state of affairs which the party "intending"—I will call him X—does more than merely contemplate: it connotes a state of affairs which, on the contrary, he decides, so far as in him lies, to bring about, and which, in point of possibility, he has a reasonable prospect of being able to bring about, by his own act of volition.'

I do not think that anything is to be gained by trying to elaborate these words, but I must fairly add that I do not at all dissent from the explanation of them which the learned Master of the Rolls has given in this case. It is a question of fact what intention a man has at a given time, difficult, it may be, to ascertain, but still a question of fact, and I think that a jury directed in such words as these could come to a fair conclusion.

Having said so much, I doubt whether I have got much help on my way to a solution of the question of construction. But perhaps it may be said that it would, in my cases, place an unfair burden on the landlord if within a short space of two months he had to attain the fixity of intention which I have indicated. Content perhaps to await the time when he can resume possession under ground (g), he is suddenly faced with an application compelling him to form an intention, which can only be formed under a consideration of a number of factors not easily ponderable. If I felt any real difficulty in construction, I should, I think, find in this consideration an impulse to regard the date of hearing as the relevant and only relevant date for the ascertainment of intention.

Equally from the point of view of the tenant it seems essential that the court should find the intention subsisting at the date of the hearing. As I listened to the argument for the appellants and studied their formal case, it appeared to me that they regarded the date of notice of opposition as the only relevant date. But I have not been able to understand what advantage the tenants could gain from the fact of the landlords' intention at that date or from the proof of it, if at a later stage it had been abandoned. Upon this part of the case I respectfully adopt the reasoning of Romer LJ upon which I cannot hope to improve.

I return, then, to the short question of construction. Under section 26 (6) a landlord giving notice that he will oppose an application must state in his notice on which of the grounds mentioned in section 30 he will oppose the application. This is the language of futurity. The landlord 'will' oppose the application and he 'will' oppose it on such and such a ground. If the matter rested there, I should not find it possible to regard the ground of opposition as referring to anything but a state of affairs existing at the date of the hearing when its validity could be tested. It might, no doubt, be relevant for the purpose of testing its validity to know something of the precedent state of affairs: that would depend on the nature of the ground of opposition. But in regard to ground (f), which we are immediately considering, nothing more is required of the landlord than that he should state that he will oppose the application on the ground that on the termination of the current tenancy he intends to do certain work and so on. All is still in the future and, except for the purpose of challenging his *bona fides*, which is not here in question, nothing that has happened in the past has any relevance. At the hearing he will oppose and prove his avowed intention. This seems to me, with all deference to those who take a different view, to be the plain English of section 26 (6) and section 30 (1) (f). I have already pointed out that it appears to accord also with the general purpose of the Act. It harmonises also with the language of section 31 (1) which contemplates the landlord satisfying the court upon any of the grounds upon which he is entitled to oppose the application.

In **Cunliffe v. Goodman** [1950] 2 KB 237, (a decision on the meaning of intention for the purposes of section 18 (1) of the Landlord and Tenant Act 1927) ASQUITH LJ said:

The question to be answered is whether the defendant (on whom the onus lies) has proved that the plaintiff, on 30 November 1945 'intended' to pull down the premises on this site. This question is in my view one of fact. If the plaintiff did no more than entertain the idea of this demolition, if she got no further than to contemplate it as a (perhaps attractive) possibility, then one would have to say (and it matters not which way it is put) either that there was *no* evidence of a positive 'intention,' or that the word 'intention' was incapable as a matter of construction of applying to anything so tentative, and so indefinite. An 'intention' to my mind connotes a state of affairs which the party 'intending'—I will call him X—does more than merely contemplate: it connotes a state of affairs which, on the contrary, he decides, so far as in him lies, to bring about, and which, in point of possibility, he has a reasonable prospect of being able to bring about, by his own act of volition.

X cannot, with any due regard to the English language, be said to 'intend' a result which is wholly beyond the control of his will. He cannot 'intend' that it shall be a fine day tomorrow: at most he can hope or desire or pray that it will. Nor, short of this, can X be said to 'intend' a particular result if its occurrence, though it may be not wholly uninfluenced by X's will, is dependent on so many other influences, accidents and cross-currents of circumstance that, not merely is it quite likely not to be achieved at all, but, if it is achieved, X's volition will have been no more than a minor agency collaborating with, or not thwarted by, the factors which predominately determine its occurrrence. If there is a sufficiently formidable succession of fences to be surmounted before the result at which X aims can be achieved, it may well be unmeaning to say that X 'intended' that result.

Where there were a number of such fences. The approval of the London County Council, as the town-planning authority for London, had to be obtained, and was refused in respect of the first rebuilding plan. A building licence had to be obtained from Hammersmith Borough Council. The first plan never reached the stage at which such a licence could usefully be applied for. As to either plan, a licence, if forthcoming, might have been granted on terms, and those terms might have deprived the project of all commercial attraction—deprived it of the character of a 'business proposition.' Such licences are often granted conditionally on a maximum selling price for the structure as rebuilt, or—if it be not sold, but let—conditionally on a maximum rent: and in respect of the second scheme a maximum rent of an unattractive level was in fact proposed by the local authority.

This leads me to the second point bearing on the existence in this case of 'intention' as opposed to mere contemplation. Not merely is the term 'intention' unsatisfied if the person professing it has too many hurdles to overcome, or too little control of events: it is equally inappropriate if at the material date that person is in effect not deciding to proceed but feeling his way and reserving his decision until he shall be in possession of financial data sufficient to enable him to determine whether the project will be commercially worth while.

A purpose so qualified and suspended does not in my view amount to an 'intention' or 'decision' within the principle. It is mere contemplation until the materials necessary to a decision on the commercial merits are available and have resulted in such a decision. In the present case it seems to me that (assuming that the plaintiff was, both before and after 30 November 1945, disposed to demolish and rebuild if she could do so on remunerative terms) she never reached, in respect of the first scheme, a stage at which she could decide on its commercial merits; nor, in respect of the second scheme, the stage of actually deciding that that scheme was commercially eligible—unless indeed she must be taken not merely to have repudiated her architect's authority but to have decided that it was commercially ineligible. In the case of neither scheme did she form a settled intention to proceed. Neither project moved out of the zone of contemplation—out of the sphere of the tentative, the provisional and the exploratory—into the valley of decision.

The *dicta* of Asquith LJ in the foregoing case was applied in:

REOHORN v. BARRY CORPORATION

Court of Appeal   [1956] 1 WLR 845

The tenants of land used as a car park applied for a new tenancy under the 1954 Act. The town corporation, the landlords, resisted the application on the ground set out in section 30 (1) (f). At the hearing, the corporation produced resolutions for a proposed comprehensive development scheme on the land, an outline plan, evidence of consultations with an architect and a letter from a development company stating that the company was agreed 'in principle' to start work at a certain date 'subject to the approval of the council' and the conclusion of satisfactory building arrangement. No plans had been prepared or agreed, nor any terms as to a building lease, nor was any proof produced that the proposed developers, who did not give evidence, were financially in a position to carry out the work.

Held: The landlords had failed to establish the quality of intention required by the 1954 Act.

DENNING LJ: Such being the facts, the question is whether the intention required by the Act is satisfied. In the recent case of *Fisher* v. *Taylors Furnishing Stores Ltd*, I pointed out that the intention must be 'a firm and settled intention, not likely to be changed; ... It must be remembered that if the landlord, having got possession, honestly changes his mind and does not do any work of reconstruction, the tenant has no remedy.' In considering whether the court should be satisfied of the landlord's intention, I think that it may readily be satisfied when the premises are old and worn out or are ripe for development, the proposed work is obviously desirable, plans and arrangements are well in hand, and the landlord has the present means and ability to carry out the work. Such was the position in *Fisher's* case, and in several other cases which have come before this court. But the court will not be so readily satisfied when the premises are comparatively new or the desirability of the project is open to doubt, when there are many difficulties still to be surmounted, such as the preparation and approval of plans or the obtaining of finance, or when the landlord has in the past fluctuated in his mind as to what to do with the premises. In those circumstances, even though he should assert at the hearing that he has a firm and settled intention, the court is not bound to accept it because of the likelihood that he may change his mind once he gets possession. Such was the position in *Herbert* v. *Blakey (Bradford) Ltd* (under section 30 (1) (g)).

In the present case, the premises are ripe for development and the proposed work is obviously desirable: but the difficulty is to be satisfied that the corporation have the present means and ability to carry out the work. 'Intention' connotes an ability to carry it into effect. A man cannot properly be said to 'intend' to do a work of reconstruction when he has not got the means to carry it out. He may *hope* to do so: he will not have the *intention* to do so. In this case the corporation contemplate turning this land into a splendid estate by the sea. They are exploring the possibilities of it; they are discussing the ways and means, in the shape of a building lease; but that is as far as they have got. Their ability to do the work, or to cause it to be done, is, I think, open to question.

I desire to say at once that there is no objection to their doing it by way of a building lease. Indeed, as I have indicated, it is the only way in which the corporation can develop this land; and no one would wish to hold up development because a building lease was chosen as a means of doing it rather than doing it through independent contractors. The decision of this court a little while ago in *Gilmour Caterers Ltd* v. *St Bartholomew's Hospital Governors* shows that it is permissible for a landlord to cause the work to be done by way of a building lease. But in that case the building lease was already executed; the premises were old and ripe for development; the landlords had complete control of the work to be done: it was all specified and ready to be done at once. In this case, however, it is very different. There is no building lease, no lessee in existence at the moment, no plans with any details, no knowledge of any financial backing. There is so much still to be explored and discussed, there are so many factors outside the control of the corporation altogether, that I do not think that there is here that 'intention not likely to be changed' which is required before the tenant is to be deprived of a new lease. I can well see that in the course of the next few months difficulties may arise which might lead to the abandonment of this plan, or, at all events, to its suspension for an indefinite period. It would not be right that the tenant should be turned out by the landlords on such an uncertain and unsettled intention. It seems to me that, to apply Asquith LJ's words in *Cunliffe* v. *Goodman*, the matter is still in the region of 'the tentative, the provisional and the exploratory,' and has not yet reached 'the valley of decision.'

In **D.A.F. Motoring Centre (Gosport) v. Hutfield and Wheeler** (1982) 263 EG 976, the landlord intended to reconstruct the premises comprised in the holding. As regards the financial feasibility of the landlord's plan, the trial judge was not shown a detailed scheme such as might have been necessary to place before a finance house in order to obtain a loan but the landlord had provided letters demonstrating that his bank manager was willing to increase his borrowing facility and had adverted to the possibility of borrowing from other sources of credit.

Held: There was sufficient material for the judge to conclude that there was a reasonable prospect of raising the finance to enable the landlord to develop the premises.

A formal resolution expressing an intention to demolish is not essential to establish the existence of that intention by a local authority.

POPPETS (CATERERS) LTD v. MAIDENHEAD CORPORATION

Court of Appeal   [1971] 1 WLR 69

The Corporation served a notice terminating a tenancy of warehouse premises and giving as grounds for opposition to its renewal that it intended to demolish and reconstruct the whole or a substantial part of the premises. However, the Corporation had passed no formal resolution to that effect but the development had been approved in principle in committee and noted in the committee's minutes.

Held: An intention of a local authority or any body corporate could be ascertained from any relevant evidence and was not confined to a formal resolution expressing their intention. In the present case, the intention to demolish was sufficiently ascertained from the committee's minutes and from the evidence of the Corporation's officers.

BUCKLEY LJ: In my judgment, the intention with which a local authority or any other corporate body acts is an intention which can be ascertained by any relevant evidence. It can no doubt be clearly established by a resolution passed by the body to the effect that its intention is such as is set out in the resolution, but the circumstances may be such that as a clear matter of inference the intention with which the body is acting can be discovered without any resolution having been passed at all. For myself I see no logical ground for saying that when the intention of a corporate body is in question such intention can only be discovered from a resolution passed by that body.

I do not pause to consider cases decided in relation to companies incorporated under the Companies Acts because in the case of such companies the directors of the company normally have a very wide delegated authority and can act as the company with the full force and authority of an act of the company itself. I am considering cases where that sort of situation does not exist but where the question is whether a corporate body, such as the local authority in the present case, has acted with a particular intention.

In the present case the minutes to which I have referred demonstrate, in my judgment, that this was a project which had been maturing for a long time and which had not only been before the relevant committees of the local authority, but the local authority had itself confirmed the decisions of those committees on the three occasions I have mentioned, and the notice given by the town clerk determining the company's tenancy would appear to have been in pursuance of that maturing project. When one comes to read the judge's note of the oral evidence given before him one finds that that, in fact, is what the witnesses say was the position.

The motive for effecting the intended work is immaterial.

FISHER v. TAYLORS FURNISHING STORES LTD

Court of Appeal   [1956] 2 QB 78

The landlords of a retail shop gave notice to the tenant determining his tenancy. The tenant applied for the grant of a new tenancy and the landlords opposed this on the ground stated in section 30 (1) (f) of the 1954 Act. The landlords' object was not to occupy the old building but to rebuild on the site and to occupy the new building for the purposes of their business of furniture retailers.

Held: The fact that the landlords intended to occupy the rebuilt premises themselves did not deprive them of their right to possession under section 30 (1) (f) of the 1954 Act.

Morris LJ: If the landlords' real reason for wanting possession was that they wanted to occupy them, then they failed to prove that their reason was that they reasonably required possession for purposes of demolition or reconstruction. The phrases which have their origin in the judgment of the county court judge in *Smart's* case and which were repeated and were employed in *Atkinson* v. *Bettison* are only of assistance where employed in the process of deciding whether necessary proof is forthcoming. Where, as in section 30 (1) (*f*), proof of an intention is to be supplied, and of an intention related to a particular time, then the genuineness of a declared intention may have to be decided. Considerations as to what may be a landlord's 'primary purpose,' or his 'real intention,' or his 'main purpose,' or his 'secondary purpose,' or his 'real reason' (to quote phrases which have been used), are only of relevance and assistance in the course of deciding whether the landlord has proved that he genuinely has an intention of doing one of the things specified in section 30 (1) (*f*), and of doing it on the termination of the current tenancy. If the landlord proves his intentions and proves them to the satisfaction of the court, and proves that in order to carry them out he must have possession of the holding, then his opposition succeeds, and it matters not that after demolition or reconstruction or construction according to his proved intention he proposes himself to be in occupation; but his intentions under section 30 (1) (*f*) must be genuine and not spurious or specious, and they must be to do what the words of the section describe, and to do it at the time denoted.

If a case occurs in which it appears that a landlord had a desire to obtain possession for his own occupation, and had no thought at all of making any alteration to the premises, but if, after realizing that because he had not owned for five years, he could not oppose an application of his tenant for a new lease, he then proclaimed an intention to reconstruct, the court would have to decide whether the newly proclaimed intention was genuine. It certainly could be entirely genuine even though it owed its birth to a realization of the effect of section 30 (2) upon a desire and intention coming within section 30 (1) (*g*); but the circumstances would call for careful examination. Intentions can easily be asserted: their genuineness must be established. In such examination the only inquiry would be and must be as to whether the landlord had proved an intention which brings him within the language of section 30 (1) (*f*). Any consideration of primary and secondary purposes, where any such consideration can occur and is helpful, must always be subordinate to an inquiry directed to the actual words of the section.

Note: The foregoing was applied in *Craddock* v. *Hampshire County Council* [1958] 1 WLR 202, where the landlord's intention to demolish was not made ineffective because it was ancillary to incorporating the premises in a tenant's agricultural holding.

The intended method of carrying out the work is also immaterial.

GILMOUR CATERERS LTD v. ST BARTHOLOMEW'S HOSPITAL GOVERNORS

Court of Appeal [1956] 1 QB 387

The tenants applied for the grant of a new tenancy which was opposed by the landlords relying on section 30 (1) (f) of the 1954 Act. The landlords had made an agreement with a third party to grant him a building lease of the business premises in question for a term of 48 years upon condition that he cleared the site and erected a new building.

Held: The terms of section 30 (1) (f) were satisfied by the proposed demolition and reconstruction of the premises under the terms of the agreement.

DENNING LJ: The argument before us is that the hospital have not made good their ground of opposition. It is said that in section 30 (1) (f) the words 'the landlord intends to demolish or reconstruct the premises' mean that the landlord must intend to do it himself or by his immediate servants and agents, and that that excludes a case of this kind where the landlord intends to get it done under the terms of a building lease.

In my judgment that is much too narrow an interpretation of section 30 (1) (f). The landlord intends to demolish or reconstruct the premises even though he does it through the hands of a building lessee. In a way, the grant of a building lease is a means of paying for the work. Just as when you employ a building contractor you pay him in money, so you pay the building lessee by granting him a period of years of occupation. It seems to me that, whether the work is done directly by a building contractor or less directly through a building lessee, the landlord intends to demolish or reconstruct the premises. He intends to have it demolished and reconstructed, and that is sufficient. The judge so held, and I see no reason to interfere with his decision.

21.4 (b)   The nature of the intended work

The removal of topsoil and clay and the in-filling of the excavated space with refuse and a fresh layer of clay and topsoil are not activities within the scope of section 30 (1) (f) of the 1954 Act.

BOTTERILL v. BEDFORDSHIRE COUNTY COUNCIL

Court of Appeal (1985) 273 EG 1217

SIR JOHN ARNOLD P: Now, the section, in its relevant subsection, (f), permits the landlord to oppose the tenant's application for a new lease on the ground:

'that on the termination of the current tenancy the landlord intends to demolish or reconstruct the premises comprised in the holding or a substantial part of those premises or to carry out substantial work of construction on the holding or part thereof and that he could not reasonably do so without obtaining possession of the holding.'

There is no doubt that the last part of the condition is fulfilled, and all that this landlord has to do is to demonstrate the relevant intention.

Originally the case was put under all three elements in the condition as to intention. As the learned judge said, 'The applicants'—that is to say, the gun club—'say that all three of these things are concerned in one way or another with something *on* the land'; that is to say, demolition, reconstruction and carrying out substantial work of construction. Demolition, they say, is taking down something that is already on the land; reconstruction is reconstruction of something which is already on the land; and carrying out substantial work of construction is constructing something on the land which was not previously there. On the other hand, the county council argue that 'to carry out substantial work of construction on the holding or part thereof' is an expression wide enough to cover anything which can be described as construction work in the ordinary engineering sense; and a great deal of the hearing of this appeal has been occupied by a consideration of what can be described as construction work in the ordinary engineering sense.

The learned judge thought it was necessary to consider separately reconstructing on the one hand and carrying out substantial work of construction on the other. In relation to the first part of it, reconstructing, he said this:

'During the course of argument I raised the question whether it could be said that the county council were proposing to reconstruct the land in the sense that they are proposing to remove the existing clay and topsoil and to replace it with waste and fresh clay and topsoil. Mr Berry's answer to this is'

Mr Berry was appearing for the applicants

'that you cannot sensibly speak of "reconstructing" something that was never "constructed" in the first place, and that you cannot therefore "reconstruct" the land itself. He argues that the whole of section 30 (1) (f) is concerned with things that can be said to be constructed on the land, such as buildings, roads, runways, bridges, dams, etc.'

Then he says that the solicitor who was appearing for the county council [Mr J A Kerce] was inclined to agree with Mr Berry's argument that you cannot 'reconstruct' something unless it was 'constructed' in the first place. The learned judge says Mr Berry had been right and Mr Kerce was right to agree with him. Then he referred to a passage in *Housleys Ltd* v. *Bloomer-Holt Ltd* [1966] 1 WLR 1244, in the judgment of Diplock LJ (as he then was), when he said at p 1252:

'It is, I think, plain, on the true construction of paragraph (f), that "the premises" there referred to must be limited to that part of the holding which is capable of being demolished and capable of being reconstructed.'

So there one finds a general agreement, in my judgment, that there has to be something that was constructed if it is to be reconstructed. If construction consists of no more than the carrying out of some operation on the land, involving the putting together of more than one thing (and, if necessary, including a plan or design as to what the thing should look like at the end of the day), then it is very difficult to see why the argument which received the accolade of the learned lord justice and the acceptance at any rate by the county council was correct at all, unless one happened to know how it was that the land reached its existing condition, because quite plainly the existing contour of the land is the result of the extraction of the brick clay. If anything more was done than merely digging out, any attempt was made to reshape or grass or otherwise improve the appearance of the land at the end of the operation, if 'construction' means anything wider than the provision by building or erection of some new structure on the land, it was already constructed land and therefore would be capable of reconstruction. But that does not seem to have occurred to anybody.

Then the learned judge goes on to consider what is the prime matter with which he was concerned, namely, what is a substantial work of construction. He points out that counsel for the county council said that what they intended to do—and indeed counsel for the appellants before us said that what they intend to do—is to carry out substantial work of construction on the holding.

Then one comes to the argument which prevailed, which is thus described:

'Mr Berry argues, as I have already indicated, that the whole of section 30 (1) (f) is concerned with things constructed or to be constructed *on* the land, such as roads, runways, bridges and dams.'

The word 'on' is provided with an emphasis, and counsel for the appellants says that is to distinguish it from 'in'. My understanding is that it is to distinguish it from the conception of work 'to' the land being construction work. It seems to me, reading that passage, that 'on or in' would have been just as convenient a way of expressing the judge's intended expression of thought as the word 'on' alone. If what was being contemplated was an underground chamber, or anything else of the sort, it would have been, in the judge's mind (or in Mr Berry's mind at that stage, because it is later on that the judge accepted it), just as much a construction on the land as a building which had not been built into the land, but built merely on foundations near to but still on the top of the land.

The learned judge, having stated Mr Berry's argument in that way, goes on thus: 'What is it that the respondents propose to do in this case?' Then he gives the shorter definition that I have already read as to what they propose to do, and continues:

'I have to form a view of what Parliament intended in the paragraph. I do not think that Parliament intended to include the type of work which the county council propose to carry out here. I think that Mr Berry is right in submitting that "to carry out substantial work of construction on the holding or part thereof" involves the actual construction of something (whether it be a building or a road or whatever) on the land;'

and that is what the learned judge gave effect to by deciding the case in favour of the applicants.

Now, it seems to me that, in construing the words 'work of construction' in this section, one must construe the words in the manner most convenient and apt to fit into the context in which the words appear in the statute. We have been offered, and helpfully offered, two dictionary definitions. In the *Oxford English Dictionary* one finds the word 'construction' defined first of all as 'the action of framing, devising, or forming, by the putting together of parts'. That involves bringing within the conception something capable of being framed, devised or formed. Those are not words which are usually or conveniently applied to what at the end of the day is intended to be a field, with some trees in it, with a lightly domed contour.

The next alternative offered is 'erection, building'. That seems to me to be the one which is most convenient to import into this section to give it the natural meaning that one would expect; and it is very much what the learned judge has adopted, slightly extending the ordinary conception of 'erection' or 'building' to works built upon the land, even though themselves not often or conveniently described as a building, such as a concrete platform or a road.

Then one has a rather more abstract conception: 'the art or science of constructing; the manner in which a thing is constructed or formed'. It is the 'work of construction' which is under consideration as a composite phrase and, as counsel says—I think rightly—one is entitled to assist oneself with the interpretation of that phrase by looking at the definition of the word 'construct', because the work of construction is really the work which is done when one constructs. If one looks at that, what does one find?—'to make or form by fitting the parts together; to frame, build', again more conveniently used to describe the bringing into existence of some structure than the altering of the shape or, to some extent, the composition of a field.

Chambers' Dictionary throws up very much the same sort of result. Under 'construction' one has: 'the act of constructing anything piled together; building'; and the word 'construct' is: 'to build up; to compile; to put together the parts of; to make; to compose'. If one said 'What is it that the county council intends to construct?', what would the answer be? For my part, I think it would be that they do not intend to construct anything; they are merely altering, by putting waste in the middle and some topsoil and grass on the top, the shape of it, and giving a slightly new composition to this field. But for them to say 'We intend to construct a domed field with some trees' seems to me to be language of a most artificial kind.

The question whether the proposed works amount to 'reconstruction of a substantial part of the premises' within the meaning of section 30 (1) (f) of the 1954 Act is one of degree.

ATKINSON v. BETTISON

Court of Appeal   [1955] 1 WLR 1127

DENNING LJ: The next question is whether the proposed work is the reconstruction of a substantial part of the premises. The question what is 'substantial' is one of degree, and therefore of fact. If a judge went wrong in that he came to a conclusion which was clearly wrong or to which no reasonable man could come, then this court would interfere. But when it is a matter on which two minds can quite reasonably come to differing conclusions, then it is essentially a question for the county court judge. This seems to me to be such a case. It is a building on three floors. Nothing is proposed to be done with the first and second floors. All that is intended is the fitting of a new shopfront, and a new floor. The judge said that if [counsel for the landlords'] construction of the Act was right, any landlord could buy premises, and by means of merely altering the shop-front get the tenant out and go in himself. That shows what the judge felt about the case. He thought that this was not the reconstruction of a 'substantial part' of the premises. I think that that was a decision to which he could properly come, and that this court cannot and should not interfere with his view on the matter.

HODSON LJ: So far as the second point is concerned I think that the respondents in this appeal are right on that also, because this appeal raises the question on which the county court judge did, I think, hope to get some guidance as to how the word 'substantial' was to be approached. But I am afraid that nothing more can be said by this court than was said by the House of Lords in *Palser* v. *Grinling* in connexion with a rent case, the question there being whether the substantial portion of the rent was attributable to furniture. In that class of case, as in this class of case, the onus is on the landlord, and Lord Simon's words are applicable. He said:

'One of the primary meanings of the word is equivalent to considerable, solid, or big. It is in this sense that we speak of a substantial fortune, a substantial meal, a substantial man, a substantial argument or ground of defence. Applying the word in this sense, it must be left to the discretion of the judge of fact to decide as best he can according to the circumstances in each case, the onus being on the landlord.'

And see further:

JOEL v. SWADDLE

Court of Appeal   [1957] 1 WLR 1095

LORD EVERSHED MR: I think that in cases of this kind it is apt to be dangerous to take each individual item entirely in isolation, and then to say that each item so taken cannot itself be a work of reconstruction or a substantial work of reconstruction. One must look at the whole work which is proposed, and then say, in regard to it: Does it amount to a substantial work of reconstruction? I think that what is here proposed—and there is no question as to the facts—does, when you view it in that way, amount, within the meaning of the paragraph, to a work of reconstruction of a substantial part of the premises. I lay considerable emphasis on that part of the work which consists of the substitution of the transverse walls by the proposed girders resting on pillars; I also think, with respect to the county court judge, that he also gave somewhat too little emphasis to the floor; because what is proposed is not merely the making of a new floor, but the sinking of the floor, not a great deal, but by a distance of some eight inches, which produces an appreciable increase in the total space of what was, and is at present, the tenant's holding.

I come back now to the citations which the county court judge made from *Percy E. Cadle* v. *Jacmarch Properties Ltd.* That was a case in which the work the landlord intended to carry out consisted substantially of making internal staircases where previously there had been external means of access only, to the basement on the one hand and to the upper floor or floors on the other. The view that the county court judge had taken was that the putting in of an internal staircase was rather a matter of improvement than of reconstruction—than of interference, that is to say, with the structure, as such, of the building.

It is in that context that Denning LJ and Hodson LJ, in the course of their judgments, used the phrases which the county court judge quotes—'the word "reconstruct" here is best expressed ... by the synonym "rebuild."'

When the facts of *Percy E. Cadle* v. *Jacmarch Properties Ltd.* are considered, what the county court judge was intending to express will be apparent; the putting in of a staircase did not amount in any ordinary use of the phrase to any 'rebuilding' of the premises. On the other hand, I think, with respect to the county court judge, that you do not fail to rebuild in the structural sense because you do not substitute for a wall another and different wall, but leave a space, if you substitute girders resting on pillars for the wall, performing the structural function which the wall previously performed.

So far as the earlier case is concerned, I would respectfully adopt as being helpful in this case the rather more extensive exposition used by Ormerod LJ, which was also quoted by the county court judge in this case. Ormerod LJ said:

'the word "reconstruction" must mean ... in the first place, a substantial interference with the structure of the premises and then a rebuilding, probably in a different form, of such part of the premises as has been demolished by reason of the interference with the structure.'

I have not in the present case said anything about demolition, or what the county court judge said about demolition, because I am content for my part to rest my conclusion upon the other words in the paragraph, namely, that 'the landlord intends to reconstruct a substantial part of the premises.' In construing those words I adopt the language I have cited from Ormerod LJ's judgment. I think that what is here intended to be done does in a real sense involve an interference with the structure of the whole, or of a substantial part, of the premises, and involves a 'rebuilding,' in the ordinary sense of the word, of the premises or a substantial part, by substituting structurally something different from that which was there before.

Note: In the foregoing case, the work consisted of turning the whole of the ground floor and a yard into one enclosed space by removing various partition walls and the back wall, substituting steel girders and pillars to support the upstairs premises, lowering the floor by eight inches and putting in a new front. In *Bewlay (Tobacconists) Ltd* v. *British Bata Shoe Company Ltd* [1959] 1 WLR 45, the work involved the amalgamation of two shops into one by removing three-quarters of the dividing wall with consequential alterations to some of the pillars supporting the ceiling, putting in a new double shop front, a small amount of reconstruction of lavatory accommodation and the filling in of a recessed portion of a wall. This was held to constitute reconstruction of a substantial part of the premises. It is important to bear in mind, however, that possession may reasonably be required for *substantial* reconstruction of *part* only of the premises as in *Fernandez* v. *Walding* [1968] 2 QB 606.

In **Housleys Ltd v. Bloomer-Holt Ltd** [1966] 1 WLR 1244, Sellers LJ suggested in an *obiter dictum* that the laying of concrete—the laying of a roadway, the laying of a runway, or any other substantial work of concreting—may well be within the contemplation of the 1954 Act and may well be 'substantial work of construction'. In **Cook v. Mott** (1961) 178 EG 637, the tenant applied for a new lease and the landlord opposed the application on the ground of section 30 (1) (f). The premises consisted of a piece of land used for breeding and boarding dogs and the structures placed on the land were for the most part kennels, the majority with concrete foundations. The landlord intended to remove these, raise the level of the land, clear it, construct a road, lay soil and water pipes and electric cables and convert the land into a caravan site.

Held: The landlord's proposals involved 'substantial work of construction'.

Ormerod LJ: The learned County Court judge has found that the work of construction which the landlord proposes to carry out is, to use the words of the paragraph, 'substantial work of construction on the holding or part thereof,' and 'that he could not reasonably do so without obtaining possession of the holding.' It has been argued very fully by [counsel for the appellants] that none of the things referred to by the landlord in his evidence amount to work of construction: that it is wrong, for instance, to speak of constructing a road; it is wrong to regard the laying of electric cables, water pipes, soil pipes and so on as work of contruction; that it is not constructing so much as laying drains and making roads, or whatever the appropriate term may be. I have come to the conclusion that this is largely a matter of degree depending on the circumstances of each particular case. I think you might have proposed work which consisted of nothing more than laying a pipe or drain which could not be regarded as work of construction. On the other hand, I think it is open to any judge of fact dealing with a matter of this kind to consider the work which has to be done and the picture which the evidence creates and decide whether that is something which becomes work of construction. That is what the learned County Court judge has decided in this case: not only that this is work of construction, but (and this I think can hardly be disputed) that it was a substantial work of construction, and that, in those circumstances, paragraph (f) of the subsection applied and the landlord was justified in refusing to grant a new tenancy. It is, in my view, as I have said, largely a matter of first impression and a question of the facts and circumstances of each particular case.

21.4 (c)   The need to establish possession of the holding

The landlord will not require legal possession of the holding if the tenancy contains an access clause and the work falls within the terms of that clause.

HEATH v. DROWN

House of Lords   [1973] AC 498

The tenant occupied premises for the purposes of her business under two leases containing clauses reserving to the common landlord the right of entry for the purposes of carrying out any necessary repairs. The landlord served notices on the tenant under section 25 of the 1954 Act stating that he would oppose applications to the court for new tenancies on the ground specified in section 30 (1) (f).

Held: The expression 'obtaining possession of the holding' in section 30 (1) (f) meant the landlord's putting an end to such rights of possession of the holding as were vested in the tenant under the terms of the tenancy and in the present case it was not reasonably necessary for the landlord so to act since it was conceded that he could carry out the intended work under the reservations in the tenancies.

LORD KILBRANDON: The 'holding' referred to in section 30 (1) (f) is *ex hypothesi* one in respect of which there is a subsisting tenancy, since section 24 (1) extends the current tenancy until the tenant's application for a new lease has been finally disposed of. 'Obtaining possession of the holding' (s.c. by the landlord) must, in my view, mean putting an end to such rights of possession of the holding as are vested in the tenant under the terms of his current tenancy. This is the ordinary meaning of 'obtaining possession' in the context of the relationship of landlord and tenant. Moreover, an examination of the Act shows that when the word 'possession' is used it means the legal right to possession of land.

In the present case it was not reasonably necessary for the landlord to put an end to such rights of possession of the holding as were vested in the tenant under her current tenancies, since it is conceded that he could carry out his intended work of construction on the holding under the reservations in her current tenancies. So he could not bring himself within the terms of section 30 (1) (f).

The foregoing decision was applied in:

PRICE v. ESSO PETROLEUM COMPANY LIMITED

Court of Appeal   (1980) 255 EG 243

The landlord of a filling station served a section 25 notice on his tenant specifying section 30 (1) (f) of the 1954 Act. The lease contained a provision allowing the landlord to enter at any time to carry out 'improvements, additions and alterations'.

Held: The intended works fell within this provision and, therefore, the landlord could not rely on section 30 (1) (f).

MEGAW LJ: It has been held by the House of Lords, in *Heath* v. *Drown* [1973] AC 498, that if the terms of the existing contract between the parties—here the tenancy agreement—entitle the landlords to carry out the works in question, then the landlord cannot successfully oppose the tenant's application for a new tenancy by reliance on paragraph (f): for the word 'possession' in this paragraph means not mere physical occupation but the legal right of possession. The fact that the landlord may reasonably have to deprive the tenant of physical occupation for a time, when the landlord enters upon the premises in order to carry out the works, does not destroy the tenant's 'possession': the landlord can do the works without obtaining possession, though he may have dispossessed the tenant of occupation. Hence, as a matter of law, the landlord fails to satisfy the requirement of the concluding 14 words of paragraph (f), if the contract entitles him to carry out the works.

So the simply-stated question, by the answer to which this issue falls to be decided, is: on the terms of the tenancy agreement, would the landlords have been entitled to enter upon the Whitgift Service Station in order to carry out the intended works?

I now come to the terms of the tenancy agreement of 24 June 1976. In that agreement the landlords are described as 'Esso' and the tenant as 'the Dealer.' Clause 1, so far as is relevant, provides:

'1. The Letting. Esso agrees to let and the Dealer agrees to take: (a) the service station premises described in the Schedule hereto (which together with all buildings and erections now or at any time erected thereon are hereinafter called "the Service Station").'

Then there is subparagraph (b), which I need not read. Then the clause goes on:

'but Esso reserves the right to enter the Service Station at any time with workmen and others for the purpose of carrying out such improvements, additions and alterations to the Service Station as Esso may consider reasonable, after consultation with the Dealer.'

The schedule referred to in subparagraph (a), so far as is relevant, reads: 'The Schedule. The Service Station. All that piece or parcel of land situate at Brighton Road, South Croydon'—and then there is a description of what that piece of land is—'together with all buildings erected thereon and known as Whitgift Service Station.'

The vital words in the latter part of the clause, which have been referred to in argument in this appeal as 'the reservation clause,' are 'improvements, additions and alterations.' Of course, those words have to be read in the context of the surrounding words and of any other of the contractual provisions which may shed light on them. Are the planned works 'improvements,' 'additions' or 'alterations' or all three of them? If so, the landlords cannot rely on paragraph (f), because, if so, the landlords can reasonably do the works without obtaining possession of the holding, on the interpretation of 'possession' in *Heath* v. *Drown.* I can see no valid reason, with great respect to the sustained submissions for the landlords, why it should be said that the intended works are not, at least, improvements, and it may well be also, in whole or in part, alterations and additions. The landlords would not lose their right of entry if each of the items of the planned works fell within one or other of those heads, merely because they did not all fall within one and the same head. But, as I see it, the tenant does not need to rely on that proposition here, for the totality of the planned works are property within the word 'improvements.'

For the landlords, it is said that the words 'The Service Station,' where capitals are given to the words 'Service' and 'Station,' are a definition which relates the service station to the particular superstructures which are upon the surface of the land at the time when the application of the clause comes to have to be considered: the time when the landlords would be entering, if they have a right to enter. For myself, I do not see any magic in the use of the capitals, in the use of the words 'Service Station,' or anything particular in the form of the definition which helps here.

For the landlords, it is said that, to come within the clause, the word 'improvements' must be improvements to existing buildings and structures, not the creation of new ones; 'additions' must be additions to existing buildings; 'alterations' must be alterations to existing buildings. The clause does not, it is said, permit Esso to enter in order to carry out works which are, in effect, the demolition of all the existing structures above the surface of the land covered by the tenancy agreement and the replacement of those demolished buildings by other, fresh, buildings.

For the tenant, it is pointed out that, if and in so far as any help is to be gained by consideration of the extent to which the planned works involved demolition and new structures, the essential part of the petrol service station, as distinct from an ordinary shop or an ordinary factory, is the forecourt, with its petrol pumps and with its underground tanks and supply lines from tanks to pumps. The structures at the back of the forecourt may be important but are ancillary to the essential part of the premises for the retail petrol supply business, that is, the tanks, the lines and the pumps on the forecourt, where the customers' cars come in and station themselves in order to draw petrol from the pumps. Those essential parts will not be materially changed. The tanks will remain, the lines from the tanks to the pumps may, at any rate in some degree, be capable of being retained. The pumps themselves will change in number and location. But essentially it is the same; there will not be a material change.

For myself, apart from any help which one may gain from the context of the vital words and from the agreement as a whole, I find it impossible to regard the planned works as not falling with the ordinary commonsense meaning of 'improvements to the Service Station.' I am glad to find what I regard as being complete confirmation of that view from the high authority of the judgment of Morton J in *National Electric Theatres Ltd* v. *Hudgell* [1939] 1 Ch 553. The headnote, in its holding no. 1, at p 554, says 'that the proposed works would be an improvement on the holding in any ordinary use of the word "improvement".' The works in question there, which Morton J held were an improvement in the ordinary sense of the word, involved the demolition of what had been a theatre, and the building in its place of a row of buildings, which, when built, would be used for shops and offices. It is perfectly true that Morton J's decision was a decision, not on the words of a particular covenant nor on the words of any section of Part II of the Landlord and Tenant Act 1954, but related to provisions of the Landlord and Tenant Act 1927. There were statutory provisions there which Morton J, in his judgment, referred to as supporting his view that the planned works (in that case works to be carried out by the tenant) were properly to be regarded as being improvements. But that does not in any way affect the fact that Morton J, without reference to the consideration of the particular statutory context, expressed the view, at the outset of his judgment, in these words:

'It seems to me that these works—that is, the works I have briefly described—would be an improvement on the holding in any ordinary use of the word "improvement." When the works have been carried out, the plaintiffs can say: "We have pulled down the cinematograph theatre which was no longer of any use. We have substituted for that a row of shops with residential flats over them. The result is that the letting value of the holding has been greatly increased, both immediately and at the end of the term." It would surely be a natural use of words if the plaintiffs went on to say: "We have carried out an improvement of our holding."'

In my opinion, on the true construction of this tenancy agreement, the landlords were entitled, under the tenancy agreement, to carry out the contemplated works. Hence, on the doctrine of *Heath* v. *Drown*, section 30 (1) (f) of the 1954 Act is not available to the landlords.

The *Price* v. *Esso* case is to be contrasted with:

LEATHWOODS LTD v. TOTAL OIL (GREAT BRITAIN) LTD

Chancery Division   (1984) 270 EG 1083

The tenant applied for a new tenancy of a garage and filling station. The landlord opposed the application on the basis of section 30 (1) (f) and (g) of the 1954 Act and the tenant argued that the landlord did not need legal possession to carry out the works but merely physical occupation since there was a clause in the lease permitting the landlord to enter for the purposes of carrying out any improvement, addition or alteration which the landlord considered desirable.

Held: The works intended by the landlord required legal possession since they were in excess of the right of entry conferred by the lease.

MR VIVIAN PRICE QC: [Counsel for the landlord] referred me to the remarkable coincidence of fact between the circumstances in the *Price* v. *Esso* case and the present case. In both there is the requirement to demolish and reconstruct. In both there is the increase in the number of petrol pumps. In both there is to be a different pump layout. In both the work will take about 16 weeks. In both it is necessary to close down the premises while the work is being carried out. In the light of all these coincidences, [counsel for the landlord] submits that the present application turns, so far as paragraph (f) is concerned, on the proper construction of clause 2.16 (a) of the lease, which I have read, and he submits that on the proper construction of that paragraph it is clearly to allow Total to enter and carry out all the necessary works.

To all of this [counsel] on behalf of Total, makes essentially a short and simple answer. He submits that what is intended by Total goes beyond their entitlement under clause 2.16 (a) because in place of the old service station will be a petrol filling station with no facilities for the sale and repair of motor vehicles. Total will, so Mr Porten submits, need more than the physical occupation of the premises contemplated by clause 2.16 (a). It will need legal possession. The user covenant by Leathwoods contained in clause 2 (10) provides:

'That the premises shall not without Total's consent ... be used for any purpose other than that of a filling and service station [together with the sale and repair of motor vehicles]

[Counsel for the tenant] points out that this covenant is not only restrictive but also permissive and it seems to me that he must be correct in that submission. If, after the works are carried out, Leathwoods would not be able to carry on its business in the sale and repair of motor vehicles because the facilities for so doing would no longer be available, then, if the lease is still in force, this circumstance would constitute a derogation from Total's grant and a breach for which Leathwoods would be entitled to claim a remedy. It does not seem to me that the words of clause 2.16 (a) provide any answer and in this respect I, of course, bear in mind the words of Lord Morton of Henryton in the *National Electric Theatre* case quoted in Megaw LJ's judgment in the *Price* v. *Esso* case which I have just read. In my judgment, the circumstances in *Price* v. *Esso* were essentially different, while the teaching of *Heath* v. *Drown* and *National Electric Theatre* v. *Hudgell* provides no answer to the consequences that flow from the inclusion in the present lease of clause 2.10.

In my judgment, Total have established their second pleaded objection based upon para (f) of section 30 (1).

The tenant may be able to rely upon the provisions of section 31A of the

1954 Act (added by the Law of Property Act 1969) to resist the landlord's claim for possession of the holding.

REDFERN v. REEVES

Court of Appeal

(1979) 37 P & CR 364

The tenant occupied business premises under a lease which allowed the landlord to enter on to the premises to carry out structural repairs. The tenant applied for a new tenancy and the landlord opposed the grant on the ground specified in section 30 (1) (f) of the 1954 Act. The tenant, pursuant to section 31A of the Act, stated that she would give the landlord access to the holding for the purpose of carrying out the work. At the hearing of the application, it was found that the tenant would have to be out of occupation for two to four months to allow the work to be done. The deputy judge found in favour of the tenant on the basis that the interference with her business would not be substantial and that she would be able to carry on the business upon her return.

Held: For section 31A of the 1954 Act to apply, it had to be shown that the landlord could carry out the work without interfering to a substantial extent and for a substantial time with the tenant's use of the holding for the purpose of the business carried on by her and not that the work could be done without interfering with the tenant's business or the goodwill of the tenant's business. Accordingly, in the present case, the tenant was not entitled to rely on section 31A.

LAWTON LJ: Now, once it is accepted that the landlord could not, under the lease, go in to do the new works, the question has to be asked: what right had he to go in? He had a right given to him by the consent of the tenant. It follows that that brings into operation section 31A (1) (a) of the Act of 1954. The relevant parts of that section are these:

'(1) Where the landlord opposes an application under section 24 (1) of this Act on the ground specified in paragraph (f) of section 30 (1) of this Act the court shall not hold that the landlord could not reasonably carry out the demolition, reconstruction or work of construction intended without obtaining possession of the holding if—(a) the tenant agrees to the inclusion in the terms of the new tenancy of terms giving the landlord access and other facilities for carrying out the work intended and, given that access and those facilities, the landlord could reasonably carry out the work without obtaining possession of the holding and without interfering to a substantial extent or for a substantial time with the use of the holding for the purposes of the business carried on by the tenant; ...'

The first problem that arises is: what is meant by the words 'the work intended?' Now, the 'work intended' is the work that cannot be done by the landlord without obtaining possession of the holding, and, in the context of this case, this means the new work and not the work that is covered by clause 2 (9) of the lease.

[Counsel for the landlord's] submission is that these words, in the context of section 31A, mean the whole of the proposed works. I do not accept this view. The next problem is, however, 'the' work, that is to say, the new works: could this reasonably be done without obtaining possession of the holding and without interfering to a substantial extent or for a substantial time with the use of the holding for the purposes of the business carried on by the tenant?

The position, on the evidence, is not all that clear, but, having regard to the nature of the new works and what the defendant's [sic] architect said about them, it seems to me that the deputy judge must have taken the view (although he did not say so in terms) that the new works would interfere to a substantial extent and for a substantial period of time over and above the extent to which and the period of time for which the works that were covered by clause 2 (9) of the lease would do so.

[Counsel for the landlords] says that, if that is the right construction of the judgment, his client has established that he requires lawful possession within the meaning of section 30 (1) (*f*) and that, therefore, he is entitled to resist the grant of a new tenancy.

[Counsel for the tenants] on the other hand, says that that is not so, for two reasons. One is that the whole object of section 31A is to safeguard the tenant's business. If, therefore, on the facts it can be shown that the tenant's business will be safeguarded notwithstanding having to give up occupation of the premises while the proposed work is being done, then she is entitled to the protection that is given to her by section 31A. [Counsel for the tenants] argued (and rightly argued) that section 31A was brought into the Act of 1954 in 1969 to give tenants further protection. He pointed out that, on the evidence that there was, the deputy judge found that, by transferring her business to nearby premises temporarily, the tenant would be able to safeguard her business.

[Counsel for the landlords] on the other hand, submitted that that did not come within the wording of section 31A (1) (*a*) at all, and the reason that he gave was this. The words are that, if the works are to be carried out, they must be carried out without interfering to a substantial extent or for a substantial time with the use of the holding. [Counsel for the landlords] submitted that the court must look to the physical effects of the work and not to the consequence of it from a business point of view. He submitted that that must be so by reason of the words 'with the use of the holding.'

In my judgment, that submission is well-founded, and, as the deputy judge, by necessary implication, found that there would have been an interference to a substantial extent and for a substantial time with the use of the building—with the holding—because of the new work, it follows that the tenant is not entitled to the protection given by section 31A (1) (*a*).

Note: The decision in *Redfern* v. *Reeves* was approved in *Mularczyk* v. *Azralnove Investments Ltd* (1985) 276 EG 1064, (CA), where the landlord was held unable to rebuild without obtaining possession of the premises and substantially interfering with the tenant's business of a dog kennels. The court considered that a relevant factor was the frightening effect the building operations would have on the dogs and, in the circumstances, held that section 31A did not apply and that the tenant's application for a new tenancy would be refused.

Section 31A of the 1954 Act does not give the court power to limit the work the landlord intends to carry out.

DECCA NAVIGATOR CO. LTD v. GREATER LONDON COUNCIL

Court of Appeal   [1974] 1 WLR 748

The landlords, a local authority, let half an acre of land to business tenants with a provision that the tenancy could be determined if the land was required for a fire station. The landlords decided to build a fire station on the land and the tenants applied under section 31A (1) (b) of the 1954 Act for a new lease of part of the holding on the ground that a satisfactory fire station could be built on the remainder of the land.

Held: The words 'intended work' in section 31A (1) (b) of the 1954 Act meant the work which the landlords intended to do and the court had no jurisdiction to decide whether the landlords' purpose could or should be achieved by doing some different work. Accordingly, since the local authority's 'intended work' required the whole of the holding, they were entitled to recover possession of the whole.

LORD DENNING MR: In *Fernandez* v. *Walding* [1968] 2 QB 606, this court held that the word 'holding' could not be read to mean 'part of the holding.' Accordingly the landlord was entitled to recover possession of the whole though he only intended to reconstruct part.

Soon afterwards the legislature amended the law so as to reverse that decision. It enabled a tenant in an appropriate case to get a new tenancy of *part* of the holding. It did so by the Law of Property Act 1969, section 7 (1), which inserted a new section 31A into the Act of 1954. I will not read the whole of the section. It is complicated; but I will seek to summarise it in so far as it applies to the present case. It enables a tenant to get a new lease of part of the holding, if he shows that the landlord could do his intended work on the remainder of the holding. The tenant, of course, must be willing to accept a new tenancy of the part and to pay a fair rent for it. And the severance must not be such as to prejudice the landlord financially. The rent of the two portions let separately must not be substantially less than the rent of the property would be if let as a whole.

On the new section, the question arises: can the court inquire into the actual needs of the landlord? Does he really need all the holding, or ought he to be able to make do with only part of it? Decca say that the council could build a perfectly good fire station on part of the premises. The council could alter the plan by moving the proposed fire station a few feet further to the west. That would leave a strip of 15ft wide down the eastern side available for Decca. On it Decca could have a car park which would be most valuable for their business and their employees. So Decca say it is entirely unreasonable for the landlord to have the whole of the premises. It seems to me that the question depends on the meaning of the words 'intended work' at the end of section 31A (1) (*b*).

[Counsel for the tenants] submitted that the test was to see what was the general nature of the work which the landlord intended to do—that is to say, what was the description of it—and then, so long as the general nature or description of it was satisfied, the court would inquire whether he needed *all* the land for the purpose. If he ought to be satisfied with part, then the court could say so.

I cannot accept [counsel for the tenants'] submission. I think that in this section 31A, as in the other parts of the Act of 1954, the court has to look into the actual intention of the landlord. It is sufficient if it is a fixed and settled intention held in good faith which he is able to carry out and will doubtless carry out if he obtains possession. If the carrying out of the work so intended is such that it requires the whole of the holding to do it, then the landlord is entitled to recover possession of the whole. If the work so intended only requires part, in law he is only entitled to possession of the part, and the tenant is entitled, on proper terms, to have a tenancy of the remainder.

The county court judge put it well when he said:

'... the words "the intended work" in section 31A mean the work which the landlord in fact intends to do, and leave no room for a tenant to argue, or the court to decide, that it would be in his interests, or the interests of the tenant, or the interests of the public generally, or that it would be sensible for him to achieve his purpose by doing some different work.'

In this case the evidence showed that the council *bona fide* intended to build a fire station on the land and to surround it by a drill yard of large dimensions. The work so intended would occupy the whole of the area. The judge held that in these circumstances the council was entitled to the whole. It was of no avail for Decca to argue that the council might construct an adequate fire station in a different way. I entirely agree.

21.5   Intention to occupy the holding for business or residence—section 30 (1) (g)

21.5 (a)   Proof of intention to occupy

In deciding whether a landlord intends to occupy the holding himself, not only must he genuinely intend to do so but he must, on an objective test, have a reasonable prospect of bringing this about by his own volition.

GREGSON v. CYRIL LORD LIMITED

Court of Appeal   [1963] 1 WLR 41

The landlords of premises in Harley Street, London, opposed an application for a new tenancy of a suite of rooms occupied by osteopaths on the ground specified in section 30 (1) (g) of the 1954 Act. It was clear that they wished to occupy the rooms as offices but they had not applied for planning permission and there was a conflict of evidence as to the likelihood of getting any necessary planning consents.

Held: The landlords had to establish a reasonable prospect of being able to bring about their occupation of the premises by their own act of volition. The test to be applied was an objective one, namely, would a reasonable man, on the evidence before him, believe that there was a reasonable prospect that he would be successful in obtaining any necessary planning consents. In the present case, the landlords had satisfied that test.

UPJOHN LJ (read by Diplock LJ): The question whether the landlords intend to occupy the premises is primarily one of fact, but the authorities establish that to prove such intention, the landlords must prove two things. First, a genuine *bona fide* intention on the part of the landlords that they intend to occupy the premises for their own purposes. So far as this head is concerned, it is not in dispute that the landlords are genuinely intending to occupy the premises for their own purposes. The landlords already occupy 70 per cent. to 80 per cent. of the whole building and obviously, on the evidence, genuinely require to occupy this extra half floor to house some of their senior executives and their staff. Secondly, the landlords must prove that in point of possibility they have a reasonable prospect of being able to bring about this occupation by their own act of volition. This is established by Asquith LJ's well-known observations in *Cunliffe* v. *Goodman*, where he said:

'An "intention" to my mind connotes a state of affairs which the party "intending"—I will call him X—does more than merely contemplate: it connotes a state of affairs which, on the contrary, he decides, so far as in him lies, to bring about, and which, in point of possibility, he has a reasonable prospect of being able to bring about by his own act of volition.'

Now it being established and, indeed, admitted, that there is a genuine intention on the part of the respondents to occupy the premises for their own offices, the whole question that the county court judge had to determine was whether or not the respondents established a reasonable prospect of being able to bring about their occupation of the premises by their own act of volition. In this case no question arises as to difficulties of finance or anything of that sort, and the sole point that is made against the landlords is that they have not established a reasonable prospect of being able to obtain possession because they have not obtained planning permission and, furthermore, have not established a reasonable probability of obtaining planning permission; therefore, they fail to establish the requisite intention for the purposes of section 30 (1) (*g*). Upon this question the county court judge had before him the evidence of an expert for the landlords, who called their evidence first, the onus admittedly being upon them, an experienced surveyor, who testified that in his view, first, that planning permission would not be required in all the peculiar circumstances of this case; secondly, if, contrary to his view, planning permission was necessary, there was a reasonable prospect that it would be obtained. This witness was perfectly candid and, of course, took into account the fact that the tenants' suite of rooms on the third floor in question was not an isolated hereditament but that the landlords were already in occupation for their office purposes of something over 70 per cent. of the house and they merely required this extra accommodation for the same purpose.

For the applicants, the tenants, a chartered surveyor was called. He testified to the view that the proposed change in occupation from that of medical practitioners to office use, which was not ancillary to use by the landlords of the whole building, would be a material change of use, for it involved a change from Class XV to Class II of the Town and Country Planning (Use Classes) Order 1950. He said he would advise the landlords that planning permission was necessary, and he expressed the view that the prospects were that planning permission would not be obtained.

[Counsel], for the landlords, argued before us with great persuasiveness that the sole question was whether the landlords had a *bona fide* intention to occupy and if it could be established that a reputable firm, such as that to which the surveyor who gave evidence on behalf of the landlords belongs, advised them that planning permission was not required or that, if it was, it could probably be obtained and that they accepted that advice (as I am sure they did), that was an end of the matter, for such evidence alone established a genuine intention, for the purposes of the Act, to occupy the premises.

For my part, I am not able to accept this argument. It seems to me that the test under the second heading mentioned at the beginning of this judgment is not subjective, that is to say, purely a matter of the state of mind of the respondents, no doubt acting on the *bona fide* advice of their experts. In my judgment it is essentially an objective test, that is to say, would a reasonable man, on the evidence before him, believe that he had a reasonable prospect of being able to bring about his occupation by his own act of volition? This, of course, is a question of fact to be determined on all the evidence that is before the court.

The county court judge, in his judgment, rightly eschewed the idea that he should endeavour to sit in the seat of judgment as though he was either the planning authority deciding whether to give permission or not, or, on the other hand, the Minister of Housing who might be asked to rule under section 17 of the Town and Country Planning Act 1947, whether planning permission was required, or, secondly, who might on appeal have to decide whether the planning authority was correct in its decision. For my part I entirely assent to the county court judge's view upon this matter. The Court of Appeal pointed out in a recent case, *Simpsons Motor Sales (London) Ltd* v. *Hendon Corporation*, though dealing with a different subject-matter, that it is quite impossible for a court to decide what a planning authority or the Minister would decide, for the court has not before it the materials, such as, for example, the advice or reports of inspectors who have held inquiries and inspected the *locus in quo*, nor the expert knowledge nor knowledge of the general or local background or the relevant national or local policies, all of which matters properly affect the decision of the planning authority or of the Minister, as the case may be. I, therefore, so far, agree entirely with the county court judge. The test to my mind is entirely different. It is an objective test upon the evidence before the court: have the landlords established, not what the planning authority or the Minister would determine but the different and practical question: would the reasonable man think he had a reasonable prospect of giving effect to his intention to occupy? On the facts of this case, and subject to one further point mentioned below, this amounts to an inquiry whether the landlords on the evidence have established a reasonable prospect either that planning permission is not required or, if it is, that they would obtain it. This does not necessitate the determination by the court of any of the questions which may one day be submitted to the planning authority or to the Minister; it is the practical appraisal upon the evidence before the court as to whether the landlords, upon whom, let me stress, the onus lies, have established a reasonable prospect of success. In many cases, no doubt, proof of this may be so doubtful that the wise landlord will buttress his case by previously testing the matter in the sense that he will have obtained a decision of the Minister whether planning permission is necessary, and if that decision is against him, he will have then applied for and obtained planning permission and so put an end to the question.

For my part, however, I reject the argument of counsel for the tenants that this is the necessary and proper course in all cases. Each case must depend on its own facts, and a landlord is perfectly entitled to come before the court and endeavour to establish by his own evidence that on the balance of probabilities planning permission is not necessary or that if it is, he will probably obtain it.

The foregoing case was approved and applied in:

WESTMINSTER CITY COUNCIL v. BRITISH WATERWAYS BOARD

House of Lords   [1984] 3 WLR 1047

The appellants, who were the tenants of Nos 33, 35 and 37 North Wharf, Paddington, which were used by them as a street cleansing depot, made an application for the grant of a new tenancy. The respondent landlords opposed the application on the ground specified in section 30 (1) (g) of the 1954 Act. The tenants, who were also the local planning authority, regarded the premises as vital to their cleansing services in that they had no suitable alternative site, and indicated that they would refuse planning permission for change of use to a marina, the landlord's intended use.

Held:
(1) The test of whether the landlords had established their ability to implement their intention to bring about an occupation of the premises was an objective one, namely, whether a reasonable man, on the evidence before him, would believe that there was a reasonable prospect that he would be successful in obtaining any necessary planning permission.
(2) The test had to be applied on the assumption that the landlords were in occupation.
(3) Since the objection to the landlord's proposed use (which was a perfectly acceptable one) was for the purpose of protecting the occupation of an existing occupier and not for preserving an existing planning use, it was not a legitimate planning objection.
(4) On the assumption that the landlords were in possession, there was no evidence that the tenants would be able to resume possession of the premises for use as a street cleansing depot, since if the landlords were refused planning permission for their proposed use there would be a range of uses available for the premises which did not require planning permission.
(5) Accordingly, the landlords had established a reasonable prospect of success in the notional planning appeal which had to be contemplated in deciding whether they had established their case under section 30 (1) (g).

LORD BRIDGE OF HARWICH: In these circumstances the test to be applied by the court trying the issue raised by the landlord's opposition to the grant of a new tenancy is not in doubt. As it was put in the judgment of Upjohn LJ, read and agreed to by Diplock LJ in *Gregson* v. *Cyril Lord Ltd* [1963] 1 WLR 41, 48:

'It is an objective test upon the evidence before the court: have the landlords established, not what the planning authority or the Minister would determine, but the different and practical question: would the reasonable man think he had a reasonable prospect of giving effect to his intention to occupy? On the facts of this case ... this amounts to an inquiry whether the landlords on the evidence have established a reasonable prospect either at that planning permission is not required or, if it is, that they would obtain it. This does not necessitate the determination by the court of any of the questions which may one day be submitted to the planning authority or to the Minister; it is the practical appraisal upon the evidence before the court as to whether the landlords, upon whom, let me stress, the onus lies, have established a reasonable prospect of success.'

My Lords, I believe this test has been consistently applied ever since and it is, if I may respectfully say so, clearly right.

The essence of the argument for the Appellants, which was accepted by Walton J but rejected by the Court of Appeal, may be summarised in the following propositions: (1) the established existing use of the premises is as a street cleansing depot; (2) the desirability of preserving an existing use of land may by itself afford a valid planning reason for refusing permission for a change of use; (3) there is no suitable alternative site for use as a street cleansing depot, which serves a vital public purpose; (4) therefore it is desirable to preserve the existing use of the premises; (5) these considerations afford a sufficiently weighty planning objection to the Respondents' proposal to change the use of the premises to prevent them discharging the onus of proving a reasonable prospect of success in obtaining the planning permission necessary to the implementation of their intention to use the premises for their own business purposes.

For my part, I find it difficult to see how this argument can be sustained at all, once it is appreciated that the Respondents' prospects of success in a notional planning appeal must be considered on the assumption that they, not the Appellants, are in possession. The Appellants have given no indication of an intention to excercise any power they possess to acquire the premises compulsorily for a necessary public purpose. As it seems to me, the preservation of an existing use (which is temporarily suspended) cannot afford a ground to refuse permission for an otherwise acceptable change of use, unless it can be shown that the refusal may reasonably be expected to lead to a resumption of the suspended use. This raises questions as to the true scope, for·planning purposes, of the established existing use of the premises to which I must shortly revert.

First, however, I should advert to the second of the five propositions, as I have summarised them above, on which the Appellants rely. This is a proposition of law which I fully accept. It is supported by the decision of the Court of Appeal in *Clyde & Co.* v. *Secretary of State for the Environment* [1977] 1 WLR 926. In that case it was held that the desirability of preserving for residential use, in an area suffering from a shortage of residential accommodation, part of a new block of flats, hitherto unoccupied, was a valid ground for refusing permission for a change of use to offices. The correctness of the decision is, in my respectful opinion, beyond argument. Counsel for the Appellants in the instant case much relied on a passage from the judgment of Sir David Cairns in that case at p 936 where he said:

'The fact that the refusal of planning permission for a change of use cannot ensure that a current use which is a permitted use will continue was as already indicated the ground of the refusal of planning permission in the case of the Dartford cinema. It is equally true that whereas in the present case the permitted use has not been started, the refusal of an application to change of use cannot ensure that permitted use will ever be started. This was a point strongly relied on. I do not find it a compelling argument. The need for housing is certainly a planning consideration. If permission is given for office use, the permission will almost certainly be implemented and the building will be unavailable for housing. If permission for office use is refused, there is at least a fair chance that the building will be used for housing rather than being allowed to stand empty.'

I respectfully agree with this passage in substance, though I do not accept every nuance of its language as expressing the law with perfect accuracy. The refusal of planning permission for office use of part of an unoccupied block of purpose-built flats in an area suffering a shortage of residential accommodation must, I should have thought, as a matter of overwhelming probability, lead to the consequence that the accommodation would in due course be put to use for its designed residential purpose. Thus, in the concluding sentence of the passage quoted, the phrase 'at least a fair chance', on which counsel in this appeal particularly relies, suggests, in my respectful opinion, an unduly and, on the facts, unnecessarily lax criterion. In a contest between the planning merits of the two competing uses, to justify refusal of permission for use B on the sole ground that use A ought to be preserved, it must, in my view, be necessary at least to show a balance of probability that, if permission is refused for use B, the land in dispute will be effectively put to use A. But, this apart, *Clyde's* case [1977] 1 WLR 926, was concerned with a contest between two of the broadest classes of use, residential use versus office use. It is so far removed from the character of the present dispute that I doubt whether we can derive much assistance from it.

To determine the scope, for planning purposes, of an existing use of land established by *de facto* user for a sufficient period to put it beyond the reach of enforcement procedures (as opposed to a use commenced pursuant to an express grant of planning permission), it is necessary to answer two questions which are primarily questions of fact. First, what is the precise character of the established use? Secondly, what is the range of uses sufficiently similar in character to the established use to be capable of replacing the established use without involving a *material* change? Behind this second question lies a potential question of law in that there may be some uses of such a character that a reasonable tribunal of fact, directing itself correctly in law, must necessarily conclude that they lie within that range, or beyond it, as the case may be.

The evidence bearing upon the issue of the scope of the Appellants' use of the premises was again given by their area planning officer, in his affidavit, immediately following the passage I have quoted earlier. He added:

'But I submit that the Plaintiffs may use the premises for any of their departments provided the existing use is not materially changed. *In planning terms, the identity of the occupier who carries on such use is irrelevant. Accordingly the expression "local government depot" is not intended to imply that there is any relevance in the fact that the occupier is a local authority. It is the activities which it carries on at the depot which are relevant* and it is merely a matter of convenience and brevity that these can be described as "use as local government depot".'

In this passage I have italicised the words which seem to me of importance. Even though the witness may have strayed from his proper province of fact into an area of law, what he said was clearly correct. So long as the mixture of uses *on the premises*, which the judge held to be the relevant planning unit, remain substantially unchanged, there would be no material change of use. Those uses, as already indicated, included workshops, offices, stores, messing facilities and parking for a variety of vehicles both under cover and in the open. This is just such a mixture of uses as would be required by a wide variety of undertakings whose business was the operation of some kind of vehicular transport and who required a base from which to operate. Whether, in any particular case, the proposed use of the premises by such an undertaking would involve a material change of use would depend on the detailed nature of the proposal. But it would be of no relevance to the use *of the premises* to inquire for what purpose the vehicles parked there were to be used when they left their base. It seems to me to follow from this that the Appellants cannot sustain the first proposition on which their contentions essentially depend, *viz.* that the established use of the premises is properly defined, in planning terms, as use as a *street cleansing* depot.

Walton J, in discussing the question (now no longer in issue) as to whether planning permission was required for the Respondents' proposed use of the premises, expressed himself in terms which disclosed a misapprehension on this point. He said:

'In the existing state of affairs, those uses [*sc.* the various uses presently being made of the premises by the Appellants] are ancillary to the cleansing of the highways in the City of Westminster, and the maintenance of the highways in that city.'

The concept of a single planning unit used for one main purpose to which other uses carried on within the unit are ancillary is a familiar one in planning law. But it is a misapplication of this concept to treat the use or uses of a single planning unit as ancillary to activities carried on outside the unit altogether.

These considerations lead to the conclusion that, whatever be the correct description of the established existing use of the premises in planning terms, use as a street cleansing depot is only one of a substantial range of uses which could properly be carried on without involving a material change of use. It follows that in the notional planning appeal which your Lordships must contemplate the Respondents have established, by the test laid down in *Gregson* v. *Cyril Lord Ltd* [1963] 1 WLR 41, 48, at least a reasonable prospect of success for two substantial reasons. The first is that the objection to the Respondents' proposed use of the premises, in itself a perfectly acceptable use, is not based on the desirability of preserving the existing planning use of the premises, which would be a legitimate planning ground of objection, but on the desirability of protecting the occupation of the present occupier, which is not a legitimate planning ground of objection. The second is that, on the assumption that the Respondents were in possession of the premises, refusal of planning permission for their proposed use would leave the premises available for a range of uses not requiring planning permission, and there is no evidence to establish the probability that, in these circumstances, the Appellants would be able to resume possession of the premises for use as a street cleansing depot.

Accordingly, I propose that the appeal be dismissed with costs.

The landlord must establish a fixed intention to occupy the holding for the purpose of his business.

CHEZ GERARD LTD v. GREENE LTD

Court of Appeal   (1983) 268 EG 575

The landlords opposed the grant of a new tenancy relying on section 30 (1) (g) and in support adduced evidence of the resolution of its board of directors, of available finance, absence of any need for planning permission, a draft agreement with a restauranteur and an undertaking offered to the court that the landlords would enter into and run the business as a restaurant.

Held: The landlords had established the necessary intention.

SIR JOHN ARNOLD P: That it is necessary for a fixed intention to be shown in order that a landlord may bring himself into a situation in which he can justly claim an intention to occupy premises himself so as successfully to resist what would otherwise be the right to a new tenancy is amply established by authority. I take as the leading authority on this, because it recites the relevant part of the earlier authority, *Betty's Cafés Ltd* v. *Phillips Furnishing Stores Ltd* [1959] AC 20, where in the leading speech Lord Simonds deals with the matter thus. He says at the bottom of p 33: 'My Lords, as a preliminary to determining the date', which was the point in that case, 'when the requisite intention must be proved to have been formed, there was much discussion upon the meaning of the word "intends" in section 30 (1) (f)'. I should interpolate at this point that there is ample authority not in contest in this appeal that the intention under section 30 (1) (f) and the intention under section 30 (1) (g) require a common fixity of purpose.

He goes on:

'It might be regarded as somewhat academic in this case: for it is conceded that, whatever the meaning of the word, an intention had not been formed at the date of notice of opposition but had been formed on 23 April 1956' [which was the hearing date] 'But the question has this degree of relevance, that the greater the fixity of intention and the less the mental reservation, the greater the difficulty in supposing that the landlord is to form that intention within two months of receiving the tenant's request or for ever hold his peace'

that being of course the period within which the counternotice of the landlord must be lodged.

'In this context your lordships have the advantage of a judgment delivered by Lord Asquith (then Asquith LJ), than whom there have been few greater masters of the English language in judicial interpretation or exposition, in *Cunliffe* v. *Goodman* [1950] 2 KB 237. I will content myself with a single short passage, though much more might be usefully cited: "An 'intention', said the learned lord justice, "to my mind connotes a state of affairs which the party 'intending' ... does more than merely contemplate; it connotes a state of affairs which, on the contrary, he decides, so far as in him lies, to bring about, and which, in point of possibility, he has a reasonable prospect of being able to bring about, by his own act of volition." I do not think that anything is to be gained by trying to elaborate these words, but I must fairly add that I do not at all dissent from the explanation of them which the learned Master of the Rolls has given in this case.'

This was a reference to an exposition on this topic of Lord Evershed, which is reported in [1957] Ch 7 but is not relied upon in the present appeal as differing from the conclusions of Asquith LJ, and it is not necessary therefore, I think, to cite it.

'It is a question of fact what intention a man has at a given time, difficult, it may be, to ascertain, but still a question of fact, and I think that a jury directed in such words as these could come to a fair conclusion.'

To ensure a full exposition of authority, I will add to what extract from Asquith LJ's judgment a further passage which has been cited to us. The reference is to *Cunliffe* v. *Goodman* [1950] 2 KB 237 at p 254.

'Neither project [these were two alternative ideas of the landlord] moved out of the zone of contemplation—out of the sphere of the tentative, the provisional and the exploratory—into the valley of decision.'

With those elegant words did Asquith LJ sum up his understanding of the case, and those are the very words which are quoted in the notice of appeal in this case.

The principle item of evidence in the present case was a resolution which had been passed on 6 March 1983 by the board of directors of the respondent company, which is before us in its full text. Leaving out inessential items, after noticing that the company opposed the application of the appellants for a new tenancy and authorising two officers of the company to represent the company in court proceedings in that regard, it was resolved 'That the company do open a restaurant on the premises on termination of the current tenancy.' Then there is borrowing authorisation which in the event turned out to be unnecessary. The resolution goes on: 'That David Kolstoe and/or Michael Aspden' the two named people 'be and each of them is hereby authorised to enter into discussions with a restaurateur with a view to' obtaining his recommendations about the nature of the restaurant, ascertaining to what extent the existing equipment would be of any use and what alterations would be desirable, his advising—that is the restaurateur advising—about staff and licences.

'Negotiating, agreeing and executing any agreements or such other documents as may be required in regard to the employment of a supervising manager for the intended restaurant and who shall be responsible for the planning, development and running of said restaurant on behalf of the company'

and, finally, a knitting-up paragraph

'Generally dealing with any other matter which might arise in connection with the resolutions to open a restaurant on the premises and the legal involvement so required.'

It is not questioned on this appeal that that resolution was duly passed. It is not questioned on this appeal that that resolution embodied within it the honest intention of the company. But what is said is that too much was left uncertain and too little had been done to ensure that it is demonstrated that, to quote again the language of Asquith LJ, they had a reasonable prospect of being able to bring that intention about. The learned judge cited in that context that the freehold was unencumbered, that there was money available in the bank, no planning permission would be needed, the restaurateur with whom they had negotiated had got to the point of a full draft agreement, which, as the learned judge said, the restaurateur was willing to sign subject to approval by his solicitor of the form in which it was set forth, and the general policy of the company to diversify from, broadly speaking, a shipping connection into wider fields.

Those were the other aspects, to which he adds: 'Mr Kolstoe', who was the duly authorised plenipotentiary for the respondents, 'has offered to give an undertaking on behalf of his company that the company would enter into and run the business.' He weighs all those factors, or perhaps—and I shall come to this in a moment—all those factors less the one concerning the undertaking, aginst the factors on the other side: that the resolution was dated as recently as 6 March, that is to say three weeks before the hearing, that the company's inquiries and investigations had been carried out in an unbusinesslike way, that the costings of Mr Betti, the restaurateur were vague and that Mr Betti had put nothing in writing to back those up. He came to the conclusion that the positive factors outweighed the negative factors and the requisite fixity of intention was shown and that there was a reasonable prospect that the intention would be carried out.

For my part, I should be disposed to think that even without the factor of the undertaking those matters had been effectively demonstrated. The recent date of the resolution might of course have been the subject matter of an investigation designed to negative its good faith. It might have been suggested that it would be credulous to regard a piece of evidence so *ben trovato* in relation to the date of the hearing as being reliably undertaken in good faith. No suggestion of that sort is made. Once that aspect is to be ignored, as it must be, then there is no more than the date, and it is fair to say that the date was a better date from the point of view of the landlords than the date in the *Betty's Cafés* case. It does not seem to me that the recent date by itself is a potent factor.

I do not think it is right to say that the company's inquiries and investigations had been carried out in an unbusinesslike way. What had they done? They had shown the proposition to their expert, Mr Betti, who was more than an expert; he was a would-be participant. He had expressed from a lifetime of experience the view that the restaurant was a 'go', that it would generate a substantial, although exactly how substantial he could not at that stage say, trading profit, which, after deducting his own take, would be likely to leave what the company was fully entitled to regard as a sufficient surplus before one comes to net profit to take account of other non-trading profit deductions. The costing of Mr Betti was certainly vague, in the sense that he put the trading profit at the worst at £8000 or so and at best at about £15,000. But it does not seem to me that it was demonstrated that that was too vague, having regard to the stage at which the project had got, to be a reliable factor in coming to the conclusion that the prospects of the intention being put into effect were perfectly feasible. As to the proposition that Mr Betti had put nothing in writing to back these up, that really seems to me to be a matter of choice. The conclusions which Mr Betti had reached, whether orally as he remembered or partly orally and partly in writing as Mr Kolstoe remembered, were in the judge's judgment perfectly clear conclusions, and the form in which they were enshrined seems to me to be quite inessential. So, even without the factor of the undertaking, I would think that the learned judge must have come to the conclusion in this case that the fixed intention and the necessary prospect of success in carrying it out were established.

But there was in addition the factor of the undertaking. An undertaking in these cases is a perfectly permissible element to consider along with the other factors in relation to whether a fixed intention has been made out. It is put thus by Harman J (as he then was) when deciding at first instance the case of *Espresso Coffee Machine Co. Ltd* v. *Guardian Assurance Co. Ltd*, reported in the Court of Appeal [1959] 1 All ER 458, where in the course of the judgment of Lord Evershed MR, at p 462 the learned trial judge is quoted thus:

'If these landlords give an undertaking, there is no question but that they have the power to honour it, and I think that there is no doubt that they will honour it. They are not the sort of company whose undertakings in a suitable case the court would hesitate to accept. It is not suggested that they could not carry out the undertaking. Therefore, as counsel at the Bar today is still authorised to make this offer to me and to the tenants, I must take the offer at its face value. If that is the case, I do not see how I can any longer doubt that the intention today exists. Whether by the end of the year it will exist any longer, I do not know. The tenants may so harass the landlords that they will change their mind ...'

That plainly shows that the way that the learned judge was using the offer of an undertaking was as an element in the evidence, and that it was a legitimate use of it is demonstrated by the fact that the appeal against the learned judge's conclusion did not succeed.

In the present case, having listed under numbered heads what the learned judge calls a number of aspects to show in the case of the respondents that it had moved from the tentative to the settled and under numbered heads a number of matters to which counsel for the appellants (applicants) referred, he then (unnumbered) offers this paragraph:

'Mr Kolstoe has offered to give an undertaking on behalf of his company that the company would enter into and run the business. In my judgment, weighing up all the factors, Greene Ltd has moved from the tentative to the settled and I find it has a settled intention to run a restaurant there,'

and then he refers to some of the particular features.

Had the matter stopped there, there really could not have been any construction available for that judgment, save one which indicated that he had taken the numbered factors on the one side into account, the numbered factors on the other side into account and the offer of an undertaking all as relevant evidential factors from which he had derived his judgment. But having finished with the balancing exercise, he then went on thus:

'In order to ensure justice I will find in favour of the landlords only if an appropriate undertaking is given by Mr Kolstoe and Mr Ashton. It is essential for the protection of the tenant that this should be [and by that he means that his decision should be] only on the undertaking that has been proffered.'

The presence of that paragraph at that stage gives rise to three possible constructions. One is that all the way through—in the first paragraph to which I have referred and in that last paragraph—what he is really saying is: 'This is one of the matters which I have taken into account for its evidential value in reaching my conclusion as to a settled intention.' The second is that the first paragraph to which I have referred is to be treated thus in an analysis of the judgment, while the last paragraph is using the same factor again to demonstrate that added justice and protection is afforded by the circumstance that the landlords are placed in a degree of peril which the giving of an undertaking necessarily imports. The third is that it is the latter only which is the niche which should be afforded to both references to the undertaking in that part of the judgment.

For my part, I favour the first of those interpretations. In the first place that would be in accordance with the law, and it does not seem to me to be necessarily the consequence of the circumstance that such cases as *Expresso Coffee Machine Co. Ltd v. Guardian Assurance Co. Ltd* were not mentioned in the judgment or, for that matter, cited at the hearing that the learned judge was unaware of the law on the subject. Secondly, it is desirable to give consistency to the different parts of the judgment if one can, and it does not seem to me to be extravagant to construe the words 'in order to ensure justice' as indicating an intention on the part of the learned judge to show that finding in favour of the landlords if an appropriate undertaking is given is a way of making sure that his judgment on that point is correct and if it is correct that ensures justice to the defeated party. Comparably, the second sentence of that paragraph, 'It is essential for the protection of the tenant ...' can be regarded as a view that it is the protection of the tenant against a possibly unjust decision which is being afforded by the learned judge on the giving of the undertaking, without which its evidential value would be diminished. If that is right then there is nothing in that part of the judgment to affect its validity. But even if that is wrong and it is the second of the suggested interpretations which is right, all that it means is that that last paragraph is a piece of unwarranted surplusage, indicating, if one will, an imperfect understanding of the law, but not detracting from the correct evaluation and use of the offering of the undertaking at the earlier stage. It is only if the third interpretation is right that this would carry the judgment down, or might carry the judgment down. For my part, I reject that interpretation.

The judgment of Asquith LJ in *Cunliffe* v. *Goodman* [1950] 2 KB 237 (see page 429, earlier) was also applied in:

EUROPAK (MIDLANDS) LTD v. TOWN CENTRE SECURITIES PLC

Chancery Division   (1985) 274 EG 289

A new tenancy of a multi-storey car park sought by the tenants was opposed by the landlords on the ground that they intended to occupy the premises for the purposes of a business to be carried on by them therein. The landlords were the lessees of a large development of retail shops, banks and leisure facilities for which the car park provided the parking accommodation. The landlords claimed that it would be advantageous for them to operate the car park themselves and submitted evidence from the minutes of their board meetings, from quotations for parking control equipment obtained from a supplier and by an affidavit sworn by their property director to show their intentions.

Held: The landlords had established a firm and settled intention to occupy the premises for the purpose of their business.

WARNER LJ: The issue that I have to decide today is whether in fact the defendant does have a present intention—and that means, as [counsel], who appears for the plaintiff pointed out, a fixed and settled intention—to occupy the premises for the purposes of a business which it intends to carry on.

The evidence as to that consists of an affidavit sworn by Mr Whitehead, the defendant's property director, on which he has been cross-examined, and also a few documents in an agreed bundle.

It appears from Mr Whitehead's affidavit that the multi-storey car park in question is in a complex in the centre of Leeds known as the Merrion Centre. The defendant is the lessee of the Merrion Centre under a number of building leases from the Leeds City Council, all of which are due to come to an end on 30 April 2087. The Merrion Centre is a large development of retail shops, banks and leisure facilities, for which the multi-storey car park in question provides the car-parking facilities. The defendant provides the management, maintenance and ancillary services for the various undertenants and, in a sense, for the public, at the Merrion Centre. I say 'in a sense' for the public because, as Mr Whitehead accepted in cross-examination, the defendant does not actually carry on at the Merrion Centre any business providing a direct service to the public, though it does things like cleaning the access roads and so forth.

The conclusion that, according to Mr Whitehead, the defendant has reached is that it would be of advantage to it to operate the car park itself, either because the car park could itself provide a profit for the defendant (and Mr Whitehead referred in that connection to a car park in Manchester which the defendant operates and which he described as very profitable) or because, so Mr Whitehead said, even if the car park were run at a loss, there might be an advantage in it to the defendant, for this reason: the car park is at present, so he told me, running at about 40 to 50% occupancy and, if the defendant were able, by adopting an appropriate pricing policy, to increase that substantially—possibly to double it—the effect would be to increase the rental value of all the shops in the Merrion Centre, and that would enure to the benefit of the defendant company as their landlord.

[Counsel for the plaintiff] submitted to me that the evidence—and in particular the documentary evidence—fell short of disclosing a fixed and settled intention on the part of the defendant to run this car park itself. He said that at most it disclosed a situation in which the defendant was contemplating the possibility of running the car park itself, and he referred me to the judgment of Asquith LJ in *Cunliffe* v. *Goodman* [1950] 2 KB 237 at pp 253 to 254, which, he told me, had been approved by the House of Lords.

Leaving aside, for the moment, the memorandum of association of the defendant, the documentary evidence consists of two categories of documents: first, a few minutes of board meetings of the defendant and, second, some quotations obtained by the defendant from suppliers or potential suppliers of such articles as parking control equipment, signs and electrical fittings, and for works to the lifts at the car park.

The board minutes, [counsel for the plaintiff] submitted, did not disclose a fixed and settled intention on the part of the defendant, until one came to a minute of the 12 December 1984. That is headed 'NCP Lease Negotiations' and it reads:

'Notwithstanding approaches from NCP for a new lease, it was resolved that we should pursue our court application for possession in view of the continuing and definite intention to occupy the premises for our own use.'

That minute, however, [counsel for the plaintiff] pointed out, was very recent and was clearly formulated with an eye on these proceedings.

The earliest relevant minute is one dated in September 1983. That reads:

'NCP Lease. No further progress had been made with Richard Parker of NCP but it was agreed that to preserve our position a notice should in any event be sent to NCP that we were proposing to take back the car park at the end of the lease for our own occupation.'

Mr Whitehead told me that, at that time, the defendant, although it had been approached by Mr Parker of NCP about a new lease, had in fact already decided to take the car park over itself. I think, however, that [counsel for the plaintiff] was right in suggesting that the minute itself did not disclose such a firm intention.

Then there is a minute in April 1984, headed 'NCP Lease' and recording that: 'Mr Whitehead reported that we were presently looking into setting up our own management with a view to running the car park ourselves.' That, [counsel for the plaintiff] suggested, evinced that the defendant was examining the possibility of running the car park itself, rather than implementing a firm decision to do so.

As to the quotations, [counsel for the plaintiff] pointed out that, except in the case of those for parking control equipment, they had been obtained simply from one supplier in each case. There appeared to have been no attempt to obtain competing quotations. That, he said, was surprising if there really was a firm intention to take over the management of the car park. Moreover, although the defendant's architect had been involved in the correspondence with those suppliers, there were no plans drawn by him for the implementation of the alleged decision to introduce new lighting and other equipment on the premises.

[Counsel for the plaintiff] also stressed the fact that the defendant had not begun recruiting staff. I find that point less impressive, first because, until these proceedings are over, the defendant cannot be sure of recovering possession of the premises, and second because, as is common ground, even if the plaintiff fails, as a result of the proceedings, to obtain an order for a new lease, it will be entitled to remain in possession of the premises for three months. That will give the defendant ample time to recruit staff.

As to the points made by [counsel for the plaintiff] on the documentary evidence, I have to bear in mind that what, in the end, matters is the intention of the defendant now. More importantly, I have to bear in mind that to accept [counsel for the plaintiff]'s contention would involve my saying that I disbelieve Mr Whitehead. Mr Whitehead did not, as it seemed to me, retreat at all in the course of his cross-examination from his position that there was a firm decision by the management and indeed the board of the defendant to take over and run this car park themselves. Mr Whitehead did not strike me as the sort of person who cannot be believed on his oath. It seemed to me that he remained totally unshaken and that the more points were put to him in an endeavour to shake him the more convincing his evidence became.

Finally, [counsel for the plaintiff] relied on a point based on the wording of the memorandum of association of the defendant. He confessed that he did not think it his strongest point. [Counsel] on behalf of the defendant accepted that the paragraph in its memorandum of association that could most appropriately be invoked as conferring power on it to run the car park was para 3 (2), which reads:

'To carry on or acquire any businesses similar to the businesses above-mentioned or which conveniently or advantageously be carried on or combined with them, or may be calculated directly or indirectly to enhance the value of or render more profitable any of the Company's property.'

The 'business above-mentioned' were, putting it shortly, the business of property owners and managers. [Counsel for the plaintiff's] submission was that the directors of the defendant could not, when they decided to carry on the business of a car park at the Merrion Centre, know whether it would prove to be one that could conveniently or advantageously be carried on or combined with its business as landlord of the Merrion Centre, or whether it would be calculated directly or indirectly to enhance the value or render more profitable any of the company's property.

I reject that submission. It amounts to saying that, on its true interpretation, para 3 (2) of the memorandum of association of the defendant means that its directors can never tell, when it embarks on a particular enterprise, whether or not that enterprise will be *intra vires*. That cannot, it seems to me, be right, particularly bearing in mind that in any business venture there is almost always an element of risk.

For those reasons I propose to declare, on the issue directed by the master's order to be tried, that the defendant has proved that it intends, if and when it obtains possession of this multi-storey car park, to occupy it for the purposes of running it itself.

The intention of a landlord company can be derived from the intention of its officers and agents.

H.L. BOLTON (ENGINEERING) CO. LTD v. T.J. GRAHAM & SONS LTD

Court of Appeal   [1957] 1 QB 159

DENNING LJ: The second question is whether the landlords have proved the necessary intention to occupy the holding for their own purposes. This point arises because the landlords are a limited company. [Counsel for the tenants] says that there was no meeting of any board of directors to express the landlords' intention, and that therefore the landlords—the company—cannot say that it has the necessary intention.

[Counsel for the tenants] says that there must at least be a board meeting. In view of the recent decision of this court in *Austin Reed Ltd* v. *Royal Assurance Co. Ltd*, he has to concede that the decision of the board need not formally be recorded in a minute, but he says that, even though not formally recorded, there must be a board meeting by which there is a collective decision, and it is not sufficient that individual directors should individually be of one mind.

A company may in many ways be likened to a human body. It has a brain and nerve centre which controls what it does. It also has hands which hold the tools and act in accordance with directions from the centre. Some of the people in the company are mere servants and agents who are nothing more than hands to do the work and cannot be said to represent the mind or will. Others are directors and managers who represent the directing mind and will of the company, and control what it does. The state of mind of these managers is the state of mind of the company and is treated by the law as such. So you will find that in cases where the law requires personal fault as a condition of liability in tort, the fault of the manager will be the personal fault of the company. That is made clear in Lord Haldane's speech in *Lennard's Carrying Co. Ltd* v. *Asiatic Petroleum Co. Ltd*. So also in the criminal law, in cases where the law requires a guilty mind as a condition of a criminal offence, the guilty mind of the directors or the managers will render the company itself guilty. That is shown by *Rex* v. *I.C.R. Haulage Ltd*, to which we were referred and in which the court said:

'Whether in any particular case there is evidence to go to a jury that the criminal act of an agent, including his state of mind, intention, knowledge or belief is the act of the company ... must depend on the nature of the charge, the relative position of the officer or agent, and the other relevant facts and circumstances of the case.'

So here, the intention of the company can be derived from the intention of its officer and agents. Whether their intention is the company's intention depends on the nature of the matter under consideration, the relative position of the officer or agent and the other relevant facts and circumstances of the case. Approaching the matter in that way, I think that, although there was no board meeting, nevertheless, having regard to the standing of these directors in control of the business of the company, having regard to the other facts and circumstances which we know, whereby plans had been prepared and much work done, the judge was entitled to infer that the intention of the company was to occupy the holding for their own purposes.

In **Birch Ltd v. P.B. Sloane Ltd** (1956) 167 EG 283, His Honour Judge Daynes pointed out that proof of the landlord company's intention could not be given by the oral testimony of the secretary and directors and he adjourned the hearing in order to enable the landlord to put their house in order by convening the necessary meetings of the board of directors and passing the necessary resolutions. In the course of his judgment he said:

'I pointed out it was no good one director or one secretary going into the box and saying what the Company intended. The intention of the Company is shown by a resolution either of the directors, or, if it is beyond their powers, by the Company in general meeting. In this case a resolution by the Company in general meeting is not necessary. This is within the powers of the directors, who have power to manage the Company's business.'

This decision is, therefore, authority for the view that a landlord cannot intend a course of action requiring approval at general meeting if such approval has not yet been obtained. But if the directors have the necessary power, proof of a board resolution is unnecessary where there is other evidence of a firm decision: see the *Bolton Engineering* case, above, where work had already begun on adjoining property.

In **Manchester Garages Ltd v. Petrofina (UK) Ltd** (1974) 233 EG 509, the landlords opposed the grant of a new tenancy on the ground that they intended to occupy the premises for the purpose of their own business. The only evidence of their intention was given by the landlords' regional manager who had full authority to make such decisions and was totally responsible for the landlords' affairs in the region.

Held: If a contemplated act was within an agent's authority, then his intention was that of the company for that purpose, unless shown to be inconsistent with a contrary intention in a superior authority.

BUCKLEY LJ said: The contention in support of the appeal had been that since the landlords were an incorporate body, their intention must be found either in the form of a decision of the board, or of an intention in the minds of the members of the board, or, it was said, an intention formed by an authorised agent of the board provided he was what counsel described as 'a head-office mind representing the mind or will of the company.' Counsel argued that Mr Moodie was a regional manager, that he was not at the nerve centre of the company, and that his decision could not be regarded as establishing the intention of the company, because it could be over-ridden by the board. He (counsel) submitted that the intention of an agent of the company, acting within his authority, was not the intention of the company so long as his decision could be over-ridden. Reference was made to a number of authorities bearing upon the way in which an intention of a corporate body could be established in evidence. Those authorities showed that the question to be decided in such a case as this was whether the landlord at the date of his notice of opposition and at the date of the hearing had a firm and settled intention to carry out whatever particular activity it was said that he did intend to carry out, whether it be occupying premises for the purpose of his own business, demolishing them, or whatever it might be. Particular mention might be made of the decision of the Court of Appeal in *H L Bolton (Engineering) Co. Ltd* v. *T J Graham & Sons Ltd* [1957] 1 QB 159, in which, Mr Maddocks submitted, the agents of the company, whose minds were said to constitute the mind of the company, were agents at a directorial level.

He (his Lordship) thought that the agents in that case were acting not as directors in what they did, but as managers. Denning LJ in his judgment appeared to be considering their actions and their states of mind in their managerial capacity. There certainly was evidence before the court in the present case that Mr Moodie had complete responsibility for the conduct of the company's business within his region, and the question of what should be done with the Clayton Service Station was a matter which arose within his region and was within the ambit of his authority. The judge proceeded, quite properly, on that basis; indeed, it did not appear that that view of the matter was at all disputed before him. In his (Buckley LJ's) opinion, if some act which was contemplated was one which was within the authority of an agent of a company whose decision was said to evidence the intention of the company, if it was a matter within his authority to carry out without any further authority of any superior authority in the company, such as the managing director or the board of directors, then his intention was the intention of the company for the relevant purpose, at any rate if it was not shown to be inconsistent with some concurrent contrary intention in ome superior authority who could gainsay him in respect of the particular act. If the intention of the agent was shown to be a firm and settled intention—which was not, as he (his Lordship) thought, by any means the same as an irrevocable intention or one which could not be overruled—then it was the firm and settled intention of the company. In the present case, the evidence indicated that it was Mr Moodie's firm and settled intention that the company should recover possession of this service station and should carry on trade there itself. There was no indication that the decision of Mr Moodie was contrary to any policy or any project of any higher authority in the company so that he would be likely to have been over-ruled in the matter. In these circumstances, in his (Buckley LJ's) judgment, the judge was fully justified in treating that evidence as being evidence of a firm and settled intention on the part of the landlord company to use the premises, when possession of them was recovered, for the purpose of the landlord's own business.

In **Espresso Coffee Machine Co. v. Guardian Assurance Co.** [1959] 1 WLR 250, tenants of business premises applied for the grant of a new tenancy which was opposed by the landlords relying on section 30 (1) (g). The landlords' board of directors passed a resolution stating that they intended to occupy the premises and the landlords also gave an undertaking to the court that on obtaining possession they would occupy them.

Held: The landlords had shown an honest, present intention to occupy the premises.

LORD EVERSHED MR: The judge expressed his conclusion as follows. After observing that the word in the section is 'intention' (more strictly, if I may be forgiven for the slight correction, it is 'intends'; but that does not matter), without any qualifying epithet, he said that an 'intention,' to satisfy the section, must be 'honest,' 'present,' and 'real.' I do not think he left out any characteristic which he should have borne in mind. He then said:

'As I understand it, at the time of the resolution'—that is, February—'the possibility of obtaining a lease of No. 199 had already been mooted. Nevertheless, the board expressed the intention to occupy No. 227, not contingently, in the event of nothing better turning up, but absolutely, and they were willing to offer an undertaking to the court, and authorised that to be done.'

Then, after referring to *Betty's Cafés Ltd* v. *Phillips Furnishing Stores Ltd* and *Lennox* v. *Bell* in which undertakings had been offered, the judge proceeded:

'But if the Guardian Assurance Co. gives an undertaking, there is no question of its power to honour it, and I think there is no doubt that it will honour it. It is not the sort of company whose undertakings in a suitable case the court would hesitate to accept. It is not suggested that it could not carry out the undertaking if it wished. Therefore, as counsel at the Bar today is still authorised to make this offer to me and to the applicants, I must take the offer at its face value. If that be the case, I do not see how I can any longer doubt that the intention today exists. Whether by the end of the year it will exist any longer, I do not know. The tenants may so harass the landlord that the landlord will change its mind.'

The end of the year has passed, and we know that, as [counsel for the landlords] has told us, he is still instructed, if necessary, to repeat the undertaking: the same intention continues to exist. But that is not the point that has to be decided. The question is: Was the judge entitled to find as a fact (as he did) that at the date of the hearing before him—27 June 1958—the landlords did intend to occupy these premises and get into possession for their own business? and I think, for reasons which I have stated, that the judge was amply justified in so concluding.

ROMER LJ: If a landlord desires to rely on section 30 (1) (g) of the Act, he has to show that on the termination of the current tenancy he 'intends' to occupy the holding for business purposes; and it has been well established now, on the authorities, first that such an intention must exist at the hearing of the tenant's appliction, and secondly, that the intention must be a real intention, fixed and settled. Having regard to the affidavit of the deputy general manager and to his evidence in the witness-box—to which my Lord has referred—one would have thought *prima facie* that even on that alone the two requirements to which I have referred were satisfied. Nothing could be clearer than the evience which he gave, and he repeated more than once, in categorical terms, in the evidence that he gave on behalf of his company, that his company did intend, if they got possession of 227, to go into occupation. When one adds to that the fact that counsel was authorised to offer, and did offer, to the court the undertaking in the form which my Lord has read, the matter really seems to be put beyond any doubt. Some undertakings, of course, are unacceptable. There was a case—one of the cases to which Harman J referred [*Lennox* v. *Bell*]—where the court was offered an undertaking which it knew perfectly well the person who offered it was incapable of carrying out. When one gets a responsible body like one has here, no such criticism can be levelled. It was an undertaking which the judge was prepared to accept, and which he did accept; and in regard to such an undertaking I would only quote a passage from a judgment of Danckwerts J to which [counsel for the landlords] referred us, in the second *Betty's Cafés* case, in which he said: 'The undertaking seems to me to compel fixity of intention.' I know of no better way of describing it than that description that Danckwerts J gave; and it appears to me that, that undertaking having been given and accepted, it is perfectly decisive of the fixity of intention which I agree is a requisite element.

In **Lightcliffe and District Cricket and Lawn Tennis Club v. Walton** (1977) 245 EG 393, a cricket club applied for a new tenancy of three and a half acres of the landlord's property, the remainder of which was used as a farm. The landlord opposed the grant on the ground that he intended to use the land for his business as a farmer. He gave an undertaking to that effect to the county court judge who, on the other hand, heard evidence that the landlord's existing land was only farmed to 50 per cent. capacity.

Held: The landlord did not have a present, fixed and genuine intention to farm the land.

STEPHENSON LJ: The question in this case for this court is that which was stated by Lord Evershed MR in the *Expresso Coffee* v. *Guardian Assurance* case [1959] 1 All ER 459 at p 463. The question was 'Was the judge entitled to find as a fact, as he did, that at the date of the hearing before him ... the landlords intended to occupy [*this site*] for the purposes of their own business?'

In my judgment, the judge asked himself the right question and he was entitled to arrive at the answer at which he did. There was evidence before him which supported an honest or genuine or settled or fixed intention. There was the undertaking, and there was undoubtedly the ability of the landlord to carry it out. But there was also evidence to the contrary. There was evidence that he had no need whatever for this field. There was evidence that he had taken no preparatory steps to carry it out, such as the steps which were taken by the resolutions of the companies in the cases to which [counsel for the appellants] has referred us. [Counsel for the appellants] has failed to satisfy me that the judge discarded the undertaking because of the language which he uses about it to which my Lord Shaw LJ, has referred, or that the learned judge failed to consider the ability of the landlord to carry out his intention simply because the learned judge did not mention it; nor has he satisfied me that the judge regarded the absence of need as conclusive simply because it was the reason which he gave in that manuscript note at the end of his judgment.

Finally, he has not satisfied me that the learned judge regarded the intention as genuine in the sense of being *bona fide* and fixed simply because he was kind enough not to say everything which he thought about it. It would, in my judgment, be quite wrong for this court to hold that giving an undertaking, whoever gives it and in whatever circumstances, creates any legal presumption in favour of a landlord. Equally, it would be wrong to hold that uncontradicted evidence of a landlord's ability to carry out his intention creates such a presumption. Nor are we bound by any authority which has been cited to us so to decide against commonsense and to treat as a matter of law what is, it seems to me, quite clearly a question of fact.

Support for the view that an undertaking is not conclusive cannot possibly be derived, as [counsel for the appellants] sought to derive it, from the observations of Romer LJ in the case of *Expresso Coffee*. It is quite clear from what that learned Lord Justice said at p 463 of the report that when he is talking about an undertaking being perfectly decisive of fixity of intention, he is referring to the kind of undertaking which had been given by a responsible body like the landlords in the case of *Expresso Coffee* and in the earlier case decided by Danckwerts J of *Betty's Cafés Ltd* v. *Phillips Furnishing Stores Ltd.*

Equally, I find it impossible to draw the conclusion which [counsel for the appellants] asked us to draw, that the ability to carry out an intention proves its existence, from the decision or observations of the Lords Justices in the case of *Reohorn* v. *Barry Corporation*, reported in [1956] 1 WLR 845 to which he also referred. In that case, Denning LJ said at p 849 that '"intention" connotes the ability to carry it into effect.' In that case, there was no ability to carry the intention into effect and so the intention was negatived. That does not in my judgment help us to decide the converse that where there is ability to carry out intention the judge ought in the absence of any other circumstances to find that the intention is genuine and settled.

I can detect no error of law in the judgment of the learned judge.

The landlord must intend to occupy the holding for the purpose of his business 'to be carried on by him therein'.

HUNT v. DECCA NAVIGATOR CO. LTD

Chancery Division   (1972) 222 EG 625

PLOWMAN J: The defendants opposed the plaintiff's application for a new lease under the Landlord and Tenant Act 1954, on the ground in section 30 (1) (g) of the Act. They said that they required the site for the purposes of a business carried on by them, which in this case was a car-park for employees and visitors to companies in the Decca group, whose premises adjoined the site. The Decca group had between 80 and 90 subsidiaries, the radar, record and navigator companies being among them. The only issue was whether section 30 (1) (g) applied. The plaintiff said first that assuming the defendants intended to occupy the site, nevertheless they did not intend to do so for the purposes of their business 'to be carried on by them therein.' He conceded that 'therein' included 'thereon,' but submitted that the proposed car-park was auxiliary to a business which was not carried on 'therein,' or 'thereon,' but elsewhere. The court was unable to accept that submission. The business in question need not be independent—the storage or the holding of equipment manufactured elsewhere would fall within paragraph (g), for example. Any large business concern was expected as part of its general business operation to provide reasonable facilities for its employees. A staff canteen or other building for staff would come within paragraph (g), and there was no reason why that should not be equally true of a staff car-park. That was not using a car-park for a business carried on elsewhere, but using a car-park for a business carried on on the site and elsewhere as well. On the evidence, there was at present space for 225 cars, but no doubt that would more than double with the number of persons employed.

Provided that the landlord intends to occupy the entire holding on termination of the tenancy, it is immaterial that he does not intend to use the entire holding immediately for his business.

METHOD DEVELOPMENT LTD v. JONES

Court of Appeal   [1971] 1 WLR 168

The landlords held the lease of a floor of a building, using part of it for their own business purposes and subletting the remainder to tenants. Wishing to extend their own user of the premises for purposes of their business, they served a section 25 notice on the tenants stating that an application for a new tenancy would be opposed on the ground in section 30 (1) (g) of the 1954 Act. The landlords intended to use about a third of the sublet premises immediately and most of it within about a year but had no plans as to some 400 square feet.

Held: Section 30 (1) (g) covered a situation where landlords intended, within a reasonable time from the termination of a lease, to enter into occupation of all the holding and to use a part of it for the purposes of their business.

SALMON LJ: I think that paragraph (g) of section 30 (1) of the Act is not perhaps very felicitously worded. Its meaning could perhaps have been made clearer than it is. The same criticism is possible in respect of much of this Act. But I have little doubt that paragraph (g) must cover a situation such as the present where the landlords intend at the termination of the lease—which must mean within a reasonable time from the date of its termination—to enter into occupation of all the holding and use a part of it for the purposes of their business. I consider that the evidence shows that these landlords intended to occupy all the holding in the sense in which the word 'occupy' is used in paragraph (g) although they would be carrying on their business only in part of it. That seems to me to be 'occupying the holding partly for the purposes of a business to be carried on therein.'

FENTON ATKINSON LJ: Did the landlords prove that they intended to occupy the whole holding of 1866 square feet for the purposes of their business? They proved that they intended to use for their business at once some 644 square feet. They established, as it seems to me, by clear evidence a present, settled intention over the next 12 months to expand so as actually to use a total of 1466 square feet, and that meant they had no present plans as to the remaining 400 square feet. [Counsel for the tenant] says that that was not enough—that in order to succeed under section 30 (1) (g) the landlords must show an intention to make actual use of the whole of the holding. I cannot agree with this submission. It may be that it is very much a matter of impression, but it seems to me plain that you can occupy a holding for the purposes of your business under section 30 (1) (g) even though you may not intend at present to make actual physical use of the whole of the holding. There is a settled intention here to use a very substantial part, something like four-fifths, and, just as you can plainly occupy a dwelling-house as your residence even though you leave a couple of rooms empty, I think there that these landlords proved an intention to occupy the whole of this holding for the purposes of their business.

In **Willis v. British Commonwealth Universities' Assoc.** [1965] 1 QB 140, the Court of Appeal held that a landlord company may establish that it intends to occupy the holding for the purposes of a business to be carried on by it therein, notwithstanding that another body will also be occupying the holding and that the landlord company is in liquidation, so long as its activities are being preserved and will continue for a substantial time.

In **Jones v. Jenkins**, The Times, 14 December 1985, the Court of Appeal held that a landlord could not oppose the grant of a new tenancy under section 30 (1) (g), on the ground that she wished to occupy the holding for the purpose of a business to be carried on there, if that business consisted of reletting parts of the holding as residential flats since she could not then be said to be occupying them.

In considering whether the landlord intends to occupy the holding for the purpose of his business, it is necessary to have regard to the definition of 'the holding' in section 23 (3) of the 1954 Act as 'the property comprised in the tenancy'.

NURSEY v. P. CURRIE (DARTFORD) LTD

Court of Appeal [1959] 1 WLR 273

Premises, consisting of some small buildings in a yard, were let on a quarterly tenancy and were used by the tenants to store and vulcanise tyres. The landlords, served a section 25 notice on the tenants relying on section 30 (1) (g) in opposing the grant of a new tenancy. The landlords intended to demolish the buildings and develop the property as a petrol filling station for their use. At the hearing of the tenants' application, it was contended that the landlords were not within the terms of their notice because they did not intend to occupy the holding. The county court judge held that the proposed demolition of the buildings was immaterial since the holding comprised the land on which the buildings stood and the landlords intended to occupy the land. The tenants appealed.

Held: The landlords had to prove an intention to occupy 'the holding' defined by section 23 (3) as 'the property comprised in the tenancy', namely, the small buildings in the yard, which they were unable to do.

Wynn-Parry J: In paragraph (g) of subsection (1) of section 30, there is a reference, as there is in the preceding paragraph (f), to 'the holding,' and the phrase 'the holding' is defined in section 23 (3) as meaning 'in relation to a tenancy to which this Part of this Act,' namely, Part II, 'applies,' 'the property comprised in the tenancy.' In paragraph (g) the words 'the holding' must be read as interpreted in the light of that definition, and 'the holding' is one which the landlord intends to occupy 'for the purposes, or partly for the purposes, of a business to be carried on by him therein, or as his residence.' It seems to me that that language circumscribes the use of the phrase 'the holding' in that paragraph, and makes it necessary to concentrate the whole of one's attention on the particular piece of land, whether it has buildings on it or not, which is the subject-matter of the tenancy in question. So viewed, it appears to me that the contention for the landlords in the present case is too wide, and that when one is looking at the material time at 'the holding' under paragraph (g), it is not permissible to take into account the wider scheme which the landlords had in mind, and merely to treat the land comprised in the holding as land which, in one way or another, will be used for the purpose of the wider undertaking.

Willmer LJ: It is not now in dispute that the landlords here proved a case within paragraph (f) of section 30 (1) of the Act of 1954, in the sense that they proved an intention to demolish or reconstruct the premises in question. Unhappily for them, no reliance was placed on paragraph (f), and no mention of paragraph (f) was made in the notice which they served under section 25 of the Act. The only ground put forward in the notice which they served was the ground that: 'on the termination of the current tenancy we intend to occupy the premises for the purposes, or partly for the purposes, of a business to be carried on by us therein.' The words there used follow approximately, although not exactly, the wording used in paragraph (g) of the same subsection of the Act. It was contended on behalf of the landlords, and was held by the judge, that in addition to proving a case, as they admittedly had, under paragraph (f), they had, in the circumstances, also proved a case under paragraph (g), in the sense that they proved an intention, prevailing at the time of the hearing, to occupy the holding for the purposes of a business to be carried on by them therein. It seems to me, however, that so to hold does violence to the wording of the paragraph. I have said that the words used in the landlords' notice do not exactly correspond to the words used in paragraph (g). [His Lordship read the paragraph, and continued:] The important word for the purposes of the present case is the word 'holding,' and that is defined by section 23 (3) of the Act of 1954 as meaning 'the property comprised in the tenancy.'

It appears to me, therefore, that in applying paragraph (g) of section 30 (1), one must look at the particular holding comprised in the particular tenancy which is before the court in the particular case. Here the building is described in the tenancy agreement as

'the buildings forming part of premises known as No. 248, Broadway, Bexley Heath in the county of Kent, and comprising the drivers' room, can store, pump and the spirit store, together with the right of ingress and egress thereto.'

In relation to this case, therefore, paragraph (g) must be construed as though, instead of the word 'holding,' those words, which I have read from the tenancy agreement, were set out in the paragraph.

The question to be determined, then, is whether the landlords proved that on the termination of the current tenancy they intended to occupy

'the buildings forming part of premises known as No. 248, Broadway, Bexley Heath in the county of Kent, and comprising the drivers' room, can store, pump and the spirit store'

for the purposes, or partly for the purposes, of a business to be carried on by them therein. To that there can be only one answer. The only intention proved was an intention to demolish and reconstruct. It appears to me that, on what I conceive to be the true construction of paragraph (g), it is straining language to say that the landlords brought themselves within it.

The foregoing decision was distinguished in:

CAM GEARS LTD v. CUNNINGHAM

Court of Appeal   (1981) 258 EG 749

The tenants applied for the grant of a new tenancy of a car park used in connection with their business. The new tenancy was opposed by the landlord who wished to occupy the land for the expansion of his business of testing vehicles for the MOT test. The tenants contended that the landlord did not intend to occupy 'the holding' within the meaning of section 30 (1) (g) of the 1954 Act since the landlord's proposal, which included the erection of a building on the site for a workshop, office, waiting rooms and vehicle inspection pits, was the creation of a new holding and not an occupation of 'the holding'.

Held: 'The holding' consisted of the vacant site on which the landlord proposed to erect a building, so that he would in fact occupy 'the holding' plus something else.

OLIVER LJ: The appellants' contention before the learned judge and in this court was that since the only ground of opposition to the grant of a new tenancy under the Act specified in the respondent landlord's notice was that which appears in section 30 (1) (g), the landlord had to show that his intention was not just to occupy the site, but that he was to occupy 'the holding'; that the holding consisted of the present vacant site used as a car park and that the proposed erection on that site of a new building to be used for the purpose of a testing workshop constituted the erection of a new and different holding and that therefore the landlord was not proposing to occupy 'the holding' for the purposes of the business.

The erection of the proposed building was, no doubt, a major work of construction, which could be carried out only if the landlord obtained possession, and it might indeed have justified opposition to the grant of a new tenancy under section 30 (1) (f); but that was not the ground that was specified, and since the only ground relied upon was the ground in subparagraph (g), that is the ground upon which the landlord must rely.

The learned judge rejected that contention, which was based upon the decision of this court in the case of *Nursey* v. *P Currie (Dartford) Ltd* [1959] 1 WLR 273. That was a case which bears a superficial resemblance to the present case, in that the landlord's notice in that case was confined to the ground specified in section 30 (1) (g), and what the landlord company proposed to do was to demolish the existing buildings, which were standing in a yard which was occupied by the landlord, and redevelop the site as part of a petrol station which it proposed to carry on there. The Court of Appeal held that the ground of opposition was not made out; and it did so because of the limiting definition of the word 'holding' in section 23 (3) of the Act.

That subsection defines the word 'holding' as meaning 'the property comprised in the tenancy'—I close the quotation there; there is some more but it is not material for present purposes. The court held in that case that that definition included the existing buildings. The landlord, since it intended to remove the existing buildings and replace them with others, did not therefore intend to occupy 'the holding' but intended to occupy the new buildings to be erected on the land forming part only of 'the holding' viewed as a totality—at any rate, that is what I apprehend is the ratio of the decision in the *Nursey* case, and that is the view of it which was adopted by this court in the case of *Method Developments Ltd* v. *Jones* [1971] 1 WLR 168; I refer particularly to the judgment of Salmon LJ, as he then was, in that case.

I confess that the *Nursey* decision is one which I find far from easy to understand. The only argument, so far as can be deduced from the report at p 275, had been that since the landlords intended to demolish the buildings, they could not be intending to occupy 'the holding' which included the buildings. But Wynn-Parry J, who delivered the first judgment, seems to have taken the view, at any rate on one reading of his judgment, that it was fatal to the landlord's claim that the holding was to be occupied as part of a larger complex and not as a separate holding on its own. He said, at p 277:

'It seems to me that that language circumscribes the use of the phrase "the holding" in that paragraph—that being subparagraph (g)—and makes it necessary to concentrate the whole of one's attention on the particular piece of land, whether it has buildings on it or not, which is the subject-matter of the tenancy in question. So viewed, it appears to me that the contention for the landlords in the present case is too wide, and that when one is looking at the material time at "the holding" under paragraph (g), it is not permissible to take into account the wider scheme which the landlords had in mind, and merely to treat the land comprised in the holding as land which, in one way or another, will be used for the purpose of the wider undertaking.'

I cannot think that the learned judge can have intended to do more than to answer the question, which is: Is the holding which the landlord intends to occupy the same holding as that comprised in the tenancy? Construed in the wider sense that I have indicated, it would follow that a landlord who carried on a business next door to the demised premises and who wanted to occupy those premises as one with his existing shop for an expanding business, would be unable to rely upon section 30 (1) (g) and would be able to resist a new lease only if he intended to reconstruct. For my part, I cannot ascribe so eccentric an intention to the legislature. Certainly, Willmer LJ confined his judgment to the narrow ground that the definition of 'the holding' simply involved reading into the subsection, in place of the words 'the holding', the parcels of the lease—a ratio which hardly helps the present appellants, since the lease in the present case merely refers to 'all that piece or parcel of land delineated for the purposes of identification only on the plan annexed hereto and thereon edged red', and that is precisely what the landlords intends to occupy.

But even if I am wrong in the limits within which, as I think, the judgment of Wynn-Parry J must be read, and even assuming that the concurrence in that decision of Hodson LJ renders the wider construction binding upon us, it still does not seem to me to help the appellants in the instant case. There is no wider scheme here in which the holding is proposed to be incorporated. The landlord simply intends to place a building on the site and to use the whole site, together with the new building, for the purposes of his business.

[Counsel for the appellants], who has argued this appeal, if I may say so, with conspicuous frankness and acumen, seeks to steer a course midway between the construction of Wynn-Parry J's judgment to which I have referred and the very limited ratio adopted by Willmer LJ. He suggests that the ratio of the *Nursey* case is that you have to look at the holding as it is at the termination of the tenancy and to ask yourself the question: Does the landlord intend to occupy the holding for the purposes of *his* business in substantially the identical condition as it was at the date of termination? If he intends to occupy the whole of it, but to make any material alteration to its condition, then he is intending to occupy a different holding.

For my part, I find myself unable to follow [counsel for the appellants] through the gap which he thus seeks to make between the prongs of Morton's fork. Whatever may be the true ratio of the *Nursey* case, I am unable to extract that from it and indeed to do so would, I think, be to attribute a wholly irrational and capricious intention to the legislature. Accepting as I must that *Nursey* is binding upon this court, I certainly do not feel disposed to strain it beyond the narrowest limits within which it is capable of being confined.

I think that the determining feature of the *Nursey* decision was not the *purpose* for which the holdings were occupied by the tenant, or the particular condition at the time of the determination of the tenancy, but the fact that the holding consisted of the buildings which, under the landlord's proposals, were to be demolished. That may or may not have been a logical or reasonable construction of the section, and I bear in mind Salmon LJ's reservation in the *Metal Construction* case, as to whether it was correctly decided, although the combined industry of counsel has not succeeded in unearthing the inconsistent unreported case in the Court of Appeal to which Salmon LJ referred. But it cannot in any event, in my judgment, have any possible application to a case such as the present, where 'the holding' consists solely of a vacant site upon which the landlord proposes to erect a building, so that what he will occupy is 'the holding' plus something else. He proposes to occupy everything that is there at the moment, with the sole exception of two lengths of topsoil and subsoil which will be removed to sink the inspection pits. *Nursey* v. *Currie* is, in my judgment, of no assistance to the tenant in such circumstances.

21.5 (b) The intended business must be the landlord's business unless one of the statutory exceptions applies

FRISH LTD v. BARCLAYS BANK LTD

Court of Appeal   [1955] 2 QB 541

Tenants of business premises applied for the grant of a new tenancy. The freehold reversion was vested in trustees on trust for sale, the income of the proceeds of sale being held on discretionary trusts for a number of persons. One of the objects of the discretionary trust had entered into an agreement with the trustee landlords to take a tenancy of the premises at a rent in excess of that paid by the tenants. The trustee landlords objected to the grant of a new tenancy to the tenants on the ground specified in section 30 (1) (g) of the 1954 Act.

Held:

(1) Some limit had to be put on the provision in section 41 (2) of the 1954 Act, which provided that 'where the landlord's interest is held on trust the references in paragraph (g) of subsection (1) of section 30 of this Act to the landlord shall be construed as including references to the beneficiaries under the trust or any of them ...' Any person having any beneficial interest in the premises however remote was not entitled under paragraph (g) to oppose the grant of a new tenancy. The beneficiary who intended to occupy must have such interest under the trusts as either to entitle him to be put in occupation or to justify the trustees on his application in letting him into occupation.

(2) Since the trustee landlords were proposing to grant a tenancy to an individual, who happened to have a beneficial interest as one of the objects of a discretionary trust, and that individual's occupation would have no reference at all to his beneficial interest, which could not of itself give to him any right of occupation, the landlord's objection based on section 30 (1) (g) as applied to a trust under section 41 (2) was not made good.

JENKINS LJ: I agree with [counsel for the tenant] that some limit must be put upon the meaning of the words 'the beneficiaries under the trust or any of them.' In my view it is impossible to hold that any person having any beneficial interest in the premises, however remote, can oppose the grant of a new tenancy under paragraph (g). I think that the interest of the beneficiary must be an interest under the trust on the strength of which he intends to occupy.

If [counsel for the landlord's] argument were accepted, the most remarkable consequences would ensue. One might, for example, have a case where the landlord's interest was settled on trust for one person for life, with remainder to another. If [counsel for the landlord's] argument is right, the reversioner could come forward and meet the tenant's application for a new lease on the ground that he, the reversioner, being a beneficiary by virtue of his interest in remainder, intended to occupy the holding, and thereupon, provided the trustee could be prevailed upon to grant him a new tenancy and, I suppose, to announce to the court his intention of granting such a tenancy, an objection under section 30 (1) (g), to the grant of a new lease would be made good.

Again, one might have a case where the interest of the beneficiary, although in possession, was an interest wholly irrelevant to any right to occupy the premises; as, for example, the case of a mere annuitant.

I find it unnecessary to attempt any exhaustive definition of the kinds of beneficial interest which would suffice to satisfy the section, but, as I have said, some limit must, in my view, be put on the wide meaning of the words 'the beneficiaries under the trust or any of them.' As some limit must be placed upon the words, it seems to me that in the context, and having regard to the manifest intention of paragraph (g), the limit must be, broadly speaking, of the nature suggested by [counsel for the tenant]. That is to say, the beneficiary, who intends to occupy, must have such an interest under the trust as either to entitle him to be put in occupation, or, at all events, to justify the trustees on his application, if they think fit to do so, in letting him into occupation. That would cover, besides the case of an absolute beneficial owner with the legal estate outstanding in a trustee, such interests as that of a life tenant.

In cases of settlements otherwise than by trust for sale no question could often arise, for in general the tenant for life under such a settlement combines in himself for a purpose of this sort the character of trustee and beneficiary. Again, I think, the class of beneficiaries with which paragraph (g) is concerned might well include a person entitled to a life interest in the proceeds of sale of the premises, the premises being held on trust for sale as in the present case.

This is a case of a trust for sale, but the person claiming as beneficiary has not got a life interest in the income of the fund. He merely has during his life the possibility of receiving such payments, if any, as the trustees may from time to time think fit to make to him in exercise of their discretion. That nebulous right or *spes*, as one might almost term it, clearly could not of itself give to this beneficiary any right to occupy the premises. It might conceivably be possible that if the trustees, in the exercise of their discretion, had decided, until such time as they might decide otherwise, to pay Mr Parnes the income of the holding in question and had further determined that for the time being they would allow him to be in occupation of the premises, treating the rent which the premises would otherwise have realized as set off against payments made, or notionally made, to him in exercise of their discretion, and if Mr Parnes had then expressed his intention of occupying in accordance with that arrangement, he could have been brought within section 30 (1) (*g*), as applied to trusts by section 41 (2), precarious though his right of occupation might be. But no such arrangement has been proposed by the trustees in the present case. They have not taken the view that they could properly let Mr Parnes into occupation on terms such as those to which I have referred. Their proposal is simply to grant to Mr Parnes a tenancy of the premises, and they say that because Mr Parnes happens to be a beneficiary under the settlement, in the sense that he is one of the objects of the discretionary trust, their intention to grant him a tenancy, and his intention to occupy as tenant, suffice to support the objection under paragraph (*g*). I find it impossible to accept that conclusion. This not a case where a beneficiary intends to occupy in right of his beneficial interest; it is a case in which trustee landlords propose to grant a tenancy to an individual who, it so happens, has a beneficial interest as one of the objects of a discretionary trust in the proceeds of sale in the premises under the trust for sale. That intended occupation, as it seems to me, would have no relevance at all to the beneficial interest, such as it is, of Mr Parnes under the settlement—an interest which could not of itself give him any right of occupation whatever.

Accordingly, I take the view that, on the true construction of the section, the objection based on paragraph (*g*) of sub-section (1) of section 30, as applied to the case of trusts by sub-section (2) of section 41, is not made good.

Note: This decision was applied in *Carshalton Beeches Bowling Club* v. *Cameron* (1979) 249 EG 1279, CA. See also: *Sevenarts* v. *Busvine* [1968] 1 WLR 1929.

The other two statutory exceptions are:
(1) Where the landlord has a controlling interest in a company and it is intended that the company will occupy—section 30 (3): see: *Harvey Textiles Ltd* v. *Hillel* (1979) 249 EG 1063.
(2) Where the landlord is a company and the business is to be carried on by another company in the same group—section 42 (3).

The carrying on of a business by the landlord in partnership with his wife is a carrying on of a business by the landlord himself within the meaning of section 30 (1) (g) of the 1954 Act.

IN RE CROWHURST PARK

Chancery Division   [1974] 1 WLR 583

GOULDING J: The defendant has given evidence and been cross-examined and I find without hesitation that he has a genuine and substantial intention for the occupation of the several premises for the purposes of a business. The real objection that is made by the plaintiff to the contention of the defendant is that in the plaintiff's submission the defendant wants the occupation of the premises for a business to be carried on not by himself alone, but in partnership with his wife.

The expressions used by the defendant in cross-examination were, as one might expect in the case of a husband and wife living happily together, not altogether unambiguous as regards partnership. On the other hand there is, in my judgment, a significant piece of evidence in the shape of a printed form of application for caravan pitches which the defendant says he has had printed with a view to using it in the business that he desires to pursue. It is headed: 'Site Application Form. To: J. P. and E. J. Simmons. Please reserve a site for my caravan at Crowhurst Park' etc. Although the point is not altogether an easy one, taking that form put in evidence by the defendant together with his oral evidence, I find that his present intention does relate to a business to be carried on by the defendant in partnership with his wife. However, in my judgment that is not an obstacle to his contention here. The defendant, in the ordinary use of language, will nonetheless occupy the premises and will nonetheless carry on business in the premises for the existence of the partnership. Where two persons carry on business in common as partners each of them occupies the firm's premises and each of them carries on business. Accordingly, the analogy between the present controversy which settles on the words 'business to be carried on by him' and the dispute considered by the Court of Appeal in *Clift* v. *Taylor* [1948] 2 KB 394, is not a false one. It was there held on a different statutory enactment relating to the rights of tenants that occupation by a firm of which the landlord was a partner was occupation by the landlord himself within the meaning of the enactment. Similarly, I hold here that the carrying on of a business by the defendant in partnership with his wife will be carrying on of business by the defendant himself within the meaning of section 30 (1) (g).

In **Tunstall v. Steigman** [1962] 2 QB 593, the Court of Appeal held that a landlord does not intend to occupy the holding for the purposes of a business to be carried on by him therein if what he intends is that the holding shall be occupied by a company, even if he and his nominees hold all of the shares.

21.5 (c)   The word 'business' in section 30 (1) (g) is defined by section 23 (2) as including 'any activity carried on by a body of persons'

HILLS (PATENTS) LTD v. UNIVERSITY COLLEGE HOSPITAL BOARD OF GOVERNORS
Court of Appeal   [1956] 1 QB 90

DENNING LJ: [Counsel for the tenants] then raised a second point: Not only must the governors intend to occupy the premises, but they have to do so for the purpose of a business to be carried on by them therein. On this point Morris LJ drew attention to the definition of 'business' in section 23 (2) of the Act of 1954, which provides: '... the expression "business" includes a trade, profession or employment and includes any activity carried on by a body of persons, whether corporate or unincorporate.' Reading those words into the section it seems to me plain that the governors intend to occupy these premises for the purposes of an activity to be carried on by them therein. Their activity is managing this hospital, and they intend, if they get these premises, to occupy them for the purpose of that activity. It is difficult to think of a parallel case. One that occurs to me, though it is not an exact analogy, is that of a building owner who employs a contractor to build a house. It is quite a proper use of language to say that the contractor is building the house 'on behalf of' the owner, but equally it is quite proper to say that the contractor 'occupies' the site, and that the contractor is carrying on his activity of building on the site.

Note: See also *Parkes* v. *Westminster Roman Catholic Diocese Trustee* (1978) 36 P & CR 22, where the Court of Appeal held that for the purposes of section 30 (1) (g), the provision and running of a community centre and church meeting room to be run by the local parish priest for members of his congregation, was a 'business'.

21.5 (d) **Ground (g) is excluded 'if the interest of the landlord, or an interest which has merged in that interest and but for the merger would be the interest of the landlord, was purchased or created after the beginning of the period of five years which ends with the termination of the current tenancy ...'—section 30 (2) of the 1954 Act**

DIPLOMA LAUNDRY LTD v. SURREY TIMBER CO. LTD

Court of Appeal   [1955] 2 QB 604

In 1949, the Surrey Timber Co. Ltd (the landlords) purchased the freehold reversion of business premises then let to Fleetwing Oil Co. Ltd for a term due to expire on 25 March 1955 and sublet to the Diploma Laundry Ltd (the tenants) for the whole term less one day. In 1953, the head lease of Fleetwing Oil Co. was surrendered for valuable consideration and in 1954 the tenants applied for a new tenancy. The landlords opposed the application on the ground that they required the premises for the purposes of their own business under section 30 (1) (g).

Held: In considering, for the purposes of section 30 (2) of the Act of 1954, whether the 'interest of the landlord' had been purchased or created within five years immediately before the termination of the current tenancy, the relevant time for determining which interest was the interest of the 'landlord' as defined in section 44 was the date when the tenant made his request for a new tenancy. At that date, the interest of Fleetwing Oil Co., had there been no merger, would not have been the interest of a 'landlord' as defined in section 44 (1) (*b*), because it was then due to expire in less than 14 months, and it would therefore have been irrelevant for the purpose of section 30 (2). The interest of the landlords, on the other hand, was the interest of a 'landlord' as defined and since it had not been purchased or created within five years of the date on which the current tenancy terminated, the landlords were not disabled by section 30 (2) from relying on the ground of objection which they had put forward.

LORD EVERSHED MR: What is meant by 'the interest of the landlord'? I shall have presently to refer to section 44, which defines the word 'landlord,' but I confess that I have no doubt as a matter of construction of this subsection that the words 'the interest of the landlord' mean the relevant interest of the landlord for the purpose in hand, namely, that of considering whether the landlord is or is not on a particular date entitled to oppose, on the ground of paragraph (*g*) of subsection (1), the tenant's request. The court is, therefore, required to consider what was the interest of the Surrey Timber Co. when the request was made, or when the opposition was put in—and for the present purposes it matters not which is the more correct date. That such is the sense of the words, seems to me to follow from the language which I have also read—'or an interest which *has* merged in that interest and but for the merger '*would be* the interest of the landlord.' Those are the words which, as it seems to me, point inevitably to the date when the landlord is saying: 'I wish to oppose this application.'

If I am right, I think there is at once to be discerned the answer to the present appeal. I have already said that, so far as the freehold is concerned, which was the interest in fact of the landlords at the relevant date, it had been acquired in the year 1949; but then come the words 'or an interest which has merged in that interest and but for the merger would be the interest of the landlord.' Apart from the definition section, the narrative which I have given would lead, I think, clearly to the conclusion that those words would be apt to cover the merged interest of the

Fleetwing Oil Co. Ltd; because, had it not been for the merger, that interest would be the interest of the landlord, meaning thereby the landlord of the Diploma Laundry Ltd. If that had been the right conclusion, the court would then have had to consider whether that leasehold interest had been purchased or created after March 1950.

The county court judge came to the conclusion that a surrender for valuable but not monetary consideration was not a 'purchase' within the meaning of the section, and he concluded also that there had been no 'creation' of that or any relevant interest within the meaning of the subsection.

On the view I take, it is unnecessary for me to express my view on those matters, and I do not do so. The question which, I think, must be answered adversely to [counsel for the tenants] and is fatal to his appeal is: what is the effect, on the language I have read and emphasized in section 30 (2), of section 44 and the definition there to be found of the word 'landlord'? [His Lordship read section 44 (1).] The extraordinary elaboration of that definition is, at first sight, surprising. It inevitably contemplates that there may, in relation to any relevant tenancy, be more than one landlord. But that is, no doubt, in order to secure that a tenant is not to be deprived of his claim to a new tenancy, or limited in the effect to be given to his application, by the circumstance that the interest immediately expectant on his existing interest is one which has but a very short time to run. In other words, the Act, as I understand it, contemplates the grant of a new tenancy which will bind not only the immediate and limited reversion, but a more remote interest as well; and so in this definition the words 'whether immediately or not' are used. At the same time it is made clear that for the purposes of this section—and, therefore, for the purposes of Part II—certain reversionary interests which have but very little time to run are excluded from relevant consideration.

I have said that the requirement of section 30 (2) is that one has to consider at the date of the application who are the landlords or the possible qualifiers as landlords, and what their interests then are. If I go back to section 44, the freehold interest of the Surrey Timber Co. Ltd was plainly the interest of a landlord within the meaning of that section, since it fulfilled the condition, first, that it was an interest in reversion expectant—in fact, immediately—on the termination of the relevant tenancy, second, that it was a fee simple, and, third, that it was not itself a reversion expectant on an interest which fulfilled both the first two conditions I have mentioned. The language makes it clear, in my judgment, that the Surrey Timber Co. Ltd are in a situation to say: 'We are the landlords within the meaning of section 30 (2), being immediate reversioners, and our interest is that of freeholders, which we acquired in 1949.' But then I have to consider the words which I have already read—'or an interest which has merged in that interest and but for the merger would be the interest of the landlord.' I must, therefore, ask the question: But for the merger, would the interest of the Fleetwing Oil Co. Ltd be the interest of 'the landlord' (as defined by section 44), or would it have been the interest of the landlord on the date of the application? The answer, in my judgment, is that it would not. It is true that it was or would have been an interest in reversion expectant on the termination of the relevant tenancy within the terms of paragraph (a) of section 44 (1); but it would not have satisfied condition (b) because it was not a fee simple, nor was it a tenancy which would not have come to an end within 14 months or less by effluxion of time. The reason is that, as I have already said, the interest of the Fleetwing Oil Co. Ltd would have come to an end by the effluxion of time in March 1955, five or six months after the date which we are considering, of the tenants' application or the landlords' opposition. Therefore it seems to me that it necessarily follows that in the autumn of 1954 the leasehold interest of the Fleetwing Oil Co. Ltd, merged or not merged, would have been an irrelevant interest for the purposes of section 30 (2). The interest of the Fleetwing Oil Co. Ltd in the hands of the freeholders or in the hands of anybody else, would not have been an interest of a 'landlord' within the relevant definition. It therefore follows, as I think, that the question whether that interest might be said to have been purchased or created by the freeholders within section 30 (2) need not be further considered. If the interest of the Fleetwing Oil Co. Ltd had by effluxion of time or would by effluxion of time have expired before the tenants made their application, the results, as [counsel for the tenants] concedes, would have been clear; and I do not think it makes any difference that it would still have subsisted in October 1954, because then it would have had but five months left of life.

For these reasons, I think, with all respect to [counsel for the tenants'] argument, that the landlords in the present case are not disqualified as being landlords whose interest for the purposes of section 30 (2) was purchased or created after March 1950.

In **Morar and Laxman v. Chauhan** (1985) 276 EG 300, the Court of Appeal held that where the landlord of business premises is a trustee for one or more beneficiaries then section 41 (2) of the 1954 Act entitles those beneficiaries as well as the landlord to oppose the grant of a new tenancy upon the ground contained in section 30 (1) (g). Moreover, the section places such beneficiaries under a similar limitation as there would be on the landlord were he alone beneficially entitled to the reversion so that if the trust under which the beneficiaries acquired their beneficial interest was created within the preceding 5 years, then they too are barred from relying on paragraph (g) under section 30 (2).

The word 'purchased' in section 30 (2) of the 1954 Act means bought for money.

H.L. BOLTON (ENGINEERING) CO. LTD v. T.J. GRAHAM & SONS LTD
Court of Appeal   [1957] 1 QB 159

In 1941, the landlords purchased the freehold of certain land and buildings and leased them to Tubes Ltd, which in turn sublet part of the premises to the tenants. In July 1954, the landlords served a notice to quit on Tubes Ltd in accordance with the terms of their lease but that notice was rendered ineffective by the coming into force of the 1954 Act. Tubes Ltd, however, moved out in February 1955, surrendering their tenancy to the landlords, which thereupon served notice in accordance with the 1954 Act on the tenants, who applied for a new tenancy. The landlords opposed the grant of a new tenancy on the ground specified in section 30 (1) (g).

Held: The interest which had merged in the landlords' freehold interest by operation of law on the surrender of the tenancy by Tubes Ltd was not 'purchased' within the meaning of section 30 (2) so as to debar the landlords from relying on paragraph (g).

DENNING LJ: The object of subsection (2) is to prevent an incoming landlord, within the last year or two of a tenancy, from buying up the premises over the head of the tenant and then ejecting the tenant on the ground that he requires it for his own purposes. In order to prevent this, the Act says that the landlord cannot rely on paragraph (g) unless he has bought the relevant interest more than five years before the end of the tenancy. In this case the current tenancy ended on 26 April 1956. The landlords bought the freehold interest in 1941, much more than five years before; but the relevant interest here, says [counsel for the tenants], is not the freehold interest, but the leasehold interest which the landlords acquired when Tubes Ltd surrendered their tenancy. That was acquired in January or February 1955—well within the five years. I think that [counsel for the tenants] is right in saying that the leasehold interest of Tubes Ltd is the relevant interest. It is an interest which has merged in the landlords' freehold, and but for the merger would have been the interest of the landlords. If the landlords 'purchased' that interest after the beginning of the five-year period, then the landlords cannot rely on paragraph (g). [Counsel for the tenants] does not suggest that the leasehold interest was 'created' after the five-year period began; indeed, it was extinguished within the five years by the merger; but what he says is that it was 'purchased' by the landlords within the five years, because they purchased, he says, in January or February 1955, when it was surrendered by operation of law.

The question there is: what is the true meaning of the word 'purchased' in subsection (2)? [Counsel for the tenants] contends that it has its old technical legal meaning and denotes any acquisition of land other than by descent or escheat; whereas [counsel for the landlords] contends that 'purchased' here has its modern popular meaning of buying for money.

In this contest I think that much help is to be gained from the fact that this Act of 1954 is dealing with a similar subject-matter to that of the Rent Restriction Acts; and in the Rent Restriction Acts it is clearly established—by *Baker* v. *Lewis* and *Powell* v. *Cleland*—that 'purchased' there is not used in its technical legal sense but is used in its popular sense of buying for money.

This meaning of 'purchased' seems to me to conform with the intention of Parliament. It was to prevent a speculator buying up the property and then getting the tenant out on the ground that he required it himself. Parliament did not intend to place a like fetter when the premises came into the landlord's hands by a surrender for no money payment at all. I would agree that if the landlords had bought out Tubes Ltd—if they had paid a substantial sum of money in return for the surrender—it would have been a purchase. But there is no such feature here; and in the absence of it I am satisfied that the interest which merged was not purchased within the meaning of this Act. My conclusion is, therefore, that 'purchased' in this Act has the same meaning as in the Rent Acts. It has its popular meaning of buying for money and not the technical legal meaning of acquisition otherwise than by descent or escheat. T. J. Graham & Son Ltd did not purchase within the five years and they are therefore not debarred from relying on paragraph (g).

The *Bolton Engineering* case was applied in:

FREDERICK LAWRENCE LTD v. FREEMAN, HARDY AND WILLIS LTD

Court of Appeal   [1959] Ch 731

In 1952, a lease for 99 years was granted to Sears Ltd subject to an existing lease vested in the tenants, which was due to expire on the 22 March 1959. By a contract, dated 30 June 1954, the landlords agreed to buy the head lease, together with other property. On 1 November 1954, the head lease was assigned to the landlords in consideration of their observing the covenants in the head lease. The landlords gave notice under section 25 of the 1954 Act terminating the underlease on 22 March 1959, stating that they would oppose a new tenancy on the ground specified in section 30 (1) (g).

Held:

(1) the landlords were precluded by section 30 (2) from relying on paragraph (g) because their interest had been purchased within five years of the termination of the underlease. For this purpose, the purchase took place on 30 June 1954 when the landlords contracted to purchase the head lease.

(2) The word 'purchased' in section 30 (2) meant 'bought for money' and did not include the acquisition of property in consideration of giving a covenant.

ROMER LJ (giving the judgment of the court): This court in *H. L. Bolton (Engineers) Co. Ltd* v. *T. J. Graham & Sons Ltd* defined the word 'purchased' in the Act of 1954 in a way which is, in our opinion, binding upon us. Denning LJ, in whose judgment

Hodson and Morris LJJ concurred, expressed the conclusion that the word in section 30 (2) of the Act of 1954

'has the same meaning as in the Rent Acts. It has its popular meaning of buying for money and not the technical legal meaning of acquisition otherwise than by descent or escheat.'

What then is the popular meaning of 'buying for money'? One of the definitions of 'buy' in the Shorter Oxford English Dictionary is 'to get possession of by giving an equivalent, usually in money; to obtain by paying a price.' In *Inland Revenue Commissioners* v. *Gribble* Buckley LJ said:

'"Purchaser" may, as it seems to me, mean any one of four things. First, it may bear what has been called the vulgar or commercial meaning; purchaser may mean a buyer for money. Secondly, it may include also a person who becomes a purchaser for money's worth, which would include the case of an exchange. Thirdly, it may mean a purchaser for valuable consideration, which need not be money or money's worth, but may be, say, a covenant, or the consideration of marriage. Fourthly, it may bear that which in the language of real property lawyers is its technical meaning, namely, a person who does not take by descent.'

Buckley LJ's judgment was a dissenting judgment but the passage which we have quoted was in no way at variance with the judgments of the other members of the court. It is clear, we think, from what was said in *Bolton's* case, that 'purchased' in section 30 (2) of the Act of 1954 falls within the first of Buckley LJ's four categories, to the exclusion of the other three, and means 'bought for money.' 'Money' in this context is not confined to cash in its strict sense, for a man who bought something and paid for it by cheque would popularly be said to have bought it for money. It would, however, exclude a covenant, for the acquisition of property in consideration of giving a covenant falls within Buckley LJ's third category. The relevance of this is that, in the transfer to the landlords of the property in question (together with other properties), the only consideration moving from the landlords to Sears Ltd were the covenants implied under section 77 (1) (*c*) of the Law of Property Act 1925, and which were incorporated in the transfer. If, therefore, the only relevant document for present purposes was this instrument of transfer it would not be possible, in our judgment, having regard to *Bolton's* case and *Gribble's* case, to say that the landlords 'purchased' the reversion in the premises. Both [counsel], however, for the landlords, and [counsel] for the tenants, were agreed that in order to ascertain the true nature of the transaction between Sears Ltd and the landlords under which the latter acquired their interest in the premises, it is permissible to look to the contract which preceded the transfer for the purpose of seeing whether the interest was 'purchased' by the landlords. This agreement was dated 30 June 1954, and is a document of somewhat special character. The third recital in the agreement is that

'Sears have agreed to sell and Freeman [the landlords] have agreed to purchase the goodwill and certain assets used by Sears in connection with (Sears') business and certain freehold and leasehold premises and interests in certain other premises short particulars of which are set out in the First and Second Schedules hereto (such properties hereinafter sometimes collectively called "the said properties") on the terms and conditions hereinafter set forth.'

In conformity with this recital, clause 1 of the agreement is expressed in terms of sale and purchase: 'Sears sell and Freeman purchase as at 1 January 1954 (hereinafter called "the sale date").' The clause then describes the items of property which are to be transferred and these include, as the third item, the leasehold interests in the properties particularised in the Second Schedule, amongst which are the interests now in question. Clause 2 provides that

'the consideration for the sale and purchase hereby agreed shall be in respect of the properties First to Eighthly in clause 1 hereof the amounts respectively attributable to such properties in such order as follows.'

There then follow sums of money ascertained or ascertainable in respect of items 1 and 2 and items 4 to 8. Two of these sums are purely nominal amounts of £1 each. To the leasehold interests comprised in the Second Schedule, however, no 'amount' is attributed at all. The consideration for those interests is expressed to be the covenant by the landlords to pay the rents reserved and to observe and perform the covenants and conditions contained in the leases under which the properties were held and to indemnify Sears Ltd in respect of any breach thereof. Apart from this covenant and indemnity no cash consideration, even a nominal one, was attributed to the leasehold interests comprised in the Second Schedule. Accordingly, just as the subsequent transfer of these interests could not, as already stated, be regarded as a 'purchase' of the interests if the instrument were taken by itself, so also the agreement to transfer them could scarcely be regarded as an agreement by the landlords to 'purchase' them, if it were to be divorced from the other terms of the contract. Perhaps, indeed, the most attractive way of putting the landlords' case on this point, as [counsel for the landlords] in fact put it, was as follows: Look first, as one naturally would look, to the instrument of transfer of these legal interests and one finds that it was not a transfer for money. Look then to the agreement for the transfer of the interests to see whether the consideration was intended to be money. One finds that the agreement is in precise accordance with the transfer in point of consideration. There is, therefore, no ground for suggesting that the consideration stated in the transfer was at variance with the intention of the parties. The landlords, said [counsel for the landlords], were buying the business and paying for it, but were merely taking over the relevant leasehold interests.

We fully appreciate the force of [counsel for the landlord]'s submission on this question but we are of opinion that it ought not to prevail. The third recital of the agreement and clause 1 and the opening words of clause 2 seem to show quite clearly that the transaction embodied in the agreement was intended by the contracting parties to be one of sale and purchase and nothing else. It is quite true that it would be difficult to say how much the landlords 'paid' for the relevant interests if the amount had to be assessed in terms of money. But to an inquiry whether the landlords bought Sears Ltd's leaseholds, along with its business and other assets, the answer, we think, must surely be 'Yes.' This would, in our judgment, be the ordinary commercial view of the transaction and it could only be negatived by splitting up what is one single and indivisible agreement into different parts and treating each part as having an existence independent of the others. This would appear to us to be an illegitimate approach to the matter. If at the instance of either contracting party the court had been asked to decree specific performance of the agreement, and had done so, the subject of the decree would have been the contract as an entirety; and the contract as a whole is, in our judgment, a contract of sale. That the ordinary or 'business' view of the transaction is that which we have indicated is we think supported by the terms of clause 9 (b) of the contract, which, as regards the property in the second Schedule, expressly stated that the landlords 'shall be deemed to *purchase* with full notice of the terms contained in the leases under which such properties are held'; and by clause 10 of the contract, which reads: 'Sears are *selling* and will convey grant transfer and assign as beneficial owners.'

We cannot refrain from adding upon this part of the case that the (by no means easy) question involved may, if this case should go to the House of Lords, have then become wholly academic if [counsel for the landlords'] argument be accepted upon the last question with which we later deal.

If, therefore, as we think, the landlords did purchase their interest in the Camden Town leaseholds, the next question which arises is, when they did so. As to this, there would seem to be three possible dates, *videlicet*: 30 June 1954, when the agreement between Sears Ltd and the landlords was signed; or 1 November 1954, when the instrument of transfer was executed; or 13 November 1954, when the transfer was registered under the Land Registration Act, 1925. The 'interest of the landlord' with which section 30 (2) of the Act of 1954 is concerned is presumably the interest by virtue of which the landlord opposes a tenant's application for a new lease. That interest in the present case was a legal interest in reversion expectant on the termination of the tenancy, and in our opinion the landlords 'purchased' this interest on the date when the agreement with Sears Ltd was signed, namely, 30 June 1954. They did not acquire the position or status of landlords until 1 November (or perhaps more strictly 13 November) 1954, when the purchase was completed and registered; but it seems to us that the relevant date for the purposes of section 30 (2) is when a landlord purchased his interest and not when he filled the character of landlord. If so, the only question in the present case is as to the date on which the landlords, as between them and Sears Ltd, became the purchasers of the interest. As to this it is well settled (see, for example, *Lysaght* v. *Edwards*) that in equity a purchaser is treated for all practical purposes as the owner of the property sold upon the signing of the contract of sale and the vendor becomes a trustee for him of the legal estate. There is nothing in the agreement of 30 June 1954, to displace this conception; and indeed it is expressly provided by clause 12 (a) thereof that until Sears Ltd should obtain licence to assign the relevant interest (amongst others) they would 'hold and retain the legal possession thereof upon trust for Freeman [the landlords].' We are accordingly of opinion that the landlords 'purchased' the relevant interest on 30 June 1954. We would add that this view is consistent with the conclusion at which this court arrived upon a similar point under the Rent Acts in *Emberson* v. *Robinson*.

Note: It was also decided in this case that the provisions of section 64 (1) of the 1954 Act (which extend a tenancy for a period of three months from the date when an application for a new tenancy is finally disposed of) were not to be read into section 30 (2) and that the phrase 'the termination of the current tenancy' in that section was referable to the date specified in the landlord's notice under section 25. The decision in *In re 88, High Road Kilburn* [1959] 1 WLR 279, (see later, page 493), was considered but held not to apply to section 30 (2).

ROMER LJ: We do not suggest that the decision of the judge was wrong. But the Act of 1954 is not a model either of lucidity or consistency, and the fact that the expression 'on the coming to an end of the current tenancy' in section 33 has the meaning which Wynn-Parry J attributed to it does not necessarily show that the words 'the termination of the current tenancy' are to have a similar meaning in the context in which they appear in section 30 (2). As we have already pointed out, there are indications in sections 30 and 31 and elsewhere in the Act that the words were not intended to have that meaning in section 30 (2), and those reasons are not applicable to section 33. We do not, therefore, regard the decision in *In re 88, High Road, Kilburn* as being inconsistent with the view which we have expressed as to section 30 (2).

The 'interest of the landlord' in section 30 (2) of the 1954 Act means the landlord's interest in the holding from the time when it originally arose by purchase or creation.

ARTEMIOU v. PROCOPIOU

Court of Appeal   [1966] 1 QB 878

The landlord had carried on a cafe and restaurant business in the demised premises from January 1960. In March 1960, he acquired by assignment the leasehold interest in the premises. By a lease, dated 7 April 1961, he was granted by the freeholder a further term of seven years from 25 March 1961. By an Underlease, dated 1 November 1963, he sublet the premises to the tenant for a term of one year from the 13 October 1963 with an option for a further year. In March 1964, the tenant exercised that option and stayed on in possession. On 29 October 1964, the landlord gave a section 25 notice terminating the tenancy on October 1965, opposing the grant of a new tenancy on the ground specified in section 30 (1) (g).

Held: The landlord had acquired an interest in the premises for the purposes of section 30 (2) since March 1960, when he obtained an assignment of the leasehold interest therein and, accordingly, was not debarred by that section from opposing the grant of a tenancy under paragraph (g).

DANCKWERTS LJ: I now turn to the other point. Here, [counsel for the tenant's] argument is more formidable. It depends on treating the landlord's acquisition of an interest in the holding as dating only from 7 April 1961 (or, perhaps, from 25 March 1961). This would be after 'the beginning of the period of five years which ends with the termination of the current tenancy' (that is, in October 1965). On the other hand, the landlord has had an interest in the property since March 1960, when he obtained an assignment of the unexpired portion of the existing term. If the object of the subsection is that which I have stated, the landlord, having been the owner of the leasehold interest in the holding since March 1960 that is, more than five years before October 1965, the terms of subsection (2) would appear to be satisfied.

In my opinion, 'the interest of the landlord' (the material words) cannot have the meaning which has been suggested on behalf of the tenant, as such a construction would produce plain injustice to a landlord who has held the holding under successive tenancies for a long period of years, as indeed it would have done in *Town Tailors Ltd* v. *Peacock's Stores Ltd* if the landlords in that case had not been able to succeed under paragraph (*f*) of section 30 (1).

An intention to produce an unreasonable result is not to be imputed to a statute if there is some other construction available. In the present subsection the result contended for would be quite irrelevant to the mischief which the statutory provision was intended to meet, namely, the prevention of exploitation of tenants by speculators. The provision cannot have been intended to defeat landlords who have been landlords of the holding or a long period, even if their title has been renewed within the last five years. There is a perfectly reasonable construction available which avoids such an unfortunate result.

In my view, 'the interest of the landlord' means the interest of the landlord in the holding from the time when it originally arose by purchase or creation. This construction covers equally an interest of a landlord under one long period by one lease or under a series of leases. In my opinion this construction makes sense and the other construction does not.

For the purposes of section 30 (2), a landlord's interest is created on the date when the lease is executed and not on the date when he went into possession.

NORTHCOTE LAUNDRY LTD v. FREDERICK DONNELLY LTD

Court of Appeal   [1968] 1 WLR 562

By a lease, dated 23 September 1964, the landlords demised premises in London to the tenants for a term of 21 years from the 29 September 1964. It was formally agreed that the landlords should retain a small portion of the premises to keep a London outlet for its business. The tenants went into occupation under the lease of the 29 September and the landlords retained possession of the small portion for which it was subsequently agreed it should pay rent, so that it became a yearly sub-tenant of the tenants as from the 29 September.

On the 2 November 1966, the tenants served a section 25 notice on the landlords stating that it required the premises occupied by the landlords for its own purposes.

Held: The tenant's right to rely on paragraph (g) of section 30 (1) of the 1954 Act was not excluded by section 30 (2) since its interest under the head lease was created on 23 September (when it was executed) and not on the 29 September (when it went into possession).

RUSSELL LJ: Donnelly being for the present purpose the landlord under the Act of 1954, and Northcote being the tenant who wants an extension of its tenancy of the retained part, the question quite simply is this: when was the interest of the landlord created for the purpose of subsection (2) of section 30? That arises in this way because the landlord Donnelly requires (and has satisfied the judge that he requires) the possession of the premises for his own occupation, which is a ground under (g) of section 30. The point that Northcote, the tenant, then takes is that Donnelly is not entitled to rely on ground (g) because of subsection (2).

In the first place it is quite plain that under the first part of that subsection the interest of Donnelly, that is to say, the interest under the lease of 23 September 1964, was undoubtedly created within the five years' period that is mentioned in subsection (2). So far, therefore, the tenant rightly says that ground (g) is not open. But subsection (2) goes on to say that you can exclude the landlord from relying on ground (g) only if it is also shown that at all times since the purchase or creation of the interest of the landlord, the holding has been comprised in a tenancy or successive tenancies of the description specified in section 23 (1), that is to say, a business tenancy. The point is this: was the interest of the landlord, Donnelly, created when the lease was executed on 23 September 1964, or was that interest created at the commencement of the term? If the first is the true view, then it is not possible to say (because of the six days difference between 23 and 29 September when Northcote became sub-tenant) that at all times since 23 September has there been a business tenancy of this part of the holding, and ground (g) is not excluded. *Aliter* if 29 September is the date of creation.

I find this really not a problem of any difficulty at all. The interest of the landlord in this case is quite clearly the leasehold interest which was created by the lease, and the lease was executed on 23 September. I find it quite impossible to construe this sub-section in any way other than to hold that the relevant date for the present purposes is 23 September.

If I may venture to remark, as Megarry J has observed in The Law of Real Property (1962) 3rd ed. at p 372: 'A lease ... is a document creating an interest in land.' Here the lease, when it was created, was a reversionary lease, but when created it was nevertheless an interest in the land, and it is in respect of that interest that the landlord now claims as such.

Chapter 22

Terms of new tenancy granted by the court

22.1 The court may only determine the terms of the new tenancy in default of 'agreement' between the parties

Terms for the grant of a new tenancy which are agreed by the parties 'without prejudice' and expressed to be 'subject to contract' are not agreed terms within the meaning of sections 33 to 35 of the 1954 Act.

DERBY & CO. LTD v. ITC PENSION TRUST LTD

Chancery Division   [1977] 2 All ER 890

OLIVER J: The negotiations are expressed to be subject to contract'. Whatever else may be meant by the word 'agreed' in the sections to which I have referred, it must, I think, refer to an unconditional and final agreement. I do not mean necessarily an agreement in the contractual sense, but an agreement which is final and not subject to any suspensive or other condition.

The meaning of the words 'subject to contract' is tolerably clear now and has been the subject-matter of a number of recent decisions. I have been referred by counsel for the tenants to *D'Silva* v. *Lister House Development Ltd* and *Leveson* v. *Parfum Marcel Rochas (England) Ltd*. Those are merely, I think, examples of the same sort of situation as that in this case. But counsel for the landlords himself does not contend that the negotiations gave rise to any contractual liability on either side.

In my judgment it is not simply a question of contract. Where negotiations are carried out 'subject to contract' that means, and I think this is clear from the authorities, that they are conditional on the final engrossment, execution and a exchange of the formal lease, where the case is one of negotiation for the grant of a lease or tenancy. In the instant case there never was such an exchange. That condition was never fulfilled, and the bargain remained conditional. It does not seem to me therefore that one has, until that condition has been fulfilled, a final agreement for the purposes of the secions of the 1954 Act to which I have referred.

22.2 Property—section 32

A tenant has no right under section 32 to a new lease of premises occupied by a sub-tenant at the time of the order, but if he goes into occupation before the order, he may be able to obtain a new lease even though he did so after applying for the new lease and for the sole purpose of obtaining it.

NARCISSI v. WOLFE

Chancery Division   [1960] Ch 10

The tenant used the ground floor and basement in connection with his restaurant business and sub-let the three upper floors as furnished flats. After he had made his application for a new tenancy but before the hearing, the sub-tenant of the first floor flat gave up his tenancy and the tenant stored some food on the first floor in connection with his business. He also left some furniture in the first floor flat and on one occasion he spent the night there. The sub-tenants continued in occupation of the second and third floors. The landlord contended that the holding consisted of the ground floor and basement only.

Held:
(1) The date at which the property constituting the holding was to be designated was the date of the order of the court and not the date of the tenant's application.
(2) Since the tenant was in real need of storage space, albeit temporarily, it was impossible to say that the tenant's occupation of the first floor was not genuine and that, therefore, at the material date, the holding of which the tenant was entitled to have a new lease comprised the basement, ground and first floor.

ROXBURGH J: The purpose of the occupation of the first floor was, in part, to try to get a new lease, and the occupation was with a temporarily designed object. I do not think that it is my business to investigate the tenant's purpose; it seems to me that Parliament has invited something of this sort, that what I have to do is to see whether there is a real occupation or whether it is simply colourable.

I cannot say that it is simply colourable. It may be that the mere fact that what remained in the flat was the tenant's was enough to make the occupation revert to him when the sub-tenant left. I deliberately refrain from deciding that question, but it is a point which I cannot entirely ignore. There was this furniture on the first floor and, while it might not be enough in itself, it is an item in the schedule of points to be considered.

I propose to eliminate altogether the use of the premises as office accommodation, for that seems to me to have been almost negligible and a breach of covenant. I am inclined to accede to [counsel for the landlords'] argument that, under the Act, occupation cannot be based upon acts of occupation which are in breach of covenant. That is why I had to construe the meaning of the covenant at the beginning of my judgment. That does not, however, apply either to the one night when the tenant slept in the first-floor flat or to its use for storage; it does not seem to me that either of those acts was a breach of covenant, but that is why I have eliminated the office user. I am not going to decide whether the use of the first floor for one night's residence in several months would be enough. The really important matter, in my judgment, is one about which there is no real conflict of evidence, and that is the use of the first floor for storage purposes in connection with the tenant's business as a restaurateur.

I accept the evidence that the tenant was in real need of storage accommodation and will continue to be in such need until the basement is put into a condition in which it can be used for storing any food. It is that aspect of the case which makes it impossible for me to say, in this case, that the occupation was merely colourable.

Therefore, I hold that today, the date of the order I propose to make, the tenant is in occupation of the first floor and, accordingly, I designate the holding as being the basement, the ground floor and first floor, but excluding the second and third floors.

The court has no power to grant a tenancy of premises more extensive than the original holding.

G. ORLIK (MEAT PRODUCTS) v. HASTINGS & THANET BUILDING SOCIETY

Court of Appeal   (1975) 29 P & CR 126

STAMP LJ: We conclude that neither by the effect of a grant contained in the lease nor by the effect of any irrevocable licence or any equity have the tenants as against the landlords any such right of parking as is claimed.

If it be right that the tenants have no right of parking such as is claimed, section 32 (3) of the Act of 1954, which was relied on on behalf of the tenants and requires that where the current tenancy includes rights enjoyed by the tenant in connection with the holding those rights shall (in the absence of agreement between landlord and tenant) be included in the new tenancy, affords the tenant no assistance.

Section 35 of the Act is in more general terms. It provides as follows:

'The terms of a tenancy granted by order of the court under this Part of this Act (other than terms as to the duration thereof and as to the rent payable thereunder) shall be such as may be agreed between the landlord and the tenant or as, in default of such agreement, may be determined by the court; and in determining those terms the court shall have regard to the terms of the current tenancy and to all relevant circumstances.'

The object of Part II of the Act is to give security of tenure to business tenants by, *inter alia*, conferring power on the court to order a new tenancy of the property comprised in 'the holding,' that is to say (see section 23 (3)), of the property comprised in the existing tenancy excluding any part not used for business purposes, and, however widely expressed, section 35 cannot, in our judgment, consistently with the scheme found in Part II, be construed to enable the court to enlarge the holding, for example, by ordering the grant of an easement over the landlords' land or by conferring rights over the landlords' land not hitherto enjoyed.

[Counsel for the tenants] relied on the judgment of Upjohn J in *Re Albemarle Street (No. 1)* [1959] Ch 532, as authority for the proposition that section 35 gave the court the widest possible discretion as to the terms to be included in the new tenancy. There, the tenants under the terms of their existing tenancy had a right to exhibit advertising signs outside a part of the landlords' building of which the demised premises formed part. The right was, as Upjohn J held, one which had no connection with the demised property and was purely personal and merely a licence. Upjohn J pointing out that the great width of section 35 was shown by the fact that the court was entitled and bound to have regard not only to the terms of the current tenancy but to all relevant circumstances, held that he had jurisdiction to make an order for a new lease containing that term of the current lease. It is not necessary to comment on that decision except to point out that there the tenant had under the current lease the very right which it was sought to have included in the new lease whereas in the instant case the tenants had no such right.

In our judgment, the new tenancy ought not to contain a new term as to parking and we therefore allow the appeal to the extent of varying the order in the court below accordingly.

The *Orlik* case was applied in:

KIRKWOOD v. JOHNSON

Court of Appeal   (1979) 38 P & CR 392

A lease of business premises contained an option for the tenant, by notice to be given not less than three months prior to the termination of the term, to purchase the freehold. The tenant did not exercise that option by the due date and the landlords gave notice under section 25 on the 1954 Act to terminate his tenancy. The tenant applied for a new tenancy proposing that it should be for a term of five years and include a similar option to purchase the freehold.

Held:
(1) Section 35 of the 1954 Act did not empower the court to create a new saleable asset for the tenant, nor to enlarge the holding, nor to confer rights on the tenant over the landlords' land not hitherto enjoyed by him. In the present case, the fresh option would confer on the tenant a new saleable asset since it would extend the tenant's right to acquire the freehold for a further five years and confer on the tenant something that he had not had under the original lease.
(2) Section 32 (3) was inapplicable because the current tenancy at the date of the hearing did not include a right enjoyed by the tenant to exercise an option to purchase the freehold since such right lapsed before the tenancy expired.

ORR LJ: [Counsel] for the landlords, submits that the object of Part II is to provide security of tenure for business tenants and that it is implicit in Part II that the court can only include in a new tenancy such terms as will preserve or protect the tenant's enjoyment of the premises and of the business conducted thereon. Alternatively, he advances a narrower argument that the court has no power to grant a fresh option to acquire the reversion collateral to and outside the relation of landlord and tenant, and, additionally, he submits that it is surprising, if Parliament contemplated a grant of such option under Part II of the Act, that no guidance is given in the Act as to such matters as title to the reversion, or the ascertainment of the price payable for the reversion and for the option itself, or the mode of exercise and conditions attached to the exercise of the option.
For the tenant, [counsel] submits that it is sufficient compliance with the objects of the Act that the terms should be consistent with security of tenure, and he points to the circumstances of this case, in which the tenant, if he were to prosper, would have to invest capital, for which the option would be an inducement. He also disputes that this option was a fresh one, and he relies on the very wide words of section 35.
In support of his arguments, [counsel for the landlords] relied on the statement made by Denning LJ in *Gold* v. *Brighton Corporation* that nothing in the Act enables the court, in exercising its jurisdiction under the Act, to create a new saleable asset for the tenant, and on the judgment of this court, delivered by Stamp LJ, in *G. Orlik (Meat Products) Ltd* v. *Hastings and Thanet Building Society*, where the tenant sought to have incorporated in a new lease under section 32 (3) or section 35 of the Act of 1954 a right to park two vans in an agreed position partly on the landlord's premises. The county court judge upheld that claim, but this court on appeal concluded that the tenant had not had any right of parking such as was claimed and allowed the landlord's appeal. Stamp LJ, in the judgment of the court, observed as follows:

'The object of Part II of the Act is to give security of tenure to business tenants by, *inter alia*, conferring power on the court to order a new tenancy of the property comprised in 'the holding,' that is to say (see s.23 (3)), of the property comprised in the existing tenancy excluding any part not used for business purposes, and, however widely expressed, section 35 cannot, in our judgment, consistently with

485

the scheme found in Part II, be construed to enable the court to enlarge the holding, for example, by ordering the grant of an easement over the landlords' land or by conferring rights over the landlords' land not hitherto enjoyed.'

That reasoning is binding on this court, and, considered in conjunction with the terms of the Act of 1954 and the observations to which I have earlier referred of Denning LJ in *Gold* v. *Brighton Corporation*, has satisfied me that the deputy judge in the present case had no jurisdiction to insert in the new lease an option to acquire the freehold. It is true that in the present case the original lease had contained such an option, but, in my judgment, it is impossible to say that the fresh option confers on the tenant nothing that he did not have under the original lease. The effect of the order is to extend the right to acquire the freehold for a further five years. In that respect, in my judgment, it confers on him, in the words of Denning LJ in *Gold* v. *Brighton Corporation*, 'a new saleable asset' and also, in the words of Stamp LJ in *G. Orlik (Meat Products) Ltd* v. *Hastings and Thanet Building Society*, 'enlarge[s] the holding.'

GEOFFREY LANE LJ: It is not in dispute that in the lease of 1 September 1972, by clause 8 thereof, the landlords gave to the tenant an option to purchase the holding subject to certain conditions. Likewise it is not in dispute that that option was never exercised and, accordingly, lapsed, no notice having been given to the landlords (as the clause required) not less than three calendar months prior to the termination of the term. So, by March 1977, no option remained alive. Does section 32 (3) of the Act of 1954 apply in these circumstances? I think not. The current tenancy at the date of the hearing did not include rights enjoyed by the tenant in connection with the holding. The court was being asked to create or re-create a fresh right in favour of the tenant when none at that time in fact existed. The decision in *G. Orlik (Meat Products) Ltd* v. *Hastings and Thanet Building Society* is authority binding on us that that is not permissible.

The other possibility advanced by the tenant, *viz.* section 35, is in my view equally of no avail to him. The decision in the *Orlik* case makes this clear, as the passage already cited by Orr LJ makes apparent. I do not accept [counsel for the tenant] submission that the *Orlik* case was decided *per incuriam* on the basis that the court had overlooked the effect of section 62 of the Law of Property Act 1925 on section 32 (3). I agree that the deputy judge's order should be varied accordingly as my lords have indicated.

22.3   Duration—section 33

The court has full discretion to order a short term where the landlord fails to establish grounds (d)–(g) of section 30 but persuades the court that he is likely to be able to establish such grounds in the near future.

UPSONS LTD v. E. ROBINS LTD

Court of Appeal   [1956] 1 QB 131

Tenants of shop premises applied for the grant of a new 14-year tenancy on the expiry of their current tenancy. The landlords, who had only one shop, which there was a real risk they might have to leave, had purchased the premises in question intending to occupy them on the termination of the current tenancy for the purpose of carrying on their own business therein. However, they were unable to establish any right to oppose the grant of a new tenancy under section 30 (1) (g) because the period during which they had been the landlords was two months short of the five year period required by section 30 (2).

Held: The words 'in all the circumstances' in section 33 of the 1954 Act conferred a discretion wide enough to entitle the court to take into account all such grounds of opposition as the landlords had failed to establish as of right under section 30 and in the circumstances of the present case (including greater hardship) the grant of a new tenancy for one year only was justified.

DENNING LJ: When it became clear that the landlords could not resist the grant of a new lease, the only matters for the county court judge to determine were the rent and the duration of the new lease. He determined the question of the rent at a figure which is not in dispute; but he decided that they should have only one year's extension, and it is against that decision that the tenants appeal. They say that they should have seven years.

The first point taken by [counsel] on behalf of the tenants was that the judge ought not to have had regard to the fact that the landlords required the premises for their own purposes. The landlords proved here that they wanted to carry on their business of outfitters on the premises; and they said that there was a risk that they would have to leave their present premises. They asked, therefore, that the term of the lease should be as short as possible. [Counsel for the tenants] asked us to say that the fact that the landlords wanted the premises for their own purposes was an irrelevant consideration, and not one to be taken into account by the judge.

I cannot accede to that view. Section 33 of the Act of 1954 provides that the new tenancy

'shall be such a tenancy as may be determined by the court to be reasonable in all the circumstances, being, if it is a tenancy for a term of years certain, a tenancy for a term not exceeding 14 years, and shall begin on the coming to an end of the current tenancy.'

Those words 'in all the circumstances' are amply wide enough to cover the present situation. I see no reason for cutting them down by reference to the earlier section—section 30 (1) (g)—which deals only with rights, and not with matters which come within the discretion of the court.

[Counsel for the tenants] referred to section 31 (2), where a limited extension of the tenancy is in certain circumstances given to the tenant for a definite period, and after that the landlord gets possession. That section, too, concerns rights, and does not affect the scope of section 33, which states that the court has to consider 'all the circumstances.' I think that the judge here was entitled to have regard to the fact that the landlords require the premises for their own purposes.

[Counsel for the tenants] then said that the judge considered the greater hardship in the case, and that he ought not not have done so because that came into the temporary Act of 1951 and did not appear in the new Act. In my judgment the words 'in all the circumstances' enable the court to consider hardship as well as other circumstances.

Then, said [counsel for the tenants], the judge founded himself on the ground that the landlords would have quit their present premises on 1 February 1957, whereas there was no admissible evidence to that effect. The judge did not say that they *would* have to leave their present premises; he said that there was a danger or a real risk that they would have to leave them. There was ample material on which the judge could so hold, and there was no reason why he should not take that into account.

[Counsel for the tenants] then argued that the judge was wrong because he took into account the fact that Upsons Ltd have a chain of some 250 shops, and that the loss of one would be a comparatively small matter for them, whereas the landlords have just this one shop and they would suffer much more. I see no reason why the judge should not take that into account.

It seems to me that none of the criticisms are well founded. The judge seems to have said to himself:

'The landlords bought these premises not quite five years ago. They bought them in order to get possession for their own business purposes. There is a real risk that they may have to leave their own premises. These tenants (Upsons Ltd) are a large concern. They have been there, it is true, for a number of years, but they have had one year's extension of the contractual term already. If they have another year I think that that is reasonable in all the circumstances.'

I see no error in point of law in the judge's reasoning. The width and scope of section 33 are such that he was entitled to take into consideration all the matters which he did, and I would dismiss the appeal.

The court may grant a short term where the tenant requires only enough time to make an orderly departure from the premises with a view to moving to a new location.

C.B.S. UNITED KINGDOM LTD v. LONDON SCOTTISH PROPERTIES LTD

Chancery Division   (1985) 275 EG 718

The tenants applied for a new tenancy of factory premises. The main issue concerned the length of the term to be granted, the tenants asking for a very short term expiring on the 31 August 1986 and the landlords submitting that the term should be of 14 years duration. The tenants were in the process of moving to a new location and required only enough time to make an orderly departure. The landlords who were themselves tenants, having a head tenancy for 150 years at a substantial rent, argued that the capital value of their interest would be materially diminished if a shorter term than 14 years were granted.

Held: In all the circumstances, it would be reasonable to grant the shorter term asked for by the tenants.

HIS HONOUR JUDGE MICKLEM (sitting as a Judge of the High Court): I turn to the submissions of counsel for the landlord. He submitted that the question was at large. He said that one of the factors was the 10-year existing lease and that it was right to weigh the advantages on both sides. On the one side, there was the tenant's requirement for a short period and, on the other side, there was the proper regard of the landlord to maximise the marketability of his asset. Under section 33 he submitted that the tenant was not to be protected from market forces and he submitted that the practice of the market was important and I ought to have regard to what would happen if there was no protection under the Act. Weighing the factors, his submission was that there was a significant detriment to the landlord which could not be compensated because, although the investment value was affected, rental value was not. Therefore, he said that he ought to be entitled to grant a 14-year lease. On the tenant's side he said that he accepted that the tenant's need was only for a short time. It is a present need, but not a certain need. There is no real disadvantage in a longer lease. After all, it would be a marketable lease and the chances were that it would be readily marketable on the evidence before me; it would be at a rent which was less than the rent which could be demanded of any new tenant and there was a demand for the property; it would be marketable within a year, and he submitted that there was no real disadvantage in the comparative inflexibility of the position of the tenant through only having a particular lease of the balance of 13 years (or nine years, if it were a 10-year lease) to market, and that really all that the tenant could complain of here was the minor irritation of having to instruct agents and get on with disposing of the lease. His submission was that the balance came down heavily in favour of a 14-year term.

All that was disputed, not surprisingly, by counsel for the tenant. He submitted that the market forces should only have a very limited effect on the present issue and that they were not really an important factor. He pointed out that the evidence is such that the landlord will, in practice, know by the end of September of this year whether the tenant is actually going out. The tenant has given an undertaking to keep the landlord informed as to the progress of its move. It is prepared to give an undertaking to allow the landlord every facility for showing people round the premises, and he says that the landlord will have, effectively, 11 months in which to find a new tenant and that the prospect of a void with negative cash flow is a comparatively small one, and that further the tenant offers to pay £50,000 if, in the event, the tenant is not out on 31 August 1986. He says that there is a substantial difficulty for the tenant in dealing with what will then be a 13–year lease. The evidence is that the market wants at least 15 years—not only the landlord wants it, but tenants of this sort of property want it—and it is not so easy for him to dispose of that lease as it would be for the landlord to deal with the premises with complete flexibility, which it will have. He says that the purpose of the Act is to protect the tenant and that is a very important consideration and what ought to be given is the protection that he needs and no more. He points out that the supposed diminution of market value is to some extent a paper transaction, because he points out, with force, that the evidence is that there is no intention of the landlord to part with this property and he says that if a short term is granted the landlord is adequately protected by a rent of £260,000, which is more than his expert said it is worth; that there is unlikely to be a long void, and, although there is some uncertainty, it is an uncertainty which will be quickly resolved and, once that is resolved, the experts who, under terms of market sentiment, have valued the property down will be able to value it up again. It is a postponement of a realisation of an advantage rather than any actual loss.

I hope I have, perhaps imperfectly, summarised what has been said on both sides. I have come to the conclusion that, in all the circumstances, it would be reasonable for the tenant to have the tenancy for which it asks to 31 August 1986. I am persuaded by the arguments on behalf of the tenant. It will give him the protection which he actually needs, which the Act is there to provide him with, and I do not attach great weight to the 'market forces' argument. In the absence of any suggestion that there is going to be a sale, it seems to me that, for the reasons put forward by the tenant, which I will not repeat, the landlord is properly protected and it would be reasonable to grant the shorter term which is asked for and that is what I propose to do.

The court has power to insert a break clause allowing the landlord to determine the lease when ready to demolish or reconstruct the premises.

McCOMBIE v. GRAND JUNCTION CO. LTD
Court of Appeal   [1962] 1 WLR 581

ORMEROD LJ: In the circumstances I propose to say nothing about the merits of this case, because the question has been before the judge and the case is going back to him to make a new determination of the term which should be granted in the light of the knowledge that he has the power to introduce a 'break clause' into the lease, if he thinks fit so to do. It seems to us that the proper course is for the case to go back to the judge, who is apprised of the facts, and for him to consider the whole of the evidence and come to what conclusion he thinks proper about the term of the new lease, having regard to his power to include a 'break clause' in it.

Where the premises are dilapidated and ripe for development and the landlord intends to demolish and reconstruct in the near future, any new lease granted under section 33 of the 1954 Act must be short.

LONDON AND PROVINCIAL MILLINERY STORES LTD v. BARCLAYS BANK LTD

Court of Appeal [1962] 1 WLR 510

The landlords let part of certain premises owned by them to tenants as a millinery shop for a term of seven years. After the lease expired, the parties conducted negotiations for a new tenancy over a period of four years, during which time the tenants remained in possession at the original rent reserved in the lease. The shop was in a fair state of repair but the remainder of the premises was in a very dilapidated condition. The landlords had contracted to sell their interest in the premises to a development company, who genuinely proposed in the near future to demolish and reconstruct the premises, but they had no fixed present intention to develop as at the date of the hearing. The tenants applied for the grant of a new tenancy and the county court judge granted them a lease of nine years. The landlords appealed.

Held:
(1) Where premises were in a dilapidated condition but ripe for development and the landlord genuinely proposed to develop them in the near future, any new tenancy must necessarily be of short duration.
(2) The length of the original lease and the enjoyment by the tenants, since its expiry, of a further period of possession at the original rent were material factors to be considered in determining the duration of the new tenancy.
(3) In all the circumstances, the tenancy granted would be for one year only.

WILLMER LJ: The tenant's application for a new tenancy was made in pursuance of the Act of 1954, and it is, I think, useful to start by considering what was the purpose of that Act. It is, of course, clear that the purposes of Part II was to confer on tenants of business premises in proper cases a measure of security of tenure. But I think it is equally clear that the Act was also designed to secure some protection for landlords. Thus, it is provided by section 31 (1) that where a landlord can bring himself within any of the seven paragraphs of section 30 (1), the court shall not make an order for the grant of a new tenancy. If, as in the present case, a landlord is not able to bring himself within section 30 (1), and a new tenancy has to be granted, it is provided by section 33 that the duration of the new tenancy shall be such 'as may be determined by the court to be reasonable in all the circumstances.' It is implicit in this provision that the new tenancy, while giving proper protection to the tenant, must not be such as would be unfair or oppressive to the landlord. This accords with what was said by Birkett LJ and Parker LJ in *Reohorn* v. *Barry Corporation*. Moreover, both these lords justices, and indeed all the members of the court, emphasised that the Act of 1954 was not to be used as an instrument to defeat development. It is thus the duty of the court to have regard to all the circumstances, both as they affect the tenant and as they affect the landlord, and to make such order as will reasonably protect the interests of both.

The most important circumstance from the point of view of the tenants in the present case was the fact that they held the premises under a seven years' tenancy, and were thus well established with a prosperous business in a main shopping centre of Chester. Against this, however, it is to be remembered that, thanks to the intervention of protracted negotiations, they had by the date of the hearing already had the benefit of an extension of over four years—a circumstance which seems to me of some materiality when considering the duration of any new tenancy. It was so held by Russell J, rightly in my judgment, in *Frederick Lawrence Ltd* v. *Freeman, Hardy and Willis Ltd*.

From the point of view of the landlords, the circumstance principally relied on was the fact that most of the building, other than the part which formed the subject of the tenants' tenancy, was in a deplorable state of repair. [His Lordship then referred to the evidence and continued:]

The experts who gave evidence for the landlords were unanimous in expressing the opinion that for practical purposes the premises were beyond repair, and that the only sensible course would be to demolish the existing structure and replace it with a modern building. One of those experts, in cross-examination, went so far as to express the fear that if repairs were attempted, the whole building might tumble down, so that in his view a full repair would in effect involve a rebuilding. All three experts for the landlords agreed that the site was ripe for immediate redevelopment. This was not a matter of serious controversy. The two expert witnesses for the tenants agreed that the obvious thing would be to pull down the whole of the building and re-erect a new building, provided that the local authority would allow it, though one of them expressed the view that any redevelopment should include the adjacent site. The fact that the site is ripe for redevelopment is a most material circumstance to be considered when fixing the duration of a new lease—see *Reohorn v. Barry Corporation.*

Not only was the site ripe for redevelopment, but it was proved that the landlords in fact intended to redevelop it. It was for this very reason that the landlords, who held the property as trustees, sold it to the development company. A director of the development company gave evidence that his company bought the property for the express purpose of demolition and redevelopment. He was not challenged on this. He further said that plans had been prepared and submitted to the local authority, and that he believed the plans would be approved and planning permission granted. Having regard to the condition of the property, I can hardly think that planning permission was likely to be refused. It is true that, since the contract between the landlords and the development company had been entered into only a few days before the hearing, neither the landlords nor the company were in a position to prove such a fixed intention as would have entitled them to invoke section 30 (1) (*f*) of the Act of 1954 and prevent altogether the granting of a new tenancy. Nevertheless, the fact that the intention existed at the date of the hearing was a most material circumstance to take into consideration when fixing the duration of the new tenancy—see *Upsons Ltd* v. *E. Robins Ltd.*

Having regard to all these circumstances, it appears to me that all the evidence pointed to one conclusion, namely, that the new tenancy should be one of short duration—long enough to allow the tenants a reasonable time in which to find alternative accommodation without disrupting their business, but not so long as to delay unreasonably the work of redevelopment, which was so obviously desirable.

In **Amika Motors Ltd v. Colebrook Holdings Ltd** (1981) 259 EG 243, the tenants of motor premises applied for a new tenancy and the landlord did not oppose but asked that only a short term be granted with a break clause to enable the landlord to redevelop the premises in the near future. The county court judge granted a term of five years with a break clause at the end of the third year. The tenant appealed on the ground that the judge had found that the proposed works could have been carried out (albeit inconveniently) with the tenant in occupation and that the tenant would suffer grave commercial disadvantage by the result.

Held: It was impossible to say that the judge had erred because he had considered all relevant matters.

WALLER LJ: The learned judge's judgment was a very full and careful judgment. He set out fully all the relevant facts; in particular, as I have already mentioned, he explained in detail the possible consequences to the tenant. The fact that the learned judge found it was feasible to do the work while the tenants remained in possession does not necessarily mean that it was reasonable—particularly, as the learned judge found in the passage which I have already quoted, that the landlords needed access to the whole building.

Again, the fact that the learned judge set out in full the grave difficulties in which the tenants would be is, in itself, an indication that he had them in mind. In order to interfere with the discretion of a judge it would be necessary to find that he was wrong in law, in that he failed to take into account matters which he should have taken into account, or he took into account matters which should not have been considered (see Ormrod LJ in *London & Provincial Millinery Stores Ltd* v. *Barclays Bank Ltd* [1962] 1 WLR 510).

I do not think it is possible to say on either of the matters which I have mentioned that the learned judge was wrong in law. Furthermore, I do not think that the learned judge's decision was so manifestly wrong that it must have been based on an error of law. He was faced with a very difficult problem, considering on the one hand the great hardships which might arise for the tenants, and on the other hand the underlying policy of the Act not to restrict landlords in redeveloping their property. Accordingly, I am satisfied that the judge was not in error in any of those respects.

In **J.H. Edward & Sons Ltd v. Central London Commercial Estates Ltd** (1984) 271 EG 697, the main issues in dispute concerned the length of the new term and as to whether the lease should include a break clause to enable the landlords to determine the tenancy for redevelopment. The county court judge ordered a new lease for 12 years without a break clause for redevelopment.

Held: It was wrong in the circumstances of the case to grant a substantial term of 12 years without such a clause. A fair solution was the grant of a seven year lease with (1) a rent review at the end of the fifth year and (2) a redevelopment break-clause not to take effect until the end of the fifth year of the term.

Fox LJ: It is clear, as a matter of law, that the 1954 Act is not to be used to inhibit development (see, for example, *Reohorn* v. *Barry Corporation* [1956] 1 WLR 845; *London & Provincial Millinery Stores Ltd* v. *Barclays Bank Ltd* [1962] 1 WLR 510). In the present case it is a matter of importance to determine whether the two shops may be required for redevelopment purposes. It is the landlords' case that they may be so required and that, therefore, either a fairly short lease or a lease with a redevelopment 'break' clause is appropriate in each application.

The landlords' original intention was a comprehensive development of the whole site. That, the judge found, was the reason why they inserted redevelopment 'break' clauses in the leases of some of the shops. The local authority were, initially, favourable to such development, but in 1978 they withdrew their support and no comprehensive scheme is in view.

It is said, however, that nos 131 and 131A may be required for development of the hotel.

On 20 July 1982 the board of the hotel company resolved that it would be necessary to obtain vacant possession of nos 127 to 131A Tottenham Court Road 'in order to carry out substantial alterations to the ground floor layout of the hotel to provide the necessary facilities essential to the proper functioning of a hotel of their standard and size'. And it was resolved that the architect be instructed to draw up plans for incorporating the area of the shops within the ground-floor layout of the hotel.

Now, as I have indicated, it seems to me that the evidence establishes that the superior landlord for the time being may wish to develop nos 131 and 131A as part of the hotel. In that connection it is important to bear in mind that, in view of the agreement of June 1982, the company is likely soon to be the superior landlord of the tenants of the shops for the purposes of the 1954 Act. It is not satisfactory to look at the matter simply from the point of view of the appellant landlord.

If it is likely that the superior landlord for the time being may wish to develop the property, then (since it is not the policy of the 1954 Act to inhibit development) he should not be saddled with a lease which may prevent such development. In that connection a present intention to redevelop immediately is not necessary: (see *Adams* v. *Green* (1978) 247 EG 49; *Amika Motors* v. *Colebrook Holdings Ltd* (1981) 259 EG 243). Accordingly, it seems to me that it must be wrong in principle, in the present case, to order the grant of new leases for such substantial periods as 12 and 10 years respectively without development 'break' clauses. That has the effect of preventing development without the consent of the tenants during the period of the leases. I conclude, therefore, that the judge's decision was wrong and that the matter is at large before us.

For a further case on the subject, see *Adams* v. *Green* (1978) 247 EG 49, CA.

The grant of a new tenancy is governed by section 64 (1) of the 1954 Act so that a new lease does not commence until the expiration of a period of three months after the termination of all proceedings relating to the tenant's application.

IN RE No. 88, HIGH ROAD, KILBURN

Chancery Division   [1959] 1 WLR 279

WYNN-PARRY J: That leaves me with the last point to consider, namely, from what date is the new lease to begin. Section 33 of the Landlord and Tenant Act 1954, provides that, where the court makes an order for the grant of a new tenancy, the tenancy, as regards term, shall be 'for a term not exceeding fourteen years, and shall begin on the coming to an end of the current tenancy.' In order to find out what is meant by the phrase 'current tenancy' it is necessary to progress backwards to section 26 (1), where it is said:

'A tenant's request for a new tenancy may be made where the tenancy under which he holds for the time being (hereinafter referred to as "the current tenancy") is a tenancy granted for a term of years exceeding one year ...'

The result of that in the present case is to make the current tenancy the lease dated 5 December 1921. Again, in order to ascertain how the current tenancy, that is the lease of 1921, can be terminated, it is necessary to look at section 25. By sub-section (1) of that section it is provided that

'The landlord may terminate a tenancy to which this Part of this Act applies by a notice given to the tenant in the prescribed form specifying the date at which the tenancy is to come to an end (hereinafter referred to as "the date of termination").'

If subsection (1) stopped there there would be no difficulty at all in coming to the conclusion that the lease in question here came to an end on 24 June 1958. But there is added to subsection (1) this proviso: 'Provided that this subsection has effect subject to the provisions of Part IV of this Act as to the interim continuation of tenancies pending the disposal of applications to the court.' I have therefore to consider Part IV, where the relevant section is section 64. The sidenote to that section is: 'Interim continuation of tenancies pending determination by court.' [His Lordship read section 64 (1) of the Act and continued:] The effect of the proviso to section 25 appears to me to be the same as if section 64 (1) had been written in at the end of the first paragraph of section 25 (1) instead of the proviso. I am quite unable, in view of the force of the language used, to come to any conclusion other than that, once the conditions stated in paragraphs (*a*), (*b*) and (*c*) of section 64 (1) are fulfilled, the notice given by the landlord under section 25 (1) ceases to be of any effect so far as terminating the tenancy at the date specified in his notice is concerned, and that the tenancy will be continued and will only be terminated under section 64 (1).

The result is, therefore, that the new tenancy must begin at the earliest three months from today, but its commencement will, of course, be further delayed if the tenants (as they have every right to do) decide to test this matter before the Court of Appeal.

I consider that the result at which I am compelled to arrive is one which is unjust to the landlord. But I cannot mitigate that injustice as regards rent, for the new rent can only operate at the end of the period determined by section 64. I can, however, intervene so far as the term of years is concerned, and I do not propose to grant a term of 14 years, but to direct that, when the lease comes to be executed—that is, when the matter is finally disposed of—the term of the lease to be executed shall be for a term ending on 24 June 1972. I shall also direct that there be included in the lease a right in the landlords at such point of time as it eventually emerges shall represent half of that term to apply to have the rent reviewed.

The decision in *88, High Road, Kilburn* was applied in:

MICHAEL CHIPPERFIELD v. SHELL U.K. LTD
WARWICK AND WARWICK (PHILATELY) LTD v. SHELL U.K. LTD

Court of Appeal   (1981) 42 P & CR 136

The landlords opposed two applications by stamp dealers for new tenancies in the 'Bourne' at Shell-Mex House in the Strand on the basis of section 30 (1) (g) since they wished to use them for their own business purposes but later accepted that they could not maintain their opposition on this ground at the present. The county court judge ordered three-year terms 'to commence with reference to the provisions of section 64'. The landlords appealed both as to the length of term and the uncertain commencement date.

Held:
(1) Section 64 terminated the old tenancies three months after the final disposal of the action or four and a half months thereafter in the event of an appeal. Accordingly, it was advisable for the trial judge in such cases to follow the example of Wynn-Parry J in *In Re No. 88, High Road, Kilburn* whereby a specific date by reference to the three-month limit was specified for the duration of the term at the date of the order.
(2) The judge had exercised her discretion as to the length of the term properly, taking into account the landlords' argument that this was a 'near-miss' case of landlord's opposition.

O'CONNOR LJ: The existence of this problem was recognised as long ago as 1959 by Wynn-Parry J in *Re No. 88, High Road, Kilburn*, and a solution was found. That case was heard in February 1959. The landlords did not oppose the grant of a new tenancy, and the issues before the court were as to duration and rent. Having construed the effect of sections 33 and 64 of the Act, the judge said:

'The result is, therefore, that the new tenancy must begin at the earliest three months from today, but its commencement will, of course, be further delayed if the tenants (as they have every right to do) decide to test this matter before the Court of Appeal. I consider that the result at which I am compelled to arrive is one which is unjust to the landlord. But I cannot mitigate that injustice as regards rent, for the new rent can only operate at the end of the period determined by section 64. I can, however, intervene so far as the term of years is concerned, and I do not propose to grant a term of 14 years, but to direct that, when the lease comes to be executed—that is, when the matter is finally disposed of—the term of the lease to be executed shall be for a term ending on June 24, 1972.'

It seems that this admirable formula has been overlooked by the profession. The case was not cited to the county court in the present cases. We think that it is in the interest of both landlord and tenant that the end date of the new tenancy should be established when the order is made even though it is not possible to make sure when it will start. The shorter the time, the more important this is. We think that the duration of the new tenancy should always be expressed in this way.

In the present cases we think it apparent by her reference to section 64 that the judge was intending to grant new tenancies of three years ending in July 1983. Had there been no appeal, that is what would have happened. It is for this reason that, when we dismissed the appeal on 10 October we varied the order as to duration by ordering that the new tenancies should end on 31 July 1983.

The duration of a new tenancy determined by the court under section 33 of the Act is a matter of discretion; it is for the judge to decide what is 'reasonable in all the circumstances.' This court will not interfere unless it is shown that the judge in exercising her discretion has taken into consideration matters that she ought not to have done and/or failed to take into consideration matters that she ought to have done.

We turn to the substantive complaints that are found in the notice of appeal. In the first place, the landlords say that the judge failed to take into account or to give proper weight to the circumstances in which they consented to the grant of new tenancies. The gravamen of this complaint is that it was only a technical defect in their notices to Cameo that made it impossible for them to oppose the grant of new tenancies to the tenants and that but for that they would have opposed the grant successfully. They submit that this is a 'near-miss' case and rely on the decision of this court in *Wig Creations Ltd* v. *Colour Film Services Ltd*. In that case, the tenants occupied two floors under separate leases each of 21 years' duration, in the one case from 25 March 1947, in the other from 25 March 1959. The landlords, who occupied another floor in the building, bought the reversions on 1 March 1965, as they foresaw expansion of their own business. When the first lease fell in, notices were given for March 1968. Although they wanted the premises for their own business, the landlords could not rely on paragraph (*g*) of section 30 (1) by reason of subsection (2) the five-year rule. The tenants, who also wanted the floor for their business, asked for a new tenancy to expire in March 1980, the same date as their lease of the other floor. The judge granted a tenancy of three years; he took into account the five-year rule and said that, but for that factor, he would have acceded to the tenants' request.

The tenants appealed. Dismissing the appeal, Lord Denning MR said:

'Section 33 is in very wide terms. It empowers the court to do what is "reasonable in all the circumstances." Suppose a landlord bought five years ago, *plus* one day. He could resist a new tenancy altogether on the ground that he wanted the place for his own business. Suppose he buys it five years ago *less* one day. Should he be kept out of the place for several years simply by the two-day difference? I think not. The policy of the Act is to give a landlord (who has purchased more than five years ago) an absolute right to get possession for his own business: leaving it to the court to do what is reasonable if he has purchased *less* than five years. In doing what is reasonable, the five-year period is a factor which it is permissible for the judge to take into account. The weight of it is for him.'

In the present cases, the landlords submit that, by a parity of reasoning, the duration of the new tenancies should have been such as to enable them to get possession of the Bourse by serving fresh notices to coincide more or less with the Cameo case. They submit that the grant to July 1983 produces a leap-frogging situation cutting the ground from under their feet in the Cameo case.

I do not think that these complaints are well-founded. The judge said: 'Although the landlords have failed in opposing a new tenancy they are entitled to have their intentions and the evidence given in respect of their opposition taken into consideration.' Then she gave herself the following direction:

'Dealing with the issue of duration and other terms, where there is no agreement section 33 of the Act of 1954 comes into operation. It provides discretion to grant terms reasonable in all the circumstances and entitles me to take into consideration all factors. It includes the grounds of opposition of [the] landlords under section 30 (1) (g), their intentions and plans and the hardships and needs of each party. I must give proper protection to the tenants but not be unfair to the landlords, nor allow the grant of a new tenancy to defeat development or reduce the value of the building, and must weigh up and reasonably protect the interests of both parties.'

We can find nothing wrong in this direction. It is true that there is no express reference in the judgment to the possible effect on the future Cameo case, but the judge was well aware of Cameo and in the end we do not think that it matters. If it was reasonable in all the circumstances to grant new tenancies to these tenants up to July 1983, then that exercise of discretion is not made unreasonable by the fact that the result may be a factor for consideration if and when the Cameo case comes before the court. Further, we do not think it right to conclude that the judge had forgotten and thus paid no attention to the reason for the landlords abandoning their opposition to the grant of new tenancies: she recorded it accurately in her note of the proceedings before her on 9 July 1979; he had earlier set it out in her judgment. We think that the landlords are driven to asserting that the grant of three years demonstrates that she cannot have given any weight to this topic. To this assertion we can only say that we do not agree. We think that the judge had it in mind and that the terms granted do not show that she must have disregarded it.

In **Turone v. Howard De Walden Estates Ltd** (1983) 267 EG 440, the county court judge wished to grant a seven-year new tenancy so that its termination would be near that of leases of adjacent premises forming part of the same estate. His first order was for a tenancy of seven years which was expected to commence in January 1981 but owing to an appeal to the Court of Appeal and the possibility of a further appeal, the new tenancy could not commence until May 1982, thus expiring in May 1989, much later than the other leases in the estate. In an attempt to correct this result, the judge varied his order by fixing the commencement of the seven year term as 15 January 1981, overlooking the fact that the new tenancy could not commence before the 11 May 1982.

Held: The order would be corrected so as to provide that the new tenancy should expire on 15 January 1988, adopting the formula of Wynn-Parry J in *In Re No. 88, High Street, Kilburn* (above).

DUNN LJ: This kind of situation is one which has given rise to difficulty in the past. It is a difficulty which was dealt with in the case of *Chipperfield* v. *Shell UK Ltd*, to which I have already referred. The difficulty is that it is impossible to say with precision at the time when the judge of first instance makes the order granting a new tenancy when that new tenancy will commence; and if one does not know when it will commence and nothing is said, it is equally impossible to ascertain when it will expire.

The existence of this problem, as this court said in the *Chipperfield* case, was recognised as long ago as 1959 by Wynn-Parry J in the case of *Re No. 88 High Road, Kilburn* [1959] 1 WLR 279, and a solution was found. That case was heard in February 1959. The landlords did not oppose the grant of a new tenancy, and the issues before the court were the duration and rent. Having construed the effect of sections 33 and 64 of the Act, the learned judge said at the top of p 284:

'The result is, therefore, that the new tenancy must begin at the earliest three months from today, but its commencement will, of course, be further delayed, if the tenants (as they have every right to do) decide to test this matter before the Court of Appeal.

I consider that the result at which I am compelled to arrive is one which is unjust to the landlord. But I cannot mitigate that injustice as regards rent, for the new rent can only operate at the end of the period determined by section 64. I can, however, intervene so far as the term of years is concerned, and I do not propose to grant a term of 14 years, but to direct that, when the lease comes to be executed—that is, when the matter is finally disposed of—the term of the lease to be executed shall be for a term ending on 24 June 1972.'

The Court of Appeal said in the *Chipperfield* case:

'It seems that this admirable formula has been overlooked by the profession. The case was not cited to the county court in the present cases. We think it is in the interest of both landlord and tenant that the end date of the new tenancy should be established when the order is made even though it is not possible to make sure when it will start. The shorter the time the more important this is. We think that the duration of the new tenancy should always be expressed in this way.

In the present cases we think it apparent by her reference to section 64 that the learned judge was intending to grant new tenancies of three years ending in July 1983. Had there been no appeal that is what would have happened. It is for this reason that when we dismissed the appeal on 10 October we varied the order as to duration by ordering that the new tenancies should end on 31 July 1983.

That case was cited to the learned judge on the application for correction of the order, but the order in the form in which it was drawn does not follow it. It is difficult to know why the judge did not do so. However, it is plain, both from his judgment on 14 October 1980 and his judgment on 20 July 1982 when the matter went back to him, that his intention was that any new tenancy should expire early in 1988, and in my judgment the order ought to be brought in line with that intention.

22.4   Rent—section 34

In default of agreement, the rent payable under the new tenancy is that at which the holding might reasonably be expected to be let in the open market by a willing lessor.

NEWEY & EYRE LTD v. J. CURTIS & SON LTD

Chancery Division   (1984) 271 EG 891

In an application for a new tenancy of a warehouse, the parties agreed that the new lease should run for 14 years, with five year rent reviews and a restriction of user to the storage, repair and wholesale warehousing of electrical goods. The premises consisted of two floors, each of 3590 square feet. A detailed analysis of the comparisons between the demised premises and adjoining premises was made, which were the nearest comparables.

Held: The result of the calculations was to produce for the demised premises a ground floor rent of £2.40 per sq. ft and a first floor rent of £1.20 per sq. ft. This gave a rounded–up total rent for the premises of £13,000.

Mr E.C. Evans-Lombe QC: The issue in this case has now been reduced to the correct level of rent payable under the proposed new lease. The court's power to fix such rent derives from section 34 (1) of the Landlord and Tenant Act 1954, which reads as follows:

> 'The rent payable under a tenancy granted by order of the court under this Part of this Act shall be such as may be agreed between the landlord and the tenant or as, in default of such agreement, may be determined by the court to be that at which, having regard to the terms of the tenancy (other than those relating to rent), the holding might reasonably be expected to be let in the open market by a willing lessor, there being disregarded—'

And there then follow a series of disregards which it is common ground do not have any application in the present case.

In the course of the argument before me, there was brought to the court's attention comparables by both the plaintiffs and the defendants. The plaintiffs' comparables consisted of three properties: first Unit 29 itself, which I have just described; secondly, 128 Bullingdon Road, in Oxford; and, thirdly, 55 St Thomas's Street, in Oxford. Having heard the evidence adduced on both sides as to nos 128 and 55 and having seen a plan of those premises, I take the view that neither no. 128 nor no. 55 assist me at all in coming to a view on the proper rent chargeable in respect of Unit 28. Both those properties are situate in different areas of Oxford and are of a general state of repair and layout which renders them, in my view, not comparable to Unit 28.

The defendants put before me a list of comparables, nine in all. These comparables consist in fact, with two exceptions, of a series of subdivisions of a large 17,000-sq. ft unit on the estate which some two years ago was subdivided into a number of sub-units. The two exceptions to that are, firstly, Unit 19 on the estate, a very modern unit recently constructed and let, of rather less than 3000 sq. ft; and some bungalow offices, again recently let. It seems to me that the bungalow offices are of no assistance in the calculation which I must make. I also take the view, for reasons which I will dilate on later in this judgment, that the rental agreement made in respect of Unit 19 was somewhat of a special case.

The one surviving comparable of the defendants, which was put forward by them as their best comparable, is Unit 29, and I propose to deal with this comparable and apply it as far as possible in the calculation of the rent appropriate to Unit 28. The similarities between that unit and Unit 28, and the reasons why the agreement made in respect of this property assists me are as follows. It is, of course, on the same estate; it is next door. On that estate it has exactly similar problems and advantages of access to it as those appertaining to the subject property. I am prepared to treat it as of similar floor area. It is accepted on all sides that warehousing space on a first floor is of only half the value of warehousing space on the ground floor, and when I suggested to [counsel for the plaintiffs] that it was, therefore, reasonable to treat Unit 28 as if it consisted of rather mor than 5000 sq. ft of ground-floor space, he did not demur from that approach. The rent-review period under the leases is precisely the same in each case, five years. The same agents negotiated the rent between the same parties. Finally, the rent has been recently reviewed, the negotiations taking place in June 1983. Neither of the surveyors called by the landlords or the tenants was prepared to advance definite evidence that the rent market had varied significantly since that date in respect of a property such as this.

I now set out the differences which will have to be accounted for in applying the rent agreed on this property to Unit 28. Firstly, this is a new building, some five years old, by comparison with Unit 28, which was put up in the late 1950s, as I have said. Secondly, it has a modern clearspan layout, by comparison with the subject property which, because it has two floors, has a row of six stanchions to support that floor; it has a lift-space which has to have space left round it and stairs which again have to have space left round them. Thirdly, the lease upon which Unit 29 is let contains a full repairing covenant. Fourthly, the user clause in this lease is very much more liberal than the user clause contained in the lease of the subject property. The user clause in the case of Unit 29 does not restrict the use of the property to the business currently being carried on by the tenant. Fifthly, by comparison with Unit 28, and for historical reasons, there are lavatories and ablution facilities comprised in the demise of Unit 29 of which there are none in Unit 28. It appears that by agreement between the landlords and the tenants a short time ago the lavatory facilities attached to Unit 28 were demolished and an annex (which I will call 'the lavatory annex') was constructed between units 28 and 29, producing a triangular-shaped abutment. In that annex was constructed a lavatory block sufficiently large to cope with the work force in both units 28 and 29. It was, therefore, larger than that required by Unit 29. There is access to it from both buildings. The lavatory complex occupies approximately half the annex and would seem to preclude any form of commercial use for that annex at all. The annex was constructed at the request of the tenants, and the construction was financed roughly 50-50 between the landlords and the tenants.

I now turn to the sixth difference. The rent agreed in June 1983 in respect of Unit 29 was, of course, a reviewed rent, agreed between a landlord and a sitting tenant, whereas I must attempt to arrive at a rent obtainable in the open market. The rent agreed in respect of Unit 29 was £12,000. When that is reduced to the rent per sq. ft of floor area of the property there is a conflict on what the proper figure should be. The tenants contend that it should be £2.34 per sq. ft, the landlords contend it should be £2.48. The reason for the difference is that the tenants in their calculation take in the floor area of the lavatory annex, whereas the landlords do not. In my view, on this issue the landlords are right. It seems to make no sense, if one is seeking to calculate a rental by square footage, that one should bring into that calculation square footage which as a result of the tenants' own requests and actions has no commercial usage at all. Accordingly, the base rent should be created as being that which results from the landlords' calculations, namely £2.48 per sq. ft.

It is common ground that a reviewed rent agreed between an existing tenant and a landlord is in general lower than a rent negotiated in the open market. Neither side adduced any evidence as to how much of a discount there usually is in such circumstances. It seems to me that if I am to apply Unit 29 as a comparable, I have first to come up with some figure which represents this discount. Looking at the defendants' schedule of comparables, there appears to be a rough base rental of the order of £2.50 to £2.51 per sq. ft. Those figures arrive from the lettings of the various subdivisions of Unit 15. Standing out from that was the letting of Unit 19, which was let on 1 September 1983 at a rent of £2.51, but with the addition of a premium of £3000, and I should say that that letting was for a period of 15 years with three-year rent reviews. I received a certain amount of evidence as to the nature of that letting. These are the first tenants of a brand-new set of premises. It appears that the transaction was something of a special transaction. The lease contains an upwards-only review clause, and I think it is of note that, whereas it is possible to absorb the premium so as to make it represent annual rent, thereby converting the rental figure from £2.51 per sq. ft to £2.84 per sq. ft, when one is dealing with an upwards-only rent review provision the impact of £2.51 per sq. ft with a premium is entirely different from a bargain with £2.84 per sq. ft straight rental. I, therefore, take the view that there is evidence before me which justifies my coming to the conclusion that the approximate estate rental figure for premises that are not brand new is of the order of £2.50 to £2.51.

Unit 29, of course, is much newer than Unit 15 or the subdivisions of that unit, although those subdivisions were produced as a result of a conversion of those premises some two years ago. They none the less remain a conversion. It seems to me that I would be justified, doing the best I can, to come to the conclusion that the rental that would have been charged or arrived at in respect of Unit 29, had this been a fresh letting as opposed to a review, would have been £2.55 per sq. ft. This reflects the greater modernity of Unit 29 and also the somewhat better vehicle access which it has compared with the Unit 15 conversions.

It was pressed upon me that there is a break in the demand for warehouse lettings, which takes place at approximately 3000 sq. ft, and that demand for warehouses of less than that is in fact greater than warehouse space in units greater than that and that, accordingly, it would be justified to discount rent for units of greater than 3000 sq. ft. I am not satisfied that any evidence was brought to the court which justified the court in taking such a view. I accordingly take the view that no discount is necessary where one is comparing rents for premises of approximately 3000 sq. ft and those of approximately 5000 sq. ft. It may well be, and I think there was some evidence of this, that for very much larger units a lower rent per sq. ft is usually obtained. But as between those relatively small units no evidence was produced which justifies a differential.

I now come to consider what adjustments should be made to the rent of £2.55 per sq. ft, which I think would be the proper rent for Unit 29, if it had been negotiated in the open market, if one is looking for the appropriate rent for Unit 28.

It was common ground between the parties that there should be an adjustment to the Unit 29 rent to take account of the fact that Unit 29 was on a full repairing covenant, whereas Unit 28 was on a landlord's repairing covenant; and it was common ground that that adjustment should be effected by adding 5% to the rent. It was contended that the age of Unit 28 made the burden of the interior decorating obligation of the tenants more severe than that for a modern building. I do not think that any evidence was brought to this court which justified this being treated as a substantial, additional burden, and I accordingly take the figure of Mr Thomas (the landlords' surveyor) of 1% as an appropriate deduction or reducing of the rent figure to take account of this. The third matter was the general appearance of the premises and the layout. I have already described how the layout of the ground floor of Unit 28 contained six stanchions and other obstructions, and the fact that it was on two floors, and was an old building and perhaps not appearing to be in its first youth. I propose to deal with general appearance and layout as one matter. It was conceded on behalf of the landlords that there should be some reduction in respect of this. I do not take the view that the disadvantage flowing from these matters is anything like as serious as that which the tenants' surveyor suggested; and, accordingly, I again take Mr Thomas' figure of a 5% reduction to take this into account. Fourthly, the absence of lavatories from Unit 28. It is clearly a disadvantage to warehouse premises that they do not contain lavatories which can serve the persons working in the warehouse. It is a disadvantage if those premises are treated, as they must be treated, as separate premises, even though lavatories are in fact available next door. Accordingly, *prima facie*, one would think that there should be a reduction in the rent by comparison with premises which have such accommodation. However, in the present case the comparable is Unit 29 where, at the request of the tenants, lavatory accommodation to accommodate both those working in Unit 29 and Unit 28 was constructed. Furthermore, it was constructed in an annex built on to Unit 29, which is comprised in the lease of those premises and which might otherwise have been used for commercial purposes. It effectively neutralises that annex. It seems to me, therefore, that if one is going through the process of comparing Unit 28 and Unit 29, these two factors cancel each other out and there should be no adjustment of the rent of Unit 29 to take into account the absence of lavatories in Unit 28.

Finally, I turn to consider the impact of the difference in the user clauses between these two properties. The respective surveyors on either side gave widely differing answers to the question of what the appropriate reduction in this case should be. On the one hand, Mr R D Gough [ARICS, partner, Chesshire Gibson & Co.] suggested it should be as much as 20%. On the other hand, Mr E D J Thomas [FRICS, partner, Adkin] for the landlords suggested it should be only 5%. On behalf of the landlords it was urged upon me that there was no indication from any of the evidence of lettings on the estate, where a variety of restrictive clauses (including clauses such as the one in the draft lease) have been agreed and imposed, that the presence or absence of such restrictions had any effect whatsoever on the rent. I cannot take quite that view, but equally I do not think that there is any evidence which justifies the court in reducing substantially the rent when comparing it with Unit 29. I accordingly take Mr Thomas' figure of 5% as the appropriate deduction. According to my calculations, the resulting reductions and increases cancel each other out at a net reduction of 6% on the figure of £2.55, which is approximately and to the nearest penny 15 pence per sq. ft. This throws up a ground-floor rent of Unit 28 of £2.40 per sq. ft, and applying the rule, which is common ground, that first-floor accommodation should be half that of the ground-floor accommodation, this throws up a rent per sq. ft for the first floor of £1.20 per sq. ft. Calculating those figures out against the floor area, it throws up a figure of £12,924, which I propose to round up to a figure of £13,000 per annum; and it is accordingly that figure which, in the exercise of the power conferred me by section 34 of the 1954 Act, I fix as the rent applicable to Unit 28.

Accordingly, I propose to order that the rent for Unit 29 should be a rent of £13,000 per annum.

Where there are no suitable comparables, reference may be made to the general increase in rents in the area.

NATIONAL CAR PARKS v. COLEBROOK ESTATES LTD

Chancery Division   (1982) 266 EG 810

In this case, the judge was concerned to assess under section 34 of the 1954 Act the amount of rent payable for a basement car park in London under a new lease of 14 years, with provision for the landlord to terminate the lease after 7 years should they wish to demolish or reconstruct the building. The judge considered expert evidence of rental values by the landlords' and tenants' valuers and determined the rent at £29,000.

FOSTER J: *The rent:*

This is, I find, a most difficult question. It is governed by section 34 of the Landlord and Tenant Act 1954, which provides that the rent payable shall be

'determined by the court to be that at which having regard to the terms of the tenancy (other than those relating to rent) the holding might reasonably be expected to be let in the open market by a willing lessor'

and then there are four subparagraphs which may be disregarded, since they are not relevant to this application.

I heard two expert witnesses, Mr H M Berney FRICS for National Car Parks, and Mr David Harris, also FRICS, for the landlords. There was, to say the least, a difference between these two valuations, the former saying the new rent should be £26,500 and the latter £50,000. The most impressive witness, and, if I may say so, the only one who had intimate knowledge of the garage business both as landlord and tenant, was Mr R S Durrant, who was also FRICS, and he has been estate surveyor to NCP for 13½ years. He gave evidence that the premises could only be used for block parking and that he had had no demand from any car hirer for the premises even as a park for their vehicles, or from any other operator. It was in an area in which there were no hotels and few large shops. It was only used by local workers in a very congested one-way street and the ramp made it difficult for two-way driving through it, though it was possible. In fact the parking at the premises was only open from 8 am to 9 pm for five days a week. I cannot think that he would not have put the premises to better use if there was any demand. Mr Harris' estimate is, in my judgment, based on the premise that the premises could be better used than at present. In his report he says this:

'The type of business which now requires such a full garage use in central London includes such as car-hire businesses, car concessionaires, taxi service, a business or public body operating a fleet of vehicles (the GPO, the police etc).'

The comparables produces by both experts are, in my judgment, in no way comparable. There seems to be a ridiculous idea that in W1 one is in central London and the conditions are the same throughout. Nothing could be more untrue. Mr Harris would compare the premises with premises at Marble Arch and at Kingston House North in SW7. In any event, they are all self-parking and it is like comparing chalk with cheese. Mr Berney produced three comparables which are equally totally different. First, the rents were all fixed as long ago as 1979 and, again, the first and third are self-parking and the second is block and self-parking. I am sure that NCP would not use the premises as block parking if there was a way more profitable to use it. As for car-hire firms taking the premises to garage and repair their fleet of cars, the premises are too near the centre of London and they look for premises further out which are cheaper, retaining only a few cars at their office for immediate hire. Mr Berney arrives at his figure by applying £2 per sq. ft per annum. Mr Harris arrives at his value by applying a sum per annum per car space.

I cannot think that either of these approaches can be right in this particular case, since there are no comparables. I would prefer to apply the general increase in rents in the area, which varied between 10% and 15%. I will take 20%. This means that if the rental on 25 December 1980 was £20,000, on 25 December 1981 it would be £24,000 and on 25 December 1982 it will be about £29,000, and in my judgment, and having taken 20% rather than 15% for a five-year period, £29,000 per annum would be a rent which, in my judgment, might reasonably be obtained in the open market.

The amount of the new rent may depend on the nature of the restriction on user to be inserted in the new tenancy.

ALDWYCH CLUB v. COPTHALL PROPERTY CO.

Chancery Division   (1962) 185 EG 219

A club applied to the court for a new lease of its premises. Evidence was given that the premises were appropriate for use as offices and the landlords, under the existing lease, could not reasonably refuse consent to such use.

Held: It was not open to the court to fix the new rent on the footing that the would–be tenants in the hypothetical open market were limited to clubs.

PENNYCUICK J: It is not disputed by the landlord that the tenant is entitled to a new tenancy of the premises. The main and indeed the only significant issue is whether the rent to be determined in respect of the new tenancy shall be the rent appropriate to a lease on the footing that the premises may be used either as offices or as a club, or on the footing that the premises may be used as a club only. It is quite clear from the evidence that the premises are now suitable for development as offices and that they could be most advantageously let as offices. It is common ground between the witnesses that the landlord under the existing lease could not reasonably refuse consent to the use of the premises as offices, and the landlord deposes that it would in fact have given such consent if asked for it.

The issue of substance is that of the rent, the amount of which must depend upon the nature of the restriction on user to be inserted in the new tenancy. Under sub-clause (8) of the existing lease which I have read the restriction is not to use or allow the premises to be used for any purpose other than as a club without the previous consent of the lessor and not to be unreasonably refused. The tenant has in fact used the premises throughout as a club, but, as I have said, the premises are appropriate to be used as offices; planning permission has already been obtained for that purpose; and the landlord accepts that it could not reasonably refuse consent to such an offer. The premises would be likely to command a higher rent for use as offices than as a club. This being the position, it seems to me that, having regard to the terms of the current tenancy and the other relevant circumstances, the corresponding provision in the new tenancy should permit use as a club or as offices without any exception on the part of the landlord. It will then follow as a matter of course that the rent is that obtainable in the open market on the footing that the premises may be so used, namely, £5200.

[Counsel] for the tenant contends that the proper course, having regard to the terms of the current tenancy and the relevant circumstances, is to retain in the new tenancy sub-clause (8) of clause 2 in its existing form, or to restrict the use of the premises still further by confining it to use as a club with no exception for any other purpose with the consent of the lessors. The rent would then be fixed on the footing that the would-be tenants in the hypothetical open market were limited to clubs. The rent fixed on this basis has been described in argument as 'club' rent. I do not see any ground upon which the Court at the instance of the tenant and contrary to the wishes of the landlord could thus sterilise the use of the premises to their present use with the consequences that there would be excluded from the hypothetical open market the class of would-be tenants most likely to pay the best rent, namely, those wishing to use the premises as offices. The point hardly admits of elaboration. In support of his contention, [counsel for the tenant] cited one authority only, namely, *Gold* v. *Brighton Corporation* [1956] 1 WLR 1291, in the Court of Appeal, but that case merely decided that the Court will not fix the terms of the new tenancy so as to preclude the tenant from carrying on the business which in fact heretofore was carried on by it. See per Denning LJ, at page 1293, where he said:

'Turning now to the Act of 1954, I think it plainly intends to protect the tenant in respect of his business. Section 23 says that the Act applies to premises which are occupied by the tenant "for the purposes of a business carried on by him." Inasmuch as the tenant is to be protected in respect of his business, the terms of the new tenancy should be such as to enable him to carry on his business as it is. They should not prevent him from carrying on an important part of it. At any rate, if he is to be prevented from using the premises in the future in the way in which he has used it in the past, it is for the landlord to justify the restriction: and there ought to be strong and cogent evidence for the purpose.'

Then Parker LJ, at page 1296 said this:

'Undoubtedly under section 35 of the Act the county court judge is given a very wide discretion, but in the ordinary case, at any rate, it is difficult to think of any considerations which would justify changing the restrictions on use in such a way as to alter or limit the nature of the business which the tenant has lawfully carried out on those premises and which it is clearly the object of the Act to preserve.'

There is nothing in that judgment which would support the contention that the Court should impose a new restriction at the instance of the tenant which would have the effect of reducing the lettable market value of the premises.

The zoning method of valuation may be appropriate in determining the new rent under section 34.

JANES (GOWNS) LTD v. HARLOW DEVELOPMENT CORPORATION

Chancery Division   (1979) 253 EG 799

HIS HONOUR JUDGE FINLAY QC: The major problem, on which the others, in my judgment, to a large extent turn, is what rent should be paid under the lease? Here again there is a certain measure of agreement between these parties as to this problem. Both experts—and I say both, not for the moment taking account of a third expert who gave evidence on behalf of the plaintiffs, because he did not make an initial but merely certain corroborating evaluations—both experts who gave evidence before me, that is to say P F Jones [MA FRICS], who was called by the plaintiffs, and D J Green [BSc (Est Man) ARICS], who was called by the defendants, were agreed that an appropriate approach is that which is referred to as a zoning method. This is a process whereby a notional superficial area of the premises is determined with a view to ascertaining the proper rent by applying to that notional superficial area the rent per sq. ft appropriate to the part of the premises which is designated as zone A. Zone A is that part of any premises which is bounded by the front of the premises and is to a depth of 15 ft therefrom. If zone A is to be let at the rate of £X per sq. ft, then the next zone is the next 25 ft in depth, which is, it is agreed, to be charged at the rate of half of £X per sq. ft. And the next zone, which is the remainder of the shop depth (apart from the two zones which I am about to mention), is to be charged at one quarter of the rent per sq. ft appropriate to zone A, ie £¼X per sq. ft. There are therefore three zones, all differentiated according to the depth from the front of the shop. A fourth zone is that comprising ancillary accommodation within the shop, the interior ancillary accommodation of offices, lavatories and the like, and that is charged at the rate of one-sixth of the rent appropriate to one sq. ft of zone A. And finally the fifth zone is that of outside ancillary accommodation, and that is charged at the rate of one-tenth of the rent appropriate to zone A. The notional superficial area is accordingly ascertained by adding together the area of zone A, that is the part of the premises within 15 ft of the frontage, to one-half of the actual area of the part which falls within 15 and 25 ft in depth from the front and one-quarter of such area, if any, as falls more than 40 ft from the front, and further adding one-sixth of the area of any ancillary interior accommodation and one-tenth of the area of any outside ancillary accommodation. When all these various areas are added together one has a notional area which, when multiplied by the ascertained amount appropriate to one sq. ft of zone A will yield the basic rent. It is further agreed that although this is a proper approach particular circumstances may require modification either upwards or downwards of the basic rent thus arrived at. In determining whether any such modification should be made it is appropriate, in my judgment, and I do not think that there was disagreement with this by any of the experts, that regard should be had to any user covenants which there may be in the lease.

The covenant as to user contained in the lease which I have mentioned and which is, it is agreed, to be maintained in the new lease was a covenant by the tenant to use the demised premises for the purposes only of a retail lock-up shop and offices in connection therewith for the sale of fashions, ladies' and children's wear and accessories 'provided that the main characteristic of the shop is fashion' and subject to a further proviso that the user should be conducted so as not to contravene the provisions of a covenant contained in the lease, in common form, against the use of the premises in such a manner as to cause nuisance and noise or the like.

Applying these principles as to how the area of the premises in terms of zone A is to be ascertained, both parties arrived at the conclusion that there are 1628 sq. ft in terms of zone A. Mr Jones for the plaintiffs took the view that the appropriate rent per sq. ft of zone A was £17. Mr Green for the defendants said the appropriate rent was £8.59 per sq. ft. The difference of £1.59 gives rise to a basic difference of £2588.52 *per annum* for the area of £1628 sq. ft. These differences, which I should say are not the only differences between the two experts, arise from four matters. The first is this, that both experts arrive at their conclusion as to what the appropriate rent for one sq. ft of zone A should be by comparing the rents of other premises in the neighbourhood. But the comparables, if I can so call them, to which Mr Jones has had regard include four properties, nos 2, 3, 4 and 5 The Rows, which are not included among those considered by Mr Green. The second point is that Mr Jones did and Mr Green did not make an allowance for the return frontage which one finds in two properties, namely nos 1 and 2 Market House and nos 6 and 14 The Rows. Both Mr Jones and Mr Green made allowance for the return frontage of no. 11 and no. 15 Adams House. The point about a return frontage allowance as I understand it is this, that if there is a return frontage it is regarded as advantageous to the tenant and accordingly should result in some increase in the rent. If therefore one is considering the rent that has been agreed in respect of premises which have a return frontage and endeavouring to arrive at what is the rent per sq. ft of zone A of the premises, it is necessary first to deduct from the rent payable the allowance for the return frontage and then to divide what is left by the notional zone A area to arrive at the rent per zone A sq. ft.

The third point of difference is that Mr Green has treated one of the properties which is regarded as comparable by both himself and Mr Jones, namely 10 The Rows, as being notionally two properties and not one only; and he has done so because at some date since the new lease of 10 The Rows was granted, that lease being one dated 3 May 1976, there has been an assignment of the lease, and on the assignment a premium was paid. Mr Green took the view that it would be appropriate to regard that premium as indicating that as from the date of the assignment the premises should be treated as let at a rent equal to that reserved by the lease plus an addition representing the annual value throughout the residue of the term of the premium that had been paid. Accordingly he treated 10 The Rows as furnishing evidence not only of the rent at which it was let by the lease dated 3 May 1976 but also as let by the joint effect of that lease and the assignment upon which the premium was paid. Mr Jones did not view the matter in that way, and accordingly there is in effect an additional comparable in Mr Green's calculations that does not occur in Mr Jones's.

The fourth point of difference was that Mr Jones made no allowance in his calculations for the fact that rents have risen since the dates when the comparable rents selected for comparison were arrived at, that being at the end of 1976 or early in 1977, although the exact dates when the various agreements were made was not in evidence before me and some may have been made at dates later than 1977. Mr Green on the contrary made an allowance of what appears to have been a little over 15 per cent because his basic rent in terms of zone A is £7.44 and he increased that, as I indicated, by an addition to allow for a rise in rents to £8.59. There is a further point that I should mention as to the manner in which Mr Green arrived at the rent of the basic £7.44 per sq. ft of zone A. He did so by taking (i) an average of the comparable properties in Market House betwixt and between, that average being £7.53; (ii) an average of the four properties (treated as five) in The Rows, the average being £7.36; and (iii) an average of the five properties in Adams House, that average being £7.46. He then added together the three averages and divided the total by three to arrive at £7.44. I am not satisfied that that is an appropriate way to arrive at the average. It appears to me that the proper way would be to take the rent per sq. ft in terms of zone A for each of the 12 properties, or, if it be right—and I have not yet come to this point—to treat one of them as two, the 13 properties, and then divide the total by 12 or 13. That would produce a slightly different answer.

As to the points of difference, it is said that it is wrong to include the properties 2, 3, 4 and 5 The Rows. They are in a side street that leads off Market Square. It is said that they are properties let for quite different purposes than those that we find in the Market Square, and in any event they are not part of the enclave of properties that front on to Market Square. There is I think some force in that argument and I have come to the conclusion that the proper course is to exclude from consideration two of these four properties, namely 2 and 3, but to include 4 and 5 The Rows. I do so for this reason. The two properties I have last mentioned front on to The Rows and do so opposite the return frontage window and the return frontage of the premises with which I am concerned, 4 and 5 Market House. They are in my judgment properly to be regarded in comparing rents in the neighbourhood because in a very real sense they are adjacent to 4 and 5 Market House. I do not think, however, that the same can be said of 2 and 3 The Rows, which are removed from it not only by being on the other side of the road but by being in effect beyond the areas on which the side windows of 4 and 5 Market House look.

As to the second point, in my judgment it is proper to make allowance, as Mr Jones has done, for the return frontages, not only to the premises 6 to 14 The Rows, occupied by McHarris Motorcycles, but also the return frontage of the premises 1 and 2 Market House occupied by Eastern Electricity Board. So far as the McHarris Motorcycles property is concerned, that return frontage appears to me to have no features that would entitle one to disregard it. It is said in relation to 1 and 2 Market House that the return frontage looks only upon an alley way. I do not regard that as a reason for disregarding the return frontage and making no allowance for it, because a return frontage may be of utility to the occupier and an attraction to his customers, not merely because the paths along the thoroughfare pass the return frontage but also because the customers are attracted to the side window by looking first at the window in front.

As to the third point, in my judgment it is not right to treat 10 The Rows as two properties and to introduce a second comparable by reason of the consideration of the terms of the assignment on which a premium was taken. I have no evidence before me as to the reasons or basis on which that premium was paid or calculated. And in my judgment the proper course is to have regard to 10 The Rows as furnishing evidence of the state of the market so far as rents are concerned by considering the terms of the original letting for the lease dated 3 May 1976 and not speculating upon the reasons for the payment of the premium at some later stage.

As to the fourth point, it is in my judgment proper to make some allowance for rising rents. I have come to the conclusion, however, on the evidence which I have heard that the allowance of 15 per cent is too much. Mr Jones accepted that some allowance should be made for rising rents, and, having regard to the evidence he gave and also the evidence of Mr Green as to this matter, I have come to the conclusion that the appropriate allowance for the rise in rents is an allowance of 10 per cent.

Bearing in mind what I have said about making allowances for return frontage, a matter which affects not only 6 to 14 The Rows and makes the appropriate sq. ft rate in respect of that property a rate of £6.72 and not the £6.78 shown in Mr Green's schedule, an allowance should also be made for the return frontage in respect of 1 and 2 Market House, which means that the appropriate rate per sq. ft in terms of zone A is £7.50 and not £7.84 as shown in the schedule. Further, the appropriate terms to consider in relation to 10 The Rows are those in the original letting. That results in my view in a rate per sq. ft in terms of zone A of £6.68 and not a rate of £6.89 as shown in Mr Green's schedule, because I calculate, as apparently does Mr

Jones, that to take the average of the rents reserved over the first five years results in a figure of £6.68. Bearing these various circumstances in mind, I find that the rent per sq. ft indicated by the comparables that can properly be regarded, that is to say the properties shown on Mr Green's schedule and also 4 and 5 The Rows, and taking the average of the various rents per sq. ft in respect of all these properties, is in terms of zone A £7.23. 1628 sq. ft at such a rent gives a figure of £11,770.

I now come to the further matter of disagreement which arises not in arriving at the basic rent per sq. ft but in the view taken as to whether any deductions should be made from the figure thus arrived at in respect of two matters. Mr Jones gave evidence that he thought deductions should be made in respect of the quantity of the property demised and also in respect of its shape or configuration. So far as the latter point is concerned, his evidence is not supported by that of the other expert called on behalf of the plaintiffs, R A Childs [FRICS], who did agree that some deduction should be made for quantity. I do not think, although Mr Green contended that no such deduction should be made, that he did so with quite the enthusiasm with which he differed from Mr Jones's view on certain other matters. I find that it is appropriate to make some deduction for quantity. It is a matter of advantage to a landlord to let property in larger units rather than in a number of small units, and the tenant is in my judgment entitled to some allowance for that advantage which the landlord has. I accept Mr Jones's evidence that an appropriate deduction for quantity is 5 per cent.

So far as the question of the shape of the premises is concerned, I am unable to accept the evidence that a deduction of 15 per cent should be made for that. It is I think to be noted that there is no suggestion that, in the course of a period of more than 20 years that the plaintiff company has occupied these premises, they have made any attempt to alter the internal arrangements in any radical way. The shape of the premises, having, as it has, a large frontage and not perhaps a correspondingly large depth, may well be apt for the nature of the trade carried on by the plaintiff company. The trade of selling ladies' and children's wear and fashion goods is no doubt one where facilities for display play a prominent part in the success of the venture, and I am not satisfied that it is appropriate to make any deduction by reason of the fact that there is a large frontage to this property and not a relatively large depth to go with it. I do not overlook the fact that the result of the large frontage is that a large part of the premises falls to be charged at the zone A rate, or rather I should say that a large part of the premises falls within zone A. That is no doubt disadvantageous to the tenant, but the disadvantage is of course compensated by the amenity produced by the large display area.

Accordingly I consider that there should be deducted from the figure of £11,770, which I have stated is arrived at in the way I have indicated, 5 per cent for quantity. That amount is £588, leaving a balance of £11,182. Furthermore it is appropriate in my judgment to add the figures for the return frontage, and I think the appropriate figure is £190, being £10 per ft for a return frontage of 19 ft. So far that produces a figure of £11,372. However, I have already indicated that there should be an addition to that of 10 per cent to allow for the rise in rents in the period between the time when the comparable rents were arrived at and the date when the new lease will commence, which is in February 1980. That produces a figure of £12,509, which I propose to call £12,500.

In my judgment, therefore, the appropriate rent under the new lease is £12,500.

Note: The zoning method of valuation was also applied in *U.D.S. Tailoring Ltd* v. *B.L. Holdings Ltd* (1982) 261 EG 49.

The court has power under section 34 to determine a rent increasing by fixed amounts at specified times and that power includes the power to determine that the rent should not commence or should be at a lesser rate until repairs are effected.

FAWKE v. CHELSEA (VISCOUNT)

Court of Appeal   [1980] QB 441

GOFF LJ: The next question of construction which was argued, although in the events which have happened it is probably now academic, is whether the court has any such power when determining a rent under section 34 for a new tenancy. Here in my view the answer is free from doubt. I am satisfied that section 34 (3) authorises nothing more than the inclusion of a rent review clause, but what of subsection (1)? The judge thought that he could not make any such order because this would be 'not a variation of the determined rent for the new tenancy, but the determination of two rents.' With all respect I do not agree. If supported by evidence that this would be the manner in which 'the holding might reasonably be expected to be let in the open market by a willing lessor' I see no reason why the court should not determine a rent increasing by fixed amounts at specified times. By the same token the court has, in my judgment, power to provide that the rent shall not commence, or shall be at a less rate, until repairs are effected, or shall cease to be payable or be reduced as from the time, albeit later than the commencement of the new lease, when they are in fact started and until completed. This does not in any way conflict with section 34 (3) or render that subsection otiose, because under a rent review clause the court would not itself be determining the rent but delegating that function.

BRANDON LJ: On the footing that the market rent of premises in general may be affected by the situation with regard to their state of repair in the manner which I have described, the questions whether and how the market rent of the premises concerned in any particular case are so affected must depend on the evidence on that case. If the evidence showed that the market rent would be a rent which varied during the period of the tenancy according to whether the premises (a) remained out of repair, (b) were in the course of being put into repair and (c) had been put into repair, then it seems to me that the court, applying the principle of determination prescribed by section 34 (1) would not only have power to determine, but would be obliged to determine, a differential rent accordingly. If, on the other hand, the evidence showed that the market rent, though affected in amount by the present and future situation with regard to state of repair, would nevertheless be a normal fixed rent over the whole period of the tenancy, then the court's duty would be to determine a fixed rent in accordance with that evidence.

STEPHENSON LJ: I agree with both Goff and Brandon LJJ that on its true construction section 34 as amended authorises, by subsection (3), what has been called a variable rent—that is a provision for the parties varying the rent by a rent review clause—and, by subsection (1), what Brandon LJ has termed a differential rent—that is a provision by the court varying the rent payable at different periods during the term of the new tenancy.

Note: In *Family Management* v. *Gray* (1979) 253 EG 369, the Court of Appeal decided that on an application for a new lease under the 1954 Act, a tenant is not entitled to set up in reduction of the rent to be paid under the lease the defects in the premises arising from his own breach of covenant to repair.

Both the *Fawke* and *Family Management* cases were considered by Warner J in *Harmsworth Pension Funds Trustees Ltd* v. *Charringtons Industrial Holdings Ltd* (1985) 274 EG 588, in the following terms:

'It seems to me that the real issue between [counsel for the plaintiffs] and [counsel for the defendants] is in which of two fairly recent decisions of the Court of Appeal I should look for guidance. The first of those decisions in point of time was

Fawke v. *Viscount Chelsea* [1980] QB 441, on which [counsel for the defendants] relies. The second was *Family Management* v. *Gray* [1979] 253 EG 369, on which [counsel for the plaintiffs] relies.

[Counsel for the defendants] accepts that, as [counsel for the plaintiffs] points out, *Fawke* v. *Viscount Chelsea* was a case that arose out of the failure of the landlord to carry out his obligations to repair the exterior of the property. It was held that, in determining an interim rent for the property under section 24A of the Landlord and Tenant Act 1954, it was proper to have regard to the actual condition of the premises at the date when the interim rent was assessed. That, of course, would diminish the rent receivable by the landlord. There was no question in that case of any breach by the tenant of his repairing obligations, so that no argument of the kind that has been addressed to me was addressed to the Court of Appeal on behalf of the landlord. However, it is fair to say that both Goff LJ and Brandon LJ expressed themselves in their judgments as if the consequences of a breach by the tenant of his repairing obligations would have been the same as the consequences of the breach by the landlord of his.

[Counsel for the plaintiffs] concedes that, if his argument in the present case is right, those passages in the judgments of Goff LJ and Brandon LJ were, to say the least, inappropriately worded in so far as they did not differentiate between the consequences of a breach of an obligation to repair by the landlord and those of a similar breach by the tenant. [Counsel for the plaintiffs] invites me to disregard those *dicta* not only because, in so far as they related the consequences of a failure by the tenant to repair, they were plainly *obiter* (and uttered without the Court of Appeal having had the benefit of hearing the relevant argument) but also because they are inconsistent with the later decision of the Court of Appeal in *Family Management* v. *Gray*.

The learned judge preferred the view in the *Family Management* case and held that in determining the fair market yearly rent for the purpose of a rent review, there should be disregarded any diminishing effect on such rent of any failure by the tenants to repair the demised premises in breach of their obligations under their covenant.

The open market rental under section 34 falls to be determined without regard to tenant's fixtures.

NEW ZEALAND GOVERNMENT PROPERTY CORPORATION v. H.M. & S. LTD

Court of Appeal   [1982] QB 1145

The parties negotiated a new lease of business premises for 21 years at a rent of £25,000 per annum for the first seven years and for the next seven years at the open market rental of the demised premises. The parties disagreed about the appropriate rent for the second seven-year period and the matter was referred to arbitration. The arbitrator decided that the open market rental value was to be determined on the basis that the lease had ended, the tenants had vacated and removed any tenant's fixtures annexed after the expiry of the old lease.

Held: The open market rental of the demised premises was to be determined without regard to tenant's fixtures.

LORD DENNING MR: I hold that when an existing lease expires or is surrendered and is followed immediately by another, to the same tenant remaining in possession, the tenant does not lose his right to remove tenant's fixtures. He is entitled to remove them at the end of his new tenancy.

Improvements

But then it is said that section 34 of the Landlord and Tenant Act 1954, as amended by section 1 of the Law of Property Act 1969, shows that Parliament proceeded on a different course. That section says that in fixing the rent payable under a new tenancy, there is to be taken into account any 'improvements' carried out within the last 21 years, but not those carried out more than 21 years past. But the answer is that that applies to improvements made by the tenant which are 'landlord's fixtures'—which the tenant is never able to remove. It does not apply to 'tenant's fixtures.'

Time of fixing rent

Finally, coming back to our present case, the rent to be assessed for the second seven years was, and would have to be, fixed by agreement or by the judge during the period when the original lease was automatically extended by the Landlord and Tenant Act 1954. During that automatic extension the tenant would certainly have a right to remove the tenant's fixtures. So the new rent should be assessed on that basis.

'Demised premises'

The meaning of 'demised premises' is also elucidated by reference to the repairing clause which is to keep 'the demised premises and the appendages thereof', including the 'landlord's fixtures' in good repair. That indicated that 'tenant's fixtures' are not part of the 'demised premises'.

Conclusion

After this long discussion, I think that in this court we should free ourselves from the shackles of the past. It is time that the law about removal of tenant's fixtures was brought up to date. This case gives this court the opportunity to do so. I think the rent of the Haymarket Theatre should be assessed on the basis that the tenant's fixtures could have been removed by the tenant if he wished—and that they should not be regarded as part of the 'demised premises' for the purpose of fixing the rent.

In fixing what a willing lessor would be prepared to accept, all the circumstances of the case, including the fact of any existing sub–tenancy, have necessarily to be taken into consideration.

OSCROFT v. BENABO

Court of Appeal   [1967] 1 WLR 1087

WILLMER LJ: It seems to me that, if he is a tenant and if his tenancy is a protected one, that must be a relevant circumstance to consider when deciding the rent at which the premises as a whole might reasonably be expected to be let in the open market by a willing lessor; which is what the judge has to decide in pursuance of section 34 of the Landlord and Tenant Act 1954. In fixing that rent, it seems to me that all the circumstances of the particular case, including the fact of any existing sub-tenancy, must necessarily be taken into consideration. In those circumstances, I am not persuaded that the point sought to be taken in this court, even if it is open to the appellants, is a good point.

HARMAN LJ: The point is whether, when finding the market value, the county court judge is to take into account all the factors. If, for instance, there is a statutory tenant in possession of part of the premises, is that a matter which he can take into account in arriving at the open market value? It seems to me that he clearly is entitled to look at the open market value of the premises in the condition in which they are and with such disadvantages as they possess as between a willing lessor and a willing lessee. There is no rule, so far as I can see, to debar the judge from taking into account the fact that there is a statutory tenancy.

In fixing the rent under section 34, the court may in certain circumstances admit evidence of the tenant's trading accounts as an indication of the earning capacity of the premises to a potential lessee but not for the purpose of estimating at what rent the premises might be let in the open market.

HAREWOOD HOTELS LTD v. HARRIS

Court of Appeal   [1958] 1 WLR 108

ROMER LJ: I only want to add a very few words on one aspect of this case which appears to me to be the only point of any general importance that has arisen. It arises out of [counsel for the landlords'] submission that the judge was in error in looking, for any purpose, to the accounts of this hotel company which were placed before him in the quest which he was undertaking for the proper rent to be fixed under section 34 of the Act of 1954. [Counsel for the landlords'] contention is that the accounts of the company were, by inference, barred from consideration as irrelevant under paragraphs (a) and (b) of section 34. I cannot take that view of the matter at all. It seems to me that paragraphs (a) and (b) are really directed to saying that (for example) the fact that the sitting tenant has been in occupation for some time past and has built up a goodwill is to be disregarded in assessing the rent which he is to pay under his new lease. Normally, of course, a man who is in the position of sitting tenant and has built up a business and been there for some years and established himself would be prepared to pay a higher rent than anybody else then coming in for the first time. It is that kind of thing, in my view, to which paragraphs (a) and (b) are directed. But I cannot find anything in the language of those provisions which renders it irrelevant to look at such material as the accounts of this company as part of the material on which the judge must make up his mind as to what rent might reasonably be expected to be obtained for the premises in the open market. I should have thought that one of the first things that anybody who was going to set up a hotel business in this type of premises in this locality would want to know would be what prospects he had of making a good thing out of it, and, therefore, what rent he would be prepared to pay for the premises—if, indeed, he decided to take a tenancy of the premises at all. I cannot see any ground, either on common sense or the language of the section, upon which that consideration should be relegated to the realm of the irrelevant. I do not think that the judge would be entitled to look at the accounts for the purpose of seeing what the company could afford to pay. [Counsel for the landlords'] suggested that that really was what the judge did in the present case—that he looked to see what profit they made in one year and what loss they made in another year, and so on, and said that this company, having regard to those figures, ought not to be expected to pay more than a particular rent. I should be disposed to agree that that was wrong, if the judge did it; but I do not think that he did it at all. He came to the conclusion that this hotel was being run efficiently; he came to the conclusion—and indeed it was agreed on all hands—that the premises could only be used as an hotel, and then, for the purpose which I have mentioned of seeing what a new person, an outsider, would pay as rent for these premises, he looked into the question of what kind of prospects, having regard to the law of supply and demand, this hotel would have. I am quite in agreement with the Master of the Rolls that the judge was justified in looking at the accounts for that purpose. It is not suggested that he dismissed all other considerations from his mind. He shows in the judgment that he did take into account other matters—the evidence of the experts and the offers which had been made for the adjoining property, which, although comparable in some sense, could hardly be described as completely comparable, and were certainly not offers in relation to these premises themselves. The weight which the judge should attribute to those respective considerations—so long as he bore them all in mind—appears to me to be primarily a matter for him; and I cannot see that he went wrong on any point of law in this case either in disregarding matters which he ought to have regarded, or in having regarded matters of which he ought to have taken no notice at all.

The foregoing decision was distinguished in:

W.J. BARTON LTD v. LONG ACRE SECURITIES LTD

Court of Appeal   [1982] 1 WLR 398

The tenants applied to the court for the grant of a new tenancy which the landlords were willing to grant subject to agreement about rent and certain other terms proposed by the tenants. Valuers' reports were exchanged indicating the availability of comparable premises in the vicinity. The tenants also carried on business under a lease of other premises about seven miles away, which lease had been renewed at an agreed rent. The landlords applied for an order that the tenants disclose by way of further discovery all accounts for the past three years in respect of the premises in suit and the premises seven miles away.

Held: In order to determine the open market rent of premises for the purposes of section 34 of the 1954 Act, the best evidence was the rent traders carrying on business in the same area were prepared to pay for similar premises. There was no general proposition of law that the tenants' business accounts were always relevant although such accounts might be relevant when comparable premises were not available and the premises were peculiarly adapted for a particular purpose. In the present case, since there were comparable premises in the area of the shop in suit, discovery of the tenants' trading accounts should not be ordered.

OLIVER LJ: The inquiry upon which the court is directed to embark in applications for new tenancies under the Act is set out in section 34 of the Act, the relevant provisions of which are as follows:

> 'The rent payable under a tenancy granted by order of the court under this Part of this Act shall be such ... as, in default of ... agreement, may be determined by the court to be that at which, having regard to the terms of the tenancy (other than those relating to rent), the holding might reasonably be expected to be let in the open market by a willing lessor, there being disregarded—(a) any effect on rent of the fact that the tenant has or his predecessors in title have been in occupation of the holding, (b) any goodwill attached to the holding by reason of the carrying on thereat of the business of the tenant (whether by him or by a predecessor of his in that business) ...'

There are two additional matters specified in the section which fall to be disregarded, but they are irrelevant to any issue raised by this appeal and can be ignored for present purposes.

So what the court has to look for is the open market rent of the premises simply as premises at which a business of the type carried on by the tenant can be carried on, but that rent is not to be enhanced, reduced or otherwise affected by the tenant's own actual occupation of the holding or by any goodwill created as a result of the business which the tenant has carried on. To put it broadly, the rent is to be arrived at on the hypothesis that the premises are empty and without regard to the tenant's previous trading.

This immediately raises the question in one's mind—of what relevance to such an inquiry are the tenant's trading results? The court is not concerned with the tenant's ability to pay rent but with the rent which a willing lessor could command for these premises in the hypothetical open market and there is a perfectly well recognised way of arriving at that by reference to the rents payable for similar premises in the vicinity.

Indeed, if one is to take into consideration the results of the tenant's trading as a relevant factor in arriving at the open market rent, the elimination from that consideration of any effect on rent from the tenant's occupation and from the goodwill involves an extraordinarily difficult practical exercise.

In his judgment the judge observed 'It is highly material to know, in order to ascertain the open market rent, what the trading position is'; and a little later he said: 'In a case of this sort where the open market rental value is in dispute, evidence of trading is relevant and admissible to consider and show what the open market value is.'

We confess that, for our part, we are entirely unable to follow this in the case of a property such as this where there are, as it is conceded that there are, plenty of comparable premises in the vicinity from which the open market value of premises of this type can be deduced. No doubt evidence of the tenant's trading would indicate whether his business had been successful or unsuccessful and so might be a pointer to the rent which this particular individual tenant might be prepared to pay in order to spare himself the disruption of moving to other similar premises in the area, but that has nothing to do with the open market rent which the court is directed by the Act to ascertain. That it is for this purpose that the discovery is sought is, we think, tolerably clear from the statement of the landlords' valuer submitted by [counsel for the landlords] which contains a frank avowal that if these tenants, in the light of their turnover in their Tufnell Park shop, have been prepared to pay a particular rent there, the disclosure of that turnover and of the turnover of the business in the premises in suit will be an indication of the sort of rent which it might be prepared to agree to for these premises.

[Counsel for the landlords] sought originally to justify the judge's order, not on any general principle that a tenant's trading records are relevant in every application for a new tenancy under the Act, but on the special ground that they were relevant in the instant case because of the fact that the tenants carried on a similar business in another area in premises rented from, in effect, the same landlord.

It is, however, difficult to see why the trading records of a similar business carried on in a totally different area, miles away from the premises in suit, should be thought to be any guide at all to the open market value of the latter. Why, it may be asked, stop at Tufnell Park? Why are the trading results of business carried on in Croydon or Piccadilly or Burnham-on-Crouch not equally relevant?

Ultimately [counsel for the landlords] felt compelled to fall back on a general proposition that the accounts of a tenant's trading in business premises—and, we suppose, also in other premises—are always relevant to any application under the Act as providing a guide to the open market rent. Support for such a proposition is said to be found in *Woodfall, Landlord and Tenant*, 28th ed. (1978), vol. 2, para. 2–0740, p 2441, where it is said:

'Evidence of the trading accounts of the existing business is admissible for the purpose of showing the earning capacity of the premises but not for any other purpose.'

The authority cited in support of this proposition is the decision of this court in *Harewood Hotels Ltd* v. *Harris* [1958] 1 WLR 108. That case was concerned with some rather unusual hotel premises in Tunbridge Wells catering largely for retired people and consisting of three adjoining houses in a terrace of six. It is not entirely clear from the report, but it rather looks as if the only comparable premises in the area were the three adjoining houses belonging to the same landlords which were, of course, not strictly comparable since they remained as private houses and had not been adapted for use as a hotel. It was in these circumstances that the tenant tendered and the judge received evidence of the tenant's trading for the purpose of showing what sort of profit a tenant of this hotel might expect to make and thus what level of rent a prospective tenant would be likely to pay. The landlord appealed on the ground that the evidence was irrelevant and that, in any event, the judge was precluded from considering it by the provisions of section 34 (*a*) and (*b*) to which reference has been made above. This court dismissed the appeal. We cannot, however, read the decision as supporting any general proposition that evidence of this type is relevant and admissible in every application under the Act. It was relevant in that case because of the absence of any comparable premises and of the nature of the business under consideration; and the effect of the decision appears to us to be only this, that where such evidence is required in order to establish the open market rent there is nothing in section 34 which prohibits its reception for this limited purpose. But to extract from that some more general proposition that evidence of trading is always to be admitted seems to us to be a quite impermissible extension of the ambit of the decision.

[Counsel for the landlords] relies particularly on the following passage from the judgment of Lord Evershed MR, at p 111:

'If the evidence was led for the purpose of showing that these tenants ought to be granted some concession because of some particular hardship that they had suffered, that might be another matter; and I agree also that the terms of the paragraph serve to exclude the consideration that a tenant might be expected to be willing to pay rather more than an outsider because he would not wish to be disturbed in his occupation. But, in my judgment, it is plainly legitimate for a judge to hear evidence which bears upon the question which he has to decide, namely: what would the particular holding reasonably be expected to be let at in the open market? Plainly, I should have thought, in arriving at a conclusion upon that question, it is legitimate to hear evidence of what similar premises which are being let for a particular purpose (as the one in suit is) can be expected to earn for a potential lessee in the market in the place where the premises are; and, if so, then similar evidence is, in my judgment, admissible for proving the same point about the premises in suit. In other words, if the purpose of the evidence of the figures was for that limited objective, then I think for my part that they were perfectly admissible and that no objection can be made to them.'

Now that, on the face of it, appears to be a statement which at least is capable of general application, but it has, in our judgment, to be read in the context of the particular facts which rendered the evidence relevant in that case, namely, that the premises were capable of being used only as an hotel and that the only physically comparable premises appear to have been private houses. This, we think, appears rather more clearly from the judgment of Romer LJ.

Certainly the decision shows that there may be cases where the production of trading figures may be both relevant and admissible and that where that is so section 34 does not inhibit the consideration of such evidence for the narrow limited purpose described even though the exclusion of any consideration of the effect of the tenant's occupation and of goodwill may present the judge with a very difficult task.

It is, we think, clear that there are several types of premises, of which an hotel is only one example, where the ascertainment of an open market rent may depend upon an assessment of the likely profitability of the business for which the premises are peculiarly adapted. Other instances might be a petrol-filling station, a theatre or a racecourse, in all of which the market rent may well depend upon the average takings. It is both unncessary and would be unwise to seek to define or limit the categories of premises where such evidence would be relevant for the limited purpose described in the *Harewood Hotels* case [1958] 1 WLR 108. But that is a far cry from saying that such evidence is always relevant and, in our judgment, considerations of this sort do not apply in the ordinary case of shop premises with no peculiar features in a business area such as that with which the instant case is concerned and where there are plenty of comparable premises from which the open market rents can be deduced.

There is no peculiarity in the premises themselves or the business carried on there which would lead to the conclusion that trading records would be of any assistance and it cannot, in our judgment, make any difference that the landlord, for his own purposes, seeks to restrict the user of the premises by a covenant in the lease. Such a restriction may, no doubt, decrease the obtainable rent by restricting the market to those engaged in the particular specified trade, but it cannot alter the nature of the relevant evidence from which the open market rent is to be ascertained.

In the ordinary way, the best evidence of the open market rent is what traders carrying on business in the area are prepared to pay for premises of this type and evidence of the successful or unsuccessful nature of the particular tenant's business would, in our judgment, generally be not only irrelevant but also positively confusing. Nothing in the circumstances of this case suggests that the discovery sought by the landlords could be of any assistance in determining the open market rent. It would, in our judgment, be very unfortunate and would greatly increase the expense and length of proceedings under the Act if the statement which we have referred to in *Woodfall, Landlord and Tenant*, 28th ed.—which is perfectly accurate so far as it goes in relation to the case cited in the footnote—were thought to justify a general proposition that the tenant's business accounts are always relevant material or the notion that orders for discovery of the type sought in this case ought as a matter of course to be made in applications under the Act for new tenancies.

Note: See also Chapter 9, section 9.3, entitled 'Taking trading results into account', at page 195, earlier.

The court may insert a rent review clause in the new lease so as not to prejudice the landlord where a long term is granted.

IN RE No. 88, HIGH ROAD, KILBURN

Chancery Division   [1959] 1 WLR 279

WYNN-PARRY J: I have to consider first the question of the term for which this new lease should be granted, disregarding for the moment that which I shall have to decide later—a question of law as to the date from which the lease is to begin, and a question which has not yet formed the subject of any judicial decision in the High Court, although there is a decision of a judge of county courts. The tenants ask that the new lease should be for a term of 14 years, and they ask for that because naturally they want security of tenure. The landlords, on the other hand, understandably, would like the shorter term of seven years. There is no likelihood of their wanting to use the premises themselves—they are a private family company which buys properties for investment and do not propose to embark on any retail trade themselves—but they say that if the tenants are to have security of tenure in the shape of the longer term, then a guard against inflation should be provided for them, and that a provision should therefore be included in the lease that, at the end of the first half, a right should be given to the landlords by the lease, to have the rent reviewed, provided that any review shall not have the effect of lowering the rent but only of increasing it, if on a review it is considered that, in the circumstances then obtaining, the rental value of the property has increased.

My inclination is to provide the tenants with the longer term of years, provided that I do not prejudice the landlords. [Counsel for the tenants] asked that a further term should be put in, giving to the tenants a right to break the lease at seven years if the result of the review of the rent, in their opinion, resulted in too high a figure. I think, on the whole, that they are asking for the best of both worlds, and I propose to grant to the tenants the equivalent of a 14-year term, but to direct that there be included in the lease a provision for the review of the rent at the end of the first half of the term for which the landlords ask.

Note: The tenants subsequently applied under section 36 (2) of the 1954 Act for an order revoking the new tenancy granted under the Act. In making the order of revocation, Wynn-Parry J ordered the tenants under section 36 (3) to pay the whole of the landlords' costs including those of the application.

The court may insert a rent review clause in the new lease which provides for review of rent downwards as well as upwards.

STYLO SHOES LTD v. MANCHESTER ROYAL EXCHANGE LTD

Chancery Division   (1967) 204 EG 803

CROSS J: Finally there was the form of the rent revision clause. For many years now it had been almost common form to introduce into a lease of more than seven years a provision in the interests of the landlord for a stepping-up of the rent after seven years if it then appeared that it was too low. A provision of that sort was inserted by Wynn-Parry J, in a new lease applied for under the Act as long ago as 1959. In that case it was argued on behalf of the tenants that the tenants ought to have the right to get out of the lease after seven years if the rent was substantially increased and they did not like paying a higher rent. Wynn-Parry J, rejected that argument, and the tenants were not of course asking for that now. They were asking that there should be a corresponding right in them to apply for a reduction of the rent after seven years if, and it seemed a very unlikely supposition, market conditions then were such as to warrant a lower rent. I do not think that the courts had ever hitherto addressed themselves to that question. It was a rather academic matter, but I see no reason why sauce for the goose should not be sauce for the gander. I propose to insert a corresponding right for the tenants in the rent revision clause.

The decision in *Stylo Shoes* (above) was applied in:

JANES (GOWNS) LTD v. HARLOW DEVELOPMENT CORPORATION

Chancery Division   (1979) 253 EG 799

HIS HONOUR JUDGE FINLAY QC: I turn now to the question whether there should be provision, not only for a rent review, which it is agreed there should be at five-yearly intervals, but for a review down as well as up. It was decided by Cross J, as he then was, in *Stylo Shoes Ltd* v. *Manchester Royal Exchange Ltd*, reported in (1967) 204 EG 803, that in determining the terms appropriate under a new lease granted under this jurisdiction the court could in its discretion provide for a rent review clause which provided for review of the rent downwards as well as upwards.

In my judgment it is appropriate that the rent review clause should deal with the possibility of rent being varied downwards as well as upwards. And I reach that conclusion because of the evidence which I have heard about the development of what is called the Harvey Centre in the near neighbourhood of the demised premises, a development which may well have the result of rendering a rent calculated prior to that development taking place inappropriate in future years. In short the rents may in the neighbourhood of the Harvey Centre go down; equally they may go up. Having regard to that possibility, I think it appropriate that the rent review clause should provide for the review in either direction. It is submitted, however, that if such provision is inserted in the lease then some *quid pro quo* by way of increase in the rent should be allowed, because the provision of such a clause is an advantage to the tenant. It is said that the comparable rents which have been considered in arriving at the appropriate rent for these premises were all contained in leases which contained rent review clauses providing for revision of the rent upwards, and that no doubt was an advantage to the landlords which should be taken into account in arriving at these comparable rents. I am not satisfied that that is the right approach to take to this matter. In my judgment the only way to find out what is the appropriate rent is to have regard to the rents of neighbouring property and in doing so to arrive at a view as to what rent the holding might reasonably be expected to be let at in the open market. In conditions where it is expected that rents will over the period of the lease continue to rise it is no doubt common to insert rent review clauses to provide for an upgrading of the rent at appropriate intervals. I am by no means satisfied that the insertion of such a provision leads to any reductions in the rent paid under the lease. It is in my view more likely that in a particular state of the market leases are simply only granted on the basis that the rent review clause is inserted. Twenty-five yars ago it was a provision that was rarely if ever come across. In the last 15 years it has become so common as to be a matter of common form. I am not satisfied on the evidence before me that the insertion of rent review clauses for review in one direction only have affected the rents which have been payable, and accordingly I think that the appropriate course to take is to insert a rent review clause in this lease to provide for variation in either direction but to make no consequential adjustment to the rent which I have already indicated is the appropriate rent.

The date from which the rent is to be determined under section 34 is the date of the hearing but taking account of matters which could reasonably be expected to happen between that date and the date of commencement of the new term.

LOVELY AND ORCHARD SERVICES v. DAEJAN INVESTMENTS (GROVE HALL)

Chancery Division   (1977) 246 EG 651

HIS HONOUR JUDGE FINLAY QC: I am not persuaded that the proper date for determination of the rent is the date upon which the tenancy comes to an end as specified in section 25. Section 34 requires the rent to be ascertained as being that at which the holding might reasonably be expected to be let in the open market by a willing lessor, there being disregarded various matters set out in section 34 (1). The tenancy in respect of which that rent falls to be determined is one which under the provisions of the Act is not to commence until after the date of the hearing. In these circumstances, it appears to me to be very likely, upon the reading of the words in the section, that the notice thereto is contemplating that the market will be regarded as at the date of the hearing. But there is this consideration to be borne in mind that, since the tenancy is not to commence until a date after the date of the hearing, it would be likely that the provisions should contemplate that the court would take into account changes which might be reasonably expected to take place between the date of the hearing and the date when the term commences. It seems to me to be *prima facie* unlikely that the section requires the court to determine the rent as at the date which may be long past if there be the possibility that in the meantime circumstances may have radically changed so that what was a reasonable rent as at the date specified at the termination of the tenancy in the section 25 notice may no longer be a reasonable rent at the date of the hearing.

There is no direct authority on it, but in the case heard by Megarry J, as he then was, in 1972, *English Exporters (London) Ltd* v. *Eldonwall Ltd* [1973] 1 Ch 415, there fell to be considered certain questions as to the principles to be applied in determining the interim rent on an application under section 24A. In the course of dealing with that matter, Megarry J also determined the substantive rent to be paid in respect of the new tenancy, and in dealing with that it is evident from the report that his determination proceeded on the footing that the witnesses, whose evidence was heard as to the duration of the lease, were giving evidence, as at the date of the hearing, relevant to a tenancy which was to begin at a future date, the parties there being agreed as to the date at which the tenancy should commence. Having referred to those difficulties, as he did, at p 419, Megarry J says at p 431:

'A determination under section 34 alone is necessarily prospective, fixing a new rent as from the future commencement of the new tenancy, whereas a determination under section 24A will usually, if not always, be in some degree retrospective, applying in part to a period that has already run.'

and then he goes on to consider the section 24A point. He then says:

'The facts that section 34 is prospective, and that under section 24A (3) there is a hypothetical yearly tenancy, seem to me to provide sufficient grounds for holding that the values to be applied should be those existing when the interim period begins to run.

There appears to have been no argument in that case as to the date at which the section 34 determination should be considered or, to put it another way, as to the appropriate date for the purposes of the section 34 determination, but the clear statement made by Megarry J in the passage which I have read that a determination under section 34 alone is necessarily prospective appears to me to indicate clearly the view, which accords with my own, that under section 34 what falls to be done is to ascertain what would be the rent at which the premises might reasonably be expected to be let in the open market as at the date when the tenancy is going to commence. If that be so, then it is submitted on behalf of the landlords that the result of that is that because of section 64 and the uncertainty introduced by that section as to when the tenancy will commence (having regard to the possibility that the proceedings may not be determined at the hearing at first instance but may then go to appeal) that uncertainty introduces a complication which renders this mode of approach to section 34 highly impracticable.

I do not accept that that result follows. The duty of the court in determining the rent under section 34 appears to me to be to determine the rent under that section as at the date of the hearing, but having regard to such evidence as there may be that indicates that any changes may have to be taken into account, being changes that the evidence shows are likely to occur between the date of the hearing and the date when, assuming that the court's order stands as it is made by the court, the new tenancy will commence. That will be the period of three months from the date of the hearing, plus any time that falls to be allowed under section 64 (2) for an appeal being instituted. The court cannot, it seems to me, reasonably determine the rent for the purposes of section 34 on the footing that proceedings are going to be prolonged for an indefinite and unascertained period. The duty of the court is to determine the rent as at the date of the hearing, but it must do so having regard to what is the likely date of the commencement of the tenancy. Accordingly, I must reject the submission made on behalf of the landlords that the proper date to have regard to for the purpose of section 34 is 14 October 1975 and I hold that the date is that which I indicated.

22.5   Other terms—section 35

The landlord is not entitled without justification to the insertion of terms in the new tenancy which are more onerous than the terms in the current tenancy.

GOLD v. BRIGHTON CORPORATION

Court of Appeal   [1956] 1 WLR 1291

The tenant of shop premises in Brighton, dealing in new and secondhand furs and clothes, applied for the grant of a new tenancy. The landlords agreed to grant a new 14 year lease but proposed that the new lease should contain a clause prohibiting the sale or purchase of secondhand goods save with the consent of the landlords.

Held: The restriction on selling or purchasing secondhand goods should be struck out as this activity was an important part of the tenant's business. Accordingly, the terms of the new tenancy should be such as to permit her to use the premises for her existing business, including dealings in secondhand clothes.

DENNING LJ: The tenant says that it was wrong for the judge to restrict her from selling secondhand clothes, because that would deprive her of part of her existing business. She says that the secondhand clothing was the main part of her business. She said it was a very highclass secondhand shop, and it was the main part of her business. She asks for the restriction to be removed, on the ground that that was not a proper order for the judge to make. It is common ground that the rent of £650 is not affected by the restriction one way or the other.

The reason why the corporation seek to impose this restriction is because they say that to use these premises in North Street, Brighton, for secondhand clothes would lower the tone of the street: and would hamper them in their efforts to keep up the character of the street. There was very little evidence in the court below to support this contention—it was only hinted at—and since the decision, the corporation have acted in a way that is hardly consistent with it. It has been disclosed to us that the very next door premises, No. 40A North Street, which are also owned by the corporation, have since been the subject of a similar application for a new tenancy. A new lease has been ordered whereby the tenant of those premises (a relative of Mrs Gold) is permitted to continue to sell secondhand clothes there as she has done for some years.

Turning now to the Act of 1954, I think it plainly intends to protect the tenant in respect of his business. Section 23 says that the Act applies to premises which are occupied by the tenant 'for the purposes of a business carried on by him.' Inasmuch as the tenant is to be protected in respect of his business, the terms of the new tenancy should be such as to enable him to carry on his business as it is. They should not prevent him from carrying on an important part of it. At any rate, if he is to be prevented from using the premises in the future in the way in which he has used it in the past, it is for the landlord to justify the restriction: and there ought to be strong and cogent evidence for the purpose. I find no such evidence here. The mere suggestion or hint that the tone of the street would be lowered is not enough. On this ground I would allow the appeal.

It seems to me that the new tenancy ought to be such as to permit the tenant to carry on her existing business of a furrier and seller of ladies' wear, and the additional business of selling children's wear, and that it should not be confined to new clothes, but should extend to secondhand clothes as well.

A question has arisen before us as to whether the tenant should not be allowed more liberty still. It was suggested that she should be left unrestricted to the same extent as in the former lease, with the result that she should carry on any kind of shop there. I do not think that would be right. The judge, when he gave his judgment, said that he thought it was reasonable to make some restriction. It is to be remembered that the object of this Act is to protect the tenant in respect of his or her business, and not to put a new saleable asset into her hands. The clause which I have proposed enables Mrs Gold to carry on her existing business, and, indeed, in respect of children's wear, enables her to expand it. That is, I think, sufficient. After all, if in the years to come a change of user was reasonable, no doubt the corporation would give their consent. It seems to me that this appeal should be allowed and the terms of the new lease ordered by the judge should be varied in the way I have said.

The *Gold* case was applied in:

CARDSHOPS LTD v. DAVIES

Court of Appeal   [1971] 1 WLR 591

The tenants of business premises applied for a new tenancy at the same rent for 14 years and on the terms of the old tenancy, which contained a covenant against assignment without the landlord's consent. The landlords did not oppose the new tenancy but proposed a term of 21 years, a higher rent (with periodic reviews) and other terms which included an absolute covenant against assignment. Later, the landlords offered to accept a covenant against assignment without consent provided that the covenant included a proviso to the effect that in the event of the tenants contemplating an assignment they would first offer to surrender the term for no consideration. The trial judge approved a form of lease which included the covenant and proviso suggested by the landlords.

Held: The judge ought not to have approved the covenant and proviso because the proviso was so novel and burdensome a departure from the terms of the former tenancy as not to be permissible under section 35 of the 1954 Act, in the absence of special reasons. Accordingly, the lease should be amended so that it included such a covenant against assignment as was in the original lease.

EDMUND DAVIES LJ: The particular term in the old tenancy that is here directly material is, of course, that the undertaking in relation to assignment was accompanied by or subject to merely a qualified prohibition. [Counsel for the tenants] has submitted—with, I think, a great deal of justification—that the clause substituted by the judge in this regard was so markedly different from, and so much more burdensome upon the tenants than, the old term in relation to assignment that it ought not to be tolerated. It is a very big thing for a tenant who is contemplating an assignment—the landlord being required to consent to that assignment if it be reasonable in all the circumstances—nevertheless to be obliged to offer to surrender the tenancy.

[Counsel for the tenants] says that this is putting the tenant at risk, according to the landlord's whim, of having his goodwill destroyed. He relies, and in my judgment effectively, upon the decision of this court in *Gold* v. *Brighton Corporation* [1956] 1 WLR 1291, a case different in its facts from those of the present matter, but nevertheless so basically similar that the decision arrived at and the reasons expressed therefore afford me considerable help in relation to this appeal. Denning LJ was there dealing with a case where shop premises in Brighton had for some little time been used for dealing in new and secondhand furs and clothes. The landlords agreed to the tenant's request to grant a new lease, but they proposed that it should contain a clause prohibiting the sale or purchase of secondhand goods save with the consent of the corporation. This court held that the additional requirement was not a proper term to impose.

For my part, I think that the new clause 2 (11) approved of by the judge was a far more drastic change in the terms of the tenancy than was involved even in *Gold* v. *Brighton Corporation*. It imperilled the whole existence of such goodwill as these tenants had built up. They could not assign even to the most responsible person without first offering to surrender their tenancy to the landlords. I think that that was so novel and burdensome a departure from the terms of the former tenancy as not to be permissible under the Act. In my judgment the judge was wrong in imposing it, and I would be for excising all those parts of the new clause which went beyond requiring the tenants to seek the landlords' permission and placing upon the landlords the obligation of assenting thereto unless, upon some reasonable grounds, such an assignment could be objected to.

In **Charles Clements (London) Ltd v. Rank City Wall Ltd** (1978) 246 EG 739, the landlords proposed that an existing covenant against user for purposes other than the business of retail cutler without the landlords' written consent be modified to include 'such consent not to be unreasonably withheld'. This proposal was likely to increase the rent by £1750 per annum and was opposed by the tenants.

Held: The covenant should not be so modified in the absence of any special reason.

GOULDING LJ: The proposal in the present case, submits [counsel for the landlord], will not only provide a higher rent for the landlord, it will have advantages to the tenant, too. First of all the existing lease (in the positive portion of the subparagraph that I have read) obliges the tenant to continue to carry on the existing type of business throughout the term, and it prevents the tenant, either by itself or through an underlessee or assignee, from carrying on a different business. That limitation would in effect be removed by the proposed change. Again, although the landlord cannot under the existing provisions unreasonably refuse consent to an assignment or underlease of the whole of the premises, the restriction as to user would prevent any such assignment or underlease being made on reasonable terms if the trade of a retail cutler were to become unprofitable. There again the relaxation of the restriction, it is said, will confer a valuable benefit on the tenant. All that will be given to the tenant, in return for the advantage of a higher rent to the landlord, if the landlord's proposal is accepted. Conversely, it is submitted, if the landlord's proposal is rejected the court will be preventing the landlord from getting what it was meant to get under the Act as the condition of a renewed tenancy, namely a truly open market rent by current values for the landlord's property.

In my judgment those contentions are ill-founded. I have been referred to a number of authorities and I rely in particular on *Gold* v. *Brighton Corporation* [1956] 1 WLR 1291, *Aldwych Club* v. *Copthall Property Company* (1963) 185 EG 219, and *Cardshops* v. *Davies* [1971] 1 WLR 591. Of those the first and last are decisions of the Court of Appeal, the *Aldwych Club* case is a decision of Pennycuick J. Approaching the Act with the guidance derived from those authorities I find it clear that the protection intended to be given by Part II of the Act is to the tenant in his character of an occupying business tenant carrying on his trade on the premises. The advantages promised to the tenant as delineated by [counsel for the landlord] are advantages that would benefit the tenant if and when it wishes to discontinue the present business. The obligation to continue the business, the restriction on carrying on some different business, is no burden to the tenant while it continues to do what it was the policy of the Act to protect it in continuing to do. Thus those advantages are to be regarded, I think, for the purpose of exercising the court's discretion as essentially collateral. On the other hand the correlative burden on the tenant of paying a higher rent to the landlord is something that immediately affects the tenant in the carrying on of its business because there is a further outgoing, perhaps £1750 per annum (it matters not what is the exact figure) that has to be met before any profit can be arrived at. Thus the argument that the landlord should not be prevented from conferring a benefit on the tenant by modifying the restriction is one that seems to me unpersuasive.

Similarly I think there is an error of reasoning in the argument that, in the circumstances of this case, the landlord, if its proposal is not accepted, will be prevented from getting the open market rent intended by the Act. Section 34 of the Act says that the rent under the new tenancy, in default of agreement, is to be that at which, having regard to the terms of the tenancy, the holding might reasonably be expected to be let in the open market by a willing lessor. That, as Widgery LJ pointed out, presupposes that the terms are known, and under section 35 the terms of a tenancy granted by order of the court are, in default of agreement, to be determined by the court having regard 'to the terms of the current tenancy and to all relevant circumstances'. That does not mean that the terms of the current tenancy are necessarily decisive, because there may be other circumstances that outweigh them, but it is a guide to the court that Parliament wanted the terms of the current tenancy to be considered in the forefront in every case, along with any relevant circumstances of the particular case. Here I have no evidence of any special facts affecting the property that are not common to all retail premises in high-class business areas. If the parties are to be at liberty to insist on changes in the terms of the existing tenancy simply because they consider them beneficial to themselves, a field would be opened which I think the court would find it bewildering to traverse. Every tenant could volunteer to accept increased liabilities as to this or that matter for the purpose of getting, on terms that he thought might ultimately profit him, a lower rent; every landlord might press this or that concession on the tenant because it would enable him to say the open market rent was a higher rent. It therefore appears to me, for the purposes of the present case, that the right course is to take the terms of the existing lease as a sufficient guide in this respect, and not to make the alteration desired by the landlord since no special reason is shown for it and the tenant objects to it.

The court has power to require the tenant to provide a guarantor of his obligations, but when exercising its discretion to grant a new lease should not generally require the tenant to pay the costs of the landlord in the preparation of the new lease.

CAIRNPLACE LTD v. C.B.L. (PROPERTY INVESTMENTS CO. LTD)

Court of Appeal   (1983) 269 EG 542

The original lease contained provisions that the tenant should pay the landlord's costs of the lease and that on an assignment to a limited company the tenant should procure guarantees of the company's performance of its obligations under the lease. Following such an assignment, the tenant company sought a new lease. The landlord proposed a term in the new lease requiring comparable guarantees to those in the old and also payment of their costs of the lease.

Held:

(1) There was jurisdiction to make an order as to guarantees.

(2) In view of the Costs of Leases Act 1958, it was wrong to require the tenant to pay the scale costs of the landlord in the preparation of a new lease.

CUMMING-BRUCE LJ:

Jurisdiction

The first question raised by the appellants is whether the learned judge had jurisdiction under section 35 of the Landlord and Tenant Act 1954 to impose the term set out in the first paragraph of the schedule to her order. They submit that the whole object of the Act is to provide the tenant with security of tenure, which in the context means that the tenant must be granted a new tenancy without any further security for the performance of his obligations other than his own promise to perform them. They seek to derive support from the provisions of section 41A (6) because if the court already had jurisdiction to include a term for guarantors the subsection would be unnecessary. And they contend that some limitation must be put as a matter of construction upon the wide terms of section 35. The Act deals with the contractual relationship of landlord and tenant only, and the court has no power over third parties. Whatever else is negotiable, security of tenure is not. They seek to rely upon the reasoning of the speeches in *O'May* v. *City of London Real Property Company Ltd* [1982] 2 WLR 407, *Barclays Bank Ltd* v. *Ascott* [1961] 1 WLR 717, and *Kirkwood* v. *Johnson* (1979) 38 P & CR 392.

We reject these submissions. The words of the section in their ordinary meaning are clearly wide enough to include all those provisions which will become contractually binding on the parties when the lease is executed. The term imposed by the judge is not a condition precedent, and we find nothing in the cases relied upon by the appellants to support the proposition that it was outside the powers conferred by section 35. There are many terms included commonly in leases which depend for their efficacy upon the cooperation of third parties: an obligation to insure is a ready example. And we do not accept that it is a relevant distinction that in such common terms there is a market into which the tenant may go to fulfil his obligation as compared to the difficulty which may face him if required to obtain guarantors specifically identified as individuals or members of a small class such as directors of the tenant company. In our view that distinction is relevant to discretion, not to jurisdiction. There is a simple explanation of the inclusion of subsection (6) in section 41A. The section contemplates, among other situations, the determination of the obligations of one or more of the joint tenants or partners who were parties to the old lease. The old lease therefore afforded the landlord a different security for the performance of the obligations of the business tenants from that available in the new lease. It was to meet this situation that the Act provided that although there might be no provision for guarantors in the old lease, the court should have specific power to impose a term requiring them in the new lease between parties who were not identified with the parties in the old lease. We hold that there was jurisdiction to impose the term in the first paragraph of the first schedule to the order.

Discretion

We consider that on the facts, the case for the exercise of discretion in the way in which the learned judge exercised it could hardly be stronger. Clause 15 (h) of the lease made between the landlord and Tartan Textiles Ltd on 8 May 1972 expressly provided for guarantors being directors of satisfactory standing of the limited company seeking assignment of the demised premises for all or part of the term of 10 years granted by the lease. When Tartan Textiles Ltd and Cairnplace Ltd and the directors, Lester and Rifkin, negotiated licence to assign the tail end of the lease, all parties, including the two directors, agreed that in consideration of licence to assign granted on 25 February 1981 the two directors, as sureties, would covenant in the terms set out in clauses 3 and 4 of the licence. That instrument was signed and sealed by the two guarantors. The assignment followed on 6 March 1981 and included the covenant by the two directors in clause 2 thereof. Six months later, following the landlord's contractual notice to quit at the end of the term, the assignees applied to the court for a new lease for a term of 10 years. Obviously that application was contemplated by the assignees when they entered into possession for the purpose of establishing a new business in the parcels assigned for a term expiring at the end of year. The appellants submit that the term proposed by the landlord is a new term. The lease of 8 May 1972 only required guarantors on assignment of the term assigned. Those guarantees lasting a year were duly given. There was no provision in the lease of 1972 for guarantees to be given extending to the term of any new lease sought by the assignees pursuant to the provisions of Part II of the Landlord and Tenant Act 1954. But, as we understand the appellants' arguments, even that would not have availed the landlord because they have strenuously argued here and below that the court would have no jurisdiction anyway. Then the appellants' argument proceeds: term for guarantees for a year odd is a different and much less rigorous obligation than a guarantee for 10 years.

This is an unattractive submission. The term of 10 years is a term proposed by the tenant. The practical effect of the argument is that if there are greater risks of tenant's default over a 10-year term than over the year for which the assignment was contractually effective, the landlord, not the directors of the company, should bear the risk. As the whole adventure was promoted by the two directors who, we were told, by their voting rights control the company, it is not an argument which might be expected to stimulate sympathy on the part of the learned judge. In our view there is no ground for disturbing her exercise of discretion.

In the foregoing, we have deliberately confined our reasoning to the facts of the instant case. But the judge's decision upon the exercise of discretion is only an illustration of what is fair and reasonable having regard to the existing lease and to all the circumstances. Thus the principle which we have affirmed is wider than the application of the principle to the facts of this case. We only add this observation in case our judgment is interpreted more narrowly than is the case. Each case, as the section makes clear, must be decided on its own facts; there may be many other circumstances, differing widely from those in the instant case, in which it would be fair and reasonable for the court to determine that there should be guarantors of the tenant's obligations in the new lease.

The cost of the lease

The appellant company also appeals against the term determined by the learned judge pursuant to section 35 of the Act, which provided that the costs clause was to remain as in the original lease. Clause 4 (31) of the existing lease was a covenant by the tenant. 'To pay the scale costs of the landlord's solicitors in respect of this lease and the stamp duty on the counterpart thereof.' As there are now no relevant scales, it is common ground on this appeal that if the order is upheld in principle, the obligation upon the tenant should be varied to an obligation to pay the landlord's reasonable costs rather than a simple repetition of clause 4 (31) of the existing lease.

The point is a short one. By the Costs of Leases Act 1958—

'1. **Costs of leases** Notwithstanding any custom to the contrary, a party to a lease shall, unless the parties thereto agree otherwise in writing, be under no obligation to pay the whole or any part of any other party's solicitor's costs of the lease.
2. **Interpretation** In this Act—
(a) 'lease' includes an underlease and an agreement for a lease or underlease or for a tenancy or sub-tenancy; ...'

Therefore, if the terms of the new lease had been negotiated between the parties, neither party was under an obligation to pay the other party's solicitor's costs of the lease unless otherwise agreed in writing. The learned judge dealt concisely with this issue. She gave a summary of the submissions made by counsel for the tenant and for the landlord, and decided that she saw no reason to vary the costs clause and preferred the argument of counsel for the landlord. This argument was to the effect that section 35 of the Act confers on the judge the discretion to determine other terms, which was not supplanted by the Costs of Leases Act 1958.

With respect to the learned judge we do not accept her decision on this issue. In 1954 there was a custom that the tenant should pay the landlord's costs of preparing a lease which was a practice generally followed by conveyancing solicitors in the absence of express agreement in the agreement for a lease. So when in 1972 the lease between the landlord and Tartan Textiles (the existing lease) included clause 4 (31) the clause was consistent with the general practice, and before the Costs of Leases Act came into operation there is no doubt that the court had the power to embody it as 'another term' in the new lease pursuant to section 35 of the 1954 Act. But in 1958 Parliament relieved the tenant of the usual obligation which conveyancing custom and practice had imposed upon tenants. Thereafter it was only if there was express agreement in writing whereby the tenant agreed to pay the landlord's costs of preparation of the lease that the tenant was under an obligation.

Where Parliament has enacted a later Act designed to relieve tenants of a specific obligation, it is not in our view a correct exercise of judicial discretion to use the wide power conferred upon the court by the general words of section 35 of the 1954 Act to deprive the tenant of the protection conferred upon him by a later Act dealing specifically with this very obligation. It is perfectly correct to say that section 35 deals with the powers of the court and not with the agreement of a term by the parties. But it does not follow that the court when exercising discretion in determining other terms pursuant to section 35 can fairly and reasonably deprive the tenant of a protection that Parliament conferred upon him in 1958.

For those reasons we allow the appeal in respect of the order respecting the costs of the lease made by the learned judge and delete that clause from the new lease.

The burden of persuading a court to change the terms of a business lease on its renewal is on the party proposing them and the court must be satisfied that they are fair and reasonable in all the circumstances.

O'MAY v. CITY OF LONDON REAL PROPERTY CO. LTD

House of Lords   [1983] 2 AC 726

The landlord demised premises in a modern office block to the tenants for five years. The landlord provided services and the tenants paid a service charge. On the expiry of the term, the landlord agreed to the grant of a new tenancy but proposed to vary certain terms whereby the landlord would covenant to provide all the services to the building and, as and when advised by the landlord's surveyors, to repair, maintain and decorate it and recover, under a service rent, such proportion of the money spent on the services and repairs as was certified by the landlord's accountants. The landlord further proposed to recover an estimated annual sum to provide for depreciation of lifts, boilers and other equipment. To compensate the tenants it was proposed that the annual rent of £10.50 per square foot would be reduced to £10 per square foot. Those proposals created a 'clear lease' resulting in the building becoming commercially more valuable and more easily disposable.

Held: Since in deciding the terms of a new tenancy under the Act of 1954, the court was required by section 35 to 'have regard to the terms of the current tenancy' the burden of persuading it to change them rested on the party proposing the change, which had in the circumstances to be fair and reasonable and, since in the case of an office block in multiple occupation the cost of managing the exterior, the common parts, the lifts, the boilers and the miscellaneous services, which fluctuated enormously, normally fell on the landlord, the owner of the freehold interest, as it did under the current tenancy, the court should not sanction a departure from its terms so as to impose the obligation on the tenants, whose interest was limited.

LORD HAILSHAM: A certain amount of discussion took place in argument as to the meaning of 'having regard to' in section 35. Despite the fact that the phrase has only just been used by the draftsman of section 34 in an almost mandatory sense, I do not in any way suggest that the court is intended, or should in any way attempt to bind the parties to the terms of the current tenancy in any permanent form. But I do believe that the court must begin by considering the terms of the current tenancy, that the burden of persuading the court to impose a change in those terms against the will of either party must rest on the party proposing the change, and that the change proposed must, in the circumstances of the case, be fair and reasonable, and should take into account, amongst other things, the comparatively weak negotiating position of a sitting tenant requiring renewal, particularly in conditions of scarcity, and the general purpose of the Act which is to protect the business interests of the tenant so far as they are affected by the approaching termination of the current lease, in particular as regards his security of tenure. I derive this view from the structure, purpose, and words of the Act itself. But, if I required confirmation of it, I would find it in the passages cited to us in argument from the judgment of Denning LJ in *Gold* v. *Brighton Corporation* [1956] 1 WLR 1291, 1294 and of Widgery LJ in *Cardshops Ltd* v. *Davies* [1971] 1 WLR 591, 596 (also cited with approval by Shaw LJ in the instant case). The point is also emphasised by the decision in *Charles Clements (London) Ltd* v. *Rank City Wall* (1978) 246 EG 739, where the court rejected an attempt by the landlord as a means of raising the rent to force on a tenant a relaxation of a covenant limiting user which would have been of no value to the particular tenant, and *Aldwych Club Ltd* v. *Copthall Property Co. Ltd* (1962) 185 EG 219 where the court rejected an attempt by the tenant to narrow the permitted user with a view to reducing the rent.

A further point which was canvassed in argument, and with which I agree, is that the discretion of the court to accept or reject terms not in the current lease is not limited to the security of tenure of the tenant even in the extended sense referred to by Denning LJ in *Gold* v. *Brighton Corporation* [1956] 1 WLR 1291. There must, in my view, be a good reason based in the absence of agreement or essential fairness for the court to impose a new term not in the current lease by either party on the other against his will. Any other conclusion would in my view be inconsistent with the terms of the section. But, subject to this, the discretion of the court is of the widest possible kind, having regard to the almost infinitely varying circumstances of individual leases, properties, businesses and parties involved in business tenancies all over the country.

It is obvious that in the case of an office block in multiple occupation by different tenants the actual management of the exterior parts, common parts, lifts, boilers, and ancillary services will ordinarily rest in the hands of the landlords who will ordinarily covenant to provide them. Some of these items are very readily calculable or may readily be made the subject of insurance. Some may fluctuate enormously and the extent of fluctuation will, as the tenants' witness said, only ultimately be ascertainable at the end of a lease. Obviously it is to the advantage of the landlord to transfer the financial risk of fluctuation to the tenant, and there can be no possible reason why, if the tenant agrees (and the evidence was that many do), he should not do so. But the crucial question is, if the current lease does not so provide and the tenant does not agree, by what possible reasoning the court should impose the burden on the tenant against his will as a condition of his receiving a new tenancy under Part II of the Landlord and Tenant Act 1954. It may be granted that the transfer of the risk from the landlord to the tenant is a perfectly legitimate negotiating aim for the landlord to entertain. But the argument is two edged. It is equally a legitimate negotiating aim of the tenant to resist the change. Granted that a reduction in the rent of 50p from £10·50 per foot to £10·00 per foot is, in the limited sense described, an adequate estimate of the compensation which a landlord will offer if the risk is to be transferred. But the argument is again two edged. It may equally be argued that an additional 50p is the adequate estimate of the rent rightly payable to the landlord if the risk is to be kept where it is under the current lease. But neither of the two statements assists to answer the question where, in the new lease, is the risk of fluctuation to lie. If I am correct that the inference from the authorities is that the language of section 35 requires that the party (whether landlord or tenant) requiring a change must justify as reasonable a departure from the current lease in case of dispute about its terms, the answer must be that prima facie it must lie where the current lease provides, and that a mere agreement about figures based on either or both of two rival hypotheses does not shift the burden in any way.

Chapter 23

Compensation for disturbance and improvements

23.1 Disturbance—section 37

The phrase 'the premises' in section 37 (3) (b) of the 1954 Act does not bear the same meaning as the phrase 'premises being or comprised in the holding' in section 37 (3) (a), but refers to the particular part of the holding that has been ascertained under section 37 (3) (a) as having been occupied for over 14 years.

EDICRON LTD v. WILLIAM WHITELEY LTD

Court of Appeal   [1984] 1 WLR 59

The landlords demised to the tenants the first floor of a building which the tenants occupied continuously from the 21 June 1967 to the 24 May 1982 for the purposes of their business. The tenants surrendered the lease of the first floor on the 6 December 1976 and were granted by the landlords a new lease of the first, second and third floors of the same building for a term of 20 years. The tenants sublet part of the third floor from 23 December 1976 to 4 December 1981.

The question arose as to the amount of compensation payable by the landlords under section 37 of the 1954 Act.

Held: Since the first floor of the building had been occupied for over 14 years and there had been no change in such occupation during that period and it had been used during that period for the tenants' own business the tenants were entitled to double compensation for the holding they occupied, namely, the first, second and part of the third floor of the building.

SLADE LJ: Section 37 (2) of the Act of 1954, as amended, specifies the amount payable by way of compensation under section 37 (2):

'(a) where the conditions specified in the next following subsection are satisfied it shall be the product of the appropriate multiplier and twice the rateable value of the holding, (b) in any other case it shall be the product of the appropriate multiplier and the rateable value of the holding.'

For the purposes of subsection (2), the phrase 'the rateable value of the holding' is defined by subsection (5). It is common ground that, in accordance with the latter definition, on 17 July 1980 (which is taken as the relevant date), the rateable value of the holding, as it then stood (that is to say the first, second and third floors, less the sublet part of the third floor) was £9972. By virtue of the Landlord and Tenant Act 1954 (Appropriate Multiplier) Regulations 1981 (SI 1981 No. 69), the appropriate multiplier is two and a quarter.

On this appeal, the dispute between the parties turns solely on the question whether the conditions specified in section 37 (3) are satisfied. If they are not, as the judge decided, the compensation payable can only be two and a quarter times £9972 (£22,437) which, with interest, was the sum which he actually awarded to the tenants. If the conditions are satisfied, then the sum payable is twice that amount.

The conditions specified in section 37 (3) are as follows:

'(a) that, during the whole of the 14 years immediately preceding the termination of the current tenancy, premises being or comprised in the holding have been occupied for the purposes of a business carried on by the occupier or for those and other purposes; (b) that, if during those 14 years there was a change in the occupier of the premises, the person who was the occupier immediately after the change was the successor to the business carried on by the person who was the occupier immediately before the change.'

There is no dispute that the tenants can bring themselves within condition (a). They occupied the first floor of Redan House for the purposes of their business from 29 September 1966 until the termination of their tenancy of the three floors. Accordingly, they did occupy 'premises comprised in the holding,' albeit not the entirety of the holding, for the purposes of their business for the whole of the 14 years immediately preceding the termination of their tenancy. The judge, however concluded that condition (b) was relevant and not satisfied. He considered that the phrase 'the premises' referred to in condition (b) meant the same as 'premises being or comprised in the holding,' referred to in condition (a). He pointed out that the tenants' occupation of the second and part of the third floors began much less than 14 years before the termination of their tenancy. There was therefore during those years a change in the occupation of *some* premises 'being or compromised in the holding.' It was common ground (as he pointed out) that when the tenants went into occupation of the second and third floors, they did not succeed to the business of the previous occupier. Accordingly, he concluded that the tenants did not satisfy condition (b).

The correctness, or otherwise, of his ultimate decision must turn entirely on the correctness, or otherwise, of his interpretation of the crucial phrase 'the premises,' which appears in section 37 (3) (b). As I have said, he regarded this phrase as bearing the same meaning as the phrase 'premises being or comprised in the holding' used in condition (a). He did not amplify the reasons which led him to this conclusion but [counsel] on behalf of the landlords has submitted that the judge's construction was not only in accordance with the intention of Parliament, but was grammatically correct. He pointed out, clearly correctly, that the phrase 'the premises' in condition (b) must refer back to something. He submitted that this short phrase is simply a form of shorthand used by the draftsman, instead of repeating in condition (b) the longer phrase 'premises being or comprised in the holding,' and that the short phrase bears exactly the same meaning as that longer phrase.

With all respect to the argument and to the judge's conclusion on this point, I do not for my part think that this construction of the subsection is sustainable on a fair reading of the words used. It seems to me that, as [counsel] has submitted on behalf of the tenants, paragraph (a) of subsection (3) postulates the ascertainment of particular premises as being the relevant premises 'being or comprised in the holding' for the purposes of condition (a). As the words 'comprised in' make clear, these relevant premises need not necessarily constitute the entirety of the holding and, on the facts of the present case, they do not constitute the entirety. As the judge rightly held, the relevant 'premises being or comprised in the holding' for the purposes of condition (a) in this case were the first floor of Redan House in respect of which there had been no change of occupier.

In my judgment, on a fair reading of the relevant wording, [counsel for the tenants] must be right in submitting that the brief phrase 'the premises' in condition

(b) in its context means those particular premises which have been ascertained under (a) as premises 'being or comprised in the holding' and as having been occupied for the purposes of a business carried on by the occupier.

The judge seems to have regarded the phrase 'the premises' in (b) as meaning '*any* premises being or comprised in the holding.' But this interpretation seems to me to ignore the use of the definite article 'the' in the phrase 'the premises.' This use of the definite article, coupled with the repetition of the word 'premises,' rather than 'holding,' seems to me to make it clear that the premises referred to are those particular premises which have been referred to in condition (a) and ascertained in accordance with that condition.

The purpose of condition (a) in section 37 (3), as I read it, is to ensure that a tenant shall not qualify for compensation at the double rate unless *at least part* of the relevant holding has been occupied for the purposes of a business for a continuous period of 14 years immediately preceding the end of his current tenancy—during which period it may fairly be assumed that a substantial goodwill will have become attached to that particular business.

Condition (a), however, does not by itself render it necessary that the relevant occupation shall have been by the same person for the whole of the 14-year period, to enable the ultimate tenant to qualify for compensation at the double rate.

What then is to happen if there has been a change in the occupation? Condition (b), as I see it, is designed to deal with that situation. Under that condition a change of occupation of the relevant premises during the 14-year period need not disqualify the quitting tenant from receiving compensation at the double rate, *if* the same business has been carried on on those premises throughout the 14-year period. If, however, during this period there has been change of occupation, in respect of the premises identified under condition (a), compensation at the double rate is not to be available unless the person who was the occupier of those premises immediately after the change succeeded to the same business as that carried on by the person who was the occupier immediately before the change; in this contingency there must be identity of the relevant business throughout the 14-year period if there is to be a qualification for double compensation.

To summarise my conclusions, therefore, they are these. The phrase 'the premises' in condition (b) means the same particular premises as are referred to in condition (a), that is to say, on the facts of the present case, the first floor of Redan House. During the relevant period of 14 years, there was no change in the occupation of that first floor. It was occupied for the purposes of the tenants' business. Accordingly condition (b) is, on the particular facts of this case, not in point at all; it does not require to be satisfied because there was no change in the occupier of the relevant 'premises' during the 14-year period. Condition (a), as I have already said, is satisfied. Accordingly, in my judgment, the tenants are entitled to compensation at the double rate provided for by section 37 (2), since they bring themselves within subsection (3). The rate at which they are entitled to compensation is the product of the appropriate multiplier and twice the rateable value of the holding, namely twice times two and a quarter times £9972, that is to say £44,874, together with interest.

A tenant's right to compensation for disturbance only arises on quitting the premises and falls to be computed according to the law which applies at that date.

CARDSHOPS LTD v. JOHN LEWIS PROPERTIES LTD

Court of Appeal [1983] QB 161

In January 1980, the landlord of business premises served a section 25 notice on the tenants terminating their tenancy and stating that it would oppose the grant of a new tenancy on the ground specified in section 30 (1) (g). The tenant served a counter–notice and applied to the county court for a new tenancy commencing on the 25 December 1980. On the 18 February 1981, the judge dismissed the tenants' application and ordered compensation under section 37 to be paid by the landlord on the tenant quitting the premises on the 28 June 1981 and rejected the tenants' submission that the assessment of compensation should not be the rateable value of the premises but two-and-a-quarter times that value in accordance with the Landlord and Tenant Act 1954 (Appropriate Multiplier) Regulations 1981, which was to come into force on the 21 March 1981.

Held: Since the 1981 regulations had come into force by the time the tenants had to quit, compensation payable was to be assessed at two-and-a-quarter times the rateable value of the premises.

WALLER LJ: Section 37 (1), having set out the conditions which have to be fulfilled, goes on:

'... then, subject to the provisions of this Act, the tenant shall be entitled on quitting the holding to recover from the landlord by way of compensation an amount determined in accordance with the following provisions of this section.'

In *International Military Services Ltd* v. *Capital and Counties PLC* [1982] 1 WLR 575, 582–583 Slade J expressed this view about the meaning of those words:

'The word "then" in my judgment, merely means "in that event" that is to say, if the earlier conditions specified in the subsection are fulfilled. The entitlement arises on the quitting of the holding *and not before*. In my judgment, therefore, it is quite plain that the amount of the entitlement must be assessed in accordance with the law as it stands at the date of the quitting.'

I agree with the words of Slade J. In my opinion provided that the conditions set out in the earlier part of the subsection have been fulfilled the words I have quoted above indicate that the entitlement only arises 'on quitting' and the natural construction that would arise is that the entitlement should be assessed in accordance with the law at that time. The only other possible interpretation of section 37 (1) would make the hearing of the application the relevant date because the subsection starts with the words: 'Where on the making of an application ... the court is precluded ...' In my opinion the fact that section 37 (5) (*a*) refers to the valuation list in force at the date of the landlord's notice does not invalidate this conclusion. It is the valuation list in force at the date of the landlord's notice which has to be multiplied by 2¼ under the new legislation. The giving of the landlord's notice is simply an initial step in the proceedings.

It was submitted before this court that to adopt the construction that it is the date of quitting which is crucial would be adopting a construction with retrospective effect and we were referred to the decision of Brightman J in *In re 14 Grafton Street, London, W1* [1971] Ch 935. The facts of that case were quite different from the present case. There it was sought to set aside an indefeasible right to recover possession by virtue of the passing of the Law of Property Act 1969. In the present case no such right exists. When the matter came on for trial before the judge in the county court there were three possibilities: the landlord might not be able to establish that it intended to occupy the premises for its own business purposes; the landlord might have changed its mind and have decided that the cost was too great; or the landlord might establish its intention and be required to pay compensation on the tenant quitting. I see nothing retrospective in saying that the compensation would be on the basis of the law current at the date of quitting. In the *International Military Services Ltd* case which I have already mentioned, the landlord's notice was given after the passing of the Act of 1980. In the course of his judgment Slade J considered an argument based on the suggestion of retrospective legislation and, quoting in the *14 Grafton Street* case, said, at p 586:

'Nevertheless, subject to the points arising on section 47 (5) of the Act of 1980, with which I have already dealt, the language of the relevant statutory provisions seems to me plain and unambiguous. When they are read together, sections 47 and 193 of the Act of 1980, paragraph 4 of Schedule 33 to that Act, and the Regulations of 1981, in my judgment make it quite clear that as from 25 March 1981 the new amendments to section 37 (2) (*a*) and (*b*) of the Act of 1954 are to apply in the case of every tenant who thereafter quits a holding, provided only that the other conditions of section 37 (1) have been satisfied. It would have been easy for the legislature in the Act of 1980, or for the Secretary of State in the Regulations of 1981, expressly to provide that the amending provisions should not apply in cases where the landlord's section 25 notice had been served before 25 March 1981. No such exception was made, and I can see no sufficient grounds for implying one.'

We were also referred to a decision of Walton J in *Garrett* v. *Lloyds Bank Ltd* (unreported), 7 April 1982. That was a case like the present one where the landlord's notice was given before the Act of 1980 was passed and Walton J dealing with the suggestion that to make the date of quitting crucial would be retrospective legislation used words apposite to the present case:

'... in the *14 Grafton Street* case the tenant could not possibly have brought any proceedings for a fresh lease since his time for so doing had expired. Hence, there was no possibility of a fresh lease being granted. In the present case such proceedings were on foot and could very well, in not impossible circumstances, have succeeded; in particular, had such an application been fought out, the defendant would have had to establish that its intention to use the premises for its own purposes persisted at the date of the hearing. It might well have changed its mind before then, or it might have failed to convince the judge that this was really its true intention. I do not see how a right which depends upon the landlord having to persuade a court that it has a certain intention can in any way be said to be a vested right unless and until it has persuaded the court that its intention is as it says it is.'

I respectfully agree with both those observations.

In my judgment the law to be applied in cases such as the present is the law at the date on which the tenant is obliged to quit, in this case 29 June. I might add that I do not see any injustice to the landlord in such a conclusion. The policy of the Landlord and Tenant Acts is to hold the balance between landlord and tenant with an obligation on the landlord to pay compensation (and I assume fair compensation) when the tenant is dispossessed. If the unamended law was not achieving fairness I do not see that the landlord suffers injustice by having to pay what Parliament views as proper compensation.

Note: This case was applied in *Sperry* v. *Hambro Life Assurance* (1983) 265 EG 233 by Goulding J.

A tenant who is unwilling to accept the offer of a new tenancy of part of the originally demised premises is entitled to leave to discontinue his application, without the imposition of a condition that he should not apply for compensation under section 37 of the 1954 Act.

FRIBOURG AND TREYER LTD v. NORTHDALE INVESTMENTS LTD

Chancery Division   (1982) 44 P & CR 284

The landlords of business premises served a section 25 notice on the tenants stating that they would oppose an application for the grant of a new tenancy. The tenant served a counter notice under the Act and the landlord, being entitled to offer a new tenancy of part of the originally demised premises within section 31A, offered the tenant a new tenancy of the part. The tenant was not prepared to take a tenancy of part only and decided to move. The tenant applied for leave to discontinue the proceedings unconditionally and the landlord contended that a condition should be imposed that the tenant should not apply for compensation under section 37 of the Act.

Held: There was no reason to impose on the tenant any condition for the granting of leave to discontinue his action.

FOSTER LJ: For the landlord reliance is placed on *Young, Austen & Young Ltd* v. *British Medical Association*, where Whitford J granted leave to discontinue but only on terms that the tenant should not seek compensation under section 37 of the Act. He said:

'I am bound to say it does not appear to me that the court is in any way precluded from consideration of the question as to whether a term should or should not be imposed. The tenants come to this court, having started the proceeding, seeking an indulgence, and RSC, Order 21 rule 3, specifically provides that in considering whether such an indulgence should be granted, the duty is thrown on the court of considering all the circumstances of a case and of considering whether, in justice, it would be right that leave to discontinue should be granted and, if so, the terms upon which such leave should be granted. Indeed, it is not really denied by the tenants, as I understand it, that the imposition of some terms may be appropriate in cases of this kind. Graham J has recently so held in another proceeding relating to a notice under section 25 ... namely, *Covell Matthews and Partners* v. *French Wools Ltd.* Graham J was referred to a number of cases, and in his judgment he observes: "The principles to be culled from these cases are, in my judgment, that the court will, normally, at any rate, allow a plaintiff to discontinue if he wants to, provided no injustice will be caused to the defendant. It is not desirable that a plaintiff should be compelled to litigate against his will. The court should therefore grant leave, if it can, without injustice to the defendant, but in doing so should be careful to see that the defendant is not deprived of some advantage which he has already gained in the litigation and should be ready to grant him adequate protection to ensure that any advantage he had gained is preserved."'

In that case the tenants sought leave to discontinue their application merely because they had changed their mind and no longer wanted a new lease, and accordingly Whitford J made the grant to discontinue the action subject to an undertaking not to apply for any compensation under the Act. And it is on this case which the landlord heavily relies.

In *Ove Arup Inc.* v. *Howland Property Investment Co. Ltd.* Mr Michael Wheeler, QC distinguished the case before Whitford J and came to the conclusion in all the circumstances of that case that there should be no undertaking not to seek compensation under the Act.

The landlord also relies heavily on a letter which the tenant wrote to all its customers in November 1981 in which it said:

'... After 261 years at 34 Haymarket it is with the greatest of regret that we are having to make a move. We realise that progress must continue, but the inflation of rents and rates has finally defeated us. However, we are going to continue in alternative premises not far from here.

As from January 4, 1982, we will be trading in our usual way from 214 Piccadilly, London, W1 (and a telephone number is given). It is situated opposite Swan and Edgar and very handy for public transport ...'

In this case it seems to me that the tenant cannot succeed in its application unless it is willing to take a part only of the premises included in this lease, and that it is not prepared to do. It follows that its action cannot succeed. Whether the reason that it does not want to take part is because the premises offered are so truncated as to make the business impossible to carry on I know not. But the offer of part means it could not possibly succeed in this action to get a tenancy of the whole.

In those circumstances even if the tenant had come to the conclusion that the offer which was made, being an offer of the truncated premises at a rent of some £45,000 per annum exclusive was far too high and would be in any case outside its financial ability, it cannot be forced to accept a part. In those circumstances it is clear that this case can be well distinguished both from Whitford J's decision in *Young, Austen and Young Ltd* v. *British Medical Association* and from Mr Wheeler's decision in *Ove Arup Inc.* v. *Howland Property Investment Co. Ltd.* In my judgment there is no reason whatever why the tenant should be put on any term as a condition of this court granting it leave to discontinue. I have come to the conclusion that I shall grant it leave to discontinue the proceedings for a new lease and am not prepared to give leave on condition that it does not apply for compensation.

When a landlord withdraws his opposition to the grant of a new tenancy and the tenant has meanwhile chosen not to pursue his application, the landlord is still liable to pay compensation unless he can show that he would be prejudiced.

LLOYDS BANK LTD v. CITY OF LONDON CORPORATION

Court of Appeal   [1983] Ch 192

The tenants applied to the landlords for the grant of a new tenancy under section 26 of the 1954 Act and the landlords opposed the same under section 30 (1) (f). The landlords later informed the tenants that they would abandon their opposition and two weeks later the tenants decided not to renew the lease. The landlords only agreed to consent to a discontinuance of proceedings if the tenants undertook not to seek compensation under section 37. The tenants did not agree.

Held: In the absence of any prejudice to the landlords, the tenants would be given unconditional leave to withdraw their application.

TEMPLEMAN LJ: On the present wording of section 37 of the Act of 1954 as amended the tenants are entitled to compensation if they withdraw their application for a new tenancy. The section provides for compensation if a landlord serves a notice opposing the grant of a new tenancy on the ground of section 30 (1) (*f*) and the tenant either makes no application for a new tenancy or withdraws his application. But, as [counsel] on behalf of the landlords pointed out, the tenants cannot withdraw their application without leave and the question is whether, in the exercise of its discretion under Order 21, rule 3, the court should allow the tenants to withdraw their application without imposing terms on the tenants.

Section 37 of the Landlord and Tenant Act 1954 as originally enacted only provided compensation where the court dismissed a tenant's application for a new tenancy because the landlord had established a ground of opposition within section 30 (1) (*d*), (*f*) or (*g*). The tenant could not claim compensation if he withdrew his application. The Act of 1954 was amended by the Law of Property Act 1969 so as to enable a tenant to claim compensation if the landlord served a counter-notice and the tenant either did not apply to the court at all or, after making an application, withdrew that application before it came on for hearing before the court. One object of the amendment was to save the time and expense involved in initiating or continuing an application to the court, an application in which the tenant no longer had any confidence in the face of the landlord's counter-notice, but an application which the tenant was compelled to continue in order to obtain compensation when the court ultimately refused his application. [Counsel for the landlords] submitted that the amendment was never intended to allow a tenant to claim compensation if he withdraws his application for a new tenancy after the landlord has withdrawn his opposition to the grant of a new tenancy.

If the tenant proceeds with his application after the landlord has withdrawn his opposition, the tenant will be entitled to an order for a new tenancy; by section 36 (2) of the Landlord and Tenant Act 1954 the tenant can apply within 14 days from the order for the order to be revoked and can thus refuse to take up the new tenancy, but in that event no provision is made for the tenant to receive compensation. [Counsel for the landlords] submitted that the discretion conferred on the court by [Order 21, rule 3] should be exercised so as to preserve to the landlords the advantage they had already gained. The landlords, he said, obtained an advantage in July 1980 when they abandoned their opposition to the grant of a new tenancy and thus made it certain that, if the tenants continued with their application for a new tenancy, the landlords could not be obliged to pay compensation.

In my judgment, where a landlord serves a counter-notice based on grounds (*e*), (*f*) or (*g*), he is asserting a right to inflict loss or damage on the tenant by requiring the tenant to quit the premises. That counter-notice creates difficulties for the tenant who cannot know whether the landlord will succeed in his opposition or not. The prudent tenant must, therefore, cast around for alternative courses open to him if he is obliged to quit the premises and must then decide whether it is safer to adopt one of those alternative courses or to take the risks inherent in proceeding with an application for a new tenancy. The tenant's difficulties do not disappear if the landlord withdraws his opposition. In the present case the landlords, by their counter-notice in March 1980, asserted that they intended to carry out redevelopment on the premises and required possession for that purpose. The withdrawal by the landlords in July 1980 of their opposition on these grounds left alive the possibility that the landlords remained anxious to redevelop and would be able to prevail on the court to grant a new tenancy to the tenants of a short duration or a tenancy which could be determined by the landlords as soon as they were in a position to carry out works of redevelopment. When a landlord serves a counter-notice under section 30 (1) (*e*), (*f*) or (*g*) he brings to bear influence and pressure on the tenant to consider the advisability of quitting the premises. That pressure and influence are not removed as soon as the landlord withdraws his opposition. By then the tenant will, in most cases, have made investigations and inquiries which he would not have made if the landlord had not served a counter-notice in the first place. The prudent tenant must consider his alternatives and will have reason to fear that his days of occupation are numbered and will not be reassured by the withdrawal of the landlord's opposition to the grant of a new tenancy.

In my judgment, a landlord who serves a counter-notice opposing the grant of a new tenancy under (*e*), (*f*) and (*g*) presents the tenant with a choice between the doubtful possibility of a new tenancy or the certainty of compensation under section 37. Once such a counter-notice is served, the landlord has no right both to recover the demised premises and to avoid payment of compensation. It is not right to treat the tenant as being in no different or worse position than he would have occupied if the landlord had never served a counter-notice.

In the present case it is not just to deprive the tenants of compensation because of the accident that the landlords in July 1980 completed their inquiries and investigations which satisfied them that they could not, or no longer wished to, persist in opposing the grant of a new tenancy, whereas it was not until August 1980 that the tenants completed inquiries and investigations which satisfied them that, having regard to the landlords' conduct or to other factors, the tenants no longer wished to persist in their application for a new tenancy. If the tenants had repented of their application to the court in June 1980 before the landlords repented of their counter-notice in July 1980 the tenants would clearly have been entitled to compensation. I do not accept that the fact that the landlords happened to repent one month before the tenants enables the landlords, who made themselves liable to pay compensation by serving a counter-notice, now to recover possession of the demised premises without compensation.

In my judgment, when a tenant applies for leave to discontinue an application for a new tenancy, the correct judicial principle which the court ought to apply in considering the exercise of its discretion under Order 21, rule 3 involves the court in inquiring whether the landlord has been prejudiced. The fact that the landlord will be obliged to pay compensation is not in itself evidence of prejudice because the Landlord and Tenant Act 1954 provides for compensation to be paid if the landlord has served the counter-notice. The tenant should be allowed unconditionally to withdraw his application for a new tenancy even if the landlord has withdrawn his counter-notice unless the landlord has been prejudiced by the delay or by the events which have occurred between the date when the landlord withdrew his opposition to the grant of a new tenancy and the date when the landlord is informed that the tenant does not propose to proceed with his application for a new tenancy.

Compensation payable under section 37 (1) of the 1954 Act on the expiry of a business tenancy is not chargeable to capital gains tax.

DRUMMOND (INSPECTOR OF TAXES) v. AUSTIN BROWN

Court of Appeal   [1984] 3 WLR 381

Fox LJ: The sum of £31,384 paid to the taxpayer by the bank was twice the rateable value of the premises and was the sum payable pursuant to section 37 (2) (a).

The taxpayer was assessed to capital gains tax on the £31,384. He appealed to the special commissioners who allowed the appeal. The Crown's appeal to the High Court was dismissed by Walton J and from that decision the Crown now appeals.

The matter is governed by the Finance Act 1965. Section 22 (1) provides that 'All forms of property shall be assets for the purposes of this Part of this Act ...' Section 22 (3) is as follows:

'Subject to subsection (6) of this section, and to the exceptions in this Part of this Act, there is for the purposes of this Part of this Act a disposal of assets by their owner where any capital sum is derived from assets notwithstanding that no asset is acquired by the person paying the capital sum, and this subsection applies in particular to—(a) capital sums received by way of compensation for any kind of damage or injury to assets or for the loss, destruction or dissipation of assets or for any depreciation or risk of depreciation of an asset ...'

The Crown advanced the following contentions: (i) that the £31,384 was a capital sum derived from an asset, namely the lease of 27 January 1975; (ii) in the alternative, that the £31,384 was compensation for the loss of an asset.

In our opinion the £31,384 was not derived from the lease. The word 'derive' suggests a source. The right to the payment was, in our view, from one source only, namely the statute of 1954. The lease itself gives no right to such a payment. It was the statute, and the statute alone, which created the right to the payment. The statute simply created an entitlement where none would otherwise have existed. And in creating that entitlement it did not require that any provisions were to be written into the lease. Thus, there is no deeming provision which would in any way require one to treat the lease as being the source of the entitlement. We do not think the sum can be said to be derived from any asset. It was, as Templeman J said in *Davis* v. *Powell* [1977] 1 WLR 258, 260—a case in which he rejected the Crown's claim to capital gains tax on the compensation payable to an outgoing tenant under the Agricultural Holdings Act 1948—simply a sum which Parliament said should be paid. Further, Parliament has not said that the tenant is to be entitled to the payment just by proving the lease. He must also prove that the premises were occupied by him and were so occupied for the purposes of a business carried on by him or for those and other purposes; and the right to the double compensation payable in the present case depended also upon the fact that the tenant and his predecessors in the business run between them occupied the premises for business purposes for the previous 14 years. Thus, compensation is not the inevitable result of the lease. No doubt the right to compensation impinges upon the landlord and the tenant. And no doubt the provisions of Part II of the Act of 1954 apply to all tenancies within section 23 (1). But the right to compensation is still only a right given by Parliament. If Parliament chose to take it away, the lease by itself would not have conferred it. We do not think that it is accurately described as an 'incident' of the lease. It does not attach to the estate as such. It is a right given by statute to certain tenants in certain circumstances and the lease by itself did not confer a right to it. It was as Brightman J said in *In re 14 Grafton Street, London W1* [1971] Ch 935, 942, 'a debt created by statute, upon which the tenant may sue in other proceedings if necessary.'

On the termination of his current lease the tenant of business premises may get one of three benefits. Thus he may get either (i) a new lease, or (ii) alternative accommodation, or (iii) compensation. Neither of the first two of these seems to me to derive from the lease any more than does the compensation. The alternative accommodation will be provided by a new lease, negotiated between the parties, of different premises. Similarly the new lease granted by the court is quite distinct from the old. It need not be of exactly the same premises or at the same rent or subject to the same provisions. It is true that the tenant would not have the opportunity of getting either if he had not obtained the original lease. But any right to get them—and the legal right to get compensation—comes wholly from the statute.

For the reasons which we have given, we are unable to accept that compensation derived from the lease. We come to the alternative contention, namely that the sum was paid as compensation for the loss of an asset. There was certainly no 'loss' of the lease. The lease came to an end by the effluxion of time. That was inherent in the nature of the estate. It was given a limited exension by the statute, but that was never 'lost.' It determined under the statutory provisions. It was said, however, that what was lost was security of tenure. We do not accept that. The taxpayer was never entitled to a security of tenure in the events which happened, i.e. that the National Westminster Bank required the premises for its own occupation. The scheme of the Act is that it provides for a tenant to make an application for a new tenancy but also provides, in section 30, for grounds on which the landlord may object. Those grounds fall into two categories. Even if ground (*a*) or (*b*) or (*c*) is established, the court retains a discretion in that it must consider whether the tenant ought not to be granted a new tenancy. There is no such discretion in relation to the other grounds. In the present case, the landlord having established ground (*g*), the court could not have made an order for a new tenancy. And it does not seem to us to be justifiable to assume that the compensation was given for loss of security of tenure. We do not know for precisely what purpose Parliament gave the compensation. The sidenote to section 37, if that be admissible at all, merely says 'Compensation where order for new tenancy precluded on certain grounds.' It might be for 'disturbance' (see *Connaught Fur Trimmings Ltd* v. *Cramas Properties Ltd* [1965] 1 WLR 892, 898, *per* Lord Reid) or for loss of goodwill (see *Edicron Ltd* v. *William Whiteley Ltd* [1984] 1 WLR 59, 66, *per* Slade LJ) or for the expenses of removal (as under the Agricultural Holdings Act 1948) or for a combination of reasons. All we know for certain is that it is a sum which Parliament, for whatever reasons, has directed to be paid. In the circumstances we do not accept that it is established that the compensation was for the loss of any asset.

23.2   Improvements

A notice of intention to carry out works of improvement may be made by implication and completed by service of an architect's final drawings.

DEERFIELD TRAVEL SERVICES LTD v. WARDENS AND SOCIETY OF THE HISTORY OF ART OF THE LONDON LEATHERSELLERS OF THE CITY OF LONDON

Court of Appeal   (1983) 46 P & CR 132

The landlords demised business premises to S.L.A. Ltd. The lease contained a full repairing covenant and a covenant not to alter or add to the premises without the landlords' consent in writing. S.L.A. Ltd assigned the lease to the tenants, who wished to alter the layout of the premises which consisted partly of repairs and partly of improvements which came within the terms of the Landlord and Tenant Act 1927. The tenants instructed an architect and wrote to the landlords enclosing a set of outline plans, asking the landlords' consent to do the work and requesting to be told what amount the landlords would be prepared to pay by way of reimbursement on the termination of the tenancy. The landlords knew that the work was in hand but took no steps to prevent its continuance.

Held: The tenants, by their letter, by implication made it plain to the landlords that they were making a claim under section 3 (1) of the 1927 Act for a contribution to be paid to them when the tenancy terminated. The letter was completed when the architect's drawings were sent to the landlords and, accordingly, there was jursidiction under the 1927 Act to certify that the work had been duly executed.

LAWTON LJ: There are provisions in the Act relating to the service of notices and what a notice has to be. It has to be in writing but there is no prescribed form in which the tenant should indicate his intention to make improvements. I do not consider for the purposes of this judgment that I need go into detail about any other provisions of this Act, because everything turns, so it seems to me, on whether or not the tenant gave notice of intention within section 3 (1).

The tenants intended to spend a considerable amount of money on refurbishing the leased premises and the defendants knew that they so intended. Then on 23 June 1978, the plaintiffs' solicitors wrote to the defendants a letter which is said to be the notice. They started by referring to an earlier letter and to the way in which they proposed to sub-let the premises and to whom. Then they went on as follows:

'We are also instructed in respect of various modernisations and improvements which, it is proposed, be carried out at the building with particular regard to the fire precautions. We enclose a set of plans prepared by the architects to the lessees and no doubt the Leathersellers' surveyors will note the proposed alterations. It is intended that a considerable amount of money be spent on these improvements and alterations and therefore in addition to advising that consent to the alterations being made is, in principle, available, we would be pleased to know what proportion of the monies spent the Leathersellers will be prepared to reimburse on termination of the tenancy.'

As I have already indicated, everything turns on the letter of 23 June 1978. [Counsel] on behalf of the plaintiffs said that the letter did give notice to the defendants that the plaintiffs intended to make improvements together with a specification and plan showing the proposed improvements and the part of the existing premises affected thereby. In those circumstances, the essential step which a tenant has to take before he can hope to get any compensation for improvements on quitting the tenancy was in fact taken.

[Counsel] on behalf of the defendants said that was not so; that the letter, when read by a reasonably sensible businessman who was a landlord, would not have conveyed to him, and did not in fact convey to the defendants, that the plaintiffs were intending to make a claim under the provisions of the 1927 Act. Further and alternatively, he submitted that, even if it was a notice which did intimate an intention to make improvements, it was an inadequate notice, because the outline plans which went with that notice did not constitute a specification. A specification, he submitted, should be a document which sets out in detail what work is to be done and what materials are to be used for the purposes of that work. Undoubtedly the plans which went with the letter dated 23 June 1978, did not constitute a specification of the kind which [counsel for the defendants] submitted was essential. But it was, as I have already recounted, an outline plan. To Savills it would have been obvious that it was an outline plan which was likely to be supplemented by detailed drawings at a later date. Indeed, they asked Mr Levy for more detailed drawings and they got them. In my judgment, that which they got on or about 30 August 1978 constituted plans and a specification for the purposes of this Act. [Counsel for the defendants] accepted that, for the purposes of section 3, there need not be a contemporaneous sending of plans and specifications with the notice, because, as a matter of common sense, very often in these cases the tenant is able to give notice of intention to make improvements but he may have to wait some time for detailed plans and specifications to be drawn up. [Counsel for the defendants] accepted that section 3 (1) should be construed so as to allow for that kind of situation; but he submitted that, because of the time lag and the inadequacy of the original plans, there was no proper connection or linkage (as he put it) between the outline plan and the detailed drawings which came on or about 30 August 1978.

In my judgment, the linkage is provided by the nature of the outline plans, the inevitable expectation that there would be further detailed plans and the request by the defendants' agents for them. In those circumstances, I find that there is nothing in the point that there is no linkage between the notice of intention and the detailed drawings which came later.

The next problem is whether the letter of 23 June 1978 was sufficiently clear. I do not find it necessary to decide that point which was taken by [counsel] on behalf of the plaintiffs, that, for the purposes of section 3, all a tenant need do is to say that he intends to make improvements, without saying whether or not he is doing so for the purposes of staking his claim for compensation under the 1927 Act. [Counsel for the defendants] for his part, submitted that this is what a tenant has to do. Whether he has to do it or not, the problem in this case is, did he do it? In my judgment, on the proper construction of the letter of 23 June 1978 the plaintiffs, by implication, made plain to the defendants that they were making a claim under the 1927 Act. The last paragraph of that letter seems to me to be bringing two matters to the attention of the defendants' solicitors: first, that they wanted consent to be given to the making of alterations—that consent was necessary before the work could start, having regard to the provisions of clause 2 (*l*) of the lease; and secondly, they were making it clear that they looked to the landlords for compensation at the termination of the tenancy. They were not saying 'We are going to spend a lot of money on modernising these leasehold premises and therefore we would ask you to make a contribution to the cost'; they were expecting, not hoping for, a contribution to be paid at the end of the tenancy. That expectation could only arise under the 1927 Act.

In my judgment, the defendants' solicitors, on receiving that letter, would have been put on notice that the claim was in a form which complied broadly with the provisions of section 1 of the Act. The only way it did not comply completely with section 1 of the Act was that the plaintiffs' solicitors had omitted any reference to the compensation being payable only on quitting the premises. In my judgment, a reading of this letter by a reasonably sensible business man would have alerted him to some sort of claim which was going to be made at the end of the tenancy. A business man must be taken to know what his rights are and in any event a sensible business man, on getting a letter of this kind, would take advice. Advice was readily available to the defendants, because the claim was made to their solicitors. In my judgment, the solicitors were in a position to advise the defendants forthwith that they could expect that at the end of the tenancy a claim would be presented in the prescribed form for compensation for improvements.

The letter of 23 June 1978 however, was incomplete. It was, in my judgment, made a complete valid notice when Mr Levy, the architect, sent Savills the full detailed drawings. It follows, in my judgment, that as from on or about 30 August 1978 the three months' period during which the defendants had an opportunity of objecting began to run. For the purposes of clarity, I have assumed that the letter of 29 August arrived in Savills' office on 30 August so the three months' period ran from 30 August 1978. During that period, which would have ended on 30 November 1978, the defendants did not object to the notice. The defendants say that their letter of 6 December was a valid objection. The plaintiffs say that it was not, because they did not object to the work being done. All they objected to was the legal nature of the work, which was a matter likely to be investigated when the claim came to be considered at the trial. In my judgment, as the period for objecting ended on 30 November 1978 it is not necessary for me to come to any decision about the effect of the letter of 6 December 1978.

Works of 'improvement' in section 3 (1) of the 1927 Act include demolition and rebuilding.

NATIONAL ELECTRIC THEATRES LTD v. HUDGELL
Chancery Division [1939] Ch 553

The demised premises had been used as a cinema. The tenants submitted to the landlords a plan and specification for shops with flats above to be built on the land after demolishing the cinema.

Held: The proposed works would be an improvement of the holding within the meaning of section 3 of the 1927 Act.

MORTON J: I now turn to section 3, which is the section I have to construe. Sub-section 1 is: [His Lordship read it, and continued:] The plaintiffs in this case have not thought fit to go through that procedure with regard to the improvements which they were contemplating in 1937; they have come to the Chancery Division asking for the declarations which I have mentioned. The questions which arise in regard to the first declaration are, I think, questions of construction, and the parties are entitled to come to this Court and to obtain a decision whether the proposed works are an improvement within the meaning of the section.

The first comment which I have to make on this sub-section is that what is being dealt with is an improvement *on* the holding, that is to say, work which it is desired to carry out on the holding. I do not think that the sub-section can refer only to alterations of buildings, otherwise the erection of a new building on an unoccupied piece of land could not be an improvement; and I think it is clearly contemplated by Part I of the Act that the erection of a new building on an unoccupied part of the land may be an improvement. [Counsel] for the defendant relies strongly upon the words 'and plan showing the proposed improvement and the part of the existing premises affected thereby.' He says these words show that the improvement contemplated cannot extend to the demolition of all the buildings on the land demised. I cannot accede to this argument. It involves construing the words 'existing premises' as meaning, and meaning only, 'existing buildings,' and I do not think it would be right to give this limited meaning to the words. It is true that I can see no good reason why the phrase 'the part of the existing premises' is used instead of the phrase 'the part of the holding,' but I do not think that this Act draws any clear distinction between the word 'holding' and the word 'premises.'

Reading the Act as a whole, I see no reason for reading into the words 'an improvement on his holding,' in section 3, any condition that some part of the original bricks and mortar of the buildings upon the holding must be retained. Such a construction of the section gives rise to grave difficulties. For example, assume that a tenant of a grain–store first of all removes a defective wall and replaces it with a new wall, then treats each of the other three walls, which in turn become defective, in the same way, then replaces the roof which has become defective, then takes up the existing floor and replaces it by a new one. Each of these acts must, I think, be an improvement, yet in the end the building which was there has been replaced by something quite new. It appears to me that, in their ordinary meaning, the words 'an improvement on this holding' would cover what is intended in the present case, and I cannot find anything in the Act which limits the meaning of these words in the manner suggested by [counsel for the defendant]. [Counsel for the defendant] further contends that, if a demolition, and rebuilding can be an improvement, the rebuilt premises must be premises on which is carried on the same business as that which was carried on in the demolished premises. That would be a most important limitation on the power to make improvements, and, if it had been intended by the legislature, I think it would have been set out in the Act in plain terms. I do not find anything in the sections to which I have referred, or in the other portions of the Act, to lead me to the conclusion that such a limitation exists.

[Counsel for the defendant] points out that the construction of the Act for which the plaintiffs contend may lead to grave hardship. For instance, an investor might invest a modest sum in buying the freehold of a small property, subject to a lease, and the lessee might pull down this small property and erect an expensive block of shops with flats over them, and thereby impose upon the landlord, against his will, the obligation to pay a very substantial sum by way of compensation at the end of the lease. That may be the result of the Act, in certain cases, but I have simply to interpret the Act as it stands. Further, there is a safeguard inserted in section 3 itself, because the improvement cannot be carried out under the section unless the tribunal is satisfied that it is reasonable and suitable to the character of the holding. I do not propose to express any view upon the construction of the word 'reasonable' or upon the construction of the words 'suitable to the character of the holding' for reasons which I shall shortly state, but the landlord has this safeguard, which is of some importance.

Under section 1 (1) of the 1927 Act, the right to compensation is conferred upon 'the tenant of a holding' in respect of improvements 'made by him or his predecessors in title'.

PELOSI v. NEWCASTLE ARMS BREWERY (NOTTINGHAM) LTD

Court of Appeal   (1983) 43 P & CR 18

The landlords granted to W.R. Cox Ltd a 21 year lease of certain business premises. W.R. Cox Ltd granted a sub–lease for 21 years less three days to Louis and Triestina Pelosi who carried out extensive structural works. They in turn assigned their sub–lease to the tenants who acquired the three days reversion from W.R. Cox Ltd. The landlords gave notice terminating the tenancy and the tenants gave notice of their claim for compensation of £60,000 for improvements.

Held: Louis and Triestina Pelosi were the tenants' predecessors in title and, accordingly, the tenants had the benefit of their entitlement to compensation under the 1927 Act.

ORMROD LJ: To prove their title to the lease, the tenants would need to refer only to the assignment to them of W.R. Cox Ltd's reversion. To prove their right to possession, they would need to refer also to the assignment to them of Louis and Triestina Pelosi's sub-lease to account for their being in possession of the holding. They must prove their right to possession because the word 'tenant' is defined in section 25 (1) as 'any person entitled in possession to the "holding".' On this view Louis and Triestina Pelosi were their predecessors in title, in the sense that it is through them that the appellant tenants are tenants entitled in possession to the holding. Moreover, as a matter of fact, the appellant tenants did derive their title through Louis and Triestina Pelosi and so comply with the literal meaning of the words of the definition.

This construction seems to me to give effect to the purpose of the Act and to avoid the anomaly which arises under the alternative construction supported by [counsel for the landlords]. The Act is not concerned with proof of title, as such, but with entitlement to and liability to pay compensation. The scheme of the Act is to pass this liability back eventually to the person who benefits financially from the improvement. This is achieved by [counsel for the tenants'] construction, but it is frustrated by [counsel for the landlord's]. His argument comes to this. The tenants destroyed their right to compensation as successors in title to Louis and Triestina Pelosi by taking an assignment of the reversion to their sub-lease. I think that if it is possible to find a way of avoiding such a freak and unintended result the court should adopt it.

Chapter 24

Landlord's application for interim rent

An interim rent under section 24A falls to be assessed on the basis of what was a reasonable rent for the tenant to pay as a yearly tenant on the date for commencement of that rent, having regard to the actual condition of and state of the premises at that date and the terms of the contractual tenancy so far as they were applicable to a yearly tenancy. In some circumstances, the court has power to fix a differential rent pending completion of necessary repairs.

FAWKE v. CHELSEA (VISCOUNT)

Court of Appeal   [1980] QB 441

The tenant carried on business at premises held under a sub-lease which after its expiry, continued by reason of section 24 of the 1954 Act. The premises were found to be infested with dry rot caused by neglect of the exterior so that extensive repairs were required to both the exterior and interior. The landlord served a notice of termination and the tenant applied for an order for an interim rent under section 24A.

The county court judge held that the landlord was subject to a covenant to repair but that lack of repair should not be taken into account in assessing the interim rent. The tenant appealed.

Held:
(1) The present state of repair of the premises was relevant to the assessment of an interim rent;
(2) The court had power to fix a differential rent pending completion of necessary repairs, such power extending to the fixing of an interim rent.

GOFF LJ: In my judgment the valuation should be made not, as was argued for the landlord, upon that knowledge of the state of the premises at the commencement of the interim period which a reasonable prospective tenant properly advised and having such survey, if any, as might be reasonable, would or should have discovered, for that imports a large measure of uncertainty, nor yet upon the actual knowledge of the actual parties, for that is subjective whilst the test ought to be objective, but upon all that is known at the date of the hearing as to the condition that the premises were actually in at the commencement of that interim period. I do not see anything in section 24A which requires the court, in determining what rent it is reasonable for the tenant to pay, albeit by reference to a hypothetical letting, to shut its eyes to known facts.

Before considering the evidence in this case and the judge's findings, there are certain other questions of construction to be decided. First, has the court jurisdiction under section 24A to award a rent which is not to come into operation until repairs have been effected or is to be increased when they are or which commences at once but is later to become subject to a moratorium or reduction for a certain period? I have had the advantage of reading the judgment which Brandon LJ proposes to deliver, and with which I understand Stephenson LJ agrees, and they take the view that the court has such jurisdiction. The question is, I think, a very difficult one, and I confess with all respect to them that I have some hesitation in accepting their views on this point, notwithstanding the referential incorporation of section 34 (1) and (2) in section 24A of the Act. It seems to me that the words 'a rent which it would be reasonable for the tenant to pay while the tenancy continues by virtue of section 24 of this Act' in subsection (1), and the words in subsection (2) 'shall be deemed to be the rent payable under the tenancy from the date' etc. may well be too strong to admit of such a construction, especially so when one remembers that section 24A is conferring a power to substitute an interim rent for the contractual rent, which otherwise would continue uninterruptedly until a new lease be ordered or refused, and that in the absence of a provision in that behalf in the contractual tenancy the tenant holding over under sections 24 and 64 would not be entitled to any reduction or suspension of rent during repairs. I am, however, not prepared to dissent on this point and content myself with expressing my doubts.

The next question is how the valuers should regard want of repair and breaches of covenant when assessing an interim rent, and it seems to me they should consider what would be a reasonable rent for the tenant to pay from the date for commencement of that rent as a yearly tenant, having regard to the actual condition and state of the premises at that date, and having regard to the terms of the contractual tenancy so far as applicable to a yearly tenancy. This will mean that the hypothetical tenant will have the benefit of any covenant to repair on the part of the landlord and the burden of any on the part of the tenant, or there may be no covenant to repair on either side.

The judge in his judgment said:

'a term of the hypothetical yearly tenancy obliged the landlord to well and substantially repair, maintain and keep the premises in good and substantial repair and condition. In determining the interim rent the court must have regard (inter alia) to that term. Likewise the court must have regard to the tenant's covenant to decorate the premises. When the state or condition of the premises is regulated by such terms, in my judgment, lack of repair or want of decoration albeit a lack of repair, is not an element which the court should take into account in assessing interim rent because the landlord by the term of the tenancy is under an obligation to effect necessary repairs and if he does not the tenant has the right to enforce the covenant to repair against the landlord and claim damages. This is the correct procedure for dealing with lack of repair to the premises and consequential damage suffered by the tenant.'

He was, of course, right to take into account the landlord's and tenant's covenants to repair, but with respect, in my judgment, not to treat the lack of repair as an element not to be taken into account in assessing interim rent, on the ground that the tenant will have an action for damages or indeed for any other reason. The valuation being on the basis of a new yearly tenancy, it must in my view be assumed that these covenants will be duly performed. There can at this stage be no question of breach.

The fixing of an interim rent will not, however, affect the right of either party to sue the other for any breach of the repairing covenants in the contractual tenancy, which may have already occurred or may subsequently occur, save that in assessing damages for diminution in value with respect to any period after the determination of the contractual tenancy, credit must be given for the amount by which the interim rent was reduced on account of the want of repair from what it would have been if the premises had been in the state of repair required by the covenants. This may be considerably less than the actual diminution in value during the period of breach, since the valuation postulates prompt repair. The fixing of an interim rent would also not affect a claim by the tenant for damages for extra disturbance on the ground that the landlord's failure to repair after notice had made more extensive repairs necessary.

In cases where the interim rent so determined is less than the contractual rent the court must then consider whether, in the light of its duty to have regard to the rent payable under the terms of the existing tenancy, it should increase the interim rent up or near to that rent, or should in the exercise of its discretion refuse to determine an interim rent at all, which would leave the contractual rent payable. In determining these matters the court will, of course, bear in mind that section 24A of the Act of 1954 is a section obviously designed by Parliament to improve the landlord's position, as is shown, if in no other way, by the fact that he alone can apply under it; and certainly, where the low valuation is due to breaches by the landlord of his repairing covenants, it would I think have to be a very special case in which the court would determine an interim rent less than the contractual rent. Different considerations will apply if the low valuation is due to a fall in property values.

BRANDON LJ: I agree in general with the judgment of Goff LJ. There is, however, one question in respect of which he has expressed doubts. That question is whether the court has power, not only when determining the rent of a new tenancy under section 34 (1) of the Act of 1954, but also when determining an interim rent under section 24A, to determine what I shall for convenience call a differential rent, by which I mean a rent which varies from time to time during the period of the tenancy according to the situation with regard to the state of repair of the premises. Although I have found the question a difficult one, I do not in the end share the doubts which Goff LJ has expressed, and I shall accordingly set out my views on the matter and the reasons on which they are based.

I consider, first, the power of the court when determining under section 34 (1) of the Act of 1954 the rent payable under a new tenancy. The rent to be determined is the rent at which, having regard to the terms of the new tenancy other than those relating to rent, the holding might reasonably be expected to be let in the open market by a willing lessor, in other words the market rent. It is clear that the market rent of premises may in general be affected not only by the terms of the tenancy concerning the obligations of the lessor and lessee in relation to repair, but also by the actual state of repair of the premises at the commencement of the tenancy.

To take an extreme example, let it be supposed, first, that, under the terms of the tenancy, it is the obligation of the lessor to put the premises into repair; secondly, that the premises are, at the commencement of the tenancy, so seriously out of repair, by reason of previous fire or flood, that they are of only partial use to the lessee; thirdly, that an appreciable period must necessarily elapse before the lessor can begin to perform his obligation of putting the premises into repair; and, fourthly, that, while the lessor is performing that obligation, the disturbance will be such that the premises will be virtually of no use to the lessee at all. In those circumstances it may well be that the market rent of the premises, which would be appropriate after they had been put into repair, would be appreciably reduced during the period which would necessarily elapse before the work of putting them into repair was begun, and even more reduced during the further period which such work was being carried out.

Similar considerations would, as it seems to me, apply if the premises were seriously out of repair at the commencement of the tenancy, not by reason of previous fire or flood, but by reason of the failure of the lessor or the lessee or both to perform their previous obligations to repair. The cause or causes of the premises being out of repair are not, for this purpose, significant; the fact that they are out of repair, for whatever cause or causes, is so.

I consider, secondly, the power of the court when determining under section 24A of the Act an interim rent payable during the continuation of a pre-existing tenancy. The rent which the court has to determine in this case, subject always to its additional duty to have regard to the rent payable under the pre-existing tenancy, is the rent at which the holding might reasonably be let, having regard to the terms of such tenancy other than those relating to rent, from year to year in the open market by a willing lessor, in other words the market rent on a year to year basis. Here again it seems to me, for the same reasons as those discussed above in relation to section 34 (1), that the market rent may in general be affected by the situation with regard to the state of repair of the premises at the date when the interim rent is to commence, and that the questions whether and how the market rent of the premises concerned in any particular cases are so affected must depend on the evidence in that case. So, if the evidence showed that the market rent would be a differential rent in the sense in which I have used that expression, then the court would have both the power and the duty to determine a differential rent accordingly. On the other hand, if the evidence showed that the market rent, though affected in amount by the present and future situation with regard to state of repair, would nevertheless be a normal fixed rent, the duty of the court would be to determine a fixed interim rent.

In what I have said so far I have been considering whether the court has power to determine a differential rent first under section 34 (1) and secondly under section 24A, and I have concluded that it has power to do so in either case if the evidence warrants it. I should not, however, wish to encourage the view that this is a power which the court should exercise at all frequently. The cases in which the evidence may support a differential rent on the basis of the situation with regard to state of repair are likely, in my view, to be limited to cases in which the state of disrepair at the commencement of the new tenancy, or the commencement of the period of interim rent, is of a very serious character. In any other case it seems to me that the evidence will be very unlikely to do so.

A further question could in theory arise as to whether, in a case where the situation with regard to the state of repair was such that the premises would, in effect, be worthless to a lessee for a certain period, the court would have power to determine a nil rent for that period. That question does not, however, arise for decision in the present case for, although the tenant's valuer gave evidence that the premises were, in their original state of disrepair, incapable of being let at all, the judge did not accept that evidence. In these circumstances, I should prefer to reserve this further question until there is a case in which the facts found make a decision on it necessary.

There is one other matter which I would mention. It might be thought that, because a rent determined under section 24A is an interim rent, it can only be applicable for a short time, and ought therefore to be in every case a fixed rent rather than a differential one. In practice, however, the period for which such a rent may be applicable, having regard to the provisions of section 25 (1) and section 64 (2), may well be of considerable length (by which I mean up to two or even three years), either because of delay in the trial of the proceedings in the county court, or because of prolongation of the proceedings by one or more appeals, or both. It would be wrong, therefore, to approach the interpretation of section 24A on the basis that the period for which a rent determined under it will apply is bound to be short, and to construe the section as not giving the court power to determine a differential rent in a proper case on that account.

STEPHENSON LJ: I have had the advantage of considering in draft the judgments of Goff and Brandon LJJ. I have had many doubts in the course of the case, but of one thing I feel reasonably certain: namely that Parliament in enacting section 34 in 1954 and in amending section 34 and enacting section 24A in 1969 never considered the problem raised by this appeal: the impact of disrepair in the property comprised in a tenancy on the court's power to determine a rent under either section.

I long shared Goff LJ's doubts whether section 24A, on its true construction, permitted a differential interim rent.

However, the reasoning of Brandon LJ has resolved those doubts and driven me to his conclusion that, if the court has the power to give effect to disrepair of the property during the new tenancy and to determine a differential new rent, there is nothing in the language or the purpose of section 24A which prevents the court from giving effect to the disrepair of the premises which the current tenancy continues and 'differentiating' the interim rent in a case where the evidence justifies it.

The cases in which the court could fix a differential interim rent must, I would think, be extremely rare, even where the period when interim rent is payable is prolonged by the operation of section 64. But like Brandon LJ with whose judgment I am in complete agreement, I would not like to rule out the possibility of admitting expert evidence which could lead the court to take the exceptional course of determining a differential interim rent.

On all other points I am in agreement with the judgment of Goff LJ.

Whilst the power of the court to determine an interim rent was discretionary and not obligatory, in most normal cases the discretion ought to be exercised in favour of determining such a rent.

ENGLISH EXPORTERS (LONDON) LTD v. ELDONWALL LTD

Chancery Division   [1973] Ch 415

MEGARRY LJ: On the issue of discretion, [counsel for the tenant] pointed to the provisions relating to what I may call the permanent rent. Under section 29 (1) subject to the provisions of the Act, on an application under section 24 (1) for a new tenancy

'the court shall make an order for the grant of a tenancy comprising such property, at such rent and on such other terms, as are hereinafter provided':

the lame punctuation is that of the statute book. Section 34 (1) provides for the ascertainment of the rent at such amount as may be agreed between the landlord and the tenant, 'or as, in default of such agreement, may be determined by the court.' Plainly, said [counsel for the tenant], this is the language of obligation. The court 'shall' make the order; the 'may' goes only to quantum. This is to be contrasted with section 24A (1), under which the landlord in the cases cited:

'may,—... apply to the court to determine a rent which it would be reasonable for the tenant to pay while the tenancy continues by virtue of section 24 of this Act, and the court may determine a rent accordingly.'

Clearly the landlord is under no obligation to apply to the court, and his 'may' must be merely permissive. The court's 'may' seems equally permissive: it relates not merely to quantum but to whether or not a determination is to be made at all. Thus ran the argument.

In my judgment, this argument, in its essentials, is sound.

Section 24A was introduced in order to meet the mischief of tenants seeking to drag out proceedings under the Act of 1954 because it continued their existing tenancies at their existing rents until three months after the application was finally disposed of; and under market conditions in recent years the rents under the existing tenancies were in many cases far below the current level of rents. The court's power to fix interim rents meets the justifiable complaint of landlords under this head. Nevertheless, there may be many cases in which proceedings for the fixing of an interim rent might be unreasonable or even oppressive. Thus the gap between the rent being paid and the rent sought by the landlords may be small: or the proceedings may have marched on apace, so that the period for which any interim rent could operate would be trivial. Furthermore, once the court has ordered a new tenancy to be granted and has fixed its terms, under section 36 (2), the tenant can within 14 days require the court to revoke the order, as, for instance, he may well wish to do if the rent has been fixed at a level far above what he can afford to pay; yet in the case of an interim rent the Act provides the tenant with no such means of escape. Nor is it always the tenant who delays proceedings under the Act. Considerations such as these seem to me to support the view, based on the language of the statute, that the jurisdiction is merely discretionary. I may say that, on behalf of the landlords, [counsel] did not contest that this was the case.

In those circumstances, it seems to me that the court ought in this case to determine an interim rent. The choice lies between leaving the tenants to pay their existing rent, which is admittedly far below the value of what they are getting, and requiring them to pay a rent which, by statutory definition, is the rent 'which it would be reasonable' for the tenants to pay. In the absence of considerations pointing to any different conclusion, why should the court prefer the inadequate to the reasonable? Without laying down any formal rule that the onus lies on the tenant to show why the discretion should not be exercised, I would say that in most normal cases the court's discretion under section 24A ought to be exercised, in that to do so will usually promote justice.

Interim rent is payable from the date of the landlord's application under section 24A and not from the date of the tenant's application for a new tenancy.

STREAM PROPERTIES LTD v. DAVIS

Chancery Division   [1972] 1 WLR 645

PENNYCUICK V-C: As I understand it, the parties are at one that the amount of the interim rent should be the amount of rent provisionally agreed as payable under the new tenancy when granted, that is to say, £10,250 plus something for radiators. What they are not agreed on is the date from which the new rent is to be payable. That depends wholly on the construction of the new section 24A.

Counsel for the landlords contends that under subsection (2) the relevant date is that on which the originating summons was issued, namely, 31 December 1970, or the date specified in the landlords' notice, that is 25 March 1971. That is the later of the two dates and, therefore, it is contended on behalf of the landlords that the rent should run from 25 March 1971. Counsel for the tenant contends that the date on which the proceedings were commenced, within the meaning of subsection (2), is the date of the present summons, namely, 26 November 1971, so that the new rent will run only from that much later date. There is a significant difference between an annual rent of £4000 and an annual rent of £10,250 over a period of some eight months.

It seems to me that the construction of section 24A is perfectly unambiguous. It will be observed that section 3 of the Law of Property Act 1969 introduces this new section as a substantive section and not as an addition to be written into section 24 or any other section of the Act of 1954. That appears from the opening words of section 3:

'After section 24 of the Act of 1954 there shall be inserted the following section'; and then subsection (2): 'In section 24 (1) (*a*) of the Act of 1954 for the words "the next following section" there shall be substituted the words "section 25 of this Act".'

I will read again subsection (2) of section 24A:

'A rent determined in proceedings under this section shall be deemed to be the rent payable under the tenancy from the date on which the proceedings were commenced or the date specified in the landlord's notice or the tenant's request, whichever is the later.'

In the opening expression the words 'proceedings under this section' necessarily mean the application to determine interim rent because such an application is the only form which proceedings under section 24A can take. Then in the subsequent expression 'the date on which the proceedings were commenced' the word 'proceedings' can only, as a matter of grammar, refer back to the word 'proceedings' in the opening expression i.e. the application under section 24A. It seems to me quite impossible to construe subsection (2) so that the word 'proceedings' in the subsequent expression denotes the proceedings started by the substantive originating summons. That involves construing the words 'the proceedings' in the subsequent expression in subsection (2) as something different from 'proceedings under this section' in the opening expression in the same subsection. I find that an impossible construction. It is worth pointing out that there is no reference to proceedings in section 23 or section 24 of the Act of 1954 or in subsection (1) of the new section 24A. So there is nothing anywhere to which the words 'the proceedings' in the subsequent expression in subsection (2) could relate back except the words 'proceedings under this section' in the opening expression.

One may consider how Parliament would naturally have expressed the view contended for by counsel for the landlords. It would have been easy to include the word 'application' instead of the word 'proceedings' in the opening expression and then make clear in the subsequent expression that 'the proceedings' there referred to the substantive originating summons. Parliament has thought fit to adopt a different course. It is said by counsel for the landlords that on that construction the new provision only partially, if at all, alleviates the hardship which is pointed out by Wynn-Parry J. It seems to me that the section does alleviate that hardship to the extent that if the landlords take note of the true effect of the new section 24A and make application under the section at the earliest available date, then the new rent will relate back accordingly, i.e. to the date of that application or to the alternative specified date, whichever is the later.

Note: This decision was applied by Mr Michael Wheeler QC (sitting as a deputy High Court judge) in *Victor Blake (Menswear) Ltd* v. *City of Westminster* (1979) 38 P & CR 448.

There is a conflict of authority on whether the ability to consider the rent payable under the current tenancy authorises the court to 'cushion the blow' to the tenant by awarding less than the market rent under section 24A.

FAWKE v. CHELSEA (VISCOUNT)

Court of Appeal   [1980] QB 441

(For the facts of this case, see earlier, page 543.)

GOFF LJ: Section 24A of the Landlord and Tenant Act 1954 (as inserted by section 3 (1) of the Law of Property Act 1969) is, as has been stated by Stamp J in *Regis Property Co. Ltd* v. *Lewis & Peat Ltd* [1970] Ch 695 and by Megarry J in *English Exporters (London) Ltd* v. *Eldonwall Ltd* [1973] Ch 415, extremely difficult to construe and apply because it is not easy to reconcile subsection (1) with subsection (3) or to see the true relationship between the opening words of subsection (3), requiring regard to be had to the rent payable under the tenancy, and the later part of the section, incorporating subsections (1) and (2) of section 34 by reference; because the very general expression 'shall have regard to' necessarily imports a large degree of uncertainty; and finally because, as Megarry J said in *English Exporters (London) Ltd* v. *Eldonwall Ltd*, at p 430:

'I would only add that the process of applying section 34 to a hypothetical yearly tenancy is one that, at least under present conditions, may often have an air of unreality about it that would puzzle the most expert of valuers.'

In the *Regis Property* case [1970] Ch 695 Stamp J construed the words 'shall have regard to the rent payable under the terms of the tenancy' in section 24A (3) as merely amending section 34 (1), as applied to the determination of an interim rent under section 24A, by in effect striking out the words 'other than those relating to rent' and substituting 'including those relating to rent.' So he held there was only one operation to be performed under section 24A (3), that is to say, the assessment of the rent as a matter of market value in accordance with section 34 as, in effect, so amended, and, of course, on the basis of a yearly tenancy. He held that one could have regard to the rent under the existing tenancy if, but only if, it had evidential value for the purposes of ascertaining the market value, and he considered that but for the opening words of subsection (3) it could not have been regarded at all, because of the words of exclusion in that subsection.

Once the valuation exercise has been performed, however, in his view the matter is at an end and the figure arrived at cannot be modified either by the provision in subsection (1) that the landlord may 'apply to the court to determine a rent which it would be reasonable for the tenant to pay' or by the direction in subsection (3) to have regard to the rent. That is to say he rejected what was described as the cushion argument.

In the *English Exporters* case [1973] 1 Ch 415 Megarry J, taking a different view, accepted that argument. According to him the direction to have regard to the rent and the reference to section 34 are two separate things so that one must first provisionally determine the interim rent in accordance with the terms of section 34 but, of course, as if the court were ordering, not a term of years, but a yearly tenancy, and then review that against the actual rent payable under the current tenancy in the light of the direction in subsection (1) that the rent is to be reasonable. Megarry J considered that Stamp J was wrong in thinking that unless his construction were adopted one could not refer to the existing rent even in the examples given by him where it would have evidentiary value.

In the result, therefore, both agreed, though for different reasons, that the court and the expert witnesses appearing before it may, and should, have regard to the existing rent if it has evidentiary value, but the difference between them lies in Stamp J's view that, apart from that, it is irrelevant and the matter ends with the valuation, whereas in Megarry J's view it then has in any event to be considered in order to determine whether it is reasonable to adopt the valuation without modification.

Unfortunately no argument was addressed to us as to which of these views we should adopt, or whether, indeed, neither affords the correct solution to the problems posed by section 24A, as both parties were prepared to accept Megarry J's decision. We must, therefore, proceed on that basis, and this case cannot be regarded as a binding decision on this particular question of construction, but I must say that, as at present advised, I prefer the reasoning and decision of Megarry J. With all respect to Stamp J, I think he fell into error, because he overlooked the fact that there are two tenancies and two rents involved, not one. The rent to which the court is directed to have regard under section 24A (3) is the rent payable under the contractual tenancy, which is continuing by virtue of the Act, but when one applies section 34 to the determination of an interim rent, as directed by section 24A (3), one is considering a new hypothetical yearly tenancy, and one can no more consider the rent appropriate to such a tenancy when determining that rent than one can consider the rent under a new tenancy when determining that rent.

Note: The decision in *English Exporters* v. *Eldonwall*, referred to in the above judgment, was applied by Dillon J in *Ratners (Jewellers) Ltd* v. *Lemnoll Ltd* (1980) 255 EG 987, and by Judge Finlay QC in *Janes (Gowns) Ltd* v. *Harlow Development Corporation* (1980) 253 EG 799.

A summons to determine an interim rent under section 24A must be served promptly.

TEXACO LTD v. BENTON & BOWLER HOLDINGS LTD

Chancery Division   (1983) 267 EG 355

In proceedings by the tenant for a new tenancy, the landlord issued an originating summons for an interim rent on the 20 March 1981. The solicitors then acting for the landlord failed, by an oversight, to serve the summons until the 5 May 1982. On the 26 May 1982, new solicitors served a fresh summons.

Held: Such a summons must be served promptly. Accordingly, the first summons was invalidated by the delay for over a year and the interim rent could only run from the date of the second summons.

FALCONER J: It would be a very strange situation if an originating application under section 24A of the Act issued without a specified return date except for the words 'On a date to be fixed' could be issued and made valid though not served until well over a year after issue and without any intimation of its existence to the plaintiff tenant, which is the situation here.

That, in my judgment, cannot be right. In the absence of a specific provision in the rules specifying the time for service of an application under Order 97, rule 9A, subrule (1), paragraph (a), the matter, in my judgment, is governed by the Practice Direction, which requires the application, if made by summons in the tenant's proceedings for a new tenancy to be served promptly. Promptly means promptly. Solicitors acting for landlords in such proceedings should ensure that a landlord's summons under Order 97, rule 9A, subrule (1), paragraph (a), for interim rent should be served promptly, and in the ordinary way it seems to me that there should be no reason why such a summons should not be served immediately after issue.

In this case, in my judgment, in view of the long delay before service, a delay of over a year, the summons was invalid by the time a copy of it was eventually sent to the plaintiffs' solicitors. It follows that the earliest date from which the interim rent can run is that of the application on the second summons, that is to say 26 May 1982.

The court has jurisdiction to hear an application under section 24A notwithstanding that the applicant was no longer the landlord of the premises when the application is heard by the court.

BLOOMFIELD v. ASHWRIGHT LTD

Court of Appeal   (1983) 266 EG 1095

The landlord applied for an interim rent under section 24A of the 1954 Act, but assigned his reversion before the hearing of his application. The question arose whether the county court had jurisdiction to determine the interim rent notwithstanding the assignment.

Held: The county court judge had retained his jurisdiction despite the assignment and the fact that the benefit of the proceedings had not been expressly assigned.

LAWTON LJ: Then comes section 24A. The sidenote reads as follows: 'Rent while tenancy continues by virtue of section 24.' Subsection (1) is as follows:

> 'The landlord of a tenancy to which this Part of this Act applies may,—(a) if he has given notice under section 25 of this Act to terminate the tenancy; or (b) if the tenant has made a request for a new tenancy in accordance with section 26 of this Act; apply to the court to determine a rent which it would be reasonable for the tenant to pay while the tenancy continues by virtue of section 24 of this Act, and the court may determine a rent accordingly.'

The jurisdiction is to determine a rent which it would be reasonable for the tenant to pay while the tenancy continues. The rent so determined by the court applies to the tenancy as long as the tenancy continues. In the circumstances of this case the tenancy continued up to 19 February 1982 and indeed would go on continuing until the term created by the new lease started, which was in the late spring or early summer of 1982. Subsection (2) is as follows:

> 'A rent determined in proceedings under this section shall be deemed to be the rent payable under the tenancy from the date on which the proceedings were commenced or the date specified in the landlord's notice or the tenant's request, whichever is the later.'

Once again it is the rent which is attached to the tenancy which is to be determined and it is to be a rent payable from the date on which the proceedings were commenced or the date specified in the landlord's notice or the tenant's request. It seems to me that the whole purpose of section 24A is to fix a rent for the premises.

The ownership of the reversion to the premises may pass from one person to another for various reasons, but when there is such a transfer the tenancy goes on and the rent which is payable in respect of the tenancy continues to be payable. The court is concerned with determining that which is to be paid for the tenancy. When Ashwright Ltd made their application for the determination of an interim rent they were undoubtedly entitled to do so. We do not know whether they specifically assigned any rights they may have had to an interim rent to Shelgate Property Co. Ltd. It seems to me it matters not, because when they did assign their reversion to Shelgate Property Co. Ltd they had a duty to the reversioner to safeguard his interest. They had started the proceedings. The proceedings were for the benefit of the reversion, although, as [counsel for the appellants] pointed out, the benefit was not specifically transferred to the new reversioner under the provisions of section 141 of the Law of Property Act 1925. Nevertheless, Ashwright Ltd were, in my judgment, in good conscience, bound to do what they could for their assignee. In the circumstances of this case, albeit by good luck rather than planning, they did remain in the litigation so as to be a party to it on the date when the judge came to determine the interim rent. So it is not a situation such as [counsel for the appellants] outlined in the course of his submission, that from the date of their assignment they had no interest whatsoever in the proceedings which were then under way. It is also clear that Shelgate Property Co. Ltd were before the court in a position to get the benefit of any order which the judge might make on Ashwright Ltd's application. So the pair of them were before the court and every aspect of the matter was covered by their presence. It is also pertinent to repeat what I have already said, that the county court judge did not make a money order at all. He merely determined the rent payable in respect of the tenancy. If Ashwright Ltd and Shelgate Property Co. Ltd could not agree as to who was to receive the benefit of the order made by the judge, that was a matter for them to litigate among themselves. It was not a matter for the county court's jurisdiction under section 24A of the 1954 Act.

In those circumstances, it seems to me that the court did have jurisdiction to determine the rent notwithstanding the assignment to which I have already referred.

The landlord's application under section 24A is not affected by the tenant's withdrawal of his application for a new tenancy since such an application is not parasitic on the tenant's request.

MICHAEL KRAMER & CO. v. AIRWAYS PENSION FUND TRUSTEES

Court of Appeal   (1976) 246 EG 745

STEPHENSON LJ: The landlords' application of 30 April is, in my judgment, not parasitic to the tenants' application of 25 July 1974, but a wholly distinct claim for independent relief. It is a claim distinct from the tenants' proceedings for relief independent of those proceedings. It does not drop or fall with the discontinuance by the tenants of their own application, but it survives. It must be treated separately, and it cannot be discontinued simply by the discontinuance of the tenants' proceedings. However described, and whatever its form, the landlords' application is in substance an originating application. However labelled, it originates, or starts, or initiates a claim, in some sense countering the tenants' application though affording no defence to it, and has its own distinct and separate life just as much as if it had been initiated by what was in form an originating summons or application or had been ordered to stand as a counterclaim, which in substance it was. By making the application in the form in which it was made in the course of the tenants' proceedings for discontinuance, instead of by a differently headed and worded application alongside those proceedings, the landlords have not turned it into a perpetual parasite. It can be detached and stand alone in its present form without any alteration of its heading or its wording. It would be unreasonable and unjust if by abandoning your attack you could compel your opponent to call off his counterclaim, particularly if it is mounted to attain an objective of its own. I do not find myself compelled by any arguments, rules or authority put before us to treat this counter-attack, if it is correctly so described, as called off by the tenants' abandoning their attack. To do so would be, I think, to disregard the realities of these two applications. They are quite distinct in the relief which they claim. The one is, in the form in which it has been made, and understandably made, independent enough of the other to survive its discontinuance.

Note: The observations of Stephenson LJ are equally applicable to an application by a landlord under section 24A in the High Court: see Falconer J in *Artoc Bank Trust Ltd* v. *Prudential Assurance Co. Ltd* [1984] 1 WLR 1181 when he said:

'In my judgment, the defendants' application by their counter-summons made pursuant to and in accordance with the provisions of Ord. 97, r. 9A, is not parasitic to the plaintiffs' application for a new tenancy but "is a wholly distinct claim for independent relief" and "is in substance an originating application," which, like the landlords' application in the *Kramer* case, is in substance a counterclaim.

Accordingly, I hold that the defendants' counter-summons for interim rent has survived the plaintiffs' discontinuance of their application for a new tenancy and it follows that the defendants succeed on the preliminary point.'

Appendix

Recent cases

An application for the appointment of an expert is valid even though manifestly made only to comply with time limits while negotiations continue (see also section 1.3 (b) page 28)

STAINES WAREHOUSING CO LTD v. MONTAGU EXECUTOR & TRUSTEE CO LTD AND ANOTHER

Chancery Division (1985) 277 EG 305

A lease contained a rent review clause with a strict timetable which extended to the time allowed for application to the President of the RICS for the appointment of a valuer. While negotiations were in progress for the fixing of a revised rent, the landlords' surveyors (without notifying the tenants), wrote to the President of the RICS stating that negotiations were still continuing and that the application was an 'in time only application' for the appointment of an expert valuer to determine a new rent. The application was, *inter alia*, not accompanied by the necessary fixed fee which the RICS required for the processing of the application (and which was contrary to RICS Guidance Notes). The tenants contended that the application was invalid (and that the time limits had accordingly been breached) because (i) they had received no notice of the application, (ii) no fee had accompanied the letter, and (iii) the application was stated to be 'an in time only application'.

Held: The application was valid because: (i) the lease did not require notice of the application to be given to the tenants; (ii) the absence of a fee which should have accompanied the application did not prevent the application from being actually made and received notwithstanding that it would not be 'processed'; (iii) the letter did amount to a genuine application in compliance with the time limits laid down in the lease, even though the party applying hoped that implementation of the procedure would not be necessary in order to fix a new rent.

KNOX J: Finally, and critically, the first defendant was required to make an application to the president for the appointment of such a surveyor by 29 June 1984. What in fact happened was that there were some negotiations. While those negotiations were still on foot and on 30 May 1984, the surveyors to the landlord wrote a letter to the President of the Royal Institution of Chartered Surveyors. That is, of course, just short of a month before the last date for the landlord to comply with the obligation to make an application. As the issue in this action depends entirely on this letter, I propose to read it in full:

'The lease is for a term expiring on September 29 2095, at a current rent of £43,400 per annum, with provision for a rent review at September 29 1984.

The second schedule to the lease requires that application be made to the

554

President of the RICS for the appointment of an Expert Surveyor to determine a revised rent failing agreement between the parties six months prior to the review date. The application to the President is to be made not later than three months prior to the review date.

Whilst no rent has yet been agreed in this case, negotiations are continuing between ourselves and the tenants, and we are, therefore, writing in accordance with the terms of the second schedule to the lease to make an in time only application for the appointment by the President of an Expert Surveyor to determine a revised rent for the above premises at September 29 1984.

We should be grateful for your acknowledgement of this letter.'

The question before me is: was that, or was it not, an application within the meaning of the second schedule to the lease?

No notice was in fact given to the tenant by the landlord or its agents of that letter having been written to the president of the Royal Institutional of Chartered Surveyors, and it remained in ignorance of that fact until very much later in the year 1984, when the landlord filled in a form which is issued by the Royal Institution of Chartered Surveyors for use on applications for the appointment of either an arbitrator or an independent expert. That form was in fact signed by, again, the landlord's agents on December 4 1984. ...

There is provision at the end of the form for the fee to be paid to the President of the RICS. Before I read that, I should refer to *Guidance Notes* which the RICS has issued to persons who are applying to it for the appointment of arbitrators or experts. The particular paras which are relevant to this case are contained at paras 2-1, where it is said: 'Application to the President for appointment. Application to the President for the appointment of an Arbitrator or Independent Expert should be in writing and preferably made on the form obtainable on application to the RICS.' Second, 'Document(s) and fee on application. The application will not be processed until the appropriate non-refundable fee, currently £40 plus VAT, has been received together with a copy of the lease or other document conferring on the President power to make the appointment'. Then there are various provisions which set out what the president will do in selecting an arbitrator or an expert as the case may be, and when those things have been done it is stated in the notes that the appointment takes effect from the date on which the president signs the appointment, which he will not do until he has satisfied himself that the person he proposes to appoint is suitable and not in any way disqualified.

So far as the fee was concerned, the facts are that no fee was paid when the letter of 30 May 1984 was sent, but a fee appears to have accompanied the document that was signed on 4 December 1984.

On those facts, argument has been addressed to me as to the validity of that letter of 30 May 1984. [Counsel for the tenant] has taken the following points. First of all, he says that this has to be construed in a commercial way. That is not, I think, seriously controverted. Second, he says that there are essentially three defects in this letter as an application. The first is that it was not accompanied by the fee. That does not seem to me to be a valid objection. It is of course plain that the lease itself says nothing more than that the landlord must make an application, and there is no description or further elaboration of what is involved in the making of an application.

Second, it is clear that so far as the RICS's Notes have relevance—and they were relied on by [counsel for the tenant]—they do recognise that the application exists and has an objective existence by the way in which they describe the effect of the payment of a fee. The particular turn of phrase is 'the application will not be processed until the appropriate non-returnable fee has been received'. That seems to me to recognise the existence of the application. In a sense this is not directly relevant to the decision I have to take, in that the views of the Royal Institution of Chartered Surveyors, though no doubt worthy of serious consideration, cannot be binding upon me, but they do seem to me to accord with the reality of the matter, in that the application is actually made when the president is approached and told that an application is being made. No doubt it may be that the president will not take steps to process (as the expression is) that application until he receives the proper fee, but nevertheless the application is there and, so to say, on the table.

Third, [counsel for the tenant] relied on the fact that no notice had been given. Here again I feel that this is not a point of any substance, because there is no requirement for notice to be given in the lease. The provisions of the lease are, of course, detailed, and where a party is required to do something the lease says so. [Counsel for the tenant] argued that there could be difficulties if no notice was given, and a tenant might be prejudiced if he took steps which he would not have taken had he realised that a notice had been given. Those are arguments *in terrorem* as it seems to me. There is a theoretical answer to them, in that the tenant could perfectly safely inquire whether a notice had been given, since, time being of the essence, there would be no risk in his doing so. But equally, of course, there is no obligation in the lease on the tenant, as [counsel for the tenant] forcefully pointed out, to make any such inquiry. The matter is left entirely neutral.

Next—and as it seems to me by far and away the most serious point—is the way in which the letter was actually phrased. It will be recalled that the critical expression was 'We are ... writing in accordance with the terms of the second schedule to the lease to make an in time only application for the appointment by the President of an Expert Surveyor', etc. The three words 'in time only' have been the subject of argument before me. It was submitted by [counsel for the landlord] that they are capable of having two meanings: (1) that the agents were asking the president effectively not to take any further steps on the application because it was only a nominal application. The second meaning relied on by [counsel for the landlord] is that they were making an application now because, as was in fact stated in terms earlier in the letter, there were negotiations on foot. [Counsel for the tenant], on the other hand, submits that this is really not a genuine application at all and that it was not calculated to or indeed intended to put the machinery into effective operation. In support of that, he relied on the decision in *Aly* v. *Aly*, reported I think only in *The Times* newspaper on 27 December 1983, where, in relation to the provisions of Order 12, rule 8 of the Rules of the Supreme Court, there was a requirement that a defendant should apply to the court within a specified time-limit and an application had been made in that case, in the sense that a letter was sent by the litigant to the appropriate court authority, but the summons on that letter was not issued until the time-limit had expired. In those circumstances, the Court of Appeal held that the time-limit had been complied with, and they applied the following test:

> 'One had to interpret the rule in question in a way that made sense of the whole procedure laid down. It did not make sense to penalise a party who had done everything required of him by the rule, on the basis of something not done in time by the court. Therefore, one could only say that "apply to the court" meant "do all that it is in your power to do to set in the motion the procedure necessary for the relief sought"'

[Counsel for the tenant] says that in this case the landlord's agents have not done all that it was in their power to do to set in motion the procedure necessary for the relief sought, in that they had written a letter which indicated, perhaps not in very clear terms, that they did not want any action to be taken on the letter and that it was merely a piece of paper which would preserve their rights. This is a very short point. In my judgment, the true construction of this is that the landlord's agents were taking the step that they understood to be necessary to comply with the time-limit and that it was in that context that they used the words in the phrase 'an in time only application'. In my judgment, having set out the framework of the clause and made it clear within what limits they were operating, the landlord's agents indicated that they were making an application, but that it was an application on which they hoped it would not be necessary for the president to appoint an expert surveyor who would then determine the rent, simply because there were negotiations on foot. It really comes down to this, in my judgment: whether or not this was a genuine application. In my judgment, it just passes the test.

'Without prejudice' notices are inappropriate for triggering rent reviews (see also section 4.1 (b) page 80 et seq.)

NUNES AND ANOTHER v. DAVIES LAING AND DICK LTD

Chancery Division   (1986) 277 EG 417

SIR NICHOLAS BROWNE-WILKINSON V-C: But the authorities disclose two possible tests. The first is that the alleged counternotice must constitute 'a clear indication' to the landlord as to the tenant's intention, or must make it 'clear to the landlord that he proposes to go to arbitration' (see per Lawton LJ and Templeman LJ in *Amalgamated Estates Ltd* v. *Joystretch Manufacturing Ltd* (1980) 257 EG 489). However, in two later cases the test has been expressed to be that the letter alleged to constitute the counternotice must be 'unequivocal' (see per McNeill J in *Edlingham Ltd* v. *MFI Furniture Centres Ltd* (1981) 259 EG 421 and per Nicholls J in *Sheridan* v. *Blaircourt Investment Ltd* (1984) 270 EG 1290). It may be that in those two cases the learned judges were not meaning to apply any more stringent test than that of clarity laid down by the Court of Appeal in the *Amalgamated Estates* case.

This case discloses that there may be a difference between what is clear and what is unequivocal. If the expression 'unequivocal' means 'incapable of bearing any other meaning' then the way is open for arguments based on remote possibilities of construction, however unlikely they may be, in construing the counternotice.

In my judgment, the test is that applied by the Court of Appeal in the *Amalgamated Estates* case, namely that the counternotice should be in terms which are sufficiently clear to bring home to the ordinary landlord that the tenant is purporting to exercise his right under para. (c), and that is the test which I propose to apply.

It is clearly established that a letter which merely disagrees with the rent proposed by the landlord, with or without a request for additional information as to the basis on which it has been fixed, does not constitute a valid counternotice (see *Bellinger* v. *South London Stationers Ltd* (1979) 252 EG 699, *Oldschool* v. *Johns* (1980) 256 EG 381 and the Court of Appeal decision in *Amalgamated Estates*). Such a letter is equally consistent with a mere attempt to agree the new rent operating the provisions of para. (b).

In the present case the letter of 6 December 1984 goes much further than that. It was a letter written in response to the landlords' trigger notice, which expressly referred to clause 2 of the lease. The letter of 6 December is itself headed up 'In the matter of the Rent Review'. Most importantly, to my mind, the letter is described in itself as being a 'formal' notice and asks for confirmation that it is 'due' notice. That is to say, the letter on its face is a document which purports to be a notice which is formally required by and is due under some legal requirement. Now, proviso (iii) envisages only two notices: the landlords' trigger notice under para. (a) and the tenants' counternotice under para. (c).

In my judgment, it must have been clear to anyone receiving the letter of 6 December that the tenants' agent was giving a formal notice and, knowing the terms of the lease, must have known that the only provision for a formal notice under proviso (iii) was a counternotice under para. (c).

When ascertaining the revised rent, the general rule is that effect must be given to the underlying commercial purpose of the lease (see also section 6.4 (a) page 124 *et seq.*)

The general purpose of a provision for rent review is to enable the landlord to obtain from time to time the market rental which the premises would command if let on the same terms on the open market at the review dates. The purpose is to reflect the changes in the value of money and real increases in the value of the property during a long term. Therefore, where a lease contains a review clause, in the absence of clear words or surrounding circumstances, the lease should be construed so as to give effect to the basic purpose of the rent review clause when deciding the basis on which the revised rent should be valued. It should not confer a windfall benefit on the landlord by providing him with a reviewed rent at a higher level because the reviewed rent is fixed in disregard of the existence of a review clause in the lease, unless there are clear indications to the contrary.

Sir Nicholas Browne-Wilkinson V-C in *The British Gas Corporation* v. *Universities Superannuation Scheme Ltd* (6 February 1986—see below) said that the correct approach when construing such a lease was as follows:

(a) Words in a rent exclusion provision which require *all* provisions as to rent to be disregarded produce a result so manifestly contrary to commercial common sense that they cannot be given literal effect.

(b) Other clear words which require the rent review provision (as opposed to all provisions as to rent) to be disregarded (such as those in the *Pugh* case (see earlier, page 127)) must be given effect to, however wayward the result.

(c) Subject to (b), in the absence of special circumstances it is proper to give effect to the underlying commercial purpose of a rent review clause and to construe the words so as to give effect to that purpose by requiring future rent reviews to be taken into account in fixing the open market rental under the hypothetical letting.

The case of *British Gas*, which expressly approved of the approach taken in *Datastream International Ltd* v. *Oakeep Ltd* (1986) 277 EG 66 and *MFI Properties Ltd* v. *BICC Group Pension Trust Ltd* (The Times, 7 February 1986—see below) has, it is to be hoped, reduced the number of cases in which the valuer has to review the rent disregarding the existence of the review clause in the lease because of the clumsy but often common form of words in the document, as was done by Walton J in *National Westminster Bank Plc* v. *Arthur Young McClelland Moores & Co* (1985) 273 EG 402 (see above page 128), and followed in different circumstances by Peter Gibson J in *Equity & Law Life Assurance* v. *Bodfield Ltd* (1985) 276 EG 1157.

Since the decisions turned on the construction of the particular words of a particular lease, a previous decision could not bind a judge interpreting a differently worded document in a different case. However, in *Datastream, MFI Properties* and *British Gas*, the judges chose to adopt a different approach to interpreting the documents to give effect to the commercial reality of the situation. The latest decision of *British Gas*, in which the previous decisions were reviewed and in which the Vice-Chancellor laid down principles of guidance as to interpretation, must now be regarded as having superseded and rejected the approach taken in the *National Westminster Bank* case and others decided on the same principles of construction.

The literal approach in construction was rejected in the cases of *Datastream International Ltd* v. *Oakeep Ltd* and *MFI Properties* and conclusively by Sir Nicholas Browne-Wilkinson V-C in the *British Gas Corporation* case. Extracts from all these cases are set out below in chronological order.

DATASTREAM INTERNATIONAL LTD v. OAKEEP LTD

Chancery Division   (1986) 277 EG 66

WARNER J: [The] question is whether the hypothetical lease by reference to the terms of which 'the market rental value' of the property at the review date is to be fixed is or is not to include the provisions for rent reviews themselves that are contained in the actual lease. The answer to that question turns on the meaning of the words in brackets in para. 2 (1) of the Second Schedule, that is to say the words 'other than the amount of rent hereby reserved'. The defendant contends that the effect of those words is to exclude the provisions for rent reviews from the hypothetical lease, with the result that the lessee must pay a rent enhanced by the fact that, upon this hypothesis, he will be enjoying the privilege of occupying the property for 20 years at that rent. The plaintiff on the other hand contends that the words in brackets are not apt to exclude from the hypothetical lease the provisions for rent review in the actual lease and that therefore it gets the benefit of a lower rent because account must be taken of the fact that in five years' time there will be another rent review and so on.

I have no doubt that if the question were free from authority I would decide it in favour of the plaintiff. The crux is really this. Does the word 'amount' in the parenthesis mean only a fixed amount or does it include also any amount to be ascertained by means of a formula? Obviously if it includes only a fixed amount it includes for the purposes of the present review only the peppercorn (if one can call that an amount at all) and the £360,000. If it can include an amount to be ascertained by the application of a formula then it will also include so far as para. 1 (3) is concerned the 'yearly sum equal to the market rental value of the said property at the expiration of the immediately preceding period' and so far as para. 1 (4) is concerned the 'yearly sum equal to the market rental value of the said property at the expiration of the said preceding five-year period'. Of course, on the narrow construction, according to which 'amount' means only a fixed amount, at the next rent review the amount fixed at the present rent review would fall to be treated as an 'amount'. Faced with that choice as to the meaning of the word 'amount', I prefer the meaning that does not produce an unreasonable and unfair result, that is to say does not require the lessee to pay over the next five years for a benefit it will not be enjoying, namely the benefit of a lease with no rent review clause in it.

The judge then reviewed the authorities, in particular *Pugh* v. *Smiths Industries Ltd* (1982) 264 EG 823 (see earlier at page 127), remarking that, having regard to the wording of the particular lease, Goulding J could not have come to a different conclusion. He then referred to *Lister Locks Ltd* v. *TEI Pension Fund* (1981) EG 827 (see earlier at page 152) which, so far as it went, was in the plaintiff's favour. Adopting the reasoning of Vinelott J in *Pearl Assurance Plc* v. *Shaw* (1984) 274 EG 490 (see earlier at page 174 and in particular, page 176):

WARNER J continued: The next authority is also in the plaintiff's favour. That is the judgment of Vinelott J in *Pearl Assurance Plc* v. *Shaw* (1984) 274 EG 490. That was again a case about a rent review clause, but the ambiguity there arose in relation to a provision concerning user. The passage in Vinelott J's judgment that is relevant to this case is as follows:

'The purpose of a rent review clause in general is to enable a landlord to bring the rent originally negotiated up to date and to substitute for it the rent that the parties might have been expected to agree if the rent had been negotiated on the same basis as before, but in the light of market conditions prevailing at the time of the review and, of course, for the shorter term then unexpired. Looked at in that light I think the court should lean against a construction which requires the rent fixed on a revision to be ascertained without regard to the use which, under the lease, the tenant is to be entitled to make of the demised premises, unless, of course, that intention is spelt out in reasonably clear terms. Otherwise, the effect of the review might be to impose on a tenant an obligation to pay a rent appropriate to a very profitable use, but one very obnoxious to the landlord, and one which he had been careful to forbid in the strongest possible terms—the effect, that is, of making the tenant pay for something which he not only has not got, but which he cannot require the landlord to give him.'

Transferring that reasoning from a provision about user to the rent review clause itself, it suggests that I should lean against a construction which requires the tenant to pay for something which he has not got, that is a lease which is free from any rent review clause.

Warner J then distinguished the decision of Walton J in *National Westminster Bank Plc* v. *Arthur Young McClelland Moores & Co* (1985) 273 EG 402 (see earlier page 128). In the *National Westminster* case Walton J, instead of leaning against a construction that would require a tenant to pay for something he was not going to get—namely a lease free of reviews until the end of the term—had imposed on the tenant a lease with rent reviews which were to be determined on the basis that they were to be disregarded. Warner J declined to follow Walton J's example in his construction of the material review clause:

At all events, I do not feel the need to insert words into this clause in the same way that Walton J felt a need to insert words in the clause that he was considering. It seems to me that 'subject to the provisions of this lease (other than the amount of rent hereby reserved)' is perfectly intelligible English and that it would be too pernickety to say that the amount of rent is not a provision of the lease. It is obviously something provided for by the lease. From there to say that it may be referred to as a provision of the lease is not a difficult step, and I decline to alter, or possibly to alter, the meaning of this clause by inserting words in it that there is no compelling reason for inserting.

Warner J lastly considered *Equity & Law Life Assurance Society Plc* v. *Bodfield Ltd* (1985) 276 EG 1157 (see above, page 130), a decision of Peter Gibson J, which he considered a 'rather special case because, in the rent review clause in the lease there in question, there was an elaborate provision, clause 4 (2), the effect of which was to limit the rent payable following any rent review to the greater of £28,500 and 85% of the "net rental value" as ascertained on the rent review. There was no indication at all as to the reason why that provision had been inserted. The reason was unknown.'

WARNER J concluded: So Peter Gibson J regarded the case before him as stronger in favour of the landlord than Walton J's case, and each of them regarded his decision as turning on the precise terms of the lease before him. I do not therefore feel constrained in any way by their decisions, and that all the more so because I am told that in the *National Westminster Bank* case Walton J refused to certify under section 1 of the Arbitration Act 1979 that there was in that case a question of law of general public importance. So, obviously, he did not think that his decision would be applicable to other cases. In the result the authorities do not bring me to depart from the view that I would have formed myself independently of them.

The originating summons seeks a declaration that:

'Upon the true construction of paragraph 2 of the Second Schedule to the above-mentioned lease and in the events which have happened the rent to be paid by the Plaintiff with effect from the 24th June 1985 is the greater of (a) the clear yearly rent of £360,000 or (b) a yearly sum equal to the rent at which the property comprised in the above-mentioned lease is worth to be let in the open market as a whole at the best rent reasonably obtainable without taking any fine or premium subject to the provisions of the above-mentioned lease (other than the amounts of rent specified in paragraphs 1 (1) and 1 (2) of the said Second Schedule) but including the provisions for the revising of rent contained in the said Second Schedule for a term equal to the residue then unexpired of the term granted by the above-mentioned lease but having regard to the Plaintiff's rights under the Landlord and Tenant Act 1954, and, otherwise upon the bases set out in paragraph 2 of the said Second Schedule.'

I propose to make that declaration.

A common sense commercial approach similar to that taken in *Datastream* was used by Hoffman J in *MFI Properties* below.

MFI PROPERTIES LTD v. BICC GROUP PENSION TRUST LTD

Chancery Division   The Times, 7 February 1986

An underlease and a reversionary underlease contained identical terms; they provided for five yearly rent reviews. The relevant provisions were that 'the rent . . . reserved shall be revised so as to equal the rent at which having regard to the terms of this sub-underlease (other than those relating to rent) the demised premises might then reasonably be expected to be let in the open market by a willing landlord to a willing tenant for a term of 20 years with vacant possession ...'

The issue was whether the words in parenthesis—'other than those relating to rent'—required an assumption that the hypothetical letting contained no rent review clause. The landlord contended that the rent review clause was plainly a term relating to rent, which must therefore be assumed to be excluded. The tenant argued that while that might be the literal meaning, the consequences of such a construction were so contrary to common sense that the words should be construed more narrowly, so as to include only terms concerning rent which the review was intended to revise.

Held: A review clause was designed to deal with a particular commercial problem, namely that of a tenant who wanted security of tenure for a lengthy term, and a landlord, who in times of inflation or a rapidly changing property market, did not want to commit himself to a fixed rent for the whole of that term. It therefore permitted the rent to be periodically revised to an amount calculated on the assumption of a fresh rent at the relevant date.

The terms upon which such hypothetical letting had to be assumed to take place would naturally depend in each case on the particular language of the rent clause. *Prima facie* the parties had to be assumed to intend the hypothetical letting to be for the residue of the actual lease, and in the circumstances existing at the relevant date. But the language might show that a departure from reality was intended.

Where the language was capable of more than one meaning, the court was entitled to select the meaning which accorded with the apparent purpose rather than one which appeared commercially irrational.

Here, precisely the same words were used as in section 34 of the Landlord and Tenant Act 1954, and it seemed clear that in that context they had been treated as bearing the meaning contended for by the tenant, rather than the wider meaning suggested by the landlord. The exclusion of the rent review clause from the hypothetical lease was an assumption which had no apparent commercial justification, and which gave rise to practical problems.

It was common knowledge that in practice landlords did not nowadays grant long leases of commercial premises at rack rents without rent reviews.

In this case the animal was not so much fabulous as extinct, but the problem was the same.

A valuer asked to determine the rent at which premises could be let in the open market for a lengthy term without a rent review had no comparables in the real world to which he could refer. All he could do was to make an arbitrary adjustment: it was improbable that the parties could have intended the rent to be determined in that way.

The only plausible alternative to the literal construction was the narrower construction advanced by the tenant. That was the construction which his Lordship preferred, and there would be a declaration accordingly.

The approach to construction taken in *MFI Properties* and *Datastream* (above) were expressly approved and applied by Sir Nicholas Browne-Wilkinson V-C in *The British Gas Corporation* v. *University Superannuation Scheme Ltd* (below). He went out of his way to lay down general guidelines with regard to the approach to be taken in the construction of rent review provisions in leases. The literal approach adopted in *National Westminster Bank Plc v. Arthur Young McClelland Moores & Co.* and *Equity & Law Life Assurance Society* was not followed.

THE BRITISH GAS CORPORATION v. UNIVERSITIES SUPERANNUATION SCHEME LTD

Chancery Division   6 February 1986

A lease of very substantial office premises was granted by the landlord's predecessor in title for a 35 year term commencing from 25 March 1980. The rent reserved (defined in the lease as 'the Yearly Rent') was a peppercorn until 1 July 1980 and 'thereafter throughout the remainder of the term the rent of £1,150,000.00 p.a. ... or such other rent as may from time to time be substituted therefor pursuant to the provisions of the Second Schedule ...'

The Second Schedule provided that the landlord could give the tenant a review notice in which event the 'Yearly Rent' payable as from the review date 'shall be the higher of (i) the Yearly Rent payable immediately before such Review Date and (ii) the rack rental value of the Demised Premises at the relevant Review Date'. The material paragraph of the Second Schedule provided, *inter alia*, that the market rent should be the best yearly rent at which the premises could reasonably be expected to be let 'in the open market by a willing landlord to a willing tenant for a term equal to the term hereby granted by means of a lease containing the same provisions (other than as to the yearly rent) as are herein contained on the following assumptions ...'

The question before the court was whether under the terms of the lease the new rent had to be based on the assumption that there were provisions for five yearly reviews or whether the review clause fell to be disregarded when determining the rent payable.

Held: Although other cases concerned with this point had been decided earlier, they did not bind a judge from construing a differently worded document so as to produce a different result.

However, there was a clear difference in the fundamental approach adopted by Walton J in *National Westminster Bank Plc* v. *Arthur Young McClelland Moores & Co* (1985) 273 EG 402, applied by Peter Gibson J in *Equity & Law Life Assurance Society Plc* v. *Bodfield Ltd* (1985) 276 EG 1157, on the one hand, which was to construe the wording of the document literally without regard to the underlying purpose of the lease, and by that subsequently taken in *Datastream International Ltd* v. *Oakeep Ltd* (1986) 277 EG 66, per Warner J, approved by Hoffman J in *MFI Properties Ltd* v. *BICC Group Pension Trust Ltd* (The Times, 7 February 1986). The approaches taken in *Datastream* and *MFI Properties* took account of the commercial reality of the situation and should be followed.

A literal interpretation of the words of the clause produced a result which defied common sense, namely, that it required the valuer to ignore *all* provisions in the lease which related to rent. There had to be some limitation implied by the court into the words actually used in the lease. In order to decide how the clause should be construed, it was necessary to have regard to the general purpose of the rent review provisions and give effect to it. In the absence of clear words or surrounding circumstances to the contrary, the lease should be construed so as to give effect to the basic purpose of the rent review clause and not so as to confer on the landlord a windfall benefit which he could never obtain on the market if he were actually letting a premises at the review date, *viz* a letting on terms which contains provisions for rent review at a rent appropriate to a letting which did not contain such a provision.

No distinction should be drawn between those cases where the rent exclusion provision (as in this case) excluded *provisions* as to rent on the one hand, and on the other, cases where the rent exclusion provision excluded *the amount* of rent (as in the *Datastream* case). Once the truly literal approach to construction was dispensed with, there was no alternative, save in special circumstances, but to give effect to the underlying commercial purpose of the clause: *Pearl Assurance* v. *Shaw* (1984) 274 EG 490, *Datastream* and *MFI Properties* approved; *Pugh* v. *Smiths Industries* (1982) 264 EG 823 and *Equity & Law Life Assurance* v. *Bodfield* considered; *National Westminster Bank Plc* v. *Arthur Young McClelland Moores & Co* disapproved and not followed. Guidelines as to approach to construction of review clause set out above at page 558 and below in the extract from Sir Nicholas Browne-Wilkinson V-C's judgment:

SIR NICHOLAS BROWNE-WILKINSON V-C: This is yet another case raising the question whether or not a valuer, in fixing the new rent under a rent-review clause in a lease, should take into account the fact that the lease in question contains provisions for further rent reviews in the future.

Shortly stated, the problem arises in this way. For many years now, in the overwhelming majority of cases landlords granting long terms of years have insisted on the insertion of a rent review-clause in the lease whereby the rent payable is periodically adjusted to reflect changes in the value of money and property. The most common machinery is to provide for the new rent to be fixed by a valuer as being the rack rental which would be obtainable in the market at the review date if the demised premises were to be let on that date. Such rent-review clauses usually lay down the formula by reference to which such rack rental is to be fixed by the valuer. The formula commonly takes the form that the valuer is to assume a hypothetical letting of the premises on the open market on the terms of the actual lease but subject to certain artificial variations. A very common variation is that the valuer is to assume that the hypothetical letting is on the terms of a lease containing the same provisions as the actual lease 'other than as to rent' or 'other than those relating to rent' or 'other than the amount of rent hereby reserved'. I will call such words 'the rent exclusion provision'. The question is whether in any particular case the effect of the rent exclusion provision is to require the valuer to ignore the fact that the actual lease contains provisions for future rent review, on the footing that the rent review-clause is itself a provision relating to rent. The answer to that question may be of great financial importance. In the present case I was told that, if the valuer had to disregard future reviews of rent, the new rent might be as much as 20% greater than the rent which would be fixed if the future reviews are taken into account.

The present case concerns a lease of very substantial office premises granted by the predecessor in title of the defendant to the plaintiff for a term of thirty five years from 25 March 1980. The rent reserved (defined in the lease as 'the Yearly Rent') was a peppercorn until 1 July 1980 and 'thereafter throughout the remainder of the term the rent of £1,150,000.00 per annum (and so in proportion for any lesser period) or such other rent as may from time to time be substituted therefor pursuant to the provisions of the Second Schedule ...'. The Second Schedule para. 1 (a) provides that the landlord may give the tenant a review notice in which event the Yearly Rent payable as from the review date 'shall be the higher of (i) the Yearly Rent payable immediately before such Review Date and (ii) the rack rental value of the Demised Premises at the relevant Review Date'. 'The Review Dates' are defined as the dates of commencement of the 6th, 11th, 16th, 21st, 26th and 31st years of the term, i.e. at five yearly intervals. Paragraph 3 of the 2nd Schedule provides as follows:

'Rack rental value of the Demised Premises means such rent as may be agreed or determined as hereinafter provided to be the best yearly rent at which the Demised Premises could reasonably be expected to let in the open market by a willing landlord to a willing tenant for a term equal to the term hereby granted by means of a lease containing the same provisions (other than as to the yearly rent) as are herein contained on the following assumptions ...'

A review having been required by the landlord at the first review date (25 March 1985) and the parties having failed to agree the new rent, under the terms of the lease the new rent has to be fixed by an independent valuer. The question is whether such valuer in assessing the 'rack rental value' should assume a hypothetical letting on terms which include provisions for review of the rent every five years.

The question is one of construction. Accordingly I will first consider the matter apart from authority and then turn to see whether I am precluded by the decided cases from giving effect to my own views.

Despite the definition of 'the Yearly Rent' to which I have referred, the draughtsman of the lease was not careful in his use of the terminology. In various clauses he uses the phrases 'yearly rent' (i.e. without capital letters) and 'the rents hereby reserved' (in the plural). It is common ground that such variations in terminology disclose no method and can be ignored. The question therefore turns entirely on the words 'containing the same provisions (other than as to yearly rent)' in paragraph 3 of Schedule 2 construed in the context of the lease as a whole and the surrounding circumstances. There is no evidence of any special circumstances applying to this case which might affect the question of construction.

Counsel agreed that there were three possible constructions of the rent exclusion provision in this case, *viz*:

(1)   that it requires the valuer to ignore *all* provisions relating to rent in the lease;
(2)   that it requires the valuer to ignore those provisions which relate to the quantification of rent i.e. the rent payable immediately before the relevant Review Date *and* the provisions for future rent reviews;
(3)   that it requires the valuer to ignore the rent actually payable before the Review Date only i.e. he must take into account the provisions for future reviews of the rent.

The first of these constructions is the only one that the words literally bear. But the result of such a literal construction is so surprising as to offend common sense. The covenant for payment of rent is a 'provision . . . as to yearly rent'. So is the right of re-entry reserved for non payment of rent. Accordingly, if the literal construction were right, the valuer would be faced with the wholly unrealistic (and I would have thought impossible) task of fixing the open market rental for a large office block on terms which contained no covenant for payment of rent nor any right of re-entry in the event of non payment of rent. [Counsel] for the landlord to my mind rightly did not contend for this fully literal construction.

Only one departs from the literal meaning of the words, one is necessarily implying some limitation into the words actually used in the lease. The only question is whether such implication should be that inherent in construction (2) or construction (3) above. At this stage, in my judgment one is necessarily forced to seek to discover the underlying purpose of the provisions for rent review so as to give effect to that purpose.

There is really no dispute that the general purpose of a provision for rent review is to enable the landlord to obtain from time to time the market rental which the premises would command if let on the same terms on the open market at the review dates. The purpose is to reflect the changes in the value of money and real increases in the value of the property during a long term. Such being the purpose, in the absence of special circumstances it would in my judgment be wayward to impute to the parties an intention that the landlord should get a rent which was additionally inflated by a factor which has no reference either to changes in the value of money or in the value of the property but is referable to a factor which has no existence as between the actual landlord and the actual tenant i.e. the additional rent which could be obtained if there were no provisions for rent review. Of course, the lease may be expressed in words so clear that there is no room for giving effect to such underlying purpose. Again, there may be special surrounding circumstances which indicate that the parties did intend to reach such an unusual bargain. But in the absence of such clear words or surrounding circumstances, in my judgment the lease should be construed so as to give effect to the basic purpose of the rent review clause and not so as to confer on the landlord a windfall benefit which he could never obtain on the market if he were actually letting the premises at the review date, *viz* a letting on terms which contain provisions for rent review at a rent appropriate to a letting which did not contain such a provision.

Therefore, apart from authority I would hold that on the true construction of paragraph 3 the rack rental value has to be fixed on the basis that the hypothetical letting is on the terms of the actual lease excluding only the rent actually quantified and payable before the Review Date but including the provisions for five yearly rent review.

Does authority preclude me from reaching this result? In my judgment it does not. The authorities were recently reviewed by Warner J in *Datastream International Ltd* v. *Oakeep* (1986) 277 EG 66; I gratefully adopt his analysis. I add to the cases there considered, the recent judgment of Hoffmann J in *MFI Properties Ltd* v. *BICC Group Pension Trust Ltd*, [see pages 561-2], decided since the conclusion of the argument in this case. In the latter case, the words of the rent exclusion provision were 'other than those relating to rent': Hoffmann J held that in fixing the hypothetical rent the provision for rent review had to be taken into account by the valuer. His reasoning closely accords with my own and I gratefully adopt it.

Although each of the decided cases is a decision on the construction of the lease in question (and therefore not directly authority on the meaning of the lease I have to construe) they do disclose a marked difference of approach to the construction of these clauses. On the one side are Vinelott J (in *Pearl Assurance Plc* v. *Shaw* (1984) 274 EG 490), Warner J (in the *Datastream* case) and Hoffmann J (in the *MFI* case) who, like myself, treat the literal construction or any intermediate construction as offending commercial common sense and therefore give effect to the underlying commercial purpose. On the other side are those cases in which either the words were given their literal meaning (see *National Westminster Bank* v. *Arthur Young McLelland Moores & Co.* (1985) 273 EG 402) or the judge rejected the view that one should approach the construction of a rent review clause on the basis that it is intended only to give effect to the normal commercial reason for including a rent review clause: ibid; *Pugh* v. *Smiths Industries Ltd* (1982) 264 EG 823; *Equity and Law Life Assurance Society Plc* v. *Bodfield Ltd* (1985) 276 EG 1157. I am far from suggesting that the *Pugh* case and the *Equity and Law Life* case were wrongly decided. In the former, the words used in the rent exclusion provision were so clear that imputed intention could not override them and the literal construction did not produce an absurdity. In the latter, the other terms of the lease in question were very unusual. But neither Goulding J nor Peter Gibson J thought it right to give any effect to the underlying commercial purpose of such clauses.

In these circumstances, there are in my judgment conflicting decisions as to the correct approach to the construction of these clauses. I am accordingly free to adopt the approach I prefer. In my judgment the correct approach is as follows:

(a)   words in a rent exclusion provision which require *all* provisions as to rent to be disregarded produce a result so manifestly contrary to commercial common sense that they cannot be given literal effect;

(b)   other clear words which require the rent review provision (as opposed to all provisions as to rent) to be disregarded (such as those in the *Pugh* case) must be given effect to, however wayward the result;

(c)   subject to (b), in the absence of special circumstances it is proper to give effect to the underlying commercial purpose of a rent review clause and to construe the words so as to give effect to that purpose by requiring future rent reviews to be taken into account in fixing the open market rental under the hypothetical letting.

I am conscious that such an approach is perilously close to seeking to lay down mechanistic rules of construction as opposed to principles of construction. But there is an urgent need to produce certainty in this field. Every year thousands of rents are coming up for review on the basis of clauses such as the one before me: witness the growing tide of litigation raising the point. Landlords, tenants and their valuers need to know what is the right basis of valuation without recourse to lawyers let alone to the courts. The question cannot be left to turn on the terms of each lease without the basic approach being certain. It is in my judgment most desirable that this, or some other case, should at an early stage be taken to the Court of Appeal so as to resolve the conflicting judicial approaches that have emerged.

Finally, I must deal specifically with the submissions which [counsel for the landlord] made on the basis of the existing authorities. He submitted that a distinction should be drawn between those cases where the rent exclusion provision (as in this case) excluded *provisions* as to rent on the one hand and, on the other, cases where the rent exclusion provision excluded *the amount* of rent (as in the *Datastream* case). He submitted that in the former case the rent review provisions had to be disregarded whereas in the latter they did not. In my judgment such narrow semantic distinctions are both legally and commercially undesirable. Moreover since [counsel for the landlord] made the submission, it has become inconsistent with the decision of Hoffmann J in the *MFI Properties* case. Once one departs from the truly literal construction (which [counsel for the landlord] did not contend for) in my judgment there is no alternative, save in special circumstances, but to give effect to the underlying commercial purpose of the clause.

I will therefore make the declaration asked for in the originating summons.

Note: Contra-indications to the general rule expressed in *British Gas* (above) are found in *Pugh* v. *Smiths Industries* (see earlier on page 127 for facts and extract). The judge there did not approach the construction of the lease bearing in mind its general commercial purpose, but nevertheless Browne-Wilkinson V-C said that it fell into an exceptional category and that he would not go so far as to say it and the *Equity & Law Life* v. *Bodfield* decision (page 130 earlier) were wrongly decided.

Table of Cases

Table of statutes

Index